Peregrine Books
The History of Germany Since 1789

Golo Mann, son of the novelist and Nobel Prize winner
Thomas Mann, was born in Munich in 1909. He read history,
modern languages and philosophy under Karl Jaspers at
Heidelberg, where he received his doctorate in 1932. From
1933 to 1937 he taught at various French universities and, for
three years, until 1940, was editor of the Zürich literary
monthly *Mass und Wert*. He then went to America, where
from 1943 to 1946 he served in the United States Army. For
the next decade he held the Chair of Contemporary History at
Claremont Men's College in California. On his return to
Europe in 1958 he was Professor of History at the University
of Münster and at Stuttgart (1960–64).

Professor Mann's previous books include *Secretary of Europe*
(1946), a study of Friedrich von Gentz. His monumental biography of Wallenstein was published in Germany in 1971. In
1962 he was awarded the Fontane Prize by the city of Berlin,
and in 1964 the Schillerpreis by the city of Mannheim as well
as the Büchner Prize (1968), the Gottfried Keller-Preis (1969),
the Schiller-Gedächtnispreis (1977) and the Order Pour la
Mérite. He is a member of the American Academy of Arts and
Sciences. Professor Mann now lives in Switzerland.

D1146956

Golo Mann

The History of Germany
Since 1789

Translated from the German by Marian Jackson

Penguin Books

PENGUIN BOOKS

Published by the Penguin Group
27 Wrights Lane, London W8 5TZ, England
Viking Penguin Inc., 40 West 23rd Street, New York, New York 10010, USA
Penguin Books Australia Ltd, Ringwood, Victoria, Australia
Penguin Books Canada Ltd, 2801 John Street, Markham, Ontario, Canada L3R 1B4
Penguin Books (NZ) Ltd, 182–190 Wairau Road, Auckland 10, New Zealand

Penguin Books Ltd, Registered Offices: Harmondsworth, Middlesex, England

First published in German under the title
Deutsche Geschichte des 19, *und* 20, *Jahrhunderts*
Translation published in Great Britain by Chatto & Windus Ltd 1968
Published in Pelican Books 1974
Reprinted 1985
Reprinted in Peregrine Books 1987
Reprinted 1988

Made and printed in Great Britain by
Richard Clay Ltd, Bungay, Suffolk
Set in Monotype Times

Contents

Preface to the English Edition

The history of Germany here presented in English was written between 1953 and 1957. Since the completion of the German text new material has appeared, some of which has been taken account of in the English edition. Nevertheless it is impossible to hide when – in the intellectual climate of which decade – a book was written. Nor are all the much discussed new contributions to recent German history of real importance.

For example, the question of who set fire to the Berlin Reichstag in 1933 is a minor problem, of interest more to the detective or the incendiary specialist than to the historian. Nevertheless, I have revised my original account of the affair in the light of the most recent research.

Nothing has come to light or can ever come to light that will substantially change the historian's first verdict on the launching of the Second World War. The course of events was public from the beginning, unique in its simplicity. This fact cannot be altered by any secret document which those who claim that Hitler was innocent, or only partially guilty, hope to find when the British and French archives are eventually opened. Anyone who expects something of that kind merely shows that he ridiculously over-estimates the significance of a single document, of a word spoken or written at some time or other, compared with the mass of clearly available evidence as to cause and effect; either because he has learnt no historical method or – which is probably more often the case – because he uses his intelligence to serve his own doubtful purpose. The casuistry of A. J. P. Taylor's *Origins of the Second World War* deserves only a short, not very respectful refutation which I have tried to give elsewhere. The follies of the

American, Hoggan, who transformed Hitler into a prince of peace and benefactor of mankind deserves no refutation. It may be regrettable but it is not surprising that Anglo-Saxon writers, because of stupidity or enjoyment of a paradox, should irresponsibly stab in the back those Germans who are striving to spread the truth.

Anyway, no one has ever claimed that Hitler had wanted or planned exactly the war that he got in the end. What he wanted, what his ideas on nature, man, state and race inevitably produced was war or ventures which could not be pursued without war. War is an abstract noun; any real war will always differ from the idea. If there is some truth in what Taylor says about Hitler's opportunism, about the way in which he seized chances that surprised even him, it does not in any way disprove the bellicose character of Hitler's state and Hitler's policy. Hitler really wanted to murder the European Jews and to destroy Czechoslovakia and Poland, and he had always said so. He had no idea when and how he would do it, or how far he would succeed. Politicians, says Taylor, act from one day to the next, from one year to the next; their improvisations are what historians later mistake for a grand design. The observation is not without wit and may serve to correct excessively narrow interpretations. Only it happens to apply to no person less than to this one. 'I admire your Führer', a French soldier said to me in 1940. 'I must admire him because he has done everything that he promised himself he would do.' This simple boy saw the issue more clearly than our sophisticated historical philosopher. By and large I do not think that my account of Adolf Hitler's twelve years is out of date, however many new little bits of research, especially German research, have since contributed towards the completion of the whole horrible mosaic.

If anything it was the chapters on the period of the Kaiser and the First World War that needed revision. Since they were written undeniably important new material has been published on those periods, intelligent general works in which the emphasis is put in a different place – such as Theodor Schieder's *Das Deutsche Kaiserreich von 1871 als Nationalstaat* or Michael Balfour's *The*

Kaiser and his Times – as well as the results of impressive specialized research. Among the latter are Gerhard Ritter's examination
of the *Schlieffen-Plan*, Günther Zmarzlik's *Bethmann Hollweg als
Reichskanzler*, Morsey's and Matthias' great volumes on the
Interfraktionelle Ausschuss and the *Regierung des Prinzen Max von
Baden*, but above all Fritz Fischer's hotly debated *Der Griff nach
der Weltmacht*. Not that these publications upset accepted views
and replaced them by new ones. This is unlikely to happen in
relation to events about which we have long had thousands of
documents and hundreds of books of every kind and quality;
events which, moreover, in contrast to eighteenth-century policy,
were public from the start. Any intelligent newspaper reader
could see from the headlines what the game was in 1914 or 1917
while it was being played. It remained for research, old and new,
to confirm, to emphasize and to qualify in this or that respect
what had always been known. We have always known that, in
spite of the antiquated structure of the constitution, the importance of the Reichstag grew continuously under William II, that
the Chancellors came to depend a little on parliament, a state of
affairs which became noticeably more marked during the war;
that the spontaneous establishment of such bodies as the Inter-
party Committee during the reign of William II prepared the way
for the Republic or at least for a more parliamentary form of
constitution. We have always known what forces resisted this
process and why, and how it was that it did not reach its goal in
time. As regards German diplomacy every schoolboy has known
since 1919, or should have known, that in June 1914 it was fully
conscious of the possibility or even the likelihood of a European
war. One could not help but know this, unless one was prepared
to believe that Bethmann and his advisers were complete idiots,
which they were clearly not. Equally well known were the fantastic
war aims of various substantial sections of German society and
how these received whole-hearted approval from the military
leaders and half-hearted approval from the government. How
could it have been otherwise? These issues were discussed in the
press and in public.

Fischer has diligently collected the evidence of a conscious responsibility of German diplomacy for the outbreak of the First World War and has shown the continuity of German war aims during the four years of the war, tracing them back to the time before the war and following them up to Hitler's conquests. His book is an impressive testimony of national self-criticism, of the kind which German academic historians of the inter-war period unfortunately failed to produce. But the book is one sided and inadequate. It knows nothing of the dialectic of events, of the effect of pressure and counter-pressure. It completely ignores the war aims of the Entente. It does not ask whether Germany during the four war years could have had a *status quo ante* peace – a point which is far from certain – nor to what extent the most expansionist aims arose from the dim awareness of the fact that in any case there could be no return to 1914. Nor does the book give sufficient weight to the inter-play between war aims and internal German constitutional and social conflicts. There is no need to complicate simple things; the start of Hitler's war is a simple story. On the other hand one must not simplify complicated issues. I personally still cannot see any direct, conscious sequence of cause and effect between the German policy of expansion before 1914 and German behaviour during the July crisis of that year. Naturally there is a connection, but it is subconscious and repressed. It has nothing of the highly conscious, ideological shamelessness of 1939. Hitler acted in complete freedom, the Kaiser under semi-blind, semi-desperate constraint; anyone who fails to see this difference confuses the issue instead of clarifying it.

As it happens Fischer's view has been corrected or balanced by other books which appeared at the same time. Ritter's *Schlieffen-Plan* emphasizes the terrible pressure of time under which the German diplomats were acting in the last days of July; their initial mistake having been to subordinate their policy to the ideas of a politically ignorant and innocent strategist who, if it came to war, was prepared to have only the one that he had planned in advance, day by day, hour by hour. The decisive influence of the army in 1914, and its complete lack of influence in 1939, confirm that the two occasions were profoundly different. The attempts, though unsuccessful, clumsy and half-hearted, to eliminate one of the opponents in the war and to achieve a partial peace – attempts which Fischer has almost ignored – have been described by Egmont Zechlin. Hantsch's new biography of the Austrian Foreign Minister, Berchthold, does not give us the picture of a belligerent imperialist but of a long-standing 'appeaser' who in 1914 – too late? – adopted a daringly stubborn attitude, just because he had *not* taken it for so long, and was reputed at home to favour peace without honour; this would represent a parallel, though the only one, between the tired Habsburg grand seigneur and the English bourgeois, Neville Chamberlain. Although the arguments and counter-arguments, the quotations and counter-quotations of recent years may have increased our knowledge of the period of William II, Bethmann and Ludendorff, they have not really altered it.

What is new, however, is what has happened since this book was written and what at the time I wisely refrained from predicting. The frontier between 'history' and 'the present' is indefinable. 'The dense web of the fortunes of man is woven without a void', says Lord Acton. In the German edition the events after 1945 were only briefly referred to; the 'post-war period' was that year, that day. Since then the feeling has grown that we no longer live in a post-war period, that the conditions and tensions which followed almost immediately on Hitler's war, those of the Cold War or East–West conflict, have changed. At any rate their origins lie sufficiently far back in the past to make it possible to recount them. The same also applies to the German components of this development, the foundation and development of the Federal Republic, the hardening of the accidental military frontiers of 1945 into the 'two German states'. Therefore I have rewritten the last chapter and tried to tell a story which can, of course, only end in questions. The Bonn Republic has already lasted longer than the Weimar one and still survives. Indeed the forms created by the East–West conflict have survived in Germany more markedly than anywhere else. Connected with this is the fact that Germany's existence since 1945, in spite of the country's tremendous economic recovery, in spite of the prompt re-emergence of a considerable German military power, has in the main been passive. Passive even if it were true, as an American politician once said, that American foreign policy was determined for eight years by the German Chancellor, for in that case Adenauer decided or helped to decide the foreign policy of America, not of Germany. German foreign policy was completely dependent on that of America on the one hand and on that of Russia on the other. What we are dealing with in these twenty years is not the history of an independent centre of energy but of a province or of two provinces, one of which became rich without becoming powerful. Maybe it will translate its wealth into active power again one day. It would then cease to be a province and our last chapter would be given the conclusion which it lacks today.

However 'provincial' post-war Germany was, its fate was passively tied up with that of the world. The historian really needs to write the history of the world when writing the history of Germany after 1945; this, however, would miss our purpose. In a history of the world of the last twenty years, Germany deserves only a small place. Therefore this story becomes very fragmentary towards the end. It deals only with a narrow sector of world events, the German one, and assumes that all the rest, which is the main part, is known. Equally it must break off *infectis rebus*, losing itself in the undecided issues of the moment.

G.M.

Part One
Cardinal Factors in German History

The genius of Europe has given much to the world: things good and evil, generally things that are both good and evil – among them the state and the nation. Elsewhere, in Asia and in Africa, nations and states did not exist in the past. They are being produced and reproduced there today, and the forms invented by Europe are used as weapons against Europe. This is not unjust or humiliating provided we do not misunderstand it.

Ever since society began to take shape in Europe the Continent has been divided into nations: there has been one European civilization but many nations. The identity of Europe may be denied because there have always been different forces at work and many links with non-European civilizations such as Islam. But similar arguments can be used to deny the existence of nations. Let us not deny the obvious: as the embodiment of fruitful communities, as a force which explored the earth and gave continents and islands names which they still possess, as the mainspring of the world today, there has been an entity called Europe – Europe with its Catholic religion, its nobles and bourgeoisie, its towns and medieval estates, its crusades and voyages of discovery, its science, its art, its music and its politics.

But from the beginning there was something more than a great Christian Europe. The notion that this Europe was destroyed by the nations is a myth. The society that gradually emerged from the dark ages of the post-Roman era was already divided into nations, and although the complete development of the nation-state was still to come, England and France at least were definitely moving towards the nation-state as early as the thirteenth century. But states and nations remained interdependent; their rivalries, their friendships and their entities made Europe great. Later, when the situation became critical and times changed, they brought Europe to self-destruction, but it often happens in history that the forces that make us grow also destroy us. Originally the concepts of Europe, state and nation did not conflict; they presupposed each other. Even the nationalism of the nineteenth and twentieth centuries was a highly international affair. Different nationalisms stimulated and aped each other using the same words in the same cause. Even the worst nationalism with which people tried to destroy and deny Europe proved nothing against Europe, for it was a European disease.

The history of each European nation is unique, but related and similar to the histories of the others. All nations have been in close friendly or hostile contact and have affected each other: Germans and Italians, Italians and Spaniards, Spaniards and Frenchmen, Englishmen and Frenchmen, Englishmen and Spaniards, Frenchmen and Germans, Scandinavians and Germans and Englishmen, Germans and Poles and Czechs and South Slavs and Hungarians. No particular national history can serve as a model in the sense that one might regret that others did not take the same course.

Historians have often regretted that in the Middle Ages Germany and Italy did not become nation-states like France, that in Germany the idea of the Empire prevented such a development. But everything depends on everything else. Who can say whether France could have become a nation-state if Germany had become one early? Nations have assumed certain forms because others did not. Even if one admits – as I think one must – that Britain's history has been happier than that of the continental peoples, one must point out that Britain itself was able to be happily different only because the Continent was not like Britain.

Unique too has been the fate of the ethnic group which the God of History placed in the centre of Europe, unique but at the same time tied closely to that of other ethnic groups, great and small.

The student of the history of the German nation easily gets an impression of restless oscillation between extremes. At times there is a wide gap between idea and reality, as in the medieval Empire when German kings and self-styled Roman Emperors fought for a fantastic *imperium* extending far beyond linguistic frontiers while Germany disintegrated into countless little territorial states; at other times the nation indulges in a long orgy of self-destruction, as during the Thirty Years War. At times Germans reach the highest spiritual heights ever scaled by men, even though public life is dominated by a dreary mediocrity. Disinterest in politics gives way to hectic political activity, variety to complete uniformity; from prostration Germany rises to aggression, collapses again into chaos and then with incredible speed recovers a new and hectic prosperity. It can be receptive, cosmopolitan, admiring of things foreign; at other times it despises and rejects everything foreign and seeks salvation in the exaggerated cultivation of its national characteristics. At times the Germans seem a philosophical people, at others the most practical and most materialist; at times the most patient and peaceful, at others the most domineering and brutal. Their own philosopher, Nietzsche, called them the '*Täusche-Volk*'* because time after time they have surprised the world by things least expected of them.

It has often been said that Germany, unlike more fortunate countries, has no natural frontiers. There is something in this claim, although it must at once be qualified. It would credit Nature with too much political foresight to believe that by means of oceans, mountains and rivers she neatly partitioned Europe into regions in which the wandering nations could assemble and find permanent homes. 'The Rhine, Germany's river, not Germany's frontier,' wrote Ernst Moritz Arndt, and this is true to the extent that nobody can say why on earth a river should be a frontier; that mountains are not necessarily political frontiers can be seen by a glance at the maps of North America, Switzerland or Austria. The sea in particular has always been a line which it was a temptation to cross, to trade, to colonize, to conquer and to found empires, rather than a frontier. States are historical structures that have almost nothing to do with the Will of Nature. It was not the Will of Nature that Portugal should remain independent but not Catalonia or Brittany; that Britain should become a world power

* A pun on *deutsch* (German) and *täuschen* (to deceive) (Tr.).

instead of remaining a Roman or a French province. The disappearance of the great city leagues of the Middle Ages, the Lombard and the Rhenish, and the development of a much smaller and weaker league on the Lake of Lucerne into the Swiss nation-state had nothing to do with natural frontiers. The French were the first to confuse the facts of history with the facts of nature and in the seventeen-nineties began to speak of the natural frontiers of their republic; they paid dearly for it. Later the Americans decided that it was the Will of Nature that the whole of the North American continent should belong to them. They managed to establish their claim against the unfortunate Red Indians, Spain and Mexico. But the frontier between the United States and Canada is artificial from the Atlantic to the Pacific, and this frontier the Americans have respected, not because it was natural but because it was politically right. Nature has not prescribed to any state how great or small it should be.

What then do we mean when we say that Germany has no natural frontiers? Only this: that in its frontiers, or lack of frontiers, it differs somewhat from other states. Britain is surrounded by water. France has the Atlantic to the west, mountains and sea to the south and a few mountains to the south-east – all of which the French have crossed several times; to the north and the north-east the country is open. Germany has mountains to the south, sea to the north, open country to the east and west; that is the whole difference. It is centrally situated like Poland, Persia and other countries. There is no need to maintain that Germany is mysteriously destined to lack frontiers because of its central position.

It lies midway between Latins and Slavs, and this factor has indeed been of great importance for the Germans. At certain times the Germans were less civilized than their Latin neighbours. Their society developed later and more slowly. European civilization spread from the west and the south to the east and the north, with the result that in the Middle Ages western and southern Germany showed more developed forms of economic, political and intellectual life than eastern Germany. But the latinized West did not keep its slight lead. At the height of the Middle Ages

Cologne was as much a capital of Christianity as Paris, and the Hohenstaufen court as much a centre of civilization as the Capetian. If much later the Germans again fell behind their western neighbours, if in the seventeenth, eighteenth and even in the nineteenth century they were still in a sense imitating the more advanced West, the explanation is not to be sought in their barbaric origins, which went no further back than those of the British. The explanation lies in more recent economic, political and intellectual developments. On rare occasions the Germans were even ahead of their Latin neighbours. By and large the two were well balanced and if there were conflicts, such as those between the Popes and the German Emperors, they arose from the very fact of a common civilization.

In the East the position was different. On the whole – not always and not everywhere – the Germans were more civilized than the Slavs. Here they were both threatened and themselves threatened others. Until the late Middle Ages they were confronted by something fundamentally alien, and even more recently by something intrinsically different. We need not go into the question of what a race is. Races tend to mix, particularly in places where they meet and fight, and the Germans mixed with the Slavs in the East long after they had amalgamated with the conquered Celts in the South. When we speak of the German and Slav races we are not referring to biological entities, but to historic forces divided by language, custom and possibly religion. Such forces clashed in the East, one trying to expand at the expense of the other. But German penetration in the East consisted more of peaceful settlement and less of racial and religious struggles than Slav and German nationalism was later prepared to admit. German colonists were in demand in Poland and Bohemia; brutal oppression such as that of the heathen 'Prussians' was the exception and not the rule. Yet the fluid situation in the East greatly influenced the character of the Germans as a nation. In more recent times Germany's two eastern states in particular, Austria and Prussia, were affected by the nature of their contact with the Slavs. As a result there was a difference between them and landlocked Germany, which lacked such contacts and looked to the West.

Here are some of the cardinal factors in German history: the comparative unimportance of Germany's sea communications; the extent of its overland communications in the west, the east and the south-east; and the proximity of the Slavs. After history had once made these factors no historical activity could change them.

The Empire, later called the Roman Empire, later still the Holy Roman Empire and finally the Holy Roman Empire of the German Nation, was important in the history of Germany not for what it achieved – its practical substance never amounted to very much – but for two reasons. First, because it was an obstacle and so generated positive reactions and developments, and secondly because it was the basis for a legend, an idea and a memory. (These points do not apply to the Frankish Kingdom whose ruler, Charlemagne, had the title of Roman Emperor bestowed upon himself. At that time there were no Germans or Frenchmen.)

As early as the Ottonian period the empire had its centre of gravity in Germany. The situation remained the same ever after, however far-flung and ill-defined the frontiers of the Empire were in the south and west, and however Christian and universal the idea became. Reality always fell short of the idea, approaching it only at brief moments. In the Middle Ages there could be no Caesars in the style of Augustus; nor could there be presidents of a free community of Christian peoples. Europe was too vast, too fragmented and soon also too deeply divided between nationalities. What the phantasmagoria of the Empire produced was a curiously tense, often unhappy liaison between Germany and Italy. It was also responsible for the division of Germany into territories whose rulers in the end acquired and represented such political reality as there was. The Emperor was either the greatest territorial lord or nobody at all. The Empire should have been a beautiful dome to the edifice formed by the countries of the Christian world. In the end it was only a brittle German political complex which barely managed to serve as a bridge. Other nations gradually developed towards unity; Germany, which had begun with the Empire, ended up with indissoluble particularism. When the idea and practice of the modern state spread from Italy, Spain, France and Britain, there was no nascent central power in Germany to benefit. It was therefore the territorial princes who benefited; and such the situation remained until well into the nineteenth century.

This was not altogether a misfortune; all nations need not take the same road. Germany took a different road, and one that led past strange places. At the beginning of our story, let us say in 1789, the Empire was made up of 1,789 territories, of which some were independent states and European powers, but most just consisted of a few castles and villages.

Germany's political multiformity has nothing to do with its nature and geography, or with its historical beginnings. It is true that there is great regional variety; the German who feels himself at home in the Black Forest, on the Main or the Neckar or in the Alps, will feel a stranger on the Lüneburg Heath. But the same is also true of the old provinces of France, like Provence and Brittany. Germany has no greater variety of scenery and climate than other European countries. It has been said that one of the causes of the division of Germany was the Roman *limes*, the fact that for hundreds of years the Romans occupied the country south of the Danube and west of the Rhine, whereas they were soon forced to abandon the region between the northern Rhine and the Elbe, and never got beyond the Elbe. I cannot persuade myself to regard this as a reason for the German political system in more recent times. The Roman occupation was really more likely to split the country in half than to divide it into 1,789 principalities. The fact that the Romans had once been there may well have made a difference for a long time, but it cannot make a permanent difference. Nor were the various tribal groups in which the Teutons entered history as important for the development of Germany's political system as even the Constitution of 1919 would suggest. The old duchies had disappeared early. The territorial princes who emerged in the course of the Middle Ages had originally been servants of the king and feudal lords, holders of numerous offices and beneficiaries of many feudal privileges which they gradually transformed into territorial overlordships vested in their persons and families. In the case of Bavaria territorial rule coincided with part of the old tribal region; elsewhere, for example in Hesse and Saxony, little remained of the old tribal character but the high-sounding name. In modern times the largest principality, Prussia, was named after an exterminated heathen tribe. Even the names of the majority indicated that they were feudal domains with a castle or the ruler's place of residence as their centre. This was not something that was there at the beginning; it is a historical development. The Austrians were Bavarians by descent; history, and modern history at that, has made them into something different.

But why then the political division of Germany? The historian is often unable to distinguish cause from effect. He can only say that this is what happened and therefore it happened in this way. Description and explanation become one. The reason for an event lies in the event itself. We are merely rearranging words if we say, for example, that something in the Germans drove them towards political multiformity and made them reproduce the divisions of their old tribal organization in completely changed circumstances. As far as the human, personal aspect goes the type of the aggressive politician is later found among the princes and not among the representatives of the Empire. Master politicians like Maurice of Saxony, Maximilian I of Bavaria or Frederick William of Brandenburg did not serve the idea of the Empire. The only politician of genius who for a time had great plans for the Empire, Wallenstein, regarded himself as the representative of the Austrian territorial power and later as a ruler in his own right. The question then would be why the most intelligent political energy was absorbed by the principalities. To this there is only one answer: the Empire was always more a figment of the imagination than a reality, and after the fall of the Hohenstaufen it became a mere dream. But in a dream there is no place for *Realpolitik* – though *Realpolitik* may use the dream for its own ends. Thus from the sixteenth to the eighteenth century the House of Habsburg used the idea of the Empire to advance its own power and glory.

The Empire and the system of principalities went together – the open but ill-defined nature of the one, the petty but realistic nature of the other. For the political existence of the Germans both were of importance. The memory of the Empire delayed and impeded the development of the modern nation-state; in the end it contributed to its establishment and deformed it. Much of the nation's combination of political superiority and inferiority complexes stemmed originally from that memory. Germans felt superior to other people because the Empire had been theirs and because they believed themselves to have inherited the civilizing mission of the Romans; they felt inferior because for many years the antiquated, cumbersome machinery of the Empire had been outmanoeuvred by the more versatile western nation-states, and because German political reality was usually confined to small principalities with no great historical mission. This is what happened and one can only marvel that it did. None of the nations that came into being in the early Middle Ages could claim to be the heir of Rome, the Germans even less than their Latin-speaking neighbours to the west and south, and Europe never did entrust them with Rome's civilizing mission.

The Empire was Germany's western face. It was the form which Germany tried to give to its relations with its western and southern neighbours. In some way or other the Low Countries, Lorraine, Burgundy and Italy were to be parts of the Empire, which was conceived as a static system. The purpose of the German Emperors' Italian campaigns was not to extend the Empire but to restore an existing system, to force perverse reality to conform to the idea. With those expeditions the Emperors wanted to establish in Italy the authority which they lacked in Germany and with which they hoped to subdue Germany – an intention that was never fulfilled. In the East, where the Germans were threatened and threatened others, the role of the Empire was small. Here there were unrest and oppression, new things were created on new ground, not an old dream revived. Here German princes, the dynasties of the Babenbergs, the Ascanians, the Guelfs, the Teutonic Knights, the Habsburgs and the Hohenzollern, acted on their own. One result was that in the East the German nation outgrew the Empire first in fact and then also in form. In the West and the South the Empire included regions which were not, or which gradually ceased to be, German; in the East it excluded regions which gradually became German. The two most powerful German states in modern times, Austria and Prussia, thus came to have some of their centres of gravity outside the Empire. Independent of the Empire, independent even of the German principalities, members of the German nation lived among Poles, Czechs and Magyars, lived in the towns as artisans and traders – a *Deutschtum im Ausland* (Germans living abroad) centuries before the expression was invented. The involvement of the Germans in the life of eastern Europe gave rise in the era of imperialism, in modern times, to the false belief that the East was the Empire's true sphere of activity. The legend of the supra-national structure preserved and directed by Germans, which was supposed to be a national system as well, was transferred to regions outside the medieval *imperium*. In our day this delusion, this claim, finally led to a terrible defeat of the Germans in the East, the consequences of which cannot be assessed even now.

Another cardinal factor – a cardinal event – in German history is Luther's rebellion.

Let us leave aside the question of the origins of religion and the extent to which it may be affected by other, non-religious factors. Everything in life has a bearing on everything else. It is enough to say that religion was a determining influence everywhere. How could it be otherwise? Man's idea of himself, of his place in the world, of his relations with his fellow men, of the meaning and purpose of existence, his beliefs, hopes and fears inevitably affect the organization of the community. Karl Marx commented sarcastically that even in the Christian Middle Ages man was not able to live by religion alone, and he was obviously right. But the Christian Church helped to decide how man lived, and how he was governed, what he feared, what gave him comfort and what were his economic, moral and aesthetic codes.

As for Protestantism, the modern variety of Christianity, all the peoples and states of western Europe began to come into conflict with the Roman Church in the sixteenth century. In some places - in Spain, Italy, Hungary and Poland - the Counter-Reformation triumphed, although it was the Catholic states, particularly the Spanish Empire, rather than the Papacy that benefited from its success. In France after bitter religious wars the Protestants remained a minority, at times very powerful, then tolerated, then persecuted, finally to become a small but indispensable part of the life of the modern state, active in industry, science, philosophy and politics. There is a slight resemblance between them and the Catholic community in England, another numerically small, suspect minority which won equality of civil rights only in the nineteenth century.

In Germany the nation was nearly split in half by the religious quarrels of the sixteenth century. This split did not happen elsewhere and all one can say is that it did happen in Germany, although it was apparently by no means inevitable. Protestantism was originally a German affair. It was born in Germany and there – to use an abused expression since we have no other – it became a popular movement within a few years. In Germany Protestantism found its incarnation in a man unique among the spiritual leaders of the day, not because of the power of his mind – in that respect Calvin was superior to Luther – but because of his popularity, his magnetic strength and depth of character. Why was Martin Luther, the poet and writer, the mystic, the inspiring preacher, the born politician and demagogue, unable to give the nation new spiritual and temporal unity, why did he fail to achieve what a few clever English rulers accomplished without much difficulty? The problems that faced Luther were too hopelessly entangled; he could not unravel them.

The German Emperor of the day would have liked to bring the Empire under the control of his dynasty. But he was also King of Spain and had long ceased to be a German. The unity that he would have brought, had he been allowed a free hand, would not have been spontaneously German but imposed from abroad. Charles V could not put himself at the head of the Protestant movement which, if victorious, would have divided his multilingual *imperium* into Protestant national states; he was bound to fight it. The result was a new form of division. The Counter-Reformation was victorious in Austria, Bavaria, on the Rhine and here and there in central Germany; north and east remained Protestant. Once more it was the princes who benefited from the confused revolution – the Protestant ones who enriched their states with church property and each of whom now became his own Pope, as well as those who had remained Catholic. Henceforth a man's religion was determined for him by his territorial ruler.

Class wars embittered the issue. Whenever in the history of Europe the simple people have come in contact with the original texts of the New Testament there has been social unrest because its message is one of human equality and justice and is hostile to the rich. Luther's interpretation was different. The malevolent attitude which he adopted during the Peasants' War, and the brutality with which he called for the destruction of the rebels, did much to rob his cause of its attraction and the public of their hope. The man who had caused so much confusion was basically a conservative, and it emerged that he stood for order at any price.

An achievement like Luther's has many aspects and contains political and non-political elements, liberating and repressive ones. One selects from it what one can use and one employs it for purposes for which it was never intended. Nevertheless, the idea that every Christian could look after his own soul and needed no ordained priest to intercede for him, and that the thousand-year achievement of the Roman authority should no longer count when confronted with the living interpretation of the Scriptures, was revolutionary and released both good and evil influences. But the freedom which Luther preached was only spiritual and had nothing to do with political freedom. The good Christian was completely passive. He was free – spiritually – even when in chains, and he owed complete obedience to authority, any authority. But authority must be armed with a sharp sword because the people could not be relied upon to be disciplined voluntarily. Luther, who was optimistic enough to break the authority of the Pope and to believe that the individual, or at any rate he personally, could interpret the Bible correctly, was at the same time profoundly pessimistic about human nature. As a result, Luther's activities strengthened the authority of the princes and worked against the responsibility of the Estates as it had developed in the late Middle Ages. Luther was despotic and superstitious and soon – as soon as he was himself no longer threatened by persecution – became a persecutor.

How then do the first two cardinal factors in German history affect the third, Luther's Reformation? It was the Empire, cumbersome, complex and entangled in non-German affairs as it was in 1520, that decided the fate of Protestantism and alone explains the religious partition. It was the German princes who gained by it. Since the eastward-looking, newly German or colonial parts of Germany – Brandenburg, Pomerania and Prussia – became Protestant while the old Empire to the south and the west remained predominantly Catholic, the Reformation once again strengthened the dividing line between the two regions of Germany. Many are the forms – terrible war and peaceful competition, the establishment of states, cultural agreements and political alliances – in which this confessional dualism has manifested itself; it still exists today.

The period of Charles V and Luther was the last in which the Empire was the centre of the spiritual and temporal storms that shook Europe. Thereafter its importance declined. Protestantism itself hardened and fruitless disputations took the place of the tremendous, vital experience that had found expression in the young Luther. There is something questionable about petrified, officially sponsored, organized protest. A movement like Protestantism must continually be reborn, must search ever deeper and grow beyond itself, as it did periodically in the Anglo-Saxon countries into the twentieth century. In Germany, too, individual Protestants were creative in intellectual and public life, but the Lutheran state churches soon ceased to be a source of creative unrest. The greatest German Protestants were those who, though of Lutheran descent, outgrew all ecclesiastical and even Christian restriction – Leibniz, Lessing, Hegel, Nietzsche.

The hardening of the Lutheran revolution is not the only, or even the main, reason why around 1600 the Empire no longer occupied the same place in the world as a hundred years earlier. Germany, which so far had shared all Europe's great experiences – the Roman occupation and Christianity, feudalism and the crusades, the monastic movement and the universities, cities and middle classes, Renaissance and Reformation – now failed to share the greatest of them all: the incipient Europeanization of the world. German ships ploughed neither the Atlantic nor the Indian Ocean. Germany's trade declined, its cities grew poor and its middle class became fossilized. Of the matchless education provided by colonization, the widening of horizons, the increase in material wealth and the quickening rhythm of life, Germany had only a small share. The big decisions were made elsewhere. While the Dutch were founding their republic, the first free active federation of states in modern times, and while England was fighting its heroic duel with Spain, German Protestant and Catholic princelings waylaid each other, and now and again one of them annexed some impoverished imperial city. At the time when the most fateful development of modern history, the Anglo-Saxon colonization of North America, began in earnest, Germany started its Thirty Years War.

Great wars and historical crises in general can be looked at from different angles. It has been said of the so-called First World War that it was primarily a duel between Germany and Britain, or between Germany and Russia, a new chapter in the age-old struggle between Teutons and Slavs, a war between democracy and autocracy, the last in a long series of conflicts between Germany and France, and so on. Perhaps it was all these things and more. Perhaps it was really none of them and was completely devoid of sense, nothing but – nonsense. Nations have always managed to find some rational necessity, some ideological reason for murdering each other.

Of all the great wars of modern times the Thirty Years War was the most confused, the maddest, a mass of cross-currents, clashing ambition, fanaticism and fear. It was a religious war between Catholics and Protestants in which the Catholic states led by Bavaria took the side of the Catholic Habsburgs. It was also an attempt by the Spanish–Austrian dynasty to subdue the Empire, resisted by an alliance between the Catholic princes led by Bavaria, and the Protestant ones. The intervention of France was aimed less against Germany than against the great international power of the Habsburgs which had its centre of gravity in Madrid. The intervention of Sweden, on the other hand, was not aimed against Spain but against the danger of a revival of the German Empire in northern Germany and on the Baltic. Wallenstein, the man who strove for that revival, who dreamed of a German navy, who wanted to dethrone the princelings and to transform Germany into a state like France and Spain, was not a German but a brilliant Bohemian financier and adventurer who corresponded with his intimates in Czech. The German Emperor did not understand his plans and dropped him. The war began as a chapter in the Austrian Counter-Reformation and a conflict between the Habsburgs and the estates of the kingdom of Bohemia, whose relationship to the Empire was uncertain. It ended as a war between France, Sweden and Holland on the one side and Austria and Spain on the other, with Germany in the middle and on both sides, while nobody cared any longer about the liberties of Bohemia. Great wars usually finish up as something completely different from what they were at the beginning and people forget how and why the conflict began. But such wars also speed up, and in retrospect confirm, new developments. They stimulate the rise of nations, or classes, or ways of life that were emerging anyway; they hasten the disappearance of those that were already on the decline. The Thirty Years War confirmed a long-standing trend in the development of the German Empire.

The victors – if there are any victors at all in such prolonged struggles – were the new western powers, France, Holland and also Sweden. The German princes were victorious to the extent that they gained by the Peace of Westphalia the independence which they wanted. Even the House of Habsburg might be described as a victor. Although it had failed to conquer the Empire, it emerged from the chaos of war as a European power, detached from the Empire and based on the Austrian provinces, Hungary and Bohemia. It was detached from the Empire partly because in reality the Empire no longer existed. The loser therefore was the Empire, and hence the people, because hitherto the Empire had been a source of law and legal protection. Henceforth the princes ruled by absolute right. The main loser, however, was

German civilization. Recently historians have tried to minimize the horrors of the Thirty Years War by disproving the statistical basis of the accepted view of the terrible decline in the population, the sacking and destruction of cities and the sufferings of the rural population; in short they have presented the whole war more or less as an invention of Prussian anti-Habsburg propaganda. There may be something in this. Even Schiller in his description of the fall of Magdeburg based himself on Protestant reports and even on him these made the impression which had been intended. But the reality of this catastrophe, of Europe's material and moral crisis, is obvious. It reveals itself in the magnificent dirges, poems and songs of the day, in Grimmelshausen's *Abenteuerlicher Simplicissimus* (Adventures of a Simpleton), and even in the stilted exchanges of the diplomats. A country still rich and flourishing was gradually destroyed by annual armed clashes, shrewd scheming in the face of almost continuous negotiations and by much hypocritical talk about the desirability of peace. As Wallenstein wrote: 'In the end, when all countries are reduced to ashes we shall have to make peace.' Reconstruction took decades, in a sense centuries. People had not in those days achieved our scientific perfection either in destruction or in reconstruction.

Compelled in the sixteenth century to give up its place in the front line of history, Germany was henceforth relegated completely to the background. This situation was emphasized by the rapid rise of its neighbour, France. The French *Grand Siècle* began as the Thirty Years War ended. German, which had earlier had a hard struggle with Spanish and Italian, was now superseded by French as the language of politics, art and science. The German writers of the next hundred years, with the exception of Leibniz, were insignificant by comparison with their French contemporaries.

In human terms a century and a half is a long time and, although these years were unusually peaceful, the western world in 1789 was strikingly different from that of 1648. Scarcely a single great change of this period took place inGermany or was initiated there. France rose to the heights of a Catholic absolutism reminiscent of the Roman Empire and fought for hegemony in Europe. Intellectual freedom made headway in Holland; republicans, materialists and atheists began to make themselves talked about. The English kings who had wanted to emulate the French Bourbons failed; out of the medieval estates there developed a parliament and government by parties, a cabinet and a prime minister. Locke advanced his concept of the limited, liberal state, of the social contract and of popular representation in reply to Hobbes's theory of the divine right of kings. Russia appeared in western politics and became a power on the Baltic and a major force in Europe. Britain and France fought for India and North America; hardly had the French been defeated than the British Americans began to make difficulties for their mother country. The Bank of England was set up, paper money was introduced, and speculation flourished on the Stock Exchange; financiers, wealthy members of the middle classes, journalists and demagogues exerted their influence. The steam engine and the spinning jenny were invented and the production of coal increased. Defoe, Swift and Fielding wrote satires, Voltaire wrote stories and pamphlets. But in 1750 the abbots of Salmansweiler, an abbey under direct imperial control, ruled as they had ruled in 1650 and continued to send their contingent of twelve men to the Imperial army. Nothing changed in the country of Laubach except when some reigning count added a rococo wing to his medieval castle, or another, moved by the spirit of the Enlightenment, founded an orphanage. The Empire remained unreformed and unadapted and gradually acquired the reputation of being something very old and very comic. Thus in the end the German nation could imagine that it was younger than other nations. It was youthful in so far as its antiquated, fossilized institutions were no longer suited to the nation and the age.

The break between Austria and Germany established by the Peace of Westphalia was confirmed by Austria's expansion south-eastwards and by Prince Eugène's victories over the Turks. The old Bavarian *Ostmark* became the great Danubian monarchy, an independent empire governed instinctively by ancient Roman and Byzantine traditions, the product of conquest and inheritance but still historically 'more logical' and geographically more fitting than its expansionist politicians realized. There were Germans in this Empire, but they were fewer than the Slavs, Magyars and Italians.

Less logical historically, more artificial and more violent was the state that developed in the north-east, the rise of which represents the most important German political event of the eighteenth century. Even at that time this development seemed revolutionary, though not as portentous as it was to prove in the nineteenth century.

We have spoken of the cardinal factors in German history, of Germany's position between East and West, of the Empire and of the Reformation. Prussia is no such cardinal factor; it only existed for a hundred and fifty years, from the early days of Frederick the Great to the early days of William II. There was no Prussia as an historically active factor before Frederick's Silesian wars, and long before the Prussian state disappeared formally in our own days it had been absorbed by Germany. Whatever the future may bring, Prussia will never reappear, and given the quick pace of modern life, its name will soon be forgotten. Prussia's history was brief. But its function, its unpredictable role, the unwanted opportunity assigned to it by the caprice of history, was to give the German nation its modern political shape – a task which it accomplished in its own characteristic and not very happy way. Then it disappeared.

An old French encyclopaedia describes Prussia as 'a kingdom that has grown by war and robbery'. That can be said of all kingdoms – and of most republics. Frederick the Great did the same as Louis of France or Peter of Russia or President Polk of the United States of America. But in the case of these others the meaning of their conquests becomes clear in retrospect: they gave the nation its state. The kings of France, though petty rulers at first, were always the Kings of France; the history of their aggrandizement is the history of the growth of France. The same is not true of the Prussian state, which only served its own interests. It did not exist for the German nation – the marriage between the two came very much later – nor did it exist for the good of its subjects, although it made great demands upon them. Sociologists tell us that there really is no such monstrosity as a state and that people who talk about the interests of the state mean certain social classes, bureaucrats, landowners or soldiers, the sum of whose material interests make up the 'state'. Such sensible theories do not give us the whole truth. The hapless barrack kings who created the Prussian state could have enjoyed life like any German prince as Margraves of Brandenburg; to do so they did not need Prussia. They did not work for themselves, they worked for the state and almost killed themselves with work. We must also qualify the old legend that Prussia was a Junker state. Junkers – privileged landowners – existed elsewhere, east and west of the Elbe, and elsewhere they were better off than in Prussia. They were, and remained, the masters in Mecklenburg. They were, under the patronage of the Tsar, the masters in the Russian Baltic provinces. They were the masters in Poland. They were the masters in Hanover because the Elector, who was also King of England, was away and left the aristocracy of his native country to its own devices. They were not the masters in Prussia. Only after it had destroyed the rights of both the Junkers and the cities did the state reach an unwritten compromise with the aristocracy in the reign of Frederick the Great. The nobles were allowed to continue to rule the countryside, to sit in judgement over their peasants and monopolize the senior careers in the army and the administration. As long as they allowed the King to govern. These concessions gradually reconciled the Junkers to the absolute state which later provided them with profit and protection. Nevertheless one cannot say that they made Prussia; the Prussian state made itself. Or to put it in a less mystical way: it was the creation of a few kings possessed by the fury of *raison d'état* and of the servants whom they commanded.

If Bavaria, and even Württemberg or Hanover, gave distinct groups of Germans something resembling political organization, such was not the case in Prussia; there was no Prussian ethnic group. At times the Prussian state had almost as many Polish as German subjects, at others there were as many from western and central Germany as from east of the Elbe. The number of subjects was more important than their nationality or character. Austria was later called the Danube monarchy because the great river was its lifeline. Prussia had a small share in several parallel river systems: there was a reasonably compact region east of the Elbe and some stretches of land between the Elbe and the Rhine. Prussia could just as well have spread elsewhere and there were times when it sought to lay its hands on places deep in southern Germany, on Ansbach, Sigmaringen and even the Lake of Neuchâtel. 'Other states,' wrote Mirabeau, 'have an army, in Prussia the army has a state.' He should have said: other nations have a state, in Prussia the state has a number of territories, fragments of one or more nations.

Even what is said about the army is not true. Prussia was not ruled by a brutal soldiery and by arrogant generals. Discipline among the soldiers was extreme and frightening and the officers were modestly paid and non-political. Although the army represented by far the greatest item of expenditure in the budget and although the whole administration was geared to the army, the purpose of the army was to serve the state, to maintain, to preserve and to extend it. Military considerations determined economic policy: the everlasting taxes, government monopolies and tariffs, the protection and encouragement of industry which the king used to fill his exchequer. All this was later called militarism, although *étatisme* would be a more accurate word. Romantic glorification of war did not appeal to the kings of Prussia. They were as parsimonious with war as with everything else. An artificial state surrounded by old, genuine and menacing states needed a strong army as a machine needs a motor.

As far as the eighteenth century is concerned we shall do well to forget the old idea of 'reactionary' Prussia. In those days Prussia was looked upon not as reactionary but as progressive and enlightened. It was thought to be well ruled because it was ruled in the interest of the state by a strict professional king and a reliable, professional bureaucracy. Its administration was rational, logical and honest, its justice prompt and impartial, approaching what was later called the reign of law. This picture of a progressive sensible Prussia, almost republican despite its absolute monarchy, survived in France even after Frederick's death and only gradually gave place to another in the nineteenth century.

The focal point of all pro-Prussian sympathies was the monarch who had managed to transform some fragments of north German territory into a great power on which the peace of Europe depended. Frederick astonished the world and kept it in suspense, and this people liked. The Empire was *gemütlich* and, from a political point of view, almost comic. Prussia was not *gemütlich* but its king was taken seriously. His alliance with Britain brought provincial, neglected Germany back into world politics. His seven-year struggle with the three greatest military powers earned him the admiration of even those Germans – they were in the majority – for whom the centre of the nation was still Vienna and not Berlin, which to them was a long way away, anti-imperial, new and foreign. Moreover Frederick was not only a soldier and man of action but also a 'philosopher' and man of letters – an unheard-of combination. He was tolerant and permitted freedom of thought. He permitted it in the religious and metaphysical sphere, which did not interest him, but not in politics. This fact tended to be disregarded because even the French were interested not in political but in philosophical freedom – and in philosophical, strong, efficient, absolute government, which Frederick appeared to provide. Learned and would-be learned men from all over the world made the pilgrimage to visit him.

What a great man, curious, lovable and repulsive! The founder of Prussian Germany spoke and wrote poetry in French and mocked the German way of life. King by the grace of God but without a religion, philanthropist and misanthropist, free-thinker and despot, citizen-King and protector of the Junkers, still the idol of the nationalists many years later, by nature a cold, unhappy cynic who had no contact with the people, cultured, musical, yet superstitious, stubborn and morose – that is how Frederick II appears in retrospect and how he stands at the centre of Prussian–German history. His legend was bad for the Germans because it first gave them the idea that great men must perform great deeds, that the magician can do what he likes, and that there is no need to pay attention to his methods provided ne continues to bring success.

The division of Poland to which Frederick agreed in the seventies was more than a German affair. It was an audacious, shameless piece of east European politics, a division of spoils between three independent powers, Prussia, Austria and Russia. But it was approved by left-wing intellectuals like Voltaire and Mirabeau because the Polish peasants had suffered wretchedly under their own masters and would be much better ruled by the enlightened King of Prussia.

Mirabeau the younger liked the whole German federal system and sang its praises in the last volume of his work on the Prussian monarchy. In his view a number of interrelated small states was preferable to a great single, centralized state. A nation organized on those lines had no capital or artistic centre, but this loss, if it were a loss, was counterbalanced by the wealth and variety of numerous small competing centres. There was freedom in Germany because what could not be said or done in one state could always be said or done in another; emigration to a new home never involved more than a day's journey. The German princes kept an eye on each other, many of them were excellent rulers and only a small minority actually did harm. They vied witn each other to promote learning and to train a good civil service.

It is impossible to make serious comparisons between one age and another. We are the children of our time, and to say, as we sometimes do, that we would rather have lived in another century is empty talk. Every age has its fears and privations as well as its achievements and pleasures, the enjoyment of which is rarely distributed justly. Those of our contemporaries who would like to have lived in the eighteenth century see themselves as sons of Frankfurt patricians or as Austrian counts and patrons of Mozart, not as persecuted free-thinkers languishing in the gaols of the duke of Württemberg or as serfs in Mecklenburg. But it is safe to say that whereas at the time of the Thirty Years War it was a misfortune to have been born a German, generally speaking this was no longer true a hundred years later. Although the political system was still what had emerged from the treaties of Westphalia, there was a new spirit transcending the old forms where it could not fill them with new life; and much of the literature and architecture of the times conveys a feeling of contentment.

Mirabeau was probably right in thinking that some of the German rulers were excellent. Baden, Brunswick, Weimar and Dessau had rulers who were abreast of the Enlightenment, which they tried to apply for the welfare of their subjects; they did not merely pay lip-service to it like Catherine the Great. Alongside these there still existed some ugly caricatures of French absolutism. In retrospect it is easy to reject a form of government whose success depended so much on the accident of personality. But every period has its own ideas and the ideal of the later eighteenth century was good government, not democratic government as an end in itself, nor even government safeguarded by democracy. Gradually the feeling grew that the days of the prince-bishoprics, that strangest form of government of the old Empire, were numbered – but not because they lacked democratic foundation. If anything, the fact that the prince-bishop was elected and that the cathedral chapter had certain rights made the ecclesiastical territories a little more democratic than the hereditary states. They were considered out-of-date because they belonged to the Church and the trend of the age was rationalistic and secular; hence the fate which befell them was aptly described as secularization. The functions of the ruler-priests were to be taken over not by the 'people' but by bigger and more rationally organized monarchies.

The most radical political theorist of the seventeen eighties was certainly no democrat, nor even a representative of the aspiring bourgeoisie, but the elected 'Roman' emperor, the ruler of the Austrian hereditary lands, Joseph II of the House of Habsburg-Lorraine. This talented fanatic did more in the way of levelling, centralizing and rationalizing than would have occurred to the most progressive professor. He tried to transform the Church into an obedient state institution, looted the monasteries, suppressed 'useless' orders, and his Prime Minister, if not he himself, made a laughing stock of the Pope during his desperate visit to Vienna. He rejected all coronation ceremonies as antiquated nonsense and presented himself to his peoples as the industrious head of a bureaucracy which was clearing away the remains of the old corporate institutions. He rode roughshod over national differences and intervened benevolently in the lives and deaths of his subjects. The Emperor accepted the idea of freedom or spiritual tolerance to the extent that he abandoned for a time all control of books – an act which he came to regret. On the whole, however, freedom was confined to the kind of discussion which did not affect his own monopoly of power. He did not for one moment doubt that he and his heirs would remain masters of the great, reorganized bureaucracy which worked for the good of all his subjects.

Aufklärung, the German word for enlightenment made famous by Immanuel Kant, was later also used in other languages to describe a basic spiritual trend of the eighteenth century. The Germans now took a leading part in a supra-national, western intellectual movement. They did not begin it; enlightenment was already at work in the English revolution and in the French opposition to Louis XIV. Nothing in history really starts at one particular moment; the spirit of the enlightenment can be traced back to the Renaissance and to rebellious scholars in the Middle Ages. But by the second half of the eighteenth century enlightenment had become the triumphant, sometimes the reigning, philosophy.

Enlightenment, whatever else it meant, signified active freedom of ideas, criticism of tradition and authority – benevolent criticism for creative and not for destructive purposes. Existing values were brought before the tribunal of reason which either supported the requirements of expediency, the interests and passions of the present against the dead weight of the past, or was confident of its ability to recognize eternal commands of God or of Nature. These two attitudes existed in Germany; the second, and better of the two, was the more prevalent. Yet they lacked the backing of a self-assured middle class. No one doubted that John Locke spoke for the old oligarchy and the new English upper middle classes. The demands of the Third Estate in France were the product of a strong, prosperous bourgeoisie. By comparison the German middle class was weak; the proudest cities, Nuremberg and Augsburg, seemed like shadows of their glorious past. The German enlightenment did not have its roots in any particular class. The cause of this is to be found more in the character of the middle class with its deep respect for authority and in the egotistical sense of self-preservation of the patriciate than in economic backwardness. Anyway the enlightenment did not become a movement of political protest as in France. Its representatives were senior civil servants and ministers close to the rulers, and even, as we have seen, some of the rulers themselves; or they were writers, poets, publishers of journals in Berlin or Göttingen, and professors. The first group was interested mainly in the problems of improved administration and not in the constitution or the political rights of the citizen. The second indulged in great scientific, moral and metaphysical speculations but took care not to make political demands. The most outstanding of them, Immanuel Kant, remained an obedient subject of the King of Prussia.

Never in recent times has Germany been in such complete harmony with the best qualities of its western neighbours or reached such heights of European genius as in the person of this unique man. In vain has he been presented as a purely German phenomenon by stressing for example the 'Prussian' character of the somewhat austere theory of duty which he advanced in his old age. In vain has he been presented as an un-German cosmopolitan, the last in a line of an English philosophical tradition, whose family was of Scottish origin. He was certainly cosmopolitan because his concern was with man. Contemptuously he pushed aside the novel 'appeal of fools in Germany to show national pride'. He who himself became such a powerful influence was open to foreign ideas, French – those of Rousseau – as well as English. Philosophy and science know no political frontiers. But he was also German without being aggressive about it. His simple, beautiful language was German, as were his old-fashioned politeness and reticence and also his passionate interest in what was happening abroad, in the reforms of Joseph II, in the American and then in the French Revolution.

Kant was no optimist. He took mankind and its history very

seriously and had a lofty conception of man's tasks and of the demands made on him. But he did not expect too much, least of all from politicians. He knew much more than John Locke about the future dangers springing from the wickedness of the human heart and from technical progress uncontrolled by a sense of truth and justice. He knew this not because he was born later but because he had a more incisive mind and a more acute sense of observation. Kant thought that learning had made man cunning but that he lacked morals to make him civilized; man was always ready to fight, but not for justice. Even if he went to war for a just cause it soon developed into an unjust one. It was better to go to war honestly for purposes of conquest than for punitive reasons. Crusades for justice logically pursued must end with internecine destruction 'in the universal graveyard of mankind'. Such an end was probable anyway if one remembered how much progress military science had made and would certainly continue to make: a hell of evils, a barbaric destruction of civilization by civilization itself. Kant refused, however, to believe in such an end. It was impossible to believe something that was an insult to all religion and to the whole purpose of human existence. Man was free to escape self-destruction and to raise himself to a truly moral, truly republican state. It was possible that he might be helped by Nature herself, by the hard facts that were not concerned with morals. Perhaps Nature was using human injustice and aggressiveness to accomplish what could not be accomplished in the modern military state: the free development of all man's dormant talents, the establishment of eternal peace. Had Nature not used these forces to create the state towards which the individual savage adopted the same attitude as the state would one day adopt towards world federation? People who started political intrigues were unaware of this; perhaps the purpose of all wars was the final end of such intrigues and eternal peace. The turning point would come at the moment of greatest distress and extreme danger. This might take some time yet, but man had no need to save time. The individual could never reach the goal of mankind; perhaps the species might, or at any rate it could get closer to it. Meanwhile one ought at least to acquaint nations with the idea and write history 'with world citizenship in mind' because without awareness of a common past and a common task there could be no community of interest in the present. Kant was a hard-headed naturalist; no wickedness or stupidity, nothing that happened in life surprised him. He could be sarcastic like Voltaire and realistic like Hobbes, but he was less dangerously one-sided than either. In spite of the most bitter knowledge he could be as enthusiastic as Rousseau or Schiller. A veil of shyness concealed faith, charity and hope. Many pronouncements made since his day have become stale but Kant's speculations about history, politics and the position of man as a political animal are as alive today as they were almost two hundred years ago.

Our reflections have reached the moment in time when we must take up the story in greater detail. 'Modern' can mean many things. To us the Germany of the Emperor William II appears old-fashioned and far away. But some readers will still have known it and William died only in 1941. Anglo-Saxon historians date the beginning of modern history from the discovery of America and the early sixteenth century. German historians usually start with the French Revolution. There are even some writers who think that modern history ended a short while ago and that we are now living in the 'post-modern' age. Such classifications are misleading; they serve practical purposes and disappear with them.

However, the period of the French Revolution and perhaps even more the years immediately preceding it can be called 'modern' in two senses. From our point of view because we have ever since been a prey to conflicts, hopes and fears which emerged at that time. Some of the things that existed then are still 'topical' today, such as the philosophy of Immanuel Kant. But the men of the late eighteenth century were modern also in the sense that they regarded themselves as modern, as different from everything in the past. They were hopeful, even exuberant, and sure of their cause. They despised the dark past, the Middle Ages, which even Kant called an 'incomprehensible aberration of the human mind'; nor did they think highly of their own political institutions. For the first time in history everything would now be sensibly arranged and this arrangement would last.

In Germany the change was one of attitudes far more than of institutions. The economic life of the country at the end of the century does not seem very different from what it had been at the beginning. Cities were small and had not expanded for centuries, if they had not actually shrunk in size. The vast majority of the population continued to earn its living by agriculture and town and country continued to be closely linked. Traffic continued to be slow and small in volume, roads were few and forests large. Part of the aristocracy and some merchants in Hamburg or Frankfurt were rich; bourgeois and officials lived in respectable modesty; the peasants produced almost everything needed for life. Industry as the word came to be understood was in its infancy. But the spiritual life of a nation is more spontaneous, freer, and its sources are more mysterious than certain writers are willing to admit. It was not the growing prosperity of the middle class which inspired Friedrich Schiller to write *Die Räuber* or *Kabale und Liebe*, but the restless spirit of the age and Schiller's own genius. What would happen now, what would the future bring?

Looked at from the seventeen-eighties the future did not present any insoluble problems, no terrible wars, no venomous religious struggles, no last stand by the defeated ruling classes, least of all a rebellion of Germany against Europe. Never was Germany more European and popular, never was there more hopeful good will and less fear. Of course another diplomatic crisis was imminent, but that was nothing unusual. The Turkish Empire in the Balkans seemed ripe for dissolution. Two eastern powers, Austria and Russia, were about to become its heirs, partitioning it after the Polish example and fighting over it. The same fate could be prophesied for the sad remains of the Polish elective monarchy. And what would become of the German Empire, that galaxy of imperial knights and imperial cities, of abbeys, bishoprics, margraves and landgraves, that baroque system which was clearly no longer suited to the age but which would not die? Here too the most likely solution seemed the application of the new system of partition, with the two great German, or semi-German, powers acting as executors. Joseph II had wanted to acquire Bavaria by barter but his attempts had been foiled by the King of Prussia acting as protector of the German princes. Perhaps the King's successor could be paid off with a comparable gain in the north? How would France which had been forced to swallow the partition of Poland, react to a violent solution of Germany's domestic problems? How would England react to a Russian drive for Constantinople? These were the questions which diplomats asked themselves pessimistically. Such chaos had not threatened since the Thirty Years War. But it would be confined to the diplomatic and military spheres which, according to eighteenth century conceptions, affected only a few.

The crisis did in fact come in the fourth year after the death of the great Frederick. But, as so often happens, it came from a direction and in a way which no one had expected.

Part Two
Stormy Beginning (1789–1815)

At the beginning of modern German history lie twenty-five restless years.

*Das Jahrhundert ist im Sturm geschieden
Und das neue öffnet sich mit Mord . . .**

was Schiller's comment on the turn of the century. Still, even then
most Germans probably tilled the land as they always had and
only occasionally looked up from the plough when a neighbour
told them that they were no longer citizens of Fürstenberg but of
Baden, or that the Emperor Napoleon had set out for Russia with
an army the like of which had never been seen before. Young
noblemen made their grand tour, their educational journey to
France and Italy, just as in peace time. In those days only a few
people were completely caught up in political events. The great
majority was only partially affected, by being compelled to do
military service, by economic changes, blockade and inflation, or
by the development of new industries. But there was much unrest
and profound changes took place. During the first quarter of the
century the nation certainly did not lack creativeness; in philosophy, literature and poetry it possessed a greater wealth of genius
and talent than ever before or since. Nevertheless Germany was
essentially passive during the great political crisis of the Revolution and the Napoleonic period. It watched neighbouring nations,
Frenchmen and Britons, fight a prolonged duel with unprecedented energy and bitterness, and was forced to pay a good part
of the costs which should not have been its concern. Things
happened to Germany, but they were done to it by others. The

* The century went out in a storm and the new one opens with murder . . .

country adapted itself, not without a sense of constructiveness in southern Germany, not without creative genius in Prussia after 1807, not without diplomatic elegance in Austria. But it was only a process of adaptation, voluntary or compulsory, to great happenings elsewhere. The French Revolution was hot, the German cold. Traditions were abandoned, political frontiers, laws and living beings shaken up, but only in the way in which eighteenth century oligarchy might have done; there were no public meetings, no storming of Bastilles and no guillotines. The storm blew elsewhere, Germany only felt its effects. As a result the Germans had in years to come no wish to look back and be proud of the great political and social transformation that occurred at the beginning of the nineteenth century; they saw it as a time of shame, however lasting or positive its achievements. The Germans became active – against France – only during the last act of the long revolutionary drama, in 1813. Even then they did not play a really glorious role comparable with that of the British or the Russians. Though the 'War of Liberation' was a notable effort on the part of the Germans it was not the popular uprising that contemporary, and even more later, imagination wanted to make of it.

It was not in 1813–14 that Germany took revenge for its passivity during the Napoleonic drama. The real reaction to that experience came later, in the second half of the century. What psychologists teach about the individual also applies to the nation: it can harbour old, unpleasant memories, transform them in strange ways and derive aggressive energies from them.

1. Germany and the French Revolution

The incidents which had begun to alarm the French kingdom in the spring of 1789 were followed with the greatest interest east of the Rhine. After the autumn they were called 'the revolution in France', a name which this curious sequence of events has kept, and which we still use to describe various basically distinct things.

Originally no one had thought of 'revolution'. The aim of the French rulers was to make use of the ancient institution of the Estates General for moderate reforms. Not one of the elected representatives came to Versailles thinking of violent change. But soon the world heard of the transformation of the assemblies of the three Estates into a single national assembly; of the revolt of the city of Paris; of the compulsory move of the King from his fairy castle in the country to the heart of the capital frighteningly teeming with democrats; of the great, enthusiastic or forced renunciations of the two privileged classes, the clergy and the aristocracy. Then things quietened down. For a time it seemed as though it might be possible to set up in the Old World a grandly conceived constitutional state parallel to the one recently established in the New World. A national state, indivisible but sensibly divided into small administrative units, in which there was equality for all before the law, in which the King as hereditary president ruled through ministers responsible to parliament, in which the church was a state institution, in which everybody contributed according to his means to cover public expenditure and in which all careers were open to everyone. A state with a peaceful foreign policy – with such a lofty conception of the dignity of one's own people how could one wish to enslave others? – in which speech, scholarship and religion were free and everything was transfused by the spirit of civic virtue and charity.

But men fail most easily when they are too enthusiastic. The idea is spoilt by its exponents, who are creatures of flesh and blood and egoism. Excess produces reactions against which it in turn reacts, assuming even more extreme forms. The clash of many mixed and changeable aims produces the most unpredictable situations, as it did in France at the beginning of the seventeen nineties. The winds blowing through the country became a hurricane destroying human beings and things. Half-hearted co-operation and secret resistance by the *ancien régime* hastened the revolution. The greatest politicians quickly exhausted themselves. Inexperienced theorists tried their hand at that most difficult of all games – playing with power in times of revolution. The most vocal doctrinaires in Paris became more uncompromising and more defiant. After two and a half years the King was still on his throne, a figure of misery, a prisoner, pushed about, looking for help from beyond his frontiers but fearing it; the party in power openly wanted war with traditional Europe.

The Revolution had long ceased to be an internal French affair and had become an adventure in which the rest of Europe had to take part; certainly the nation that lived next to the French, and in certain regions – in Alsace and Lorraine – with the French. By 1792 the revolutionary doctrine had developed into a declaration of war on the whole of old Europe, its monarchs, its privileged classes, its churches, and even those of its states that were baroque creations established by historical accident and held together by dynasties instead of being republican nation-states. Europe's internal unity showed itself at that time, as it has often done since then. The drive of the democratic revolution could not stop at paper frontiers; countless self-appointed propagandists made sure that it would not.

There was no lack of mutual provocation: French emigrants were allowed to pursue their activities on German soil; German property was confiscated in France. The revolution became a war desired finally by both sides, the rulers of France and traditional Europe. But once a great war has come it follows its own law, becoming an end in itself instead of a means, a dominating force which changes all those involved.

The surprising thing now happened: France was victorious. An army of former royal troops and revolutionary volunteers pushed back the Prussians and Austrians. Then the French went over to the attack and a few months later they controlled the Rhineland and Belgium. There followed declarations of war on Britain, Spain and Holland, together with an appeal by the French National Convention to the peoples of the world to rise against their rulers and the promise of help if they did so. Sensationally unexpected victories encouraged the revolutionary rulers to further annexations. Occasional defeats precipitated developments in France. War was confused with civil war; French peasants allied themselves with the King of England, and while French towns were reduced to rubble on the orders of the rulers in Paris, this suffering land made tremendous efforts abroad. Under the dictatorship of a Committee of Public Safety France kept the European alliance in check. The minor German potentates, ecclesiastical princes and secular rulers, thronged – dispossessed – into the interior of the Empire. Gradually the German nation realized that something had happened that could not be undone, at least not the destruction, and that for better or worse Germany was involved.

The scholars, poets and writers who had gradually emerged in Germany saw their intellectual ability to assimilate experiences put to the test. They owed it to themselves and to their public to make judgements, but the situation they had to judge remained fluid, producing ever greater surprises and disappointments.

Among the older generation it was Immanuel Kant who clung most loyally to his belief in the republic as the only true form of government. In an article entitled *Über den Gemeinspruch: ' Das mag in der Theorie richtig sein, taugt aber nichts für die Praxis'* *
he showed that the right theory rightly used was undoubtedly practical too. If republicanism, the form of government in which people decided their own fate, was good in theory it must also be good in practice. Disappointing experiences proved nothing except that one had made a false start. 'There can be nothing more damaging and less worthy of a philosopher,' he had written earlier, 'than vulgar reference to experience, since there would be no sad experiences if one behaved in accordance with the correct theory at the right time, and if crude notions, for the very reason that they were taken from experience, had not thwarted everything.' What interested him in the revolution, he now emphasized, were not the actions of the leaders but the idealism of the masses, which had proved, in spite of everything, that there was a desire for good in man. How else to explain the enthusiasm with which thousands of young Frenchmen had sacrificed themselves for freedom and equality? Against that individual misdeeds mattered

* Concerning the popular saying: 'It may be right in theory but is useless in practice'.

little. Bad people were found under other forms of government but not the patriotism which the French had shown during the revolutionary war. Those were Kant's views. Others, more cautious, were never more than interested spectators like Wieland and Goethe, or turned away with contempt after the first waves of democratic terror had hit Paris.

The young, the unsettled, were overwhelmed by what they read in the papers. Some pursued the revolution to Paris, like Friedrich Georg Foerster, who died there deeply disappointed. To others the revolution came as it did in Coblenz to Joseph Görres, who rejoiced and mocked at the collapse of the old system of government. In his periodical *Rotes Blatt*, he announced the sale of 'three electors' caps of tanned buffalo-hide together with lead-filled crosiers, furnished with daggers and encircled by artificial snakes. The eye of God mounted on top is blind. – Two bishops' mitres, richly trimmed with tinsel, somewhat stained by cold sweat, but otherwise in good condition; hence very useful as red caps on trees of liberty. – A ducal hare skin hat, embellished with cocks' feathers, trimmed with a precious stone distilled by a clever alchemist from the tears of ten thousand widows and orphans . . . A barn-full of patents of nobility, written on asses' skin, but badly moth-eaten in parts and giving out a strange smell of decay . . .' Even distant onlookers like Hegel, then a theological student in Tübingen, or the newly appointed civil servant Friedrich Gentz in Berlin, were affected for life by this experience. Whether they ceased to support the revolution and became its enemies, nationalists instead of cosmopolitans, whether they escaped into the ivory tower of a political philosophy or took up ingeniously thought-out, conciliatory positions avoiding the controversial issues of the day – they never quite succeeded in freeing themselves from their early experiences.

What is true of those who were young in the seventeen nineties is probably true also of the nation as a whole. In some sense Germany itself was young, impressionable and receptive in those days. The events of the French Revolution left an indelible mark on German affairs and German thought.

2. Reorganization from Above

The war of the German powers against France, begun in 1792, continued with short intervals until 1807. There then followed five years of peace – the real 'Period of the Empire' – a peace which, on closer inspection, was and could be no peace. The war was a duel between Britain and France over traditional problems, the European balance of power, the Dutch coast and control of the Mediterranean and the Near East. Britain, which ruled the seas but was weak on land, found allies on the Continent who joined in the struggle now and again, partly in the interest of their own security, as they saw it, and party to seize opportunities and to reap unfair gains. They were all against France, which had learnt in the Revolution a new strategy of mass armies, long fronts, annihilating blows and psychological warfare, but which was tempted by military superiority into making intolerable claims and conquests. At the same time, however, they were against each other, and did not trust each other; neither Prussia and Austria nor Austria and Russia trusted each other, while the small German states trusted neither Austria nor Prussia. They were all therefore persuaded once or more than once to leave the Grand Alliance and to come to terms with the enemy, France. Prussia did this as early as 1795 and gained ten years of apparently advantageous neutrality, which in the end proved all the more disastrous. Austria did the same in 1797, in 1801 and again in 1805. Russia came to terms with France in 1807. The small German states did so whenever there was an opportunity or they were forced to, which in their case amounted to the same thing. This willingness to desert, this lack of solidarity, was one of the sources of French superiority; thus when in the summer of 1813 all the European powers came together in a reasonably firm alliance for the first time, France could not hold its over-extended lines in Germany, Italy and Spain for as much as three months.

Even fifteen years earlier the French front had been far too extensive. The situation had not been created by General Bonaparte; he had inherited it when he became dictator and was forced by the dangerous, extreme character of this heritage to go further still. It was impossible to stabilize the situation as it was, with the Netherlands French, the Rhineland French and Switzerland, Italy and Rome all ruled in one way or another by France. Bonaparte went on because he could not stop where he was and because the others, Britain in particular, would not allow him to stop there. He wished for peace and an opportunity to strengthen and enjoy his acquisitions, and was not conscious of lightly starting wars; he always regarded himself as being attacked, provoked and coerced. But when he made peace it was no more than an armistice; either he caused new unrest by ruthlessly sharing his spoils with his enemy, as he did with Austria in Italy as early as 1797, or he imposed conditions which the vanquished were forced to accept for the moment but would certainly evade in the long run.

The armistice periods after the Peace of Lunéville in 1801, the Peace of Pressburg in 1805 and the Peace of Tilsit in 1807 were intervals of political experiment and domestic change which were mostly in line with Bonaparte's ideas; even where reforms were carried out without his help and were secretly aimed against him, they were necessarily influenced by France. Bonaparte or, as he was called after 1804, the Emperor Napoleon, therefore played as central a role in German history as in that of France. The shape of Germany's political, legal and administrative life, which was preserved through the nineteenth century and in many cases until well into the twentieth, was moulded under his spell. Napoleon also gave the Germans new notions of politics, the state, power, war, success and greatness; they accepted these. If it were possible to measure such things at all one might be tempted to claim that the Napoleonic myth later flourished more strongly in Germany and was more effective there than in France. At the end the French saw the Emperor as the loser – an illustrious menace that had been disposed of. For at least a century the Germans thrived on greater hatred of Napoleon and more glowing admiration for him.

Napoleon became curiously deeply involved in German affairs, partly as a result of his own dreams and party because somehow

Germany and France have always been deeply involved with one another. An Italian by birth, he got on well with the Italians; he flattered their patriotism and ruled them either directly as King of Italy or through his family. Spain was foreign to him; his attempt to intervene in the life of the Spanish people proved a bad mistake. With Russia he grandly sought to divide Europe and those parts of the Near East that belonged to Europe. In the end he tried to impose his will on Russia by war, probably without knowing how he would have used a victory in 1812. Because Russia was more alien to him even than Spain he was tempted into his mad march to Moscow. His influence on Russian history has been small; what had a lasting influence was not the fact that Napoleon reached Moscow but that the Russians paid him a return visit in Paris, and became the leading continental power. Britain with its well-established, free political life was also foreign to him. Britain remained almost untouched by the French Revolution and afterwards as before went its own way which had been confirmed rather than called in question by the long, victorious duel with 'Boney'. Napoleon felt less at ease with the Germans than with the Italians, but preferred them to the Spaniards and understood them better than the Russians or the British. He respected the Germans but found them weak and malleable in politics; the vision of the 'Empire', its name and its baroque decrepitude, lured him deep into the country where many glittering courts flattered his snobbishness. The old Empire was dissolved on his orders but he immediately created a substitute, the Confederation of the Rhine; and as he ruled on the Rhine and in Italy he could see himself as the true and mighty heir of the medieval Reich, or better still – as his capital lay in Frankish country – as the new Charlemagne. This was a misunderstanding. Nineteenth-century Europe did not want a supranational 'empire' but nation-states – a development greatly accelerated by the imperial adventure.

In 1801 Austria, and with it the Empire, finally recognized the French Republic and all its conquests in the Rhineland and the Netherlands. The need now arose to compensate those German princes and landowners who had lost their possessions west of the

Rhine. This became the occasion for a basic reorganization of the Reich. The ecclesiastical states, the electorates, the prince-bishoprics and the imperial abbeys and monasteries were secularized. The imperial cities disappeared, and with them – after a new war and a new defeat of Austria in 1806 – a Milky Way of imperial princes, counts and knights. The operation was called 'mediatization' because these curiosities which had been under direct imperial control were now incorporated into the larger states of the Empire; but as the Empire itself ceased to exist in 1806 the term 'mediatization' soon lost its meaning. The victims of 'mediatization' were allowed, as privileged subjects, to remain in their castles, where many of their descendants still live today. The victims of 'secularization' were made to leave their monasteries, which either went to ruin or became private property. Churches were closed and looted, works of art were sold at give-away prices or gathered together in local museums. The spirit of the age was irreligious and anti-clerical; often the number of monks expelled from the monasteries was pathetically small. But if decline begins at the zenith recovery starts at the nadir. In the long run the Catholic Church benefited from the loss at the beginning of the century which transformed it from a rich but often very worldly institution into an impoverished one. The strange clearance sale, formally an internal German affair, was really controlled from Paris. The result was the German states as we have come to know them, and as with a few changes they still exist today: Bavaria, Württemberg, Baden, Hesse.

The programme, looked at through Napoleon's eyes, had much to be said for it. Something had to be done with Germany; the rotten feudalism of the Reich was anyway incapable of holding out against the new century – a truth of which politically conscious Germans had long been aware. But what at one time had seemed the probable solution, a partition of the German states between Austria and Prussia, was contrary to French policy; even more was the establishment of a German nation-state. As yet the pseudo-emperor could rule southern and western Germany, directly, as he ruled Italy. A small number of German monarchies, artificial enough to be weak, but solid and dignified enough to satisfy German pride, planets around the imperial sun – that was the plan, and given the situation it was the best possible one. The choice of salvaged dynasties was not inept. In view of the past it was sensible that Bavaria should emerge from the liquidation of the Empire as the greatest of what were later called the *Mittelstaaten*, and even Württemberg, Baden and Hesse had more historical *raisons d'être* than the principalities of Hohenlohe, Fürstenberg or Leiningen which were now under the administration of their more fortunate neighbours. Yet some frontiers were just drawn arbitrarily; there was no need to amalgamate the Palatinate on the right bank of the Rhine with Baden, or Franconia with Bavaria. If for a long time the link between the German states and their ethnic origins had been slight, this legendary character of theirs now vanished completely. Dialects, districts, creeds and historical traditions were intermingled in the new states which could not claim to be anything more than the fulfilment of an abstract political principle.

Some things that owe their existence to accident and arbitrary action stand the test. The German states established by Napoleon stood the test in several ways in the nineteenth century: as administrative units, as training grounds for governments and for parliamentarianism, and as intellectual centres. Yet they were not genuine states in the sense that Switzerland or Holland are. Not one of them ever fought for its existence, not one of them ever dared to go its own way in a crisis. The Bavaria of the Thirty Years War was a genuine, if somewhat limited, political force manoeuvring with caution and deadly earnest between the European powers. After Napoleon, enlarged by countless splinters from the Empire, it was a fair-weather state; it never again dared to venture into a storm or to put itself to the test. It has remained thus to our day.

Napoleon later said that the Germans had been readier for a nation-wide organization than any other European people and that any strong man who felt so inclined could have placed himself at the head of thirty million Germans. It is very understandable that he himself did not want to be this strong man. It was the French tradition to play off the German princes against the

'Empire' or, alternatively, to support the Empire against the most powerful principality. It was also in the dictator's personal interest to surround himself with satellites whose court ceremonial he could imitate as they could imitate his; a procedure which gave the new imperial position a more solid foundation. The paradoxical situation in which Napoleon found himself was that France, which had staged a great national revolution and wanted to set an example for other countries, once it had become an Empire had no use for national revolutions in other countries. But the pseudo-emperor, fumbling for conservative protection and anxious to make his peace with Europe, had no use for real monarchs either. The German princes served his purpose; they appeared to be genuine, legitimate rulers, they bore ancient names, but they were his creatures, who reigned over artificial states and who had all forfeited their claim to be legitimate rulers by their spoliations. Napoleon's dilemma was that in an emergency he could not rely on those who were most useful to him just because they were useful to him in their existing state. Bavaria and Württemberg and Baden, artificial creations, fair-weather states, supported him as long as he brought fair weather. They betrayed him with alacrity, and had no alternative but to betray him, as soon as the 'sun of Austerlitz' ceased to shine.

Napoleon liked to see himself as the man who quelled great storms and settled great historical issues as he chose. But at the turn of the eighteenth century there was no storm in Germany strong enough to sweep away all the rubbish of the past - as patriots of the stature of Freiherr vom Stein were to learn. What happened between 1801 and 1806 was roughly what had already been in the air at the time of Frederick and Joseph: another application of the 'system of partition', a deal between the great princes at the expense of the weak ones. France's newly acquired superiority merely ensured that the main beneficiaries were not, as in the partition of Poland, the two Great Powers, Prussia and Austria, but the new *Mittelstaaten*.

When in 1805 Austria and Russia made what for the time being was the last attempt to check the expansion of the Bonapartist Empire, motivated in equal measure by domestic conflict, recklessness and fear, easy opportunity and serious threat, the German Reich no longer existed. The armies of the new central German states fought for France. Their rulers renounced their imperial allegiance and assumed the title of King or Grand Duke. This was sensible enough as they could hardly remain Electors when there were no more Roman emperors to elect. But these new kings were even less independent than their predecessors had been. They now depended on the ever-watchful, energetic, clever, merciless Emperor in Paris. No sooner had they proclaimed their independence than they had to take part in proclaiming something else: the foundation of the 'Confederation of the Rhine', a permanent alliance of German states under Napoleon's protection. In practice their armies became units of the great French army; their diplomacy was confined to rivalry for the dictator's favour and to efforts to strengthen their ties with him by family bonds, through which they hoped to acquire still more land, still further illusionary gains in the event of new peace treaties.

The Confederation of the Rhine was intended to be the old Empire without the German Great Powers. Napoleon, always anxious to cloak his rootless power with the magic of age, vainly used various institutions and ceremonies to stress this continuity. How in the long run could Germany and Italy allow themselves to be ruled from Paris? How could post-revolutionary, bourgeois Europe believe in Charlemagne's imperial mantle which a foreign general, a product of the Revolution, claimed to be wearing? The great realist was also a great dreamer. He mistook passing opportunities and advantages for final achievements, confused the tinsel with which he covered the craziest by-products of the war with real gold, and became increasingly entangled in romantic dreams.

On the other side the inevitable happened, not without tragic dignity. The last 'Roman Emperor', Francis III, proclaimed the dissolution of the Empire, released all his former vassals from their obligations and took the title of 'Emperor of Austria', created in 1804. In his *Annalen*, a brief chronological autobiography, Goethe says drily:

'Meanwhile the Confederation of the Rhine had been set up and its consequences were easy to predict; on the way home we read in the newspapers that the German Empire had been dissolved.' More detached still is the spirit of the entries in his diary for 6 and 7 August 1806:

Seven o'clock in the evening at Hof. Announcement of the proclamation of the Rhenish Confederation and the French Protectorate. Reflections and discussions. Good dinner . . . Quarrel between servant and coachman on the box which excited us more than the dissolution of the Roman Empire.

This was Goethe's general attitude. He had little faith in politics on a big scale and believed only in small, observable spheres of life; to him the burning-down of a farm was more real than the collapse of an 'Empire'. But the historical situation probably contributed to Goethe's indifference. Sentimentalists and students of antiquity might have been moved by the formal end of the 'Roman Empire', but it brought nothing new. Secularization and 'mediatization' had rendered the dead institution a last service, because the ecclesiastical states and imperial cities which vanished in the process had been its only surviving dependencies. For intelligent people the whole institution had long been a joke.

> *Das liebe Heilge Römische Reich,*
> *wie hält's nur noch zusammen?**

For centuries it had not held together for any serious purpose. On the other hand the establishment of the Confederation of the Rhine made it clear that the German states, apart from Austria and Prussia, would have to continue to exist together in some form; and the Confederation of the Rhine was followed less than nine years after the dissolution of the Empire by the 'German Confederation'. To draw a modern parallel one might say that the German Confederation was to the old Empire as the United Nations is to the League of Nations, the same thing only a little more effectively organized. Therefore closer inspection shows that the end of the Holy Roman Empire was not the decisive

*The dear old Holy Roman Empire, how on earth does it still hold together?

event which it was later claimed to be. However, purely symbolical factors also play a part in history, and the memory of past imperial glory later did things to the German spirit that the Empire had been unable to do while it was still a pathetic reality at the Diet of Ratisbon. The end of the Empire was associated with the disappearance of old forms and ways of life. It became the symbol for the end of the good old times and the beginning of new ones.

A later generation of nationalistic historians cursed the 'princes' revolution' of the Napoleonic era as an arbitrary, soulless, megalomaniacal, treasonable enterprise imposed by foreign rule; but with the same breath they praised it as progress towards unity and modernity. There is something to be said for both points of view.

Speaking generally, there are three spheres in which the French Revolution affected Germany. The Rhineland was part of France for twenty years and was reformed directly from Paris with firmness and intelligence. The states of the Rhenish Confederation imitated France, though not without adding some local peculiarities. Napoleon left his satellites considerable freedom in the choice of means, provided there was no conflict with his own interests. In Prussia one cannot really speak of imitation, though the French influence was strong. Here the reforms were also an independent, imaginative reaction against the misery of the defeat which necessitated them. In this way the Prussian state proved that it really existed, in spite of all its contradictions and artificialities. It attracted ideas and their originators, men of enthusiasm and ability who came to the rescue from different parts of Germany.

In Cologne, Bonn, Mainz, Speyer and Trier the French ruled, and ruled well. They were not popular, but even the best foreign rulers rarely are. They were not popular as they were in Milan, but they were not hated as they were in Madrid. Sensible, well-organized administrative units replaced outmoded imperial cities, minute feudal states and theocratic principalities. Napoleon's government was both absolute and liberal. Absolute because orders came from above, because the immense bureaucratic machinery was directed by the Emperor and his ministers; liberal because everybody was equal before the law, Christian and Jew, knight, burgher and peasant, and because under the law everybody was free to live the way he liked. Absolutism of this kind must in the end defeat itself. Successful citizens, industrialists, merchants, bankers and landowners will sooner or later want to take part in Government. In the long run the influence of France's liberalism and not its absolutism predominated in the Rhineland – as Prussia discovered when after Napoleon's fall it established its own government in Cologne and Coblenz. Twenty years, and such eventful years, are a long time. The Rhineland has never again been simply 'German' like some small provincial town in Thuringia.

In southern Germany the surviving states, Bavaria, Württemberg and Baden, set to work with a will. Nothing remained undone that might serve to destroy established institutions: schools were taken over by the government, churches were placed under state control and transformed into national churches on the French pattern, class privileges were abolished, the newly acquired territories became administrative districts or departments in the style of French *départements*, legal systems were simplified and modelled directly on the *Code Napoléon* or revised in its absolutist yet bourgeois spirit, expert ministries with administrative hierarchies were set up, old universities reorganized and new ones founded, and Protestant scholars were brought in to annoy ultra-Catholic populations. In short, everything that still remained of the old *Reich* and might have affected the sovereignty of the new 'empire' was completely eradicated. Parliamentary representation of the kind tolerated by Napoleon in Paris was promised but did not eventuate because of the war.

The peoples of Europe have always learned from each other, and imitation is not necessarily foolish. The state founded by the Normans in England in 1066 was a Franco-Norman one but it became the basis of the English state. Therefore it is a mistake retrospectively to condemn the new German *Mittelstaaten* because they were created during the French period and in the French spirit. Among their founders were violent and grotesque personalities like the first king of Württemberg, as well as noble men like the Prime Minister of Baden, Reitzenstein, and the Bavarian lawyer Anselm Feuerbach. The 'princes' revolution' was not as barren of ideas nor as brutal as Heinrich von Treitschke claims. Someone had to start it and even in southern Germany someone had to introduce a sensible system of government; given the way in which German history had developed the 'people' could not do it. Subsequently the south German states fulfilled their duties tolerably well and became centres of a liberal movement for which the achievements of the first ten years provided at least the framework. Yet they never completely overcame the strange conditions of their beginning; a slightly foreign air continued to pervade the new groupings, the new hierarchies and the cultural splendour of the restored capitals. This may help to explain the weakness which the *Mittelstaaten* demonstrated in every future crisis. Just over a century after the 'princes' revolution' its beneficiaries, the dynasties, were forced to retire without a hand being lifted in their defence; long before, they had lost any real influence over the shaping of the nation's destiny. Generally speaking, therefore, the end of the old Empire was the beginning of the nation-state, though the road to it first led to the complete, if ephemeral, triumph of the principalities. They became too important, too modern for the old dynastic system, but they were incapable of ever becoming popular states in their own right.

Very different was Prussia's history during this period. Prussia had retired from the war in 1795. Since then, under the peace treaty of Basle, it had enjoyed a neutrality together with the rest of northern and central Germany. For the capital, Berlin, and for smaller capitals, like Weimar, this was an intellectually fertile period. It was the beautiful period of the friendship between Schiller and Goethe, when every year brought a play by Schiller, a story by Jean Paul, and when Berlin society accomplished some tremendous intellectual feats. It was the great decade of German literature. This creativeness undoubtedly had something to do with the long period of peace in the midst of wars. 'The world was on fire everywhere', Goethe reported in his *Annalen*, 'Europe had changed shape, cities and navies were being destroyed on land and sea, but central and northern Germany profited from a certain feverish peace which enabled us to enjoy a doubtful safety.' The state itself used its neutrality as states were wont to do: at the beginning for another joint piece of robbery with Russia which brought it vast Polish territories, including the capital Warsaw, and later to make big profits from secularization.

Suddenly these doubtful advantages were lost again. Having made the mistake of not taking part in the resistance against French expansion for eleven years, Prussia made the mistake of joining it at the most unfavourable moment, in the autumn of 1806; whereupon Napoleon destroyed the antiquated Prussian war machine with incredible rapidity. He regarded the Prussian system as more dangerous than the south German one, though at the same time sufficiently artificial to be easily destroyed. This is what he wanted to do after the Prussian defeats of 1806–7, but even then he was not free to play the game entirely as he wished. He now decided to come to terms with Russia, the power which only a few months earlier he had accused of being non-European and barbarian. The Tsar preferred to preserve a rump-Prussia between the two Empires, his own and that of his new friend. The result was not a success. Prussia's Polish loot became the 'Grand Duchy of Warsaw' which was part of Napoleon's system and contained the promise of a future Polish nation-state; therefore it could not fail to be doubly unwelcome to the Russian imperialists. The Prussian territories west of the Elbe also came under French influence and were consolidated into a new satellite state. Between French Poland and French Westphalia there came to lie a bisected Prussian state, substantial enough never to become reconciled to existing conditions, and able to reform itself and to salvage for better days what remained of its old tradition. It is easy to say that Napoleon's arrangement was a serious mistake. In retrospect his whole history is a succession of mistakes; there was no 'right' course of action.

The Prussian collapse of 1806 and the unkind treatment meted out by the victor to the victim had an unfavourable effect on Franco-Prussian or Franco-German relations. Because Prussia had lost where the south German states had gained and because it continued to be tormented by the victor, the reform of the state took on an anti-French accent. Whereas southern Germany was officially on most cordial terms with Napoleon Prussia was barely on speaking terms with him; its best citizens secretly began to dream of a war of liberation. As at the moment there were no territorial gains for Prussia to assimilate but only losses to be put up with, the Prussian reform was devoid of hate and violence. The state was there, a state already put on a rational footing by Hohenzollern absolutism; it could therefore afford to adopt a creative approach.

The chief factor was that outstanding individuals chose to serve Prussia. 'Men make history', said a German historian. Sometimes this is true and sometimes not. In this case it is more or less true. In Prussia no changes were brought about by the masses; they came from above or not at all. They came from enlightened bureaucrats and soldiers, East Prussians who had been influenced by Kant or men from the *Reich*, from Hanover, Westphalia and Nassau, who for one reason or another had been attracted into the Prussian civil service. The best among them, after whom all the reforms are usually called, was Freiherr vom Stein. He deserves his reputation, this powerful, proud, warm-hearted and good man. Born an imperial knight in a region where the tradition of the *Reich* was comparatively strong, he felt that his only obligation was to the Empire which no longer existed. This state of affairs Stein regarded as temporary and illegal. He was interested in Germany's two Great Powers because for the time being they alone could be real German states. The rest, the 'sultans' as he called them, from Bavaria to Nassau-Usingen, he looked on with characteristic intolerance. They must all disappear – he did not exactly know how; nor did he know how the survivors, Prussia and Austria, could exist side by side. Stein was no diplomat and was contemptuous of the skills of the diplomat. He had begun as a practical man, as an inspector of mines, and had for many years been in close touch with industrial development; mere theorizing and penmanship he regarded as unworthy of a man. He never missed an opportunity of thundering against the 'overvaluation of the speculative sciences'. 'The strange, the incomprehensible attracts the attention of the human mind which indulges in idle brooding instead of taking firm action.' As he grew older, Stein the technician, the administrator and founder of industries did not lack tremendous political ambition. He was what many think they are but only few manage to become: a patriot. For him Germany was something noble and precious. For the liberation of Germany from French rule he was ready to sacrifice his money, his possessions and his life. The reforms which he was allowed to make in Prussia in 1807–8 were in the last resort intended to serve the cause of liberation.

There are many aspects to Stein's reforms. Politicians are not ideas incarnate or walking textbooks; woe betide us if they claim to be anything of the kind. Doctrinaire statesmen will always bring with them two things: tyranny and defeat. Stein was no doctrinaire but he had strong yearnings and sympathies, one of which drew him to the Holy Roman Empire and the Middle Ages. He was attracted by the idea of the old system of estates, of well distributed privileges and obligations, of a Christian aristocracy patriotically doing its duty, of self-governing cities, of corporations, churches and universities administering their property in the common interest. He may have idealized all this in the fashion of those days but he was also a modern man who believed in the educational and moral function of government. The purpose of good government was to educate citizens to educate themselves, or at any rate to take an organized part in public life so that the state lived from within and so that there could be no repetition of the deplorable collapse of 1806. People should be able freely to follow their occupations as in France. Stein's appreciation of both medieval corporative and modern liberal ideas need not be regarded as contradictory. Many lines of development converged in the trend which in the later nineteenth century was called 'liberal'. It is possible to trace one such trend back to the Middle Ages: modern English parliamentary government grew out of the old system of estates. Stein admired England and would have been very upset if it had been demonstrated to him, as it could have been, that his actions were influenced by French revolutionary ideas.

Stein's ideas crossed with other, newer ones: the demand for free trade as it had come from England, the concept of man as *homo oeconomicus* whose urge for profits needed only to be freed from all government restrictions in order to produce ever greater quantities of wealth and happiness in free competition. This emphasis on free trade became more marked when after a year Stein had to resign and to leave the country. In his letters he had carelessly referred to a future war of liberation. His successor, Hardenberg, lacked Stein's idealism.

The peasants were emancipated, but the landowners kept their police powers and the right to deal with minor offences in their districts; in order to provide compensation for the old services and payments in kind the land was divided up, with the result that hundreds of thousands of peasants were unable to find an independent existence. Against Stein's wishes, but in line with the aims of his free-trade assistants, this policy (*Bauernlegen* – 'laying the peasants flat' – was the German term) made serfs into farm workers and their sons and grandsons into urban labourers. The Prussian aristocracy emerged from the period of reform un-broken, in the long run enriched and made politically conscious. Henceforth all occupations were open to its members, they were allowed to acquire any kind of property, not just land, and preserved some of their written privileges as well as some of those which were unwritten; service in the army, administration and at court was no longer exclusive to them, but their chances of advancement were better than those of others.

Stein's personal attitude towards the aristocracy was ambi-valent. He belonged to it himself and was proud of his ancestry and arrogant. On the other hand, his experiences with the Prussian aristocracy filled him with contemptuous impatience and there came a time when he would have liked to do away with it altogether. His ideal was the English aristocracy, rich but with a sense of responsibility, continually revivified by the elevation of members of the middle class to the peerage, rendering valuable political service in the House of Lords, and so constituted that titles passed only to a single heir, while younger sons joined the ranks of the middle class. In Germany every son inherited a title, even if there was nothing else to inherit – a circumstance which

now made itself all the more painfully felt because the expropriation of the Catholic Church had deprived the aristocracy of the
richest source of income for its younger sons.

In the city democracy begins with Freiherr vom Stein, though
the word was still taboo. He was the founder of self-administration by elected town councils. Of his achievements this one has
proved the most enduring. Even in the twentieth century Prussian
cities aroused the admiration of the world, and were models of
the way in which public welfare services should be run. But even
at the beginning of the twentieth century – and particularly then –
the contrast between municipal democracy and the semi-absolutism of the state was striking. Historically it is due to the fact that
less than half of Stein's reforms were successful, that he was able
to reorganize the cities but not the state. National representation,
which he saw as the crowning achievement of his work, was not
introduced.

The great soldiers who now took charge of the army also set
out to make this institution more democratic, or perhaps we
should say, to give it a national basis, to imbue it with patriotic
spirit and to put merit before hereditary privilege. The principle
of universal conscription was proclaimed though not fully applied,
because of the restrictions which Napoleon imposed on the Prussian army, which were, however, cunningly and secretly defied
whenever possible. Mass armies had been the creation of the
French Revolution; Napoleon had disciplined them and used
them for his strategy of destruction. In the long run the new spirit
and the new means could not remain the exclusive property of
France. Intellectually the Prussian military reformers, Scharnhorst, Gneisenau, Clausewitz, are the equals of Carnot and Saint-
Cyr; they had greater respect for the human being than Napoleon.
It was probably inevitable that, having taken over the people's
army, they should also take over Napoleon's strategy of destruction, the whole new, uncompromising philosophy of politics and
war as a 'continuation of politics by other means'. We may consider
it a misfortune that they went to school with Napoleon, but it was
Napoleon who built the school and forced the pupils to attend.

It is doubtful how much of Scharnhorst's and Gneisenau's

basically humanitarian spirit was absorbed by the army and survived. An outstanding individual can make suggestions, but whether they are realized is another matter. This is particularly true if his ideas concern the army, an institution whose purpose is to kill and which is and must always remain based on brutal customs, on command and obedience. Napoleon's philosophy of war, impressively summarized in General von Clausewitz's famous *Vom Kriege* (On War), remained the philosophy of the Prussian general staff, more so after the middle of the century. The long-term effect of Scharnhorst's liberal and humane ideas is less clear. Old Prussian class traditions later re-emerged in the army and blended with new forms of discipline, new technical skills and brutalities.

What survives, in the history of states, of the intellectual efforts of outstanding men? If they write books, then books survive, appeals by one individual to other individuals which sometimes produce an effect even centuries later. But what happens when they leave their study and become involved in the difficult, always disappointing work of political leadership? The same question might be asked about the school and university reform which constitutes one chapter of Prussian innovations after 1807 – though this is by definition an intellectual sphere, in which the influence of an eminent minister or organizer ought therefore to be more effective than in the army. Wilhelm von Humboldt, who was Minister of Education in the years of reform, was almost too good to be true. He was a great humanist, an active philologist, a political philosopher, experienced in the ways of the world and cosmopolitan in outlook – his patriotism came late and never really suited him – a pleasure-loving egoist who wanted to make his life a work of art and did not grudge his fellow citizens the things that he had himself. Such a man at the head of the educational system is difficult to fit into the conventional picture, or caricature, of Prussia. It was an extraordinary time and it gave extraordinary men a chance. Under Humboldt's guidance there developed the Prussian school system as it remained to our day: elementary education for all, classical education for the middle classes and the civil servants, universities as institutions for scientific research and teaching. Education was not thought of as what it later tended to become in Germany, a means of hardening class differences, nor was it thought of as vocational training, but simply as free, classical education. How far it was ever possible to achieve this aim is open to question. But it was more nearly achieved in the first half of the nineteenth century than in the second, and more nearly in either half than in the twentieth century.

The Prussian educational system was intended as the antithesis of the strict, highly centralized and militarized hierarchy of the Napoleonic school system, just as Stein's municipal order was intended as the antithesis of French central government control of local authorities. In the same spirit the new Prussian army was more democratic than the French, which permitted substitution or buying-out, and which had lost its original character through conquest, occupation and the addition of foreign units. Stein's reforms were not mere copies of French revolutionary innovations; they were creative even when they borrowed from the enemy. But after a time the reforming movement largely came to a halt. The moments in history in which noble enthusiasm reigns are short and one must be grateful for any lasting achievement from such a period.

3. Cosmopolitans and Nationalists

European politics in the nineteenth century fed on the French Revolution. No idea, no dream, no fear, no conflict appeared which had not been worked through in that fateful decade: democracy and socialism, reaction, dictatorship, nationalism, imperialism, pacifism. The same can be said of Germany's intellectual history in the nineteenth century in relation to these ten or twenty years. What came later signified development, variation, imitation, or decline, by comparison with the creative originality of the turn of the century.

This creativeness was not a consequence or product of the Revolution; to regard it as such would mean attributing too much importance to political events. Kant, Goethe, Herder and the young Schiller had appeared long before the great wave of unrest swept across Europe. The connections between the one and the other are mysterious, but it cannot be pure coincidence that, while France was enacting its political drama and its youthful generals and organizers were conquering the Continent, an unprecedented wealth of intellectual talent appeared all over Germany, in Prussia and Silesia, in sterile Berlin itself, in the Rhineland and in Swabia. Even if we regard the potentialities as given, the form in which they realized themselves was affected by the events of the day, by the *Zeitgeist*, the spirit of the age – a term which was first used and whose significance was first felt at this period. Though the country was still sparsely populated and news travelled slowly – in that technical sense we are today subject to incomparably greater pressures – men like Fichte, Schleiermacher and Hegel, Görres and Arndt, Gentz, Adam Müller and Kleist, Brentano and Arnim took a serious and intense interest in their time; without its fateful events they might have chosen other roads.

For the great neo-humanists, or classicists as they were later called, the degeneration of the Revolution confirmed the opinions which they had come to hold. When the Committee of Public Safety ruled in Paris Schiller was no longer the poet of *Die Räuber* and *Kabale und Liebe* nor Goethe the young German patriot of 1770. Goethe as Minister of State had good judgement and sound political instincts but he was not a theorist; he was most at home in the era of late, highly enlightened, benevolent princely absolutism. He found the drama of the Revolution interesting, but strange and repulsive; there was nothing in it that he wished either to identify himself with, or to oppose. He was more interested in Napoleon and his legal order in Europe, while it lasted.

> *Zur Nation zu bilden, ihr hofft es, Deutsche, vergebens.*
> *Bildet statt dessen, ihr könnt es, freier zu Menschen*
> *euch aus . . .* *

* In vain do you hope, Germans, to make yourselves into a nation. Make yourselves – you can do it – into freer human beings instead . . .

Schiller turned away from the Revolution after the execution of Louis XVI, but one cannot say that he ceased to regard politics as the greatest of all human concerns. The Wallenstein trilogy, that noble masterpiece, contains profounder thoughts about the struggle for power, leadership, rebellion, order and chaos, war and peace, than any other German play. And *Wilhelm Tell*, the last play which he finished, is still a hymn of praise for tyrannicide, freedom, nation and fatherland.

Nineteenth-century national-democratic rhetoric found plenty of material in all these things, although Schiller was no longer a democrat when Bonaparte's star rose and no longer primarily interested in the social order. His main concern now became education, the purpose of which to him was to train not nationally conscious but noble, free human beings, educated by recreation, art, beauty and philosophy to become better citizens. Schiller spent his most productive and his most settled and most celebrated years under the protection of Prussian neutrality. He died before it collapsed and we must not ask how he would have behaved during the subsequent times of humiliation and revolt.

The development of his friend, Wilhelm von Humboldt, might give us a clue. For a while Humboldt continued to devote his attention to education as a means of turning the individual into a nobler human being, and to improving his own in Spain or in Rome, wherever interest and opportunity took him. In those days he claimed that he was not interested in Germany and that his true home was a small circle of like-minded friends. The Prussian collapse of 1806 does not appear to have moved him greatly. Later, Humboldt became a politician, first as Prussian Minister of Education and then as a diplomat. As such he defended the interests of his state – vigorously when it became a question of translating victories into territorial gains and power. He adopted a decidedly anti-French attitude and admitted that Prussia had a role to play in Germany, although at the time of the Congress of Vienna he did not regard the establishment of a single German state as desirable. The cosmopolitan had become a patriot. It is possible to be both, because both ways of thinking relate to the human being and the human community, the one directly, the other through the nation. For a long time yet it was taken for granted that free nations would live better together than unfree principalities, and that a confederation of peoples would crown the work of liberation. The French Revolution itself was both cosmopolitan and nationalist. It needed a succession of unhappy concatenations – the absolute state and the national state, class rule and the democratic army, the competing claims of several nationalities on the same territory – to transform the patriotism of the early nineteenth century into aggressive, oppressing nationalism. Perhaps we should simply say that up till now man has distorted every idea by his all too human actions, and that this is not the fault of the idea but of man himself; just as he misused the Christian religion of charity for the most horrible persecutions, the careful cultivation of national characteristics degenerated into a murderous undertaking.

Of all this almost nothing was noticeable in Napoleon's time. The first who steeped themselves in their own people's history and national character were pure in spirit; they did not cease to be cosmopolitans because they came to believe in the nation.

Joseph Görres for example had begun as a revolutionary and delighted in the collapse of the rule of church and aristocracy in the Rhineland; he had rushed to Paris as the representative of his countrymen to arrange the union of the Rhineland with France. What he saw there disappointed him, as he had already been disappointed by the reality of French military rule in Coblenz. Napoleon's government and character disappointed him still further, even though they made a deep impression on him. He gave up politics temporarily and devoted himself to scientific, philosophical and philological research and speculation. In Heidelberg he met a talented pair of friends, Clemens Brentano from Frankfurt and the Prussian Achim von Arnim. The three threw themselves into the study of the German Middle Ages, folk songs, fairy tales, sagas and paintings. In the fruits of their research, Görres's *Deutsche Volksbücher* and *Des Knaben Wunderhorn* by Arnim and Brentano, they wanted to open new horizons to their countrymen, to offer them comfort and beauty. The periodical which Arnim published in Heidelberg was called *Tröst*

Einsamkeit (Comfort in Solitude), a 'paper for hermits, old and new sagas and prophecies, stories and poems'. There was something of a protest against the prosaic, violent, military present in such intellectual adventures. Later the word 'romantic', which was used loosely to describe the poets and thinkers of the period, came to mean escape from the present, longing for a better bygone age, absorption in dreams, and immersion in the depths of the past and of the soul, and spiritual freedom.

> *Mondbeglänzte Zaubernacht,*
> *die den Sinn gefangenhält,*
> *wunderbare Märchenwelt*
> *steig auf in der alten Pracht!**

Novalis, Brentano, Arnim and Tieck wrote beautiful poems. They created a magic garden for the Germans in which new gardeners continued to labour until the middle of the century. But this was another world from that of society and politics, and for our purposes we should not be discussing it. Except that even here there were links with politics. It was the German Middle Ages that attracted the poets, German songs and epics that were republished – of a kind that Frederick the Great would still have scornfully rejected as 'barbaric stuff'. Frederick knew of no German fatherland, but Görres, Arnim and Heinrich von Kleist were patriots, and their activities, however exalted they were and sounded, were a denial of Napoleon's international military rule. What began as a flight from the present, therefore, affected them as well, and subsequently affected them very profoundly. We see Görres later as a powerful nationalistic publicist, Kleist as a perspicacious politician, though emotionally unstable, and the proud, handsome von Arnim as the founder of a 'Christian Round Table' in Berlin, hostile to Stein's reforms, hostile to the French – and even hostile to the Jews. The mind of the individual is not a textbook, it is full of contradictions. In times of excitement writers change faster than in normal times (if normal times

---

*Moonlit magic night which captivates the senses, fairy-tale world, arise in pristine splendour!

have ever existed), and the dividing line between what is reprehensible and what is noble is frequently not very clear.

The Germans certainly could not remain as innocently peaceloving and cosmopolitan as they had been in Kant's day. Napoleon had taught them too roughly what power was and what the reward of weakness. The misery of state and nation made them discover state and nation, though they still approached the new problems with high idealism. Johann Gottlieb Fichte, that profound thinker and argumentative but touchingly honourable man, presents a curious example of this.

Fichte believed in man and humanity and probably also in God with a seriousness that only a few no-longer-Christians have shown. He believed in the spirit as creator of all things which are nothing without it, and in the right of the individual to develop himself properly in freedom. At the beginning he believed with stern enthusiasm in the French Revolution. From the right of the individual he came to the state as the omnipotent agent which alone could guarantee that right, and from there he quickly arrived at what today is called the totalitarian state, the state as unrestricted ruler of education and economic life. From the all-powerful state he finally came to the nation and the nation-state. Fichte reached this point in his *Reden an die deutsche Nation* (Addresses to the German Nation), delivered in Berlin at the time of the French occupation. He was still an idealist, and he still thought it the nation's task to promote human welfare and regarded a league of nations as the final goal. But now he saw as the media of the *Weltgeist*, world spirit, the nations and above all the German people whom he regarded as the only genuine, original people in a corrupted world. This was nonsense; Fichte did not know the world, and what he told the Germans about their task in it was pure invention. But he was a great orator and made a deep impression on his audiences and later on his readers. The superficial, brazen phrases about the German nature that would save the world, in vogue a hundred years later, were late consequences of the work begun by Fichte and his friends – consequences which his inflexible character would certainly have rejected with scorn.

Others were less subtle thinkers than Fichte, and their road to nationalism was less steep, for example that of Ernst Moritz Arndt who was nevertheless an honest man and a good writer. Others again were imbeciles, like Friedrich Ludwig Jahn, who carried Teutomania to ludicrous and nauseous extremes, although there may have been a sound element in his gymnastics. Another was a great storyteller and dramatist, but he was a sick man – and sick he would probably have been even without Napoleon. Yet men readily blame their times for the demon in their own soul and transfer their self-hatred to a political object. It was thus that Heinrich von Kleist hated the French conqueror, calling upon the Germans:

> *Schlagt sie tot! Das Weltgericht*
> *Fragt Euch nach den Gründen nicht!**

The Emperor in his distant capital did less to stop this incipient German nationalism than one would expect in our age of 'ideological warfare'; in fact he did nothing. Whereas Paris journalists had to write what he wanted, the German metaphysicians – 'the Kants and the German enthusiasts', as he called them – could do what they liked. As long as his actions did not run counter to the spirit of the age – and he had confidence in himself in this respect – these men could not harm him.

The desire to read and to study [said Joseph Görres] is not checked, and the government is afraid only of material opposition; literature has long been looked upon as the nation's toy which nobody will even try to take away from her. To suppress national character is not the Emperor's way ... It is the fact that he cannot find any true national character in the Germans that has puzzled him about this nation.

Fichte could make speeches and Jahn take his gymnasts for walks as long as they did not openly incite to rebellion. In Napoleon's opinion they were not the stuff that political destiny is made of .

---

*Strike them dead! At the last judgement you will not be asked for your reasons!

4. The Fall of Napoleon and his Legacy

Napoleon's empire with its annexed provinces, its petty kingdoms, its satellites and compulsory allies was an interlude that could not last, a weird by-product of the factors which created it and then destroyed it again. By far the most important of these was the Anglo-French duel. Because Britain refused to recognize the frontiers established by pre-revolutionary France, the annexation of Belgium and the conquest of Holland, the duel went on. Again and again Britain found allies on the Continent whom Napoleon was compelled to defeat, and subject to conditions designed to make it impossible for them to begin again; the very kind of conditions to which they could not become reconciled. He then tried, in vain, to live in peace and friendship with them. Unable to hit Britain directly he wanted to hit the British economy by closing the markets of Europe to British industry. To carry out this unnatural programme he believed that he needed direct control over coasts and ports – Holland, Hamburg, Italy and Dalmatia – and to make them part of France. The 'Continental System', the source of much violence, hatred and corruption, caused more misery on the Continent than in Britain. So did the war against Austria in 1809, the never-ending Spanish war, and the strain on Napoleon's compulsory allies of having to be everlastingly prepared for war. Yet the Emperor was not conscious of being an oppressor of nations. He did not wish to torment and exploit them, least of all the Germans, for whom – or for whose rulers at any rate – he had genuine feelings of friendship and obligation. He thought he knew the middle classes, for whom he provided modern institutions. The ephemeral episode of the 'Empire', the unification of Europe under a new Charlemagne, he regarded as something permanent. Opposition – the revolt of the Spaniards, the papal excommunication, the diplomatically careful refusal first of Austria and then of Russia to fall in with his plans, the anger of the Germans rumbling secretly under the surface of obedience – he regarded as mere ideology, revolutionary nonsense, an irritating misunderstanding of the course of history. In

1812 when he led his Grand Army against Russia he believed that as a good European he was waging war to end war; after this there would be peace. What such a man himself believes in such a situation is of little importance historically.

Neither are we here concerned with his much-admired personal achievement: how one man controlled Europe, the object of his selfish extravagant imagination, through his officers, how he ruled from Madrid to Moscow, how he mobilized vast armies with no better means to move them about than the Romans, and how, in giving his orders, he always kept an eye on the propaganda effects. Nothing fitted in his system; one tear and it fell apart everywhere. What defeated him? Britain did. And also Russia, its people and its geography and climate. Then there was Austrian diplomacy which determined his defeat in the summer of 1813. Further, he was defeated by himself, because he was not prepared to make concessions, because, to use Metternich's phrase, he 'would not let himself be saved'. Austria would glady have let him off lightly if he had been prepared voluntarily to abandon control of Germany, Italy and Spain. Finally, Germany too was responsible for his defeat. His collapse occurred on German soil; in the decisive battle of Leipzig the vital part was played by Prussian and Austrian troops.

Nevertheless Germany did not play a main role in the War of Liberation, which was a European, primarily a joint Anglo-Russian enterprise. Napoleon's disaster in Russia was the inevitable beginning; the next decisive event was the Tsar's decision to carry the war beyond his own frontiers into Germany. In this, however, he was influenced by the advice of the great German emigrant at the Tsarist court, Freiherr vom Stein, and the Convention of Tauroggen by which a Prussian auxiliary unit of the French army under General Yorck proclaimed its neutrality, the revolt of East Prussia and Prussia's gradual move towards the Russian camp – all these are vital links in the chain. Afterwards diplomacy regained the upper hand. In Prussia east of the Elbe there was enthusiasm, and there it is possible to speak of a popular rising. Coolly calculating, Austria joined the alliance in order not to be left out and in order to remain master of the situation and so prevent the real change desired by the patriots round Stein. The states of the Confederation of the Rhine stayed with Napoleon until just before the battle of Leipzig or after it. Then, willingly or reluctantly, they made a dignified move into the victors' camp, where they were received politely in spite of their sinful past; each side needed the other and each could after all accuse the other of much the same things. Non-German historians have sometimes commented sarcastically on the quiet attitude of the Germans during the crisis of Napoleon's final agony, so unlike the popular fury of the Spaniards or the Russians. How difficult it is to please everyone. If the nation had really followed Kleist's call: 'Strike them dead! At the last judgement . . .' it would be accused of typically German barbarism and treachery instead of typically German timidity and civic obedience.

The Prussian army proved its mettle. It was now a popular force, the great reserve army of the *Landwehr* which many volunteers flocked to join; new patriotic and xenophobic songs were heard and, though belatedly and restrained by diplomacy and the habit of obedience, war was waged against the oppressor. These factors gave the war of 1813–14 a new character, symbolized by the Order of the Iron Cross. It was an adventure which stimulated the imagination – that wintry march 'across the Rhine into France' under the spectacular leadership of the aged Marshal Blücher. Napoleon's last stand against merciless superiority, his incredible return from Elba, and the battle of Waterloo – decided by the Prussians – seemed to the Germans like a last judgement and increased their national self-confidence.

There was a difference between the aims of the patriots, the leaders of the Prussian army, Stein and his propagandists, and the achievements of the diplomats. This difference became more obvious as the day of final victory approached. Stein, Görres, Arndt and the many other enthusiastic readers of the new *Rheinischer Merkur* wanted a great German empire with an emperor at its head and with corporative institutions. They wanted to chase away the princes of the Confederation of the Rhine, of Bavaria, Saxony and Württemberg. They also demanded that as a punishment France be made to return at least the former imperial provinces of Alsace and Lorraine, insisting on the severest possible terms to cure once and for all the desire for war. The diplomats did not want this; neither the cool-headed Clemens Metternich who now directed Austria's foreign policy with masterly skill, nor the south German rulers, nor even the Prussian Prime Minister, Hardenberg. None of them regarded a new 'Reich' as either desirable or obtainable, or wanted to complement the French Revolution by a German one. The order which they established after the collapse of Napoleon's system was called a 'restoration', which fundamentally it was not; indeed on closer inspection restorations usually prove to be merely on the surface. The fact that some of the princes deposed by Napoleon were allowed to return to their thrones did not affect the social, or even the diplomatic changes of the Revolution. What happened at the Congress of Vienna in 1815 was not that pre-Napoleonic Europe was restored but that Napoleonic Europe was divided, with the result that Austria now ruled where France had ruled in Italy, Prussia ruled where France had ruled on the Rhine, and Russia ruled where France had ruled in Poland. There had been many partitions, but the country which for twenty years had taken the lion's share now had to give back everything to be divided so as to establish an equilibrium of power. Napoleon, who quickly saw through the true war aims of his opponents, had reason from his point of view to be indignant. They pretended to be fighting for justice against the great criminal but wanted to continue his system after their own fashion and to benefit from it.

It was impossible to return to pre-1792 conditions or to create democratic nation-states in Germany and Italy. The emergence of such states would have entailed the self-destruction of Prussia and Austria and an internal movement of Jacobin energy and scale which did not exist. What did exist were disappointed, angry patriots, among them influential writers, but no popular movement to realize their dreams. Not only did the old powers, headed by Austria and Prussia, triumph once again but they needed to do almost nothing to suppress the disappointed nationalists. They had only discreetly to establish *faits accomplis*. The result was that the German states remained as Napoleon had created them.

The 'princes' revolution' of 1801–6 was neither undone nor continued.

It would have been excellent if at Napoleon's fall Germany had
become a state, a national republic, a democracy; the nineteenth
century would then have taken a different course and we
should not be where we are today. But to speak of missed
opportunities is meaningful only where genuine opportunities
existed, which was not the case in 1815 either in Germany or in
Italy.

But because the recent past had shown how easily a divided
Germany could become a temptation for its neighbours, a battle
field and a place for oppression, and probably also because some
small concession to the nationalists was felt to be expedient, the
Congress of Vienna set up the German Confederation. The Confederation was at least better planned than the old Empire in
which there had been no question of plan or purpose. What was
dissolved in 1806 was a very badly organized federation of German states, with all kinds of useless and antiquated encumbrances.
What was recreated in 1815 was a better organized federation of
German states whose constitution took account of realities instead of concealing them beneath fiction. For this reason the
Confederation was intended to preserve not only the 'external and
internal safety of Germany' but specifically also the 'independence
and inviolability of the individual German states'. There was to
be a Federal Diet in Frankfurt – formerly the town where the
Emperor was crowned and now once more a Free City – to which
governments would send their representatives and which would
be so constituted that the two biggest states could not outvote
the smaller ones, nor the other way round. If it chose to, the
Federal Diet should be able to determine joint economic and tariff
policy, assimilate judicial systems and organize joint defence. The
Federal Act provided member states with advice of a somewhat
vague mandatory nature on internal government and the political
rights of citizens. These member states were now 'sovereign',
although in fact they were more loyal to the Confederation in the
decades to come than they had been to the Empire in the eighteenth century. The federal constitution met their interests and

views. The equation between the written word and reality was correct – for a time.

Some inter-German territorial changes had preceded the preparation of the constitution, though only one was sufficiently important to be worth mentioning here: the reconstitution of the Prussian state. Because the victor of 1812, the liberator of Europe, the Russian Tsar, wanted to have Poland, Prussia once more had to surrender its Polish share of the booty of 1795. However, as one of the victors it was entitled to rule over at least as many 'souls' as before 1806 and therefore compensation had to be found in Germany. Because the Rhineland could no more remain part of France than return to its pre-revolutionary, antiquated constitution its people were simply told that henceforth they were Prussians. The same news was given to the inhabitants of the western part of Saxony. Only as a result of these two acquisitions, the 'Rhine Province' and the 'Province of Saxony', did Prussia become a predominantly German state straddling diagonally across the country and stretching far to the south, and was thus put in a position to preside over German history in the nineteenth century. Whether this could or should have been foreseen in 1814 is difficult to say. A few Cassandras did foresee it.

In 1814, however, the issue was not to protect Germany against Prussia or Europe against Germany, but Germany and Europe against a new French revolutionary attack. This aim was served by a strong Kingdom of the Netherlands – the union of Belgium and Holland – and by a strong Prussia on the Rhine.

In retrospect it is easy to prophesy and to show diplomats where they went wrong; working under the pressure of the moment their task is more difficult. In the longer run they can never do the right thing, for at some point their decisions always have unwelcome consequences. The situation is particularly difficult after the victory of allies over their former conqueror. If their new system is aimed against the vanquished enemy so as to prevent a recurrence of danger from that direction, they are later blamed for failing to see that the threat came from another direction. Yet if they turn at once against the new danger it will be said that as soon as they had achieved their first paltry objective they destroyed and betrayed the great alliance which could have maintained lasting peace and happiness. The 'horsetrading in provinces' that went on at the Congress of Vienna later became the object of liberal loathing. It was said that the people were not consulted before their states were divided and territorial losses were made good by territorial gains. Later experience has shown that plebiscites are not an infallible way of drawing frontiers or creating states, and mass expulsions even less. The methods of 1815 compare reasonably well with the artificial ones of 1919 and the barbarous ones of 1945. In 1815 no ethnic group was asked which state it wished to belong to, but none was expelled. What was consulted were the interests of both European and internal German equilibrium or peace; after all there were other ways of taking account of popular feeling without misused plebiscites. The majority benefited from the change or remained unaffected; a minority later found it annoying or almost unbearable. The second effect had not been foreseen by the peacemakers of 1815; any more than they foresaw a revision of their work. They regarded the new order as static and sensible, not as dynamic and 'historic'. After years of chaos they wanted at last to establish permanent order, even a kind that did not satisfy everybody. Our world is not, after all, such that any one order could ever satisfy everybody.

Of the three German political systems the Austrian, the Prussian and the 'third' (that of the *Mittelstaaten* or the Confederation of the Rhine) the Prussian emerged as the most popular from the Napoleonic catastrophe. This is curious, because most of the time, that is until 1809, Austria rather than Prussia had been the centre of German resistance against Napoleon and could most validly claim the old imperial legacy. At first, however, it was not a question of time but of the impact of recent events. What had aroused enthusiasm in the War of Liberation had worn Prussian and not Austrian colours. The Prussian army leaders overshadowed the cunning Austrian generalissimo. Stein himself, although he was and in his heart remained stateless, had once, at the right moment, served Prussia. The headquarters of Blücher's so-called 'Silesian' army were also the headquarters of national literature; it was here that the demands for a severe punishment of France and for the 'Rhine, Germany's river, not Germany's frontier' were most vigorously raised. At the time, however, the Prussian state did not avail itself of this quickly acquired opportunity. Austria now put its European interests far above its German ones, gave up the recovery of its former west German possessions and recouped its losses in Italy instead, behaving like a European power with only a limited stake in German affairs. Similarly, official Prussia acted like a state, not like part or leader of the German nation and quickly fell out with the 'Teutomanes' who had put their faith in it. The condition for the success, even the existence, of the 'German Confederation' was that Austria and Prussia should get on together as two European states; a silent agreement which both the Prussian and the Austrian governments recognized in 1815. The memory of what the Prussian state had briefly achieved never died completely and was revived in very different times and conditions; it was then coupled with the legend that in 1814 a great hope had been betrayed, and that the omissions of the past must now be made good.

5. Interlude

No new principle is ever immediately and completely victorious; the world must always tolerate various trends, various realities and dreams simultaneously. Who anyway would want to live in a period in which everything is organized in accordance with a single idea? The French Revolution meant the breakthrough of new liberal, democratic and nationalist aspirations that were henceforth always at work. The liberal demands freedom for the individual to live without state interference. This demand sounds splendid but it will always come up against boundaries which are sometimes more widely and sometimes more narrowly drawn. The democrat demands the equality of all and the rule of the majority, which he makes into something intrinsically just, almost sacred. Yet the majority is not a sure means for discovering the true and the good. Democracy and liberalism moderate one another. The liberal principle combined with the democratic means the protection of minorities against the majority, and the protection of the individual against state interference; the democratic principle combined with the liberal means the protection of the majority against the powerful or successful individual who disregards the interests of the community. Similarly the two principles can destroy each other. Liberal catch-phrases readily hide the rule of numerically small but economically strong groups; government by the majority may well conceal the tyranny of a single will, a committee of public safety or dictator to whom the masses have entrusted themselves. Democratic military government in particular is anti-liberal, first because it forces everyone to do what only very few want to do, and secondly because it gives the whole state a military stamp and subjects popular education, the pursuit of knowledge and economic policy increasingly to military interests. The principle of the nation-state was meant as a just principle intended to strengthen not run counter to older, cosmopolitan hopes of peace. Nations would not do to each other what despots had done to each other; one nation's right of self-determination sanctioned that of another and established democratic peace between the two and everywhere. The experience of the age of revolution, however, was disappointing. The democratic military nation-state revealed itself as a state based on force at home and abroad. It used Machiavelli's principles as much or more than any absolute prince, with a clearer conscience and with greater effectiveness.

That was the lesson of the Napoleonic age, a first concentrated lesson that had to be learned and repeated many times in the course of the nineteenth and twentieth centuries. It had not exhausted the new ideas; these now existed and were and remained powerful. But they were unreliable, on paper because each of them carried to its logical conclusion cancelled itself out and led to absurdity, and in practice because ideas depend on men to realize them and because there is no relying on men. Men make of ideas what they want or consider appropriate under the pressure of circumstances.

Though the Congress of Vienna took place twenty-five years after the beginnings of the French Revolution its spirit was pre-revolutionary. It was a meeting of the old Europe after a new one had already made a noisy appearance. In Vienna there was talk not of popular sovereignty but of legitimate monarchies, however 'illegitimate' the conditions, for better or for worse, they had taken over. They spoke not of nations but of states, which all represented more or less the same thing. They spoke not of national interests but of European interests. The German Confederation was a main product of this spirit, its constitution a chapter of the Congressional Act which itself was meant to be something like a European constitution. As in the old days Germany was again part of Europe, greater than the others because it was involved with foreign destinies and because it was recognized as the heart of Europe. On the other hand it was less important than the others because it lacked the full force of a national state. Foreign rulers were members of the Confederation, the King of England as King of Hanover, the King of Denmark as Duke of Holstein and the King of the Netherlands as Duke of Luxembourg. Conversely some German rulers were not members in relation to all their possessions: East Prussia and Posen, though Prussian, were outside the Confederation and so too were Hungary and much of Italy, although they were ruled by the Habsburgs. In spite of formal isolation, however, the fate of Poland and Italy was closely connected with that of Germany. Poland remained partitioned between Russia, Prussia and Austria; Austria, which presided over the Federal Diet, was the chief power in southern Germany and in Italy. If separation from other nations is a condition of national existence, then the Germans had failed again to achieve such a separation and to realize themselves. The German Confederation was still European, intended to preserve European, as well as internal German, stability; it was not meant to do more.

One must never forget the real purpose of the German Confederation in so far as it is connected with European politics [wrote Wilhelm von Humboldt]. Its purpose is to ensure tranquillity. The whole existence of the Confederation is consequently designed to preserve the equilibrium of the Continent through natural gravity; it would be quite contrary to this purpose to introduce a new collective state into the ranks of the European system in addition to the bigger individual German ones, not through a disturbance of that equilibrium but as the result of arbitrary action. No one could then prevent Germany, as Germany, from becoming another conquering state, a situation which no good German can want. While it is well known that the German nation has derived great advantages in intellectual and scientific education from having no foreign policy, it is not certain what effect such a policy might have . . .

That was the idea. Germany was too great, too varied to become a state like the others. As a unified power it would be too great for the rest and too strong for its own happiness. But it could be something better – Europe's trustee, unassailable and yet unfeared, united in defence, unsuited to expansion, diverse and content, devoted to science, education and development. This was a beautiful idea but also an artificial one, artistically expressed – an entirely static, conservative idea that could never inspire enthusiasm. If an age of tranquillity was approaching – and that was the intention of the peacemakers – the idea was a good one. However, if an age of dynamic simplification was approaching, the idea would be difficult to defend.

6. Hegel

The man who told the Germans most emphatically in what age they were living was the philosopher Georg Wilhelm Friedrich Hegel. He joined together in his mind the whole of current experience and ideas, everything that had ever been thought. This powerfully wrought fabric, the Hegelian 'system', later fell apart, but its individual tenets could never again be what they had been before Hegel; they remained shaped and coloured as he had left them. What Napoleon was to the political history of the period Hegel was to its intellectual history.

He was only one year younger than Napoleon but took longer

to become what he was. The intellectual usually takes more time to mature than the man of action; moreover Napoleon made the German philosopher's life difficult. While the Emperor ruled Europe Hegel earned his living as a provincial journalist and schoolmaster. Fame only came to him after the last bulletins from the front and after the last new state had been founded. His most influential period as professor of philosophy at Berlin was the fifteen years after Napoleon's fall. Therefore we might regard him as the philosopher of the Restoration rather than of the Napoleonic era; but eras follow each other without a break and clear divisions exist only in our minds. Hegel's philosophy was mature when Napoleon fell. What he did thereafter was merely to develop it, to apply it to different spheres of knowledge and to adapt new experiences to it as best he could. A man's fame and influence do not usually coincide with his essential achievement.

Born in Württemberg, educated at the seminary in Tübingen, Hegel started as a theologian, God-seeking and self-searching. He reflected with painful wonderment on the experience of solitude, separation and the fact that every being must be an entity by itself. But this gentle Swabian seeker after God also had an acute political sense of what a state is. He developed his philosophical ideas by studying German philosophy, Kant, Fichte and Schelling; his historical and political sense found ample food in the happenings of the times. From both sources, and from his vast learning, he created the Hegelian philosophy of history.

It was a fantastic, almost mad, almost successful attempt to give an answer to every question ever asked, and to assign to every answer ever given to every question a historical place within his own great, final answer – an attempt to create being dialectically from thought, to reconcile idea and reality and to overcome the cleavage between self and non-self. It was this cleavage – the existence of the self in an alien world – that Hegel made his starting-point. What he found was the identity of everything with everything, of God with the world, of logic with reality, of motion with rest, of necessity with freedom. The world spirit is everywhere, in nature, in man, in the history of man. The spirit, alienated from itself in nature, comes into its own in man. This process takes place on the one hand in the true history of peoples and states, and on the other in art, religion and philosophy. All these spheres correspond to each other; what is accomplished in each individual sector belongs to the whole and fits into it or nothing will be accomplished. 'As far as the individual is concerned each person cannot in any event help being the child of his time. So too philosophy is the expression of its time in ideas.' 'He who expresses and accomplishes what his time wills is the great man of his time.' Every present is always a single whole, just as the history of mankind is in its general lines a whole. It finds expression in peoples, states and civilizations, of which the west European or, as Hegel calls it, the Germanic is the highest so far attained. Will there be higher ones? On this point the philosopher is silent. One can only understand the past, and the present to the extent that it is the final product of all pasts which are preserved in it. The future cannot be explored or understood; it does not exist for the spirit. No other historical thinker was so little concerned with the future as Hegel. What he hinted at, or what followed from his doctrine, was that the future would be something entirely different from the past. For philosophy comes late, at the end of an epoch. It does not come to change or improve, but merely to understand and to express; it constructs in the realm of the spirit what has already been constructed in the realm of reality. 'When philosophy paints its picture in grey on grey, it means that a form of life has grown old, and by painting it grey on grey it cannot be restored to its youth, but only recognized . . .' This applies to all true philosophy, and is most valid for the philosophy of all philosophies, namely the Hegelian, which brings to an end the epoch of all epochs; the age of Protestantism, enlightenment and revolution. What was still to come? Hegel shrugged his shoulders sadly at this question. Perhaps America, perhaps Russia, perhaps nothing at all. His philosophy gave no answer, and given its nature could not venture to attempt one. 'The spirit is in its full essence in the present . . .' But this philosophy of fulfilment, this song of praise of Man-God contains an element of pessimism: after 1815 nothing further is to be expected.

Though Hegel's philosophy as a whole constitutes rest, fulfilment and finality, it is full of unrest and struggle, both in the realm of the spirit and of reality. The spirit is never content with what has been achieved, it always seeks new conflicts, it must struggle to find and express itself anew. States and peoples are never at rest, they come into conflict and one of them must give way. The world spirit advances by catastrophes, and its path is marked by forms that are used up, emptied, and jettisoned. Quiet is only apparent quiet, lull before a new storm; as mere rest it is of no interest to the historian. 'Epochs of happiness are empty pages in the history of the world.' History does not exist for the happiness, the idyllic contentment of the individual. The goal is set high: the reconciliation of all contradictions, absolute justice, complete knowledge, the incarnation of reason on earth, the presence of God. The road to it is one of exertion and ever new confusion. But what has happened is the only thing that could have happened and how it happened was right. Terrible things occurred; the rise of the Roman Empire was terrible and terrible was its fall. But everything had a purpose and was as it should be. Julius Caesar was murdered after he had done what the age wanted from him; the Roman Empire collapsed after it had completed its historical mission. Otherwise how could it have fallen? It is useless to lament the abysses of history, the crimes of power, the sufferings of good men. The world spirit is right in the end, its will will be obeyed, its purpose fulfilled; what does it care about the happiness or unhappiness of individuals? 'The real is the rational and the rational is the real.' When something ceases to be rational, when the spirit has already moved on, it will wither away and die. The individual may not understand his fate because he is liable to over-estimate himself and believes that history revolves around his person at the centre. The philosopher who perceives the kernel in the multi-coloured rind of what occurs will provide the insight too.

Power, and war, which creates and enhances power, cannot be omitted from all this. Man only realizes himself in the state and the state exists only where there is power to defend and attack. Might gives right. It is unlikely, it is in fact impossible, that the state without right on its side will win. What sort of right? Not a universally valid, pale right invented by stoicist philosophers, but historical right, the superiority of the historical mission. Thus right was on the side of the Spaniards against the Peruvians, in spite of all their cruelty and deceit; right was on Napoleon's side against the antiquated German Empire. Later, on the other hand, right was on the side of allied Europe against Napoleon only because, the professor concluded after much puzzling over this problem in his study, the arrogant Emperor, himself now out-dated, gave the Allies the right to conquer him, and only because he put himself in the wrong could he be conquered. Success, the outcome, provide the justification; in power there lies truth. When he began, Hegel wrote:

Men are so foolish that, blinded by their ideal vision of unselfish conceptions of freedom of conscience and of political liberty, and by the inward ardour of enthusiasm, they do not see the truth that lies in power . . . It is the philanthropists and moralists who decry politics as a human endeavour and an art, and who look on striving for one's own interest at the expense of what is right as a systematic work of injustice, while the ranting, non-party public, i.e. masses who have neither interest nor fatherland, whose idea of peace is the beer-hall, denounce politics for its fickleness and insufficient devotion to what is right . . .

But to Hegel the interests of the state alone are the force that decides what is right. That was what he thought at thirty, and he still thought so at sixty. In his late *Rechtsphilosophie* he still mocks at pacifists. 'And yet wars do occur whenever they lie in the nature of things; the crops grow again and idle talk ceases as soon as history recurs in real earnest.'

All this was developed with great force and originality, illustrated with a wealth of examples and produced in a language of creative force which German philosophy has never since attained. It was not narrow – it was as wide as the universe, a 'History of the World from a Cosmopolitan Point of View' in twenty volumes for which Kant had suggested the idea. Hegel's ideas were not anti-liberal; the state which he outlined in his philosophy of right was a constitutional though not a parliamentary state. He was very serious, not cynical, and took a very earnest view of history, man and his task. His ideas were not intolerant or misanthropic. If Hegel sacrificed the individual, especially the great individual, to his 'world spirit' he nevertheless had a very clear sense of individual greatness and tragedy; if he looked upon the individual primarily as citizen and member of a community, he nevertheless wished to recognize his claim to a secure private sphere. He was contemptuous of the sentimental egoists, the unreliable romantics who merely toyed with God and the world and art, and of intellectual capriciousness and speculation, but only because he himself had experienced similar temptations. He had started with the loneliness of the individual in the tumult of life and though he ended by glorifying the state, his original feeling for the conflict between Self and World, Self and Other, lived on in his writings. His work is one of conflicts overcome and preserved. It is the richest, most subtle, most powerful philosophical edifice that has ever been erected.

It is also the most dangerous. The great professor presumed to tell us what the world is, to construct it from nothing or from 'pure being' in a system of equations that promised to omit nothing, neither the stars, nor the stones, nor science nor reality. He presumed to understand the origin, course and purpose of history. The philosopher knew what game was being played, the players themselves did not. Misused pawns, miserable puppets, they hung on strings held by the world spirit and moved according to its wish, but believed that they were following their own will. For Hegel everything fitted; he nodded grim confirmation over every piece of news that reached his desk. Once again the inevitable and the comprehensible had occurred.

Pretentious scholars and quack prophets have often nursed similar notions in Germany and outside. But they did freely what Hegel avoided doing: they applied their doctrine to the future, predicting its inevitable course. They were smaller men than he. In the beginning they were second-rate, inflated geniuses, in the end they were evil-minded littérateurs. But the vice they practised was brought into the world by Hegel. He it was who first discovered that all who had failed in life had deserved their fate, that there was no need to feel sorry for them, and that only those who fulfilled the demands of the world spirit were destined to remain on top. He was the first to have the audacity to claim that he understood all that happened, approved of it, called it by universal names, and assimilated the reality to the idea. He defended power and Machiavellianism, the art of the ruthless use of power. He despised the moralists, the wiseacres who wrung their hands, the 'intellectuals' who told history what course to take instead of recognizing goodness and truth in reality itself. Even Kant had been one of these when he sadly remarked: 'It is not to be expected that right comes before might. It ought to do so but it does not.' Hegel rejected this dualism and doubt, again only after heavy spiritual conflict – in the highest sense. But how easy it became for others to ape this gesture which, without Hegel's living genius, became pure impudence. He spoke much of freedom, in the civil and in the philosophical sense, of the 'being-by-itself' of the spirit, of reconciliation of the ideal with the real, and he meant it all seriously. Yet he helped those who after him falsified the concept of freedom, as Rousseau had before him. Since the citizen finds his freedom only in the state, and the state must not lack the means of coercion, freedom is in the last resort found only in being coerced. According to Hegel, the criminal who is sentenced to death thus merely has freedom and human dignity bestowed on him. It was these casuistries of the Hegelian dialectic that were later used by German and non-German sophists to present the worse cause as the better and to proffer mad fantasies in the guise of political philosophy.

It was Hegel also who made the German world aware that 'history' is continuously in the making, that people live in history and that there are great decisions to be made. But this was not his doing only; his ideas were flood-gates through which the whole stream of the thought of his time forced its way. Even in the later eighteenth century men believed that they were living in unusual times; but they conceived of it as a single, unique step from a medieval irrationalism to a rationally ordered world. Now there were continuous crises, now every age had its own law which it struggled to fulfil, as did every nation, every *Volksgeist*. A great boost was thus also given to the science of history, and to the view that every product of the human mind, state, law, custom and civilization can be understood in terms of its historical conditions. So-called Historicism has its good and its dangerous aspects. It separates the nations by recognizing their right to an existence of their own, as well as the absolute right to achieve that existence. Universally valid things make way for relative, historically conditioned things: 'world history is the world court of justice'.

Most of the innovations that our book deals with will have to be qualified by saying that they have their dangers. Man is his own friend and enemy. He uses his noblest and best intentioned ideas to produce means of destruction. So uncertain are all his creations that it only needs a little exaggeration, intensification and falsification to turn Rousseau's teaching into Robespierre's murderous practices, or to use Hegel's philosophy to create nationalist totalitarianism. Must we therefore say that it would have been better if this great thinker had not lived? If man did not live dangerously would he ever have achieved anything?

Part Three
Old Gods and New (1815–1848)

Napoleon described the old Continent as a tiresome molehill which did not satisfy his conception of grandeur. Yet Europe was pleasant and spacious in his time, and its German-speaking regions were extensive. The reader of Napoleon's letters or conversations is surprised by how modern they are. But an attempt to visualize what the countries which he ruled for a few years were then like, yields a picture more reminiscent of the Middle Ages than of our own day. Towns were still days and weeks apart. Those who had seen Europe, their country, or even a part of it and who were not confined to the vicinity of their town or village all their lives were still a tiny minority. For a moment, Napoleon had lit the flame of European unity, and its light continued to glow. But his means had been those with which the Romans had kept their empire together, the horse and the cart.

The main occupation of the German nation was what it had been a thousand years earlier – agriculture. Three-quarters of the population lived on the land and most townspeople got their livelihood from it. Towns were small and their way of life differed little from that of the country. Agricultural products were Germany's most important export, followed by craftsmen's products. There was no industry in the modern sense; manufacture was a matter of handicraft and home work. In town and country life was patriarchal. At table the farmer presided over the farmhands, the master over the journeymen; prayers were said at meals and only the senior farmhand or journeyman was allowed to speak without being addressed.

Class divisions were as uncomplicated as economic life. There were the 'nobility', the 'middle class' and the 'people'. Nobles were landowners and held privileged positions in the army or the civil service. The middle class was composed of members of the academic and liberal professions, middle-rank civil servants, merchants, successful promoters of home industries and townsmen who had bought land. The rest was 'the people' – peasants, artisans and tradesmen, soldiers and journeymen, who began – but only in the forties – to be called 'proletarians'. At the top were the princes: those who still ruled and those who had been 'mediatized' and had ceased to rule at the beginning of the century, but who still had certain rights and enjoyed special status in their former territories. The Germans were a loyal people who clung to traditions; how loyal almost defines description. When the Elector of Hesse returned in 1814 after eight years of banishment he was enthusiastically welcomed, though almost everybody knew that he was a particularly bad prince who had once sold his subjects as soldiers to Britain and whose character had hardly changed subsequently. This fact did not diminish his subjects' enthusiasm. The wicked prince's carriage was pulled in joyful oblivion by citizens who included learned and liberal men such as the Grimm brothers.

Such a society, divided into thirty-six states, was easy to rule, provided it remained as it was. The history of the next thirty-three years is not primarily a history of the progress of ideas. Ideas are powerful provided they fit in with the changing climate. What gave the ideas new force, new meaning and different emphasis, and what finally led the 'people' to active participation in politics, was the slow, irresistible change in society. It has been said that it is impossible to fight ideas, but while they are only ideas they can be fought. Conservative statesmanship is powerless, however, against the hidden and automatic social process which, day by day, year by year, transforms small towns into cities and artisans into employers and employed. Today men attempt to plan and master the social process; there was no thought of that in the early nineteenth century when things were allowed to take their course. Thus it happened that a political order which in 1816 was reasonably suited to social realities lost more and more of its usefulness, until, in the middle of the century, there was profound unrest. A steady drip, not a cloudburst, wears down the stone. From the stage-coach to the railway, the steamship and the telegraph, from the faith of an earlier generation to unconcealed atheism and materialism, from Goethe to Heine, from Hegel to Marx, from *Faust* to the *Communist Manifesto* – this is a story of tremendous social and intellectual upheaval.

1. Congress Europe

The coalition against Napoleon produced at first something like a European system, a lasting alliance of the Great Powers, Britain, Russia, Austria and Prussia, to which defeated France was allowed to adhere. The German Confederation was not as such a member of this pan-Europe, though it was represented by its two main powers; it was itself the creation of the first of the congresses by which the Great Powers sought after their fashion to ensure the peace of the Old World. It was a memorable attempt. Periodic meetings were held in suitably situated German, Austrian or Italian towns, not at regular intervals but when a sufficient number of problems had accumulated. The congresses settled disputes between the smaller states, saw that everything was as it should be in France, and even dared to touch upon such moral problems as the abolition of the slave trade. The idea was to nip in the bud the threat of new catastrophes, to serve peace and prosperity. For a short time all went well. Soon it became clear, however, that rulers, though they professed to have the welfare of mankind at heart, had their own interests which they hoped to satisfy under the cloak of the general good. Statesmen pretended to be concerned only with justice and major questions, but they could not avoid being themselves merely a part of the whole, and unjust; they confused their own interests, often only imaginary, with those of Europe as a whole.

The main power in Germany and Italy, the Habsburg multi-national state of Austria, had nothing but peace and quiet in mind. Outstanding among the men who spoke and acted for this state was the Foreign Minister, or Chancellor, Clemens von Metternich. He was a man of the old school, handsome, vain, cultivated and intelligent; happy and pleasure-loving as far as his own person was concerned, but pessimistic as a statesman and interested only in defending the *status quo*; a west European serving the great, diversified state that bordered on Russia and Turkey, a German from the Rhineland, aristocratically brought up, educated in the French manner and European in outlook. If anybody could claim to have the interests of the Continent at heart it was Metternich. The state which he served and on whose existence his own brilliant life depended was inextricably connected with Europe as a whole, for it was part of Germany, of Italy, of Poland and of south-eastern Europe. It was a structure that trembled dangerously as soon as anything moved on the Continent. Therefore Metternich was an enemy of any movement, any sudden, noticeable 'progress'. He disapproved of the 'new ideas', of the national state, of popular sovereignty, of constitutional monarchy. Should they triumph, the Austrian Empire would cease to exist. Britain, Russia, France and even Prussia might gain something by new movements, but not Austria, nor the social order that reigned in the Austrian Europe and under which he, Prince Clemens, prospered so well.

There are things to admire in Metternich. He foresaw the destructive chaos which nationalism would bestow upon the Europeans and had a clear feeling for joint European responsibilities. It was his doing that a sensible peace was made in 1814. Yet he expected nothing of the future and was frightened of it; he did not want to create anything new but merely to delay for a while what he himself regarded as inevitable. He had little faith in the judgement of his fellow men though much in his own, and described himself as 'doctor in the world hospital' – as though all historical activity, particularly all doctrinaire and idealist enterprise, was nothing but disease and folly. By nature tolerant and friendly, though callous, he became cruel for political reasons; he was not unduly worried by the knowledge that noble visionaries were lying in chains in Austrian prisons. He was opposed to any form of dramatization: 'above all no pathos', he wrote under his own portrait. Yet because of his fear he created tragedy where none would have occurred if events had been allowed to take their natural course. After a long period during which he was hated by most historians and was anathema to all progressives it has now become customary to stress Metternich's achievements. On balance, making allowance for the fact that there is little that statesmen can really achieve, Metternich has more to his debit than to his credit.

The policy of the European congresses, to the extent that it was influenced by Metternich, was given a static, frightened, vindictive emphasis. This result was regrettable because it discredited the principle of joint European action and made the egoism of particular states appear comparatively progressive. While the Tsar would have liked to suppress Spanish liberalism and the South American independence movement he helped the Greek rebels against their Turkish rulers because he was planning to make himself the heir of Turkey and master of the Balkans and Constantinople. Austria was ready for joint action against revolution everywhere, but especially in Italy where its own frontiers were threatened. In Italy Austria took action, with or without Europe's mandate, and restored the absolute power of evil princelings. France did the same in Spain. Britain alone did not admit the principle of intervention. Though prepared to prevent the return of Napoleon and of revolutionary imperialism, Britain was unwilling to intervene in the internal affairs of foreign states, or to fight liberalism without asking for whose benefit action was being taken or whether there was anything worth saving. Britain opposed Prince Metternich on moral grounds but safeguarded British interests at the same time, because it had little to fear from liberal or national demands. It had no objections to the independence of South America, or to the independence of Greece provided that Greek independence was not a gift from Russia.

Because every power wanted something different and bent principles to suit its own interests, the congress system collapsed. At first it broke into two parts, with the two western powers on one side and the 'three eastern despotisms', Russia, Austria and

Prussia, on the other; then it broke into smaller parts which, like planets in a system without a central sun, circled around each other in confusion, formed brief attachments and broke away again, pulling away from and against each other while still being held together. The most steadfast country was Prussia, which remained loyal to Austria as well as to Russia, the reason being that Prussia was the smallest of the powers, without major European interests, still less overseas ones; moreover Prussia was deeply engaged in its own internal development.

2. Metternich's Germany

Germany was a piece of Congress Europe, with the difference that here the Metternich system lasted much longer. The Austro-British agreement ceased to exist at the beginning of the eighteen-twenties, and Austro-Russian agreement collapsed over the conflict about Greek independence and was revived only occasionally. Up to the forties and beyond, Prussia and Austria found more to unite than to separate them. The framework of their joint existence was the German Confederation, which survived until 1866.

The Confederation was a miniature Congress Europe; led by the same power, Austria, ruled by the same spirit and, unfortunately, equally unproductive. What little action it took was negative, concerned with defence. Fruitless attacks were made on the 'new ideas'. Topical questions were not tackled on a federal basis, and the provisions of the Federal Act, under which constructive action affecting all Germany in the sphere of law, economic life and defence might have been accomplished, remained unused. This was all in line both with the spirit of the Metternich era and with the federal constitution, whose voting system seemed arranged to prevent decisions. To the present day no positive answer has been given to the question of what a federation of sovereign states can achieve. If its achievements are great its members will soon cease to be sovereign, as in the case of the American states. The German states remained preoccupied with their sovereignty. The confederation which they formed was at best suited only to be a guardian – a preventive, not a creative force. This meant that it was historically unsuitable, because, above all, history is movement. What that movement cannot absorb, what falls apart when movement takes place, is not alive.

If people subsequently looked back with a certain nostalgia to the days of the German Confederation, it was because those were comparatively harmless, quiet times. For almost fifty years Germany was not involved in any serious wars – a rare blessing. The *Zeitgeist*, the spirit of the times, was not militant, and it alone produces the conflicts which, it is claimed, make war inevitable. It is futile to speculate how a federal army consisting of state contingents would have behaved in an emergency.

Politically the old Empire had fallen into three parts, Austria, Prussia and the Empire 'proper'; the same was inevitably true of the Confederation. In the Confederation 'proper' one has to distinguish between the three south German states (which since 1818–19 could boast of being constitutional) and central Germany, Saxony, Hanover and the small north German states. There were profound differences within each group: between Hamburg which was advanced and anxious for contact with England and medieval arch-conservative Mecklenburg, between Baden, which was politically alive and looked across the Rhine towards France, and Bavaria, ostensibly a constitutional state and a patron of the arts, but uninterested in power politics. Germany was still without a centre and still presented a picture of colour and variety.

It is impossible to say when exactly 'Austria' ceased to be regarded simply as 'German'. Humboldt's wife wrote as early as 1815:

Austria is so varied and its component parts, its nationalities, are so heterogeneous that I would wager anything that it will cease to be a German power in this century. German national feeling appears to be growing and Austria is not keeping in step. There is apparently no force strong enough to halt the spirit of the times . . .

Thirty years later Austria's noblest poet, Franz Grillparzer, made a sharp distinction between Germany and Austria. He declared proudly that he had never published anything abroad and had never written for German journals, thereby contrasting his country as an entity with the rest of Germany. Not all were as Habsburg-minded or as unreceptive to the claims of a national state as Grillparzer, not all succeeded in cutting themselves off from Germany so easily and naturally. Metternich himself regarded the Habsburg monarchy as a predominantly German political system, without attaching much importance to the fact; the capital was German, the dynasty was German and the language of the army and the senior civil service was German. At the same time Metternich encouraged the efforts of the Czechs and Croats to cultivate their languages; he wanted the old provinces of the Empire to have a life of their own so as to preserve its equilibrium. Hungary went its own way, an empire in itself, the property of a native aristocracy, unconcerned with German and European affairs.

The Danubian Empire was separated from the 'rest of Germany' by the barriers of tariff walls and a strict censorship of books and periodicals. In Austria there was no political literature apart from that initiated by the government and ably produced by educated foreigners. There was no stimulating intellectual life; indeed one might say there was no public life at all. The police were omnipotent and omniscient, the universities were conceived as schools for training civil servants, and the Catholic Church was controlled by the state. No constitutional restrictions affected the power of the monarchy. Austria behaved, or tried to behave, as though the French Revolution had never been. At the top of the pyramid there was the Emperor, Francis I, a hard-working, honourable man as he saw himself, not without patient political shrewdness, but cold and heartless, a man who unhesitatingly identified the welfare of his subjects with the splendour of his dynasty, and who was untouched by any trace of 'modern ideas'. 'I don't need scholars but obedient subjects,' he said to the professors of Graz University. 'Those who disagree with me can find themselves another master.' There were the Emperor's numerous relatives with their sinecures, vice-kingdoms and Italian thrones; then came the nobility, international or inter-Austrian, German, Czech, Hungarian, Italian, Belgian and Spanish, but always and above everything Austrian, rich, pleasure-loving and urbane; next followed the senior civil servants, the clergy, the provincial notables, and then the 'people'. Music flourished, and a little later – but this was already a sign of nascent unrest – comedy as well. Austria was a beautiful country and though the government was in constant financial difficulty, not a poor one. Yet there was no active community life, no state in the sense which the word had acquired in the previous fifty years. Austria took little part in the intellectual life of western Europe. The writer Börne, from Frankfurt, called it 'Europe's China', an allusion to its isolation, its immobility and lack of history. Could that state of affairs continue, was it possible in the nineteenth century to govern European peoples in this way and for this kind of Austria to rule the German Confederation? A Frenchman wrote in the thirties: 'The nineteenth century will spell death for the Austrian monarchy.'

It is also impossible to say exactly when a few prescient men first began to hope or fear that Prussia might one day unify Germany. In the eighteenth century this would have been a laughable idea; Prussia was the mischief-maker, the destroyer of imperial unity. During the later years of the Revolution Prussia went its own selfish way while Austria fought on, for itself and the Empire, and showed remarkable staying power in spite of all defeats. It was during the years of reform that Prussia first showed signs of a national and humane spirit transcending its narrow interests. As yet Stein did not think of Prussians as more 'German' than Austrians; he still hoped that the two would share the leadership of their common country. It was the men at Prussian headquarters during the War of Liberation who were the first to regard themselves as more nationalistic, better and more forward-looking than the Austrians. At the Congress of Vienna experienced diplomats, like Talleyrand and even Gentz, uttered warning words about Prussia: it was about to make an alliance with the nationalists, it aspired to conquer the whole of Germany. The new territorial divisions made no provision for thwarting this ambition;

they took Prussia far to the west and the south, and gave it the Rhine, the river of which it now began to make a curious heathen cult. Then there was quiet; the reformers disappeared, the old Prussian nobility came to the fore again and there was a close understanding between Metternich and the King of Prussia. Yet even during these years of peace Prussia's tariff policy was consciously directed towards the economic domination of Germany. Thinking people in the twenties realized that Prussia's problems were soluble whereas Austria's were not, that it was the better ruled, more modern, more active state, a miniature Germany, whereas Austria was only a miniature Europe – and from that almost everything followed. After 1830 the prophecies became more numerous: Prussia would expel Austria from the German Confederation and unite the nation, either peacefully or by force. That was not the conscious aim of the Prussian leaders. Nor on the other hand can it be said that the subsequent events and actions were surprising, unnatural improvisations. The opportunities became gradually more numerous. There was much speculation, some of it correct, about the shapes which gradually began to appear on the distant horizon.

Whereas in Austria the problems of the modern state were officially unknown, in Prussia they were not disputed. A strong wind blew in Prussia and there were restless spirits there, particularly in the newly acquired western provinces. Repeatedly – five times, as people calculated bitterly – the monarch had promised to give representatives of the people some share in the government. The promise was neither kept nor withdrawn and this imprecision created a provisional atmosphere. There was corporative representation in the provinces, but it was weak and predominantly aristocratic, suited to keeping political demands alive, not to implementing them. As a source and centre of intellectual stimulus Berlin University towered above that of Vienna, and though the great professor of philosophy, Hegel, now defended the state as it was and taught obedience, his complex philosophy was inherently one of movement and unrest. Universities also existed in Königsberg, Breslau and later Bonn; there were aggressive academic teachers like Ernst Moritz Arndt and influential journalists like Joseph Görres. King Frederick William III, a north German variant of the Habsburgs, was a wholehearted supporter of Metternich and of his son-in-law, the arch-reactionary, the despot of all despots, Grand Duke, later Tsar, Nicholas of Russia. Yet it was more difficult in Prussia to behave as though the French Revolution had never happened than in Austria. Consequently oppression took a more violent form, as well as being more futile.

In the German Confederation the two Great Powers made common cause – an inevitable condition for its success, for its very existence. Negation united them, the fight against the liberalism of south German constitutional life, new, artificial and harmless though it was. With greater determination they fought the universal 'spirit of unrest', the 'passion for change', the 'demagogues'. That is the real political theme of the years around 1820. It must be said that it was unproductive, that period in which statesmen chose to make the persecution of romantic students, of courageous if not very bright youths, their chief preoccupation.

What Metternich and his allies offered the Germans was peace and order, customary, ordinary, unhistorical things. A long period of stirring history was now to be followed by uneventful times in which the individual's sole concern with the law was to obey it. He was to concentrate on the economic struggle for existence; the rest would be done discreetly by a congress of diplomats in Frankfurt, by rulers and ministers, councillors and chiefs of police. The prospect did not please the young men back from the war. Thrilled by their common experience and by the songs of the poets of freedom – some of them excellent – they expected other things. They did not know themselves exactly what; it is characteristic of such youth movements that they generate noisily assertive energies and create a community feeling without having a rational programme. 'We are here, we are better than the old ones, we want to stay together' – that is what it amounts to. On the other hand it is characteristic of political activity that in the long run it can never satisfy such large, vague hopes and demands. Metternich knew this and took pleasure in his wisdom. The old men who were in power had experienced the

French Revolution, and their one aim was to prevent its repetition. The young men had experienced only the War of Liberation and had enjoyed it.

The *Burschenschaften*, the student associations which spread from Jena to northern and central Germany, were Christian and national, in favour of a united, great German fatherland, against foreign, particularly French, influences, and against the Jews, who had recently become conspicuous in literary life and whose civil status was in question. The students were not 'liberal' in the sense which the word acquired a little later, in the eighteen-twenties. They were not interested in constitutions of the south German type; on the contrary, they felt that such popular representation was an artificial product, imported from Britain and France, a feeling that was not entirely unjustified. On the other hand they were not in favour of absolute monarchy; among the books ceremonially burned at the great student rally at the Wartburg in 1817 were works of absolutist political philosophers, as well as the liberal *Code Napoléon*. This twofold hostility indicates how difficult it was to bring the political views of the *Burschenschaften* into line with the ideas and conflicts of the times. Their ideal lay in the past; they thought that their choice of dress, their beards and long hair were Teutonic and they believed their black, red and gold colours to be the colours of the old Empire. They hated the French who had wanted to force them-selves on the world as the nation of progress; they hated Germany's pre-revolutionary past of rococo, pigtails and fancy uniforms, not for being the past as such but for symbolizing a perverted, Frenchified period. From Jahn they took the enthusiasm for physical fitness as well as a strong feeling for equality, a protest against inherited class distinctions. Jahn and his followers in the *Burschenschaften* carried their Franco-phobia to absurd, repulsive extremes: 'If you let your daughter learn French you might just as well teach her to become a whore.' Other *Altburschen*, Arndt, Luden and Fries, taught the students more worthwhile things, a feeling for the seriousness of life, a sense of what is fitting, faith in God and faith in man; indeed the whole move-ment must have been an indissoluble mixture of the noble and the absurd, of sane and distorted ideas. This first German youth movement was unique, and more confused than anything that had appeared in European politics since Rousseau. Above all it could not be identified with French or English, or even southern European, political concepts, and did not want to be. Görres, close to this movement though towering above it, sought to make its activities comprehensible to the French public in the following words:

> In Germany it was not the Third Estate that made the revolution but governments under the protection of a foreign power (Napoleon's) ... With us it is the supporters of despotism who use Jacobin forms and practices, whereas some of the friends of freedom defend the principles of the French reactionaries. That is the confusion which presents the foreign observer with a puzzling problem ...

The clear-cut concepts of French politics – reactionary, conservative, progressive, revolutionary, left, right – were useless for the understanding of German problems.

These boys were really harmless, if devoid of taste; they might have been left in peace. What happened was that one of them, a morbid youth, took too seriously the dagger which they all carried in their belts. He assassinated a minor dramatist named Kotzebue who earned some pocket-money by sending reports to the Tsar. It was a fortunate period in which such a stupid crime could make 'history' and stir passionate feelings among the populace. The murderer, Karl Ludwig Sand, who was beheaded, became a martyr of the national cause, a misguided saint. Prince Metternich made the murder into as great a threat as the storming of the Bastille, calling for extreme measures if Germany was to be saved from chaos. His generation of rulers was always scenting danger and was forever on the defensive. It thought that the French Revolution could have been prevented if only the King had struck in time, and it wanted to do better.

There now began an unpleasant period of political persecution. Its guiding principles were called the 'Karlsbad Decrees', because it was in Karlsbad that Metternich in confidential ministerial discussions pushed through the programme which was later enacted law by the Federal Diet. A commission was set up to investigate subversive activities; individual states could use its reports as they thought fit. The *Burschenschaften* were dissolved, the universities were placed under political supervision and advance censorship of all printed material of less than twenty pages was introduced. Again one is tempted to say what harmless, happy times in which such actions could be regarded as terrible despotism. Yet every age must be judged by its own yardstick. In the early nineteenth century men everywhere in Europe and America strove for civil liberties, which included the free discussion of political questions. To attempt to stifle this desire was to sin against the spirit of the age. So much the worse if the attempt was successful; it then involved what in legal language is called a 'crime against unborn life'. Prince Metternich succeeded only in part. He was too civilized, at bottom too 'liberal', to insist that the decrees be strictly applied. Moreover, he had nothing positive to offer, no faith to press on people; what he offered and demanded was moderation. But it is hard to fight for moderation with immoderate means. The acquisition of what is now called 'totalitarian' power requires fanatical determination and faith, which Metternich and his friends lacked. The fact that Germany was so divided also helped the cause of freedom. Some German states, particularly the southern ones, regarded the decrees of Karlsbad and Vienna as conflicting with their sovereignty and did not carry them out. Nevertheless there was persecution and innocent people were ruined. Intellectuals were restricted in their activities, intimidated and driven out of the country.

The fact that the German Confederation accomplished nothing except the Karlsbad Decrees amounted, even at this early stage, to bankruptcy. On paper it appeared insignificant; in reality its only achievement was a narrow, philistine negation.

3. An Example: Joseph Görres

We have already met Görres as a young, high-spirited intellectual adventurer at the time of the French Revolution, and as a mature but angry man during the dramatic months of Napoleon's fall. Now we meet him again. Without reaching a very advanced age he lived through the whole of the period covered by this chapter. One generation sees many historic figures and tries to understand them as best it can. Let us take Görres as an example of how a powerful lively mind sought its way through the labyrinth of the times.

He belonged to those who were deeply disappointed by the outcome of the last Napoleonic crisis. He had hoped for a German empire, strong abroad and free within. Instead there was Metternich's aristocratic caution, supported after brief hesitation by Prussia. The men who had dreamt of a strong Prussian leadership of Germany were compelled to retire into private life, first Stein, then Humboldt and then Görres, whose *Rheinischer Merkur* was banned after he had dared to attack reaction in Prussia.

Görres was now a Prussian subject; his home, the Rhineland, had been amalgamated with Prussia at the Congress of Vienna. The reshaping of the province, its unification with old Prussia, whose character was so different, did not take place without serious troubles in which Görres constituted himself the defender of his Rhenish countrymen. His thesis was that the Rhine province had not been conquered but had become part of Prussia by treaty, and that the King was therefore obliged to concede to its citizens their rights in matters of popular representation, economic interests, and religious freedom and equality. He took up the cause of disappointed hopes, of suppressed unrest. His pamphlet *Teutschland und die Revolution* appeared in 1819, after the assassination of Kotzebue and after the Karlsbad Decrees.

In it Görres said that in 1815, at the Congress of Vienna, historically false decisions had been made. Germany had been cheated out of a new form. The German Confederation was worthless, it was merely the 'Holy Alliance' on German soil; Europe was playing a game of make-believe; in fact the Confederation had no genuine life of its own.

The current theory is that in noble universality the German must belong to all nations; Swiss, Jewish pedlar, lackey and ruffian of the whole world all in one, he must never, at the risk of severe punishment, think of his country, which they have torn to shreds. He is allowed to ape all foreign follies, but when the young generation tried to bring back old German customs it was accused of Teutomania.

The freedom just tolerated in southern Germany was not 'that German variety which added the much hated unity to real freedom', it was only 'French liberality come to terms with Napoleon'. The rulers of Bavaria, Württemberg and Baden hated the memory of the old Empire; their states were cold mechanisms which eradicated everything traditional, everything that had developed naturally.

Their constitutions are not social associations set up by independent men to involve and to liberate each other; they are books whose leaves had once grown green, then were torn to shreds, pulverized and made into paper on which their vulgar thoughts were written, numbered, bound and given a gilt edging; when out of print they are reissued in a new edition. Thus their activity is not blessed because it is based only on vanity . . .

Austria thought that it could lead a quiet life and keep completely apart from Germany's intellectual movement 'but nobody can break off an historical association as easily as that and just pocket the profits'. Because of its glorious achievements, Prussia might have played its part in reshaping the nation in the eighteenth century and again in 1813. But the men in Berlin pursued a selfish, purely Prussian policy, and, like Austria, saw ghosts everywhere and were terrified of revolution. Their clumsy, wicked oppression merely strengthened what they were hoping to destroy.

After four years of bitter party struggle, of senseless resistance against the demands of the times, of partial concessions by one side and exaggeration by the other, the situation has reached the point where the whole of Germany is in a state of spiritual ferment and its mood is such as usually precedes great historical catastrophes. The busiest intrigues and the cleverest demagogic efforts from below could never alone have succeeded in arousing and embittering the quiet, peace-loving, sober and moderate German people to its very depths; that has been successfully accomplished by those at the top who control the long arm of the lever . . .

And further:

Not for this have such terrible storms swept across Europe, that while they still rumble on the distant horizon the empire of mediocrity which they destroyed should rise again – the empire in which all force is discord, all talent dangerous power, in which all thought is regarded with distrust and all enthusiasm is treated as dangerous folly. Henceforth history has no use for vapid, threadbare courtiers who study triviality and make futility their business . . .

Görres described the student movement as a natural reaction against everything false and as an attempt to achieve, in the academic sphere at least, what had failed miserably in the political. He was even prepared to understand Sand's action and to approve of the motives, if not of the deed. For the Karlsbad Decrees he showed even more contempt than hatred: 'The noise of boxes being broken open', 'the comings and goings of policemen', 'hasty abrogation of all legal forms', 'interrogation, arrest and release'. By such means, he prophesied, the course of history could not be stayed. Revolution could and should be prevented, for revolutions were terrible. A German revolution would be at least as frightful and violent as the French. It would

inevitably end with the expulsion of all ruling dynasties, the destruction of all ecclesiastical forms, the extermination of the aristocracy and the introduction of a republican constitution; then, when it has found its more fortunate Wallenstein, it will step beyond its frontiers and destroy Europe's whole rotten political system as far as the frontiers of Asia, because every revolutionized nation necessarily becomes a conquering one . . .

That must not happen, neither must there be foolish resistance to the Will of the Age. Reform there must be, a return to the position of four years earlier when the wrong road was taken in Vienna. Its aim would not be to put into practice any one theory, like that

of Rousseau; that was not what the Germans, or men in general
were likely to do. '. . . theory cuts like the blade of the sword and
spreads like the flame of the fire; but human beings are a mixture
of contrasts, modified by gradual change, and all extremes are
poison to their nature.' Görres did not want a Jacobin state based
on a single plan. Germany needed monarchy and aristocracy, just
as it needed a strong, free middle class, corporate representation
of the whole nation, and freedom of thought and expression. It
needed moderation, not revolutionary excess, reconciliation not
conflict. However, it takes two to produce reconciliation. After
Görres had made his powerful plea the King of Prussia ordered
his arrest and he was forced to flee. Since he was not safe in any
German state he went to France, to Alsace.

In Görres' thought there is much that is characteristic of the
period and also much that is characteristically German. He was
liberal but not in the sense of the liberalism practised in France
under the restored monarchy, which he regarded as a corrupt
comedy. He wanted to see Germany reformed, but on the basis of
old traditions – with a peasantry, an army, a teaching profession,
and a parliament representing the middle class, the aristocracy
and the church. But were such estates still in existence, after
hundreds of years of absolutism, in the century of the middle
classes, and if they still existed, would they be the future leaders of
society? Was Görres, with his firm belief in the flow of history,
not demanding a reversal of this flow? It is characteristic of him
that he wanted 'progress' and an admixture of democracy, but
certainly not something modelled on what was gradually developing in France; he wanted a Germanic democracy, a national
community. This would have needed great public spirit, not only
in the individual publicist but also in the mass of the people who
made up 'Germany'. The political philosopher can hardly count
on such lasting enthusiasm or such control of all selfish interest –
Görres demanded that the aristocracy should voluntarily and
happily pay as much in taxes as it possibly could.

In Strasbourg, where he spent several years of exile, Görres
returned to the faith of his childhood. He who as a young man
had made fun of the 'profitable foolery' of the 'black magicians'

became the champion of the Catholic Church. Homeless, he longed for firm support both in this world and in the next. The return was made easier for him by a democratic Catholic movement initiated in France, though not welcomed in Rome. The new Catholic character of his activities finally took him back to Germany. In 1827 he was given an appointment at the University of Munich. Prussia protested against the appointment of this 'demagogue' and demanded his extradition, but Bavaria refused to listen. Görres thus learned to appreciate the advantages of German particularism. It was possible to be wanted by the police in Berlin and to be a highly respected man, a professor and even ennobled, in Munich.

In his old age Görres worked for many years on a vast four-volume work entitled *Die christliche Mystik* (Christian Mysticism). It was full of both profound and strange things, so strange that the church itself regarded him with suspicion. Görres was fighting against what seemed to him the strongest trend of the period 'impertinent beggar's pride', 'the dreariest, shallowest ignorance'. What the natural sciences could comprehend gave no meaning to life and had no right to claim universality. There was another, higher type of knowledge, which was as susceptible of proof as physical knowledge. 'If you deny what the best and most credible people in all ages have repeatedly found I shall deny the whole of world history . . .' He was referring to apparitions of the devil and of ghosts, to the good and the evil eye and the proven effect of holy water. The rationalist and worshipper of revolutions of 1793, the enthusiastic German romantic of 1806, became a mystic in his old age; not only a mystic but the teacher of a mixture of science and hair-raising speculation that can only be called superstitious. He had gone from one extreme to the other, and yet always remained the same, an honest fighter for justice and a seeker after truth.

4. Periods and Events

Thirty-three years is a long period both in the life of a nation and of an individual; they bring change. It has been said that these thirty-three years, 1815–48, were an uneventful period, which is true if one means that there were no wars, revolutions or major conflicts. Before 1815, and again after 1848, the papers were able to offer more exciting news. Yet Europe and its German-speaking part changed in those years, just as they did before and since. The changes were of the kind against which governments are power-less unless they seal off their country from world history, as Japan did for two hundred years. Prince Metternich tried to do this in Austria, though not seriously. He encouraged the building of roads and railways and during his rule Vienna became a great industrial city. How in the long run could the 'defence of the *status quo*' be successfully maintained against such developments? Metternich and his friends were sufficiently clear-sighted to recognize that their policy was essentially one of rearguard action. 'Time storms ahead,' wrote the Chancellor; 'to halt its violent advance by force would be a vain undertaking . . . To soften the disastrous effects is all that remains for the protectors and friends of peace to do . . .' There was economic progress; factories, banks and insurance companies were founded. The nation grew. In the three decades after Napoleon's fall the population of Germany, excluding Austria, rose from twenty-four to thirty-six million. There were developments in fashion and modes of life which became increasingly middle class – if an absence of colour, monotony of dress, lounge-suits and boots, spectacles and cigars are middle class. There was advance in the intellectual sphere, and the German language became more flexible.

If we say that there was 'advance' we do not necessarily mean that things improved. The word 'advance' has a positive, happy connotation which probably originates from war, where advance is better than retreat. Because time moves only in one direction – we think of it as 'advancing' – we are tempted to regard the changes that time brings as 'progress'. Faith in progress was never stronger than in the nineteenth century. It originated in the seventeenth and eighteenth century and was connected with the progress of science which was clearly developing at a tremendous rate. Faith in progress was also connected with political history, where there was an advance in the direction of freedom and self-government. Furthermore, we tend to equate progress with desired increase, and in the period under consideration energy increased with ever-growing rapidity: production rose, traffic became faster and the population multiplied. To that extent there was undoubted 'advance'. As regards the progress of human happiness every change brings losses and gains. In that sense there can be no straightforward advance, but in 1840 this proposition was not as axiomatic as it is today.

The fundamental changes are the slow and undramatic ones, which happen every day and finally add up to something big. Sudden revolutions, if they are of use at all, can only release forces that have accumulated day by day for years. More or less the same is true of the so-called change of generation, which does not really occur in public life, although the death of some outstanding personality or other might create such an impression. At the beginning of the eighteen-thirties two Germans died who had been dominant in their spheres for many years, Goethe and Hegel. At the time it was felt that with them an era had ended and that another, less important as well as more active, was beginning. The deaths of two individuals, however, cannot make, though they may symbolize, a turning point. The men who next came to the fore in German literature had already been there and had long regarded the 'poet prince' as old-fashioned.

It can never be determined to what extent the revolution of 1848 was caused by social change and to what extent it was spontaneous, an affair of the 'intellectuals' stimulated by foreign countries, by France, by anticipation and false comparisons. Certainly foreign influence was strong. The old leaders were men of the Napoleonic era whose ideas were those of the Germany of 1818. The young generation thought differently and was different. German society, too, was different and more modern, and since systems of government had remained almost unchanged, they were obviously more antiquated in 1848 than in 1815. Even in 1848, however, industrialization was still in its infancy; towns on average had only just kept in step with the increase of the population as a whole, and those who, like Karl Marx, simply transferred to Germany ideas derived from the French experience were mistaken.

In July 1830 workers and students in Paris rose against the Bourbon King, Charles X, who was about to overthrow the constitution. Fighting on the barricades was followed by the flight of that incorrigible old gentleman. Clever citizens for whom the revolt seemed to be going too far raised Louis Philippe of Orleans, a relative of the royal house, to the throne. These events made a deep impression in Europe. The expulsion of the Bourbons was the end of the 'restoration', a blow against the work of the Congress of Vienna. If the rulers of Europe allowed it to happen, a precedent would be created, of which the consequences could not be foreseen. They did allow it to happen; after fifteen years they could not make war to put the Bourbons back on their throne. Britain had no such intention, and neither had Austria or Prussia; perhaps the Tsar had, but he was soon involved elsewhere. The conflagration spread from one centre to another. In August there was a revolution in Brussels and the Belgians rose against the alien bureaucracy of the King of the Netherlands; in November the Poles rose against Russian rule, in February the Romans against their old-fashioned sovereign, the Pope. In Britain in the course of 1831 there was growing, often violent, agitation for parliamentary reform. The old order seemed to be collapsing everywhere. However, it was not international liberalism that was destined to be victorious in Europe but other forces more difficult to describe. In Belgium some clever political manoeuvring prevented a catastrophe; the Great Powers decided to create an independent, permanently neutral kingdom of the Belgians. The new state soon became a model of central and local self-administration. Here the constitution made the king, not a gracious king the constitution. The Poles were left to their fate, the guns and gallows of Tsar Nicholas; Prussia actively helped the Tsar by mobilizing on its eastern frontiers to prevent the rising from spreading to its Polish province of Posen (Poznan) and to drive Polish refugees back into the Russian fire. In Rome there was the Austrian army and good advice to the Pope to experiment with a few modern ideas. In 1833 Europe was back to 'normal'. Soon the legality of the new French government was doubted only by a few pedants.

Germany too was part of the world in which this sequence of events took place. In several states of the Confederation, in Hesse, Hanover and Saxony, popular pressure led to the enactment of a basic law in the modern sense. There was much enthusiasm for the liberation struggle of the Poles, and also for the reappearance in Paris of the old heroes of the legendary revolutionary past – while it was not yet clear that the citizen-King, Louis Philippe, intended to steer a very sober, not to say ignoble, course. In contrast to the celebrations of the *Burschenschaften* twelve or fourteen years before, the tenor was now more radical, more international, more in keeping with European liberalism as a whole. Once more, as around 1790, France became the model. The speeches that were made at a political meeting in Hambach in the Palatinate in 1832 might just as well have been made by French or Italian popular leaders.

As soon as German popular sovereignty is given its legitimate place there will be the closest federation of peoples, because the people love where kings hate, the people defend where kings persecute, the people do not grudge brother nations what is most precious to themselves and which they seek to acquire with their life-blood – freedom, enlightenment, nationhood and popular sovereignty. The German people therefore does not grudge its brothers in Poland, Hungary, Italy and Spain these great, invaluable benefits . . . Three cheers for the united free states of Germany! Three cheers for federated, republican Europe!

Theirs was the easy optimism of men concerned only with ideas, without any experience themselves, who never thought about the great experience of the French Revolution. People are good, let them be in charge and chase away the princes; the rest would follow. For example, as someone suggested at Hambach, the French might give the Germans Alsace and Lorraine and recompense themselves with the French-speaking part of the Netherlands. Only a small minority thought and spoke like this and penetrated beyond the demands of constitutionalism to the idea of a democratic republic. The road to it seemed smooth because the case was logical and appeared to be dictated by common sense. The obstacles in the path, however, were anything but logical. They had been created by History, and History cares little about common sense.

The Radicals were taken seriously enough to be feared, and there was a new wave of persecution in Prussia, Hesse and even in easy-going Bavaria, more vicious than that of 1819. Hundreds of people were sentenced to death, and although they were re-prieved from execution their spirits were broken in prisons and fortresses. German refugees met in foreign capitals, in London, Paris, Brussels and Zürich. Some, not the worst, turned their backs for ever on their homes and emigrated to America. The contrast between the existing political system and the intellectual resources of the country was great. Those who thought about these things at all – always a mere minority – did not doubt that there would have to be a change, that a monarchical, bureau-cratic military system was no longer in keeping with the spirit of the age. But who would bring about a change, how and when and what form it would take, nobody really knew.

It was in other spheres and by other people that creative action was taken. In 1818 the Prussian state became a unified customs area. The policy of the Prussian Ministers was to present the German Confederation with *faits accomplis*, to force the small states surrounded by Prussia to join the Prussian economic system by imposing high transit duties, and to promote agriculture by low import duties. One by one they joined the *Zollverein*, beginning with various small north German states, then Hesse, then Bavaria and Württemberg, and finally Baden and Saxony. Internal German customs barriers disappeared and the govern-ments of the *Mittelstaaten* left the direction of their trade policy largely to the Prussian rulers, although they were formally entitled to be consulted. Only a few north German states, orientated towards the sea or towards Britain, like Hanover and Hamburg, kept apart. The aims of the *Zollverein* were economic; they corresponded to the facts of the situation and were propagated by such an un-Prussian, imaginative, progressive and freedom-loving writer as the Württemberg economist, Friedrich List. How could Germany's economic life catch up with that of Britain, France and America as long as Anhalt-Köthen and Anhalt-Dessau were separated by frontier posts?

Political consideration also played a part. The importance of the customs union between Prussia and southern Germany, wrote the Prussian Minister of Finance, lay in the fact that 'unification of these states in a customs and trading union leads to the establishment of a unified political system.' Metternich fully appreciated this fact, realized the significance of Austria's exclusion from the unified Prussian-led economic area and tried to prevent it; his diplomacy was no more able to stop the flow of goods than his police were able to stop the flow of ideas.

Economics are not identical with politics and we must be wary of saying that from that moment, 1 January 1834, the course of German history was prescribed. In every crisis, however, the fact of economic unity and dependence was henceforth a powerful, secret influence. Nothing irremediable had been created but the new union weighted the scales heavily on one side. The southern German liberals, incidentally, were opposed to the customs union, which they saw as a conquest of the South by reactionary Prussia – which in a certain sense it was. Yet might economic unity and progress not in the end operate against the very powers that the liberals were afraid of? History prepares many surprises, often disagreeable ones, for the victor.

The framework created by the *Zollverein* was filled in by the railways. Again it was Friedrich List who was their great advocate, and the construction of the first big line, from Leipzig to Dresden, was due to his persistent initiative. Other lines followed, from Munich to Augsburg, Frankfurt to Mainz, Berlin to Anhalt. In 1845 Germany had about 1,250 miles of track; only ten years later there were almost 5,000 miles and the construction of the major lines was in full swing. Is this not the secret, the essence of the history of this and subsequent decades? Is it not this which changed Germany more profoundly and more irresistibly than all revolutions, wars and political intrigues taken together? The railways produced, consumed and reproduced capital which was invested in more railways, they encouraged the establishment of banks and stock exchanges and gave a decisive stimulus to the mining and machine industries. They created the new types of men who built and operated them, industrialists, workmen, engineers and office-workers. They displaced people and speeded up news services before the days of the electric telegraph, and raised the volume of passenger and goods traffic – literally a thousandfold. They revolutionized the art of war, changed the face of towns and the rhythm of rural life, and brought lonely villages within the reach of the towns. They created wealth, they created poverty and transformed the poor into what were now called 'proletarians'. They reduced the size of a country that had once been spacious and beautiful.

Of all this only the very first beginnings were felt in 1840. In Germany it was mainly private capital that built the railways and drew from them annual dividends of fifteen per cent and more; in Austria it was the state. Once the railways were there, however, Austria could not remain Metternich's Austria. Heine revealed this secret in a poem, the fable of the horse and the donkey. The two animals watch a noisy steam train push past, billowing black smoke. The horse is dismayed, his day is over, man will no longer need him or feed him, and will send him to the devil. The donkey remains cheerful; he, the homely, unassuming, useful beast of burden, has nothing to fear from the new age, man will always want him. The moral: the age of chivalry is over, the proud horse must go hungry, but the wretched donkey will always have his hay and oats.

The age of chivalry was over – the refusal of the 'knights', the rulers of Germany, to recognize this fact lay at the root of the political struggles of the next decades. However, things happen very, very slowly in real life. The *Zollverein* no more created instantaneous political unity in Germany – though it laid the foundations for it – than the new industry which grew up round the railways produced the instantaneous change in the class structure which some theorists had expected. Meanwhile in

Barmen, his native town, the schoolboy Friedrich Engels passed daily by factories where in low, uninspected rooms, workers – among them six-year-old children – 'breathe in more coal smoke and dust than oxygen'. To him and others came the idea that was bound to come to people at such a time: that the essence of all history is economic history; that political struggles are merely the expression of what takes place in the economic sphere; that politicians are only puppets on strings which they themselves do not feel.

In 1837 a minor ruler, the King of Hanover, an Englishman by birth brought to Hanover by a dynastic accident, revoked the basic law proclaimed a few years earlier in the wake of the July revolution in Paris. He wanted to make his own decisions undisturbed by the modern disease of parliamentarianism. Seven professors of the University of Göttingen protested, among them such famous scholars as the liberal historian Dahlmann and the celebrated philologists and collectors of fairy tales, the brothers Grimm. Thereupon the King dismissed them. This was another relatively harmless incident compared with what later generations became accustomed to. However, the effect of an element depends on the chemical solution in which it is mixed. So great was the respect for law in Germany and so profound the veneration for great scholars that the dismissal of the 'seven' unleashed a tremendous storm of indignation.

People fought for copies of the Grimms' and Dahlmann's letters of protest. An association was formed which went on paying their salaries. The excitement was so great that the southern German states appealed to the Confederation to restore the Hanoverian constitution. The royal Don Quixote had wanted to show the professors who was the master: 'Professors, actors and whores can always be had.' Now the professors showed that they were the masters, the most respected class in the land; that the power of public opinion was greater than that of traditional authority. The middle class, the young Friedrich Engels remarked at this period, ruled directly in Britain and France and indirectly in Germany, through public opinion. There was some truth in this statement, in spite of newspaper censorship and supervision of universities, and in spite of the absence of a great forum like the parliaments of western Europe.

The dismissal of the 'Göttingen seven' was overshadowed in the same year by an event which roused public opinion even more: the arrest by Prussian police of the Archbishop Droste of Cologne. This act had been preceded by long negotiations between the state and the Archbishop on the subject of the training of priests. The state wanted this training to take place at its new University of Bonn, where there were liberal theologians sympathetic to historical research, whereas the Archbishop insisted that the priests should be educated at his seminary. The state was to keep its hands off these matters, which were the closest concern of the church. Another subject of dispute was the question of mixed marriages. The Bishop, on papal instructions, wanted to give his blessing only if couples were prepared to bring up their children in the Catholic faith. The state wanted some relaxation of this rule and had got it from Droste's predecessor. Prussia was unaccustomed to tolerating a foreign, independent power within its frontiers. The recalcitrant Archbishop was removed from his See and taken to the fortress of Minden. Not since Napoleon had kidnapped the Pope and taken him to France had anyone dared to do such a thing to a high church dignitary. Now it was done not by a revolutionary dictator, but by the pious, conservative Prussian state. A wave of indignation swept across Catholic Germany. Public opinion seized eagerly upon a conflict which concerned the whole German nation and made national discussion possible, although it was confined to the spiritual plane. Dozens of pamphlets were published. In Munich the aged Görres made a powerful intervention; his leaflet *Athanasius* was the revenge of the Rhinelander on the Prussian state which had persecuted him and would have broken him had he been less resilient. What Görres now elaborated contained internal contradictions. He wanted the church to be free from the state, mistress of its own sacred house, and yet recognized at the same time by the state as the great spiritual force in the life of the nation. The state must not control the church, nor must the two be separated, because life cannot be neatly divided into compartments and because such a separation must lead to control of the state over the church and then to control of revolution over the state. The absolute Prussian state, the bureaucratic kingdom, rationalism, atheism and revolution – Görres saw them all as the same threat, as one and the same enemy, the enemy of German freedom, piety and order. His words struck home and powerfully affected people in the same way as did all the writings of this great publicist. In the following year he founded in Munich the *Historisch-Politischen Blätter für das Katholische Deutschland* (Historical and Political Journal for Catholic Germany), a journal that was conservative and nationalistic as well as strongly pro-Bavarian and anti-Prussian. Later it fought against the unification of Germany by Prussia, as long as it could do so with an atom of hope.

In 1840 there occurred the death of the last ruler of the Napoleonic era, the aged Frederick William III of Prussia He was succeeded as absolute ruler of fifteen million Prussians by his eldest son, Frederick William IV – a change of historic importance. The oppressive symbol of the old age was dead and buried, the new man was known to be more gifted than his predecessor and no friend of his father's 'enlightened' bureaucratic system.

There was universal agreement [wrote Karl Marx] that the old system had had its day and would have to be abandoned, and what people had silently endured under the old King was now openly pronounced to be unbearable . . . In dilettantist fashion he [Frederick William IV] had acquired some knowledge of the elements of most branches of learning and therefore considered himself sufficiently informed to regard his judgement on every matter as decisive. He was convinced that he was a first-class speaker and there was certainly no commercial traveller in Berlin who could surpass him in supposed wit and volubility . . . No sooner had his father's death loosened the glib tongue of the new King than he began to make countless speeches proclaiming his intentions . . .

The picture is drawn with Marxian malice, but Marxian malice sometimes hits the mark.

Frederick William IV was one of those personalities who accidentally find themselves at a parting of the ways in history. He could have turned one way or another. He was far from being a great man, but he was so placed that his character had a decisive influence, whether he acted or not. He was intelligent, full of good intentions, educated, longed for affection and was appreciative of beauty. But he was weak and a prey to temporary influences, a complacent improviser, dependent on advisers whom he liked to dupe, superstitious, arrogant and faithless. In the end he became insane. His ideas were those of the romantic at odds with his age. He wanted to rule with the consent of the people, but this consent must find medieval expression, and society must be a hierarchy consisting of happy peasants, honest townsmen, pious clergy, faithful nobles, the prince among his vassals. In 1845 there could be no such society. The liberals wanted something different and the monarch was disgusted to find that they despised his noble aim.

The contemptible Jewish clique [he wrote to a friend] strikes daily by word and example at the root of the German character; it does not (unlike myself) want to distinguish between the estates which alone can form a German nation; it wants to throw all the estates together . . .

Frederick William IV dreamt also of a united Germany – which he usually spelt *Teutschland* after a patriotic fashion which had sprung up around 1813. The Empire must be re-established in its former glory, under the Habsburgs, and in it there would be a suitable place for the King of Prussia as *Reichs-Erzfeldherr*. Such ideas were even more foolish in the eighteen-forties than they sound today. Our age is confused and devoid of ideas; it does not know what it wants and therefore anything seems possible. But in 1845 people knew exactly what they wanted. They had ideas in which they believed, eminently bourgeois and sober ideas.

The new reign began well. There was an amnesty for political prisoners, and the victims of the persecutions of 1819 were rehabilitated. Towards France, which had just revived an unfortunate demand for the Rhineland, Frederick William adopted a markedly nationalistic attitude. Concessions, which put a temporary stop to the conflict between church and state, were made to the Catholic Church. Archbishop Droste was allowed to return to Cologne. The provincial parliaments and the press were given greater freedom. Metternich and the Tsar were no longer Berlin's polar stars. For the first time since 1815 Prussia seemed to deserve to be Germany's political and moral leader. Then nothing happened. The King temporized, feasted and talked. 'The child is happy,' commented one of his friends, 'when the bird which it holds fluttering by a string behaves as though it were a free bird; but at no price would it cut the string and turn illusion into reality.' Six years passed in this fashion, years of oracular pronouncement, promise and retraction, years of development; years also of bad harvests and famine.

In 1843 the *Rheinische Zeitung*, edited by a Dr Marx in Cologne, was banned 'because of licentiousness of expression and opinion'. It is easy to ban newspapers; sometimes, however, it is less easy to suppress what finds expression in them. In the summer of 1844 the linen-weavers of the small Silesian town of Peters-waldau acted in a strange and frightening fashion. They ganged together, two thousand of them, destroyed the houses of rich manufacturers, demolished factories and demanded higher wages. Investigations revealed the dreadful conditions under which they lived. The fault lay with the world market and the labour market which favoured the employers. *Blutgericht* (Blood Judgements), the anonymous song, describes how the weavers' employers used their advantage.

> *Ihr Schurken all, ihr Satansbrut,*
> *Ihr höllischen Dämone,*
> *Ihr fresst der Armen Hab und Gut,*
> *Und Fluch wird Euch zum Lohne . . .**

There are another twenty-four verses in similar vein, the strongest indictment of early capitalism ever written in verse.

Frederick William was moved by reports of the misery and gave from his privy purse. Charitable organizations also helped, but the root of the evil remained untouched. The Prussian bureaucracy failed to grapple with this problem or with that of the famine that raged in Silesia and East Prussia in the winter of

---

*All you scoundrels, you brood of Satan, you demons of hell, you gobble up the goods and chattels of the poor: a curse shall be your reward . . .

1847. The state had no parliamentary institutions, but in the economic sphere it was all too liberal. Wages, like other prices, were governed by the law of supply and demand. What was really happening and was really needed was not understood. It was grasped, after a fashion, by the sinister individuals whom people had taken to calling the 'Communist Sect', a loose group with extreme aims.

In 1847 the King of Prussia decided to make a move on the constitutional question. He convened representatives of the nation in Berlin. They were not, however, the type of popular representatives from whom public opinion expected salvation, nor even the modest enough type to which the southern Germans had been accustomed for decades. They consisted merely of representatives of the provinces, the 'United Estates', heads of former imperial, 'mediatized' noble families, and elected representatives of the minor nobility, the towns and the peasants. In addition, the King formed the aristocracy into a separate *Herren-kurie*, an imitation of the House of Lords. Only questions of finance were to be discussed jointly by all the estates. In fact, however, it probably does not matter much how a parliament is elected, its better members will always represent, if not the 'people', the opinions current at the moment. Public opinion did not like the 'United Diet'. The Austrian Ambassador in Berlin reported: 'The arrangement is out of tune with the needs of the age, if only because the statute establishing the estates lacks the prerequisite of a modern constitution.' More important was the fact that the United Diet did not like itself, and in that way its members demonstrated that, though chosen in a bizarre manner, they basically represented the politically interested classes of the nation. The United Diet was composed of senior civil servants, mayors, merchants and bankers – 'Rhenish travellers in wine', a Prussian landowner forced to work with this rabble, called them scornfully – as well as of liberal aristocrats. All in all it was an assembly of high calibre, for indeed the period was characterized by a high level of education. Except in the Upper House only a very few members spoke and voted in line with the King's ideas. The majority presented classical liberal demands, maintaining that they were not the estates which the late King had often promised, and that as long as their rights, particularly those of being convened at regular intervals and of approving taxes and loans, were not clearly defined they could not accept responsibility in whole or in part. The decisive vote was on the so-called *Ostbahn*, the railway line from Berlin to Königsberg, which the government intended to build itself, since, in spite of state guarantees, no private company could be found for this unprofitable enterprise. A loan of thirty million thalers was required which the assembly refused to approve; even a majority of the East Prussian delegates put principles above the material interests of their province. A little later the King ungraciously dissolved the Diet. It had discussed and prepared a good deal; the mere fact that uncensored reports of its deliberations were permitted to appear in the press considerably increased the tempo of public opinion. But nothing was solved; the prophecy of the French Minister, Guizot, that the United Diet in Prussia would 'change the world' remained unfulfilled.

What did shortly change the European scene – to the extent that politics can – was a series of events which originated once again in Paris.

5. Germany and its Neighbours

In the nineteenth century 'history' meant mainly diplomatic history; Leopold Ranke, the great initiator of archival studies, was a master of this subject. The European peoples or states were regarded as a group of powers who perpetually measured themselves against each other, who fought one another and, while fighting their battles, proved themselves in 'the realm of ideas'. Catholic powers faced Protestant powers, despotic states confronted liberal states, and the principle of hegemony faced the principle of multiple independence. For Ranke and his disciples the conflict was not senseless: God was at work and the leader who created a new great power achieved a degree of immortality. Spain, Austria, France, Britain, Russia, Sweden, Bavaria, Holland and Prussia were majestic figures on God's chessboard. The virtuosos of militant foreign policy, Richelieu, Wallenstein, Oxenstierna, Mazarin, Louis XIV, William III, Eugène of Savoy, Marlborough, Pitt, Kaunitz and Frederick the Great were heroes whose thoughts and actions needed scientific investigation. Purely social and economic factors were trifles, means to the end which lay in foreign policy.

During the years under discussion foreign policy was not, however, the main preoccupation of the European states. They were tired of war; after 1815 they lost the feeling, which governments had had before and were to have again, that they were playing a continuous, dangerously enjoyable game against each other. Judged by the standards of our own times it is truly remarkable for how long there was no major diplomatic crisis. At first there was the European congress system. Later people spoke of an Anglo-French 'liberal' front against the three absolutist powers of the East, Austria, Prussia and Russia. But these fronts were vague and there was no question of irreconcilable differences or ideological crusades. Britain and Russia sometimes joined forces – for example over the question of Greek independence – and so too did Britain, Austria and Prussia. Interests varied and changed without the deadly seriousness which had characterized European politics at the beginning of the century.

Three powers above all acted as the guardians of peace, the three main conquerors of Napoleon: Britain, Russia and Austria. Britain flooded the Continent with its industrial products and ruled on the seven seas. It decided the dispute over the independence of South America but allowed France in Spain, and Austria in Italy, to do as they liked. Tsar Nicholas I watched over the graveyard quiet of eastern Europe and he in turn was watched by the German and Italian princes. The capital of the European monarchies, their stronghold and the model for their way of life, was not Potsdam or Vienna but St Petersburg. In 1830 the Tsar dearly wanted to arrange things in his own way in France and the Netherlands, but the Polish rising stopped him. Austria was another guardian of the existing order, but not dynamically. Russia could and wanted to expand and had tremendous potential strength. After 1815 there was no lack of prophets who in horror imputed to Russia both the will and the ability to dominate the world. With Austria there was never the slightest question of this. The Empire of the Habsburgs had no centre, served no nation, was constantly in need of money, and had for its leader the intelligent, pessimistic Metternich who was only interested in preserving the existing system. He was the last person to want to follow in Napoleon's footsteps. Austria ruled in Italy through its armies and led in Germany through its prestige and the skill and intrigues of its Foreign Minister. But it only wanted to preserve the *status quo*. Where there was a threat of change, Metternich intervened if he safely could, as in Italy. The revolutions in South América, Greece, France and Belgium he allowed to happen. Towards the end of his long rule, old, haughty and despairing, he allowed almost everything to happen.

The fact that Austria regarded the policing of Italy as its main military task and otherwise permitted its military machinery to rot, might have given the better-ruled Prussian state certain opportunities in Germany. The Prussia of Frederick William III, however, was as reluctant to embark on adventures as Metternich's Austria. Prussia also looked to the Tsar whenever it moved, and the Tsar did not tolerate revolutionary experiments in Germany. Twice events in France forced the Prussian army to adopt an attitude which amounted to the protection of all Germany: in 1830 when it was uncertain how the beneficiaries of the July revolution in Paris would behave on the European stage, and again in 1840. Louis Philippe was neither a revolutionary nor an imperialist but a frightened and very peace-loving statesman. He preferred to belong to the councils of the conservative powers rather than to challenge them. Yet during the whole of the eighteen years that he wore the constitutional crown of thorns the citizen-King was in a delicate position. The national revolution had made him king and had been disappointed by his upper middle-class system of government. He was therefore anxious to flatter French nationalism, if it was possible to do so without much risk. Hence the diplomatic crisis of 1840. It centred in the East, a forerunner of later crises. France made common cause with the Pasha of Egypt, who was about to rise against his Turkish overlord and to take Syria from him. Britain reacted; it no more wanted France in Egypt now than in Napoleon's time. Louis Philippe's eastern policy achieved what the July revolution had failed to do: at once France, as in 1814, faced the united Great Powers, Britain, Russia, Austria and even Prussia. The ways of foreign policy are strange. Russia and Britain now threatened France with war over Turkey, and fourteen years later Britain and France went to war against Russia, again over Turkey.

The Rhineland had nothing to do with Egypt and Syria, but then there is no connection either between militant attitudes and reason. Forced to give way in the eastern Mediterranean, French nationalism let it be known through its press that the Rhine was still France's natural frontier and that there could be no lasting peace in Europe until it was also France's frontier on the map. Thiers, the Prime Minister, a professional admirer of Napoleon, did not dissociate himself from this opinion. The German reaction was surprising. There was an upsurge of nationalism, a feeling of being threatened, an enthusiastic readiness to defend the threatened territory, such as there had not been since 1813 – and even then it had not affected the whole country in the same way. Topical songs voiced the general feeling: 'They shall not have it, the free German Rhine' and 'Like thunder rolls the cry, to the Rhine, to the German, German Rhine ...' These were new sounds, shriller than those of 1813. In those days a few writers had tried to make the Rhine into a kind of national deity, a majestic symbol of German splendour – 'the Rhine, Germany's river, not Germany's frontier'. Now this attitude caught on among the masses. The new German river cult conflicted with the older French idea which, while claiming to be more sensible, was no less curious, namely that the Rhine was France's 'natural', strategically vital frontier. The events of the war of 1814 ought to have disillusioned the French; the Allies had crossed the Rhine, then France's frontier, without difficulty, and had marched straight to Paris. Fixed ideas, however, are not defeated that quickly. If superstitious faith in 'strategic frontiers', rivers and chains of hills exists even today, what can we expect from our great-great-grandfathers?

The French were hurt and surprised; they had not meant to give offence. Least of all the liberals who had always regarded German liberalism as their ally. Why become so excited over a piece of land which Nature happened to have given to France? Could Prussia not find compensation on the North Sea or in Lower Saxony, and Germany as a whole on the Danube? Lamartine wrote the *Marseillaise de la paix*:

> *Nations! mot pompeux pour dire barbarie!*
> *L'amour s'arrête-t-il où s'arrêtent vos pas?*
> *Déchirez ces drapeaux; une autre voix vous crie·*
> *L'égoïsme et la haine ont seul une patrie,*
> *La fraternité n'en a pas!*

He sent his well-meant product to Nikolaus Becker, author of *They shall not have it, the free German Rhine*, who, unmoved, sent the French poet his own song by way of thanks. It was an unfortunate coincidence that both nations should have chosen the Rhine as their symbol of national feeling, as both could have chosen many other beautiful things not threatened by anyone, forests, rivers and mountains, in the interior of their country. As a result the Rhine became the symbol of Franco-German enmity, later called an 'hereditary enmity'. As Prussia was the German military power on the Rhine and used firm language during the crisis of 1840, it was Prussia and not Austria which earned national glory for the *Watch on the Rhine*. This time the danger passed by. Louis Philippe, a born pacifist, drew back and dismissed his militant Prime Minister. But an echo of the excitement lingered on. Or was it the distant sound of future trouble? Emotionally there was something amiss between the two nations which had such close ties and which had existed side by side from the beginning of time. The discord was only emotional, but so essentially is foreign policy. Without the likes and dislikes which individuals invent and transmit to the masses, without sportive competition, pride, fear and hatred based on sheer ignorance, there would be no international political conflicts. It is claimed that they are of an 'economic' nature. But this is nonsense, a rationalization of the irrational. What economic interests set the French and the Germans against each other?

The story of the relationship between the two neighbour nations and their opinion of each other is a curious, bitter story. Most of the time France did not regard Germany as its enemy. In the sixteenth and seventeenth century the enemy was the House of Habsburg, representing the union of Spain, Italy, Burgundy and Austria, whereas Germany proper, particularly Protestant Germany, seemed a natural ally. In the eighteenth century the enemy was Britain, mistress of the seas, as well as the Habsburgs. Prussia appeared as the progressive power whose alliance was sought. The situation remained the same during the Revolution and Napoleon's day. What other nation was such an apt pupil of the harsh Emperor, or rose so late and so hesitatingly against him? After 1814 French patriots blamed the British and the Russians for their fall from the imperial heights, but not the Germans. The influence of German civilization in France was never stronger than after Napoleon's fall, a development which may have been connected with France's confusion and exhaustion after Waterloo and which received considerable stimulus from books like Madame de Staël's *De l'Allemagne*. The French threw themselves on German philosophy, Kant and Hegel, Goethe, Schiller and the Romantics. Germany was seen as the country which had produced these great men, a philosophical, poetical, musical, non-political country. And as these were good qualities which France was conscious of having sacrificed to politics and activity of the intellect, the French were not at all anti-German.

After 1830 when things began to move again in Europe, there were plenty of writers in Paris who thought about Germany's future. Germany must become politically conscious, it could not remain Madame de Staël's romantic fairyland for ever. It would unite and become a nation-state like the others. But this unity, achieved nobly and freely, even if under Prussian leadership, need not constitute a threat to France. On the contrary, were not the two nations really meant for each other? Was it not their common task to be Europe's most powerful force and to keep Russia in check? In 1835 Eugène Lerminier expressed the opinion that Germany would fall under Russia's spell unless it allied itself with France. This, roughly, was the view of the most famous liberals, Lamartine, Victor Hugo and Alexis de Tocqueville. The only dissenting voice was that of the philosopher of history, Edgar Quinet. He had gone to Heidelberg in the twenties as a lover of German philosophy and had lived there for ten years and married the daughter of a German professor. When he returned to France in 1837 he was Germany's enemy. For him Germany was no longer the country described with too much affection by Madame de Staël, the country of metaphysicians and dreamers. It was a materialistic and political country, in the grip of a nationalism of which the French had no conception. '. . . The Germans, awakened by their poets, have lately made themselves the object of a self-worship which will lead to their destruction.' Particularly in Prussia the 'old cosmopolitan objectivity' had given way to an 'irritable, choleric nationalism', and thanks to its efficiency and its efforts to build a modern society the Prussian state would sooner or later make the rest of Germany conform to its pattern. Everything was ready, only the great man was still missing. Once he appeared, woe betide France. An arrogant Germany, barren of lofty ideas but practically superior, would attack its western neighbours and demand back all the provinces lost since the Middle Ages.

Was Quinet right? Was the Germany of the end of the *Biedermeier* period as malevolently self-idolatrous as he claimed? The disappointed lover must have seen something, because we who came after him know all too well how his predictions came true. Those who make accurate historical predictions perceive something which exists but which most people fail to see because it is as yet barely visible. Especially in the eighteen-thirties, Germany's development did not seem a threat to its neighbours. On the contrary, whereas the *Burschenschaften* after 1814 had been anti-French, German liberalism was not, and radicalism, as expressed for example at the gathering at Hambach, least of all. The radicals wanted a republic in the style of the French one of 1792, and a

European, republican league of nations. They looked upon France as the great friend and teacher. 'Long live the Franks, the brothers of the Germans, who respect our nationality and independence' – ended one of the most striking speeches at Hambach. This was the kind of thing both French and German radicals liked to hear. Those who envisaged other alliances or other conflicts were few in number.

6. *Philosophy and Politics*

No single figure or group of figures dominates the thirties and forties. The quiet, independent writers, Franz Grillparzer the dramatist or Adalbert Stifter the novelist, may mean more to us today than the political, philosophical authors who played such an important role in Germany around 1840. Yet while the former can hardly be accorded a mention in a political history, the latter, often inferior as human beings, indicate what was happening. Moreover, there were men of genius among them such as Heinrich Heine and Karl Marx and, later, Nietzsche.

In the official Germany the King's people felt happy and reasonably secure; the study of German and Greek was cultivated, grand opera and romantic poetry encouraged; and provincial capitals were beautified with Greek temples, Italian Renaissance palaces and collections of medieval pictures. This Germany looked to the distant past, to antiquity, and to more recent times in which the greatest name was Goethe. In the eighteenth century monarchs like Frederick the Great and Joseph II had been in advance of their age, a situation which probably had done the monarchical principle no good. Kings should be representative of the traditional aspect of their time, rather than of what points to the future.

Close to the royal sphere were the conservative scholars, the advisers of the kings, the historian Leopold von Ranke, the political theorist Friedrich Julius Stahl; thinkers who were

Christian and monarchist without necessarily being against constitutional government. Ranke lived to a very old age, to the end of the century, but by education and mental make-up he belonged to the beginning of the century. He was opposed to violent contrasts; at once cosmopolitan, patriotic and loyal to Prussia and Bavaria, the states which he served, he was a royal servant through and through, tolerant, eager to understand, open to the world, anxious to avoid the ultimate and most difficult questions, always prepared to believe that history was doing the right thing and that victory and power went to good men. As a historian he knew that the political systems of his day were the result of historical development. However, since they were there, they must be upheld and must be changed only gradually and wisely.

Nineteenth-century Germany produced no great conservative philosophy of state and society such as Britain had possessed since Edmund Burke. This was partly because the German nation had no state. A thinker who spoke in the name of all Germans and offered a nationalistic programme, ceased at once to be 'conservative' because he aimed at something that did not exist, like the great thunderers of the time of the War of Liberation, Stein, Arndt and Görres. In those days the conservatives had been the circle round Metternich, and its surviving members were still conservatives. But this circle was so Austro-European and international that it is hardly possible to speak of German conservatism. Then there were journalists, professors and writers whose influence was largely confined to a particular German state, to Austria, Bavaria, Prussia or Württemberg. Görres for example, the Rhinelander who late in life had become a Bavarian, was now a conservative thinker who exerted himself for Bavaria, not for Prussia. Görres the Catholic valiantly fought with his pen against the encroachments of the Prussian state on the Catholic Church. Indeed, the religious issue was another obstacle to the formation of a nationalistic conservative school of thought. While in Catholic monarchies like Bavaria and Austria Catholics could be happy and conservative-minded, it was more difficult for them under Prussia's Protestant authority, where conflicts were frequent and Catholics were tempted to form unreliable alliances of convenience with other rebel elements. Religion binds people with established beliefs and authority. To that extent all religion is conservative, even substitute religions like Communism, once they are established. Liberalism as such was not anti-religious, though it was anti-authoritarian. It tended to act as a liberating force and in the last resort to make religion a private matter. Above all it believed in science. Once men put their trust wholly in positive knowledge it is impossible to say where they will end up. In that sense religion in all its ecclesiastical manifestations was at war with liberalism. But Germany's religious division prevented the establishment of clear fronts. When Protestant Prussia, which the aged Frederick William wanted to be a religious, authoritarian state, came into conflict with the Catholic Church, Catholic Germany rebelled against Prussia – a state which was, or should have been, its ally in the fight against liberalism. The two parties accused each other of recalcitrance, lawlessness and aggressive bids for power. Inevitably both came into contact with the common enemy. Prussia did so, because it defended the control of the church by the state and the supremacy of the state in the sphere of morality – a late liberal thesis – and Catholicism did so because it rebelled for one reason or another against the authority of the King of Prussia.

In the predominantly Protestant parts of Prussia, in the hierarchical structure of the kingdom, Luther's heritage constituted a conserving element; it conserved the state to which the subject owed blind obedience, even if the state did things that were illegal and not at all conservative. Luther had taught that the Christian is directly responsible to God. Authority had a different responsibility; it must wield a sharp sword in this world where ideal ends are unattainable and order must be preserved, even at a high price, because men are disobedient and wicked. This was no developed political philosophy but a simple and instinctive faith which expressed itself more strongly in the self-assured, threatening speeches made by the young deputy von Bismarck in the United Diet than in books on political philosophy. It came instinctively to those who believed in it. Fundamentally conservatism must be instinctive; it can only become a conscious developed philosophy when there is danger of revolution, when it is being questioned and must defend itself.

This it was now forced to do, against the liberals. Although speaking *ex officio* only in the southern German constitutional states, the liberals could speak for the whole of Germany because they were not committed to the existing system and wanted the German Confederation to become a closer union. In Baden they looked to France, in northern Germany more towards Britain. The basic demands were the same: the nation must help to shape its fate through some suitable form of representation, not so much in order to guide a strong, active state but in order to limit the state's activities so that its citizens were as far as possible left in peace to follow their own interests, protected but unrestricted. The ideal was freedom from state interference even more than power for the people. The ancestors of the liberals, the eighteenth-century 'philosophers', had believed that man was good and that God was also good, so good that man could leave Him to look after Himself and concentrate on the practical problems of this world. This was not an unchristian attitude, but it no longer contained the Lutheran fear of God and belief in the sinfulness of man. The liberals expected great things on earth, without too much hard fighting and without tragedies. The offshoot of liberal Germany was radical Germany – republicans, democrats and, as we have seen, international nationalists.

Less in evidence but no less important were the activities of solitary social thinkers and philosophical writers. Not given to pomp and circumstance, they lived alone or in small groups, often in insecurity and poverty, often at odds with each other.

We have referred earlier to the state professors, the most celebrated of whom from the forties to the seventies was Leopold von Ranke. In the twenties and until his death in 1831 this position had been occupied by Hegel, Professor of Philosophy at the University of Berlin. The heritage of this great thinker, the 'Prussian political philosopher' as he has often been called, fell into strange hands. He who in his lifetime had been the exponent of obedience, became after his death the exponent of revolution. This was no mere caprice of the history of ideas, rich though it is in surprises and paradoxical allegiances. Hegel's work was ambiguous and explosive. So was the age which it claimed to express in philosophical terms, and .on which, in spite of all extravagance, it really had a direct bearing. Hegel was aware of his time. He is the precursor of all those who make it their profession to talk about their times and who try to understand what is happening.

Moreover his later publications are characterized by a profound sadness. His work was intended to mark the end of a prolonged development, not of one epoch but of a succession of epochs, of an eternity; it was intended as climax, fulfilment and end. Religion had spent itself, art had spent itself. Not they but philosophy now satisfied man's noblest desires. But as philosophy had said its last word in Hegel's writings, what then remained to be done after him? Nothing, or something completely different, for which Hegel with the egoism of the great man made no attempt to prepare his pupils. He himself was gloomy, particularly after the July revolution. He felt that he was taking the glory of a thousand years with him into the grave. However, if his philosophy was right, then his forebodings must apply also to reality because his thesis was that historical reality and philosophy matched each other, that they were one and the same thing. People were living on the brink of a new age. The French Revolution itself had been only a prologue to other unimaginable changes.

It was left to the disciples after the master's death to interpret the new age. If Hegel's philosophy had been true, then it could not remain true: it must be treated as Hegel had treated all earlier philosophy, 'set aside', affirmed and denied at the same time. Hegel had started life as a Protestant and had somehow managed to bring Christianity even into his mature philosophy. His disciples or their disciples broke with Christianity and became atheists – an attitude which could be derived from Hegel's philosophy, if it was followed to its logical conclusion. They took it upon themselves to explain Christianity, like all religious belief, historically, as a reflection of social reality, as a self-misunderstanding. Hegel had spoken much of the reconciliation of idea and reality, but he had achieved this reconciliation only in the mind, through his philosophy; it was for philosophy to recognize retrospectively that what happened in reality was reasonable. Hegel's successors, however, claimed that reality was not reasonable but must be *made* reasonable, not by dreams but by political action. Politics, understood rightly, was thus in the end the true philosophy. Hegel had spoken of the 'truth of power', and had meant the power of the state, of kings, of victorious armies. His followers spoke of the truth of revolutions, of majorities, of mass action. There was no need to fear the masses as Hegel had feared them. The rights of the private individual were not as important as the liberals believed. The state could not be too powerful, provided it was a scientifically directed state, free from all superstition. Such a state would do away with the remains of the Middle Ages and make men equal.

Thus, very briefly, the 'Young Hegelians', Ludwig Feuerbach, Arnold Ruge and Bruno Bauer. It is difficult to say whether Hegel's philosophy did them and their cause any good. Faith in the liberating power of the natural sciences, republicanism and socialism existed in Britain, in France and elsewhere in Germany. To the modern reader the works of a socialist of the eighteen-thirties, like the medical student Georg Büchner who despised Hegel's dialectic, have a much greater appeal than the writings of the Young Hegelians. Büchner, a poet of genius, went straight for his goal; in his *Hessische Landbote*, realities were discussed forcefully and directly. The Young Hegelians knew everything; thanks to Hegel they held the key to all mysteries. But they had not forged the delicate intellectual tools which they used and had not suffered the creative agonies of the young Hegel. Their intellectual and human achievement therefore fell short of their claims. They were self-confident as disciples of a great master are, dogmatic, anxious to outdo one another, either close friends or bitter enemies. A new type developed with them, that of the 'intellectual', the writer who is at odds with the public, the state and the existing system. Later, when Germany was liberal, such people were left alone. In the thirties they struggled with the censor, and their publications were banned because governments were sufficiently intelligent to notice signs of sinister happenings;

whereupon they were forced to find a new home for a few years.

The 'Communist' sect was intellectually more modest and at first had no connection with the Young Hegelians. Its members were workers and craftsmen who from their experiences and observations, from Christian tradition and the writings of French and English socialists, drew their own simple conclusion: the terrible misery of the industrialized world must be redressed by the abolition of private property. This idea was in the air. People were afraid not so much because there was a strong Communist organization – which there was not – but because the idea was in the air; because the misery of factory workers cried out for redress and the state provided none. The fear of Communism in the forties came from the bad conscience of society.

7. Heinrich Heine

The poet Heinrich Heine is usually regarded as a member of the literary movement known to its members and to others as 'Young Germany'; it was referred to as such, for example, in a decision of the German Confederation of 1835 threatening members of the group with punishment because of 'their unconcealed attempts in bellettristic writings accessible to all classes of readers, to make the most outrageous attacks on the Christian religion, to denigrate existing conditions and to destroy all decency and propriety'. Young Germany, which started a little earlier than the Young Hegelians, blossomed in the thirties. Its members were more successful, less ascetic and less scientific than the Young Hegelians. Its means of expression were political journalism, lyrics, travel books, novels and plays. Little of the work of this school has survived. Only Heinrich Heine is immortal and anyone concerned with modern German history must try to describe as best he can his character and his ideas.

It is true that there have been purer German poets. His

contemporaries, Rückert, Eichendorff and Uhland, were more innocent than Heine, closer to the ordinary people and happier; as artists they were more unassuming, but more reliable. Heine, to whom writing verse came easily, was occasionally guilty of lapses of taste. Towards the end of his life he proved that, in spite of all human limitations, he was equal to the great task entrusted to him; for six years he lay on his sick bed dying slowly and painfully of spinal consumption and during this time he wrote his most brilliant prose, his most profound, sad and beautiful poems.

He was a Jew from the Rhineland. Shortly after the July revolution he came to Paris as a born rebel delighted by the great news. There he remained until his death. As one cannot live from poetry he earned his living mainly as a journalist, by contributing daily or weekly reports from Paris to the big, liberal south German newspaper, the *Augsburger Allgemeine*. In addition he interpreted German literature and philosophy for the French public. Journalism lends itself to unpremeditated, irresponsible observations; the journalist must take into account the taste of his readers and not make things too difficult for them. Heine simplified complicated issues and he has therefore been accused of frivolity, perhaps not quite without justification. Frivolous he was, or let us say modern, in concerning himself with the most serious issues without making up his mind on them. He was highly intelligent and shrewd, but he did not take sides. One day he was a German patriot, the next an emigrant who warned France of the German danger; at times he was a conservative, at others a revolutionary; now a socialist and now an aristocrat who dreaded the plebian future. He spoke eloquently on two philosophies, the enjoyment of life, the hedonism of the Greeks, and the serious, ascetic faith of the Jews (among whom he counted true Christians), and was himself attracted by both. His friends and critics and those who envied him, fanatical republicans and stout-hearted progressives, accused him of vacillation. Heine, who refused to take certain problems seriously, was perhaps more serious in his deliberate flippancy than others whose seriousness was unsullied by doubt or by understanding. They spoke for the moment, Heine for a century. Moreover he spoke exquisitely. Fifty years later

Friedrich Nietzsche said: 'How well he handles German. One day people will say that Heine and I were by far the greatest artists in the German language ...' Heine enriched and modernized German prose.

As a social critic he was influenced by Saint-Simon, one of the earliest modern socialists, who confidently believed in the future of humanity. For him the golden age lay not in the legendary past but in the future. It would become a reality by harnessing the natural sciences for the needs of man. All men would find work, all would be well housed and clothed and would eat and drink to their hearts' content. The best would rule, an élite of scholars and scientific planners – technocrats as we should say today. This vision appealed to Heine, who enjoyed his food and drink and felt sorry for the poor.

He foresaw the inevitable annihilation of the rich and their state by the poor, the 'dangerous classes' as they were called in France at the time. His prescience did not make him happy, yet he despised the existing social order; his attitude was that of one who was above or outside it. It was as though Heine was bewitched by Communism. In his articles he constantly talked about it at a time when only a very few people concerned themselves with it. He spoke of it more with dread than hope, as of an elemental movement of the age, immune to politics.

Communism is the secret name of the terrible antagonist who confronts the present-day bourgeois regime with proletarian domination and all its consequences. There will be a terrible duel ... Though Communism is at present little talked about, vegetating in forgotten attics on wretched straw pallets, it is nevertheless the dismal hero destined to play a great, if transitory part in the modern tragedy ... (20 June 1842).

Three weeks later he prophesied that a European war would develop into a social world revolution from which would emerge an iron Communist dictatorship,

the old, absolutist tradition ... but in different clothes and with new catch-phrases and slogans ... Maybe there will then only be *one* shepherd and *one* flock, a free shepherd with an iron crook and an identically shorn, identically bleating human herd. Confused, sombre times loom ahead, and the prophet who might want to write a new apocalypse would need to invent entirely new beasts, and such frightening ones that St John's animal symbols would appear like gentle doves and amoretti by comparison . . . I advise our grandchildren to be born with very thick skins.

Then again he saw Communism not as a system under which men would enjoy the material benefits of life but as one under which they would slave at their jobs with dreary monotony; once he even predicted the marriage of the Catholic Church with the Communists and foresaw an empire of asceticism, joylessness and strict control of ideas as the child of this union. Heine made himself few friends by such prophecies. The conservatives, the good German citizens, regarded him as a rebel and a frivolous wit. The Left saw in him a faithless ally, a socialist who was afraid of the revolution, who took back today what he had said yesterday and who behaved like an aristocrat. It is true that Heine, the artist, was both an aristocrat and a rebel. He hated the rule of the old military and noble caste, particularly in Prussia, despised the rule of the financiers, particularly in France, and yet feared a levelling reign of terror by the people. He approved of constitutional or parliamentary monarchy and paid compliments to Louis Philippe for which the Prime Minister of the citizen-King temporarily rewarded him with a pension. The only thing that was of vital interest to him was that there should be freedom to mock as seriously as he did himself; freedom to speak the truth and to speak it well. He hated everything that was not genuine, everything that was ugly and exaggerated for partisan purposes.

Heine was rightly known as a friend of all that went under the collective term 'progressive': industry and technical science, liberalism, democracy and socialism. But while he was known as such and persecuted for it by official Germany he suddenly intimated to the adherents of the same cause that he was not one of them, because he, the artist, had different values to defend and because he saw further than they. He was a modern who did not like the modern age. He, the fighter for 'freedom', the enemy of 'reaction', had no faith in the freedom of the coming 'spring of the peoples' or in national democracy; he saw through the contraditions of the movement which to its followers seemed simple and certain to bring happiness. Would it not bring war instead of the promised peace, and brutal clamour instead of a peaceful, enduring way of life? How could his art, his song, survive if politics became increasingly important?

Heine, therefore, could not identify himself with any one of the great causes that excited his compatriots at home or in exile; the servant of beauty and the intellect cannot do this. He could only see things with gay, sarcastic or melancholy eyes, without committing himself. Yet just because he was detached, sometimes to the point of treachery, his work has remained more alive than that of his more resolute contemporaries.

Those who had no doubts, who were reliable, were equally irritated by Heine's attitude towards Germany. At times he loved it and could not do otherwise. He had been born there and spoke its language; he was only a young man when he wrote the poems which have become part of Germany's national heritage. Sick and lonely in exile, he longed for home. Yet at other times he mocked his compatriots in a manner which they could not forgive for their philistinism, their provincialism, their weakness for titles, their bureaucrats, soldiers and thirty-six monarchs. In an extremely witty poem he says that if there were ever to be a German revolution the Germans would not treat their kings as roughly as the British and the French had treated theirs:

> *Franzosen und Briten sind von Natur*
> *Ganz ohne Gemüt; Gemüt hat nur*
> *Der Deutsche, er wird gemütlich bleiben*
> *Sogar im terroristischen Treiben.*
> *Der Deutsche wird die Majestät*
> *Behandeln stets mit Pietät . . .**

No sooner had Heine written verses of this kind and mocked at the Germans for their lamb-like patience than he warned the French that the German revolution of the future would far exceed theirs in terror.

*Frenchmen and Britons are by nature completely soulless; only Germans have souls. They will remain soulful even when terror reigns. Germans will always treat royalty with reverence . . .

A drama will be enacted in Germany compared with which the French Revolution will seem like a harmless idyll. Christianity may have restrained the martial ardour of the Teutons for a time, but it did not destroy it; now that the restraining talisman, the cross, has rotted away, the old frenzied madness will break out again.

The French must not believe that it would be a pro-French revolution, though it might pretend to be republican and extreme. German nationalism, unlike that of the French, was not receptive to outside influences filled with missionary zeal; it was negative and aggressive, particularly towards France. 'I wish you well and therefore I tell you the bitter truth. You have more to fear from liberated Germany than from the entire Holy Alliance with all its Croats and Cossacks put together . . .' Heine toyed with things cleverly and irresponsibly. At the time it was thought in France, in Italy and in Germany too that nationalism was international, closely related to the republican and the democratic cause; that nations, once they were free and united at home, would join forces in one great league of nations. Heine did not share this view. He regarded nationalism, particularly German nationalism, as a stupid, disruptive force motivated by hatred.

Smilingly, as they came to him, he threw his ideas and premonitions on to the literary market; frivolously, people thought, but perhaps because he was averse to all solemnity, pathos and pedantry. He was at home only in Europe, yet Europe was no real home. A man without a home, without roots, cannot be effective, but he can see and speak, and that is what Heine did. His work, full of beauty, depth and passionate restraint and also of facile effects, heralded the crisis of the West. Fifty years later Nietzsche grappled with it and yet another fifty years later we all experienced it. The genius came early. He determined nothing, he achieved nothing, he helped only by rising above problems, by understanding, and by finding the perfect, conciliatory expression. That help Heine continues to give us today.

8. Karl Marx

Heine speaks somewhere of his German compatriots in Paris
'among whom the most determined and intelligent is Dr Marx'.
Marx was as intelligent as Heine and though no poet he was a
writer of the first rank who forced his mind into a single, narrow
track. He wanted to dominate world history and force it into the
track followed by his own mind. Marx was effective and still is,
although his work did not have the results that he expected.

Like Heine, he was a Jew from the Rhineland but twenty-five
years younger and without the experiences of the Napoleonic age.
Old men of Napoleon's generation were still in power when he
was born and when he was young and contemptuous, convinced
that the future belonged to him and his like. He studied in Bonn
and Berlin; in 1842 in Cologne he edited the *Rheinische Zeitung*
which was soon banned; in 1843 he went to Paris and in 1845 to
Brussels. Then, in 1848, he briefly returned to Germany, aged just
thirty. The political philosophy and revolutionary strategy named
after him was already complete in his mind.

A Russian who met him at a socialist gathering in Brussels
describes him thus:

> With a thick black head of hair, hirsute hands, his coat buttoned up
> crooked, he nevertheless had the appearance of a man who had the
> right and the power to command respect ... His movements were
> angular, yet bold and self-confident. His manners were directly con-
> trary to all social custom. Yet his demeanour was proud, with a trace of
> contempt, and his shrill, metallic voice was curiously in harmony with
> his radical judgements on men and things. He spoke only in imperatives
> which tolerated no opposition and which were enhanced by the tone
> which characterized everything that he said and which affected me
> almost painfully.

A few years later, Carl Schurz, an observant, intelligent German
student with strong views, commented:

> What Marx said was in fact full of substance, logical and clear. Yet I
> have never seen a man behave with such offensive, unbearable arro-
> gance. He brushed aside any opinion that differed substantially from

his own. Anybody who contradicted him he treated with barely concealed contempt. If he disliked an argument he countered with biting sarcasm at the pitiable ignorance of the speaker or with slanderous insinuations against his motives. I well remember the cutting, contemptuous, I am tempted to say spitting, way in which he uttered the word 'bourgeois'; and he denounced as 'bourgeois', as clear examples of profound spiritual and moral debasement, all who dared to disagree with his views.

There is no doubt that this is what he seemed like – there are too many witnesses and too much agreement – and there is no doubt that he was like this. He was blessed and cursed with a tremendous intelligence which isolated him and made him haughty. He certainly had love, for his wife and his children, and he also had compassion; he was nauseated by the distress which had come with industry. His spirit was inflexible in trouble, and his loyalty to the titanic task which he had imposed on himself was absolute. These are praiseworthy virtues; but they were overshadowed by his tremendous determination to have power, and to be right and to be the only one who was right. He wanted to destroy his opponents and his critics with his sword, or as long as that was impossible, with his pen dipped in poison. Such a man cannot better the world.

Marx was the son of his age and exposed to many influences. The myth which he invented was not as original as he himself believed. The expectation of the great revolution which would one day transform the world and make it a good place for ever came to him from the eighteenth century, from France. The view that politics and society must be interpreted in the light of history, as something that developed and disappeared, he shared with the German historians of his age, with the school which was later called Historicism. The preoccupation of the age with the natural sciences led to an attempt to apply their laws to the social sciences, to assume that history behaved according to a few laws or even one great law, and that this law could be discovered. Marx was far from being the only man to make the attempt. Faith in progress, so strong in his writings, was a heritage of the preceding century bourgeois *par excellence*. The idea of the 'class struggle',

that one social class would take over from another, was in the air
in Marx's youth; the Danish-German scholar Lorenz von Stein
expressed it in scientific form in a book which appeared in 1842.
The French Revolution, it was said, had brought to power not the
people but only the propertied middle class which shamelessly
ruled the people in its own interest. Next time it would be the turn
of the proletariat. We have seen how this prospect fascinated
Heinrich Heine. Atheism and the explanation of religion as based
on ignorance, superstition and human 'self-alienation'; utopian-
ism and the hope that after the last, socialist revolution, the state
itself with all its instruments of coercion would wither away to
leave a freely productive, happy, anarchistic society; the idea that
mankind was passing through a great crisis and that this crisis
could be controlled through science – all these were concepts that
were in the air in the thirties and cannot be attributed to one
particular thinker. Taken together they contain almost the whole
of 'Marxism'.

The strongest spiritual influence on Marx was that of Hegel.
This he had in common with the Young Hegelians; he was closer
to Arnold Ruge for example than might be thought from his
scornful polemics. Hegel's philosophy was seductive to a powerful, lonely, infinitely ambitious mind, because it was as clever and
full of ideas as it was violent, twisted and crazy in its claims. A man
of Hegel's intelligence who followed and corrected and improved
on him, might well believe that he had been chosen to give mankind an account of its history and to tell it how to make history in
the future. The first claim Marx took over from Hegel, the second
he added himself. Hegel, he argued, had concentrated on man's
spiritual history and had explained changes in social conditions
from it. This was a reversal of the true state of affairs. One must
start with social reality, with economic life, with the existing legal
and political situation and see spiritual matters, religion and
philosophy in relation to them. In fact one must ask why man
bothers to build such realms in the clouds. Was it because something was amiss in his real world where men ruled over men and
exploited each other, where there were rich and poor, misery in
spite of wealth, and increasing misery in spite of increasing wealth?

Man did not control the social reality which he himself had created, albeit unconsciously and without a plan – he was a stranger to himself. Therefore in his anguish he invented gods, saviours and philosophical systems designed to explain an alienated, confused, agonizing reality. But these cloud-cuckoo-lands, of which the Hegelian system was the last and most elaborate, were of no help or effect. They had to be destroyed by criticism; this, however, could not be done without an understanding of the social reality which had given rise to these ideas, without changing it and putting it in order. Therefore after Hegel's death it was no longer the task of philosophy to top the Hegelian system with another and still more elaborate system, but to recognize and change reality and to prepare the revolution scientifically; philosophy must thus no longer be pure philosophy but idea and action – action springing from the idea. 'Philosophers have only *explained* the world in different ways; what matters is that it should be *changed*.'

Marx thus arrived at a negation of philosophy which for him culminated in Hegel, and he turned from philosophy to politics. But – and this is important – his politics were based on philosophy. He rejected philosophy on its own ground, in its own jargon which he knew only too well. Later he occasionally came in contact with the working class, mainly through his friend Engels. He did not know it when he prepared the outline of his theory. He knew Hegel, the philosophers before Hegel and the Young Hegelians. The whole mumbo-jumbo of the Hegelian dialectic is present in his writings: the tension between being and consciousness, the 'coming-to-itself' of the consciousness, the 'negation of the negation', the leap from quantity to quality, and so on – all those profound ideas which frequently come close to distortion and punning.

It is therefore the task of history [writes the young Marx] when the otherworldliness of truth has disappeared to establish the truth of this world. Once the sacred figure of human self-alienation has been un-masked it will be the task of philosophy, which serves history, to un-mask self-alienation in its unholy forms. Criticism of heaven thus turns into criticism of the earth, criticism of religion into criticism of justice, criticism of theology into criticism of politics.

Biting sentences which, as one reads them, sound as Carl Schurz described Marx's language, mordant, over-clever, betraying an excessive delight in thought and power.

Hegel had not wanted power. He had been careful to make no predictions. His philosophy was only what Friedrich Schiller maintained that all art must be: play, a sublime play of ideas. Such play is not science, is neither true nor false; it is only beautiful or not beautiful, profound or not profound, it either appeals or it does not appeal to us. Marx wanted to transform the Hegelian work of art into a political science, practically applicable like the natural sciences – to use it to make predictions and to give practical guidance to the revolutionary politician. He broke up the real world of politics into general concepts: 'bourgeoisie', 'proletariat', 'petty bourgeoisie', 'revolution', 'ideology'. 'The proletariat' must 'become conscious of itself' in order to 'put an end to' itself and its antithesis, the bourgeoisie; a process which, like every process dealt with by Hegelian philosophy, must be both necessary and free. The political world, however, is not rational enough to be broken up in such a manner. It does not exist to prove one man right. Philosophy, particularly Hegel's over-clever, over-elaborate philosophy, was not made for politics.

Just as future Communist leaders sometimes – not always – pursued successful policies in spite of the mumbo-jumbo which they regarded as realistic science, Marx was sometimes – not always – a successful judge of present and future. His work, though not lacking in abstruse nonsense, was full of predictions which have come true. Prophets make mistakes and history cannot be predicted in its entirety, but Marx the prophet predicted more things correctly than most of his kind. Whether he succeeded because of his half-true, half-nonsensical science or in spite of it is impossible to say. He certainly had intuition. As a political journalist and historian of his own times his achievements were great: angry, witty, endowed with the perspicacity of hatred and overpoweringly intelligent. His achievements in this sphere have dated least.

Friedrich Engels, whom he met in the forties and with whom he formed a life-long friendship, had a different nature. The son of an industrialist from Wuppertal, he loved women and wine, was a soldier, sportsman, chivalrous and gay. Engels also began with Hegel, but in contrast to Marx soon gained practical experience as an industrialist. His first book, *The Condition of the Working Classes in England*, published in 1845, was really as the sub-title says 'based on personal experience'. Though his political predictions may have been wrong, his descriptions of social conditions were, if subjective, only too true. No more powerful accusation of unfettered capitalism has ever been written. The conditions under which men, women and children worked and lived and which Engels describes, are so shocking and heart-breaking that even today one understands and sympathizes with his false conclusion that the situation could not continue and that the day of reckoning must come and produce a terrible social explosion. In his way Engels too was conceited; he loved to hold forth and find fault even before he met Marx. Marx, whom he regarded as a genius and whom he supported and praised with chivalrous unselfishness, was the only person from whom he took orders. The two complemented each other and worked so closely together that it is often impossible to distinguish the contribution of each. Engels taught Marx something about the 'people' whom the Herr Doktor knew little about. From Marx Engels learnt how to resolve reality into concepts, the 'dialectical' approach; and later the special economic theories developed by Marx, as well as the poisonous art of polemics which, with Engels however, always retained a more human character. Together in the years 1843 to 1847 in Paris and Brussels they formed their ideas by criticism of the Young Hegelians and 'utopian' socialists. Together in the first days of 1848 they wrote the pamphlet that was to conquer half the world, the *Communist Manifesto*. It contains the quintessence of 'Marxism'; what came later was application, economic consolidation, illustration and defence, not creative development. The *Manifesto* is a work of immense persuasive force, simple and homogeneous, in spite of the complicated ideas which were worked into it. The first to be overwhelmed by it, to such an extent that they never had another idea, were its authors.

At the basis of man's history lie his economic needs, the satisfaction of his daily wants. The way in which goods are produced and distributed determines forms of government, state and law, as well as forms of thought, philosophy, morals and religion. Ever since there has been property, since the dissolution of the primitive tribal communities, there have been social classes: a class which ruled and drew economic profit from its rule and others which were ruled, though sooner or later the latter have rebelled against the conditions imposed on them. History is thus a history of class struggles. The class which had come to power in western Europe since the eighteenth century, particularly as a result of the revolutions of 1798 and 1830, was the bourgeoisie, the capitalist class. All new ruling classes begin by accomplishing the task which history has allotted to them; otherwise they cannot become ruling classes. The bourgeoisie has tremendous accomplishments to its credit.

It has been the first to show what man's activity can bring about. It has accomplished wonders far surpassing Egyptian pyramids, Roman aqueducts and Gothic cathedrals; it has conducted expeditions that put in the shade all former exoduses of nations and crusades . . . The bourgeoisie has subjected the country to the rule of the town. It has created enormous cities, has greatly increased the urban population as compared with the rural, and has thus rescued a considerable part of the population from the idiocy of rural life . . . The bourgeoisie during its rule of scarcely one hundred years, has created more massive and more colossal productive forces than have all preceding generations together. Subjugation of Nature's forces to man, machinery, application of chemistry to industry and agriculture, steam navigation, railways, electric telegraphs, clearing of whole continents for cultivation, canalization of rivers, whole populations conjured out of the ground – what earlier century had even a presentiment that such productive forces slumbered in the lap of social labour?

However, the class which had such tremendous achievements to its credit will not rule for nearly as long as the feudal aristocracy. This is because the bourgeoisie has brought into existence a class which will quickly destroy it. How? Under capitalism everything becomes a commodity, an object of barter; the love which the wife sells to the husband as much as the labour which the proletarian sells on the market. In the long run he will never get more for his labour than is needed to 'reproduce' it, that is to say to keep him and his family alive. But he produces more than this wage is worth and this 'surplus' constitutes the capitalist's profit. 'Surplus value' is the source which makes capital grow. The more capital grows, the more the big independent capitalists increase their wealth, the more the small independent entrepreneurs are reduced to the level of wage earners, to the mass of those who eke out a bare existence under conditions unworthy of human beings. At the same time periodic economic crises become more frequent because the workers are not allowed to enjoy the bulk of what they produce. Misery increases the whole time and the number of those who are poor in spite of the growing wealth of society rises. The rich become fewer in number and there are more frequent and violent economic crises, unemployment and starvation. Does it then need much intelligence to foresee the inevitable end? One day soon the great army of proletarians will topple the small band of capitalists from the pinnacles of power. The great robbers who had been about to rob the whole people will themselves be dispossessed. Private ownership of the means of production, the negation of all true partnership and freedom, will be rejected. The great revolution will be a political one because the capitalists control the state through their parliaments, their legal systems, their armies, churches, schools and even – as in the France of Louis Philippe – through their kings. But the revolution will transcend politics, it will change the basic structure of society.

This will be the last revolution. For whereas all previous revolutionary classes were small minorities and therefore became *ruling* classes, the proletariat is in an overwhelming majority, it consists of almost the whole people, or at any rate represents the people, since it is the most progressive element. The proletariat will use power not in its own interest but for the benefit of all; it will not exploit anybody. However, one must reckon with a period of resistance from those who have been overthrown and dispossessed; and while this period lasts there will have to be an 'iron dictatorship' of the proletariat. Obviously a strong hand is needed to keep down the former privileged classes, to exercise revolutionary justice and to establish the new social forms. But once this has been done not only dictatorship but the state itself, with all the means of coercion which have characterized it since the Egyptian pharoahs, will cease to be needed. What is the state but an instrument of repression whose wheels turn for the benefit of the ruling class? Once there is no more ruling class, no exploiters or exploited, the state itself must obviously disappear. Men will pursue their occupations in free partnership, unobstructed by kings, soldiers and priests, by dispute and fear and religious superstition. Science, thoughtfully applied, will take man to undreamt-of heights of comfort and happiness. All contradictions are resolved. What Hegel had accomplished only in philosophical terms, the reconciliation between consciousness and reality, is at last achieved. All is well with the world and man is himself.

The Communists are the vanguard of the proletariat, just as the proletariat is the vanguard of mankind. They are that part of the proletariat which has become conscious of itself and it is through consciousness alone that the goal can be achieved; in fact, class consciousness and revolution are one and the same thing. It is the task of the Communists to prepare the revolution scientifically. They must demolish all other socialist theories and schools with their criticism, because there is only *one* true, scientific socialism, namely their own. On the other hand they will form alliances with *any* revolutionary group – even with the bourgeoisie; this will happen in places like Germany where the bourgeois revolution is not yet complete. Capitalists and proletarians are allies against feudalism. Then, however, the bourgeois revolution will be mercilessly continued until it becomes the proletarian revolution, either immediately or after a short period of naked, shameless capitalist rule no longer disguised by monarchical or feudal forms. In any case this will not last long. 'Let the capitalists know beforehand that they work only in our interest,' wrote Engels in January 1848 in the Brussels German-language newspaper.

In Germany they will soon have to ask for our help. Go on fighting valiantly, milords of capital! For the moment we need you; in places we even need your rule. You must do away with the remains of the Middle Ages and absolute monarchy for us, you must destroy patriarchalism, you must centralize, you must transform all more or less propertyless classes into real proletarians, into recruits for us; through your factories and trade you must provide us with the basis of the material means which the proletariat needs for its liberation and as a reward you may rule for a short time . . . but do not forget: the hangman stands outside the door.

Thus runs the reasoning of the *Manifesto*. Is one to call it brilliant or marvel at the enormous presumptuousness served by so much skill? The most astonishing fact about the intellectual adventure of these two arrogant young men was its lasting, worldwide effect. The spirit of the *Communist Manifesto* never really came to life in the German social democratic movement. It came to life in the Communist parties of Russia and Asia and is alive there today. Two elements have come down from the *Manifesto* to our day with evil results: the certainty of possessing the key to the future, the complete certainty of being right while everybody else is wrong; and the readiness to make alliances with other groups – with those who are wrong – but only to use them, to cheat them and to destroy them as quickly as possible. 'We willingly support other left-wing parties,' Lenin wrote, 'but as the rope supports the hanged man.' It was Marx and Engels who brought this curse of falsity into the world.

They saw many things. Some of their statements were confirmed by the next hundred years and some very strikingly by the next six months. The class struggle between the bourgeoisie and the proletariat was indeed a key to the understanding of contemporary events, particularly in France, which they regarded as the model for Europe's history as a whole. Others too saw this. The idea was in the air and became a terrible reality in June 1848, all the more rapidly because it was in the air. Other historical thinkers too succumbed to the temptation of applying the experiences of their age to the past as a whole and then believed that they had discovered the law governing history.

We know, however, that history did not take the course Marx prophesied and it would be useless to disprove his work by enumerating all the things which came about in spite of his predictions. Every prophet is refuted by the future. Marx was proved right more often than almost anyone else who has tried his hand at this dubious pastime. The most successful paragraph in the *Manifesto* is probably the one describing the achievements of capitalism, because what it describes hardly existed in 1848 and only came to maturity about 1900. Marx foresaw the whole significance of a capitalist world economy, and this vision alone would be enough to make him a memorable figure. But it is neither his insight nor his errors in judging the situation which need arouse passion today; they are over and done with. What were the basic errors which distorted his ideas and his political programme?

Marx despised politics and therefore failed to appreciate the opportunities it offered to mitigate the class struggle and the chances for the proletariat to improve its conditions by political action. The fact that later, in writing *Das Kapital*, he needed to rely so heavily on the reports of British factory inspectors – as Engels had done for his *Condition of the Working Classes* – should have been a warning to him. Though paid by the 'bourgeois', 'capitalist' state to discover the truth about the living conditions of the workers, these inspectors reported with merciless objectivity. Political action had been responsible for this attitude and it was conceivable that much more could be achieved in the social sphere by political pressure. There was certainly a connection between politics and the economic struggle, but the two were not identical and could be separated, a fact which Marx ignored. He not only despised politics but also the philosophy or science of politics and regarded the theory of the limitation of power or division of authority, of the constitutional state, and everything that had been thought about it and done for it for centuries, as mumbo-jumbo. He was interested only in the class which had economic power; the rest were ideological fantasies hatched in the interest of the rulers to support and disguise their position. Therefore the works of Marx and Engels contain no word on how the power of the Communist state might be limited or how it should be exercised. To them the question seemed absurd; political power, even if dressed up in legal garb, was economic exploitation, and where the one did not exist the other could not exist either. This serious error, the simple equation of politics with the 'economic basis', with property relations, also lingers on. Even today Communists will tell us that a state in which the means of production are not in private hands, is a Communist state, that it can never be imperialist, can never be despotic in domestic matters, can never exploit workers and peasants, and so on.

Marx thought little about the economic standards and rules which victorious Communism would one day devise for itself. The 'expropriation of the expropriators', the common ownership of the means of production, the liberation and scientific direction of the productive forces – that was enough for him. For years he thought intensively about the way to the goal, about the decline of the capitalist class, the struggle, the technique of the revolution. About the goal itself he did not think at all, so that after the final victory his greatest pupil, Lenin, found himself in some embarrassment; only then did people begin to consider what Communism should look like. The argument about what is true Socialism or Communism in practice has continued ever since. There was nothing on the subject in the works of the master.

In politics man reveals himself as he is, with his good and bad potentialities, with his suspicions, fear and hatred, egoism and altruism, rivalry in games, delight in lending a helping hand, lust for power, desire for security, cruelty, idealism and base passions. Marx despised politics because he reduced the human problem to a purely natural one and denied its moral side. Once the economy was settled the rest *must* sort itself out. And he dismissed as priestly talk the argument that it was man with all the failings of the flesh and the soul who must settle his economy and that he would remain even after achieving economic liberation. He could be shocked by the hard-hearted greed of the English capitalists, with good reason; systematically, however, there was no place in his philosophy for the difference between good and evil. Man acted as he must; if economic conditions changed he would undoubtedly act differently. This optimism, which Marx inherited from the Enlightenment, still permeates modern social science in the West. It regards the problem of man merely as a concrete problem which can be solved scientifically, not as a moral one which must for ever remain in the balance. To put it more simply, it overlooks the fact that those who must solve human problems are also human beings, and that there is no relying on human beings.

Another aspect of the same attitude is Marx's denial of all religion. Philosophically he regarded it as an expression of human 'self-alienation', and practically as the venal servant of the ruling system. Can one deny that there was some truth in this? The disgracefully run-down papal state, defended by Austrian soldiers and Rothschild money, the English High Church which sided with the Tories and which saw in the most modest parliamentary reforms the end of the world, the Christian Teutonic pomposity of the kings of Prussia or Bavaria, the almost universal alliance between 'throne and altar' – such things could well lead the revolutionary to hostility against all organized religion. There was a great preacher in New York who thundered from his pulpit that the worker who could not keep his family on a dollar a day did not deserve to live. This man of God was himself pocketing thousands of dollars a month and as he preached loose precious stones rattled in his pocket. He was not untypical in America. As we are speaking about Marx's basic mistakes, however, the present writer must declare himself and remind his reader of the difference between the organization and its aim or highest objective. In everything man creates there is the human element, in the organization of the church as much as in any other. Maybe, as the Romans said, corruption of the best is the worst. But the corruption of the churches proves nothing against their mission. On the contrary, the one awareness that all Christian religions have in common is that man cannot be relied upon, that he stands in need of grace. Edmund Burke, the founder of modern conservatism, was not an incorruptible politician but his views are no less true for that. It was he who wrote:

We know, and what is better, we feel inwardly, that religion is the basis of civil society, and the source of all good and of all comfort. In England we are so convinced of this, that there is no rust of superstition, with which the accumulated absurdity of the human mind might have crusted it over in the course of ages, that ninety-nine in a hundred of the people of England would not prefer to impiety . . . We know, and it is our pride to know, that man is by his constitution a religious animal; that atheism is against, not only our reason, but our instincts; and that it cannot prevail long. But if . . . we should uncover our nakedness, by throwing off that Christian religion which has hitherto been our boast and comfort, and one great source of civilisation amongst us, and among many other nations, we are apprehensive (being well aware that the mind will not endure a void) that some uncouth, pernicious, and degrading superstition might take the place of it.

Marx, on the other hand, called religion 'the opium of the people' and proposed to free us from it for ever. The present writer is convinced that Burke did more justice to the human situation – and was therefore closer to the truth – than Marx.

The *Communist Manifesto* was completed in the first days of 1848. Three months later its authors rushed to Germany, where they believed the moment had come to translate their ideas into actions.

Part Four
1848

1. THE STORY

'One morning towards the end of February 1848', the American politician Carl Schurz recalls from the days of his youth in Germany, 'I was sitting quietly in my attic working away on Ulrich von Hutten when one of my friends burst in and gasping for breath, shouted: "What are you sitting here for? Haven't you heard the news?" "What?" "The French have thrown out Louis Philippe and proclaimed a republic." I dropped my pen – and Ulrich von Hutten has not been touched since. We leapt down the stairs, into the street. Where should we go now...?' So powerful an effect did the news of the February revolution in Paris have on young Germans.

The European revolt against the established order which with diminishing faith in itself had existed for thirty-three years, began in January in Sicily and southern Italy. In February it spread to France, scarcely surprising those who had long watched the citizen-King's corrupt, unpopular regime follow its lonely downhill path. Germany, too, was ripe for a great event. It had long been the fashion among serious people to expect it, to hope for it and to fear it. What one expects usually happens because, consciously or not, one acts according to the expectation. Liberal election victories in southern Germany showed from which direction the wind was blowing. The problem of the Prussian constitution demanded a solution. In Austria Chancellor Metternich could not survive for ever; even the most dynastically faithful patriots admitted that his 'system' had become an anachronism. In Germany as a whole, particularly in the West and the

South, the demand for a reorganization of the Confederation, for a German Reich, became increasingly insistent. Then there was the Socialist or Communist movement, intangible, numerically small but much talked about and feared; Prince William of Prussia pronounced a warning against 'Liberal and Communist influence' even in the Prussian army. The year 1847 had brought one of those periodically recurring trade crises of whose nature little was known and whose consequences were combated with wholly inadequate palliatives. Something would therefore have happened, if not that year, then a little later. But as Germany was part of Europe the stimulus provided by the Latin countries started things moving in Germany and they moved easily.

1. The March Revolution

In the first weeks of March a flood of meetings and demonstrations organized by the middle class, supported by peasants, artisans and workers, swept the leaders of the liberal opposition into power in Baden, Württemberg, Bavaria, Darmstadt, Nassau, Kassel, Saxony and Hanover. The same demands were made everywhere, varying in degree according to the nature of the existing mismanagement; they were granted everywhere with the same readiness, as though the rulers had long been secretly convinced that they must change their habits. Everything was granted, freedom of the press and of assembly, arms for the people or the National Guard, trial by jury, reform of the franchise where there was one, and participation in the establishment of a German federal state. South German parliamentarians meeting in Heidelberg even decided to convene on their own initiative a German National Assembly in Frankfurt-am-Main, 'in order to protect the whole German fatherland and its rulers', as their proclamation said. The rulers too were to be protected because nobody wished to emulate the French example. No one was to be hurt by the 'March experience', as it was later called. Jubilation fraternization, reconciliation with contrite princes, flags, torches and triumphal arches – that was the mood. There was to be no terrible collapse as in France in 1792, no new beginning of German history. Force was if possible not to be used, only persuasion, strengthened by a little revolutionary attitudinizing.

But what happened in Stuttgart or Darmstadt could not decide the fate of the nation. Although the 'third Germany' as a whole carried some weight, the first and the second, Austria and Prussia, carried more.

On 13 March Metternich retired from office and slipped away to Britain, still talking, still philosophizing. Although in its unanimity the movement which brought about this departure at first seemed to resemble those of southern and western Germany, it drew its nourishment from stronger sources. Vienna had four hundred thousand inhabitants, among them a class-conscious, intelligent industrial working class, politically informed, well-led students, as well as a variety of organizations, trade and cultural associations, and a great many foreigners from the provinces of the Habsburg Empire, Poles, Czechs, Hungarians and Italians. In Austria too 'everything was granted' hastily, first the dismissal of the Chancellor, then the magic thing which in those days was credited with almost unlimited remedial power, a 'constitution'. What was not clear was what form it should take in order to give equal satisfaction to the many peoples of the Empire. Vienna was Austrian, very loyal to the Emperor as well as very German, and wanted an *Anschluss* – the word came into use then – to a greater Germany. Milan and Venice were in revolt, and nothing less than complete separation from Austria could satisfy the democratic nationalism of the Italians. A south Slav, 'Illyrian' or Croat movement threatened the predominance of the Magyar aristocracy within the kingdom of Hungary. In Prague Czech spokesmen staked their claims, directed less against the Empire than against its predominantly German character, having calculated that there were more Slavs than Germans in the Habsburg Empire. What form could be found to contain all these elements? In the spring and early summer months of 1848, when the

Austrian monarchy lurched like a rudderless ship, there were many who prophesied the downfall of this once glorious but anti- quated state.

Neither before nor after Metternich's fall was Austria capable of using the revolutionary development in Germany for its own ends or to give it direction. The kingdom of Prussia was in a better position as late as the first weeks of March. If there was to be sudden change there must be leadership, either from a strong revolutionary organization – which did not exist – or from one of the major German states and its rulers. What Paris was for France only Vienna or Berlin could be for Germany. It is true that later, in the autumn, one man attempted to proclaim a German republic in Lörrach, opposite Basle, in the furthest cor- ner of southern Baden; but Lörrach was no place for such a ven- ture. What mattered were the great cities and the Great Powers. But the liberal movement was not nearly strong enough or ruth- less enough to grapple successfully with the Great Powers. It waited, it pleaded for leadership. A delegation of liberals from the small states went to Berlin to convince King Frederick William IV of the opportunity awaiting his ambition. This psychopathic autocrat, paralysed by all kinds of untimely reveries, was, how- ever, not the man to seize the opportunity.

He was eager to perform a great historic deed, provided it could be done exactly as he wanted, leaving the pomp of kingship in- tact and avoiding danger – requirements that were difficult to fulfil. His first concession in Prussia, the periodic convening of the United Diet, was no longer enough. Prussia was part of Ger- many as Germany was part of Europe; Prussia also wanted to have its 'March experience'. There was much talk of the all- powerful 'spirit of the age'; disturbances in the big provincial cities, Cologne, Breslau, Königsberg and later in Berlin, made this spirit triumphant also in Prussia. These disturbances were harmless enough, but seemed more serious because the army be- haved as was its old, grim custom. Tension grew and Frederick William let himself be persuaded that it was high time to give way to the spirit of the age. Only five days after Metternich's fall 'everything was granted' in Prussia too – freedom of the press and a liberal constitution for the whole of Germany as well as for Prussia. This ought really to have meant the end of the 'March experience'. However, there was serious street fighting in Berlin between the people and the army. Perhaps sound political sense came to the help of the aggressive instinct, the panic or the misunderstanding of some unit. Or perhaps the Berliners wanted to show for once that they and not the army were the masters of their city. They demanded the withdrawal of the soldiers. After several hundred people had been shot dead His Majesty granted this demand too. The regiments were withdrawn from the city and a hastily organized National Guard kept order in their place. This was a victory for the liberal spirit, particularly in the capital of this state which from its beginning had belonged to the army. The triumph was confirmed by the hasty flight of Prince William, the King's brother, who had the reputation of being an archmilitarist and agitator, a 'Russian', and by the obeisance which the King was forced to make to the bodies of the victims brought into the castle courtyard – 'only the guillotine is missing now', the Queen remarked on this sombre occasion; it was further confirmed by the curious procession on horseback which Frederick William made through the city on 21 March, wearing a sash of black, red and gold (the revolutionary colours of national Germany), to announce that he was placing himself at the head of Germany. The bewildered monarch was followed by members of the National Guard, celebrated fighters of the preceding days, behind whom came the 'people' enthusiastically sweeping the state dignitaries along with them. 'Just as well your brother made peace', said a workman to one of the royal princes, 'let me tell you, otherwise things might have become sticky, very sticky. We were all for a republic if the shooting hadn't stopped. All is well though, and we think that everyone will keep their word, then we won't give any trouble.' That was the question, would everyone keep his word?

Spokesmen for the liberal opposition, two businessmen from the Rhineland, Ludolf Camphausen and David Hansemann, were summoned to lead the government. The United Diet, meeting for the last time, acknowledged only one final duty: to

sanction the latest developments and to adopt legislation providing for an election of 'the assembly to be convened in order to
draw up the Prussian constitution'. In principle the franchise was
democratic and it needed only the implementation of such royal
concessions as freedom of the press, trial by jury, an independent judiciary, the establishment of a national guard and the repeal of feudal legislation, to make Prussia a modern, middle-class
state.

In fact nothing was decided And the situation was so confused
that even a century later it is difficult to see how it could have been
unravelled.

2. Unsolved Problems

The old powers, the Courts, armies and bureaucracies, had not
been defeated. Without serious struggle there could be no serious
victory. There had been no serious contest of strength in March,
either in Vienna or in Berlin. The 'March achievements' were the
result of a momentary loss of nerve on the part of the rulers, not
their decisive defeat. Furthermore, the victors themselves did not
want a real victory; they did not want a revolution in the French
sense. The words 'everything is granted' heard so often with joy
in Germany at the time, show that people wanted freedom to be
granted by the traditional authority. Reform, compromise,
'agreement' were the German liberals' favourite terms; only a
few radical democrats raised the question of what should happen
if the two partners, 'crown' and 'people', failed to agree. After
Louis Philippe's fall someone said to a famous Westphalian
liberal that the same might happen in Germany. He replied:
'Revolution in Prussia? It's absolutely out of the question. In
Prussia we want peaceful, national reform and a liberal constitution, but in no circumstances revolution.' Similarly the
Hessian Minister, von Gagern, who later became President of the
German National Assembly, and who, with his virtues and his

weaknesses, was a typical representative of the whole movement, said:

You must proclaim the intention of this Assembly so that it echoes through Germany ... our intention of preserving the monarchy, of establishing an Assembly that wants freedom and strives for it in the interest of the people and of popular sovereignty, while remaining faithful to the principle of monarchy in the state and advocating the need for unification.

Popular sovereignty but monarchy; and, let it be noted, not the type of monarchy that Britain has today, monarchy that was crushed to rise again as a friendly, beloved symbol of national unity, but monarchy as it existed in Germany, tenacious, selfish and closely connected with powerful social forces. The German liberals wanted a thorough political change, but without the rough means employed for the purpose by other countries, because above all they hated lawlessness. Such a trusting game could only succeed if all the partners kept to the rules. There were no changes in the army and the administration. New, inexperienced ministers were put in charge of hostile staff who regretted the good old days. In March the princes – with exceptions – were probably honest about their concessions. Even one of the most conservative and a relatively intelligent one, Prince William of Prussia, believed for some weeks that the spirit of the age had defeated him and that he must accept the new situation. Men rarely have enough consistent malice to do one thing while planning something else. When the rulers noticed that the spirit of the age was not so dangerous after all and they they need not have given way, they began to listen to their reactionary advisers.

The liberals wanted peaceful reform and legal continuity, by which they set great store. They did not want to appoint themselves but to be entrusted with restricted powers by the former rulers. There was an immediate break-away by a group which did not regard such a preservation of the old legality as either possible or desirable. They were variously called democrats, republicans or social republicans. In Berlin, in Vienna, later in Frankfurt, in western and south-western Germany, everywhere, they were soon completely opposed to the liberals. A movement to the left, the emergence of a new, radical opposition by the side of the old one in power, is normal in times of revolution. It happened in France in the eighteenth century and in England in the seventeenth. In France, however, where politics were taken with passionate seriousness, one of the parties was eliminated before the remaining majority split; when Girondists and Jacobins faced one another the supporters of the monarchy were no longer a political power. In Germany the defenders of the old order still existed. The right gained the support of the liberal centre as the left became more radical. The liberals wanted constitutional monarchy, but rather than let themselves be overpowered by the democrats they surrendered to the Prince of Prussia. Radicalism therefore weakened the revolution; it could only have had the reverse effect if it had been very strong and ruthless.

In addition to the new division of the nation into parties there was the old division into states which were much healthier than was thought at the time. The fact that in March something common to all Germany had emerged, the roots of which went back a long way, did not yet mean the end of particularism. In 1848 Europe demonstrated that it was a whole in which one piece was part of the rest: there was revolution simultaneously in Paris and in Budapest, in Palermo and in Posen. This solidarity did not, however, put an end to the nations or their clamorous urge for self-realization; quite the contrary. Neither did Germany cease to be divided into states because the same liberal movement had momentarily been successful everywhere. While we associate the existence of these states with certain classes and their interests, with princes, landowners, officers, civil servants, court purveyors and so on, it would be a mistake to attribute their existence only to material interests. States have an idea of themselves which is handed down from generation to generation and has its roots deep in the past. We are sentimental creatures, proud of the community to which we belong. Austria, Prussia, Bavaria and even Württemberg, Hanover and Hamburg all had distinct notions of what the state should be. A loyal citizen of one of these states – which meant all but a few completely independent, highly intelligent and rootless individuals – who wanted German unity wanted something difficult to combine with his loyalties. In certain regions, for example in Old Bavaria – the name given to the districts that had been part of Bavaria before Napoleon – loyalty to the state was clearly stronger than the enthusiasm for a united Germany.

Not only was Germany divided politically, it was also linked by some highly complicated relationships to non-German states and peoples. The German Confederation included German, semi-German or allegedly German states which also owed allegiance to other rulers: Dutch Luxembourg and Limburg, Danish Holstein, and of the Habsburg territories, in addition to the German-Austrian regions, the Italian Trentino and the predominantly Czech kingdom of Bohemia. On the other hand there were regions ruled by a German state and inhabited at least partly by Germans – the Prussian provinces of East and West Prussia and Posen (Posznania) – that did not belong to the German Confederation. If there was to be an empire of *all* Germans – and that was the ambition – there were patriots who recalled the existence of many Germans on foreign soil: in French Alsace, in Danish Holstein, in the Baltic provinces of Russia and in the cities of the Habsburg Empire, down the Danube almost to the Black Sea. The modern, somewhat crude method of 'population exchange' or 'resettlement' was unknown in the nineteenth century. A German empire or national state could therefore only come into being if it included a great many non-Germans, or excluded a great many Germans, or if it chose a difficult middle road between these two extremes.

Finally, the emergence of a new national state in the heart of Europe was an international question of concern to all the European powers. Britain, France and Russia could be in favour or against, but they could not be indifferent to the question whether such a state should be established, what form it should take and what its frontiers should be. The Great Powers were concerned with every major change in the balance of power; they were particularly concerned in this instance because, as we have seen, the German question had always been considered a European one and the constitution of the German Confederation of 1815 had even been written into the Final Act of the Congress of Vienna.

Popular sovereignty versus historic or monarchical law, social democracy versus liberalism, dynastic states versus the Confederation, national state versus foreign nationalities, great powers versus the new Great Power – none of these problems was really thought through or fought through to the end in 1848 and 1849. In chaotic interplay they dominated, confused and wrecked the great attempt.

3. Confusion Worse Confounded

From a legal point of view the assembly of German politicians which met in Frankfurt at the end of March to prepare the convocation of a national parliament was revolutionary because it had not been invited by any of the existing authorities. Yet even this 'pre-parliament' established close relations with the Federal Diet, and the Federal Diet – still the only legal representative of the Confederation – hastened to follow its suggestions. The Federal Diet explicitly agreed to elections for a parliament which was to draw up a constitution for the whole of Germany; legal continuity seemed thus to be preserved or restored. Those who wanted to transform the pre-parliament into a revolutionary government in the French style, into a 'Convention', who were anxious to forge a programme of definite social reform while the iron of democracy was hot, controlled barely a tenth of the assembly. The general idea was that henceforth the majority would rule peacefully with the blessing of the old authority; the old privileged minority must not be replaced by a new revolutionary one. After a few stormy meetings the pre-parliament dissolved itself. A committee of fifty of its members remained behind in order to keep an eye on the old Federal Diet until the true National Assembly began its work. Elections were fixed for 1 May.

The unexpected, not provided for in the liberal textbook, began even as the Committee of Fifty performed its legally obscure but important duties.

A radical republican from Baden, Friedrich Hecker, a tough, red-bearded brigand who attracted the young, decided that nothing could be done in Frankfurt and that he must act on his own. After proclaiming a republic in Constance he and his volunteers moved northwards, hoping to win over the masses. At the same time a 'German Legion' was forming in France, composed of itinerant craftsmen, men of private means and *literati* under the leadership of the poet Georg Herwegh, a few hundred in all. These were senseless, melodramatic ventures which the committee in Frankfurt could not tolerate but which it was impotent to deal with because it lacked physical means of coercion. The result was unpleasant: the rift between liberals and radicals widened, the gathering in Frankfurt admitted the need for action against the left, and the activities of the radical writers came to be looked upon as both dangerous and ridiculous.

In addition to the anxiety caused by radical activities there was another, confusing one: the problem of the foreign nationalities.

In order to make the Committee of Fifty more representative some Austrians had been invited to join, among them the Prague historian, Professor Palacký. The assumption was that, as of old, Bohemia was part of Germany. Palacký replied that he was Czech and not German. Let the Germans establish their republic; while he had no objections it was of no concern to him as a Czech. Moreover, he was not merely a Czech but an Austrian, and Austria was the Empire which protected the small West Slav and South Slav peoples and it must not be destroyed. On the contrary, it must remain as it was; the German Austrians belonged inseparably to the great family of the Danube Empire. 'Indeed, if the Austrian Empire did not exist already one ought to hasten, in the interest of Europe, in the interest of humanity itself, to create it . . .' Palacký's letter which struck the men in Frankfurt as strange is a noteworthy document The spokesman of Czech nationalism solemnly proclaimed that the Czechs were a different nation from the Germans and that consequently the German Empire could not be the great medieval empire which included Bohemia, but at best something much more limited. Furthermore, Palacký expressed himself against the union of German-speaking Austria and the Empire. He did not want an encirclement of Bohemia by a great German empire, and while he spoke in terms of the new concept of a Czech nationality he also used the old one of an indestructible Austrian monarchy which had become an historical fact. Palacký was a politician without office or mandate and could not decide such questions, but he stirred up a wasps' nest of problems and contradictions.

Then there were the Poles, who had always been regarded as the noblest victims of absolutist territorial greed, the brotherly allies of all who strove for freedom. In March the German liberals were of the opinion that the Poles too should benefit from the revolution and at last be given back their own state, their ancient republic. But how? The great part of former Poland belonged to the Tsar and Tsar Nicholas was not to be trifled with if his authority was concerned. He would not accept the establishment of even a fragment of Polish independence on Prussian soil. The liberation of Poland could only be achieved by a war against the Tsar's well-drilled mass army. There were Germans who welcomed the idea of such a war, either because they had not thought out the possible consequences – this was true of certain liberal war enthusiasts – or because they had thought about them all too carefully and hoped that a world war would produce the true revolution. The King of Prussia, however, did not want such a war, least of all against his brother-in-law in St. Petersburg, the unbending, proud protector of all monarchy. Nor was the Russian problem the only one. The Prussian province of Posen – the so-called Grand Duchy – was inhabited by Poles and Germans, about half a million Germans and slightly more Poles, who in some areas lived completely separately and in others in close proximity. When the Prussian state granted the Poles political rights which they had not possessed hitherto they began to act as rulers of the province, establishing their own government, persecuting Germans and Jews. It is characteristic of men who have been disfranchised to take more than their share when they are liberated and to do to others what has been done to them. In the same spirit the Czech leader, Palacký, started to talk about the reconquest of Saxony, which he claimed had once been Czech or at least Slav, and where the Germans had established themselves illegally. In Prague there was only talk, but in Posen there was action, confiscation and looting. The Germans reacted and Berlin intervened. At first, still full of liberal good will, it tried to mediate and to keep the two nationalities apart in a friendly fashion. In the end it was forced into the civil war on the German side and Prussian troops suppressed the Polish rising. The Prussian general, it seems, set out to teach the Poles a lesson; the Poles, spurred on by their noblemen and their bishop, were ready to give as good as they got. The Prussian troops, who won willy-nilly, disarmed the Polish revolutionaries and restored the old system – applauded by the Germans. This was not a victory of the revolution, not even of the German revolution.

The unsolved Polish question was still causing confusion when the Danish one arose; it seemed as though Germany's neighbours conspired to make its well-meant, hopeful national effort as difficult as possible. But there was no such conspiracy. Nations clashed because the national liberal movement was a European one and because the same motives were at work in different countries. The Danes wanted their greater Denmark at the very moment when the Germans wanted their great, united Germany; hence the clash.

The Schleswig-Holstein affair was vital and simple and at the same time incredibly complicated. Since the late Middle Ages the King of Denmark had reigned over the two Duchies which, according to a very ancient treaty, were never allowed to be separated. Holstein was part of the Holy Roman Empire and, after 1815, of the German Confederation; Schleswig was not. The inhabitants of Holstein were entirely German in blood and speech, whereas in Schleswig only about three-quarters of the population were German; in northern Schleswig Low German merged into Danish. The Danes, patriots like the Germans, wanted to give their state a more modern form and demanded the incorporation of the whole of Schleswig into Denmark. The matter was urgent for a curious legal reason. The Danish king had no sons and while in Copenhagen the crown could pass to the female issue of the royal house, in the Duchies the succession was restricted to males. Therefore, if tradition was followed, the personal union between Schleswig and Denmark would cease with the death of Frederick VII. For Denmark this was a grievous loss; for nascent Germany it was an important gain, providing an opportunity of becoming a maritime power on the north Sea and the Baltic. Long before 1848 German and Danish nationalists had turned their attention to developments in Schleswig-Holstein.

In March the Duchies were gripped by the same enthusiasm for action as the other German states; because of their special position they wanted even more, namely the admission of Schleswig into the German Confederation and its virtual independence of Copenhagen. The Danish king thought otherwise: 'We have neither the right nor the power nor the wish to make our Duchy of Schleswig part of the German Confederation; rather we desire to strengthen the indissoluble union of Schleswig and Denmark by means of a joint constitution.' The inhabitants of Schleswig rebelled, a provisional government was established in Rendsburg – how many provisional governments there were in those days – and Schleswig-Holstein appealed for help to the common German fatherland and its most powerful prince, the King of Prussia. While Danish troops moved into Schleswig Frederick William IV surrendered to the national clamour for war. His liberal government wanted to use Prussia for a great action on the part of Germany and to unite the country by means of a common war against injustice. The Committee in Frankfurt called for the formation of volunteer corps. The Danes could not hold out against the Prussian attack; the victors pushed on through Schleswig into Denmark proper, to Jutland. This was a dangerous game, however much the Germans had reason to think that they were in the right. The Danes, too, thought that they were in the right. What anyway did right mean where interests conflicted, where two peoples were imbued with equal determination to survive? Denmark was a small country but Schleswig-Holstein was situated on the Baltic and the North Sea; the great power on the Baltic was Russia and the great power on the North Sea was Britain. An attack on Denmark must sooner or later lead to a clash with these great powers.

4. *The* Paulskirche

Such was the situation on 18th May when the long promised German National Assembly at last began its work in Frankfurt. The auspices were no longer as promising as they had been even two months previously; the Assembly needed to do very good work if it was to win. The revolution had been victorious without ever having won a real battle; the mass of the people – theoretically sovereign – were no longer so enthusiastic; half-disappointed, they were losing interest; the old powers were regaining their confidence and still controlled the armed forces. Triumphant liberalism was threatened from the 'left' by radical democracy, and therefore depended all the more on the old powers with which it wanted to reach an 'understanding'. How a German national state would deal with non-German nations which had close ties with Germany was an unsolved but already poisoned problem; the international situation was tense, giving rise to a number of grave conjectures; there was the *possibility* of war against Russia, the *possibility* of war against France, not to mention the war actually being fought against Denmark. The liberal planners had visualized a very different picture at the beginning of March. A Prussian assembly, which met in Berlin, was elected at the same time as the German National Assembly; and a few weeks later a constituent diet gathered in Vienna. Thus there now existed three interlocking circles, the Austrian the Prussian and the German. In theory the German was designed to coincide with the other two because the Frankfurt Assembly decided that its legislation applied without reservation to all German states, and so also to Austria to the extent that it was, or wanted to be, German. In fact the situation was very different; it was not Vienna and Berlin that were dependent on Frankfurt, but Frankfurt on Vienna and Berlin. It was also dependent on Prague, Munich and Stuttgart, Paris, London and St Petersburg, but chiefly on Berlin and Vienna. The German National Assembly had authority, or seemed to have it, only so long as the Austrian and Prussian states were immobilized by internal strife.

The Assembly which met in the bare rotunda of the *Paulskirche* was certainly a distinguished one. There has never been a more highly educated parliament: more than a hundred professors, more than 200 learned jurists, writers, clergymen, doctors, burgomasters, civil servants, manufacturers, bankers, landowners, even a few master craftsmen and small tenant farmers – but not a single worker. There were aged men from the Napoleonic era and young men who would live to see the twentieth century, worthies from provincial towns and universally beloved and famous poets, orators, historians and politicians. Much idealism and optimism, reduced to silence in Metternich's Germany, were assembled here and allowed to raise their voice. The world was good, the German people was great and good; and their old rulers were not so bad that it was not somehow possible to come to terms with them. The exponents of these noble ideas also had a high regard for themselves and the Assembly to which they belonged. The Hessian Heinrich von Gagern, a handsome, impressive man and a great orator who favoured the middle road, was elected president. He was chosen because the Assembly wanted to follow that road, the centre being by far the most powerful group.

At the beginning there were and could be no parties, but soon they emerged: the left, the right, the centre and bridges which reached from the centre to the right and to the left. The right wanted to restrict the Assembly's work to drafting a constitution without interfering with the German governments; and it wanted a moderate, balanced constitution, protecting as far as possible the rights of the princes, states and privileged classes. The left wanted real popular sovereignty and wanted the Assembly, as the representative of the people, not merely to talk but also to rule; it wanted laws to level out old inequalities. The extreme left demanded an indivisible republic, if it could be achieved. The left was also very nationalistic and aggressive in matters of foreign policy. 'What is impossible for forty million Germans?' The centre took some ideas from the right and some from the left and was itself split from top to bottom – the usual fate of centre parties. The parties treated each other with respect, their representatives spoke well, and apart from conventional views expressed distinctly personal, divergent opinions. There were real debates in the *Paulskirche*, verbal victories and defeats.

The decision to form a national government, a 'provisional central authority', before founding the German Empire, was a victory for the left. There were prolonged public and private discussions to determine the method of appointment and the composition of this authority. The right wanted a directory of princes, the left a plenary committee of the Assembly itself, pure parliamentary rule. The result was a compromise; the central authority was set up by the Assembly which elected the 'imperial regent', but the man whom it chose was a prince, a Habsburg Archduke John of Austria. Gagern and his friends were pursuing a cunning policy. They argued that the old powers would accept a prince from a famous house; that an Austrian could offer as dowry his Austria, at any rate the German part, which had proved a difficult, self-willed partner. The prince was elected by the Assembly and the individual states were not asked for permission, a move calculated to please the left. Moreover the prince was popular, had long been an enemy of Metternich's, and was a so-called liberal, who had married a postmaster's daughter whose children he wanted to see securely established. Nonetheless the choice was not a happy one. By choosing a Habsburg as ruler the German National Assembly tied itself for better or worse to Austria; henceforth Austrians controlled the unstable levers of the power which was in Frankfurt's gift, and which they would in the last resort always use in Austria's interest. John was no longer in his first youth; he had held command in the wars against the French Revolution and had lost a battle in 1800. Since then the old gentleman had learnt to hit exactly the right note of the new age and was good at playing the plain man. He will not appear many more times in our narrative because he played a false, but weak, game and accomplished nothing. Archduke John formed a cabinet which was to be responsible to the Assembly. Ministries were established, a chancellery, a ministry of justice, of foreign affairs, of war and of the navy. There were sensational dismissals of ministers, there were ministerial councillors, imperial ambassadors and imperial gazettes. But the minister of war had no army, the minister of justice no courts of law, the ambassadors were recognized only by a few small states – very warmly in Washington – and were received with the utmost caution in Paris and London; none of them dared to venture to St Petersburg. For the time being Archduke John presided over an empire in the clouds; whether it could ever become anything more solid depended on developments over which the men in Frankfurt had almost no influence

5. Setbacks

Neither Vienna nor Berlin had calmed down since the spring; in both capitals there was a succession of congresses, demonstrations and shooting incidents. In Vienna things went so far that the Emperor, the feeble-minded Ferdinand I, once fled, or was abducted by his protectors, to Innsbruck. The growing disorder in Vienna was of no help to the German liberals. It isolated the rebellious city in the midst of the conservative Austrian countryside and helped to compromise the liberal idea among the friends of order. The Prussian assembly did good work. It was younger and more radical than the National Assembly, but again this did not help the German national venture, because those

Prussians who were serious about their own new state could not be equally serious about the German Reich. There grew up something like competition between the parliaments and their methods – a thought which may well have occurred to the conveners of the Prussian assembly.

In June the European, and therefore also the German, revolution experienced its first major setbacks. A 'Pan-Slav Congress' had been established in Prague, consisting of Czechs, Austrian South Slavs and Poles. Designed to be a rival to the German National Assembly it stressed the Slav character of the Habsburg Empire and agitated for federalism within Austria. In principle this development appealed to the conservative Austrians who did not want union with Germany; because it was directed against pro-German, red Vienna. In the last resort these Austrians were prepared to work with the 'Austro-Slavs'. But the Pan-Slav Congress degenerated into a somewhat aimless rising of the Czechs, with barricades, calls for arms for the people and all the familiar demands. The city commandant, Prince Windisch-Gractz, an out-and-out aristocrat, an out-and-out soldier, a loyal Austrian imperialist even when there was practically no Emperor and no Austria, knew what he was doing. He withdrew his troops across the Moldau, began to shell the centre of the city and so forced the Czech population to a quick surrender. The Pan-Slav Congress scattered and the imperial Austrian order was restored, proving that the old weapons were still effective, if anyone dared to use them.

The Germans were not dissatisfied with the ignominious result of the Czech and Pan-Slav movement, unmindful of the threat that the means which had been used against the Czechs could equally be turned against them. A few weeks later another Austrian general, Radetzky, marched into Milan, which had been forced back into obedience. The Austrian colossus, which in April seemed to be disintegrating, began in the summer visibly to regain its old shape. It was possible to play off one nation against another, Germans against Italians, Slavs against Magyars and Germans; and the imperial Austrian tradition was tougher than the democrats believed. Anyway, the German liberals had from the start refused to recognize as their allies the Lombards who were fighting for national independence. That was Austria's affair and could be of no concern to Germany.

After Prague came Paris, where the situation was grimmer and gloomier than in Germany. Here Karl Marx was proved more or less right; the class struggle between the 'bourgeoisie' and the 'proletariat' moved more and more into the centre of events. The alliance between the bourgeoisie and the urban proletariat began to fall apart as soon as the common enemy, the old King, had disappeared. When the 'national workshops', big state enterprises for the unemployed, were closed, the long expected explosion took place. There was street fighting, the like of which modern Europe had not seen before, and the red fortress fell. General Cavaignac, dictator of the party of order, employed a new outflanking strategy which broke the barricades and ended this kind of civil war. Neither side showed any mercy and in three days more people were killed than in the whole of the German revolution. The result was the total, prolonged defeat of socialism in the country where it had been most strongly developed, and, momentarily, the dictatorship of the victor, Cavaignac. Lying in wait behind and against him there was already a more fortunate aspirant to power whose electoral slogan was shortly to decorate the walls: *Si vous voulez un bon – Prenez Napoléon!* Once again Germany was not dissatisfied with the outcome of the slaughter. A member of the Prussian assembly said that 'one of the most fortunate happenings in all Europe' was the way in which the problem of the Red Danger had been 'so brilliantly buried in France'. There were various ways of looking at the question. The fact was that the European revolution had begun in France and that there it had now visibly passed its zenith.

6. Schleswig-Holstein

Germany did not have to wait long for the crisis. The venture
which had seemed so promising for the unification and expansion of the Empire, the war over Schleswig-Holstein, had proved
a dangerous burden. Not from a military point of view, since on
land the Germans were obviously superior to the Danes, but
because there were still great powers and the peninsula was an
object of European interest. Although, as we have seen, there
were certain Germans, irresponsible liberals as well as communists bloodthirsty for philosophical reasons, who wanted war
against Russia, the Prussian cabinet decided as early as April
that such a war was not feasible. The Tsar on the other hand was
ready for a show-down and this fact alone would have been
enough to decide the nordic complications in Denmark's favour.
In addition Britain, while adopting a more liberal, objective and
conciliatory attitude than Russia, pressed for an amicable
settlement of the conflict. However complicated the legal issue,
there was no doubt that Prussia-Germany in a moment of enthusiasm had attacked a weaker neighbour and had itself broken
the law by allowing representatives from Schleswig to take their
seats in the Prussian assembly. Moreover, legal and moral
issues apart, it was politically not very desirable that the 'Dardanelles of the North' should fall under the control of what
looked like becoming a Great Power on land and sea. France
also subscribed to this view, and Prussia gave way to pressure
from the three Great Powers. After prolonged negotiations, interrupted and renewed, Prussia in August concluded the armistice
of Malmö; this left the final settlement of the issue to a future
peace treaty but stipulated the military evacuation of the Duchies
as well as the repudiation of everything that had happened there
since March in sympathy with the German revolution. Prussia
had gone to war together with other German troops, at the behest of the nascent German state. The armistice it concluded
alone, without asking the representatives of the central authority
for their views, in fact without first notifying Frankfurt.

Emotions ran high in the *Paulskirche*. The King of Prussia had insulted the National Assembly, had let himself be frightened by a diplomatic conspiracy, had betrayed the honour of Germany. If the Assembly allowed this to happen, if it abandoned the most German of all German provinces to the Danes, it might as well close the temple of German unity. This must not happen. 'Let France,' exclaimed a member of the extreme left, 'let England, let Russia dare to interfere in our just cause. We shall reply with one and a half million armed men.' But they would not dare, and why not? 'Because they are intelligent, because they know that an unjust attack on Germany would produce a German national rising the like of which history has probably never seen.' Karl Marx, observing the situation with frightening intelligence from the editorial offices of his *Neue Rheinische Zeitung*, commented:

Let the bourgeois and the Junkers in Frankfurt have no illusions: if they decide to reject the armistice they decide their own downfall, as the Girondists of the first revolution who were active on 10 August and who voted for the death of the ex-king thereby prepared ... their downfall. If on the other hand they accept the armistice they also decide their own downfall, place themselves under Prussia's sway and will have no further say in anything. Let them choose.

To present the matter in the form of these alternatives was hardly helpful. Marx thought that a people's war fought against Prussia's wish would quickly lead to the real revolution and sweep away the German middle classes, the liberals and the moderates. As, however, the armies of Prussia, Bavaria and now also of Austria were intact such a people's war lay beyond the realm of the possible. Anger unsupported by power can achieve nothing. The National Assembly did not really face the unpleasant choice between right and left which Marx thought that it must make. It had no power and could not mobilize any. The comparison with the great French Revolution did not apply: the Germans in 1848 were not what the French had been in 1793.

So the National Assembly came down first on the left and then on the right. On 4 September it decided by a narrow majority that the armistice of Malmö was invalid; this was a victory for the left. As the decision could only be justified with thundering speeches but not implemented, the Assembly decided a week later, by almost the same majority, that the armistice was nevertheless valid. What followed, while not yet the Marxist revolution, was nevertheless a furious popular uprising in Frankfurt and the Hessian vicinity. Its causes are difficult to describe. Was 'Germany's honour' as dear as all that to the rebels? Did they dimly feel that the National Assembly, though elected by the people, did not really represent them and that they, the ordinary people, would once again go away empty handed? Was there also some sheer pleasure in excitement and bloodshed, were there agitators at work, mad *literati* aping the French Revolution? It is impossible to answer any of these questions absolutely in the negative. When a member of the extreme left said that the new disturbances in Frankfurt, in the Rhineland and in Baden were spasms of an abortive revolution he probably hit the nail on the head; it was a revolution that was insufficiently strong to realize itself completely and therefore squandered itself in a number of ugly riots. Barricades were erected even in Frankfurt, the offices of some *Paulskirche* parties were destroyed, the Assembly itself was threatened, two conservative members were murdered in gruesome circumstances, while others – like the aged *Turnvater* Jahn who no longer understood what was happening – just managed to escape a similar fate. What could the unfortunate 'German government' do in these circumstances? Should it wage a people's war against Denmark, Russia and France in league with those who had just beaten the deputy Prince Lichnowsky to death with umbrellas? It sought protection from those who could give it, from the Prussian army garrisoned in the federal fortress of Mainz. Royal Prussian troops, instead of fighting the Danes, restored order in German Frankfurt.

It was the most curious situation imaginable in a revolutionary battle [noted the writer Heinrich Laube, who was present]. The insurgents fought against authorities who had only just emerged from the nation's universal suffrage. The attacked defended themselves with troops whose commanders had only recently been the adversaries of those who were now attacked – and would probably soon be again.

The troubles in Frankfurt revealed the full extent of the impotence of the National Assembly; impotence rather than weakness of character or lack of ability. The empire of the liberals was an illusion and could not decide real issues like war and peace. As long as Prussia and Austria were genuine states Germany was no state. Prussia had basically never ceased to be one; it was probable by early summer and certain by late autumn that the end of the Habsburg Empire had been proclaimed too soon.

7. *Vienna and Berlin*

In Austria the political fate of the Germans was inextricably involved with that of the other peoples of central and south-east Europe: Slavs, Rumanians and Magyars. In March Hungary had been given the rights of a self-governing state. If German and Polish nationalism were on less good terms with each other than the liberals had hoped, the situation was even worse in the old Kingdom where the traditionally ruling Magyars were in conflict with the 'subject nations' – the Rumanians, Slovaks, Slovenes and Croats. In western Europe Kossuth, the leader of the new Hungary, was regarded as a good liberal, in America even as a democrat. In reality this charismatic, conceited revolutionary was the most extreme nationalist who had hitherto appeared. He gave the non-Magyar peoples of Hungary the choice between complete submission or extermination. They chose to fight. The Hungarian spring of freedom thus quickly degenerated into a murderous war against the Magyars by the Croats and the Slovenes under the leadership of their Viceroy, Baron Jellačić. The supporters of imperial Austria welcomed this development because the war in Hungary offered an opportunity of ending Magyar separatism. All those who for one reason or another wanted to see the Habsburg monarchy preserved were against the Magyars – the generals of the imperial army, the international feudal lords, the Czechs (because they regarded Austria as a protection against Germany), the loyalists of the Alpine provinces and the conservative supporters of the dynasty generally. On the side of Hungary were those who wanted union between Germany and Austria, the pro-German Viennese who looked towards Frankfurt – and the more radical they were the more they did so. If Hungary became independent, if the Habsburg monarchy collapsed, German Austria could become a member state of the German Empire, mopping up Bohemia in the process. In the imperial diet which met in Vienna in July to prepare a constitution for Austria, the supporters of a 'greater' Germany were in the minority; the majority was with the Slavs and the loyalist Austrians. The diet, a wild, multilingual gathering, established at least one lasting claim to fame: it abolished the remains of hereditary serfdom, the surviving feudal services of the peasants, thus giving modest satisfaction to the most numerous class of the country.

Vienna, the capital, on the other hand was in the throes of a revolution and of a constantly growing German nationalism as well as social demands, and therefore sympathized vociferously and menacingly with Hungary. Nobody has ever counted the radicals or the supporters of the dynasty in Vienna. It is possible that there too the loyal Austrians were in the majority. The workers and the unemployed, hard hit by the general paralysis of the economy, the politically conscious lower middle class, the students, young and romantic – they all wanted something quite different and new: a great democratic and socially just Germany, maybe as a monarchy under good Archduke John, maybe as a republic. As the summer passed Vienna fell increasingly under democratic control. The town was administered by a revolutionary central committee, a Committee of Safety. While civic guards, student legions and workers' battalions organized themselves there was no sign of the imperial government. Newspapers like *Der Mann des Volkes* (Man of the People), *Die Rote Mütze* (Red Cap), *Der Ohnehose* (Sansculotte) and *Der Proletarier* (The Proletarian) spoke a dramatic language. In the early autumn Vienna, rather than Baden or the Rhineland, was the hope of all those who wanted to revive the flagging German revolution. Karl Marx put in a personal appearance in order to give scientific advice. The explosion came when a German regiment disobeyed an order to march against the Hungarians. The Minister of War was massacred in his office and the feeble-minded Emperor escaped for the second time. Red Vienna, under a city commandant elected by the municipal council, prepared to stand on its own feet.

But whom should it choose as its ally? Looking back on these grim events a hundred years later it is easy to talk. The Hungarians were a long way away, and between them and the Viennese were Jellačić's Croats. The National Assembly in Frankfurt felt even more impotent on the question of Vienna than on the Danish issue, it met under the protection of Prussian guns and was more afraid of radical democracy than of reaction in Prussia and Austria. The French Revolution was over and Paris was ruled by the army as protector of the conservative middle class in town and country. In the East Tsar Nicholas lay in wait with 500,000 soldiers. For the moment, however, Russia's help was not needed. Red Vienna found itself isolated in conservative German-Austrian and Slav country, isolated from a good part of its own population. From the south-east loyalist troops marched against the rebellious capital, 'wild men', as their leaders said warningly. There were regiments among them which to the Prussian ambassador 'looked more like Asiatic Turks than Europeans' – and who were to behave accordingly. Prince Windisch-Graetz, the conqueror of Prague, advanced from Bohemia to put an end to the rule of the Viennese 'gutter snipes' as he put it. The Czechs, his enemies of yesterday, gave him their explicit blessing: as long as he fought the Viennese supporters of a 'greater' Germany they would assuredly not stab him in the back. The conquest of the town was pursued methodically and without mercy; whatever hope, idealism, good will, youth, whatever extravagant folly and fury had held sway there for half a year was put down in a few days. The red terror was followed by the white which is not a whit better and often even more brutal.

The victims of the courts martial included a member of the

Paulskirche, the honest, popular leader of the left, Robert Blum. He had come to Austria at the behest of his party, to observe, to clarify and to help. Since September Blum had been deeply disheartened by the development in Germany for which he had risked everything. He thought of emigrating or of retiring forever from politics but remained from a sense of duty, without hope. Finding himself in the middle of the battle for the defence of Vienna he took charge of a unit, thus, legally speaking, committing a crime. But his execution was a political act, arranged between Windisch-Graetz and the new Austrian head of government, Prince zu Schwarzenberg, to show the German National Assembly what they thought of it and who was in control.

The fall of Vienna saved the old Austrian system. The army leaders, elegant, grey-haired, determined noblemen, Windisch-Graetz, Schwarzenberg, Radetzky and Jellačić, had forced the disintegrating monarchy together again. For whose sake? For themselves? They could probably have preserved their positions in the new national states. For the sake of the Germans? Windisch-Graetz occasionally spoke of the Germanic interest which was best served by preserving the Danubian monarchy; but these feudal Austrian Europeans were not really German patriots. For the sake of the House of Habsburg? They despised the Emperor; the Archdukes flirted with Germany and had already shared out Austria between themselves. For the sake of the world into which they had been born and which they could not imagine without the imperial state? That would probably be the most accurate reply. The new Prime Minister, Felix Schwarzenberg, was a master of the game of power politics, a man of cool audacity who was shortly to reveal his political character. He dispatched the diet to the provinces, to Kremsier, where it was allowed to go on talking for a while. As long as the Frankfurt Assembly existed it was useful to have an Austrian counterpart. In the Hungarian theatre of war Windisch-Graetz was given supreme command. As the feeble-minded Emperor no longer fitted into the new order Schwarzenberg got rid of him in December, replacing him by his nephew, the eighteen-year-old Archduke Francis or, as he was now called in memory of the good Emperor

Joseph, Francis Joseph. In the same month Louis Napoleon
Bonaparte was elected President of the French Republic with an
overwhelming majority so that Francis Joseph and Napoleon III
presented themselves to Europe together, two symbols and
supporters of the restored order.

In a special edition the *Kreuzzeitung*, the Prussian reactionaries'
paper, jubilantly told its readers of the change in Austria's affairs.

> Last night Vienna was taken by storm. Most of the university leaders
> and the mob fled in cowardly fashion, deserting those whom they had
> corrupted ... The rule of anarchy and of the red republic has been
> overthrown and the power of the law has triumphed. May the hydra
> never again raise its accursed head anywhere.

Prussia could not lag behind where Austria led the way. As soon
as the first measures of Schwarzenberg's rule by the sword became known in Berlin King Frederick William IV decided to put
an end to the revolution. Though Berlin was less radical than
Vienna it had not been possible to restore order completely
between spring and early autumn. Many factors encouraged a
coup d'état: the gifted but mentally unstable monarch still talked
of reviving the Middle Ages; weak, vacillating governments
followed one another in quick succession; and the constituent
assembly was definitely orientated more to the 'left' than the
German one. On the other side there was the traditional Prussian
army, intact, supported by the Junkers and probably also the
greater part of the rural population; there was a determined,
well-organized reactionary party, used to power, which was
learning the modern craft of propaganda; there were the middle
classes, organized in the Berlin National Guard, frightened by
the workers, with whom they had frequent clashes, and consequently driven increasingly to the right; and while the language
and behaviour of the Radicals and democratic congresses became more extreme, the political interest of the general population declined and gave way to a desire for peace and order. There
was no need for a repetition of what had happened in Vienna,
particularly as the defeat of the Viennese had provided a dis-
couraging example. On 2 November the country was presented

with an energetic conservative, General Count Brandenburg, as Prime Minister. On 9 November the Prussian assembly was transferred to the provinces, on 14 November martial law was declared in Berlin and on 5 December the ministers proclaimed a constitution, hurriedly thought up by themselves, and declared the national assembly dissolved. All this happened with only the symbolic use of force. What in Austria had been a fearful tragedy in Prussia became a tragi-comedy. The parliamentarians exercised passive resistance, allowed themselves to be pursued from building to building for a few days and appealed to the people not to pay their taxes. Then there was peace in Prussia. The 'dictated' constitution seemed at first sight more liberal than might have been expected; some of its provisions were based on the work of the national assembly.

8. Grossdeutsch *and* Kleindeutsch

So much for Austria and Prussia. But what about the German Reich? The Assembly in the *Paulskirche* had done a thorough job and until the late autumn had concentrated mainly on the basic rights of the citizen which were to be enshrined in the preamble to the constitution. These basic rights were excellent. If there was almost nothing about the social responsibility of the state there was almost everything about the guarantees of liberty, the freedom of movement and the equality before the law needed by the individual in order to look after himself. The Assembly had wanted to set up a constitutional state in which there would be freedom for political activity, science and life generally, and one must not make fun of such a serious effort. The difficulty was that whenever the Assembly wanted to achieve something real its own unreality became apparent. Although the 'basic rights' were published in the *Reichsgesetzblatt*, not one of the great German states, neither Prussia nor Bavaria not to mention Austria, adopted them. The Frankfurt deputies must really have thought highly of themselves that in such circumstances they successfully avoided for so long the painful suspicion of living in cloud-cuckoo-land.

Once the basic rights had been disposed of the Assembly valiantly went on to discuss the constitution proper. Here the inevitable question was where the frontiers of the Empire should be drawn. The members of the constitutional commission found the answer: 'No part of the German Reich shall belong to a state with non-German territories.' The German Austrians were therefore confronted with the choice of joining Germany or remaining united with the Hungarians, Southern Slavs and Northern Italians. During the winter the words *grossdeutsch* ('greater' German) and *kleindeutsch* ('little' German) came into vogue; to unify Germany without Austria was the *kleindeutsch* solution, with Austria the *grossdeutsch* solution. However, there never were any proper *kleindeutsch* or *grossdeutsch* parties, because the advocates of unification without Austria would only too gladly have accepted Austria into the new fatherland, provided Austria agreed to make the necessary sacrifice – after all, who would not be 'great' rather than 'little', whole rather than mutilated? The supporters of unification with Austria wanted precisely this, so long as the Habsburg Empire was expected to collapse. Once it had been restored they had no positive policy and merely tried to prevent or water down the alternative solution. The whole of Austria could not be united with Germany; a German nation-state which included Milan, Venice, Zagreb, Budapest and Cracow was nonsense. But such a complete unification was all that Felix Schwarzenberg offered, either because he really believed it to be possible or as a piece of sheer mockery. On 27 November he announced that the preservation of the Austrian monarchy was a European necessity, and that it would remain as it was. On 4 March 1849 he dismissed the Austrian Diet and decreed the constitution of a centralized unitary state. A stroke of the pen did away with the historic rights of the Magyars, Croats, Italians and also the Germans. Henceforth the multi-lingual colossus was to be *one* state, like France. On 9 March the Iron Prince let it be known that this state demanded to become a member of the new German federal Empire, with the proviso that it must have more votes in the federal parliament than all the rest of Germany, Prussia included.

Now the situation was clear, unification with Austria was impossible. The only alternative was the *kleindeutsch* solution – Prussian leadership, or nothing at all. Nothing at all – unless one believed in the possibility of a new revolution which would sweep away Austria and Prussia. It was certainly possible to want this, but unless there were very, very many people who did and unless they were very well organized, armed and led, it was like wanting to conquer the moon. Some Bavarian Catholics and south-west German democratic anti-Prussians amused themselves for a while trying to find clever solutions with Austria; but under any name these would in fact have been tantamount to a return to the old German Confederation.

In the early spring of 1849, therefore, the majority of the National Assembly, right as well as left, reluctantly became *kleindeutsch*; and the two sides now worked better together than ever before. A number of concessions were made to the left: universal, equal and direct male suffrage, a cabinet responsible to the Diet and a president or emperor whose veto could merely delay the Diet's decisions. The left for its part accepted with a sigh the principle of hereditary monarchy with an emperor provided by the Prussian royal house. Politics, after all, is the art of compromise, and it was impossible to get away from Prussia. Once the constitution was adopted the Assembly proceeded to elect the emperor; with an unimpressive majority it chose the King of Prussia. It was significant that the minority did not vote for anybody; the supporters of a greater Germany had no alternative to offer. The question now was whether this time the decision on paper would become a reality.

The Prussian government – set up after the *coup d'état* – had thrown out promising hints in the course of the winter; it was suggested that a closer German federation under Prussian leadership was being seriously considered, that it would then be possible somehow to come to terms with Austria in a wider federation. Such was the view of the government, of the new Prussian popular representatives and even of the arch-conservative Prince William. The decision rested with the King. Frederick William IV was attracted by the idea of doing something great and historic for Germany; he vacillated between ambition and hatred of all things modern, liberal and democratic. The second leaning predominated. To the deputation offering him the crown he made one of his more pompous speeches; the parliamentarians had to study it carefully afterwards before they discovered the 'no'. Among his friends the monarch spoke more clearly of the 'filthy crown', the 'sausage roll', the 'dog collar', the 'crown by the grace of bakers and butchers'. The drift of his speech, he said, had been: 'I cannot say yes or no. One accepts or rejects only things that can be offered – and you have nothing to offer. Such questions I settle with my peers. But before we part let me tell you the truth: against democrats soldiers are the only remedy! Farewell.'

A pathetic tale, sad to relate. Once again, for the last time, the German National Assembly discovered that its revolution had been a piece of April foolery. In vain did the Prime Minister von Gagern, implore the King to say to which articles of the constitution he objected; the Assembly was prepared for any revision. In vain did no less than twenty-eight small German states announce under pressure from their populations their acceptance of the constitution and the Emperor. Prussia remained inflexible, and following Prussia's lead Bavaria, Saxony and Hanover. Was the work of a year to end in the wastepaper basket, were the great hopes of March 1848 to end in nothing? The Assembly decided that its work was nonetheless valid and announced that there would be elections to the constitutional diet in the whole of Germany. This was a revolutionary step or none at all.

9. The Civil War

There was still so much inflammable matter in Germany, so much passion for the cause of unity, so much fury about the treachery of the governments that in May something like a second revolution came to the assistance of the helpless representatives of the people. It was the revolution which would have taken a very different course in March 1848, had the princes in their anxiety not 'granted' everything. Meanwhile the old forces had recovered and reorganized themselves and as they now took back what they had granted a year before there were popular revolts in many places, simultaneously or in quick succession; in Saxony, in the Prussian Rhineland, in Baden and in the Bavarian Palatinate. Was this a last, unexpected opportunity for the National Assembly? Some critics think that it could have placed itself at the head of this movement which was in urgent need of leadership, given it legitimacy, surrounded itself with rebellious troops and overrun the country. For the moment there was no threat of Austrian intervention because the Hungarians were still fighting a successful war against Vienna. This is what we read. The German National Assembly, however, did not take this opportunity; it acted in accordance with the law under which it had assumed power. In old age one does not change and the Assembly was old after a squandered year. It never put to the German princes the basic question of all struggle for power: can you kill me or can I kill you? The Assembly's aim, its language, its way of life had been to reconcile the old with the new. Now under much less favourable conditions it could not – or at any rate did not – risk the ruthless trial of strength which it had missed the previous year. It failed to give the hoped-for leadership and while it protested and negotiated a little, the Austrian representatives, then the Prussians and then all those of the right and the centre bolted. At the beginning of June the rest, the so-called 'rump parliament', less than a hundred men, moved to Stuttgart; the King of Württemberg, under pressure from his subjects, who were enthusiastically in favour of German union, adopted an equivocal attitude. He did not need to maintain it for long. On 18 June he ordered the closure of the council chamber and had the German National Assembly, what remained of it, chased away by mounted police.

The revolutionary energy displayed belatedly in the cause of the Reich constitution was squandered in a welter of blood and suppressed with a super abundance of military force, first in Dresden, then in the Rhineland, in the Palatinate and in Baden. Prince William of Prussia, who a year earlier had hastily escaped from the revolution to Britain, now had the satisfaction of leading two full Prussian army corps to south-west Germany. There was a repetition of what had happened in Vienna in the previous October, inviting the same kind of melancholy comment. Neither revolution nor counter-revolution is attractive. What attracts in the one is idealism and honest, unselfish hope, what offends is dilettantism, melodramatic posturing, quarrels among the leaders and the abruptness of change. What attracts in the other is the fact that it restores order, what Hegel called 'the truth of power', what offends is self-righteous brutality, the vindictiveness of the victors, and the sterility of victory. All this was experienced by tormented Baden from May to June 1849, and later. The accurate historian should mention both the bravery of the rebellious Baden troops in their fight against the Prussians and the quarrelsome and childish behaviour of the provisional revolutionary government, the chaos which it left behind. It should be stated that many inhabitants were grateful to Prussia for restoring order while others hated the north German oppressor. History rarely permits the clear-cut judgement which the reader would like.

The end was summary executions. The Prussian victor knew no mercy, not even for the people who had fought for a constitution under which the Prussian King would have become emperor. What blind injustice, what cruel confusion. The German revolution had wanted to be different from other revolutions, friendly, tolerant, legal; it suffered for it by ending in an interminable chain of treason trials.

The turn of the Hungarians came a few months later in

August, not without assistance from the Tsar. Nicholas I finally did what he had contemplated for eighteen months: he sent an army to the aid of the Emperor Francis Joseph which put an end to the revolutionary, heroic, though unfortunately not very just struggle of the Magyars.

10. The Prussian Union

After the tragedy came the satiric drama. Having betrayed all hopes put in him and crushed them with his troops Frederick William IV nevertheless wanted the glory of being the man who unified Germany, or something similar; of course without democracy, so that he would be dealing with his peers and not with representatives of the people. With this aim in mind Prussia, Saxony and Hanover concluded in May 1849 the so-called Three Kings' Alliance to which other small north German states acceded. The idea came from a member of the Frankfurt right and friend of Frederick William, General von Radowitz, a conservative but imaginative man who certainly had Germany's well-being at heart. He wanted to save what could be saved from the bankruptcy of the *Paulskirche*, if only a closer confederation of northern Germany. For a brief period the vacillating mind of the King was won over to the idea, as it had already been won over to several others. It says little for the acumen or the dignity of the Frankfurt liberals or 'Constitutionalists' that they too clutched at this straw, at the very moment when Prussian troops were conquering south-west Germany; they were once again deceived by the impostor in Potsdam. The Prussian parliament agreed; the Frankfurt constitution was borrowed and suitably improved to give the monarch more authority. In March 1850, after much humming and hawing, Prussia convened in Erfurt a 'parliament', composed of the states of the 'North German Union', in which the liberal celebrities of the *Paulskirche*, Gagern, Dahlmann and Simson, could once again bask in their importance. They were happy with little. A witty young reactionary who appeared in Erfurt, the Prussian delegate von Bismarck-Schönhausen, called the union 'a hybrid of timorous thirst for power and tame revolution'. The King wanted power provided it could be obtained without danger and the liberals had certainly been tamed. But change was no longer possible without great danger. Whereas in March 1848, even in March 1849, it might have been possible to have complete German unity now even the small part of it which Frederick William lusted after could no longer be got. Austria did what it could not have done in 1848 or even in 1849; it vetoed any 'close federation'. Behind this veto was the iron will of Prince Felix Schwarzenberg ('We shall not let ourselves be thrown out of Germany', he said) and an Austrian army reputed to be superior to that of Prussia besides Austria's powerful ally, Tsar Nicholas. Even if Austria alone could not have settled the issue the will of the Tsar was decisive. As Karl Marx, in exile in London shrewdly foresaw:

Austrian and south German troops are lining up in Franconia and Bohemia in order to force Prussia back into the federal parliament. Prussia is also arming . . . But this noise will lead nowhere . . . Neither the King of Prussia nor the Emperor of Austria, only the Tsar is sovereign. In the end rebellious Prussia will bow to his command . . .

This is exactly what happened. For reactionary Prussia the liberating 'people's war' which the German radicals had wanted to wage against Russia two years earlier was impossible. Prussia gave in and conceded all Schwarzenberg's demands, the restoration of the German Confederation as established in 1815, Austria's presidential position, Denmark's control of Schleswig-Holstein – everything. Three years after March 1848 Francis Joseph and his Minister Schwarzenberg were in a stronger position in Germany than old Metternich had ever been. The 'March Ministers' had long vanished from the small German states, the March achievements had been watered down or suppressed. Several thousand fine speeches, several thousand dead and several thousand trials – such was the harvest of 1848 and 1849. Of the great, hopeful turmoil nothing but disappointment, shame and derision seemed to remain

2. REFLECTION

1. German and French Revolution

People claim that in 1848 the revolution could have been successful in Germany if it had done this or that at this or that moment. What are 'revolutions' anyway? Is it desirable that they should occur occasionally and is it desirable that they should be successful? One must not shirk this general question if one wants to judge the events described above.

According to Marx, revolutions occur periodically; whenever the means of production become too powerful for the system in which they operate. In other words, when the political and economic ruling class is no longer equal to its task. Then it must step down. Because no ruling class abdicates voluntarily it remains in control until the whole of the old order breaks down and is forcibly swept away, administration, legal system and all that goes with it. That is revolution, and from it emerges the new ruling class . . . The Marxist view of revolution contains only a small element of truth; it is not borne out by history. Doubtless there are social or economic 'classes', but they are nothing like the distinct and clearly defined groups that Marx sees in them. Neither do they gain or relinquish power so abruptly. The rise of the European middle class was a very slow process which can be traced back to the Middle Ages. That does not mean that the great French Revolution which began in 1789 was not to some extent connected with the demands of the bourgeoisie and the peasants. However, it was directed less against the aristocracy, which had long ceased to be the ruling class, than against a system of government at once weak and annoying, antiquated and bankrupt. A modernization of the French state was certainly desirable; that the revolution degenerated into bloody civil war was at first mainly the fault of the court and its foolish resistance. As the tension grew extraneous elements entered: exaggerated idealism, fear and passion generated by the European war, collective and individual ambition and violent quackery which achieved little of real value. What the French Revolution could accomplish it had accomplished by 1792, and Napoleon essentially returned to the position of that year. Change, reform and adaptation of the law to new economic and moral conditions are necessary in history, but revolutions in the form of sanguinary tragedies, sudden violent fundamental upheavals are neither necessary nor desirable. Nor do they ever lead to what their leaders envisage. Britain, for example, has managed until now to do without revolution although there have certainly been social changes. The so-called English revolutions of the seventeenth century were definitely not revolutions in the Marxian sense; if anything they were counter-revolutions. It was the kings who tried to introduce an alien absolutism and who were defeated by the *old* parliamentary system in the Civil War of the sixteen-forties and again in 1688.

The French Revolution was such a dramatic, such an impressive event that it dominated politics and the interpretation of history even in the middle of the nineteenth century. Marx and Engels based their whole theory of revolution on it, and, although they pretended to have many examples, it is no accident that they always chose the same one, because in fact they had no other. They really only knew two revolutions, the bourgeois or French one which had taken place recently and the proletarian revolution which would take place shortly. Most German democrats and radicals were strongly under the influence of the French Revolution, whose language and gestures they copied. In Baden the form of address current during the civil war of 1848–9 was 'citizen', as in Paris in Robespierre's day.

But conditions in Germany in 1848 differed fundamentally from those of France in the late eighteenth century. There was no bankrupt administration on the verge of collapse; the Austrians were not badly governed and the Prussians were well governed. No helpless monarch convened the old estates because he was in financial difficulties. On the contrary, the Germans rebelled against the effective, often all too effective bureaucratic state. Their demand was for greater freedom of action, legal safeguards, political participation (which meant the control of the government by popular representatives), and above all for national unity, the participation of the whole nation in all important questions. This longing existed, and although today we are no longer as optimistic about the idea of the nation-state as our ancestors were a hundred years ago, we can understand the longing. The Germans felt that their standing in the world did not correspond to their strength, and that Metternich's Confederation was not the right instrument with which to acquire the position due to them. A nation becomes one by feeling itself to be one. The Germans in the middle of the nineteenth century clearly had this feeling, and because they regarded themselves as a numerous, strong people with a glorious past, they wanted to make an impact beyond their frontiers. The defeat of the revolution justified those who regarded such an attempt as nonsense and who only believed in force, the force of the Prussian army or of the revolutionary working class. It also justified those who now took even less interest in politics than before, and who turned to better things, to making money, to science; also perhaps to literature and to metaphysics which allowed them to despise history.

2. The Great Powers and the German Revolution

Historians have recently expressed the view that the attempts to unify Germany in 1848-9 failed because of external factors; that the three Great Powers, Britain, Russia and France were opposed to it, and that this opposition rather than reservations of a philosophical nature was the real reason why Frederick William IV refused the imperial crown. The argument is difficult to refute because in history one can hardly ever state with certainty that something might have happened if . . . The great coalition which proved fateful to Germany in 1914 was certainly not probable in 1848; one might even go so far as to say that Britain would definitely not have gone to war to prevent the unification of Germany if carried out with restraint. In fact it was the British Foreign Secretary who finally made the most sensible proposal on the difficult question of Schleswig-Holstein, namely to give the northern, predominantly Danish part of Schleswig to Denmark, but all the rest to Germany. Although individual voices were raised in protest in London, the opinion of some member of Parliament or other does not prove that Britain as a whole wanted to prevent German unity. The government and the country in general adopted a waiting, friendly attitude. France was itself in the throes of a revolution, and during the decisive spring months of 1848 was quite incapable of intervening. There, too, feelings varied; according to their own revolutionary and democratic theory the French should have welcomed the unification of Germany as much as that of Italy, though age-old arguments of power politics spoke against it. In the spring the French Foreign Minister and the Russian Chancellor did in fact discuss whether a united Germany of forty million or – with Austria – seventy million people constituted a threat to France and Russia. At the same time different combinations, such as France, Prussia and Britain, or Poland, Germany and France, were considered. Everything seemed possible in such confused times and the few pieces that existed on the European chessboard were moved about in all possible directions in the minds of excited diplomats and journalists. Yet nothing was thought through to the end and in fact nothing happened. Only in the war against Denmark did Prussia in the end find itself confronted by the great powers. The argument that Germany was not even permitted to have little Schleswig and would therefore certainly not have been permitted to unite does not hold water. It was unfortunate that Germany allowed itself to be provoked and began its internal unification with a war abroad. The establishment of a new great power in the centre of Europe demanded prudence and statesman-like leadership.

The view that Europe conspired against the 'good Germany' of 1848 and that thereafter the only alternative was the 'bad' Prussia-Germany created by Bismarck can therefore not be adequately substantiated. It was, moreover, rejected by Bismarck himself, who, after all, knew no small amount about European diplomacy. In his memoirs he speaks at length about the rocks on which the revolution foundered, without mentioning external relations. On the contrary, he thinks that in March 1848 and again in the spring of 1849, Prussia had the opportunity for decisive action. But Prussia did not want to act, nor did Bismarck himself, although not because of the international situation.

3. The Problem of the Nationalities

In 1848 no thought, no action was carried through to the end. But several elements appeared for the first time which were later responsible for much bloodshed and for the failure of thoughts and actions. It became clear that it was extremely difficult to isolate the destiny of Germany from that of other nations, and that it was therefore very difficult to establish a German nation-state. Until 1848 it had been thought that oppressed and divided peoples – Germans, Italians and Poles – shared a common aim and would live together in a brotherly fashion after their liberation. 'Europe is being re-shaped according to its nationalities', wrote the future Field-Marshal von Moltke in March 1848. 'All foreign elements will disappear; as long as we regain everything German we shall be richly compensated.' How to cut away everything non-German, how to regain everything German, that was the difficulty, in Posen, in Bohemia, in the whole Austrian Empire. In addition to the peoples who had hitherto been theoretically allowed their freedom there now suddenly appeared those of whom nobody had thought so far, like the Czechs and the South Slavs. When it became evident that the liberated peoples would not behave like loving brothers and that it was impossible to draw a fair dividing line between them, the German liberals readily agreed to let might come before right, or their own right before the rights of others. In the great Polish debate in the

Paulskirche the victorious party was the one which put the interest of the Germans before that of the Poles.

It is high time that we awaken from the romantic self-renunciation which made us admire all sorts of other nationalities while we ourselves languished in shameful bondage, trampled on by all the world; it is high time that we awaken to a healthy national egoism which, to put it frankly, places the welfare and honour of the fatherland above everything else ... I admit without beating about the bush that our right is only the right of the stronger, the right of the conqueror ...

This was said by Jordan, the member of the Assembly probably best acquainted with the situation in Poland. Dahlmann, a great liberal professor, spoke of the *power* for which the German people really longed. Heinrich von Gagern, the advocate of unification without Austria, personally also preferred a solution which permitted the establishment of a 'greater' Germany, or rather of an all-embracing Germany of totally unrealistic dimensions.

I wonder if in the national interest we can ... in future leave the non-German provinces of Austria to themselves and to chance. I believe that it is the role of the German people to be great, to be one of those who rule ... What kind of unity must we strive for? A kind that will enable us to fulfil our destiny in the East; a unity that will enable us to make those peoples along the Danube that have neither the vocation nor the right to independence satellites of our planetary system.

It would be wrong simply to condemn the nationalism of the German liberals. To abandon the Germans in Posen to the turbulent Polish majority was really asking a great deal. As long as power was power and the right of the strongest prevailed everywhere in the world the Germans were bound to prefer their own rule to that of the Slavs. It was not the ideas of these men, however irresponsible and lacking in awareness of the immense difficulties of the problem, that were to blame, but the really insuperable tangle of the central and east European nationalities. The problem has never been solved by anybody; therefore we must not demand a solution from the men of 1848. It was their misfortune to be the first to discover it and to rush straight into it with simple-minded optimism.

In 1848 it also became clear for the first time that the concept of the nation-state would sooner or later destroy the Austrian monarchy; a prospect which inevitably implied various dangers and dangerous temptations for Germany. Czech nationalism was an imitation of German nationalism, and was childishly unoriginal, particularly where it wanted to be very original.

It is fortunate [wrote the poet Franz Grillparzer] that Palacký's views are not shared by the majority of his countrymen but only by a small fraction, the party of the 'Germanized' Czechs. Having learned everything that they know from the Germans, as a sign of gratitude, they also imitate the Germans' latest follies. Where does this outcry about nationality, this emphasis on an indigenous language and history come from but the German universities, where learned fools have provoked the spirit of a quiet, sensible nation to madness and crime. There is the cradle of your Slavomania and if the Bohemian declaims loudest against the German he is merely a German translated into Bohemian.

How true. But if the Germans became nationalists not only in 'little Germany' but also on Habsburg territory, the Slavs were in the end forced to defend themselves by imitation. Grillparzer, an Austrian of the old stamp, logically despised German as much as Slav nationalism. He mocked in 1848:

> *O Herr, lass Dich herbei,*
> *Und mach die Deutschen frei,*
> *Dass endlich das Geschrei*
> *Danach zu Ende sei!**

and prophesied more grimly:

> *Der Weg der neueren Menschheit geht*
> *Von der Humanität*
> *Durch die Nationalität*
> *Zur Bestialität.†*

*Oh Lord, deign to set the Germans free so that their clamour for freedom shall cease at last.

†The road of modern man leads from humanity by way of nationalism to bestiality.

But a solitary Viennese poet who occupied a not very important position in the civil service could not prevent the aberrations of history.

4. The Class Struggle

According to another theory, propounded particularly by Marx and his pupils, the revolution foundered on the rock of the class struggle. The liberal bourgeoisie was frightened of the democratic lower middle classes and both were afraid of the proletariat. Therefore there was no united front against the old powers, the monarchy, the aristocracy and the army. Because black-red-gold was frightened of red it yielded to Prussian black-and-white and Austrian black-and-yellow. We must briefly examine this view, brilliantly presented by Marx and Engels in their *Revolution und Konterrevolution in Deutschland*.

The German revolution was determined by political, not by social or economic factors. Although there was some localized social unrest in the forties it did not produce the events of March 1848. The middle classes rose against the absolutism of the princes which seemed to them out of date. Shortly after the event the revolution was rightly called the 'bourgeois' revolution; more recently it has become known as the 'revolution of the intellectuals'. That expression, too, is apposite because professors and writers played an important role both in preparing the revolt and in the *Paulskirche*. Only when the revolution was under way did a number of distinct opposition groups develop: the democrats parted company with the liberals and were in turn left by a group which might be described as radical republicans or social democrats.

But one must not think in terms of a great proletarian party such as developed towards the end of the century. There was not the slightest possibility of anything on that scale in Germany in 1848. There were still far more craftsmen than factory workers and more peasants than craftsmen and factory workers together. Of these there were not more than a million at the most and many of them still regarded themselves as craftsmen and regretted losing the security and status that went with the craftsman's position. The workers' congresses which met in Berlin and Frankfurt in 1848 did not discuss the dictatorship of the proletariat but matters of direct concern: the protection of handicrafts, of apprentices and journeymen, the promotion of small-scale industry through patent legislation, export subsidies, cheap imports of raw materials, and also free education, progressive income tax, the welfare of the old and so on. Those were the outlines of a liberal social policy, no more. The most successful labour leader of 1848, Stephan Born, although he knew and respected Marx, abandoned the master's teaching as soon as it came to practical work. 'I would have been laughed at or pitied,' he says in his reminiscences, 'had I behaved like a Communist, which anyway I no longer was. What did I care about distant centuries if the hour offered an abundance of problems and work.' Born organized, if not the world revolution, a printers' trade union which quickly achieved results in the wage struggle everywhere in Germany. He also set about the foundation of a great workers' 'fraternity' whose local committees were to intervene in wage negotiations, establish building societies, and work for political and general education. Many such associations were founded, but they were all suppressed by the reaction of the fifties.

Liberal or democratic citizens really had nothing to fear from the beginnings of this practical workers' movement. The theories of Marx and his Communist League, domiciled in London, Paris and Cologne, had a few hundred German supporters at the most. Why then this fear of the 'Reds' which Engels mentions and which undoubtedly existed long before 1848?

The German middle class may have made the same mistake as Marx, who busily encouraged them in this: they transposed the conditions of the class struggle which existed in Britain and Paris to Germany, where they did not exist. Naked, shameless class war had, it is true, been fought in Paris in June 1848, and the whole theory was taken from there. Muddle-headed people easily assumed that similar things would happen in Germany or were happening already. This may explain why at certain critical moments the middle class was really frightened of the Reds, why the National Guard in Berlin refused to admit workers to its ranks, and in Vienna in October urged the surrender of the city, whereas the workers wanted to fight on. The reactionaries welcomed this fear. 'Democracy', 'socialism', 'communism' and the end of the world were muddled into a single terror – a trick successfully repeated the world over to the present day.

There was no sharp, conscious class struggle in Germany in 1848. But the Progressive Party split very early and it is obvious that this split was bound to weaken the drive of the whole movement. For the paralysing consequences both extremes must be held responsible, the docile orators in the *Paulskirche* as much as the irresponsible rioters, like Hecker and Struve, and the champagne-drinking revolutionary writers, like Georg Herwegh.

Marx and Engels did not play a happy role during the two years of revolution. The best that can be said for them is that they had almost no influence. Their whole theory that the bourgeoisie and the lower middle class would now come to power, only to be overthrown by the proletariat, did not fit into the German conditions and was highly artificial. How was it possible to support a movement that was allowed to be victorious merely in order to be immediately stamped out? Someone who was interested only in the second revolution could do nothing useful for the first. On the occasion of a trial of Communists in Cologne after the victory of the old powers, Marx protested in the *New York Tribune* against the monstrous procedure of the Prussian government: 'How can the Communists be called conspirators against the Prussian state as they are only conspirators against the state that will come *after* the present one, against the bourgeois republic ...' Nothing is more characteristic of Marxism than the twisted logic of this argument. Nine out of ten Germans at the middle of the century belonged to the 'lower middle classes', peasants, craftsmen, small businessmen, teachers and so on. Someone who despised these nine-tenths of all Germans as thoroughly as Marx and Engels did could not formulate German policy; he could only *see* the weaknesses of the bourgeois revolution, and this they both did, with eagle eyes. If their criticism was unconstructive their positive proposals were wild and questionable. In August 1848, for example, during the Schleswig-Holstein crisis, Marx asked for nothing less than a large-scale German war against the three great powers, Britain, Russia and France, from which alone a true revolution might blossom forth. By right Denmark, as well as Sweden and Norway, must be ruled by Germany because Germany was at any rate more revolutionary than those countries; their civilization Marx described as characterized by 'brutality against women, permanent drunkenness and lacrimose sentimentality, alternating with berserk fury'. For the national aspirations of the Austrian Slavs, particularly the Czechs, Marx and Engels again had nothing but contempt; they were under German rule and under German rule they must remain. If the Slavs continued to betray the revolution there would be a 'war of extermination and ruthless terrorism – not in the interest of Germany but in the interest of the revolution'. Germany, on the other hand, most of whose inhabitants he so deeply despised, was for Marx the fatherland of the abstract but terrible goddess called 'revolution' and was therefore destined to rule.

When nothing came of the world revolution for the moment the two friends were deeply disappointed. They told another friend, Techow, who saw them in London in August 1850, that they would soon emigrate to America. 'It was a matter of complete indifference to them if this miserable Europe was ruined as it surely would be without social revolution.'

5. Leaders and Led

The revolution lacked good leadership. In the *Paulskirche* there were great scholars, able administrators, a few successful businessmen and witty writers all of whom made fine speeches and uttered profound things. What the liberals did not know was that in politics there is always an element of struggle which inevitably becomes more ruthless at moments of crisis when the legal framework trembles. Only the extreme right and left senses this. Professor Dahlmann, whose agitation in September 1848 resulted in the overthrow of the 'imperial government' because he wanted to continue the war over Schleswig even without Prussia, had not thought how this could be done. A few days later therefore he shamefacedly joined the supporters of the armistice. That incident compromised the whole of the great party to which Dahlmann belonged. Bismarck drew a malicious portrait of Heinrich von Gagern, first president of the National Assembly and third 'Imperial Prime Minister'. The two men met in Erfurt in 1850; there is something ironical in the tremendously superior formality with which the unsuccessful founder of the Empire of 1848 met the successful founder of the Empire of 1871. 'The phrase gusher,' said Bismarck, 'addressed me as though I was a public meeting.'

'Phrase-gusher' – the expression might have come from Marx. In fact, the Communist and the Junker had several things in common in their judgement of the year 1848. For both it was the first great political experience, a year of apprenticeship. In March 1848 Bismarck wanted to organize a reactionary *coup d'état*, a counter-revolution, while Marx wished to push the revolution to a radical conclusion. But neither was yet in a sufficiently strong position to achieve anything so decisive; they remained in the background, men of the future. Both came to the conclusion that in future things would have to be done very differently. 'The great questions of the age,' said Bismarck in 1862, 'are not decided by speeches and majority decisions – that was the big mistake of 1848 and 1849 – but by blood and iron.' By blood and iron – that is roughly the lesson which Marx drew from the 'mistakes of 1848'. All his life he waited for the true revolution which had not come in 1848 and which, when it came, would have to be conducted very differently; with scientific thoroughness, and without mercy either for the monarchy and bourgeoisie or for the lower middle classes. The science, the strategy of revolution, developed by Marx after the collapse of 1849, was taken over by Lenin and successfully applied in 1917. Lenin's historical achievement can thus be indirectly traced back to the defeat of the men of 1848.

But that was yet to come; the immediate victors were men of a different type, soldiers of fortune in search of power, energetic, cynical adventurers with a touch of fantasy, Felix Schwarzenberg in Austria and Louis Napoleon in France. They were the beneficiaries of the general disenchantment – and also of the economic prosperity which began in the summer of 1849.

The losers were the nameless legions who had fought and hoped for a worthier life. Many of them emigrated, mostly to America. At least 80,000 people, more than a twentieth of the population, emigrated from Baden as a result of the revolt of 1849. After 1849 the number of emigrants from the whole of Germany, which in the forties had amounted to about 100,000 a year, rose to about a quarter of a million annually. Those who dared to take the plunge into the unknown were the most active and courageous; among them were born leaders of men who later achieved fame in American public life. For the United States the influx of German immigrants was an incalculable gain.

6. *What Remained*

The events of 1848–9 did, however, bring changes, both good and bad. Before 1848, in accordance with authoritarian theory, there was no political life apart from sham constitutional activities in a few small and medium size states. After 1850 politics never again disappeared from the German consciousness. However narrow and illiberal the 'dictated' Prussian constitution was on paper, it provided the basis for serious political battles, and there were developments for which there had been no provision made in the constitution. Nor did Austria return to the calm of Metternich's day. Before 1848 it had been a great historical fact questioned by no one; after 1848 the Austrian state perpetually redefined, examined and rejected itself, like a sick man tossing on his bed in search of a more comfortable position. A sickness of the state, never cured, always treated with new remedies or hopelessly abandoned to its own law – that is the history of the long reign of the Emperor Francis Joseph (1848–1916).

Political innocence was lost and with it a good deal of the idealism which had made itself heard with jubilant self-assurance in the spring of 1848. Now it was the turn of realism, though not only as the result of 1848. A revolution achieves much less than is often thought. It is merely an expression, a sudden explosive focusing of certain tendencies of the period. And some things that found expression in 1848 were then already out of date. Intelligent French observers noted even in the thirties that in politics, and also in literature and philosophy, Germany was increasingly attracted by realism and materialism. Shortly before 1848 the Prussian writer and diplomat Varnhagen von Ense noted in his diary the following striking remark made by an acquaintance:

In the capital there is as yet little sign of it but in the commercial and provincial towns a generation is growing up which is oblivious of, or even hostile to, all idealistic endeavour, which rushes headlong towards brutal reality and which will soon accept nothing that is not concerned with material needs and pleasures.

It was not in 1848 but in the fifties and sixties that this generation came into its own. It made Germany into an industrial state; and for it, in line with its ideas, was founded the Empire whose character differed so substantially from the vision of the best of the men of 1848.

Part Five

Restoration Again (1849–1862)

How did the intelligent German of the fifties see the world, Europe, his country? Let us take at random a writer who reached his full intellectual stature in those years, the Prussian historian Johann Gustav Droysen. He published an article in June 1854 when the two western powers and Russia were involved in a war in the Crimean peninsula which was prevented from spreading and becoming a European war by Germany's neutrality. Droysen argues that the Crimean War, the 'European crisis' as he calls it, was not caused by any fundamental, insurmountable difference between Britain and Russia, neither of which wanted the war. The man who wanted it was the Emperor Napoleon III who reigned in Paris and kept Europe in turmoil. Who was he? He was an adventurer, eager to destroy the European system of 1815 and therefore to humble the power which had always been the mainstay of that system, Russia. 'The Emperor of the French is like a gambler at the faro table; he always stakes his whole winnings; one more lucky throw and he will have broken the bank.' His throne was the only concrete evidence that remained of the Revolution of 1848. 'Everywhere else in Europe reaction has been victorious, only in France has the revolution taken a positive turn.' Let the old monarchies welcome Bonaparte as the tamer of the revolution, let him copy their methods of government – he could never completely deny the democratic basis of his authority. The good old days which the reactionaries dreamt of restoring were gone forever. Moreover, Napoleon was an unreliable ally; having humiliated Russia he would offer it peace and stir up new trouble in company with yesterday's enemy. Let the European states not over-estimate themselves; they had shrunk. At the beginning of the sixteenth century a European system of states had developed, in opposition to the old small-scale Italian system; likewise a system of world states was now developing, compared with which Europe would be what Florence, Milan and Venice had then been to Spain, France and Britain. There was 'rapidly growing democratic North America', 'vast continental Russia with its caesarian absolutism', and the British Empire; soon there would be China. In future those giants would fight for control of the earth. 'It is already discernible that there is a much deeper contrast between North America and Russia and between China and Britain than between the crumbling nations and states of old Europe.' Britain was aware of that development and therefore moved cautiously. Its position as a world power did not allow it to become engrossed in Europe.

Where under such new conditions stood 'our poor, tired, much divided Germany'? It was not a European power, let alone a world power. In the greatest crisis of modern history it was led, advised and represented by Austria, a state which, though recently galvanized into audacity, could never come adequately to terms with the new historical forces. Prussia, subordinate to Austria, was also ruled by the party of static reaction. But a common conservative policy was not in the interest of the nation, not even really in the interest of Prussia, which alone could give the nation up-to-date leadership. What was required was not the realization of abstract theories of equality and Jacobin rule but the establishment of an independent Germany and the creation of 'something healthy, real and promising from the tremendous changes described above, from the profound social and intellectual ferment which now affects Europe like a fever'. That could only be done by the Protestant German spirit, and, to the extent that an external agent was required, by the 'healthy authority' of the Prussian state; therefore Prussia must lead Germany.

If great changes had taken place in the political sphere, even more profound and revolutionary ones had occurred in social and intellectual life. The old European civilization based on a subsistence economy, handicrafts and feudalism had gone.

While industry had destroyed the independent artisans, the state had destroyed the old self-sufficient social units. Whereas once the state had been the embodiment of law and order, it had now become a mechanism for the creation of ever more power. It no longer needed people of independent education, it needed technically trained servants, and the spirit of the age ensured that they would be forthcoming. As a result of the triumphs of the natural sciences their methods were applied everywhere. Old beliefs were disappearing and only positive achievement counted.

Our spiritual life is deteriorating rapidly; its dignity, its idealism, its intellectual integrity are vanishing ... Meanwhile the exact sciences grow in popularity; establishments flourish whose pupils will one day form the independent upper middle class as farmers, industrialists, merchants, technicians and so on; their education and outlook will concentrate wholly on material issues. At the same time the universities are declining ... At present all is instability, chaos, ferment and disorder. The old values are finished, debased, rotten, beyond salvation and the new ones are as yet unformed, aimless, confused, merely destructive ... we live in one of the great crises that lead from one epoch of history to the next, a crisis comparable to that of the crusades on which the knights-errant embarked in the struggle for the Holy Sepulchre, or of the age of the Reformation when America appeared upon the horizon of history.

Droysen thought that it was useless to bemoan such a development or want to delay or undo it. That was the mistake that European reaction had made in Berlin no less than in Vienna and St Petersburg. These changes were historical facts, and what was a fact was right and what was historically right had power, indeed, invincible power. Resistance was pointless. Did it follow that the radical democrats and socialists were right? Not necessarily, because there were opportunist adventurers who swam with the tide. However, to swim against the tide of history was impossible. One must co-operate by trying to shape the new forces, by preserving the link between past and future, by saving the things that were worth preserving.

Such were Johann Gustav Droysen's views in 1854. He belonged to a group of moderate liberal historians who wanted to see the establishment of a 'little' Germany led by Prussia and a reconciliation of Prussia with the modern age, thus placing themselves at the service of a cause soon to be victorious. Droysen was no genius and no prophet, but just a politically minded professor. But what he discussed in his article in 1854, were the historical themes of the fifties, the exploits of Napoleon III, the conflict between Russia and the West, and the reshaping of Italy; later came the theme of the sixties, Prussia's 'great successes'; and finally the theme of the nineteenth and twentieth centuries, compared with which all purely European events pale into insignificance: the development of 'world states' and the decline of Europe as the centre of world power. Although this development was debated as early as 1850 it was lost sight of in the age of imperialism and German glory. Then there was the transformation of society, the growing omnipotence of the state, the disappearance of old religious traditions, the anarchy of values – phenomena that were to be talked about for the next hundred years. The 'crisis of modern man' goes back a long way. An age which in retrospect seems unexciting, reactionary, bourgeois and boring – Nietzsche later speaks of the 'miasma of the fifties' – was regarded by those who lived through it as a chaotic period of transition, as an anarchistic no-man's-land between yesterday and tomorrow.

1. Years of Reaction

The European reaction of which Droysen speaks lasted only a few years. In Europe something unexpected always happens to change existing conditions. It is unimaginable until it occurs, just as it is impossible to believe during bad weather that the sun will shine again; but it is certain to happen. Moreover, the post-revolutionary years were years of prosperity and growing industrialization which brought changes in every sphere of life, as none knew better than Karl Marx: changes in the structure of society, in education, in diplomacy, in war and sooner or later also in domestic policy. The fifties were a time of technical and industrial advance. In ten years the production of pig iron in the Rhineland quintupled and the output of coal trebled; the building of railways and ships also made rapid progress. The Siemens brothers laid the cornerstone of a German electrical industry and the first big banks were founded. Visitors to the Great Exhibition of 1851 in London saw the marvels of the new technical science, which, the Prince Consort said in his opening address, would lead to new, happier statesmanship and to an international community of states. How could the nations of the world remain ignorant of each other in the age of the steamship, or dangerously misunderstand each other in the age of the electric telegraph?

Eighteen fifty-one was also the year of the *coup d'état* by which President Bonaparte made himself dictator of France on the way to fulfilling shortly afterwards the dream of his youth by assuming the title of Emperor. The historian de Tocqueville, a good observer, commented that the world was a curious stage, and that a mediocre man could achieve apparently great things provided the concatenation of circumstances was right. In his brilliant political pamphlet, *Der 18. Brumaire des Louis Bonaparte*, Karl Marx explained the dictator's rise in terms of the class struggle. The bourgeoisie, no longer able to control the workers within the framework of its liberal institutions, had resigned politically and yielded to the demagogic impostor who protected it, though at a high price. Similarly, in good Marxist and Hegelian terms, the young Ferdinand Lassalle wrote: 'In their death throes the bourgeois government and private enterprise find a common denominator in military despotism and tyranny. While his uncle, with whom he confuses himself, had an outstanding revolutionary mission, this fool is nothing but the empty symbol of the dying reaction.' For the time being the 'fool' remained in power; had he been told that he was only kept by the bourgeoisie in order to postpone the social revolution he would not have understood what was meant. Fêted as the 'saviour of order' he also wanted to be fêted as Emperor of the peasants and the workers, as liberator of the Italians and, if it was possible without too much risk, of the Poles. The character of such a talented adventurer, splendour-loving sensualist, enthusiast, dreamer and fanatic eludes summing up. He came to the fore in the heyday of European reaction and desperately wanted to be accepted as an equal by the kings of Europe. A Prussian reactionary called von Bismarck said that in his heart of hearts Napoleon III gave him an unadmitted feeling of satisfaction. At the same time Napoleon was a product of the revolution – that was how Droysen saw him – the man who stood for universal suffrage, plebiscites and national liberation. Above all he stood for unrest, however much he wanted to enjoy a hedonist existence in his castles. Having been a conspirator in his youth he could not cease to be a conspirator as a crowned head. His eyes, which General Moltke described as 'lifeless', were for ever looking for opportunities to change the map of Europe, to collect triumphs and to solve unresolved problems. He needed prestige and needed to be talked about by the world. France and its new master were indeed talked about; once again France more than any other was the power which Germany watched, which set the tone in politics, as in the arts and in fashion.

Louis Napoleon's first aim was to destroy the understanding which had existed intermittently since 1813 between Russia, Austria and Prussia, the 'Holy Alliance' and thus to end Russia's semi-dictatorship over Europe – by no means a reactionary aim.

The Austrian Empire started by trying out a system not unlike the Napoleonic one: modern dictatorship, unconcerned with tradition and prejudice. Until his sudden death in the spring of 1852 Felix Schwarzenberg ruled under the nominal sovereignty of the young Francis Joseph. Like Louis Napoleon the aristocratic Schwarzenberg was an adventurer, who despised his equals and who chose curious collaborators: a Rhenish wholesale merchant who built the harbour of Trieste, Baron Bruck, and a revolutionary lawyer from Vienna, Alexander Bach. The three men tried to unify the Habsburg territories politically and, more important, economically. Hungary was forced into the Austrian customs system. The abrogation in December 1851, a few days after Napoleon's *coup*, of the constitution decreed in

1848 meant nothing in itself; the constitution had always existed on paper only. However, the active participation of the middle classes, particularly of the Austrian Germans, was needed to realize Bruck's great plan, adopted by Schwarzenberg, to make the whole of Austria part of the German *Zollverein* and create an economic unit of seventy million people. The plan was remarkable. Bruck even visualized the affiliation of Switzerland, Belgium and Denmark to such a system, saw German industry penetrating down the Danube far into the Ottoman Empire and dreamt of a second America arising in central Europe. Schwarzenberg was less interested in economic problems; the project appealed to him because it was likely to curtail Prussia's position of pre-eminence. For that very reason it did not materialize – because it ignored politics. The empire of all the Germans – and indeed much more than that – could not be reached by the back door. Europe was not prepared casually to accept such a vast concentration of power, nor were the central German states willing to become buried in it. If previously they had relied on Austria against Prussia, they now relied on Prussia against Austria. It has been Europe's greatness and its curse that its states have been determined to dominate each other. A central Europe, united economically from Hamburg to the mouth of the Danube, was a desirable objective and would have ensured better living standards for the Germans as well as for many non-Germans. But in whose interest would such a union have operated? What powers would have had reason to feel threatened by it? Austria would have benefited, whereas Prussia, and also Russia and France, would have been threatened. The empire of seventy millions did not come about and Prussia remained master of the German *Zollverein*.

After Schwarzenberg's death and Bruck's resignation Austria relapsed into an absolutism which differed from that of Metternich's only in that it was somewhat more effective. The Emperor was his own first minister, the semblance of parliamentary representation was regarded as superfluous and the country was governed by the civil service. The Concordat which Austria reached with the Catholic Church did not make Austria more attractive to Protestant Germany. It gave the church rights which it had not had since the seventeenth century, including almost complete control of education, literary censorship and its own legal system – and that at the moment when Pius IX opened his great campaign against 'liberalism, progress and modern civilization'. The unmitigated reaction that reigned in Austria was unlikely to win the future. In 1849 Austria had first subdued the disruptive elements within its own territory and then Prussia. Yet it did not exploit its success. Was it unable to do so? Was the empire of many nations, in spite of all that could be said for it, kept together in a manner that prevented creative action in Germany?

2. Reaction in Prussia

Reaction also reigned in Prussia, though that country possessed what Austria no longer pretended to have after 1852, a 'constitution' which on paper did not look too bad. The reality, however, was different. A paper constitution is not a mere nothing. It can become something if the forces that wish it to do so are strong enough; much depends on its wording, and on its provisions. But a canal without water is useless and falls to ruin. Ferdinand Lassalle once said: 'Basically constitutional questions are not questions of law but of power; a country's real constitution exists only in the actual prevailing political conditions. Written constitutions are only of value and permanence if they exactly express the existing distribution of power in society.' The distribution of power in Prussia was such that the minorities, the civil servants, the army, the landowners and above them all the dynasty, which had always regarded the Prussian state as its property, were able to exert an influence not provided for in the constitution and entirely unrelated to the numerical or economic importance of these groups.

Suffrage was universal, but indirect and neither secret nor

equal. According to the amount of tax paid the population was divided into three classes whose votes had equal weight, so that a thousand rich men counted for as much as a hundred thousand poor men. The principle that votes should not only be counted but weighed may be worth thinking about; several other criteria of selection were suggested on this occasion, such as professional achievement, distinction between married and unmarried men and so on. The Prussian three-class electoral system was simply plutocratic, for it gave more votes to those with more money, more to the successful brothel-keeper than to the doctor and the teacher. The result, more than anything a consequence of the general discouragement, was the reactionary and subservient character of the Prussian parliament in the fifties. It did what was asked of it, whenever the government did not choose to employ 'administrative means'. The noblest 'March achievements' were watered down or done away with: freedom of the press, freedom of association and assembly, the National Guard and ministerial responsibility. The First Chamber, intended to be a kind of Senate, was replaced by the *Herrenhaus*, a copy of the House of Lords, composed of the heads of the great aristocratic families and of persons nominated by the monarch. The constitution provided for a division of power, the consent of the King and of the two chambers being required for legislation; when it came to the real division of power everyone took as much as he could, in accordance with his courage, self-confidence and determination.

The greatest determination to have power was displayed by the Junkers, the old-established landowners from the eastern part of the kingdom. They achieved their aim less by party rule – it could not be said of any parliamentary party that it was in power – than by more direct methods, by their standing in the country-side, their position in the army and the civil service, and their influence at Court. They knew how to assert themselves, having always had what the middle class so far lacked completely, an instinct for power. They also knew that they were threatened, that time was working against them, and that attack was the best defence. It is wrong entirely to condemn any class of human beings. The world is not a just place and when just men reach the top they are usually not as just as they promised to be while they were oppressed. Among the Junkers there were rebels against their own class, decent men who struggled for their economic existence and whose homes in the countryside were centres of genuine Lutheran influence. But by and large, as a class, and particularly as a ruling class, the Junkers were selfish and inadequate. Their interests were too narrow to be identified with those of the state. They were too poor to be the ruling class and had to use various forms of pressure as a substitute for economic power. Most of Germany, even of Prussia, was foreign to them; they knew nothing of the Rhineland or the Catholic regions. They were not a German aristocracy in the sense that the English aristocracy was English; they were a regional class without vision whose only interest in wanting to control the whole country was self-preservation. In 1848 an abyss had opened in front of them and although they had escaped from it the experience had made them even more stubborn, even bolder.

There was also a German nobility which, since Prussia was a large part of Germany, was also to be found in the new Prussia, in the west and in Silesia. Its members were a different race of men; some of them were so rich that they had no economic worries and left the administration of their estates to revenue offices. Those who disliked complete idleness went into politics, the diplomatic service and more recently, parliament. Their estates were scattered over various German states and they could choose their nationality without feeling special loyalty to Prussia or Baden. They were therefore national in outlook, just as in the bourgeoisie were the professors who moved from one university to another. They regarded the ruling dynasties as their equals because their own houses had reigned until they had been robbed of their dwarf states fifty years previously. Among these families were men of intelligence and education, of wide horizons, ambition and good will; the Leiningens, Hohenlohes and Fürstenbergs stand out in the history of Prussia and of Germany in this period. But these aristocrats cannot be called a ruling class; they were too spoilt and too uncommitted. They had few convictions and lived in a cultivated no-man's-land, neither bourgeois nor Junker, neither kings nor vassals. Moreover, they were few in number.

One legacy of the revolution was the political parties which appeared as organized groups in parliament. The conservatives were overwhelmingly in the majority. The moderate liberals who, in the National Assembly of 1848, had sat on the extreme right now sat on the extreme left. Between the two there was a special 'Catholic group' which, by safeguarding the interests of its co-religionists, achieved good results in this predominantly Protestant state. Later it called itself the Centre Party.

For the moment the struggle between these groups was not very serious. There were fights, discussions and intrigues, but less between the parliamentary parties than between the various cliques who had the ear of the King, the government, the 'Camerilla', the bureaucrats, the arch-reactionaries and the semi-liberals, the men who thought only about Prussia and those who thought about Prussia in relation to Germany, the climbers and the doctrinaires. Almost everybody was against everybody else; Prince William was against his brother the King, the leader of the Conservative Party was against the conservative Prime Minister, the envoy to the Federal Diet in Frankfurt was against the envoy in London and the Junkers were against the strict but honest chief of police of Berlin.

Ranke said, and it is often maintained today, that foreign policy must be formulated by independent experts and that a parliamentary government, pushed about by parties and electorates, is unfitted for this important task. Such a view can certainly be justified, but so can the reverse. The government of Frederick William IV had, as far as its own people was concerned, a free hand in foreign policy; there was no interference from parliament or fickle popular opinion, and there was no lack of trained advisers. But when it came to making a decision, the various proposals, intrigues and fantasies between which the King could not make up his mind cancelled each other out. The result was that the factious parliament could not have done worse.

3. The Crimean War

The Crimean War brought the first serious test of this system or lack of system. It was the strangest of all nineteenth-century wars, a repressed world war and yet strictly localized, a never-ending, confused diplomatic game, underlined by occasional battles. It resulted from hidden, unadmitted causes and silly incidents; the aims behind it were fantastic or non-existent.

Britain and France fought allegedly to save the Turkish Empire and to drive Russia out of the Danubian countries, out of Rumania. Britain wanted to preserve the balance of power and restrict Russian expansion. Louis Napoleon on the other hand wanted to disturb the balance of power, to wage a popular war against the Tsar, to find new opportunities for action, and later to make common cause with a weakened Russia which had learnt its lesson. The German powers found themselves between the belligerents. Austria's position was that it could not at any price accept a Russian advance on the lower Danube, but was afraid of a war with Russia in which it bore the brunt in Galicia while Prussia was free to do what it wished in Germany. On the other hand Austria was afraid of making an enemy of France because it could not maintain its position in northern Italy against the will of France. Austria occupied too many vulnerable positions, in Italy, in Germany and in the South-East. The mobilization of its army in Galicia was decisive for the war because it prevented Russia from sending its main force to the Crimea. Austria compelled Russia to evacuate the Danubian principalities, into which it moved its own troops; under the peace treaty, however, Austria was not allowed to keep Rumania because Austria had done nothing in the war and because of its completely uncompromising attitude towards Italian nationalism. In Prussia there was a reactionary and definitely pro-Russian party and a liberal and definitely pro-British party, both of which tried to influence the King; there were also a number of outsiders and rebels who wanted to use the opportunity to extend Prussia's sphere of power in Germany, who strove towards a Franco-

Prussian–Russian alliance even as the French and the Russians were killing each other in the Crimea. There is no need to go into the intricacies of the various moves and counter-moves; the up-shot was more fortunate than might have been expected from such a profusion of effort. Prussia remained neutral, but unlike Austria, which fell out with everybody, particularly with Russia, Prussia remained friendly with everybody, particularly with Russia, which it supplied with war material to the advantage of Prussian businessmen. Prussia seemed insecure, excited, almost non-existent during the Crimean War; yet undeservedly it gained more from the war than the victors. Liberated from Russian tutelage, it ceased to be the junior partner in the 'Holy Alliance' of the eastern powers, now dead and buried. Russia's industrial, military and moral weakness was revealed to all the world during the war; the Tsar could no longer usurp the role of arbitrator as he had done in 1851. The most important abiding consequence of the Crimean War was the fact that developments in Europe hitherto prevented by the more terrible presence of Russia now became possible. The direct results of the war, on the other hand, were ephemeral and the wickedness of the political game is revealed by the fact that half a million young men died for such ends. The Sultan was made to promise to adopt more modern methods of government. Rumania became independent – a status which it preserved for about eighty years; the Russians were not allowed to keep a navy in the Black Sea, which was 'neutralized'. Such compulsory disarmament, however, never survives the situation in which it is dictated.

The Crimean War, revealing the decline of Europe's most reactionary great power, created the conditions for new activity a mere five years after the failure of the revolution of 1848. It signified the end of that fleeting episode, the 'second Restoration'; the almost uninterrupted trial of strength between peoples, states, classes and ideas was resumed.

4. State and Nation in Germany

To speak of states as though they were individuals – to say 'Austria felt itself threatened', 'Prussia missed its chance' and so on – is excusable because it would be clumsy to say each time 'the diplomats responsible for the foreign policy of the Prussian state'. Sometimes historians help themselves by referring to the address of the foreign ministry of the country concerned and speak of the *Ballhausplatz*, the *Wilhelmstrasse* or the *Quai d'Orsay* as of living beings. Such shorthand, however, has more than a purely practical purpose; it draws attention to the fact that states are more than just organizations of men for certain purposes. They are traditions of power, of success and triumph – over other states – of competition, threat and counter-threat, of gain or loss; traditions, the reality of which cannot be refuted by saying that they exist only in the men's mind. Of course they exist there alone and yet 500,000 Russians, Frenchmen, Britons and Piedmontese gave their lives in the Crimea for this fictitious reality.

What was Prussia? It was more than a big slice of Poland or of the Rhineland; it was an innate, permanent determination to rule and to expand. The will was particularly strong among certain classes and groups, in the dynasty, the officer corps, the Junkers, the higher civil service and the Protestant state church. Material interests were involved because these groups prospered if 'Prussia' prospered; yet it would be wrong to think that 'Prussia' was merely a cover-up for material interests; human beings are not made like that. Many men gladly gave their lives for the glory and honour of Prussia; and if the Prussian Minister to the Frankfurt parliament, von Bismarck, had 'bilious attacks' over a minor Prussian reverse, this was not because of any threat to his own economic interests or those of his class but because he had Prussia's 'glory' at heart. What was true of Prussia was also true of Austria, with the difference that Austria's determination to exist depended even more strongly on the ruling family. Prussia had at least a name, though one that happened to be borrowed from its eastern-most province and an exterminated heathen tribe. Austria had not even a name; it could most appropriately have been called 'the lands of the House of Austria'. Whereas the Hohenzollern family served 'Prussia', the Habsburgs served the glory of their House. Whereas Prussia ruled parts of only two peoples, Germans and Poles, Austria ruled innumerable peoples. But even in Austria it was not the House of Habsburg alone which kept the country together; in 1848 when the dynasty was prepared to surrender, a handful of feudal soldiers kept the Empire together, fundamentally on their own authority.

Such gods are not immortal, although in their lifetime their high priests must claim them to be so. The fact that neither Prussia nor the Austrian Empire exists today makes our story more difficult. We speak of two states which for years polarized the energies of the German nation, which competed with each other, went to war against each other, became allies, fell out again but finally vanished into thin air. It requires imagination to see Prussia and Austria as they once were, because they are no more. Even the pompous monuments of stone, the palaces and statues, which they erected to themselves have mostly been razed to the ground. Yet there were centuries when the Tsars of Russia regarded the kings of Prussia as their equals, and a king of Prussia once forced a coalition of Russia, Austria and France to make peace. We must consider Austria and Prussia – what they were like, how they defended themselves and how they attacked, how one grew and the other shrank, and how both finally disappeared – because though our narrative is concerned with Germans and not with dynastic states both Austria and Prussia occupied or controlled large parts of Germany.

Both had omitted to identify themselves in time – in the eighteenth, the seventeenth, the sixteenth century, or even earlier – with a nation. To start with, France and Spain had also been dynasties rather than nations; the House of Spain had ruled over a galaxy of kingdoms in the Old and the New World. Within the framework which the dynasties provided and were busy enlarging, the Spanish and the French nations had gradually emerged. The dynastic state became the nation state long before there was any political theory on the subject. As dynasties changed or were driven out, there remained their determination to rule, transformed into a determination to become a state; thus France still exists today. Neither Austria nor Prussia could identify itself with Germany, if only because it was impossible for both of them to do so and one prevented the other from so doing. Added to this, Austria, given its structure, could not want to identify itself with Germany only; and Prussia too, for most of the time, wanted to remain what it was. Moreover, many smaller states, Bavaria, Saxony, Hanover and so on, were opposed to the identification of Prussia or Austria with Germany. Nevertheless, there was a German nation; the fact had emerged in 1848, in 1814 and even earlier, in Luther's time. But the German states did not serve any nation: the nation had no state.

A state might of course create a nation, even where the state combined several nationalities and linguistic regions within its frontiers. This happened in Switzerland and was happening there at this very time, as the Swiss under their new, democratic constitution developed more firmly than ever into a separate and united nation. But Switzerland was a unique case, because it had always been a free, balanced federation, without expansionist ambitions. In the past such inclinations had been harboured by some of its member states, particularly by Berne, but never by the Confederation. Switzerland did not conquer or annex, it admitted; and a country which wanted to become Swiss could be refused admission to the Confederation. Switzerland had no dynasty, no ruler and subjects, only confederates. What Kant had expected from all republics came true for once: the Swiss only wanted to be left in peace and did not want to disturb the peace of others. By adopting this attitude they became a nation with distinct characteristics. The more insistent the call for the unification of all Germans became across the border the more consciously and speedily did the Swiss abandon the remains of their German origins.

The call was loud and strong, although it is impossible to say how many people wanted a German nation state and how many viewed this objective with indifference or hostility. Decisive historical achievements have often been accomplished by minorities, without or even against the will of the majority; once they have been accomplished and tested by history, it is easy for the legend to arise that almost everybody but a few traitors had wanted what had happened. This is true for example of the American Revolution. Political movements are likely to be led and stimulated by minorities because most people are usually absorbed in their own problems. To say this is not to pass judgement on the historic justification of such movements. Before so judging one must inquire if there were other people who had good reasons for wanting something different and who suffered violence at the hands of the victors. Did most Americans in 1776 passionately want to remain British subjects, and if so was it possible for their wish to be fulfilled? If it is impossible to answer this question in the affirmative the making of the American Revolution by a minority is no less of an achievement.

In Germany there was a very strong minority which wanted a nation state. How this was to be achieved, what form it should take and what its frontiers should be were hotly debated questions, but there was general agreement on the need for reform of the 'Confederation'. Therefore there was a complicated contest of wills between Prussia and Austria and also between each of these two states and the as yet only partially unified Germany. The smaller states were of no importance in this connection because they could offer no resistance.

Although there were more non-Prussians and non-Austrians in the German Confederation than Austrians and Prussians – about eighteen million compared with about fourteen million Prussians and fourteen million Austrians – their states were too small and too scattered to exert any political pressure. The idea that there must be a 'third', 'pure' Germany to offset the two German-Slav powers appeared again and again at this time without ever becoming a reality. The small states could neither direct the course of events in Germany nor successfully oppose it; they could only let themselves be swept reluctantly along. Even the most respectable among them, Bavaria, was passive.

Political awareness did exist in Bavaria; it was old and tenacious. With roots in the countryside, in the tribal origin of the population and in the religious faith of Old Bavaria, it was less dependent on the dynasty than in Prussia or in Austria, although it had close links with the House of Wittelsbach. This awareness was, as we know, strong enough to weather the worst storms and after a long night suddenly to be present again as though nothing had happened. It was not sufficiently strong politically, however, to prevail against Austria and Prussia, and not sufficiently strong morally to sever the fate of Bavaria from that of Germany. Personally the kings of Bavaria, Ludwig I and Maximilian II, were particularly unsuited to take such a step because of the tremendous enthusiasm with which they stressed the fact that they were Germans. Bavaria took the same road as Germany, then as always, and could do almost nothing to determine where it should lead.

The German states were also by now economically completely dependent on the German *Zollverein* and its leading member. They did not appreciate this fact themselves because conservative diplomacy always treated economic issues as of third-rate importance. But the truth emerged with great force in every political crisis.

This is not to say that the German states had no genuine existence. Although the nation had no overall capital, the country was studded with the capitals of the different states, which engaged in cultural and academic competition. They were eclectic in their styles, copying the Italian Renaissance, French Rococo and Empire, and Greek antiquity, but unique in their chequered abundance, and their influence on the sense of form of those who lived in them was to the good. Now that little of this remains, and that the German tribes have been thrown together and towns have come to resemble each other as much as American towns, we can look back and evaluate the wealth that Germany has lost. The administration of these states was as varied as their size, from Bavaria to the comic opera courts of Thuringia. In some, as in Hesse-Cassel, terrible things occurred periodically; in others, as in Baden, which had presented such an unhappy spectacle in 1849, successful administrative reform led to a greater degree of local self-government. There is much to be said against German particularism, but also much in its favour. It was Germany's original political and cultural creation, but time worked against it. When the chronicler comes to historical decisions he must speak of Vienna and Berlin, not of Altenburg or Karlsruhe, or even of Munich, Dresden or Stuttgart.

5. *Ideas at Work*

Political thought progressed even though reaction reigned supreme almost everywhere in Europe. The age was so much concerned with intellectual justification that even reaction clothed itself in a variety of high-sounding theories which it presented in parliaments, newspapers and learned books.

The chief social factor from the middle of the century onwards was the increasingly intensive development of industry; the chief political factor was at first the unwillingness of the pre-industrial powers to allow the middle class to play the role in public life which corresponded to its growing wealth. The game of the old powers was made easier by the terror of the middle classes of 'red revolution', by the pressure of the working class whose numbers and influence increased as the middle classes grew wealthier. So far the Marxist analysis was correct. The theory of the old powers was conservative, that of the middle classes liberal, and that of the working class – so far as it possessed a theory distinct from that of the progressive middle classes – socialist.

In reality the situation was more complex. There was antagonism not only between social classes but also between states and nations, particularly between those nations which had not yet become states; there was also religious antagonism. Then there were the ideas of those who wanted to reconcile points of difference and to create something great and constructive above them. Such ideas could be powerful or weak, honest or dishonest.

As for the unceasing, silent struggle between states, the German rulers comforted themselves for a while yet with the belief that political and social differences coincided. The three eastern monarchies, Russia, Austria and Prussia, were the conservative states and had to be united in a natural alliance because they thought alike. The France of Napoleon III was the revolutionary state which the conservatives must oppose. Britain was difficult to place in this system but in practice leant more towards France than towards the Holy Alliance. Actually there was a mistake in the calculation. During the Crimean War it became clear that the rivalry between Austria and Russia in the Balkans counted for more than the anti-liberal views shared by the young Francis Joseph and the old Nicholas; and that was the end of the alliance of conservative powers. A little later the Tsar was not ashamed, out of sheer spite against Austria, to co-operate diplomatically with the French Emperor. Anyway all was not as it should have been with the revolutionary character of Napoleon's government. He was a believer in plebiscites, the 'chosen of the seven million', as he liked to call himself, a usurper, heir to the first Napoleon and the revolutionary chaos from which the latter had emerged. But he was also a believer in order, in social peace and authority, protected by a modern army and bureaucracy; an attitude which did not at all displease the conservatives. How could they consistently oppose a ruler who was generally hated by the liberals for destroying parliamentary freedom and self-determination, loathed by the great spokesman of socialism, Karl Marx, and who was proving such a diligent ally of the Catholic Church that the Pope was not above becoming godfather to the imperial son? At times Bonaparte appeared almost as the incarnation of the conservative cause. If only he had not then proceeded to form an alliance with his arch-enemies, the liberals, as he was to do shortly afterwards in Italy. The unfortunate truth for anyone who attached importance to the ideal order of things was that reality never quite lived up to the ideal. The case of the opportunist dreamer in Paris was an extreme one; believing himself to be above classes and 'isms' he was free to move in two opposite directions at once. This happened everywhere, ideas might claim to shape reality, but reality failed to obey.

It was in these years that Pope Pius IX marshalled the forces of his church for a crusade against the spirit of the age, timing the climax of this campaign for the sixties. As the threat to the authority of the church appeared to grow this prince became more uncompromising. There was to be no reconciliation of the church 'with progress, with liberalism, with modern civilization'. That was the spiritual climate which produced dogmas such as the Immaculate Conception and later Papal Infallibility. It was an attitude of defiance, of uncompromising struggle against almost all the dominant forces of the second half of the century. Given Pius IX's support of the Italian princes and the House of Habsburg it must be said that the policy of the Roman Church was 'reactionary', if that word has any meaning at all. This, however, does not tell us everything about Catholicism in that period. During the years of revolution the liberals and the representatives of church interests in Germany had formed some kind of alliance because both wanted to be rid of the tutelage of the princes. The alliance was the result of the political situation of the moment, and would certainly have broken up if the liberals had come to power. More significant and less dependent on day-to-day politics was the attempt of some Catholic thinkers and organizers to achieve contact with the people and to broaden the social foundations of the church. Whereas the liberal principle was each man for himself, the church taught the concept of a community of Christians, and in the treasure-house of its tradition found plenty to relieve the inadequacies of an increasingly industrial civilization. In many places Catholic societies were founded, such as the organization of Catholic apprentices established by Adolf Kolping and Wilhelm Ketteler, who became Bishop of Mainz in 1850; this organization combined material care of the sick and the old with Christian education. The movement must not be called a failure merely because it was later supplanted by one of a different character. One witness to the fact that the Catholic craftsmen's societies did much good for their members was the turner-apprentice, August Bebel, who in the fifties in Freiburg and Salzburg belonged to one of them. When all is said and done, practical assistance is better than clever theory.

One of the theorists was the political philosopher Julius Stahl, who in the fifties led the conservatives in the Upper House in Berlin. Although this man is reputed to have had considerable influence events would have taken the same course had he not lived. He confined himself to reflection, but what he said was intelligent, perceptive and well expressed. Intellect was held in so much respect that even the uncouth Junkers fighting for their material interests chose as their spokesman a learned writer who into the bargain was a baptized Jew from southern Germany, a cultivated, refined and upright little man. Stahl found some truth in most attitudes, half-truths which he tried to fuse into a higher general truth. It seemed to him that this higher truth had materialized in the Prussian monarchy. The fact that this monarchy was not absolutist was good, and the fact that it was not parliamentarian either was also good, nor must it become parliamentarian. It was limited by tradition, custom and Christian faith. To have different classes was desirable, but the strong authority above them must be that of the state. Freedom, safeguarded by authority and law, was also desirable, but it must not presume to change arbitrarily the historic, natural, God-given order of society. However, Stahl did not rule out reform; 'false reaction' was almost as reprehensible as revolution and democracy. Above all the state must be Christian, a divine and human realm. 'Our political and our religious attitude are inseparable; it is impossible to be conservative in the state and destructive in the church, impossible to be both for the order that comes from God and against the faith that comes from God. Despite all gradations there are only two possible attitudes: one is to support throne and altar undivided, the other to support revolution.' Thus a man must be a Christian and a royalist, or neither; if he was neither he lacked moral purpose and was in danger of stumbling from democracy into nihilism and blackest crime. Stahl was not a great thinker, merely clever at arranging ideas. If history had stood still and none of the great changes of the nineteenth century had taken place, if the King and his servants and officials, officers and Junkers had been strict moral characters and good Christians Stahl might have been right. As it was, he spoke of a God-given order, loyal subjects and Christian humility while the Prussian Upper House gave a rousing ovation to Herr von Rochow, who during the aftermath of a scandal in a gambling house had shot and killed the Berlin Chief of Police in a duel. Poor philosopher, what a pitiful figure he must have cut at such moments among such allies!

Consistent economic liberalism, the so-called Manchester School, found no important theoretical exponents in Germany. It was obvious that the Prussian capitalists were in favour of complete economic freedom and against the modest legislation initiated by the state in the fifties. Most Prussian entrepreneurs were in favour of free trade with the rest of the world, unlike their south German competitors. But their ideas did not crystallize into a philosophy as in Britain. When the liberal middle class became politically conscious again towards the end of the period of reaction, its main concern was with national-political and constitutional demands and not with economic issues. Industry flourished in the last years of Frederick William IV's reign. If some industrialists were persecuted at the behest of the government, this was not because they belonged to a certain professional class but because they had been too active as liberals during the revolution.

Nevertheless liberal thought in Germany at this period was more original than conservative thought, which lacked all vigour. There are, however, many shades of 'liberalism', and Mill and Spencer would have refused to regard the members of the Prussian school of historians as fellow liberals. That school consisted of a group of professors which first emerged in the late fifties and from then on exerted considerable influence for several decades. Droysen, Haym, Sybel and, the youngest of the group, Heinrich von Treitschke, have real achievements to their credit. They did not make history or engage in politics, that was done by others; but when these others at last appeared on the scene, and when their game became clear the writings of the liberal professors proved of great assistance. These historians were certainly entitled to be called liberals. They demanded a constitutional state, they hated clerical Austria, the plebiscitary dictatorship of France and German particularism, and since they were not radical revolutionaries the only object of loving hope that remained to them was Prussia. They put their faith in Prussia, though not in reactionary Prussia. To become the nation's leader Prussia must change, and this required the active co-operation of parliament and the progressive parties. To the picture of the old liberals as it was before 1848 these energetic scholars added a certain intellectual or caste arrogance which distinguished them from the democrats. But there were also new features. The founders of the *Preussische Jahrbücher* and the *Historische Zeitschrift* were no longer friends of France. To them events on the other side of the Rhine after 1789 had shown that the French often chose the wrong road. They saw a connection between Latins, Papists, despots, Jacobins and ultra-democrats and rejoiced that all this was alien to the German mind. If there was a country from which they thought that they could learn it was Britain, which was also 'Germanic'. For the rest they wanted the Germans to stop casting admiring glances at other nations and be themselves, whether the world liked it or not. To achieve this objective the Germans needed a national state, ruled by law at home and strong abroad. Whereas law must prevail at home, it was strength which in the end governed the relationship of states, which created and destroyed laws; so the state must be as strong as possible. Its foreign policy must be realistic, must not rely on an opponent's sense of justice and must be free from sentimentality; it must be *Realpolitik* – a word which made its appearance as early as the beginning of the fifties. Freedom, as an obligation and an inspiration, was found only in a state which was the source of all morality, the guardian of education and the protector of the economy. To serve such a state, to find a place in it, was freedom; to pursue only one's personal interest was what Lassalle had called a night watchman's ideal.

These scholars were historians; they were not yet economists, no longer pure philosophers, but masters of the science of history. Theirs was a logical attitude: history was not the story of theories, of things that should have been, but of facts, of success and failure. The weak went under and the strong remained on top; those who put their faith in justice without strength received the fool's reward. States, institutions, legal concepts and ways of life must be seen historically, as realizations not of general eternal truths but of national characteristics under non-recurring conditions. History moreover showed conclusively that the Prussian state had long wanted to unify and lead the German nation. Those who wanted to make this point had no hestitation in distorting history to satisfy their needs.

What is important is that these historians were energetic and intelligent writers. Anybody can have ideas, but it is the writer's energy – one is almost tempted to say, his physical energy – which gives them force. Courage, strength to believe, imagination and daring are not found in ideas alone but in the development of them in articles, speeches and books. A powerful style will follow naturally because style, energy and intellect all go together. Even Heinrich von Treitschke, the most dogmatic and most prejudiced of the national liberal historians, wrote well. Today the reader is still struck by the strength of Treitschke's faith and anger, and does not find him as blind and unjust as he was later reputed to be.

These historians derived their basic ideas from the past, particularly from Fichte and Hegel, idealistic worshippers of the state, who had also found 'truth' in 'might' and in history. They united state and nation into the nation-state – which Hegel had not done. We must not blame them for taking Germany immensely seriously and for limiting their sphere of interest both as scholars and politicians almost exclusively to Germany, because nationalism was rampant everywhere. French historians too were concerned almost exclusively with the history of France, while Russian historians had recently begun to think themselves out of their wits over the question of what Russia was or was not, or should be. Whereas the Russians copied the Germans and their philosophy, particularly Hegel, who stuck in their throats, the Germans copied the French. Every nation wanted to be different from its neighbour, and succeeded only in copying his national limitations and introversion. Awareness of the fact that the European peoples were few in number and lived in a small space, and that their fate was therefore a common one, was lost in the process.

6. *Lassalle*

The conservatives too adopted the historical approach and also produced great historians. Their conclusions were different. To them existing institutions were venerable and to be touched only with great prudence just because history had made them as they were. We have said already that an idea needs only a slight twist to become something quite different. The national liberal historians found in history the spur to action. Until now things had always changed, and with the courageous help of those who understood history they would continue to change. They shared with Marx their faith in history, their excited expectation of great historical events. After all it is difficult for contemporaries not to have some thoughts in common.

Another who thought in historical terms was a young socialist and pupil of Marx who reached his full intellectual stature in the early fifties, Ferdinand Lassalle. At that moment socialism was marking time; reaction was too strong and the general discouragement too profound for it to make any outward progress. Marx in London devoted himself to the theoretical studies designed to provide the basis for future action; Engels, a textile manufacturer by occupation, looked after the membership records of the Communist League. A socially minded democrat of a completely different type was active in Berlin in the way in which it was possible to be active there even then: the founder of the German credit and co-operative movement, Schulze-Delitzsch. He was a warm-hearted, active man, very helpful within his limits. In the writings of theoretical socialists he usually comes off badly because he did not want what they wanted and did not answer the question which they asked. Schulze-Delitzsch was a democratic citizen, not a revolutionary. He did not devote himself to the problem of the new 'fourth class', or did not see it. He was concerned with immediate, modest, practical issues. He knew the small tradesmen, the craftsmen who fell victim to the competition of industry, the careworn housewives and for them he achieved something, by teaching them self-help. Large-scale philosophical and political speculation, on the other hand, he left to those with more talent for it, of whom Lassalle felt himself to be one.

Lassalle was the son of a merchant from Breslau, an ambitious young man, energetic, clever, fearless, of great presence of mind, who never forgot that he was an upstart and who liked to show off. As a schoolboy he wrote in his diary that, looked at in the cold light of day, he was an egoist. 'Had I been born a prince I should be an aristocrat body and soul. But as I am merely middle class I shall be a democrat.' Berlin society spoilt him because of his erudition and his wit; he accepted this with indifference, certain that very different triumphs awaited him in life. In Paris, at the age of twenty-one, he met Heine, who was amazed by Lassalle's talent, wit and determination. In the same year he became involved in the fate of a middle-aged, wealthy woman of high social rank, a Countess Hatzfeldt, who was engaged in a sensational quarrel with her husband. The affair with the Countess decided Lassalle's outward existence and embroiled him in a succession of grotesque scandals and intrigues the like of which no fiction writer could have invented. He became involved in endless lawsuits from which, as the protector of his lady, he emerged as a brilliant and daring speaker in court. He sacrificed years to his curious pursuit and devoted at least as much energy to it as to politics. When at last everything had been won and the Countess's husband had handed over her share of the fortune, Lassalle unexpectedly found himself the recipient of a substantial pension from the grateful Countess. Although he lived well he used his leisure for serious purposes.

At the start of the disturbances of 1848 he was in prison in

Cologne on account of one of the worst of the Hatzfeldt scandals. After his release in August he threw himself into politics. He met Marx and Engels – surrendering to the genius of Marx – and intrigued and planned with them for a democratic republic, as he had made up his mind to do as a boy. In November he went to prison again, as a political agitator. This was lucky for him because he was unable to take part in the second, more dangerous revolution of 1849 and did not have to go into exile, like so many of his democratic and socialist friends. He stayed in Germany, on the Rhine, as one of Marx's viceroys, always ready to help, working for the socialist cause in spite of the reaction and supervision by the authorities. The Düsseldorf police reported that his 'extraordinary intellectual qualities, persuasive eloquence, tireless energy, great determination, wildly left ideas, very wide circle of acquaintances, great practical adroitness and the considerable financial resources of his client' made him one of the most dangerous leaders of the revolutionary party. Nevertheless the highest authorities finally decreed 'that the police will not oppose any further the writer Ferdinand Lassalle's application to take up domicile in Berlin'. Lassalle had a talent for fighting successful battles with the authorities. They, on the other hand, did not want to break the law and therefore decided reluctantly not to pursue even such a notorious enemy of the existing system unless he could be proved to have committed an offence.

Lassalle regarded Marx as his best friend. He helped Marx whenever possible, found him publishers and markets for his articles, and regarded him unreservedly as the intellectual head of the party. Marx, on the other hand, although too good a judge of men not to appreciate Lassalle's talent, fundamentally disliked him for very personal and very impersonal reasons. Whereas Lassalle was happy and easy-going Marx made life very difficult for himself. Lassalle, however great his compassion for the poor, was drawn towards aristocratic society and, as Engels sarcastically remarked, acted the gentleman. Marx received no pension from any rich countess, far from it. Moreover, Lassalle was independent not only materially but also intellectually. Although greatly admiring of Marx, Lassalle did not

follow him blindly and in the fifties he produced more and more
ideas at variance with those of the master. This alienated Marx,
who had little sympathy for intellectual independence in others.
In his letters to Engels he liked to refer to Lassalle as 'that person' or 'that individual'. 'How that individual talks . . .' 'Just
look at that pompous person.' Although both started life as
Hegelians Lassalle did not undergo Marx's materialistic con-
version; he remained an idealist. Quite unlike Marx he believed
in free human activity and thought that man shaped history
Like Hegel, and again unlike Marx, he believed in the all-
embracing power and duty of the state. For Marx the state was
only the 'superstructure' of the social conditions which alone were
really worth studying. Lassalle thought it worthwhile to conquer
the state politically; therefore he attached decisive importance to
universal suffrage. Finally, Lassalle was a socially minded politician and a German patriot in a different way from Marx. It is
true that Marx could also on occasions suddenly emphasize the
German side of his nature, but his revolutionary thought was
international from the beginning and grew more so as he sat in
London and interspersed his German letters with scraps of
English. He was not interested in the contests of states and
nations because he saw the class struggle as the key to all history.
Hence his readiness to abandon the Danes or the Czechs to the
Germans not because he loved his compatriots but because he
despised nationalism. Lassalle lived in Germany and perforce
gave his attention to the most important problem of the day,
namely nationalism. He was not only a socialist but also a democrat, and democracy and the nation-state seemed almost synonymous at that time. Being more in touch with the strongest trends
of the age he was less lonely than Marx; and that was what Marx
could not forgive. He could establish contact with elements
which for Marx were at best indulging in confused obstruction;
and in the last resort Lassalle could even deal with men who,
according to the master, were the proletariat's bitterest enemies.
Lassalle enjoyed adventure, a pleasure unknown to Marx.

Basically the two men were rivals, a situation which Marx, the
older and more eminent, resented. They both fought for justice

and social revolution, to which Marx sacrificed his life. But no political work is completely unselfish and the greater the conception the greater is the ambition devoted to it. Marx was consumed by a tremendous determination to dominate. It was bad enough that he should sit poor and alone in the British Museum while other, smaller minds ruled the world, but this situation was bearable because it could be accounted for by his theory. Here, on the other hand, was someone who had stolen his fire, who had adopted his most important ideas, the theories of surplus value, of the class struggle, of the inevitable revolution and of the proletariat as the class which represented all future interests, and used them in a way not laid down by the master, without even asking his leave. This was against the rules of the game. 'It is well that he is gone,' said Wallenstein when he heard of the death of King Gustavus Adolphus, 'because two cocks cannot crow on the same dungheap.' Marx may have had similar feelings when Lassalle, not yet forty, was killed in a duel; to the end he was a gentleman, a man of passion, of pride, of tremendous willpower and a Don Quixote.

7. Arthur Schopenhauer

Some men who are at odds with their age show that they belong to it by the extent of their opposition to it. Some are rebels, others want to admonish and others still are eccentrics who obtain learning from ancient books and look quietly with complete detachment at their world, as though they themselves did not belong to it. The philosopher Arthur Schopenhauer belonged to the last category. For a long time nobody took an interest in his writings. When the old gentleman to his great delight suddenly became famous it was because of historical trends which he would have disapproved of if he had been clear about them: post-revolutionary disappointment of the middle class, a temporary lack of interest in politics. These trends helped Schopenhauer who despised history and politics, though he made no effort to flatter passing moods. He wrote as he had always written, because he was too old, too stubborn and much too convinced of the truth of his ideas to think out new ones. Let people take them or leave them.

He was a great writer. His language was clear and powerful and his thought thrived on living knowledge; even those who cannot accept his basic philosophy will find in his writings a wealth of wisdom and profound and true observation. His interest in philosophy started when he was a young man in the Napoleonic era and his early questions were those of classical German philosophy: what can we know, what is knowledge, what is reality? Basically, however, he was driving at something different. Of the two conceptions which appear even in the title of his main work, *Die Welt als Wille und Vorstellung* (The World as Will and Idea), we can ignore the second. The essence of Schopenhauer's metaphysics is not the strange, eternally irrefutable and eternally useless view that reality is only an idea, exists only in the mind of the observer and that there is no existence without thought; it was the idea of the world as will that was important to him. The world as the will to be and to live, which exists in every creature, which in every creature secretly regards itself as the whole, so that there is in fact no such thing as a variety of individuals in space and time although there is a struggle of all against all, a determination to survive at any price at the expense of others; the world as a place in which the choice is to eat or be eaten – that is Schopenhauer's idea. The world is the will to live. But it would be better if this will did not exist, if there was nothing. As there is more pain than pleasure on earth, all satisfaction is merely transitory, creating new desire and new distress, and the agony of the animal being devoured is greater than the enjoyment of the devourer. What is true of animals is also true of men, although man has reason, which the animal lacks. Yet reason too must serve the will and is merely a handmaiden of hunger and sexual instinct. Man too, however high his opinion of himself, is ruled by urges, be they conscious or unconscious. Only in philosophy is there salvation. Only in philosophy does the will recognize that it is in a bad state, with the result that it turns away from itself and the whole world. But this is a 'matter of grace' and happens rarely, among saints, hermits and ascetics. Most men remain eternally chained to the senselessly turning wheel of the will; they die and are followed by others who are what their predecessors were – will.

This philosophy has been called pessimism after the Latin word *pessimum*. Schopenhauer's world was not the best but the worst possible. He argued that if it were worse than it is, it could not exist, for the will to live would cease. From there 'pessimistic' has found its way into general usage, a word coined by the bourgeois age.

Schopenhauer was also a pessimist as regards history, expecting nothing from it. How could he have expected anything, since according to his philosophy the nature of the world, and man with his desires and vices, always remained the same? If one knows the history of one state one knows the history of all states and all ages, because it is always the same. Even the present, which Droysen described with such excited amazement, could not shake Schopenhauer in his conviction. Although he sent telegrams and travelled in the new railway, he denied that there was anything really new in such technical innovations. Two diametrically opposed views therefore appeared simultaneously in Germany, and both were characteristic. In the fifties it was typically German to think as Droysen and his friends did, to treat history as the Last Judgement, and to hope that the Protestant spirit, Germany and the Prussian state would bring about historic acts of liberation. But Schopenhauer, who scorned the idea of progress, was also a representative of his age and nation who was read with pleasure. He too, the anti-historical, anti-political, pessimistic, metaphysical thinker, touched a hidden string in the German soul, and his greatest pupil, Richard Wagner, became the best loved and probably the most 'German' composer.

It is obvious from what has been said that Schopenhauer was a conservative and disapproved of revolutions. A strong, unquestioned authority was needed to keep man, the beast, in check. Switzerland, he thought, should remain the only republic in Europe, as a warning example to the other peoples. He witnessed the street fighting in Frankfurt in September 1848 and was delighted by the defeat of the 'scoundrels', the insurgents. He belonged to the middle class and owned a little capital, on the income of which he lived carefully but comfortably and to which he believed that he owed his independence as a writer; he had no need to write to please a government or the public. Every day he lunched in the best hotel, being made to pay double the usual price because of his enormous appetite. He wanted to write only for the educated and spoke with contempt of the average man, the 'factory product of nature'. No wonder that Marx's circle could not stand him after he had become famous in old age. Engels scoffed at the 'mad Dr Schopenhauer', and Franz Mehring in his history of German Social Democracy still calls him a 'philistine rentier'. This hardly goes to the heart of the matter. Schopenhauer had no greater liking for the new capitalist class than for the socialists and described its members not very kindly as 'sons of the *Jetztzeit* (here and now) with spectacles for eyes, the only result of their thoughts the cigar between their bestial lips'. This meant that he was really no friend of his time and that in spite of the success which came to him in old age he was a stranger in it. He belonged to the old school, a cultivated aristocrat who read Greek and Latin as easily as German, and who liked to quote Aristotle, Horace and Cicero. Arthur Schopenhauer was one of the last of his kind, doomed to die out in the industrial, democratic age.

Let us not rashly make him into a misanthrope. He did not believe that nations could rule themselves, but, like Voltaire, wanted them to have the most benevolent, most enlightened government possible. He warmly applauded measures like the abolition of slavery in the British Empire. He hated the Catholic Church, the 'Papist fury', as a force of spiritual oppression and brutalization; in that the old man was a son of the eighteenth century. Nevertheless he was a Christian and distinguished between two basic tendencies in Christianity: an optimistic one promising paradise on earth, which he regarded as Jewish in origin, and an ascetic one proclaiming the misery and treachery of this world, teaching resignation and compassion. Something of this, which he found best expressed in the pantheism of the Indians, is present in his own work, and that is why a man who hated politics and modern society, a Christian communist like Leo Tolstoy, looked up to Schopenhauer as his master.

In the fifties he was eagerly read by the German middle class; after the disappointments of 1848 people were receptive to his ideas. But he deserves to be read even today, independently of the historical situation. Not because he offers the truth, for no one offers it. A philosophical writer, who despises history and political and social action, must be said to fall short in some respects. But Marx also fell short, he too disregarded certain values of human existence. To despise the contemplative attitude because it is not active would be as foolish as to take the opposite view. What matters is seriousness of purpose. Schopenhauer's philosophy is great art and has the truth of art. One might add that it is German art, though its creator was completely cold towards the demand for a German nation state; he felt happy in the old-fashioned Free City of Frankfurt and liked to associate with Englishmen. Yet he wrote more beautiful and forceful German than anybody who came after him; from the depths of German tradition, mysticism, romanticism and music came the moods which he skilfully combined into the four movements of his great symphony. Outside Germany his influence was greater than that of any other German philosopher – unless we count Marx among the philosophers. This he owed to his style, being for once a philosopher who could be read with pleasure. He owed it also to his profound psychological insight which discovered the sub-conscious long before Sigmund Freud, and to his unique position in the intellectual life of his time. In the age of politics, growing capitalism and rising nation-states he fought a rearguard action for true philosophy, and he fought it well.

8 Prussian Interlude

As late as the second half of the nineteenth century the monarch could still play a decisive role in Germany. He was not only the symbol of an epoch which ended ceremoniously with his death but his character could influence the life of the country. In the years before 1840 people had looked forward expectantly to the death of the King of Prussia. And because his successor, Frederick William IV, had been such a disappointment they breathed an even bigger sigh of relief at his departure than at his arrival. Frederick William's latent insanity became so obvious in 1857 that it could no longer be disguised. His brother, the Prince of Prussia, who deputized for the King, became head of the state with the title of Prince Regent after another year of fruitless delay.

For a long time Prince William was thought to be more reactionary than his brother. Before 1848 his enemies had called him the 'Russian', in 1849 the 'grapeshot prince'. In the fifties he developed a distinct aversion to the corrupt practices of the reactionary government, the infringements of the law and the official hypocrisy. During the Crimean War he sympathized with the western powers. There was a time when the members of the camarilla and the *Kreuzzeitung* nicknamed his family 'the democratic family'; a description which badly overshot the mark. The ageing heir to the throne lacked almost all the qualities of a democrat. But he was a man of honour by his lights, level-headed, practical and of simple piety; he tried to keep his word if it was possible to do so without too much sacrifice. He possessed sympathetic qualities, gallantry, reticence and gratitude; and his education was none the worse because it was strongly influenced by France and because this man, who was born in the eighteenth century, still interspersed his German with French phrases. The concepts in which he thought came from the past; the dim and distant past, if one looks closely. He saw the officials of the state as the King's servants, and the King as the man on horseback, the commander of the army, the master. The army was his, not the state's, and even the state was his in the last resort. The climax of his life was, as three thousand years earlier, in battle, in knightly victory, in conquest, increasing his glory. Hence the two things which he thought he understood were the army and foreign policy. The notion that an industrial society wanted to exist for itself, not for the state and the armour-clad, royal Christian knight, was far beyond him. He wanted to respect the constitution, not because he liked it but because the King must stand by his sacred word, even if it related to a tiresome and useless craze. 'I shall not examine whether constitutions are salutory,' he remarked. 'But where they exist they must be upheld and not distorted by artificial interpretations.' In his first speech from the throne to parliament he proclaimed these principles: 'Kingship by the grace of God, adherence to law and constitution, loyalty of the people and of the triumphant army, justice, truth, faith and fear of God.' In his simplicity he believed in such concepts and thought that they were enough to master the problems of the age. Wherein he was wrong.

When he came to the throne at the age of sixty the nation, not only Prussia, looked to him with hopeful confidence. The feeling prevailed that, if by different means, the great objective of 1848 would after all be achieved with the help of the old man who in 1849 had been so busy suppressing the revolution. A 'new era' – this was the popular expression – had dawned. Indeed William spoke of 'moral conquests' to be made in Germany, and of the protection of the law by Prussia, a reference to constitutional infringements by some small German states. He appointed a liberal government; and the newly elected Prussian parliament was also overwhelmingly though narrowly liberal. The best-known democratic politicians had purposely refused to stand in order not to frighten the new ruler who promised so much. But when the Prince Regent stressed the 'rigid limits set by me' within which Prussian politics must move, he soon learned that no ruler, constitutional or absolute, can set such limits. The first year of his reign brought a new European crisis for which his programme had made no provision.

9. The Unification of Italy

The Italian War of 1859 – France and Piedmont against Austria
– was a consequence of the Crimean War; it was the second in
that chain of curiously limited, quick passages-at-arms in which
Europe in twenty years accomplished by force what it had been
unable to accomplish freely and nobly in 1848. Napoleon III,
always anxious to keep the world in turmoil, to make old dreams
come true and to acquire new prestige, was again the instigator
of the affair. He did not, however, profit from it and was certainly not the living force behind it; this was Italian. The urge
to be free from antiquated Austrian rule and from the small
local despots who depended on Austria was now very strong in
Italy. Because the astute Prime Minister of the King of Sardinia
and Piedmont successfully identified his state with the general
cause which he persuaded the Emperor of the French to adopt,
this particular outbreak took the form of a war between states,
started according to the rules of diplomacy.

One is often told that war is a struggle of ideas, of democracy
against autocracy, of pacifism against aggression, of conservatism
against revolution, of good against evil. Reality, however, rarely
corresponds to such propaganda-fed notions. What was the war
of 1859? Was it an attack of the revolutionary party system on
good law concerned only with its defence? France and Sardinia
had attacked, Austria defended the treaties of 1815, the *status quo*.
Was it a war of land-hungry France against a German state, a
Bonapartist war that had begun on the Po but would end on the
Rhine? That Louis Napoleon was anxious to regain France's
'natural frontiers' was an open secret. Or was it a just war of
liberation of the Italian people in which the Germans, who were
in a similar position and who longed for the same changes, must
take Italy's side, even if Italy was allied with the devil? It was
possible to regard the war in that light. A passionate controversy
developed in Germany over how the war should be seen and what
should be done; and thanks to the 'new era' there was complete
freedom of discussion. The controversy cut across parties and

groups. The Prince Regent of Prussia, who as a young man had taken part in the War of Liberation against Napoleon, could imagine nothing better than a return of that great period. He was not in the least interested in Italy's freedom and had no intention whatsoever of giving Prussia the part in Germany which Piedmont now set out to play in Italy. He was supported by the old Prussian conservatives, as well as by the Catholic leaders in northern and southern Germany who championed Austria and the threatened temporal rule of the Pope. Of the men of 1848, liberals or democrats, émigrés or stay-at-homes, some were for Austria and a popular war against Bonaparte, others for France or at least for an armed neutrality which was bound to favour Italy. From London Marx and Engels sought to clear up the quarrel, but in spite of their penetrating analyses even they failed to do so. They spoke with contempt of Austria and with hatred of Napoleon, whose overthrow they regarded as the first prerequisite for the revolution. In practice the policy of the world revolution therefore coincided momentarily with that of the 'grape-shot prince'. Lassalle, on the other hand, in a brilliantly written pamphlet described Austria as the real enemy of Italian, German and all freedom. Austria must be torn to shreds, dismembered, destroyed and crushed. Once Europe was freed from the Habsburg curse the German principalities would cease to exist of their own accord, Prussia would no longer be Prussia, and a free German Reich would appear as if by magic. If on the other hand the Germans were led into a national war against France the atmosphere of Europe would be poisoned for years to come.

How is it possible that the democrats cannot see that this war would be unimaginably damaging to civilization? Good understanding ... between the two great civilized peoples, the Germans and the French, is the focal point ... of all democratic development and of civilization. ... Once the blood-thirsty tiger of national hatred is roused again from its lair it might happen that for three decades cultural flowering will be blighted, political development obstructed, intellectual confusion made possible, that the door will again be opened to every kind of sinister Machiavellian intrigue, and that the barbarism of conquest and destruction will replace internal progress. Such a development would be by far the greatest victory of the reactionary principle since March 1848.

That was Lassalle's opinion.

Everyone saw the future differently from his allies of the moment with whose practical policy he more or less agreed, everyone had something else at heart. One cared about the glory of Prussia, another about German unification, a third about social revolution. We may be passionate advocates of some cause or other and, if we are politicians, we may even be able to achieve something. But we cannot control the consequences of our actions and recommendations, although we think we can. We have our ideas and the God of History has his and he is always stronger; that is the trouble with all large-scale political action. The aim of both Marx and Lassalle was social revolution. Marx wanted to achieve it through international class struggle; he regarded Louis Napoleon both as the most dangerous enemy and as a traitor to the working class. As far as he was concerned the turn of the Habsburgs could come later. Lassalle thought that a substantial part of the revolution was accomplished if nations became free states. In that respect he was more in sympathy than Marx with the humanist, national-democratic movement of the age, particularly that of the Italians; later in fact he visited Garibaldi, the conqueror of southern Italy, to discuss revolutionary tactics. Lassalle with his imaginative, open mind, could negotiate with a variety of people even if he did not share their views or belong to their party; Marx could not and would not do this. It is impossible to say who was right because what actually happened neither of them, nor indeed anyone else, had foreseen.

For the moment the German hair-splitting was brought to a sudden stop. Louis Napoleon feared the intervention of Prussia, particularly as the Prince Regent had mobilized his army on the Rhine and spoke of armed mediation. Francis Joseph feared the price that Prussia would demand for its help. Consequently the two autocrats took a personal decision and made peace after a campaign of three months. Austria gave up Lombardy, which was united with Piedmont, but was allowed to keep Venetia, thereby demonstrating its determination to remain an Italian power. A venture with unpredictable consequences was suddenly stopped; once again it had been conducted as though Germany did not exist.

Nevertheless the Italian national movement continued. The one push which Napoleon had given it was enough to give it momentum of its own. In the small central Italian states the people drove away the princes, most of them helpless foreigners; the unification of these states was proclaimed and confirmed by plebiscites. This was the age of the plebiscite, of the consultation of the people on matters already decided, so that only obstinate characters voted no. Then came Garibaldi's journey to Sicily, the revolt of Naples and the entry there of Piedmontese troops. In the spring of 1861 Victor Emmanuel of Savoy took the title of King of Italy and with this act his Kingdom of Sardinia and Piedmont ceased to exist.

The establishment of the Kingdom of Italy was an event unprecedented in European politics. It was not the restoration of a state that had existed before, because since time immemorial there had not been a state of Italy. Victor Emmanuel himself said that Italy was no longer the country of the ancient Romans nor Italy of the Middle Ages, but 'Italy of the Italians'. It was the nation-state which revolutionary theory had demanded and the establishment of which Austria had repeatedly fought to prevent. If the Italians had managed to achieve this, or almost to achieve it – Venice and Rome, the capital, were still outside the Kingdom – why should not other peoples manage it, for example the Germans? And this was the lesson: they had achieved it not as envisaged by revolutionary enthusiasts like Mazzini but by a highly original combination of planned military diplomacy and unplanned, enthusiastic improvisation. Camillo Cavour, Sardinia's great Prime Minister, was no democrat, still less a demagogue, and not even a fanatic advocate of the unity of all Italy. He was merely a liberal who wanted free, secular education, science and industry, a strong active state controlled and stimulated by parliament, parties, a free press, freedom of thought and freedom of ownership. These objectives he achieved in Piedmont before he ventured into foreign policy, into the liberation of northern Italy from foreign rule. For this end he did not disdain to form an alliance with Bonaparte, whom he had good reason to distrust; and for the time being he had no intention of going beyond this end. The rest happened by itself, 'from below'. What was admirable was the manner in which those two movements, Cavour's liberal, diplomatic and military movement and Garibaldi's radical, democratic and national one, joined forces. The result was the liberal Kingdom – which was, however, to have a less happy future than its foundation might have suggested.

10. Nationalverein *and* Fortschrittspartei

The comparison between Prussia and Piedmont was obvious and soon became a commonplace. This did not please the Prince Regent, who issued a statement saying that Sardinia's choice of the road of revolution was one of which his government must express strong disapproval. Cavour replied that before long Prussia would be grateful for his example.

But even if Prussia had had a Cavour, the comparison between the two states was at best as true as it was false. Both the Germans and the Italians longed for unity. Both were thwarted by Habsburg Austria and both had potential leaders, one in Turin and one in Berlin. That was as far as the parallel went. In some respects the material unification of Italy was much more difficult than that of Germany because the internal geographical, educational and economic differences and the diversities of human character were much greater in Italy than in Germany. Sicily and Lombardy were two different worlds, Baden and Saxony were not. In Italy on the other hand Austria was the enemy, the foreigner, whereas in Germany it was a venerable German power; the Italians referred to their oppressors not as 'the Austrians' but as 'the Germans' In Italy Austria had almost no friends whereas it had many in Germany, probably still more than Prussia. The German states were not rotten as Modena, Parma and the Papal States had been at the end. Bavaria was not Naples; Berlin was not full of thousands of Bavarian refugees as Turin had been full of thousands of Neapolitan ones. And finally Prussia was not Piedmont, being more important and less popular, less harmless; its strongest, almost its only political traditions provided a warning against the alliance which Piedmont had formed with liberalism.

Nevertheless there had always been a close, mysterious relationship between the fates of the two nations. Now, amid the applause of the British, the Americans and the non-Catholic part of France, the Italians achieved their nation state. Could Germany lag behind?

The German *Nationalverein* (National Association), founded in the autumn of 1859, was an echo of the Italian organization of the same name. Liberals and democrats joined forces 'to promote the unification and free development of the German fatherland', as they had already done with varying degrees of enthusiasm in the last months of the Frankfurt National Assembly, and, now as then, they put their hopes in Prussia. 'The aims of Prussian policy are largely the same as those of Germany. The German federal governments will, however, have to make sacrifices for the whole, if Germany is to have a more concentrated constitution . . .' The Association was only a qualified success and its membership was confined primarily to northern Germany. It was compelled to accept the advantages of the particularism which it hoped to overcome. None of the big states, not even Prussia, tolerated the Association within its frontiers. Finally it established its headquarters in Coburg-Gotha, where the Duke, a relative who shared the views of Queen Victoria and her husband, fancied himself as a national liberal.

Of more immediate significance was the foundation in Prussia of the *Fortschrittspartei* (Progress Party) as the result of a split among the liberals. It attracted those representatives of the people who, after three years of regency, thought that the ministers of the 'New Era' could be a little quicker about making their promises come true. The programme of the Progress Party was purely liberal, urging that the constitution should be taken more seriously than was done by the reactionary civil service and asking for a more equitable distribution of taxes, particularly for the abolition of the exemption from tax on real estate enjoyed by lords of the manor; the party also advocated closer parliamentary control of the budget, reform of the upper house (whose veto had so far killed all of the government's attempts at liberalization), savings in military expenditure, freedom of trade, and so on. Originally the party was to have been christened the 'Democratic Party'. However, at the suggestion of the electrical engineer, inventor and industrialist, Werner Siemens, it was decided to call it the 'Progress Party' because, as Siemens says in his memoirs, 'it seemed to me that the name of the party should indicate its line of activity rather than its opinions'. Though the new party counted at least one democrat with a strong social conscience among its founders, namely Schulze-Delitzsch, it anxiously kept away from everything that might be held against it as radicalism. The party was middle class, and middle-class fear of the 'red revolution' was no less than it had been fourteen years earlier. The demand for an equal franchise was suppressed and there was not a single word about the industrial workers, whose interests were after all not identical with those of the middle class. The next elections, however, showed that the Progress Party claimed rightly that it represented the Prussian middle classes. It soon became the strongest party and together with the 'Left Centre' party, with which it had close connections, had an absolute majority in parliament after 1862.

The Progress Party and the National Association both wanted Prussia to pursue a nationalistic policy and Germany to be unified under Prussian leadership. All sections of the middle classes wanted a unified state, a free domestic market, the same commercial legislation everywhere, a single German currency and a merchant fleet under a German flag – all the benefits which the industries of the western powers had long enjoyed and which even the Italian middle classes now began to enjoy. Who would deny that there was also an element of patriotism involved, the determination to present as dignified a picture to the world as other nations, as well as a collective drive for power. 'The German nation,' the journalist Julius Fröbel wrote in 1859, 'is sick of principles and doctrines, literary greatness and theoretical existence. What it demands is power, power, power. And to the man who offers it power it will offer honour, more honour than he can imagine.'

Once more as in 1849, there was a difference between those who wanted 'greater' Germany and those who did not, between the *Grossdeutsche* and the *Kleindeutsche*. After all, the problem remained basically the same as long as Austria, Prussia and the central states existed. As in 1849, the *Grossdeutsche* were in the majority in southern Germany, among the Catholics, in the small towns and in the countryside. Once more the *Kleindeutsche* were more influential because they knew what they wanted and had the commercial world, as well as the most active part of the academic world, on their side. The *Grossdeutsche* were less single-minded; their aims were made up of a mixture of conflicting wishes, ideas and dreams. Among the *Grossdeutsche* there were Bavarian aristocrats who would have liked to stop the course of history because all was well as it was and should remain so; there were Suabian democrats who distrusted Prussia; socialists who wished Habsburgs, Wittelsbachs and Hohenzollerns to the devil, and princes who hoped to save more of their sovereignty in a 'greater' Germany than in 'little' Germany; there were nationalists to whom the nation-state seemed an ugly cripple without the German Austrians, and profound political philosophers who condemned the principle of the nation-state and regarded its application to central Europe as a misfortune. Konstantin Frantz was one of these and what he said about the Federation of the German peoples and the small peoples around Germany, about European federalism, moral order and social community, was well said. If everything had happened as he imagined, how happy we should all be today. But Frantz was a political philosopher, not a statesman. He only had ideas and did nothing to put them into practice, nor could he show how, given the situation, they could be realized. The Prussian nut was not the only one that could not be cracked with philanthropic dreams; Austria too had demonstrated recently that it had little sympathy for voluntary, magnanimous changes by its stubborn determination to hold on to Venice, its last purely Italian province, by basing itself on the dead letter of old robber agreements.

Today the writers who in those fateful ten years objected to the principle of the nation-state are read with admiration. They prophesied many dreadful happenings which later came true. Konstantin Frantz was one of them; Lord Acton, the great Anglo-German historian, and Jacob Burckhardt, the Swiss art historian, were others. Acton said that nationalism was against the law of God because it worshipped something natural or biological, race or a collection of human beings identifiable only by a common language. It destroyed historical evolution, destroyed European civilization, divided the peoples, set them against each other and was likely to culminate in an orgy of barbaric mutual destruction. Burckhardt, who knew Italian history and art, marvelled at the 'enormous mistake' of his beloved, idyllic Italy now becoming a commonplace state like others, that all the magnificent old cities and republics, the tremendous memories, Rome, Venice, Florence and a hundred others, should unite to become a would-be great power, at best only a caricature of France. It is easy to understand the patrician scholar's shock. In history the old is sacrificed for the new. In this case the new was as yet brash, its value unproven and its dangers obvious: the nation-state abounded in contradictions. The liberals preached freedom but the result of their efforts was to make the state omnipotent. They glorified the nation, the good, the infallible people, though in reality they distrusted the masses and represented the interests of the well-to-do who were only a small minority. They incited people but, like the Prussian Prince Regent, wished to confine their revolution to strict limits, with the result that they were afraid even of universal suffrage. Their religion was superficial and inadequate; Christian but lacking in seriousness, it knew nothing of evil, it was optimistic and peaceable and at the same time martial, rhetorical and violent. Jacob Burckhardt saw through all this, looked further ahead into a desolate future and hastily looked away again in order to steep himself in his beloved past. But the Italians could not live on the great memories of the Roman Empire or the glories of the Renaissance. However flourishing their states had been in the fifteenth century, in the middle of the nineteenth they were wretched. They gave men nothing, they only took and obstructed. Because they no longer fulfilled the needs of society they must disappear, and their citizens must organize themselves on a broader basis. But whom should they join? 'Humanity' did not exist in political reality; neither did 'Europe'. The union of all those who at least had the Italian language in common and who felt themselves to be Italians was therefore not so unreasonable, even in terms of practical aims. Nationalism was, of course, not merely a means to an end. It existed, it was an elemental force, an aggregate of feelings, good and bad. A philosopher might deplore it and think out better aims, but unless he was also a prophet who carried men along with him and created the forces needed to achieve his goal he accomplished nothing, however justified his warnings. Nor could oppression solve the problem. For long the police in both Germany and Italy had persecuted nationalism and caused much suffering; but in vain. Nationalism still existed, and having at last achieved its aim in Italy, there could be no doubt that it would soon do the same in Germany. The only question was how. A good politician had to accept this fact and make it into something as moderate, suitable and lasting as possible. The politician must work with the material available. He leaves it to the philosopher to wish that things were different and to think out ways of achieving the highest ideals.

11 Constitutional Conflict

From the beginning the 'New Era' in Prussia had been a confused affair. Prince Regent – since 1861, King – William wanted to rule legally and constitutionally. On paper the constitution was not a cut-and-dried affair which simply needed to be 'applied'. What it was, how its formal framework corresponded to social reality, was yet to be revealed. In Britain Parliament ruled through its executive committee, the Cabinet, and the King's functions were merely formal and at the most consultative. This parliamentary form of government had emerged as the result of struggles in the dim and distant past. In Austria and France monarchs ruled with the support of army, civil service and church, and the consultative bodies were there for decorative purposes. In Prussia they were to be something slightly better, although it was not clear what. Logically the middle-class liberals ought to have wanted parliamentary government, as they had in 1848. Tamed by defeat, they had meanwhile returned to older concepts of a division of power, as it had existed in pre-absolutist times between prince and estates. Crown and middle-class popular representatives should govern together and complement one another. But such a division did not correspond to the reality of the modern state which had to be one whole. Nor did it correspond to the wishes of the Crown, which basically still wanted to represent the whole, even though, as the King put it, 'surrounded by new, modern institutions'. What the purpose, the power of those institutions would be was bound to emerge as soon as the first serious issue divided the parliamentarians and the prince with his Junker advisers.

Constitutional government – the alleged division of power – was further complicated by the existence of a third partner, the Upper House. Consisting of noble landowners and dignitaries nominated by the King, it represented too obviously the old upper class to enjoy widespread confidence. Technically its cooperation in the government of the country was as necessary as that of the other two factors, Crown and people. It was the reliable ally of the Crown as long as both defended old Junker Prussia. If the government tried to fulfil certain minimum requirements of the modern state demanded by middle-class interests, the Upper House could frustrate the intentions of the Crown as successfully as those of the Lower House. The King's only remedy was to copy the English practice of creating as many new peers as were needed to ensure the adoption of a piece of legislation. By that method the Junkers' exemption from taxation on real estate was abolished in 1861. But the conflict which was about to begin concerned the Crown and the Lower House alone.

The Prussian army was in need of reform – a fact which had emerged on the occasion of the mobilizations of 1850 and 1859. The number of recruits had not risen since 1815 although the population of the state had almost doubled. Conscription existed therefore on paper only. However, those who were called up not merely served actively for two years and belonged to the reserve for another two, but they were then still liable to be called up as members of the 'first levy' of the *Landwehr* in case of war. As a result middle-aged family men went to war while young men remained at home – an impossible situation. In addition, politically, or from the point of view of the army leadership morally, there was something wrong with the *Landwehr*. The *Landwehr* man belonged to the middle class, he was an elector, a man whose civilian activity alienated him from the army, and his officers also belonged to the middle class. He did not belong as completely to his supreme commander as the regular soldier. The political argument was not publicly mentioned by those who planned the reform which was now initiated, but the Lower House quickly suspected what they had in mind, and the accuracy of that suspicion can easily be proved by what they said in private. The *Landwehr*, wrote the King's Minister of War, General von Roon, was 'a politically false institution' and in a personal letter he said: 'In the process of universal disintegration I can recognize only one organism capable of resistance, the army. To preserve it is a task which I still regard as possible, though only for a limited period.' If that was not done Prussia would drift rapidly 'into the muddy ocean of parliamentary rule'. The Regent himself may not have been as conscious of these political motives as his adviser. In any case the reform prepared with his active participation amounted to the dissolution of the first *Landwehr* levy. The plan was to increase the number of annual conscripts by about half, to raise the period of active service to three years, to make the three youngest age groups of the *Landwehr* part of the reserve and to relegate the older age groups and the second *Landwehr* levy to fortress duties only. The reform, particularly the creation of new regiments, cost money and this expenditure had to be approved by parliament.

There were several things to be said for the technical aspects of the reform. Nor did the liberals deny that the state needed a strong army, particularly when the intention was that in German-speaking Europe it should pursue the constructive, progressive policy which it had so far failed to pursue, but which the left desired. Even in the second half of the twentieth century we do not seem to have advanced beyond the old idea that a proper state must have a proper army, at least as good as that of its neighbours. The idea was certainly not questioned in 1861. 'If we are attacked we defend ourselves', Engels had written in 1859. How could Prussia or Germany defend itself against the great armies of France or Russia if it did not have an equally good, modern army? In the struggle for power one nation out-bid the other. As populations and industries grew, armies had to grow too. The question was, who would control the new army, whose brain-child would it be?

For the King and his political generals, Roon, Alvensleben and Edwin von Manteuffel, the answer was clear. The army must remain a reliable instrument in the hand of the monarch. It must be a mass army because the age demanded it, but it must strengthen the position of the Crown and not that of democracy. The army must be the real Prussian state, as of old, and the King must be the soldier-king. As long as that was the position there was no harm in allowing the middle class to play at parliament. Roon went further; he wanted to have none of the 'constitutional humbug' and hoped to achieve just that in the course of the approaching conflict. Honest William did not go so far.

It is better to believe in something than to believe in nothing, and Albrecht von Roon, was a man of principle, a Lutheran of the old kind. Words like duty, fatherland, obedience and king meant to him the essence of all that was true, alive and sacred.

His Christianity was of the militant, not of the charitable variety; he had worked out exactly how to suppress with an iron fist the resistance of the capital, Berlin. 'The action,' he remarked, 'by which demands from the Crown are won is usually fought with guns and swords, not with the pen.' He possessed a trait often found in German conservatives: he thought highly of the moral character of those who shared his views but condemned his opponents for depravity, corruption, cleverness and sophistry, all of which were aired in the 'drivel shop' of parliament which, as an institution, served no other purpose. Once that rabble was dispersed the real Prussian people, as it was still to be found in the countryside, could certainly be brought to heel. The arrogant conviction that his own cause and his alone was right made Roon and his friends indulge in unsoldierly intrigues. How could a just man err in the service of his King? After all, though the general had read Hegel in his youth, he was no sociologist; that new field he left to the liberals. It never occurred to Roon that the process which he regarded as decay was a development of the social structure and as inevitable as a process of nature. Nor could he grasp that there must be corresponding political changes, that no God could preserve or resurrect the Prussia of Frederick William I and that any such attempt, however apparently successful, could result only in unnatural contortions. All the things that his new army needed, strategic railways, mobile bridges to cross the enemy's rivers, artillery and ammunition in hitherto unknown quantities, pharmaceutical products of all kinds, all these must be produced for him by classes which did not exist in the good old days, by miners, steelworkers, chemists and engineers, entrepreneurs and bankers. Yet Roon saw no connection between this fact and the political difficulties in which he found himself. How otherwise could he have proceeded with such bold, provocative confidence?

The Lower House was the parliament of the 'New Era', liberal but moderate to the point of throwing away its own weapons. It expected great things from the new era; as it received almost nothing it became impatient. One manifestation of this impatience was the formation of the Progress Party in the summer of 1861; now the Lower House became involved in the army reform.

Lassalle wrote to Marx: 'The law is shameful. In a word its purpose is the dissolution – complete, albeit disguised – of the *Landwehr* as the last democratic survival of 1810 and the creation of a powerful weapon for absolutism and the Junkers.' Although the liberals would have used somewhat more moderate language, on the whole they agreed. They rejected the bill and insisted on the division between *Landwehr* and line, as well as on a two-year term of service. Meanwhile, being sensible men, they voted an extraordinary grant to keep the army in good condition in view of the critical international situation. Thereupon the King and his minister immediately began to carry out the projected reform, convinced that once 189 new battalions and squadrons existed, a vote of the chamber could no longer remove them.

This irritated the deputies. In the second year the military budget was passed only by a very small majority, and at the beginning of the third year members demanded that in future they should be given a detailed statement of the various items so that they would know for what they were voting. The King, still inclined to play the role of the constitutional monarch, though annoyed by the obstinacy of the people's representatives, and much more under the influence of his intriguing generals than he himself realized, was persuaded to dismiss most of his liberal ministers and to replace them by reactionary officials; that was the end of the 'New Era'. The chamber was dissolved; perhaps the King and his advisers hoped to create a more obedient assembly by resorting to the old trick of pressure from the authorities; or perhaps they wanted to irritate both sides and produce a crisis; a crisis was not slow in coming. A bigger poll than the Kingdom of Prussia had ever seen or would ever see again proved the electorate's excitement. The Progress Party had an overwhelming majority in the new chamber, whereas the conservatives were reduced to ten members. 'What next?' asked the Minister of War. 'There is no party that can govern. The democrats are out of the question, of course, but the great majority consists of democrats and those who want to become democrats . . . No party can rule in these circumstances except the democrats, yet they cannot and must not.' Who could rule, then, and how, without blowing the constitution sky high?

One does not get the impression that the government prepared a precise plan. The King wanted, if possible, both to have his own way, and to preserve the reputation of being an honest man who kept his constitutional oath. The generals wanted a *coup d'état*. In the cabinet there were still some politically shrewd members who did not think it possible to rule the country without a budget approved by parliament, without a semblance of constitutionalism. Roon himself vacillated; in the critical weeks of September 1862 he was not the man of iron he so much liked to appear. The parliamentary majority on the other hand was dominated by those who wanted nothing more than a compromise, any compromise as long as it confirmed their right to have at least a say in military matters. The new army was there and the amalgamation of *Landwehr* and line was a *fait accompli*. Perhaps it might at least be possible to save the minor point of two-year service and thus gain a partial parliamentary victory? When William refused even this the Lower House rejected the government's bill by 308 votes to 11, provided nothing for army reform in the budget, and thus presented the government with the choice of sending the new regiments home or of ruling without a budget.

Everybody to whom the rule of law mattered realized that ruling without a budget amounted to governing in contravention of the constitution. A reactionary newspaper tried to come to the rescue by advancing the theory that, whereas the constitution laid down that the Lower House, the Upper House and the Crown must jointly prepare the budget, it omitted to say what should happen if the three failed to agree. This '*lacuna* theory' was a juridical joke which the cabinet itself did not dare to take seriously. During the last 150 years Britain had evolved a procedure to be followed in such circumstances which the latest European constitutions had copied: the new government was formed from the majority in the chamber This meant the parliamentary form of government which was no less distasteful to the King than to von Roon. William found himself unable to move forwards or backwards. He could not move forwards because, although his military prompters had made the necessary preparations for suppressing a rising in Berlin, there was no sign of any such rising and guns were of no use against the chamber's insistence on its rights. Moreover, his most important ministers, the Foreign Minister and the Minister of Finance, resigned because they felt themselves unable to carry out their duties against the will of the chamber; the stubborn old King was more determined than ever not to give way. He had expert knowledge which led him to believe that a three-year term of service was an absolute minimum, given the professional armies of France and Russia. A gathering of civilians, of his subjects, was hardly likely to know more about the matter than he, the King and soldier. The vocal conservatives of the *Kreuzzeitung* issued warnings that Prussia had become great as a military state and that it must remain faithful to its inner law or go under. The King shared these sentiments. He had wanted to rule decently and lawfully, even to respect the constitution like a toy which it had unfortunately become necessary to concede to the *Zeitgeist*. But that the day would come when political parties, gesticulating phrasemongers, democrats, Catholics, Poles and Jews would be prescribing to him how the Prussian army should look in future – that he had not imagined. If that was the new age, then there was no place in it for him and it would be better if he resigned. Let his son – who was engaged in the usual crown-princely opposition to his father and had a liberal English wife – come to grips with the Progress Party as best he could. The King drafted a ceremonial instrument of abdication.

We should not over-emphasize the historical importance of the decision at stake. Prussia's social structure and its characteristics, the spirit of the officer corps, of the aristocracy, of the churches, of the civil service and of the middle class itself would not have been changed by one dramatic defeat of the monarchy. The population was still overwhelmingly royalist, whatever way it voted. In 1859 Lassalle wrote to Marx: 'After ten years away from here you seem to have no idea at all how monarchist our people are.' The embittered withdrawal of the old King who had hopefully embarked on his task only four years earlier would have affected people; some members of the Lower House might have been moved to tears and the parties would have become more willing still to make concessions. Nevertheless, in Prussia's new, uncertain constitutional life William I's abdication would have been a serious event, a clearly visible, solemn sign that the age of the soldier kings was past and that it was not the King or the Upper House or the generals on whom the burden of responsibility rested, but the citizens. Who can tell how such an event would have affected the sense of power and responsibility of the middle classes, or Prussia's relations with Germany, or Germany's relations with the non-German world?

The King did not abdicate. Instead the papers announced on the evening of 23 September 1862 that the Prussian Minister in Paris, von Bismarck-Schönhausen, had been appointed Minister of State and acting Chairman of the Cabinet.

Part Six
Prussia Conquers Germany (1861–1871)

The man who now stepped on to the political stage played a unique part in modern German history. There is no other instance in the development of western Europe of one figure who changed a nation's destiny. Certainly not in Britain, where everything took a more natural, normal course; even France has nothing comparable to offer. Napoleon I, however meteoric his career, was only an episode; when it was over France returned to its mapped-out historical road. There remained the French administrative system, completed but not invented by Napoleon, and the legend of military glory, extremism and sudden collapse. Russian history knows of a man who in the second decade of our century took personal action that was fraught with unforeseeable consequences. Lenin, though he imagined himself merely to be carrying out what was known to be scientifically right and inevitable, was himself an historical force. The Communist revolution which he believed himself to be serving was invented, forced through and led by him. Bismarck was no such force, and knew it, being basically modest. The forces which he harnessed were there already: the determination to rule of the old, upper-class Prussian nascent industrialism, nationalism, liberalism, democracy and materialism. Bismarck provided the form which gave them cohesion. In the end they broke through this form, as Bismarck in his last years recognized that they would. Yet even the manner in which they outgrew first him and then his successors was in part determined by the pressure which he had exerted on them for thirty years. Everything that he had tried to prevent or to delay, the worst that he feared, happened in the end: world wars, world revolution, the literal destruction of the state which he idolized, with the result that the younger generation growing up today hardly knows the name of Prussia. Moreover, this happened not so very long after his death. People who knew him well actually experienced it; for example the wife of his son, who poisoned herself in 1945 a few hours before soldiers of the Red Army reached the family castle. A fate which serves to illustrate the futility of all political endeavour. Or should we say the futility of false, unjust and in the last resort unnatural political endeavour? Our story must seek to answer this question, although there will not be a clear yes or no.

1. Bismarck's Portrait

The son of a nobleman from the Mark of Brandenburg, Bismarck belonged to an old, well-known, reasonably well-to-do family from east of the Elbe. His mother came from the professional classes, the daughter of a civil servant and the grand-daughter and great-grand-daughter of professors. As an old man Bismarck said that he was not really a member of the Prussian nobility and that, because of his mother, the Junkers had never really accepted him. There is some truth in this claim. Bismarck embarrassed his unsophisticated rural neighbours by his intelligence, wit, elegance of expression and choice of reading matter, as well as by an inclination to indulge in wild, unexpected action. Even as a young man he made fun of the way of life of his class as something to which he himself was far superior. On the other hand, he liked to act the simple country squire who preferred horses and trees to the artificial wealth of cities – only to betray the split in his nature by his penetrating mode of expression. To a liberal politician he said: 'I am a Junker and want to take advantage of it', a remark which no ordinary Junker would have made. Once, as a young member of parliament, he threatened that the rural population would teach the revolutionary, corrupt cities obedience, 'even if they wiped them off the face of the earth'. Often, particularly in his younger years, he demonstrated what amounted to almost a caricature of brash class arrogance, calling all bourgeois politicians to the 'left' of him 'tailors', and being scornful at finding himself sitting next to the wife of a businessman at a diplomatic dinner In exaggerating his Junker characteristics and consciously acting the hunting and shooting squire and soldier he was at the same time expressing part of his true nature. He probably owed his culture, intelligence, ambition, worldliness and business acumen to his mother's side of the family. But the qualities that integrated his talents, the strength, the willpower and brutality of which he was capable, the insatiable acquisitiveness concerned less with money than with land and forests, were part of the Bismarck nature. To present him as an intellectual disguised as a baron would be oversimplifying his complex character. He was really a creature of the country, fond of forests and animals, and his basic views of man and society remained influenced to the end of his days by the rural, patriarchal impressions of his youth. In any case, the question of what Bismarck inherited from his father's or from his mother's side has only limited meaning. His brother Bernhard was an ordinary country squire, a fact which shows that genius comes from out of the blue.

Bismarck was tall and, though slim in his youth, later became fat because he ate and drank enormous quantities, thus giving his expressive round eyes the moist brilliance induced by alcohol. He had a high-pitched, soft voice, unexpected in a man of his bulk. In public he spoke haltingly, searching for words. He despised good speakers, and later used to say to his parliamentary enemies: 'You like to speak, you enjoy speaking. For you speaking is a profession, for me it is torment.' Yet what he had to say was always interesting, personal and well expressed; the style of his letters and official documents is masterly. He always finds the right word, the striking comparison, the illuminating joke, he knows how to paint landscapes, conjure up moods, define ideas and sum up people – the last usually with more malice than justice. It will always remain true that the style is the man: in whatever a man writes there is his spirit, his will, his soul – everything. This explains why a close study of Bismarck's writings sometimes produces a feeling of surprise and even repulsion. The precision of his expression is abrupt, the rhythm of his sentences cold and disciplined. He wrote for readers whom he did not like and rarely even respected. His education was that of a well-bred middle-class child of a highly educated period. The pupils of Prussian grammar schools were made to learn a great deal in those days. Bismarck knew Greek and Latin, wrote French like a Frenchman and English not badly; later he learned Russian. His speech and his writings were liberally interspersed with foreign words, usually French, and illustrated with quotations from Latin, and from Shakespeare and Schiller, of both of whom he was very fond. However, he only read what interested him or what could be of use to him. He never, even as a rich man, collected a real library, and his houses were said to have been furnished without taste. German literature of his own age was a closed book to him, even when it again became well worth reading towards the end of the century. Being intelligent himself, he enjoyed the company of intelligent people – of Jewish journalists for example – but was forced by circumstances of class and occupation to associate mainly with people of limited horizon.

From the days of his youth he was conscious of a powerful ambition, and with it the ability to satisfy it, and he was only in his early thirties when politics became his dominating interest. Yet it would be wrong to say that it was his only interest because he was no fanatic, no ascetic. In spite of his public duties he always managed to enjoy family life. He had a happy relationship with his wife, although by all accounts Johanna von Bismarck had little distinction. Such private traits distinguish him from Napoleon, and also from Lenin, the other two political giants with whom he is sometimes compared. He also had a sense of humour and an ability to mock at himself. Although endowed with strong instincts he knew himself well and said that there were corners in his soul into which he had never allowed others to look.

Although as a young man he was attracted by the fashionable free-thinking of the age, shortly before his marriage he returned to the faith of his fathers. It was a natural, inborn faith, not that of a convert. He often read the Bible and in the great crises of his life carried edifying texts around with him, interpreting their exhortations to fit his situation. Much has been made of the contradiction between his Christian beliefs and his political practices, the lies, the cynical tricks, the wars for which he was responsible and the cruelty with which he put an end to many a career. He himself was aware of this contradiction without condemning it. In his view there was a difference between private and public behaviour; the craftsman's technique was prescribed by his material, and the politician who was responsible for the well-being of a state must not measure his actions by the yardstick of middle-class morality. Over this he parted from the conservative friends of his youth, Professor Stahl and the Gerlach brothers, who denied this difference and preached that political actions must be in accordance with Christian ethics. Yet Bismarck's policy had Lutheran roots which revealed themselves in his hard-heartedness and his respect for law, property, authority and for the God-given differences between occupations and classes, between poor and rich. Luther had demanded that authority should wield a sharp sword, and Bismarck in power followed him in recommending the retention of the death penalty. Even in his old age he remarked to his doctor that as a matter of principle there could be no extenuating circumstances in cases of murder, and that even children who had committed a murder must pay the supreme penalty. But when he approved of the execution of Robert Blum with the words: 'When I have an enemy in my power I must destroy him', he was speaking not as a Lutheran – because Blum was no malefactor – but as a merciless political enemy, a barbarian.

There was something of the barbarian in this man who was a great writer and the noble product of German and European civilization; a nervous barbarian whose massive frame and boldness did not protect him from fits of weeping. He suffered from ailments such as phlebitis, insomnia and nervous pain in the face during most of the time that he was politically active, and made a great deal of fuss about it. When he encountered opposition he suffered from cholecystitis, jaundice and convulsions. In his later years he described the visit of a leading liberal politician as follows: 'I reached such a state of nervous tension that I finally had to say to him, "Herrr ... spare me, I am ill." Then I was so annoyed that I could not sleep until seven o'clock in the morning, and I would have shot the man if he had crossed my threshold again ...' His hates were even stronger than his loves, and those whom he hated he wished to destroy; sometimes he did so in fact, probably more often in his imagination. If some photographs show him as a grave, imposing personality, there are others in which he looks very unpleasant. Experienced psychologists soon realized that he had an overwhelming thirst for power and would never be content to play second fiddle. Later he could not bear others around him to play any part, merely wanting reliable servants. He admitted himself that he never forgot insults; and in his own mind he was always being insulted and misunderstood, the victim of sinister intrigues. He himself was by no means above intrigue; he enjoyed deceiving and trapping his enemies as much as he did startling, confusing and frightening them with his brutal frankness. His own nobleman's honour was dear to him, unlike that of his partners and opponents, and the fascination of his letters is due partly to the witty but completely unjustified malice of his comments on people; even on the kings of Prussia whom he served, on Frederick William IV, then on Crown Prince Frederick and finally on William II. Only for his real 'master', William I, did he feel loyalty and affection – with a fair admixture of contempt. Throughout his public life he pursued the royal ladies with almost comic hatred, and never got over the fact that they had arts and opportunities of influencing which even the most powerful minister could not acquire. There was much hatred in Bismarck, much impatient, nervous superiority and little love; more love for nature, for animals and trees than for human beings. Nobody can answer the question which is nevertheless worth reflecting upon: to what extent his creations absorbed his characteristics.

This Junker was drawn towards political activity because he felt that he was the right man for it, and that thus he might achieve power and fame. He was drawn too, probably, because he knew that the privileges of his class were threatened and he had no faith in the ability of his uncouth fellow aristocrats to put up a successful defence. Soon his liking for country life became theory rather than reality because he enjoyed the political hustle and bustle of Berlin. In the United Diet of 1847 he was conspicuous for his audacity, wit and aggressiveness, preparing his speeches with ambitious care. As there was no abundance of such talents among the conservatives he soon became something like a parliamentary leader. He was a frequent visitor at Court and talked politics with the royal princes; convinced he knew how to treat the mob, he would have liked nothing better in March 1848 than to start a counter-revolutionary *coup*. Nothing came of this, but, even after the King had driven through the city wearing the revolutionary colours of national Germany, Bismarck did not give up the Prussian Junker cause. He denounced the Frankfurt Assembly and supported the rights of the landowners in articles in the *Kreuzzeitung*; he helped to found the Conservative Party and intrigued against the liberal governments of the year of revolution, with Frederick William IV's friends and those who had his ear. Bismarck was bold enough severely to reproach the King for his lack of firmness. This impressed Frederick William IV; an upright, intelligent but outspoken subject who merely went a little too far in his loyalty to his King appealed to the monarch's romantic taste. In 1849 we find Bismarck again as a member of the Diet, elected under the three-class franchise, and in 1850 in the assembly of the abortive Prussian 'Union' in Erfurt; he was ever provocative, relishing argument and expressing paradoxical right-wing views with sparkling brilliance. German union, with or without Austria, the principles of the Frankfurt imperial constitution, universal and equal suffrage, no one demolished these with such supreme assurance as the tall, young representative with the high-pitched voice and the goatee. When it became necessary to defend the Treaty of Olmütz, the abandonment of the 'Union', the conservatives put him forward as their strongest gun, and Bismarck-Schönhausen accomplished this delicate task with mastery. The Christian conservatives, the Gerlach brothers and Professor Stahl, regarded him as their man, their friend and pupil. He was not, however, completely their pupil because he was and considered himself superior to them; he was not completely their friend because he was never a loyal friend in politics. Had they paid more attention they would have noticed sooner that he did not completely share their views. They thought in terms of the old, universal order: Europe, Christianity, monarchy by the grace of God, the alliance of lawfully acting kings which, as Britain existed for itself alone and France was unfortunately in the throes of revolution, must remain limited to the pious rulers of eastern Europe, Russia, Austria and Prussia. That was their interpretation of the Treaty of Olmütz. Bismarck did not speak of Europe and Christianity, nor did he say that war between the conservative powers must be avoided at all costs. War was conceivable, but only if the stakes were worthwhile, not merely for a North German union. 'The only sound basis of a great state – and this distinguishes it intrinsically from a small state – is egoism, not romanticism; it is beneath the dignity of a great state to fight for a cause which lies outside its own interest.' That view had more in common with Machiavelli's ideas than those of Professor Stahl. In 1847, the very first year of his political career, Bismarck had announced: 'One only holds to principles as long as they are not put to the test; when that happens one throws them away, as the peasant throws away his slippers, and one goes barefoot...' From the start his direct intelligence despised doctrine and speechifying; he wanted to manipulate real power, which in the last resort was always the power to kill. He could certainly discuss, but mainly in order to make fun of discussion; hence the fury which he aroused at parliamentary gatherings while he had the vitality of youth and early manhood. In 1849 he wrote to his wife, 'The German question will not be decided in parliaments but in the sphere of diplomacy and in the field, and all that we say about it and decide has no more value than the romantic dreams of a sentimental youth who builds castles in the air and thinks that some unexpected event might make him into a great man . . .' In 1862, in his first week as Prime Minister, he expressed the same thought in words which achieved notoriety. A man's development is a curious thing. Bismarck was certainly capable of development; he changed his policy, his views and judgements over and over again, and at the age of seventy was an incomparably more mature, more moderate man than at fifty. But then again one finds Bismarck as a young man expressing ideas which he was still viciously repeating in old age.

The conservative romantics could easily have foreseen that such a man would desert them one day; he himself foresaw the eventuality as early as 1850.

Olmütz proved a stroke of good fortune for Bismarck personally. After Prussia had brought itself to recognize the resuscitated German Confederation he was appointed Minister to the Frankfurt parliament – an unheard-of occurrence in the Prussian civil service because he had no diplomatic experience whatsoever and had so far only made his mark as a parliamentarian. He remained in Frankfurt for eight years, enjoying his high salary, glamorous social life, travels, intrigues and the political game on and off stage. Soon he was a master of the new craft, towering above his partners by virtue of his understanding, wit, courage, willpower and unfailing presence of mind. Frankfurt was the post in which German conditions could be studied more thoroughly than anywhere else. Bismarck also visited the capitals of Europe – he had a passion for travelling by train, keeping a cigar alight throughout the journey. He managed to be on good terms with the various cliques of Prussian reaction without identifying himself with any one of them. He could have become Foreign Minister of Prussia even then, but did not wish to because he believed that he could not achieve anything great under Frederick William IV. He managed shrewdly to keep in close touch with the royal, bureaucratic centres of power without appearing responsible in the eyes of the outside world. Few people knew that he was one of the most influential men in the state; the public hardly knew him at all.

He still regarded himself as a Prussian and not as a German, and thought in terms of the state and not of the nation, particularly as there was no Prussian nation. It is difficult to see why the Rhinelanders who were Prussian subjects should have been closer to his heart than the natives of the Palatinate or of Baden. He certainly cared nothing for 'the people'. People and nation were one and the same, and a national state would sooner or later become a people's state, as the events of 1848 had demonstrated. He agreed with the concept of the state as an historic entity, as an organ of power, as a principle of order and authority, which in Prussia was exercised by his own social class. When he wrote 'we' he meant the power of Prussia, for which he was as ambitious as for himself. For Bismarck Europe was nothing but a collection of states, some independent, genuine expansionist centres of power, like Russia, France, Austria and Britain, while others, like Belgium or Bavaria, owed their existence to the European balance of power rather than to their own strength. No great power made a present of anything to any other or wished it really well; everybody wanted to take, nobody to give, Alliances were made for the sake of convenience and could not outlast their purpose, joint defence or joint plunder. His view of Prussia was that it was hampered by the German Confederation presided over by Austria and in which Austria, together with the *Mittelstaaten*, the smaller German states, could always outvote Prussia; counting votes produced a false picture of the distribution of power. Prussia, moreover, was handicapped by certain pious prejudices, transferred from domestic to foreign policy. There was the view that Prussia must not form an alliance with revolution, with the democratic Emperor Napoleon, that it owed loyalty to the House of Habsburg: this Bismarck denied. In Frankfurt he discovered that Austria was the power which caused Prussia the greatest difficulties, which restricted its activities and bore malice towards it, hypocritically using the machinery of the German Confederation for the purpose. For Bismarck one state was as good or as bad as another, and the legitimacy of Europe's ruling houses was in any case doubtful; Prussia could not pursue a strong policy if in order to please conservative whims it refused to believe that France could become an ally, at the same time declaring it impossible for Austria to be an enemy. Let domestic policy be controlled with an iron hand – in fact it needed to be, as a pre-condition of a successful foreign policy, something which 'parliamentary chatterboxes' could never pursue – but that had nothing to do with alliances. The moment might come when Prussia would make an alliance with France, just as there might come a time when it would be necessary to send Prussian armies across the Rhine. The German Confederation was a lie invented by Austria to vex Prussia, to give the galaxy of small German states an importance to which they were not entitled and to create advantages for the selfish power of Habsburg, advantages that were contrary to the rules of true power politics. If it was impossible to reform the Confederation so as to give both great powers the right of veto, it must be broken up. Anyway, if Prussia had a natural ally it was not Austria, still less southern Germany, but Russia. This was not so much because Russia was the most reactionary power, though this factor counted – the autocracy of St Petersburg gratified Bismarck – but mainly because divided and tortured Poland united the two states that profited from the partition. Never in any circumstances could Prussia tolerate a restoration of the Polish state, and Russia was in the same position.

This was the world, as the envoy Bismarck saw it; a world in which economic policy, particularly tariff policy, must serve diplomacy, a world of naked swords where to be of importance and to be feared were one and the same thing. It was not a middle-class world, not the world as the English Utilitarians, the French Positivists or the German liberals pictured it. It was not the world of the nineteenth century, of peace, science, industry and progress; much less was it the world of Karl Marx. In spite of his great intelligence Bismarck thought anachronistically, and it is rarely fortunate if anachronistic ideas triumph in reality. Yet one must not tie that great man down too precisely; he was ready to learn and to make alliances of convenience with new powers.

During the Crimean War he belonged to those who prevented a rapprochement between Prussia and the Western Powers, maintaining for the purpose a very close, almost treasonable, contact with the Russian diplomatic service. He denied energetically that Austria in the Balkans was defending German interests against Russia: 'The mouth of the Danube is of very little interest to Germany.' Prussia had no reason to help Austria 'to procure a few stinking Wallachians'. It must use Austria's difficulties to improve its own position in Germany. 'The great crises constitute the weather which encourages Prussia's growth, in that

they are fearlessly, perhaps even ruthlessly, exploited by us.'
What he began to understand as he travelled the length and
breadth of Germany was that in addition to such ruthless exploitation Prussia must sooner or later also support – in an alliance of
convenience – Germany's determination to become a nation. Not
that his heart was in the German cause. His Excellency did not
belong to the 'people', he found it annoying that 'the peoples'
should rebel and demand something they had not got. However,
they did rebel. Anyone with the slightest feeling for reality could
not have failed to realize that the unsolved problem of 1848 still
existed and would continue to exist and cried out for a solution.
But if it must be solved, could it not be solved in such a way that
Prussia's ruling class would continue to enjoy life, and that the
Prussian state would be the winner and Austria the loser? Did
common sense not demand that the wild horse should be caught,
tamed and harnessed to one's own chariot? In 1859 Bismarck said
to a liberal politician and industrialist: 'The only reliable, lasting
ally which Prussia can have, if it behaves in the right way, is – the
German people. Don't worry,' he added when the other looked
wide-eyed at the notorious reactionary, 'I am the same Junker as
ten years ago when we first met in the Chamber but I would need
to be blind and brainless not to see what the situation really is.'
Nationalism could become Prussia's ally just as well as Napoleon
III; in the end it might even be possible to detach it from its
sister movement, liberalism.

The regency of the Prince of Prussia was a blow for Bismarck
because he had been a favourite of the now insane King and had
the reputation of being a fanatical reactionary who could not
represent Prussia's new liberal policy in Frankfurt. He was transferred to St Petersburg, honourably sacked so to speak. 'He is
politics personified,' wrote his Secretary of Legation there, Kurd
von Schlözer, 'everything in him is in ferment, wants to be active
and creative. He seeks to control the political situation, to master
the chaos in Berlin, but how he does not yet know.' A little later:
'He tells me a lot, he is marvellously frank, interesting, erratic,
revolutionary, throws all theory to the winds. And that man is in
the *Wilhelmstrasse* – My God!' During the war between Austria

and France Bismarck suggested pulling up the Prussian frontier posts in central Germany and re-erecting them on the Bodensee or wherever Protestant Germany ended; if Prussia were then made into the Kingdom of Germany the population would be delighted. To King William he expressed himself more moderately, though in the same vein, arguing that Prussia must have an independent German policy, that the Confederation was in need of reform and that Prussia should propose that the nation as a whole was represented at the Federal Diet. The King could not bring himself to agree to such an experiment, particularly as he had a low opinion of Bismarck, whom he regarded as an unpredictable and eccentric fanatic.

If Bismarck was nevertheless recalled to Berlin – his last mission was in Paris – if he offered himself to the King and was appointed Prime Minister, it was not because of his new German policy for Prussia, but because of the insoluble conflict between the Crown and the chamber. Bismarck had followed the clash with great enjoyment from afar, convinced that he was the person to master it and he had corresponded busily on that score with his friend Roon, the Minister of War. Above all he needed to wait for the right moment.

The longer the affair goes on the more the Chamber sinks in public esteem . . . When it grows weary, feels that the country is bored and longs for concessions from the government to save it from the awkward situation in which it finds itself then, I think, the moment will have come to show by my appointment that, far from abandoning the struggle, the government is resuming it with new vigour. To show a new regiment in the ranks of the ministerial battle-order at that moment might make an impression which would not be achieved now; particularly if there has been threatening talk of seizing power. My old reputation for irresponsible violence will help, and people will think it's starting. Then all those middle-of-the-road and half-hearted characters will be ready to negotiate . . .

Roon called him to Berlin at exactly the right moment. He was received in audience, found the King in real despair, offered to lead the fight against parliament to the bitter end and was appointed, as he said, 'not as a constitutional minister in the usual sense of the word but as the servant of Your Majesty'. William disliked this wild and witty man and accepted him not as the experienced diplomat who had formed his own conclusions about the European situation, but in despair, because there seemed no alternative to the 'mad Bismarck', the notoriously reactionary Junker, as he had shown himself in 1849. It was the King's last attempt to teach the democrats manners, and Bismarck's appointment was interpreted by the public in that sense. Foreign observers did not believe that his government would last long. A Swiss paper commented: 'These Junkers would like to have a try, but whether they have any ability remains to be seen. There is no need to fear that fattened geese will soar like eagles.'

2. Bismarck, the Progress Party, Lassalle

The second half of the nineteenth century was a remarkably law-abiding and moderate period in Europe: many things which at the time seemed outrageous, appear harmless seen from a more brutal age; among these is the Prussian constitutional conflict. It suited Bismarck because it made him indispensable, and because he greatly enjoyed battling with and making fun of tame members of parliament acting the part of tribunes of the people. It did not suit him because he knew that it was impossible in the long run to govern without at least the semblance of a constitution. The Junker had come to know the bourgeois and the financial world well enough to be aware of this. Did not even his friend and in some respects his teacher, the Emperor Napoleon, rule with the help of a sham parliament? German policy, as Bismarck envisaged it, demanded that Prussia should set an example of legal, progressive behaviour. He would have welcomed a compromise under which the military monarchy was given the kernel while the middle classes accepted the shell, thus providing the semblance of constitutional legality. At first, therefore, he adopted an obliging attitude and let it be known that he had great plans for Germany, which required the new, stronger army; he implied that he did not take the whole affair very tragically. But when the Progress Party pressed the legal aspect of the problem he became less conciliatory. The constitution, he argued, was not a dead piece of machinery built for all eternity, but a living thing; what precisely it was remained to be seen, but all constitutional life was compromise.

If the compromise is defeated because one of the forces involved wants to put into practice its own intentions with the use of doctrinaire absolutism the chain of compromise will be broken and replaced by conflict; as political life cannot stand still, conflicts become issues of power and then those who have the power act as they wish . . .

This is what Bismarck did to the best of his ability. For him the constitution was so 'alive', so vague, that he not only governed without a budget but also violated paragraphs that had nothing to do with the conflict. The press was not allowed to criticize the government in any way; if civil servants expressed political views they were liable to be dismissed, and the power of the state was used against public opinion. On one side there was the state, the army and an obedient bureaucracy, and on the other the overwhelming majority of the electorate. If the electors or their representatives had been prepared to act on their beliefs they would have been stronger than the state. But if they had ever felt deeply about anything, they had ceased to do so after 1848. They stood on their rights in addresses, petitions and eloquent protests but avoided everything that might have seemed in the least like illegal action, pressure or threats on their part. They did not want to, they could not, mobilize democracy against absolutism. After all, they had themselves been elected under the three-class system, the earliest contravention of the constitution. But this contravention which almost disfranchised the masses, pleased them, and this original sin paralysed their opposition. Speeches were made in the chamber attacking Bismarck's lawless regime, speeches glowing with moral indignation, loyalty to the constitution and to the idea of the constitutional state; but speeches were the very thing that did not impress Bismarck. The machinery of government was solidly constructed and served the man who operated its central lever, regardless of the fulminations of liberal professors and industrialists in parliament.

There was one man who thought that he knew how to curb the power of the state: Ferdinand Lassalle. These were his last and greatest years. His ideas, speeches and actions are worth relating less because of what he achieved – because for the moment he achieved very little, though here we find at any rate an historic source of German socialism – but because they illuminate the whole critical development of the German Europe of this period as only those of a genius can.

Lassalle advised the Progress Party to call a political general strike. If parliament refused to sit as long as the government ruled in contravention of the constitution its action would reveal the true state of affairs and show up the constitution as the make-believe it was. Then right would no longer fight an unequal battle against might, but might would face might. The power of the middle classes, which on this issue had the support of the whole people, would prove superior to that of the old state. Real victory would lead to a genuine constitution, the foundation of which must be universal and equal suffrage. Did not Bismarck himself see the issue as a struggle for power? Was it a crime to fight the government with its own ideas and weapons?

The liberals' reply was that they had no intention of taking such a blackmailing line, that they were law-abiding citizens, not revolutionaries, and that a policy whose logical conclusion was revolution could merely help the reactionaries. Lassalle seemed to them a pupil of Bismarck, or else Bismarck a pupil of Lassalle. In fact Lassalle's definition of constitutional issues as issues of power quickly got about, and both Bismarck and Roon used similar expressions in parliament

Thereupon Lassalle broke with the Progress Party. Marx's able pupil had long regarded the industrial working class as the class of the future, the truly democratic class which represented the whole people. Now he decided that this class must have a party, an organized force distinct from the liberal middle class, because the middle class had betrayed its historic task. By accepting the *coup* of 1848 and the three-class franchise of 1849 the liberals had

˙bartered legality for a slice of power. And because they abandoned legality the power which they wanted in exchange naturally – as was right – only backfired on them. Legality is wholly with democracy, and democracy alone will have power.'

This was the age of national associations. The Italian National Union had successfully contributed to the creation of the new kingdom. Under its influence the German *Nationalverein* had come into being, and also, in opposition, the *Reformverein* which wanted a reform of the German Confederation, but one under which Austria would remain part of the Confederation. Could the German workers not also organize themselves into a union which, even if it had only 100,000 members, would become a great power in the state, more than a match for tame middle-class orators? Lassalle believed that they could. Asked for advice by certain Saxon radicals connected with the Leipzig workers' educational union, Lassalle said that he was the right man to ˙take over the leadership of the workers' movement'. This was his programme: the workers must obtain universal and equal suffrage by means of powerful but lawful agitation. They were the overwhelming majority of the people, and people and state must become one. Once the state had been conquered by means of the ballot paper it must do what only the state can do: it must raise the exploited, overworked and underpaid industrial working class to the level of free human beings; that is, it must fulfil the great economic and political task, the human task, of the age. How could it do that? By setting up vast 'Production Associations' of factories owned by the workers themselves, for which the state must provide the initial credit. To begin with about one hundred million thalers – less than the cost of the most paltry war, but still so much that only the state could give it. Without the state, and consequently without its political conquest by the workers, nothing could be done. There was nothing wrong with Professor Schulze-Delitzsh's self-supporting purchasing and consumer co-operatives and sick benefit schemes, except that those who benefited from them were mainly the small tradesmen, not the industrial workers. They ran counter to the trend of the age, which was towards large-scale industry and not small craftsmen's enterprises.

Let them continue to exist, those well-meant shopkeepers' institutions, but let them not claim to be solving the problem of industrial labour. Nor could the middle classes tackle the immediate task of breaking the Prussian military state because capitalism flourished under its protection, and because the middle classes were economically satisfied, though politically disgruntled. Satisfied men never risked their lives in conflicts; they only hoped against hope that the Junkers might perhaps make them a few measly concessions if only they behaved properly. The only class which could mean business, whose economic interests coincided with its political interests, was the working class. On it depended the future, the hope of humanity. Those who were now at the bottom would come to the top, a community of free producers in a free, strong German state.

Such was Lassalle's programme. It has been pointed out that parts of it were not original. Most of his ideas came from Marx: the class struggle, the relationship between economics and politics, the concept of the working class as the universal class which, after its liberation, will no longer be a class but the free people. Some of his ideas, such as the iron law of wages, came from the English economists, others from the pre-Marxist socialists, from the German political philosophers, from Fichte and Hegel. What was original about Lassalle was the man himself, the politician, what he made of the ideas, the clever and bold way in which he developed his objectives in court – he was for ever being tried for something or other – in pamphlets, in lectures to workers' meetings in Berlin, Leipzig, Frankfurt or Düsseldorf. He always remained the elegant, pampered scholar who never attempted to ingratiate himself artificially with ordinary folk, but who spoke to them as though they were his intellectual equals and who won them precisely by that method. When in May 1863 he founded the General German Workers' Association and allowed himself to be persuaded, apparently reluctantly, into accepting the dictator-like position of president (devised in fact by himself), he was breaking new ground. Let Karl Marx in London speak with disapproval and even disgust of the activities of his former pupil, Lassalle had created something which the bookish scholar, towering far above him intellectually, had so far been unable to achieve in his British Museum. For a short time Lassalle's name was on everyone's lips.

The Progress Party found his agitation embarrassing because it wanted to stand for the whole people against the wicked Bismarck. Now here there was someone who presumed to separate the workers – at the best of times a dangerous lot – from their natural leaders, the bourgeoisie, without whom they were capable of perpetrating all sorts of mischief. So the party made every effort to keep the support of the working class. Lassalle triumphed wherever he appeared personally, but failed to win over the majority of the workers' unions. They remained loyal, as became clear at a big union meeting in Frankfurt in the early summer of 1863, to the alliance with the liberal bourgeoisie – a line which had the approval not only of the older generation but also of such young and temperamental members as the master-turner, August Bebel, from Leipzig. Were the day to come for this alliance to break up and class parties to replace the one great democratic party, the fault would lie not with the workers but with the bourgeoisie. Meanwhile the Progress Party refused to incorporate in its programme even so elementary a demand as universal suffrage.

'That man works for Bismarck,' was Marx's comment on Lassalle as an agitator. It is a truism that to have enemies in common creates a bond, however unreliable. The socialist and the feudal minister were both fighting the liberal bourgeoisie. It was indeed noticeable that Lassalle treated Bismarck with consideration, as an enemy who must be respected. 'Though we might exchange shots with Herr von Bismarck, justice would demand that we admitted even during the salvoes that he is a man, whereas the others (the Progressives) are old women.' There is no doubt that the police reported such remarks to their overlord and that Bismarck took a liking to the spirited young demagogue who gave shorter shrift to the liberals than he himself could afford to. His enterprising spirit was always on the look-out for new combinations. When the alliance with the liberals, of which he had dreamt for a time, miscarried owing to the constitutional conflict, he thought of forming an alliance with the force which had begun to emerge to the left of the liberals and – what did left and right matter – which was probably more royalist at heart than the clever-clever middle class. It is not quite certain when Bismarck and Lassalle first met, at whose initiative and how often; probably it was in the late autumn of 1863. Bebel claims that they met four times a week in the course of the next six months, whereas Bismarck says that there were four meetings altogether; the truth probably lies somewhere in between. Many years later during the Chancellor's campaign against social democracy he was forced in the Reichstag to speak of his relationship with Lassalle. He extricated himself by denying the political nature of the discussions – the poor chap had practically nothing behind him, he said – but at the same time made what was almost a declaration of love for Lassalle as a human being.

> He had something which greatly attracted me as a private person: he was one of the most intelligent and charming people with whom I have come in contact, a man who was ambitious in a big way. Lassalle was an energetic and highly intelligent person and to talk to him was very instructive; our discussions lasted for hours and I was always sorry when they were over. I regret that our political positions did not allow more extended intercourse. I would have been glad to have a man of such talents and intellect as my neighbour in the country . . .

Their curious relationship was certainly not quite so innocent as Bismarck's words suggest. In 1863 he was a public figure who had no time to amuse himself, and whatever he did, said or listened to had a purpose. Perhaps he wanted to attract Lassalle into his service, as he later tried to draw even Marx. Certainly universal suffrage was mentioned, the great venture that both politicians were thinking about at the time, although they expected very different things from it. They must also have spoken of the possibility of electoral alliances between the conservatives and the socialists, of workers' production associations and of a royal dictatorship for the benefit of the masses. The workers, said Lassalle, had a natural liking for dictatorship if it were one that did something for them and the whole community. This view appealed to the struggling semi-dictator who had to waste his energy in speeches to the liberal *Kammerschwätzer*, the parliamentary gas-bags.

Nothing or almost nothing came of all this. Although Bismarck wrote 'the state can do it' when his assistants warned him that it was inadvisable to help the suffering Silesian weavers, his state could not do much. Basically it was more liberal, bourgeois and capitalist than Bismarck appreciated. His attempts to set up production associations in Silesia, as envisaged by Lassalle, met with strong resistance, and in the end he made little effort to overcome it. His experiments were nothing like on the scale dreamt of by Lassalle. Soon Bismarck became involved in foreign policy, which absorbed all his energy. His successes in that sphere enabled him to reach a compromise with the liberals which, however half-hearted, remained for a long time the basis of his policy.

Lassalle did not witness this. In August 1864 he was mortally wounded near Geneva in a duel over a question of honour and a woman. At the time his workers' union, with only a few thousand members, was not what its sanguine founder had hoped for. But a beginning had been made and, in contrast to the world-wide ambitions of the two fathers of the revolution in England, a practical limited beginning appropriate to conditions in Germany. Marx later more or less admitted this, judging the dead man more leniently than the living one. Strange is his remark from the year 1866: 'What a loss for Lassalle that he is stone-dead. He would have been just the man for Bismarck now.'

We do not know what role Lassalle would have played in Bismarck's Germany. He might have been the man to push a great socialist party into the state, to transform Bismarck's false compromise with democracy into a genuine one. It is unthinkable that he would have sacrificed the cause for his own career like another friend of Marx, Johannes Miquel, who said farewell to socialism in order to become a great man in the national state. Lassalle was made of different stuff from the ex-communist climbers who were prepared to serve under Bismarck. He was incapable of serving at all, he was intelligent, ambitious and generous. So it is likely that he would have done more to annoy Bismarck than to please him after the founder of the Reich had made his pact with the capitalist bourgeoisie. But this is mere speculation; what remained was the memory of a political genius

whose star shone briefly over northern Germany, only to disappear again like a meteor; and the like of which was never seen
there again.

3. Crisis Diplomacy

The suppressed revolution of 1848 continued to make Germany
and Europe uncomfortable. Nothing had been solved, but to
suppress a question does not mean its removal. What was not
done at one blow in 1848 was done piecemeal in the fifties and
sixties, though not so as to promote international understanding
as the men of 1848 had imagined.

The social and constitutional problem of France remained in
the balance under the dictatorship of Napoleon III. This worked
for a while and some social classes did not fare badly in the process, although politically the country was stagnating; it passed
through a period of police-controlled holiday from politics. But
the end of the holiday was clearly approaching, the time when
men must again concern themselves with their real conflicts and
responsibilities.

Italy, which in 1848 had not been allowed to become a national
state, became one nevertheless twelve years later, though no
longer in fulfilment of Mazzini's noble democratic aims. What the
revolutionary spirit had failed to achieve was now accomplished
by calculating *raison d'état* and guns. What emerged was a new
great power, or would-be great power, not an enthusiastic ally in
the struggle for human freedom. Venice was still under Austrian,
Rome under Papal rule; these relics of an antiquated legal order
also needed to be absorbed by the new nation-state. But who does
voluntarily what he can be forced to do? Francis Joseph clung
to Venice and Pius IX to the remains of his moribund church state.

Austria's order in the fifties rested on suppressed revolution. Its
three capitals, Prague, Vienna and Budapest, had after all been
conquered one after another by the Emperor's armies. The young

Francis Joseph occupied his own states like a conqueror. This may not have seemed very strange to him because he thought in the old tradition of ruler and ruled, and the provinces which he kept, reluctantly abandoned or was perhaps prepared to exchange, belonged to him or to his dynasty. But the ideas of the age were different. In 1848 this difference of attitude had led to wars and civil wars in the Habsburg Empire, and although they had all been won by the Emperor the conflict remained unresolved. Nor could Prince Schwarzenberg's enlightened rule by the sword make the empire of many peoples into a real unitary state. The sick man was not cured, he was merely firmly bandaged, and the old pains started up again as soon as the weather changed. It is unnecessary for our purposes to list the various constitutional experiments in which Francis Joseph sought the solution, only to abandon them again a few years later. If, like his ancestors, he had been master of the situation, he would have tried nothing and left well alone. Financial difficulties, middle-class unrest, Hungarian obstinacy and finally the external defeat of 1859 started the ball rolling again in Austria. In February 1861 Francis Joseph experimented with liberalism, unfortunately still in fashion. There was to be a parliament with two chambers, and a *Reichsrat* to be elected by the diets of the individual 'kingdoms and provinces', though in a way which cleverly managed to leave the leadership or majority with the Germans. The fiction of the unitary state and of the predominantly German state – the 'February Patent' knew nothing of nationalities – was maintained, and added to it there was now the fiction of the liberal state. There were several intentions behind this, one being to prepare Austria for the final struggle in Germany. A liberal Austria had better chances than a despotic one, particularly at a moment when the Prussian Prime Minister seemed to be trying to make his state hated among German liberals.

In Germany too the groupings and countergroupings were the familiar ones: *grossdeutsch* and *kleindeutsch*, liberal and democrats, reform of the Confederation or abolition of the Confederation. Even Schleswig-Holstein suddenly returned to the forefront of national interest in the autumn of 1863. A question which has been shirked sometimes ceases slowly to be topical and disappears. But this does not happen often. Usually neglected problems reappear and plague the experts until they have been solved reasonably satisfactorily.

Just as the revolution of 1848 took twenty years to complete piecemeal, so the European war which threatened in 1848 was fought piecemeal for decades. Each power was against every other power, and therefore also against those with whom it made common cause in order to overcome a third; at the same time it busily considered what joint interests linked it, or would shortly link it, with that third power. The Crimean War did not become a general European war because the German powers refused to take part. The subsequent wars were duels between two, or two and a half powers around which the others formed a ring of neutral spectators, short operations quickly broken off: between France and Austria in 1859, between Prussia and Austria in 1866. In each case what was at stake was something left over from 1848 – Russia's reactionary hegemony which had proved unbearable in 1849 and was broken in 1854–6, Austria's antiquated position in Italy, Schleswig-Holstein, and the political shape of Germany. The war of 1870 is an exception; it was fought not over any issue of 1848 but over nothing at all. Such duels between pairs of European powers ending in quick, moderate peace treaties, and even perhaps in diplomatic collaboration between yesterday's enemies, seem strange to us: the states of Europe are no longer such absolute, independent entities that a 'localized' conflict between two of them would be possible. In the sixteenth, seventeenth and eighteenth centuries, too, every war between two of the greater powers became a general war or a war between coalitions. In Europe's diplomatic history the twenty years from 1850 to 1870 are unique. Technically speaking the fact that the general balance of power never seemed threatened may explain the localization of the wars of that period. The question of who would win was of interest but not of vital importance to the neutral powers, while at the same time the very existence of powerful neutrals was a guarantee that the peace treaty would be moderate. No victor could permit himself shameless demands; usually he was forced to grasp at modest gains because a new storm was already threatening from another direction. In localized wars the rules of the game are more faithfully observed than in wars in which there are no neutral spectators or umpires.

Never indeed, in modern times, has war been so light-heartedly discussed and planned as in these years. Monarchs and leading diplomats were for ever discussing whether the situation in Italy or in Germany was 'hotting up', whether they should intervene and change the political map a little. Far more ideas and tentative suggestions were put forward than were actually translated into actions – the partition of Austria, or Turkey, the restoration of Poland, the abolition of Belgium. In the end the Europe of 1871 was more like that of 1814 than that of the vision of Napoleon III or even of Bismarck.

By far the most serious war of the period was the American Civil War. It was not a war between two states one of which might have been prepared to reconcile itself to the existence of the other, and in North America there were no neutrals to mediate. Yet this war was fought over much the same issue as a European war of the same period: new, strengthened national unity controlled by one single region. The United States abolished slavery at the same time as Russia did away with serfdom. This was also the period in which the Japanese opened their empire to the world and began its modernization. All these developments, conflicts and reforms are historically related; they were part of a process by which the world freed itself from outdated differences and restrictions, and prepared for the great tasks of the twentieth century.

4. Bismarck's Wars

From the beginning Bismarck regarded himself – rightly – as far superior to those with whom he dealt as friend or enemy: this was not saying much. Diplomats are seldom men of great intellectual stature; scientists think more deeply and artists more creatively than politicians. Napoleon III, who had reached the throne of France thanks to blind faith in his own star, to luck, fraud and audacity, was a man of only moderate talents. Had he been strong enough to remain completely faithful to his most useful ideas Europe's subsequent fate might well have been more fortunate. But people who find themselves in a completely false position seldom achieve great things. Louis Napoleon's *idée fixe* was the rearrangement of Europe into national states. In his most lucid moments he said that it was more important to find a generous solution than to make petty territorial gains; France had nothing to fear from free contented sister nations of Germans or Italians; only in universal freedom could western Europe act as a counter-weight to the powers of the future, Russia and North America. Good sense and golden words; but the dictator was weak and a prisoner of the old sins on which his dictatorship was founded. His foolhardy advisers whispered about prestige, about France's natural frontiers, about the rewards of mediation, about gains and triumphs. Napoleon, a dreamer by temperament, listened to them; he tried first this and then that, ensnared by contradictions which were his undoing but served Bismarck well.

Francis Joseph of Austria, who from long and bitter experience was to acquire a certain wisdom in old age, was a stubborn and limited man. He was unable to give up anything unless forced to do so by defeat. His representatives and advisers were average men, though the Empire which they had to represent abroad was far from average in the threats which it faced and its mounting domestic dilemmas. It was not very difficult to get round such an Empire diplomatically.

After the Crimean War Russia scarcely counted. Moreover, St Petersburg was well-disposed towards Prussia, particularly now that the Balkan conflict between Austria and Russia had begun, a conflict not to end until both Empires fell.

Britain could be disregarded as long as what it considered Europe's equilibrium did not appear threatened. Britain regarded Russia as its enemy number one and France as potential enemy number two. It welcomed the prospect of a strong central

Europe between the two restless powers in the East and the West and welcomed also the thought of liberal, Protestant Prussia uniting Germany rather than reactionary anti-nationalist Austria.

In short, the legend of a good Germany surrounded by envious great powers determined to prevent its unification, and of Bismarck with his magic wand barely restraining the wild beasts while accomplishing his task, is a legend indeed. It grew up later, in an age when Germany began to make its neighbours uneasy. That was the case in 1900 but not in 1865. If the old powers had foreseen how Germany would develop they might – perhaps – have tried to prevent its unification. But scarcely anything is foreseen in politics, which are concerned with the practical cares of the present, not with uncertain visions of the future. In the nineteenth century there was much talk of a Russian danger, of a French one, of a revolutionary one, but never of a German one.

The most stubborn opposition came not from outside but from within. Austria could not want the German nation-state, not even in the 'greater' German form which it avowedly found acceptable. Prussia had not hitherto wanted it either in the 'greater' or in the 'little' German form, and only a few Prussian politicians had recently begun to believe that the second alternative was unavoidable in the end. One of these was Prime Minister von Bismarck, who nevertheless continued to harbour the old reservations. His great achievement was not that he created German unity; that had been longed for and talked about for fifty years. What makes his achievement so very clever, daring and unnatural is the fact that he brought about German unity without the elements associated with it for fifty years: parliamentary rule, democracy and demagogy. What for half a century had been the dream of the middle classes was now achieved without, and at times in spite of, the middle classes. In the end the German Reich was proclaimed among princes and generals, at an army camp, where a middle-class deputation looked drab and timid.

Bismarck's nature had many facets. Where the forces of history were concerned he was a very modest man. He often said that the individual could do little, that one must wait until things happened and that they always happened very differently from the way one had imagined. But then again he was impatient, arrogant and inclined to bluff, both at the time and retrospectively. In his memoirs, speeches and conversations he later liked to arrange things as though he had planned and foreseen everything, whereas in fact he seized opportunities as they came. What one man does in politics depends on what another does, as in chess, with the difference that in politics there are a great many players. At the most a player can plan a few moves while another plays. When Bismarck became a minister he probably wanted roughly the following: that Prussia should remain Prussia and become more powerful, and that his class should rule in Prussia as before. A necessary minimum of concessions should be made to the middle classes, provided this could be done by a compromise acceptable to the ruling class. Let Germany be divided between Austria and Prussia if possible – if not there were other possibilities. Bismarck saw the possible when it appeared and rejected the impossible. He was capable of lying in the execution of his duties, but not of hoodwinking himself with doctrines. He called a spade a spade, seriously, wittily, or brutally, depending on the situation, and internationally he was ready to understand the interest of the other side and to propose realistic barter. If that failed and if the issue was of vital importance to Prussia, well, then it must be decided by force of arms. There was no third possibility. Bismarck's genius consisted of sound common sense, courage and ruthlessness; in addition he worked harder at politics than most people. If all but one player play a half-hearted game, the one who takes his game seriously is likely to win.

Let us deal briefly with what is usually discussed at length, the origins and results of Bismarck's wars.

The story begins with the troublesome Schleswig-Holstein affair. In 1852 the Europeans powers had recognized the Danish heir to the throne as the future monarch of the two duchies, and Denmark in return promised to keep the German provinces, with their own constitution, separate from the main state. Under the new King, Copenhagen made the mistake of disregarding this commitment and of absorbing Schleswig into Denmark. The same had happened once before, in 1848, and the effect on Germany was the same. German national feeling, recently reinforced as it had been, was aroused by the injustice done to Schleswig. There was a north German dynast who, according to learned lawyers, had a better hereditary claim to Schleswig-Holstein than the King of Denmark. This was Prince Augustenburg, who became the symbol of German right in the northern controversy. The London Protocol, a work of the period of reaction, must be invalidated, Schleswig-Holstein must be wrested from the Danes and brought home to Germany. Such was the demand of the liberals, of the *Nationalverein*, even of the majority of the states represented in the German Confederation, which decided on federal action against Denmark.

A new German Grand Duchy, founded in a moment of democratic chauvinism, was not what Bismarck wanted. He adopted an icy attitude towards the national ardour, and this behaviour was sincere; the Germans' excitement did not appeal to him. He was less sincere, however, in claiming that he was only trying to maintain the London Protocol, that it was not a matter of giving way to German demagogy but of defending the law of Europe. If the Danes were prepared to abide again by the law that would be the end of the matter for Prussia. The Danes were not prepared to do so, fortunately for Bismarck, who had secretly made up his mind that Schleswig-Holstein must be annexed, not by liberal Germany but by Prussia. This could not be done in collaboration with the despised Confederation. Yet the first decisive steps towards this end could, indeed must, be taken in collaboration with the other great German power. Bismarck succeeded in detaching Austria from its natural base in Germany, from the Confederation and the smaller states, a manoeuvre for which he used more charm and wit and secretiveness than on any other occasion in his eventful life. The Austrian politicians, clumsy, honest, commonplace men, fell into the trap. It was not the Confederation that went to war against Denmark in the spring of 1864 but the two conservative powers, Prussia and Austria, on their own; the final solution of the question of what should be done with the duchies was left for later discussion. Of course Denmark was no match for the Austro-Prussian armies. By the Treaty of Vienna it was made to renounce forever the age-old connection of the island kingdom with the northern peninsula. This was a success achieved by the statesmanship of a minister against the will of the nation, against the Prussian chamber, which had not wanted that kind of war against Denmark and with troops for which the chamber had refused to pay. (Bismarck had said: 'If it becomes necessary to go to war we shall do so, with or without your approval.') Success confuses and wins men's hearts. Perhaps Bismarck was on the right road after all? Most liberals refused to believe it, refused to be deceived by the victory, and the constitutional conflict continued. The Prime Minister did not mind because on the crisis depended his indispensability, his influence over the King whom he would soon badly need.

It would be wrong to say that Bismarck had decided on the Austrian war before the end of the Danish one. Even Napoleon was never certain that he wanted war before it was a reality. Other factors can always intervene and Bismarck, unlike Napoleon, was never master in his own house. Although he could disregard the *Landtag* there was the Conservative Party, the Court and army cliques and the King himself, an obstinate, timid old man, for legality, provided it did not cost too much; all of these Bismarck under tremendous mental strain was forced to carry along with him, and to convince anew at every single step. It is certain that he made a fool of Austria over the Schleswig-Holstein affair and that he wanted to annex both provinces to Prussia. It is also certain that for ten years he had thought of war against Austria, which was the logical result of his policy.

I have no doubt [wrote the Bavarian Prime Minister, von der Pfordten, as early as 1862] that Bismarck desires the dissolution of the German Confederation, the separation of Germany from Austria and the subjection of the German states to Prussia . . . I believe that he is not scrupulous in his choice of means for this end, and that he will not fear a little revolution at home combined with help from outside.

An ally who always took from his partner and made demands on him without offering anything in return, moved towards war, particularly if it was in the nature of his partner to be opposed to even the fairest concessions. But Bismarck, gambler that he was then, toyed to the end with other, daring possibilities.

What gradually emerged was that he was unwilling to let the duped Augustenburg have the liberated or conquered duchies, even under conditions which would have made the Duke into a Prussian governor rather than a sovereign. What also emerged was that the joint administration of the northern provinces by Austria and Prussia was a vexatious illusion. Finally it was agreed that Prussia should administer Schleswig and Austria Holstein. But that arrangement did not solve the question of what Austria was doing in that part of the country anyway, nor did it change Bismarck's intention of swallowing both duchies. Reading about these intrigues today one is continually amazed at how easily the Austrians and the French allowed themselves to be deceived by Bismarck. 'The world wants to be deceived,' says a Latin proverb, and Bismarck never tried more resolutely to gratify that desire than between the years 1864 and 1866. He was then around fifty, in his prime as it is called.

Prussia's war against Austrian Germany was not a war over the northern loot. It was a war to decide who should rule Germany, a struggle postponed rather than produced by the joint venture against Denmark; the quarrel over the loot became an additional reason to go to war. Without other problems the two powers could have come to an agreement about the northern duchies; Vienna was well aware of the fact that the duchies bordered on Prussia but were, by the standards of the age, a long way from Austria. The two powers failed to reach agreement over Schleswig-Holstein because they could not agree over Germany; and that they had been unable to do even before the Danish war. Austria, at the end of its patience, provoked, tormented and tricked, finally broke the partition agreement and appealed to the German Confederation to settle the northern question, since the Confederation had committed itself, to its cost, to let the conflict be a matter for the two great powers alone.

The question of reforming the Confederation never ceased to be discussed during those years. Nobody denied that it was overdue, although governments were not anxious to broach the matter, it was kept very much alive by a number of associations and congresses, the *Nationalverein* and the *Reformverein*, by meetings of members of various German parliaments, in fact by public opinion. The quarrel between Austria and Prussia spurred both to make offers to Germany. In the autumn of 1863 Francis Joseph convened a congress of German princes in Frankfurt at which he submitted an ingenious, basically unworkable plan for reform. Bismarck succeeded in preventing his King from attending the congress, which was therefore a failure. He did not want any reform of the Confederation, he only wanted its dissolution and replacement by something different: Austria's renunciation of its position in 'little' Germany and Prussian supremacy. This, however, he had realized as he was amusing himself with his personal war with the Prussian liberals, could only be achieved by an alliance between Prussia and German liberalism and nationalism. Prussia would be strong enough to survive this alliance. What he had therefore proposed as early as 1863, and suggested again in the spring of 1866 in answer to Austria's stratagems, was the establishment in Frankfurt of a German parliament elected by universal suffrage either within the chamber of the Confederation or in addition to it. The proposal produced a considerable commotion. How could the man who for three years had ruled Prussia in defiance of the constitution, and who for twenty years had expressed nothing but scorn and contempt for the principle of parliamentary government now appeal to free representatives of the nation? A Berlin satirical paper announced that it intended to cease publication as it could not make better jokes than Herr von Bismarck. To some extent Bismarck was motivated by demagogic considerations and a desire to outdo the feeble Austrian efforts, but only to some extent. He believed that universal suffrage would have a conservative effect, wherein he was wrong in the long run. He also felt that the bull must be taken by the horns, that the struggle for power could not be won against the main trends of the age, nationalism and democracy. They could be exploited, controlled and deceived, but no longer suppressed. Bismarck saw this; the worthy noblemen in Vienna did not.

The German question and the Schleswig-Holstein affair brought Austria and Prussia closer and closer to the point where, according to good old custom, the decision was left to the God of War. Bismarck drove the heavy, creaking rattletrap of the Prussian state nearer and nearer to this point, convinced that without war his aim could not be reached nor his position maintained. He was then hated so much in Prussia that when he was shot at and slightly wounded by a young fanatic the citizens of Berlin openly expressed their regret at the failure of the attempt.

What tipped the scales was international diplomacy. The Italian leaders still cast longing glances at Venetia, the province which was outside the new kingdom. Napoleon III still brooded over the map, devising changes, gains and fulfilments. The French Emperor put his faith in national states like Italy and Germany, not in Austria. He also saw that Prussia was the state to 'make' Germany and that it was more in France's interest to support this inevitable development than to oppose it. If only the French, on whose approbation the weak Emperor increasingly depended, could be made to see the matter in the same light. If only somehow, somewhere, in the great transformation a small gain could be obtained for France. Well, if the war lasted a long time, if the decision remained in balance, Paris might play the role of arbiter and the arbiter might be able to profit. Hesitatingly, Napoleon arranged the alliance between Italy and Prussia, uncertain whether he was doing the right thing, whether it might not be better to regard Prussia as the enemy and to mediate between Austria and Italy. All statesmen were unsure and greedy, yet frightened and vague about their aims, all except one. It was Bismarck's boast that he had brought the most conservative of kings to the point of making the cause of German nationalism his own, of concluding an alliance with revolutionary Italy and of accepting collaboration with Bonaparte. Whatever it was, this policy was certainly not conservative.

The war was preceded by a flurry of military preparations, insincere last-minute offers, and protestations of willingness to reach understanding. The pre-war crisis lasted longer than the war itself, long enough to give the German governments time to make up their minds. In their overwhelming majority they decided that they belonged on the side of the Confederation, that is to say of Austria. Only a few of Prussia's small neighbours dissociated themselves, but, to their misfortune, not even all of them. This attitude expressed the mood of the people who wanted a reform of the Confederation and a German Reich, but did not want the country to be prussianized by the wild man in charge of an unconstitutional and hated government in Berlin. Bavaria, Württemberg, Saxony, even liberal Baden joined Austria. Hanover, which would have preferred to remain neutral, was given no choice by Bismarck. When the Confederation decided to mobilize all non-Prussian and non-Austrian army corps Prussia declared that the Federal Act had been broken and that the German Confederation was dissolved. The Prussian armies marched without declaration of war.

Friedrich Engels, a military expert in his way, swore that Austria would win and wrote a lot about a revolution, an incipient rebellion of the army in Prussia. 'The war,' the Bavarian politician, Prince Hohenlohe, noted in his diary, 'will be long and bloody.' Louis Napoleon must have thought more or less the same. But people are often wrong in such matters, particularly experts. The war was as bloody as all wars, but not at all long. The armies of the smaller states moved independently without plan, and did almost no fighting. One battle in Bohemia, at Sadowa (Königgrätz), was enough for the Austrians. Just as Bismarck was superior to the diplomats, so the Prussian war-machine, newly overhauled, quick as lightning and superbly guided as it was, proved superior to the antiquated armada of the Confederation. The superior opponent attacks, and the attacker is almost always superior; but he must know how to stop while he is still superior.

Bismarck knew this. If he never acted more audaciously, one is tempted to say criminally, then during the months before this his decisive triumph, if he risked everything including probably his life, he was also never wiser than after the victory. He did not allow himself to be carried away like Napoleon I. For him, who had the good fortune to be a civilian, wars and victories never became ends in themselves. General Clausewitz's famous dictum that war is the 'continuation of politics by other means' seemed coined for his statesmanship. Having used great cunning and wearisome patience to drag his King into the war against Austria, he now expended a great deal more nervous effort on dragging him out of it again. The monarch would dearly have liked to enter Vienna as the victor, and according to old custom take a fat slice of territory from the enemy. Bismarck looked to St Petersburg, where people were becoming restless. He looked to Paris where people were becoming very restless and offering to provide the mediation which Austria requested. He thought, in spite of the momentary intoxication of victory, of the dangers and desiderata of the future. The peace which he forced through was based on simple conditions: Austria gave up the German Confederation and every legally defined influence in 'little' Germany; Prussia incorporated the principalities of Hanover, Schleswig-Holstein, Hesse-Cassel, Nassau and the Free City of Frankfurt into its territory; it also gained the right to form a North German Confederation with the remaining German states north of the Main. Let the southerners form a South German Confederation or have separate existences, just as they chose. The choice was severely restricted by the new reality.

Such was the result of the summer war, the German fratricidal strife, or whatever it is called. What had been discussed for seven times seven years, and had been shown repeatedly to be insoluble, was solved in seven weeks. It seemed like a piece of magic. And because nothing succeeds like success the Prussian Prime Minister was given a jubilant reception when he returned from Bohemia to Berlin. The constitutional conflict, the years of illegal government – one had to be very legalistic and dogmatic to worry about them now.

5. Confusion and Regrouping

The unnatural and disconcerting thing was that the German question had been decided by the will of one man who was not an idealist, nor a man of the people, nor a famous liberal. It had been solved by the hated Junker with the regiments and new infantry guns which under the Prussian constitution should not have existed at all. He alone had done this. Neither princes nor bourgeois, neither 'great' Germans nor 'little' Germans, neither conservatives nor liberals, democrats or socialists had contributed, or at least had contributed no more than the preliminary spade work. It was clear to anyone who wanted to see it that southern Germany could not long remain aloof from the North German Confederation. The German people would thus at last have its national state, pruned of German Austria. But it would not be a truly national state because it had been founded without, even in opposition to, the nation. Now the Germans were compelled to adopt some sort of attitude towards a situation which they had neither brought about nor foreseen, which fulfilled their wishes and yet did not fulfil them. The minds of politically minded Germans were strangely confused even in the months before the summer war and still more so after it.

It was as though the Prussian liberals, the Progress Party and its neighbours to the right, were celebrating Easter Sunday and Ash Wednesday simultaneously. German unity was at last within reach, but they themselves had contributed little to it and had obviously done their work badly. The pro-Prussian but definitely liberal young historian from Saxony, Heinrich von Treitschke, said:

Liberalism must take a realistic view of the modest extent of its power, it must tone down its wishes and stop thinking that this Prussia, in whose nascent political structure, crown, army and local self-administration form the strongest supports, could easily be reshaped on the Anglo-Belgian pattern.

To 'take a realistic view', to 'rethink', and to 'face the new facts', these were the demands of the hour. Another liberal historian carried self-criticism to the point of demanding an almost unconditional surrender to Prussian power politics, on the grounds that the middle classes had proved themselves incapable of political activity which should therefore be reserved for the aristocracy.

Even before the war certain liberal politicians had sought a constitutional compromise, a reconciliation with the rulers. Instead of using his triumph to destroy the constitutional party as he could have done, the Prime Minister made concessions to it. Bismarck had understood that in his day it was no longer possible to govern completely without a constitution or a parliament. He needed parliament all the more urgently because it could help in assimilating the new provinces, the conquered states. He therefore asked for an 'indemnity' for retrospective approval of all expenditure incurred illegally by the state from 1862 onwards. The request contained no admission of guilt; the King could not refrain from declaring expressly that he had acted correctly and that he would do the same again in a similar situation. What the chamber was given, or allowed to give itself, was the semblance of legality; this would settle the whole affair retrospectively.

The question of granting or not granting the indemnity proved the ruin of the great Progress Party. To say yes meant making wrong into right because it had been successful. To say no meant remaining in opposition and taking no part in the work that was now to begin, the shaping of the North German Confederation. The political realists or those who wanted to become such and who had long had doubts about the practical aspects of their position said yes. Those who upheld the legal principle at all costs said no. Thus a new party developed to the right of the progressives which later called itself the National Liberal Party. National because it wanted a German empire and its strongest following came from the new, the non-Prussian provinces. Liberal because its programme contained the classic demands of liberalism, a free economy, free trade and a constitutional state – although in that connection it was necessary to forget the recent past. In matters of foreign policy they were content for their constitutional state to pursue unrestrained power. The national liberals offered

Bismarck enthusiastic support in his foreign policy, collaboration at home and, where necessary, 'vigilant, loyal opposition'.

The same magnet which pulled apart the Progress Party also split the Prussian conservatives. They had willingly supported Bismarck while he was breaking the constitution, they had followed him into the war against Austria in spite of everything that they had preached for fifty years about the Christian-conservative alliance of the East European powers. Real sticklers for principle, however, had not supported him even then, on the grounds that conservative policy was legal policy, that anyone who adopted Machiavellian methods, who was more Bonapartist than Bonaparte and ruthlessly destroyed the European community, was no longer a conservative. That would no doubt have been the view of Professor Stahl, but he was dead and his spirit had never been really alive in Berlin. What many conservatives now blamed Bismarck for was his new game with the liberals and the nationalists. They were unable to reconcile themselves to the North German Confederation, to the 'little' German Reich for which the Confederation was the first step, and still less to universal suffrage which Bismarck, true to his promise, wanted to introduce in the new Confederation. But as other conservatives, like other liberals, were ready to face reality, there arose to the left of the Conservative Party the *Freikonservativ* Party or, as it later called itself in Germany, the *Deutsche Reichspartei*.

It was on those two groups that Bismarck mainly relied in the coming years. They were composed of professors for whom history was in the end always right, and who wanted to put Germany's glory above petty legalistic squabbles, of liberal aristocrats from Silesia and the Rhineland, of industrialists who did not care if the King remained master in the Prussian house for some time to come provided he let them be master in their house, in factories and banks, and of high-minded patriots and practically minded grasping members of the middle classes. The two Bismarck parties were not homogeneous structures. What probably characterizes them best are the words uttered by one of their ranks, the Hanoverian Johannes Miquel, in December 1866: 'The time of ideals is past. German unity has come down from the world of dreams into the prosaic world of reality. Today more than ever politicians must ask not what is desirable, but what is obtainable.' Miquel, an old follower of Marx, had meanwhile 'faced reality' and risen to the position of mayor of Osnabrück and leader of the liberal opposition in Hanover. He was not the only ex-communist to develop into so respectable a citizen.

In Prussia the storm of 1866 quickly produced new political groups which did what the victorious Prime Minister wanted and hoped for practical gratitude. The confusion was worse outside Prussia, taking Prussia not just as a physical but as a spiritual entity; because even within the Prussian state there were living interests, Catholic, democratic and socialist, which cannot be called Prussian.

Opposition to Prussia, to the *kleindeutsch* solution of the German question, had always had a Catholic flavour. The Prussian state was Protestant, in spite of the acquisition of Silesia, the Rhineland and the Polish provinces. Protestant – or heathen – was the deification of the state and its authority, which had been current in Prussia long before it received theoretical justification from Prussia's most celebrated philosophers. The defeated House of Habsburg was wholly Catholic, Austria was Catholic and south and south-west Germany were predominantly Catholic; without Austria the German Catholics became a minority. The fact that Bismarck now appeared to be reconciling himself with the liberals was a doubtful consolation. 'Liberal' can have many meanings. The Catholic Church in Germany was liberal after its fashion; it wanted freedom from the state and protection by the state to help it in the effective proclamation of its message. The state as envisaged by the national liberals was omnipotent, the sole master of popular education, the source of morality, the authority which determined all moral concepts. If Prussia-Germany now took the road of liberalism it would find many a progressive-minded companion with faith in science and a materialistic attitude of mind; and this at a time when the Pope had declared implacable war on modern civilization. Was this the moment for a state born from the marriage between liberalism and Old Prussian elements to start to rule Germany? 'It is difficult,' wrote the Catholic parliamentarian, August Reichensperger, 'to acquiesce in such divine counsels.' Another church leader, on the other hand, the wise Bishop Ketteler of Mainz, thought that one must accept whatever God permits to happen and make the best of it.

The two world revolutionaries in Britain agreed more or less with Ketteler, if with less stress on the religious aspect. At first Marx and Engels had been royally amused by Bismarck's audacious policy and thought that it would probably culminate in a victory of the Austrians followed by a revolution in Berlin. Now they tried to find such good as could be found in the new situation.

> The affair in Germany [said Engels] seems fairly simple to me now. From the moment that Bismarck carried out the 'little' German middle-class plan together with the Prussian army, and with such colossal success, Germany's development moved so decisively in that direction that we like others must recognize the *fait accompli, we may like it or not.** As far as the *national* side of the matter is concerned Bismarck will definitely establish the 'little' German empire within the limits envisaged by the bourgeoisie, that is to say including south-west Germany, because the phrases about the Main line . . . are certainly intended only for the French. Politically Bismarck will need to rely on the bourgeoisie whom he needs against the princes of the empire. Perhaps not at this moment when his prestige and the army are still enough. But he will need to give something to the middle classes even to get parliament to give him the wherewithal to govern . . . so that Bismarck, though he may at the moment not give the middle classes more than he *must*, will be increasingly driven towards the bourgeoisie. The advantage of this is that it simplifies the situation . . . In the last resort a German parliament is something very different from a Prussian chamber. The whole particularist system will be affected by the movement, the worst localizing influences will cease and the parties will at last be truly national instead of merely local. The main disadvantage, and it is a very big one, is the inevitable swamping of Germany by the Prussian spirit . . .

A clash between Germany and France was certain to follow because the French bourgeoisie could not resign itself to the German gain in power, and a war against Prussia was popular

* In English in the original text (Tr.).

'also with the peasant and the stupid labourer'. Marx replied: 'I entirely agree with you that one must take the mess as it is . . . for the worker, of course, everything is favourable which centralizes the bourgeoisie.'

Less clear about their views were the German followers or followers-to-be of the two masters. The history of German social democracy after Lassalle's death is one of confusion which for our purpose does not need to be unravelled in detail. The quarrel in the family of that divine youth who died young, the political intrigues of his mistress, Countess Hatzfeldt and of her friends and enemies, belong to a history of the party, not a general history of Germany. For some years the dominating figure in the General German Workers' Association was the south German lawyer, Johann Baptist von Schweitzer, a gruff but intelligent man who had espoused the workers' cause out of ambition more than out of love of humanity. He edited the association's journal, *Sozialdemokrat*, which was published in Berlin. There he more or less continued Lassalle's policy, though with less enthusiasm for Prussia, Bismarck and a socially benevolent monarchy than the founder had occasionally displayed in his later days. Schweitzer argued that a Prussian Germany offered better prospects for the revolution of the future than an Austrian one; if Prussian bayonets established German unity one must accept the fact and make the best of such concessions as universal suffrage and freedom to form coalitions which it was hoped Bismarck would make. During the crisis Schweitzer even spoke of 'the banner of Bismarck and Garibaldi', as though the Italian revolutionary with the red shirt and the aristocratic Machiavellian diplomat were one and the same thing. After the war Schweitzer, who was elected to the Reichstag by the supporters of the General German Workers' Association, recognized the North German Confederation as something in the development of which one must participate, now that it existed. We have seen that this was roughly Marx's view, though Marx and Engels strongly dissociated themselves from Schweitzer's too favourable judgement of Bismarck.

On the other hand there existed of old a radical democratic, 'greater' German, definitely anti-Prussian tradition. This was the real left-wing tradition, more broadly based and with deeper popular roots than Lassalle's, which was new, realistic and devious. Prussia was the enemy and could not change its character while it was Prussia; to exclude Austria was a betrayal of the German people. Such was the view of Wilhelm Liebknecht, an old fighter of 1848, and also of the turner, August Bebel, leader of the Workers' Educational Association in Leipzig, a man who had the ear of people in the kingdom of Saxony. It was the view of the Workers' Educational Associations, of the Saxon People's Party and the German People's Party, new improvised groups formed during the crisis. They claimed to be neither for the Habsburgs nor the Hohenzollerns and to be demanding a popular republic in place of a dynastic state – although in practice they laid the blame for the threatening civil war squarely at Prussia's door, rejected neutrality and were in favour of defending Germany against the Prussian attacker. Germany meant the states which in the summer of 1866 were at war against Prussia, that is Austria, Saxony, Hanover, Bavaria and so on. That was how Bebel and Liebknecht later gained the reputation of being supporters of German particularism, of the surviving principalities and even of the ones just abolished. They did not really adopt this attitude, but politics makes strange bedfellows. Some of the ideas and recommendations of the 'greater' German socialists would really have helped Austria and the princes, if they had any effect at all. As it was, theirs were no more than last-minute warnings and calls for help. So far they lacked the backing of a powerful organization and of force, the only thing that would have impressed Bismarck. Yet almost half a century later Bebel still found nothing to criticize in his attitude during the crisis of 1866. In his memoirs he writes: 'Liebknecht and I were often asked what would have happened if Austria had won instead of Prussia. It is sad that in the prevailing conditions no other alternative remained and that taking sides *against* the one was seen as being *for* the other. But that was how things were.' Though Prussia's defeat would have meant the collapse of the Bismarckian system and of Junker rule, it would not by any means have resulted in a lasting Austrian hegemony, because internally Austria was very weak and would not have held Germany together, so that after years of confusion real democratic self-determination might have been the result.

Basically the quarrel among the socialists was not unlike that among the liberals and the conservatives. None of these groups acted effectively; the socialists were still far too few to do so; the others had remained inactive for less honourable reasons. The action that was taken in spite of the parties, in spite of public opinion, in spite of Germany, in spite of his own King and in spite of the whole world, was taken by the only man who was a politician; he risked, he won and he produced a great change with lightning speed. The question for all now was whether to recognize what had happened or not.

That success is always a powerful argument is demonstrated by a glance at the Swiss press of those days. Able to observe events in Germany from a neutral vantage point it had until recently had nothing but contempt and hatred for Bismarck, but now commented with strange haste: 'Bismarck can probably no longer be regarded as an adventurer, if one considers how many great difficulties the Minister had to overcome and how he overcame them.' And again: 'Bismarck "knew his Pappenheimer" and understood more about practical politics than a few hundred parliamentary professors . . .' From the summer of 1866 Bismarck was regarded as the greatest statesman of the age. If Prussia had lost the battle of Sadowa – which it nearly did – he would have vanished, unmasked as an adventurer, in the mists of defeat.

6. *The North German Confederation*

The North German Confederation formed the basis of the German Reich as it existed until 1918, and even the Weimar Republic of the nineteen twenties was unable to rid itself of some of its fundamental characteristics. We must therefore look at it more closely. It was the creation of the Prussian state, not of the German people, which the authorities merely allowed to do some of the work. The intention of its creators was that the people should appear to have the maximum influence, while in fact having as little as could possibly be managed. Honest compromise is desirable and necessary in constitutional life, but this compromise was basically insincere and was therefore later responsible for much controversy and much confusion and failure. The conflict was not between the Prussian and the German nation, because there was no Prussian nation. It was between the German people and the Prussian state, between majority and authority, ruled and rulers.

The Confederation consisted of Prussia, the kingdom of Saxony and the small states of northern and central Germany, Mecklenburg, Oldenburg, Weimar and so on. Some of these small states were, as we have seen, simply annexed by Prussia – a characteristically ugly and completely unnecessary act even though it had few consequences in the long run. Prussia had not dominated the old Confederation in Frankfurt, because of Austria. It dominated the North German Confederation anyway; the Hanoverians and the inhabitants of Holstein would never have had any alternative but to submit to Prussian leadership. Yet they would have liked to preserve their traditional symbols and had no desire to become Prussians. The foundation of the German national state began with an act of coercion, with a conquest which took a most unpleasant form, particularly in the Free City of Frankfurt. If this act had any meaning at all it was that the Prussian state had no intention of 'merging' into Germany but wanted to continue to exist as it was, only more centralized and more powerful than ever. Perhaps, however, the act did not even mean that much, perhaps it was entirely meaningless. William I thought in age-old concepts. A victorious war without conquest, without an aggrandizement of the state seemed to him an ignominious and unnatural renunciation. Not being allowed to snip off a piece of Austria, he insisted on repainting some pieces of the north German map in the Prussian colours. And this pleased even the implacable opposition in the Prussian chamber which approved the annexations by an overwhelming majority.

In the end those acquisitions were more useful to that Prussia which was only the greater part of Germany than to the royal, Bismarckian Prussia. They were a new chapter in the process in which the Prussian state lost its identity by expanding too greedily. The acquisition of the Rhineland had been such a chapter; already then men of un-Prussian type had infiltrated into the economic, scientific, administrative and finally also into the political life of the state. This process now repeated itself. The parliamentarians who came from Hanover to Berlin were men of character: the liberals, Bennigsen and Miquel, and the Catholic, Windthorst, who shortly afterwards founded the new Centre Party. The concessions that Bismarck made to liberalism he made not least to the liberals from the annexed provinces; just as fifty years earlier the south German states had introduced their constitutions in order to link their new possessions successfully with the old. The enemies of Prussia were right though in claiming that liberalism and Prussia did not go well together. This is the curious dialectic of Prussian history. Bismarck, it is said, was a thorough Prussian and only wanted to make Prussia a great power. But there was no room for Prussia to expand except in Germany. As Prussia did so, throwing in a little German nationalism in order to simplify expansion, it finally became Germany plain and simple whether it wanted to or not.

The constitution of the North German Confederation was hastily put together from pieces of Metternich's Federal Act and the constitution of 1849, from compromises between the Prussian tradition, Bismarck's ambition and that of the national liberals. The idea behind the draft was to enable the southern German states to accept it without major change. Therein lies its importance; only for the small states, which were Prussia's allies at the moment, the effort would hardly have been worthwhile. In fact the constitution survived for fifty years, and both the Weimar Constitution and the Basic Law of the Federal Republic borrowed heavily from it, just as it had itself borrowed from the past. In spite of all the chaotic changes, one can therefore speak of a certain continuity in German constitutional history.

Sovereignty rested with the 'allied governments'. They were represented by a *Bundesrat* which was clearly the successor of Metternich's federal diet, with the difference that the new presiding power was given very different formal, and indeed actual, rights than Austria had exercised in Frankfurt. In the *Bundesrat* nothing could be done against the will of Prussia and in practice Prussia could always have its way. In addition to the *Bundesrat* there was the Reichstag, elected by universal suffrage, which represented the whole 'north German nation'. The name Reichstag indicated the aim: there was a federation and soon there must be a Reich. The Reichstag was the showpiece of the new liberal course, the redemption of the promise of 1863, the realization of a principle of 1849. The rights of this popular representation were discussed in the constituent Reichstag which sat from February to April 1867, and although Bismarck defended his project with his usual energy and could always threaten to wreck the whole enterprise, he agreed to make some concessions. The sphere in which parliament was entitled to legislate was extended considerably; the chamber was given the right to control public income and expenditure. A compromise was reached over the army to the effect that for a transitional period there would be an allocation of a fixed sum, but that thereafter army expenditure would be treated like any other budget item. After 1871 this arrangement developed into the *Septennat*, the system of fixing army budgets for a seven-year period. Of his *idées fixes* Bismarck gave up one in order to force through the other: he agreed reluctantly to allow public servants to stand for parliament, but insisted that deputies must not receive any monetary reward. If his intention had been to prevent the rise of a class of professional, salaried politicians, he failed. But those were minor issues. More important was the question whether there should be a responsible government, a council of national ministers with a chairman. Bismarck rejected the idea on the grounds that governing was the concern of the *Bundesrat*, and that a cabinet was incompatible with the federalist structure of the

Confederation. The *Bundesrat* should be responsible to no one, but should decide by majority, of which Prussia was always certain. The *Bundeskanzler* should merely be the Prussian representative in the *Bundesrat*, voting according to Bismarck's instructions. The national liberals insisted on a 'responsible' *Bundeskanzler*, whose signature was required for all laws, and who represented the policy of the Confederation in the Reichstag. Once Bismarck had in principle agreed to this office, ill defined at first but obviously important, he had no choice but to take it himself because he could not leave something like this to anyone else. The office of *Bundeskanzler*, shortly *Reichskanzler*, was thus created really against Bismarck's will. In time he came to like it much better than the office of Prussian Prime Minister. As Prime Minister he had colleagues, as Chancellor only subordinate assistants. As Chancellor he alone was the government. He was 'responsible' in name but it was not said to whom he was responsible, and there was no suggestion that he might need the confidence of the Reichstag. In fact until 1918 German chancellors were responsible to no one but the King-Emperor who appointed and dismissed them.

The whole thing was a hasty improvisation. Bismarck did not believe in elaborate constitutions. Like Lassalle he believed in the reality which alone would show what the constitution was and could be. This process he would direct himself. The two realities on which above all he kept his eye were the power of the Prussian state and his own position. As long as it was a question of mere words he was conciliatory because he had no respect for words. Doctrines he rejected with impatience; the constitution did not list any fundamental rights, did not set out any divisions of power and did not answer questions such as where sovereignty really lay. Bismarck was probably honest when he made eloquent speeches about the need for understanding between the representatives of the people and the government. But he was also honest when he said among friends that he intended to defeat parliamentarianism with parliamentarianism, that he would only allow a sham parliament. In practice Bismarck played off the various interests and forces against each other: Reichstag and people against the governments of the princes and vice versa. The Prussian diet elected under the three-class franchise was allowed to continue so that henceforth there were two big German parliaments, as in 1848; a clumsy arrangement which survived until 1933. He allowed the princes to remain, although he could have pensioned them off as he did the King of Hanover; because he did not want the Hohenzollern throne to be the only one on democratic soil and because he would thus be able to play off Prussia all the more energetically against the 'people' as well as against the 'allied' governments. He gladly accepted the collaboration of the parties and used them without identifying himself with any one of them. Although not doctrinaire, the game that Bismarck planned and played was nevertheless highly complicated. Behind all his actions were open or secret reservations, war stratagems or *arrières pensées*.

Both the constituent Reichstag and the Prussian parliament adopted the constitution by a big majority. For it voted the national liberals, the free conservatives and – reluctantly – the conservatives; against it voted the remains of the *Fortschritts-partei*, a few Poles, Danes from Schleswig, unreconciled Hanoverians and the socialist, August Bebel.

7. Southern Germany

Of Austria Karl Marx said during the summer war that it must now become Hungarian. There was something in this; the Magyars had long regarded the Germans as their allies; a German victory – a Habsburg defeat – was a Magyar victory. In 1862 Bismarck had advised the Austrian Empire to transfer 'its centre of gravity to Budapest'. Now it was ingeniously distributed between Budapest and Vienna. The 'Compromise' of 1867 gave the Magyars more or less the state for which they had fought in 1849, a 'greater' Hungary, ruled by Magyars, linked with the other half of the Empire by the person of the Emperor, and a common foreign and customs policy. The rest of the Empire remained without a name. It was called 'Austria' but incorrectly For the Germans it was still German-Austria, although the Germans were in the minority also in this half of the Empire, and the Czechs loudly announced their claim to the historic kingdom of Bohemia. The constitution was improved and in the process the Austrian citizen was given all the freedom and legal protection available in the most progressive countries. That and good, civilized administration was what Austria offered its inhabitants, all things that have since been lost almost everywhere. It was inevitable that the squabbling between the nationalities increased rather than diminished as politics was unleashed. Above the discord there was the Emperor, loyal to his duty, detached and sad, always still his own Prime Minister, in the last resort master of all decisions – in so far as Austria was still master of them.

For a time it thought that this was still the case. Between 1866 and 1870 Austria toyed with the idea of reversing the decision of Sadowa, of fighting another war against Prussia, together with France or Italy. But this did not happen, and probably not only for superficial diplomatic reasons. The Magyars who owed their new glory to the Prussian victory would not have allowed it, and Italy was not interested. And what would Austria itself have done with a victory; what use had it made of the victory of Olmütz in 1850? When the crisis of 1870 approached Austria did not act and thereby recognized as final the decision of 1866. It continued to exist because for good reason Bismarck wanted Austria to exist, but it existed within the frontiers drawn by Bismarck.

Between an insecure Austria nursing its internal malaise and a restless France forever on the lookout for change, between democratic, well-arranged Switzerland, by now a somewhat anxious observer of German affairs, and the successful, dynamic North German Confederation, there lay southern Germany. Southern Germany, left out in the cold by the Peace of Prague, was motivated by conflicting wishes, by real needs and imaginary possibilities. We know what the end was, and are therefore tempted to believe that there could have been no other end. The historian's imagination is limited and we usually in retrospect accept as inevitable what actually happened. But in this case thinking people regarded it as inevitable even before it happened. Indeed there was little to cause excitement in the union between southern Germany and the North German Confederation, the achievement of the 'little' German national state. It was a prosaic necessity because there was no longer any alternative.

When it comes to politics we must not speak of southern Germany but more precisely of the south German states of Bavaria, Württemberg, Baden and Hesse. These were regions where in the last decades life had been comfortable, where taxes were low, where there was none of the burden of an ever-ready army, where citizens were protected by the law, where monarchs were easy-going and capitals artistic, and where, compared with the north, there was as yet little industry. Baden, which in 1848–9 had played such a dismal role, had since become much more liberal. Württemberg was called in Paris a 'royal Switzerland' – not a bad expression. The Bavarian bureaucracy had the well-deserved reputation of being excellent, and Munich, the capital, had in the course of the century become one of the towns most worth seeing in Europe. The Bavarians believed that their state was a genuine one, not an arbitrary Napoleonic creation, and Bismarck agreed with them; throughout his life he always showed marked respect for the Bavarian tradition. Yet the Bavarian state was not one that could or wanted to isolate itself from the development of Germany as a whole; and in this instance being able to and wanting to amounted to the same thing.

The Prusso-Austrian conflict had drawn these fairytale states into its vortex; then, to their own amazement, they found themselves on their feet again. By the Peace of Prague the southern German states were allowed to form their own confederation and in addition to enter into some form of association with the north German one, leaving their international existence or independence unimpaired. But with sovereignty as with constitutions reality decides whether and to what extent it exists. Bismarck at once secretly concluded defensive and offensive alliances with the south German states under which they placed their armies under Prussian command in case of war. So much for reality.

Nothing came of the south German confederation. Southern Germany was not a political entity and did not want to become one. Neither was north Germany, but it was coerced by Prussia. In addition the North German Confederation had the advantage of being a step towards the German nation-state, whereas the South German one would be an obstacle on the road to it. Therefore there must be no 'nook and cranny' Germany, as the critics called the project.

Could these states exist independently? The Munich Court liked to think so, but did not dare to say so aloud, and pursued meanwhile with many reservations and stipulations a pro-Prussian policy because it was forced to. Then there was the Bavarian Patriotic Party which in 1869 achieved a tremendous electoral victory. It was the party of those who wanted Bavaria to stand alone, democratic, conservative, rural and arch-Catholic. Even today one is in emotional agreement with the speeches of their powerful spokesman, Doctor Jörg, who thundered against Prussian militarism, against the increased burdens brought by the alliance with Prussia, against the official deification of liberalism. 'We want to remain what we are' was the crux of what he had to say, and the present writer cannot but sympathize with him. But, alas, there are times in which one cannot remain what one is – if indeed it is ever possible. After all, it is in the nature of history to bring constant change and to hollow the stone even though the drop which does it is unaware of what it is doing. If the Bavarians had not wanted to be German they ought to have taken action much earlier.

The liberal middle classes were in favour of union with Prussia – for economic reasons and because here, too, the desire to be a nation-state began to make itself felt. The leading Bavarian minister, Hohenlohe, a sceptical but clever and sensible man, planned some form of union between the North German Confederation and the South, not the entry of the South into the Confederation but a further federation between the two. The national liberals in Berlin told him outright that anything other than a complete merger of both regions was out of the question. One may doubt whether Hohenlohe's plans, if carried out, would have changed the course of German history. The forces working for the establishment of a German state were many and powerful, and paid no more attention to signed treaties than to projected ones. Nor did they pay any attention to the privileges which Bavaria reserved for itself in 1870.

If in Bavaria the opposition to north Germany came from Catholic, or as they were then called, ultramontane quarters, in Württemberg it was democratic; it was an expression of the old Suabian, 'greater' German, democratic reluctance to yield to the *Pickelhauben*, the soldiers with the spiked helmets, an attitude which we know already from 1848. Here there were people who dreamt of a south German republican federation on the Swiss model; this again did not fit in with Bavarian aspirations. In Baden the liberal friends of Prussia predominated; they were led by the Grand Duke himself, one of those princes who sympathized with the middle classes and who was ready to renounce his position: he belonged to the same school of thought as the English Prince Consort, Albert of Coburg. The Prussian Crown Prince Frederick was another of the group – 'this fool of a crown prince', as Bismarck called him.

Bismarck played his customary double game with southern Germany. When in the Reichstag the liberals demanded a quick union with the South, he played the part of the patient statesman, maintaining that history cannot be *made*, that one must wait for it to happen, that in the fullness of time the South would find its way to Germany, and so on. Thus spoke the man who had shown himself to the world as a most impatient, arrogant politician, who had made history like few other men. Often we are most eloquent about the virtues we lack. Towards south German politicians he pretended indifference; Berlin did not need southern Germany and did not want it. Secretly he was fully aware that the provisional arrangement in south Germany could not last long. The nature of politics does not permit a vacuum of power. The military alliances were better than nothing but not enough while Austria and France were able to seduce or threaten the south

German states. Prussia was soon compelled to lay its heavy hand on the whole of the South. Whether this was done for the sake of power or for the sake of the 'German idea' made no practical difference. In the summer of 1867 the Federal Chancellor let it be known that a reform of the German *Zollverein* was an urgent necessity. The nation itself must participate in making tariff legislation and the north German Reichstag must therefore be expanded by a corresponding number of members from the South. However, Bismarck's enthusiasm for parliamentary discussion was not such that he attached great importance to asking the German nation ceremoniously for advice about the level of the coffee tariff. The Bavarians recognized the true purpose of the 'customs parliament' and resisted; in vain, as always against a player who knew so well how to get people into a corner. If no customs parliament was set up, Bismarck replied with cold regret, the *Zollverein* would be dissolved and southern Germany must somehow keep its economy going alone. The threat was effective. The elections to the customs parliament seemed a setback for Bismarckian and national liberal policy. The result of holding the elections according to north German law, that is to say with universal suffrage, meant that a disappointingly large number of hostile members, Catholic or democratic particularists, was sent to Berlin because in the South the poor, the workers and the peasants were more anti-Prussian than the wealthy middle classes. Yet by their mere existence the customs parliaments became effective manifestations of the national spirit. Members needed hearts of stone not to be impressed by the banquets and the speeches, by all the national pomp displayed in Berlin.

Southern Germany was linked indissolubly with the North by a joint economic policy; its military system was adapted to the Prussian one and subordinate to it in case of war; German parliamentarians met regularly, and even in the South there were strong political parties pressing for unification; the opponents of unification on the other hand could offer no viable programme for the future to arouse national German public opinion but merely wanted to preserve the *status quo*; the whole matter had been discussed incessantly for thirty years and cried out for a solution – one needed to be blind or deaf not to realize in those circumstances where the journey would end. Its end was near and certain and no great statesmanship seemed needed to reach it peacefully. Yet this did not happen.

8. *1870*

This is a stupid story with disastrous long-term consequences. The 'war guilt question' of 1870, like a later one, has been thoroughly investigated with the expected result that both sides are blamed.

Napoleon III's policy had always been nationalistic: he had been pro-Italian, pro-German and when possible pro-Polish. For years he 'connived with Bismarck', as Marx put it; he had procured the Italian ally for him in 1866 and given his blessing to the Prussian annexations. He must have known that these would logically lead to the establishment of the 'little' German nation-state; and if such a state was set up reasonably freely, without too much open force being shown by the King of Prussia, he *could* not, given his often proclaimed basic principle, do anything to stop it. As early as 1862 he had said to Bismarck that Germany could do whatever it liked with itself; the only thing which France could not tolerate was the unification of the whole Austrian Empire with Prussia. He had no objection to 'little' Germany, only to a 'greater' Germany which would control central and south-eastern Europe. Wise words, however, are one thing and a firm, clear and courageous policy another.

This was what poor Napoleon lacked, and Emperor and Empire went to pieces. The ailing man had lost his grip on the country. The whole edifice was based on bluff; public opinion was misrepresented, parliament artificially filled with yes-men, and the weak dictator surrounded by adventurers thirsting for prestige and money. Sinister activities went on beneath the surface of the glittering but dead police state. In 1870 Napoleon tried to give them legal outlets in the 'liberal Empire' by unfettering the opposition and by governing with the parliamentary majority. But this policy was no more consistently pursued than the policy of helping the nationalities; neither was really possible under the ruler whom the coup of 1851 had brought to power.

Public opinion in France was not pro-German, unlike the Emperor, who had spent his childhood in Bavaria and with a thin voice sang German songs to piano accompaniment. 'To keep the affairs of the German Reich in a state of maximum confusion' was an age-old Bourbon tradition, something of which was still alive in the spirit of the French. The nationalities policy was not understood. Sometimes Louis Napoleon did not understand it himself and acted against it – partly because of his own doubts, partly encouraged by adventurers who sounded public opinion. He posed as the real victor of 1866, as the leader of the European revolution; his argument was that popular governments approved by France had now replaced the hated despotisms of 1815. The French saw things differently. To tear up the treaties of 1815 was certainly an old ideal, provided it was in the interest of France, not in that of Italy and Germany. For France to remain within the frontiers of 1815 without receiving any thanks while having new great powers as neighbours – that was not the ideal. All the more since German nationalism had not lost the anti-French tone to which it had become accustomed after 1813. Hence – what Bismarck called the French 'policy of tipping' – the demand for compensation, for payment or favours for services rendered. Napoleon's heart was not in these demands, but his subordinates urged him to make them or announced them without him, for the Palatinate, for the Saar, for Belgium; they were made hesitantly, always too late. Payment for political services must be received in advance, not in retrospect. During the summer war France's benevolent neutrality was valuable to Bismarck and he had repeatedly offered glorious rewards for it in tempting and imprecise words. After the Peace of Prague his mien became stony. In order to register some kind of gain Napoleon made efforts to buy the small duchy of Luxembourg from Holland. It seems that this time Bismarck was prepared to look the other way but the reaction of the German public was unexpectedly strong: no square yard of ancient German soil must go to the French. The Prussian Prime Minister, not usually the servant of public opinion, toed the line instantly and the Dutch did not dare to sell. The Prussian troops still stationed in Luxembourg from the days of the German Confederation were withdrawn and the little country was 'neutralized'. It soon ceased to regard itself as 'German'. Later it was twice occupied by the Germans and tormented for many years, but never again by France – Bonaparte came away empty-handed.

Whether Bismarck's support of the candidature of a Hohen-zollern prince for the Spanish throne was from the start designed to trap Napoleon into war, as was later claimed by his admiring assistant Lothar Bucher, or whether he merely took the opportunity to increase Prussia's glory and then in July 1870 preferred, rather than diplomatic defeat, the chance of going to war which France blindly offered him – this much-debated question need not concern us. In July 1870 each side tried to outdo the other. To an unimportant though foolish French demand Bismarck replied with a press statement which to us in our violent age seems almost laughably harmless, but which according to the chivalrous code still in existence then was equal to a declaration of war. In the difficulties which it had brought upon itself the French regime wanted a cheap humiliation of Prussia, or, if that was impossible, war. Bismarck also certainly preferred war to such a humiliation; particularly as he regarded war as inevitable anyway and because it would open up a satisfactory avenue along which he could pursue policies, which would otherwise reach a dead end. However, the war of 1870 was not fought over a genuine *casus belli*. The war aims which Louis Napoleon outlined in conversation were anachronistic and pitiful. For the attainment of the Prussian goal, the establishment of 'little' Germany, no war against France was or should have been necessary.

France was weak, Prussia was strong. The Prussian army leaders knew this, whereas the French did not, although Napoleon suspected it. Three weeks after the outbreak of war everybody knew it. The precision and force of the Prussian war machine surpassed everything that had ever been seen in this field. For years Prussian staff officers disguised as tourists with brushes and paints had studied the location of future battles. In the rear of the armies came iron bridges of the right length to span the rivers which needed to be crossed. Never before was a war so lovingly prepared; never was one fought with so much enthusiasm. What had happened in 1854, 1859 and 1866 had been trivial compared with 1870. What had not been achieved by two years of revolution and fifty sluggish years of peace was achieved by three days of war against France. There was not a moment's doubt that the south German states would stand by the Prussian alliance; any prince not prepared to do so would have been swept away. Furthermore, after a few weeks of war it was certain that the South would join the North German Confederation. Such was the mood; both regions were intoxicated by the same thrilling war experience. Even those who calculated more coolly were confident about the political situation. France, which had hitherto guaranteed the Main line, could now be discounted; and as the other great powers, Britain, Russia and even Austria, left Germany and France alone in the ring without worrying about the outcome, they too could be discounted. Consequently Prussia's allies depended completely on Prussia and no less so because they were its allies. The two decisions of the King of Bavaria, first to join the war on Prussia's side and then to offer the German Imperial crown to the King of Prussia, therefore do not deserve to be called free decisions.

If Bavaria could exist alone, independent of the Confederation [Ludwig II wrote to his brother], it would not matter, but this would be completely impossible politically because of opposition from the people and the army as a result of which the Crown would lose the support of the country; therefore, however terrible, it is an act of political sagacity, even necessity . . . for the King of Bavaria to make this offer . . . it is deplorable that this has happened but it can no longer be changed.

The French were insufficiently prepared, and suffered one disaster after another. The situation changed after the capture and deposition of the Emperor. Republican France took the war desperately seriously and the old martial genius showed itself in magnificently energetic improvisations, and not without success. At the same time the rules of the game of war broke down. Until Sedan the war had been an affair between gentlemen and the attitude of the victorious monarch to the defeated enemy had been chivalrous. Now it became a struggle between peoples in their primordial state; Paris was mercilessly starved, villages were reduced to ashes and partisans shot. What the Germans remember, however, is not the hard winter campaign but the succession of victories in the summer. Other nations had their national days, France the 14 July, which recalled the fall of the absolutist King, and America Independence Day; the new German Reich chose the day of the battle of Sedan, the day of the Last Judgement for the French, of the victory of German loyalty over Latin perfidy

After Sedan Republican France wanted peace provided it could be obtained without the loss of French territory. To start with the Prussian attitude had been that Prussia was not fighting the French nation but one guilty man, the Emperor, and that it wanted nothing from France but to be left in peace by him. Yet war, once it starts, develops its own momentum. In 1859 and 1866 it had been possible to keep the war under control and to stop it in time, but not in 1870. The conflict between the Germans and the French aroused more popular passion than that between the Austrians and the Prussians which had been created for political reasons. Even in the summer the national liberals demanded the annexation of Alsace and Lorraine and this war aim soon became the generally recognized and undoubted one. It was argued that Germany's bloody sacrifices must not have been in vain, that henceforth strategically safe frontiers must protect Germany from its war-thirsty neighbour, that territory which had been German from time immemorial must be brought back into the new Reich, that Germany must make good the omissions of 1814. Whether the Alsatians wanted to return to the Reich was immaterial. Bismarck offered no opposition to this collection of historical, military, sentimental and vindictive arguments. Although he later let it be known that he had not really shared this attitude, he did nothing to counter it; on the contrary, the manner in which he managed the war after 2 September helped to encourage it

Opposition to the annexation in the North German Reichstag came from Liebknecht and Bebel, members of the *Volkspartei*, or as it had recently come to be called the Social Democratic Party. This alone, even if it had been the only achievement of their lives, would be to their everlasting credit. Marx in London also predicted the toxic consequences of an amputation of the French body politic; like Bebel Marx's 'International Workers' Association' now demanded an immediate peace. Although Marx and Engels had approved of Germany's defensive war against Bonapartist impudence and Engels had indeed been delighted by the German victories in August and by the efficiency of Moltke's army, in the autumn they wanted the war to end. To overestimate the extent to which wars can be controlled has remained a Marxist heritage. The principle that 'defensive war' is permissible but must be stopped as soon as it ceases to serve the purposes of defence is certainly a laudable one. But the frontiers between defence and attack are uncertain; and once the monster war has been born it starts a life of its own not easily controllable by party political strategy. European socialism never really mastered the problem of war; it failed to do so in 1870 when it was still weak, and again later when it was strong and had real influence.

In the late autumn, during the siege of Paris, negotiations took place in Versailles about the entry of the southern states into the Confederation. They had no genuine card left to play; all the trumps were in Bismarck's hand. But on this occasion it was his principle to demand only the essential minimum, partly because he was convinced that the rest would follow anyway and partly also because he did not want the rest: he needed a federation of monarchies in order to keep Prussia – *his* kind of Prussia – from being swallowed up by the Reich. However, the 'reserved rights' which he granted Bavaria – its own army, diplomatic service, railway and postal systems and the chairmanship of the diplomatic committee of the *Bundesrat* – were without real historical importance. Whatever efforts Bismarck made to subordinate the national movement to the state, however much he sought to ensure that in the alliance between the German nation and the

Prussian state the lion's share went to the state, in the end it was all in vain. In spite of all alliance formulas and the reserved rights of southern Germany it was Prussia which commanded the new Reich. And in spite of Prussia's commanding position designed to control the federal states as well as to preserve them in a state of semi-independence, in the end it was all the other federal states *and* Prussia which lost their identities in the German Reich, Prussia even more so than the others just because it was the centre of gravity of the Reich. The process of dissolution was delayed a little by a certain amount of clever formalism; not even a genius could prevent it now. The days of little, Spartan Prussia, the land of king, knight and liege, were over.

They would have been over if Bismarck had pursued nothing but Prussian aims. In Germany there was room only for one Great Power, and once it existed there was no room for any other genuine state. Therefore Prussia had to become Germany, even if and just because it wanted to be only Prussia, the Great Power. All that remained to be determined were the ways and means: how the country should be ruled, how public opinion should be influenced, what form the constitution and the internal distribution of power should take. But questions of this kind are never finally settled, least of all in such a dynamic state as the new Germany soon proved to be.

King William showed a sound instinct when on the day before being proclaimed Emperor he burst into tears. He said to his closest advisers that he was in the depth of despair since the next day he would have to say farewell to the old Prussia which he alone cherished. Equally curious in its distress is the letter which a prince of Bavaria wrote to his brother after the proclamation in the Hall of Mirrors:

I cannot tell you, Ludwig, how infinitely distressed I felt during that ceremony, how every fibre of my being rebelled against everything I witnessed. It was all so cold, so proud, so glittering, so ostentatious and pompous and heartless and empty. I felt oppressed and utterly dejected in that hall.

A lament for the good old days, deploring the new age which would be Prussian and German, but above all new; industrious, noisy and harsh, and alien for morbid fairytale princes. The sorrow of the kings, the depression in the Hall of Mirrors, are curiously confirmed by Marx and Engels who were in high spirits because in their view Bismarck, without realizing it, was taking an historically necessary step towards the revolution; that explained why everything had gone so smoothly for him so far. Nevertheless he was an ass.

No one has counted those Germans who approached the new constitution with secret or open scepticism. In the North German Reichstag a number of delegates voted against the constitution, but they objected not to the Reich but to Bavaria's reserved rights, the importance of which they overestimated. In the south German parliaments the voices of Prussia's opponents, 'greater' Germans, clericals, patriots and democrats, were raised once more, though in vain. The inevitable was all the more inevitable because it lay no longer in the future but had happened amid jubilation. To stand aloof now was a question of character, of obstinacy or of individual loyalty to principle, it could no longer serve any practical purpose. The new German Reich began its existence on 1 January 1871. In February there were added to it under the provisional peace treaty of Versailles the provinces of Alsace and Lorraine, intended to be *Reichslande*. On 21 March the German Reichstag, elected by universal suffrage, met in Berlin. On the same day the Chancellor was raised to the rank of prince: Prince Bismarck – a curious combination of names by which be became known to the world. If he had resigned then, like the Emperor Diocletian at the height of his glory, it would in spite of everything have remained a purer, better-sounding name. But voluntary resignation, happy retirement and contemplation were not in Bismarck's line. For another nineteen years his heavy and fidgety hand guided the work which he had created in six or eight years – a misfortune for his work and no source of happiness to him.

9. Reflection

The foundation of this new German Reich was a unique process for which one looks in vain for historical parallels. Everything connected with it is confused, nothing can be clearly labelled. The people had long wanted unification in some form or other, but it was not the people who brought it about. Unification was brought about by the states, because the one great state, Prussia, put pressure on the small ones, the pressure being disguised by the fact that a great part of the people assisted in the affair. Only a few were completely satisfied with the result. Some complained about brutal Prussian leadership, others about the privileges which Bismarck had granted to the southern Germans, and not even those in control of the power which ultimately decided everything were content.

Should it not have happened at all? Is it possible retrospectively to contemplate a different development or a better one?

Alexander von Villers wrote in the summer of 1870:

The German Confederation, the last statesman-like idea of European diplomacy and a solid work of national and international juridical wisdom, was of a defensive nature. Prussia was the yeast which started the fermentation of the well-worked dough. Germany not only lived in peace with its neighbours, it also acted as a spoke in the wheel of every other European state eager to break the peace of the world. The only, but inevitable fault in the organism was the presumption of moral greatness among all its members ... Prussia had long said that it would not allow itself to be defeated by a majority of votes. The day that word was uttered the Confederation ought to have silenced it forever. But allowances were made and because of that the Confederation was wrecked.

A thoughtful passage though still written very much in the spirit of Metternich and not to be taken as the whole truth. If a few genuine powers form a confederation with many which are not genuine the question of decision by majority vote really becomes a delicate problem. We see this today in the United Nations.

Austria's use of the Confederation for its own ends was no more ethical than Prussia's reaction. Whether this reaction was of purely Prussian origin or whether in it and through it German energies rebelled against the Confederation is a question that can be answered as one will. Prussia was not popular among the Germans but neither was the Confederation, least of all among Prussia's opponents, the left-wing liberals and democrats, because it did not help to realize the most fundamental German aspiration.

The most fundamental aspiration of the age was to achieve a free constitutional or national state in any form. It was there, it had proved ineradicable for half a century in spite of all repres-·sion. It was for that reason that Bismarck decided to make doubtful common cause with it, though the 'nationalities humbug' was basically alien to his nature. One may ask if it would not have been a blessing if the Germans had never wanted a nation-state in the French style. The historian, coming afterwards, can know better. For example he can show that the idea of the Czech nation-state was rather unfortunate, although the Czechs got their state in the end. But as far as the Germans are concerned the position is slightly different. The establishment, internal structure and external limits, of their nation-state brought problems which have never been satisfactorily solved and which defy solution even now. Yet for that reason to renounce what in the nineteenth century seemed absolutely natural politically and economically and intellectually, and what was happening at the same time in Italy, Scandinavia and America, would have required more self-denying wisdom that could be expected from a nation with as large and as active a population as the German one.

What is curious is that as soon as one accepts this premise one is mentally forced towards the 'little' German, Prussian solution, however twisted, limited and unsatisfactory it may have been. All that the mind can do is to perform the exercise which was in fact performed twice, in 1848–9 and in 1866–70. Even in the *Paulskirche* the advocates of a 'little' Germany had almost all sponsored their cause reluctantly. Heinrich von Gagern had shown as early as 1848 in occasional imperialist fantasies that he was *grossdeutsch* at heart, and he showed it even more clearly later. It was an indisputable fact that a German national state which included the German Austrians was incompatible with the existence of the Habsburg Empire. As long as there was the one there could not be the other. All the plans for reform of the Confederation, devised in the sixties by Austrians or Germans from the smaller states, therefore have something so artificial that by comparison Bismarck's solution seems the natural one. That was the view of south German politicians like Chlodwig Hohenlohe who soon surrendered without much enthusiasm to Prussian leadership. They knew that it would happen anyway in the end. The 'greater' Germans were defeated by the existence of Austria. The south German patriots, particularists or whatever they were called, who were related to them, wanted to keep their states away from the stream of German history. Could this have been done? In the sixties south Germans liked to point to the example of Switzerland, a small state occupying a respectable position in Europe. Could Württemberg and Bavaria not do the same? The Suabian democrats very much wanted to imitate the republican Swiss. It was true that Switzerland had once been as German as Bavaria and Suabia, but that was long ago. Favoured by geography and history it had very gradually developed a nationality of its own, and every step that the Germans took towards their new unity led Switzerland one step further away from Germany. Switzerland's self-confidence was no doubt based largely on that division. Old Bavaria too had at times, for example in the eighteenth century, been isolated from the rest of Germany, but it had experienced nothing comparable with the Swiss development, a process of severance which was at the same time a creative process of consolidation. Then Bavaria's new possessions had drawn it still further into Germany. After Napoleon's fall the Bavarians became very German and did not dispute for one moment that their state was a basic part of Germany and shared fully in Germany's glory and splendour. How could they now suddenly claim to be an independent European state and have nothing to do with Germany's destiny?

However one looks at the problem, one is in the end led to the suspicion that after the failure of the first 'greater' German revolution the Prussian solution was in the long run inevitable. The same is true even of the conflict of 1866. There was no mystery about its end, and this probably explains why the losers, the south Germans, immediately adapted themselves to the new situation without great mental effort.

1870 is slightly different. If a nation wants to found a state let it do so at home. To do so beyond its frontiers, in the splendid palace of its neighbour, at his expense, means a clumsy start. Prussia and Austria had at least fought for the control of Germany, a classic political issue. Prussia and France merely fought to decide who was stronger, an issue for naughty boys, not for mature nations.

The arguments pointing to Bismarck's responsibility for this calamity have been impressively recapitulated by Erich Eyck. They were sceptically re-examined recently by A. J. P. Taylor in his history of European diplomacy. In his view Bismarck later pretended to have been not more innocent but guiltier, more scheming and more omniscient than he was. In particular Taylor claims that the story of the 'trap' which Bismarck wanted to set for Napoleon with the candidature to the Spanish throne was nothing but restrospective boasting. The question will forever remain undecided. Between 1866 and 1870 Bismarck showed that he could be very wise and also very wicked. Wise phrases are as cheap as wicked ones, and a man who is both superior and talkative will not be sparing with either. By collecting one or the other he can be made into an angel of wisdom or a Machiavellian villain, and Bismarck has been represented as both. What matters is not some phrase or other but the sum of a man's life and achievements.

In 1870 there was no need for cunning 'traps' to provoke France because the country was desperately on edge. To avoid the clash between Hohenzollern Germany, spoilt by recent good fortune and bursting at its seams, and the French Empire profoundly insecure and, though outwardly still presiding over the European concert of nations, in decay; to accomplish the union of the south German states and the North German Confederation gradually without war – *this* would have required real statesmanship, the art of moderation, of tactful forbearance which Bismarck knew so well how to use if it suited him. Even today one is still inclined to believe that the situation might have been saved by honest, direct language, an appeal to the principle of national self-determination which Bonapartist France in particular could not have denied, combined with the utmost care and the offer of a guarantee that a 'little' German federal Empire would not disturb the peace. But there was no mention of this. National liberal historians have tried hard to prove Bismarck's formal innocence, although nobody has yet claimed that he used ingenuity to avoid war. In this then lies his guilt, more fraught with consequence than any other in his life; whether he set traps or not is by the way.

Instead of unifying at home the nation united against the outside world. It happened again several times that war created a feeling of togetherness with flags, brandished swords and calls for revenge of humiliations which had long ceased to count or were imaginary, with vulgar satirical songs about the defeated enemy. It was the thread not of 1848 but of 1813 that was taken up, as indeed the teaching of German history in the Wilhelminian Empire usually jumped straight from 1813 to 1870 as though nothing had happened in between, as though one 1813 had not been more than enough. The emphasis on this parallel or alleged repetition set a completely false tone, creating a permanent holiday feeling, the myth of success connected with the one great man, the ostentatious display of strength, and, in spite of all peaceful diplomacy, the permanent readiness for war. According to an entry in Prince Hohenlohe's diary Bismarck said in the spring of 1870 that Germany must be prepared not for one but for a series of four wars. This is quite possible because even eighteen years later in his comments on the Emperor Frederick's diary he writes that the general conviction at the time had been that the Franco-German war was the beginning of a series of wars, of a 'militant century'. It is debatable if this actually happened. The old generals of 1914 were the lieutenants of 1870; much time passed between those two wars and particularly in the eighties they probably did not imagine that they would again be called upon. The sequence from 1870 to 1914 is not as clear as that from 1914 to 1939. In political history one can never speak without qualification of repetition, continuation or counter-blow, particularly if forty-three years have passed between the first and the second event. In 1914 only the very old had the comfortable feeling that they were experiencing a second 1870; history quickly passed over them on to a completely new order of things.

If it was untrue and disastrous to claim a link with the Wars of Liberation, a link with the old Empire was inevitably felt. The end of the Holy Roman Empire was not so far away, the oldest generation had lived through it; in between there had been the Confederation of the Rhine, the German Confederation and the short-lived Reich of 1849, all of which represented a certain continuity; and people like to look upon new foundation as restoration. Without the words 'Emperor', 'Empire', and 'Chancellor' unification would not have been nearly as pleasurable. It must be added that these words alone linked the Reich of the Hohenzollerns with the Holy Roman Empire. There was not a breath of the spirit of the old in the new, as there still had been in the dreams of Freiherr vom Stein. Of course, Stein had not really been successful as a politician even sixty years earlier, and the cause of his failure, the principle of the state based on power, had since become stronger. It was impossible now to return to a Christian, universal institution embracing non-German elements, and Bismarck was the last person to struggle for impossible ideals. He lacked Stein's noble conception of man and of politics; as long as they were 'God-given' they could be roughly hewn, provisional and inadequate. He impatiently denied any responsibility except to his own state, and throughout his life described as fraudulent the use of the concept of 'Europe'. How could such a man create anything that had genuine links with the old Empire? How could this be done by the highly realistic, highly commercially minded nationalistic bourgeoisie with whom he had now become reconciled?

The most imaginative of Bismarck's critics, Konstantin Frantz, made a number of proposals designed to transform the sham

Reich into a genuine one: a closer confederation of west German states possibly to be joined voluntarily by Switzerland and the Netherlands; this confederation to form an alliance with the two semi-German states extending to the east, Austria and Prussia, which themselves would constitute the legal link between Hungary and Poland and the western confederation; the whole complex to have no capital and to be something between a federal state and a European league of nations, intended to overcome the narrow concept of the national state which would never do for Germany and central Europe. Today one reads these suggestions with sympathetic agreement and feels how desirable all this would have been. Frantz's criticism of Hohenzollern Germany, of the unhistorical, unnatural character of the new imperial capital, of the false façade of the federal state is justified. But it was not only Germany which sought at the time to establish a *state* with clearly marked frontiers and a strong government. In any case Switzerland and Belgium would certainly have refused with horror the invitation to join Frantz's western confederation. At the time these were dreams on paper. Today the situation is different, today it is worthwhile to return to Frantz's writings.

Bismarck's work seems complicated if one wants to fit it into the framework of conventional concepts of political philosophy. The new Reich was not the old, nor was it a genuine federal state because there was no central authority above the 'allied governments' and because the power of one of the allies made the equality of the others into a mere polite formula. Nor was it a genuine nation-state because a substantial part of the nation remained outside and was, according to Bismarck's intention, to remain outside forever. It was what it was, difficult to give a name to but uncomplicated in its origins. The foundation of the American union was preceded by splendid theoretical discussions and profound philosophical investigations. The foundation of the German Reich was preceded by nothing but – as people said at the time – Bismarck's 'great successes', the war against Austria, the annexations, the North German Confederation, the military alliances with the southern states, the 'customs parliament' set up by blackmail, and finally the 'treaties of alliance' concluded in the flush of victory in 1870. Too much elaborate theory may harm a cause, as it has probably harmed American constitutional life to the present day. Too much brutal pragmatism has the same effect. The Reich suffered because bits that did not make a whole were hastily and roughly thrown together, the Prussian military monarchy, federation and universal suffrage. Bismarck despised theory and relied on the force of facts, of growth and development which defies theoretical definition. What developed in Germany could not be fitted into the construction of 1870, with the result that there was the most damaging tension. Bismarck attracted success but basically his work was not blessed. As a politician he knew neither pity nor dreams. He only dealt with actual, urgent possibilities, and he did so mercilessly. It is this opaque quality of his political character that makes it impossible to fit either his ideas or his achievements into conventional concepts. On the other hand it also explains his success. Had he been an idealist like Stein he would not have controlled the course of events in a manner so unique in history, as he did from 1863 to 1870.

He himself often denied this control with delightful modesty, saying that the statesman could do so much less than the public believed. In any case he had no choice; some form of unification of the nation was inevitable because people wanted it and had never ceased to do so. There was, as time would show, a force in Germany which demanded organization, and free, expansive activity. Bismarck gave the minimum, the alliance of old Prussia with the liberal medium-size and small states. Although there was something unnatural and impermanent in this solution it produced the tolerable order which reigned for forty years in central and eastern Europe, the peaceful co-existence of the three empires and the many different peoples that dwelt in them. Forty years may be regarded as a long or a short period. Nowadays unfortunately we have reason to regard it as a long period. In the end nobody is right. Could the 'greater' German imperialist democracy have avoided terrible catastrophes if, difficult though it is to imagine, it had been victorious in 1848; could the idea of opening the floodgates of national revolution in Hungary,

Bohemia and Poland which Bismarck toyed with for a moment in 1866 have been more beneficial then than it proved in 1918; could Bismarck's German successors have done better than they actually did – one must not allow the positivists to prevent one from reflecting on such questions. Yet they will remain unanswered, like an instructive puzzle that can never be solved.

Part Seven
In the New Reich (1871–1888)

This was the period of the great transformation to which the labels 'industrialization', 'urbanization' and 'age of the masses' are attached. Not only in Germany but also in the rest of Europe and in America; today this transformation is taking place all over the world. It is the same everywhere and yet it differs completely from place to place, depending on what it encounters. In the France of the seventies and eighties its effects were not as marked as in Germany; the French remained a little more true to what they had been than the Germans. In Britain the great change occurred comparatively gradually and historical continuity was preserved more successfully. America was fortunate in being spacious and rich and in having broken away from its European past before the industrial revolution started in earnest. Germany lacked space and was burdened by its political inheritance, by its old virtues and old vices. The decades which in deceptive retrospect seem happy, innocent years of peace, saw an internal expansion in Germany which can be likened to an explosion: the population increased, big cities sprang up, the structure of society changed, agriculture declined and the nation became increasingly dependent on foreign trade with all the incalculable consequences of such a development in every sphere of life.

This was the really significant development compared with which ministerial changes and party intrigues were of minor importance. The last chapters dealt mainly with politics which, in the sixties, shaped the future. Bismarck's audacious game determined Germany's frontiers and the form of government under which the nation would live in future. After 1870 the situation changed. The age of dramatic decisions, of long hoped-for, finally accomplished objectives was over, and, as happens to the individual, once wishes have come true in the history of nations they fall short of what they promised. Although the clever, selfish, hard-hearted, neurotic old man remained in office for twenty more years, he no longer knew how to direct well-aimed blows to shape events as he wanted. He was only an oppressive element, juggling and vacillating while trying to remain in power. He barely understood the great change over which as *Reichskanzler* he presided. It happened according to its own law and, to the extent that he was aware of it, against his will. Bismarck now wanted peace and quiet and if it had been within his power he would have made history stand still.

The story of the great change of a nation of peasants into a nation of labourers and white-collar workers has no clearly defined beginning or interruptions which could serve as sensible dividing lines. The beginnings of German industry go back a long way. The forties, and even more the fifties, brought a leap forward. In 1870 German industry had not yet overtaken France; better military organization, not a superior industry, gave the Germans their victory. Thereafter the curve rises noticeably more steeply; first under Bismarck, and then even more so under William II. Like a speck of grease in a plate of soup the pompous imperial regime floated on the stream of prosperity created by others.

1. Society and its Classes

The soil of Germany is relatively infertile; it is rich in a number of raw materials, coal, iron, potash, but poor in others no less essential for large-scale industrial development, such as lead, zinc and copper. It was not the nature of the country that predestined its inhabitants to be a leading industrial nation. Theirs was an effort of the mind, of willpower, self-confidence, of enjoyment of successful action; as the population increased and could no longer live on the country's agricultural output, this effort became a matter of unavoidable necessity.

There had been factory workers since the destruction of the old village community by the legislation of the early nineteenth century. The landless, and precisely the ablest and most enterprising among them, were attracted into the towns. The more were needed the more followed; advances in medical science and hygiene implied that the new generations would be more numerous than the old. The increase in the size of the population was followed by industrial expansion which in turn was followed by a further increase in the size of the population. Whereas around 1800 Germany did not have significantly more inhabitants than before the Thirty Years War, around 1900 it had at least three times as many. It was not the rural population that increased but the town-dwellers. Vast suburbs grew up around the old town centres, with uniform, dismal rows of streets, named after the battles of the Franco-German wars but lived in by people who cared little about the glory of the fatherland. This was when the term *Grossstadt* was invented; as early as the seventies the Berliners referred proudly to their 'world city'. Between 1848 and 1914 the population of Berlin increased tenfold, from 400,000 to four million; the same was true of other big cities of the Reich: Hamburg, Cologne, Munich, Leipzig and Frankfurt. What, if anything, did these new towns, their shape, their way of life, have in common with the old ones whose name they bore?

The state, authoritarian in the political sphere but liberal in economic matters, gave capitalism what it wanted: a capital market, a commercial code, a single note-issuing bank, a more rational currency and a simpler system of weights and measures. Then the milliards of the French war indemnity acted like a stimulating drug in the blood of the German economy. Large sections of the middle classes and the aristocracy were possessed by mad acquisitive greed. Between 1871 and 1874 no less than 857 limited liability companies were founded with a capital of more than four milliard marks, among them many fraudulent ones. Then came the day of reckoning, a period of hard struggle for economic survival. But expansion and consolidation continued, the creation of new industries and of new demands.

This was the age of the banks. Although most of them were founded before 1870, it was only now that they developed into organizations with thousands of employees, with marble palaces in the Berlin district of Friedrichstadt, temples of the new God; there was the *Deutsche Bank*, the *Dresdner Bank*, the *Darmstädter Bank*, the *Disconto-Gesellschaft* and the *Berlin Handelsgesellschaft*. Their growth was stimulated by industry whose development they promoted; they financed industrial expansion, took part in setting up new firms and founded businesses themselves. Their directors participated in the control of industrial concerns as members of boards. In no other country, the experts tell us, did a few big banks have such a decisive influence on the direction of the economy; so much so that finally the two spheres of power, industry and finance, practically united. In America some great industrialist might own a bank. In Germany the reverse was the case; the banks controlled many industrial concerns. After 1875 the German banks were headed by the *Reichsbank*; it was the guardian of the new currency, with a monopoly or near monopoly of the note issue, and at the same time the largest, most carefully directed institute for credit creation. The founding capital of the *Reichsbank* came from private individuals who belonged to the bank's central committee; at the same time it was a state institution whose directors were appointed by the Kaiser.

This was the age of industry which was stimulated by the needs of the network of railways – completed only after 1870 – by the construction of roads and waterways, by the requirements of the army and of the growing merchant fleet, and finally – though this came later – of the navy. It was stimulated also by the growing demand of the domestic market, of the new towns, though only too soon it came to depend on export to foreign nations or governments. Industry worked closely with the banks, owned by limited liability companies or by private members of the middle classes, and in eastern Germany also by landowners who refurbished their nobility with the glitter from coal and iron. It was directed by very capable but usually harsh, stubborn factory owners, built up by engineers who were provided in large numbers by the new technical schools, and was kept going by the ever-growing millions of factory workers of both sexes. Thus German industry, which a few decades earlier had only been a dream of Friedrich List and Karl Marx, became a reality. There was a mining industry, a machine industry, a textile industry, a chemical industry, and finally, starting in the eighties, an electrical industry which later achieved the greatest concentrations of capital. Total German industrial production overtook that of France in the seventies, caught up with the British around 1900 and surpassed it substantially by 1910; by this time it was second only to the American. Around 1830 four fifths of the German population lived on the land and earned their living in agriculture; in 1860 the number had fallen to three fifths, in 1882 to two-fifths and in 1895 it was barely one fifth. The second greatest source of energy in the world was established within a period of forty years, in the state which had been thought incapable of possessing even the force of industrial organization shown by France. This is the essence of German history in that period. The rest, using for once the well-known Marxist term, is 'superstructure'. But the superstructure is important. Because the big question was how would the nation use this new energy? How would it control and harness it within the confined space of the continent in which Germany was destined to live with many neighbours? How would it adapt its political existence to the most profound social changes which it had ever experienced? Democracy, political and then also economic, is part of modern industry, and anyone who does not want the one must logically not want the other either. But the mere act of not wanting it changes little. It follows its own laws which no armchair politician can contravene.

Into this period falls the rise of the House of Krupp. One is bound to mention the name of Krupp in a history of Germany because for a time it became a symbol of German industry. For hundreds of years the history of the Krupps is that of an up-right, unassuming family. In the nineteenth century it became industrial history and finally, under William II, also political history. Industrial and political power became disastrously inter-mingled.

The Krupps were a money-making, trading line of patricians in Essen, active in local politics, who occasionally made guns but on the whole preferred trade to production. Then their family history became industrial history as a result of the great inven-tions of the age, the increase in demand, the political events, the *Zollverein* and the wars. The personalities concerned were Fried-rich Krupp, an inventive speculator, pro-French in Napoleon's day, and his son Alfred, the actual founder of the firm, a man of the nineteenth century, who was born when his father was serving Napoleon and died when it was important to gain the favour of the Prusso-German Crown Prince, William, and when his factories employed more than 50,000 workers. Alfred Krupp was unequalled as a merchant and organizer, he knew exactly where political power was rising, where good relations paid; sensitive and brutal, a merciless competitor, he was an angry patriarch among his people, good-looking with a splendid beard and a sad mouth. He was eager to supply the whole world, friend and foe alike, with guns, and claiming unsuccessfully a monopoly in Prussia-Germany, he was always prepared to threaten the state with the sale of his firm to France or with emigration to Russia, an argument which he himself described as the 'surest form of pressure' and as 'strong tobacco'. To King William I, who blamed him for supplying hostile Austria, he said outright: 'We cannot live on Prussia alone.' A leaflet distributed for him in Britain said that in the last Russo-Turkish war both parties had been supplied to their satisfaction by him. If Krupp nevertheless sometimes boasted of the patriotic rejection of non-German offers or submitted to the Prussian government projects that were of the greatest advantage to himself, pretending to be motivated by patriotic sentiments, the Minister of War, von Roon, would reply with barely disguised irony: 'Even though I abstain for the moment from examining your proposals I cannot refrain from expressing my admiration of the way in which you ignore your own financial interest in the matter.' Alfred Krupp loathed the Social Democrats. 'I wish,' he wrote on one occasion, 'that someone of great talent would organize a counter-revolt.' The housing estates which he built for his workers were well supplied with informers.

What makes for political difficulties is a situation in which the state does not, as it must and can, control the armaments industry, but in which the armaments industry interferes with the state. This is what Krupps did in the Germany of William II. At that time the greatness of the House of Krupp no longer depended on the dynamism of one personality; the last Krupp, Friedrich Alfred, was a hypochondriac who took no interest in business. It was the vast complex of the family firm that was active and wanted to grow, and on it depended an army of directors, agents, industrial spies, ambassadors, ex-ministers, ex-generals and assorted dignitaries. In Germany Krupps eliminated their most dangerous competitors by buying up their shares; the firm's main concern became the struggle, supported by the highest quarters, for the world armaments market, against British and French competition. Krupp exerted his influence on German diplomacy in Africa and Asia. He profited from the building of the German navy and also from Britain's reaction against it; as British industry also worked with Krupp licences, the firm was interested in both German and non-German or anti-German armaments production. No wonder that Krupp helped to finance the Navy League and that he was against disarmament. This was industrial power closely associated with political power; no longer the power of an individual, hardly even of a family – because these Krupps were insignificant men – but industrial power as such which must expand in peace and, still more, in war.

The young Marx described two laws in particular, that of inevitable expansion and that of inevitable, never-ending concentration. Germany now became the classic example of the truth of both prophecies. The production of hard coal rose from 34 million tons in 1875 to 74 million in 1895, 109 million in 1900 and 150 million in 1910. The production of iron and steel, machinery and equipment increased proportionately. With this expansion there came a search for new markets, pursued first at random and then with scientific orderliness given political support. More and more people worked in big concerns, fewer and fewer people controlled increasingly large combinations within particular concerns which grew and swallowed up the smaller ones by forming 'organic' or 'vertical associations'. Ore and coal mines, blast furnaces, steel mills, foundries were amalgamated into single enterprises through the controlling power of the banks, through the cartels which in the eighties started to organize almost all branches of the raw materials and semi-finished goods industries, first by means of loose price agreements and then by laying down exactly what quantities should be produced and where they should be sold. Towering above everything was the biggest concentration of all, the state, either in its 'Prussian' form or as the Reich. The fact that the state gave orders, that it owned firms, produced economic, social and tariff legislation and that there existed close personal connections between the government, the limited power of the Reichstag and the real power of the rich, made the state the central organ of the capitalist economy. Therefore it became one of the main concerns of all large-scale economic interests to influence the state. Parliament, bureaucracy or more doubtful media were used for the purpose.

How different the state now was from the enlightened *Biedermeier* officialdom of King Frederick William III with its few million thalers to dispose of; how different also from the dream dreamt by the men of 1848 of the free, popular state governed by ideas. Ludwig Uhland would have felt unhappy in the new Reich and the survivors of the *Paulskirche* felt strangers in it. The Chancellor himself, who had despised the *Paulskirche* gathering and had destroyed Metternich's German Confederation as a useless, antiquated tool, felt less and less at home in the Reich whose form he had created but whose rhythm he had imagined differently. Even in the seventies Bismarck complained that he was really no longer the right man for the new tasks as he understood nothing about the all-important economic issues. In his old age, visiting the port of Hamburg, he looked down on the mass of ships and cranes and workers and shuddered as he murmured to himself: 'this is a new age' – which indeed it was. For someone who in his youth had attended the balls at the court of Frederick William III it must have been a strange, sinister and ultimately incomprehensible age. Although new ages do not come about from one day to the next this one took only a few decades to arrive, starting gradually and then quickening its tempo until it almost resembled an explosion; since when the speed of the change has not slackened up to the present day.

The other prediction that Marx made was that the collective strength of the proletariat would grow in proportion to the concentration of capital. Ever fewer but wealthier exploiters at the one end of the scale and at the other ever greater numbers of more exploited poor. In some sense this prophesy also came true. The number of factory workers increased rapidly, from about six million in 1895 to about eight and a half million in 1907. If among the proletariat are included all those who with the labour of their hands earned a meagre wage at the bottom of the social ladder, factory workers, agricultural workers, office workers and so on, more than two-thirds of the population or thirty-five million people belonged to the proletariat at the end of the century. The rich were a tiny minority; only a quarter of the nation belonged statistically to the reasonably well-off, to the middle classes.

So far Marx was right, but only so far. His simplifying glance overlooked a good deal, did not want to see some things and could not have foreseen others. It was simply not true in the age of Bismarck, in the age of William II, that German society consisted of a very few capitalists and very, very many wretched proletarians. And even if the statements had been true from a purely economic point of view it would not have told the whole story. Man's economic position, his way of working and living, does not completely determine his political and moral existence. There are other factors, religious traditions, values, wishes, dreams and loyalties. Marx knew these influences and in so far as they made it difficult to determine what economic class a man belonged to he called them 'false consciousness'. 'False' because they did not fit in with his ideas. But 'true' in so far as they existed.

We shall come to the rise of the Social Democratic Party later on. Between 1871 and 1914 it claimed to be the only authentic political association of the working class, the party of the 'class-conscious proletariat' in the Marxist sense. After a difficult start it gradually grew until it finally became numerically the strongest party in the country. But even at the height of its success before 1914 it only won four million votes although there were eight million German factory workers. At least half of them could not be bothered to vote or voted for another party, such as the Catholic Centre Party or the Liberals. This means that the social democratic leaders never succeeded in making the German workers as a whole as class-conscious as Marx had imagined that they would become. The same tendency was noticeable in the development of the trade unions where a number of unions totally unconcerned with the ideas of the class struggle successfully competed with the 'free' trade unions which had ties with the Social Democrats.

There undoubtedly is such a thing as the class struggle. It would be there even if Karl Marx had never invented the phrase or made the concept the focal point of his political theory. The establishment of large-scale industry where none exists, with limited funds, is always paid for by what Marx calls surplus value. This had happened fifty years earlier in Britain; it happened fifty years later in Russia, whether it was the state that set up industry, or whether it was done for profit, in free competition, by private individuals. This is what happened in Germany in the last decades of the nineteenth century. People still worked eleven, twelve or thirteen hours a day and no law ensured that Sunday was a day of rest. Wages were low and prices high, highest for housing in the new towns, because capitalists were not interested in building homes for workers. Meanwhile the luxury of the upper classes grew and the rich lived like Renaissance princes, though with less taste. In 1870 the King of Prussia still travelled in an ordinary railway carriage; in 1900 a big industrialist had his own carriage attached to the train because he could not sleep in sheets that were not his own. In the Berlin Tiergarten district new millionaires built sumptuous villas; a false aristocracy given to ostentatious display of all its possessions, filling, as the newspapers readily reported, its goldfish ponds with champagne for garden parties. Some industrialists cared more for work than for pleasure and felt responsible for their workers particularly in places where enterprises had not yet assumed superhuman dimensions, as for example in Württemberg. In general, though, the average German entrepreneur was firmly determined to remain master in his own house. He only gave what he was forced to give and as the state – from which Lassalle had expected so much – exerted almost no pressure, the only alternative was for the workers to organize themselves, to form trade unions and to embark on strikes which in the early days they lost only too often. Only blind men can dispute the reality of the class struggle in all this, only hypocrites can fail to recognize on which side the power of the state with all its means of coercion was to be found. To that extent Marx was right.

There was something amiss though with the 'theory of increasing misery' to which the master attached such importance. The country became richer, and there were more, not fewer, rich men. Although poverty is relative and the standard of living of a nation of factory workers cannot be compared with that of a nation of peasants because their wants and sufferings and satisfactions differ, no one can say that around 1900 in Germany there was more misery than around 1850. Certainly not if one compares the number of those who were very poor with that of those who were not. After all there were many more people in 1900 than in 1850, almost twice as many, the overwhelming majority of whom were not very poor. How happy they were is another virtually unanswerable question; happiness and unhappiness cannot be measured. Should one rejoice because there were more people than there had been? Should one praise or blame the new industry for making the rise in numbers possible? All one can say is that a skilled worker when employed did not lead a dull, hopeless life in Germany around 1890. He still had much to gain, but he knew that he was worth something and gradually he won a fairer share of the fruits of his labour. Famine of the kind that raged in Silesia and East Prussia in 1847 no longer existed.

The structure of society did not become simplified in the sense that Marx had stated to be an historical law; it became more complex. The skilled worker was superior to the unskilled one, he was even, as far as income was concerned, often superior to the small master craftsman with an uncertain clientele. Then there were the foremen and supervisors, the managers and agents, the laboratory workers and engineers, the buyers and salesmen and heads of departments, the ever-growing mass of office workers of all grades in industry, in trade and in the vast state-owned enterprises, railways and post office and customs administration – in every sphere gradations of income, responsibility and rank developed. This was not one mass of people dominated by a few oppressors. There were hierarchies comparable to that of the army from private to general. There were countless new occupations and new titles; and countless small, personal satisfactions could be derived from professional advancement. This situation considerably complicated the social revolution as imagined by Karl Marx. It made it impossible. Highly complex and functioning set-ups cannot be overthrown; although they can be changed and certain existing trends of development can be encouraged, it. is impossible to do away with them completely or to reverse them from one day to the next. The Marxist revolution will take place in the end only in an amorphous and unformed society, and there, of course, it cannot bring what Marx expected from it. There it brings something quite different.

This was the age of capitalism during which there existed, according to Marx's theory, two classes, bourgeoisie and proletariat. They really did exist, though not so distinct, not confronting each other as abstract concepts; there were countless gradations between the extremes of rich and poor. In addition there were the classes which do not really belong to the age of capitalism but which survived because no age is completely dominated by one economic system. Peasants, artisans, shopkeepers and innkeepers were once counted among the 'people'. With the promotion of the capitalist bourgeoisie to the position of ruling class they became known as the 'lower middle classes'. Marx predicted that they would sink down into the proletariat which many of them did. But this class or group of classes was still there and for the nation as a whole it was of inestimable, predominantly conservative importance. Although much sentimental nonsense has been talked about the virtues of honest artisans and pious peasant women, there is some truth in the stories about these virtues, however much they have been exploited by hack writers. Many a bad habit of the age was defeated by the firm traditions of some Bavarian homestead, in the nineteenth and even in the twentieth century.

Within the bourgeoisie the academically trained continued to occupy a special position. In America, the country of complete, naked capitalism unmodified by a great past, scholars counted for little unless they managed to earn large sums as inventors or lawyers. There only financial success counted. Germany on the other hand, had an important pre-capitalist past which it could not just ignore. From the eighteenth and the early nineteenth century, the age of Hegel and Humboldt, came the tradition of respect for the scholar, for the pure theorist as much as for the knowledgeable expert, for the professor of philosophy as much as for the chemist. 'Property and education' were to be the two pillars of society. Of course even education can turn into something odious, into a means of differentiating between classes, which it had not been in the good old days. Fathers sent their sons to a grammar school not to give them the old humanist education but because it was befitting their station in life. Some *Herr Doktor*s remained foolish, uneducated ruffians all their lives. But some also showed independence of mind and heart and succeeded in their aim. The professors of economics, for example, were not all 'ideologists of the ruling class' as Karl Marx's unjust doctrines will have it.

Did the Kaiser's Germany have a ruling class at all, and if so which was it? Marx himself answers this question as it can only be answered by a brilliant, malicious observer from a distance. Bismarck's Reich, he writes, is 'a military despotism, bedecked with parliamentary trimmings, with an admixture of feudalism, influenced by the bourgeoisie, bureaucratically constructed and protected by the police'.

The class which now moulded the economic life of the nation was the capitalist one, the great financiers, industrialists and merchants. But this class did not rule politically, although its representatives had the ear of the government, in parliament or outside. It did not make foreign policy, it did not control the administration of the country or the army, nor could it determine what was fashionable or in good taste. In Prussian-Germany all these prerogatives still belonged to the pre-capitalist aristocracy. To preserve this state of affairs was one of the goals which the greatest of all the Junkers had set for himself, and only on that condition had the old Prussia allowed him to found the Reich and to make his limited bargains with nationalism, liberalism and capitalism. Economically the Prussian landowners lagged far behind the new industrialists; they were not well off, they were threatened by competition from larger, more fertile countries and they needed the help of the state. Of this they were all the more certain because their representatives controlled the levers of power, in the government and the administration, in the army, the diplomatic service and at Court. Particularly at Court, at the palace of the king-emperor, the place where all final decisions were nominally taken as well as some really momentous ones. The Junkers were still politically the ruling class – if there was one at all. Some of them, whose estates were suitable for the purpose, became great industrialists themselves, the Plesses, the Henckel-Donnersmarcks, the Hohenlohe-Ratibors. More frequently the opposite happened: rich members of the bourgeoisie saw the crowning of their life's work when they were raised to the peerage whose style they copied admiringly. It really became a defiant class style only now, joyfully ridiculed by the liberal satirical journals; the style of the privileged student corporations, of the officers' mess, the style of hunting and shooting country gentlemen translated into urban terms. Formerly the aristocracy had formed an estate, not a class; at the time when Germany was a state of estates not of classes, when it had neither a capital nor a society. As the bourgeoisie and the workers became classes the aristocracy also developed into a class, all the more defiant in its style because it realized that its ruling position was threatened.

Let us not condemn any historical class as a whole. It always consists of men of flesh and blood who are free to rise above the spirit of their class or to revolt against it. Great poets like Heinrich von Kleist were Junkers; active idealists and pacifists without any trace of the Junker spirit came from that much abused class. In our own times we have seen some bearers of the most famous Prussian names sacrifice themselves in vain to save their country. Even as a class the Prussian noble caste had its virtues, those of sobriety, energy, protestant piety and modest assurance. Even their marked urge towards power, egoistic as it was – what urge towards power is not? – might be regarded as a virtue or at least as a strong point, by the state. Historical power is never without historical guilt. Let us therefore grant the Junkers their merits as we chalk up their guilt.

Towards the end of the century their guilt outweighed their merits. Neither their economic policy nor their attitude of mind gave the Junkers a right to leadership in the new, industrial and democratic age. But they could not abandon their position, they did not know how to adapt themselves, how to give way and to withdraw gradually as the British aristocracy had done with as much wisdom as grace. Equally they were incapable of retiring into splendid isolation like the French, because their determination to have power was too great and their wealth too small. Relying on the King, who for his part relied on them, they became a burden to the country. They constituted an obstacle in the path of the political education of the middle classes by preventing them from assuming authority; and the middle classes were weak enough to allow this to happen and to be satisfied with economic advantages. Even their fellow Junker Bismarck did not behave as they wanted him to because he compromised with the new age in a way which they did not understand, although his compromises were designed to delay their own political downfall. Hence the unnatural, old-fashioned, problematical nature of German political life. The Junkers failed because they could not surrender the power which they had, the middle classes because they could not grasp it.

As a young man Bismarck once described the patriarchal conditions on his estate:

> The air here preserves the servants. Bellin is the son of a local peasant who started as groom with my father and has now been in service for forty years, thirty-two of them as bailiff; his wife was born in our service, daughter of the last and sister of the present shepherd; the latter and the chief bricklayer who will also soon be sixty are the second generation of servants, their fathers having held the same positions with my grandfather and father. The gardener's family unfortunately died out last year with a childless fifty-seven year old who had inherited the job from his father . . . I must admit that I am proud of this long rule of the conservative principle in this house where my forebears have lived for hundreds of years, in the same rooms in which they were born and died . . .

These words came from the Junker's heart; his strength was rooted in this experience, in these sympathies. Fifty years later, in 1895, in his inaugural address at Freiburg, a young professor of economics, Max Weber, described the 'economic death struggle' of the Junkers. The age of the patriarchal way of life east of the Elbe was past. The German farm workers were drawn towards the towns.

> The old patriarchal relationship between the landowner and the small farmer which gave the day-labourer a direct interest in agricultural production by entitling him to a share of it, is disappearing. Seasonal work in the beet districts demands seasonal labour and money wages. The farm workers face a purely proletarian existence, but without that possibility of raising themselves to economic independence which in the towns gives the locally organized industrial proletariat self-confidence.

Germans were replaced by immigrant Polish workers who were prepared to accept what the lord of the manor could still offer.

> On the sugar beet estates the patriarchal landlord is replaced by a caste of industrial businessmen – and at the top, as a result of the desperate agricultural situation, the size of the estates is diminishing, and colonies of tenants and owner-farmers of small holdings are growing up

on the periphery of the estates. The economic foundations of the position of the old landed aristocracy are crumbling; it is developing into something other than it was.

Such a development, Max Weber continues with his upright rigour, is of more than mere economic importance. 'Large estates which can only be kept up at the expense of Germany, from the point of view of the nation deserve to disappear . . .' What about the political claims of their owners? 'For an economically declining class to be in political control is dangerous and in the long run incompatible with the interests of the nation.' The Junkers could no longer solve the tasks of the present. Not even the greatest of the Junkers could do it.

The tragedy of his political achievement, however great . . . future generations will probably find in the fact that under him his creation, the nation which he united, gradually and irresistibly changed its economic structure and became something different, a nation that was bound to demand systems other than those which he could give it and into which his autocratic nature could fit. In the last resort this was what led to the partial failure of his life's work.

And the classes called upon to take over the burden of power from the Junkers? Max Weber views them with profound pessimism. The German middle classes were not ready to lead the state; if anything the great man's long rule had made them less ready.

Part of the upper middle class longs only too obviously for the appearance of a new Caesar who will protect it – against the emergence of classes from below, and from above against social and political impulses of which they suspect the German dynasties. Another part has long become submerged in the political philistinism from which the broad mass of the lower middle class has never emerged.

As for the German working class, it was economically

far more mature than the egoism of the propertied classes will admit and it rightly demands the freedom to represent its interests even in the form of open organized economic confrontation. *Politically* it is infinitely less mature than a journalistic clique which would like to monopolize its leadership wants to believe.

The workers were really part of the lower middle class. They knew nothing about power, how to obtain it or how to use it.

Max Weber saw the struggle for existence, of the individual as well as of nations, in very grim terms. For him life was a permanent, relentless war, and Germans and Slavs must fight like wild beasts for space in which to live. His views show where his generation was right and where it was wrong. His claim that Germany could only exist as a world-power with a daring grand-scale policy was all too quickly taken up by people who would have done better to leave well alone. But his analysis of the structure of German society is memorable. His inaugural lecture represents a dividing line between epochs: between the vanishing age of Bismarck and the 'pre-war period' about to begin. Weber looked into the past and into the future with the same penetrating glance.

2. Parties

In a society of the kind into which the German people now developed there is a constant struggle for the offices and benefices in the gift of the state, a struggle for power and for the things that can be achieved with power, economic and cultural standards, laws and financial advantage. This political struggle is carried on by the parties. Although they must change with the society which they represent and whose approval they seek, they are moulded by the political system with which they deal, unless they succeed in moulding the state according to their wish of the moment. This the German parties did not succeed in doing. The tradition of the state which they found was too powerful. One man was too powerful, the Chancellor, who needed them and who flirted with them but who also weakened and corrupted them whenever he could.

We are speaking of the 'Reich'. German history is complicated by the fact that Prussia was two-thirds of the Reich, but that in politics the Reich and Prussia were never identical Prussia was different, technically because of its three-class electoral system and in fact because of the nature of its society and old ruling class. The southern German states were also different; in some respects they were more liberal than the Reich and were gradually moving towards a parliamentary form of government. But these were regional developments, of little importance for the whole. There was nothing regional about Prussia. The fact that Prussia and the Reich shared the capital, the monarch, the army and a large part of the administrative machinery as well as the Chancellor-cum-Prime Minister, that – let us repeat – it was two-thirds of the Reich while being something different, governed differently, with different party structures, somehow gave the policy of the Reich a distorted, vexatious character, unlike that of any other state in the world. Nevertheless we must henceforth speak mainly of the Reich, not of Prussia and still less of the smaller German states which continued to lead a refreshingly different, harmless existence. Decisions were now taken in the Reich, from the legislation of the seventies to the declarations of war in August 1914.

Among the political parties in the Reich it is possible to distinguish between the old and the new. The old were parties of men of rank formed at a time when the number of voters was small, when the 'people' were not yet politically mobilized: Conservatives, National Liberals, and even Progressives, though in the sixties the Prussian *Fortschrittspartei* claimed with great emotion to represent the people. The new parties were genuine people's parties, vast mass organizations which played a role in the life of the masses: the Centre and the Social Democrats.

The Conservatives were predominantly Prussian. They could lay down the law in the Prussian Chamber of Deputies and the Upper House, but not in the Reichstag. They had been unhappy about the North German Confederation, about the 'Indemnity' of 1866, about the foundation of the Reich; now they were anything but happy about the concessions which Bismarck made to the principle of the liberal nation-state which tolerated no other God beside itself. Their opposition to the Chancellor, who was one of them but who outgrew them so strangely, on occasion assumed the character of extreme, slanderous malice, and Bismarck, being who he was, replied in kind.

A group broke away from the Conservatives which called itself the 'Free Conservatives'. Numerically it was small, a party of the rich, particularly of the aristocratic great industrialists. They were conservative to the extent that they wanted to preserve what had just been gained, the prerogatives of capitalism. They had no objection to the Reich and no objections whatsoever to Bismarck.

To the left of the Free Conservatives were the National Liberals, the party that had broken away from the Progressives in 1866 in order to make peace with the victor. This was the real Reich party, the heir of the *Nationalverein*. Its members came from western Prussia, from the annexed provinces and from southern Germany. Like every big party it had its fringes and its conciliatory central figures, its defenders of principles, its champions of special interests and its opportunists. Its ideal was the *Rechtsstaat*, the progressive, constitutional and national state whose federal character must not be strengthened, and latterly also the parliamentary state. Its stars were given to making grand speeches and grand gestures – heirs of the *Paulskirche*. They were not interested in social problems, a subject on which they almost shared the views of their neighbours on the 'free conservative' right, like von Kardorff and von Stumm. But undeniably they were led by good German patriots and true parliamentarians. Any statesman who seriously wanted to do so could have built up a responsible parliamentary government with the National Liberals of the seventies. But Bismarck did not want to do so.

To the left of the National Liberals were those who had remained unreconciled, the old *Fortschrittspartei*. Its members were more conscious of matters of principle than the Liberals, they remembered the conflict of 1862 and regarded the government as an alien power which must be severely restricted until they themselves took over, until Germany became a parliamentary state. Bismarck claimed that the *Fortschrittspartei* wanted a republic, but there is no evidence of this. It was just that the party disliked the Chancellor and opposed him – an attitude which Bismarck never hesitated to label as *reichsfeindlich*. Even Richter's *Fortschrittspartei* was certainly not a socialist mass party. It wanted progress, but only in constitutional questions; social progress would follow of its own accord if nature was allowed to take its course.

There were links between all these groups. The right wing of the National Liberals looked towards the Free Conservatives while the left was on friendly terms with the *Fortschrittspartei* with which it actually formed a new party in 1884, called the *Deutsche Freisinnige*. In Bismarck's later period the National Liberals, Free Conservatives and old Conservatives collaborated closely, and for election purposes temporarily with success.

Bismarck, who did not like parties, said in his memoirs that

most members of a parliamentary party find themselves in the same position as most of those who profess different religions; they are embarrassed when one asks them to describe what characteristics distinguish their own convictions from competing ones. In our parliamentary parties the real point of crystallization is not a programme but a person, a parliamentary condottiere.

Twenty-five years later Max Weber came to a similar conclusion: what kept the parties apart were not so much fundamental differences of opinion, as the technical staff which individual leading politicians had at their disposal. It is true that it is difficult to describe the ideological differences which it was claimed separated the many liberal or semi-liberal groups. Where it was a matter of concrete questions the differences of opinion usually occurred not between parties but within them, and it was with difficulty that the leaders found a workable compromise and kept their followers together. No really major issues arose. The age was undramatic once the protracted drama which led to the foundation of the Reich was, or seemed to be, concluded; a student of history today might well think that he would happily have borne the worries of that generation. Yet the seventies are regarded as the golden age of German parliamentary life. The level of debate was high; among those who raised their voice in the Reichstag were Treitschke, the brilliant prophet of the powerful nation-state, Mommsen, the antiquarian and eloquent historian of Rome, and Virchow, the noted physician, vigorous defenders of the constitutional state and positivist deriders of religion. Later when the Reichstag had more political influence its intellectual level declined; intellect and power are not necessarily identical. The *Paulskirche*, which proved politically impotent, was a gathering of distinguished men, and the Prussian United Diet of 1847 was perhaps the most dignified and intelligent parliament which Germany ever had, in spite of the uncertainty and the total insufficiency of its rights. In the end a parliament reflects the nation, its capabilities, interests and values. As the golden age of German literature falls in the first half of the nineteenth century and not in the second half or in the twentieth century, it is not surprising that the intellectual – or let us say the literary – level of the earliest parliaments was higher than that of the later ones.

Facing the old parties there were the parties which disturbed the peace. Their beginnings were small but the future was theirs. Bismarck, who may have suspected this, hated them and tried to destroy them, because he did like the future, *this* future.

The *Zentrumspartei* was a strange product of German history and also of conditions in Europe around 1870. There was no other great European country in which the Catholics were a minority but at the same time such a very strong minority. This, in the middle of the enlightened nineteenth century, was a result of decisions taken in the sixteenth. As Protestantism appeared to have won a great victory recently – it was the Protestant Prussian state that had set up the national state, and, what is more, it had done so in league with the un-Catholic intellectual strength of liberalism – it was felt that the German Catholics too must take up the new weapons of party politics so as not to lose their heritage to an estranged world. The church must remain independent of the ever more-powerful state. It must be able to teach freely in churches and schools, it must preserve its influence over men's souls by using the old methods, and strengthen it by founding modern institutions, newspapers and clubs, for the welfare of the working masses. To do all this it was necessary to enter the political arena. The Catholic Church felt that constitutions served a purpose if they were utilized properly; if the invention of liberalism was used to restrict liberalism. Religious freedom was one of the basic rights of the citizen listed in the Prussian constitution, and hitherto the Prussian state had treated all great religious communities with exemplary fairness. But there was reason to believe that things would not continue so smoothly in the 'Protestant empire'.

The Catholic Church suspected the spirit of the age in which the foundation of The German Reich was a typical event. This followed on the foundation of the kingdom of Italy, completed by the proclamation of Rome as the national capital during the Franco–German war. Only a few weeks before Pius IX had wrested from the great assembly of bishops, the Vatican Council, the dogma of papal infallibility which proclaimed with a clarity never achieved before his absolute spiritual supremacy. It was the same Pope who in 1864 had practically declared war on the *Zeitgeist* by announcing that it was an error to think that the Pope 'can and must reconcile Himself with progress, Liberalism and modern civilization'. This was one side of the medal, the other was the fall of the Papal State, the triumph of Prussia over Catholic Austria and France, and revolutionary unrest even in arch-Catholic Spain. No wonder that the church felt threatened by the liberal state and that the liberal state felt threatened by the *Ecclesia militans* reviving its claims from the distant past. The two adversaries over-estimated each other.

Such was the background against which in the late autumn of 1870 the Centre Party was founded or revived – at first only in Prussia; the party organization which covered the whole Reich was the result of many years of alliances and mergers. To start with it was not intended to be an exclusively Catholic party. Its founders, Peter Reichensperger, von Mallinckrodt and Bishop Ketteler, hoped for a Protestant wing. Christianity instead of religious indifference, religious and natural obligations instead of the neo-Machiavellianism of the state, social responsibility instead of *laissez-faire*, the historic rights of the German states instead of the increasing power of Prussia – those were the principles that inspired the party's founders. Some of them had voted against the constitution of the North German Confederation and against the treaties of alliance of 1870 because

the treaties did not provide the same guarantees for religious freedom as the Prussian constitution, because the separation between the authority of the Reich and that of the states was not sufficiently distinct and because these treaties opened the certain road to militarism and imperialism.

The threat to peace presented by militarism, stated another proclamation, was far greater than the safeguard which it provided.

The German Catholics, the old *Grossdeutsche*, those who cared about the idyll of the German principalities, were joined by a variety of protesting allies, Catholic deputies from Alsace and Lorraine, Catholic Poles, unreconciled Hanoverians or 'Guelfs', as they were called after their exiled royal house. A Guelf soon became leader of the new party. Ludwig Windthorst was the most brilliant parliamentarian whom Germany has ever possessed. A sly idealist, a devout fox, a man of principles and a very clever politician, dignified and cunning, Ludwig Windthorst took pride of place in gatherings in which there was no shortage of great names; and he went on to win for his party, a combination of minorities, the key position in German politics. He did it in the face of Bismarck's hatred, in spite of repeated blows from the Chancellor who, for the first time, experienced or could have experienced, the superiority of organized intellect; to the bitter end the great man failed to understand what was happening to him.

The cleverness of Windthorst and his friends was not the only source of the Centre's invincible strength. Working in close collaboration with the Catholic Church the party could reach the masses and offer them something to warm their souls. It appealed to human beings, not just to unilateral interests. Moreover, it stood literally at the centre, not so much because it was situated *between* the Left and the Right as because it absorbed conservative and socialist tendencies. With the Conservatives it shared loyalty to the country, opposition to the unitary state, and the belief that historical bonds were stronger than ties dictated only by reason. For the Centre the philosophy of the Liberals amounted to this: unrestricted freedom of the individual and above it, abruptly, the omnipotence of the state. Catholic policy, on the other hand, demanded a state that was more than a mere night-watchman, that protected its citizens and looked after their material and moral welfare, while at the same time recognizing the independence of the corporations and associations thriving in it, the independence for example of religious societies. One can call this conservative. But as political ideas only need a slight twist to turn them into the very opposite of what, according to current opinion, they are, the political philosophy of the Centre also had its socialist aspects. It believed in *rights*, natural or God-given. This attitude can lead either to conservative or to revolutionary demands, depending on whether people get excited about existing rights or about ones that do not yet exist. The worker has a right to work, a right to a wage which gives him a decent existence. If the mechanism of supply and demand does not give him these rights then it must be adjusted either from above by legislation or from below by trade unions. We recall that even in the early days of German socialism there were curious links between active Christians and Socialists, between Lassalle and Bishop Ketteler. Certainly Lassalle also toyed with the Conservatives, with Bismarck, but nothing came of this game. Both sides played it for tactical reasons only. The alliance between conservatism and socialism, possibly in theory and attempted again and again, did not come to anything in the reality of German bourgeois society; not even after the dissolution of German bourgeois society. Only in the Centre Party did the idea of a conservative-socialist link not remain mere speculation, only there did it not become a lie which upset all intellectual positions. Christian trade unions were founded and workers or former workers sat among the members of the Centre Party in the Reichstag.

In a society increasingly sharply divided into classes the Centre was able to appeal to all classes because there were believing Catholics everywhere. Alone among the bourgeois parties, holding strict economic theories but at the same time dominated by massive economic interests, it judged questions of economic life from the points of view of Christian ethics, ethics of moderation and common sense. Hence it had greater freedom of movement and could be selective. Bismarck called it *reichsfeindlich*, but it was only critical of the Reich. It could say yes or no, and to some of Bismarck's projects, such as the social legislation and the protective tariffs, it said yes. Moreover, where it was not a directly interested party it could sell the votes of its members in return for concessions in other fields. Although it was a minority party and could never because of its structure become a majority in Germany, in the long run it was the most successful group in the Reichstag, the party which determined the fate of the Germany of Bismarck, Wilhelm II and the Weimar Republic. Gradually it also acquired the reputation of faithlessness and opportunism. It could work with the Right or the Left and make bargains with everybody because everybody needed it. It could rely absolutely on the majority of its electors. It did not fall when its partners of yesterday fell, and its own inglorious end in 1933 heralded the conclusion of a long epoch of German political history.

Because of its close ties with the Catholic Church and the active part which priests took in controlling its local organizations the Centre contributed to the peculiarly German custom which requires a political party to have an ideology – a principle with which the parliaments of western Europe are less familiar. The other great party of the masses, the Social Democratic Party, born in Bismarck's Reich which it survived, also had its ideology. Of about the same age as the Centre it was another product of the trend of the times since the middle of the century. Its pre-history starts with the work of the young Marx, its history as a party with the foundation of the General German Workers' Association by Lassalle, with the foundation of the Social Democratic Workers' Party by Liebknecht and Bebel in 1869 and with the union in 1875 of the two groups into the *Sozialistische Arbeiterpartei Deutschlands*. It did not spread as quickly as the Centre; and although in the end it outgrew the Centre and became the biggest political organization of the people, it did not play the same role in the Kaiser's Reich as the Centre which could do either of two things, oppose the state or work with it. The Social Democratic Party, given its constitution and that of the Reich, could really only do one thing. It worked for the future, for the day of liberation which it promised. It completely disavowed Bismarck's Reich and was completely disavowed by it. On occasions the Social Democrats' attitude did them great credit, for example when their representatives protested against the annexation of Alsace-Lorraine. But as a consequence they had no chance of making political deals of the kind that the Centre was busily engaged in.

Nevertheless the Social Democrats were a vital factor in the new Reich's destiny from the start. They were the main source of the political education of the German worker; they made this new social class politically conscious and politically active. They were the negative force in the Kaiser's Reich, provoking it into its most characteristic acts: the social legislation and the persecutions under the Anti-Socialist Law. The Social Democrats forced Bismarck's Germany to reveal its true character. By performing this function for decades, and continuing to grow in the process, the party changed its own character. If it is impossible to understand the history of the Wilhelminian Reich without the Social Democrats, it is equally impossible to understand the Social Democrats of 1919 without the history of the Wilhelminian Reich. This is a unique phenomenon: a great, superbly organized party, numerically by far the biggest in Germany, deeply rooted in the people, unshakeable thanks to its theory and thanks to tens of thousands of devoted, faithful helpers – yet always outside the real political game, neither willing nor able to help positively to decide the future course of events. By the time the Social Democrats assumed the responsibility which they should have had thirty years earlier, the party was old. It resembled the heir to the throne who becomes king as an old man and in the most adverse circumstances.

The proclamation issued when the party was founded made no mention of the name of Marx. Not only did Marx not write its programmes, he even bitterly criticized that of 1875. Nevertheless its policies were permeated by Marxist ideas – thanks to Lassalle who, though differing from Marx, was yet his pupil, and also to the slowly growing influence of Marx's and Engels's writings. The two old men in London had only indirect dealings with the party. They did not belong to its executive and were often wrong about German conditions which they did not know well. But the Germans went to England to seek advice. They saw Marx as the scientific founder and critic, the great scholar of the revolution, and Engels as the ever gay, energetic, helpful friend.

When the two wings united in 1875 the Lassallians were the stronger as far as numbers and organization went. Nevertheless the Lassallian heritage gradually disappeared. Lassalle was no scholar, no great theorist, he was the personal electrifying leader who grasps opportunities, who does one thing today and another tomorrow. A man like that does not survive his own death; in the long run there could be no Lassallian party without Lassalle, although his admirers tried to keep the flag flying. Marx's writings on the other hand were made to last, they could be effective without the master. Lassalle's state-supported 'Production Associations' figured for courtesy's sake for yet a while in social democratic proclamations only to disappear in the end. Thus Marx triumphed over Lassalle.

Because the nationalization of the means of production, the 'expropriation of the expropriators', the brutal overthrow of state and society were clumsy immediate aims for a party working within the framework of the law, the programme of the Social Democrats regularly fell into two parts. The first dealt with what would and must happen one day; the second with what must be demanded at once. One day wage slavery would be replaced by the communist society; at once it was necessary to achieve universal suffrage, the eight-hour day, effective supervision of all factories, freedom of activity for the unions, a progressive income tax and death duties, and so on. The first part concerned world revolution, the second was the programme of a democratic workers' or people's party such as could have been drawn up without Marx's influence. In time the difference between the two became more rather than less marked. The practical part of the programme became more important as the Social Democratic Party grew and the time approached when it could exercise a strong influence on government and legislation. But at the same time Marx's influence became stronger not weaker, as a comparison of the Gotha programme of 1875 with that of Erfurt of 1891 shows. In 1875 the need for a fundamental change was still justified on ethical grounds: as labour is the source of all wealth and all civilization justice demands that its products be shared equally among the working members of society. In 1891 there was no more reference to what is just and desirable, but to a dynamic inevitable development of capitalism into socialism. The theoretical part of this programme offers really nothing but the Communist Manifesto of 1848. Then, 'proceeding from these principles' – but in fact unconnected with them – follow those practical points of the programme which even a non-Marxist supporter of industrial democracy can subscribe to without hesitation. The great, healthy and practical social democratic movement really misunderstood itself. It regarded itself as something that it was not, the fulfilment of Marx's old prophesy of 1848. As a result of being forced to fit into a theory it failed to become what it really was or could be. To use a simile: Marx said that revolutions are the engines of world history. But the engine for which Marx waited impatiently in 1848 never arrived. In its place came a solid train, decades later, built by other people for other purposes, German social democracy. Although the two old men in London boarded this train they never ceased to criticize the engine drivers who for their part were under the impression that their destination was the same as Marx had had in mind.

It was not a happy combination, this juxtaposition of a revolutionary utopia, of an omniscient, heavily armoured philosophy of history – and practical democracy. It made the enemies' game too easy and later produced confusion in the ranks of the Social Democrats themselves. For a long time their supporters could not decide if the achievements already obtained were worth the trouble or if the real thing, the 'great collapse' was yet to come. On the other hand it must be said that it was Marx's teaching which gave the German workers self-confidence and self-reliance.

In times of economic difficulty and unemployment, in hard times of persecution, this is not to be despised. Without Marx's faith the leaders of the German workers would hardly have found the courage needed for their task of education, agitation and organization.

The German Social Democrats of the late nineteenth century were not what the Communists came to be in the twentieth century. They were, or wanted to be, the orthodox Marxist party; there was nothing further to the Left. When one read Bismarck's comments on the 'red danger', 'these dangerous brigands with whom we share our cities', one might think that one was dealing with bloodthirsty radicals. But what a completely mistaken idea this would be. Every age has its own character and the nineteenth century was basically liberal, not totalitarian or terrorist. If Bismarck was unable or unwilling to organize white terror of the variety which the twentieth century has experienced, August Bebel was no Lenin. He was a good German of his age, clever, warmhearted, hard-working, of strong, unbending character, thoroughly honest, a man who scorned all underhand or cruel means, a quick-witted, amusing speaker who could rouse Bismarck to violent fury, but whose ways of thinking were basically straightforward. Although he succumbed to Marx's teaching, as a human being he had a very little in common with Marx, a little more with Engels, and nothing whatsoever with the tyrants and idols of a later period.

The German Social Democrats were democrats as well as socialists, and they did not use Marx's phrase of the 'dictatorship of the proletariat' in their programmes. They cared about the rights of free men and did not doubt that social justice was compatible with personal freedom. In this respect they were liberal; also in that they adopted an indifferent but not a hostile attitude towards religion which they regarded as a private matter. Learning was the property of the whole of society and the state must promote its advance and see that it reaches the people. Among the imposing list of books which Bebel studied during his imprisonment were Marx's *Kapital*, John Stuart Mill's *Political Economy*, Lorenz Stein's *Geschichte des französischen Sozialismus und Kommunismus*, Plato's *Republic*, Aristotle's *Politics*, Darwin's *Origin of Species*, Haeckel's *Natürliche Schöpfungsgeschichte*, Ludwig Büchner's *Kraft und Stoff* and Liebig's *Chemische Briefe*. Here was the urge of the German worker for education, his faith in liberation through knowledge. In the eighteenth century this had been the urge and the faith of the European middle classes, as whose heirs the Social Democrats rightly regarded themselves now that the middle classes had become aggressive and cowardly. They were humanists like Voltaire; they wanted equality between the sexes, they wanted to humanize the administration of justice and to abolish the death penalty. They were internationalists, but of a particular brand because it was the proletarians, not the middle classes, of all countries whom they wanted to unite. In practice, however, their aims were designed to moderate the differences between states: militia instead of standing armies, no armaments race, no wars of aggression or conquest, and every nation to be entitled to decide its own fate. This too was a bourgeois heritage. This was how the German Liberals had thought in 1848, before experience confused them and the great man led them into temptation.

The fact that the Social Democrats professed to believe in the ideal of international brotherhood made it easy for their opponents to accuse them first of being *Reichsfeinde* and later of being 'men without a fatherland', which of course they were not. They were good Germans, patriots, as simple people always and by nature are, without making much fuss about it. Their activity was confined almost entirely to Germany and was the result of German conditions. We saw that even Marx was in his way a German nationalist. But whereas Marx's German policy never completely lost a certain knowing conceit, the patriotism of the average Social Democrat was of a friendlier, one might say pre-Marxist, brand. After all, the memories of the old founders of the party, like Wilhelm Liebknecht, went back to pre-Marxist times, to the *grossdeutsch*, democratic idea of 1848. They were *Reichsfeinde* because for them Bismarck's Reich was too small and left too many Germans outside its frontiers, because it was too Prussian and also because it was too centralized. From of old there had been an affinity between the ideal of a 'greater' Germany and the attachment to a particular German state, the loyalty to the native land which was now derisively called 'particularism'. The old 'people's parties', the Saxon, the south German, whose followers now joined the Social Democrats, were democratic, *grossdeutsch* and particularist. This national-cum-particularist trend was to live on in the party, to reappear in a changed form and to clash with the other, centralist or unitary trend. No great living party is ever completely controlled by a single consistent will or dominated entirely by the present. Past and future also play their part. In 1880 there were older men among the German Social Democrats who remembered 1848 and young ones who lived to see 1919. What had happened before Marx, what happened because of Marx, what followed after Marx fused into a single present.

The German Social Democrats were brave, honourable men. Their lives were hard: travelling about stirring people up with limited resources, a few weeks of freedom between two periods in prison, working as artisans or small traders besides their political activities from which they neither could nor wanted to live; as there was no allowance for members of parliament they had to sit beside rich men and themselves depend on food parcels and small contributions from party members; they were hounded by the public prosecutor and boycotted by middle-class industry – sacrifice after sacrifice. Marxist philosophy denies the force of ideas but among the so-called Marxists there lived something of the old idealism which the middle classes were about to betray. To the millions, whom men like von Stumm and von Kardorff wanted for ever to remain cringing, hard-working subjects of the sovereign, the Social Democrats brought hope, self-confidence and a distinct way of life.

A healthy society should have been able to absorb this party and give it a positive task. Bismarck made no attempt to do so – how could he have done so, he who did not even want to tolerate the National Liberals as a responsible party, who wanted to repress all parties, either by brutal legislation or by subtler practices? We have looked at the German parties as though they were rigid structures whose shape was decided from within, whereas in reality they were in a state of flux. Their successes and failures, splits and alliances, submissions and rebellions were as much the result of the activities of the dictator or semi-dictator who stood at the head of the Reich, as of their own actions. It is to his activities that we must now turn.

3. Bismarck's System

Bismarck became Prussian delegate to the Federal Diet when he was thirty-five, Prime Minister when he was forty-seven; and he was dismissed when he was seventy-five. For almost thirty uninterrupted years he presided over the development of Germany. Apart from being about a fifth of the period covered by this book it is also the central period, the vital time. Before him everything was open to question, after him everything followed a set course. He was preceded by the *Biedermeier* period; he was followed by *Weltpolitik*, world war and revolution. Therefore his name inevitably appears in our story almost *ad nauseam*. There came the time when, though he was still alive, Germany had had enough of him, too late for his good name and the success of the cause which – one must assume – was dear to his heart.

He was an overbearing man. The 'great successes' which he liked to remember had made him still more overbearing. He could no longer imagine himself without power, could not imagine that others without him could make a tolerable job of steering the new Reich. As those who despise the human race often do, he surrounded himself with men who more or less deserved to be sneered at, and he repulsed those of independent mind, of firm character and intelligence. Having created the position of Chancellor for himself he did nothing to train any successors. He persecuted without mercy those whom he suspected, usually wrongly, of wanting to succeed him, because he wanted to hold the reins of government so long as he was alive. He does not seem to have wondered seriously what would happen after him. This is the egoism that accompanies greatness. Himself a man of perfect manners and great intellect, he was upset by anything common, by the way in which the tone of the political struggle gradually deteriorated. But he had his fair share of responsibility for this because he never spared the others; although he expected to be spared he attacked the others maliciously in his speeches and insulted them in articles which he wrote anonymously or had written by his journalistic assistants. What hatred there was in this great man, what vindictiveness and persecution mania, how little generosity or love! Whenever he believed his honour to be attacked he busied the public prosecutor so that the libel actions never stopped. When the opposition or the imaginary insult came from above, from the Kaiser, from colleagues, he handed in his resignation, convinced until the bitter end, that it would be refused. The study of his later years does not create a pleasant impression. Until 1870 he had been daring in his handling of the governmental engine; after that date it trundled along while he squabbled with his co-travellers, often bringing the whole thing to a halt.

He continued to prefer nature to men and spent a large part of the year on the vast estates which the King had given him, Varzin in eastern Pomerania and Friedrichsruh near Hamburg. There he led the life of the rich Junker which he enjoyed, wandering in the forests, eating enormous meals, smoking a long pipe and reading pleasant books surrounded by sons, a daughter, his in-laws and by secretaries and satellites. Those who wanted anything from him had to make the pilgrimage to Varzin. From there he threw his thunderbolts at Berlin and spun his thread to the European capitals. What if a clairvoyant had said in those days to his younger son Bill: 'Here in Varzin in 1945 your wife will poison herself a few days before the arrival of the Red Army, the end of the Junkers and the partition of Germany' – but no such prophecies are ever made.

Bismarck was determined never to rule as representative of a party and had long ceased to belong to any one of them. He was clever enough to realize that the age of popular representation would last a while and that it was necessary to come to terms with it; he was no longer as contemptuous of the 'parliamentary windbags' as in his early days. Although he devoted a good deal of energy to the Reichstag and the Prussian Landtag and found it worthwhile to make many brilliant even magnificent speeches there, he refused to accept the principle of party rule, or of majority rule, or of anything approximating parliamentary government. If he had identified himself with a majority, however servile, he would have appeared to depend on it, and if at the next election the majority had become the minority the government would also have had to change, as was the law in Britain, Belgium and France. Bismarck's aim was at all costs to prevent such a development in the Reich. It was necessary for him to have a majority, for the time being it was impossible to do without one. But not only must it be a majority of absolutely docile yes-men, the government must remain free suddenly to seek parliamentary support from another group if it felt like it. Let majorities change, the same man remained Chancellor, relying on the prestige of his name and the confidence of His Majesty. For Bismarck therefore it was at least as important to preserve this confidence as to tame parliament; to undermine by venomous plots the influence of the Empress, of the liberal Crown Prince Frederick and of a variety of real and imaginary enemies at Court and go on making himself indispensable to the old monarch. His mandate in Prussia as in the Reich came from the King of Prussia, not from parliament. The Reichstag could be sent home if it did not obey, not so the Kaiser and the courtiers. Bismarck proved better at choosing the right moment to dissolve parliament and to fight an electoral campaign with the right demagogic slogans than his patriarchal, anything but democratic, education might have led one to expect. However, if even new elections failed to produce an amenable parliament, if the *Reichsfeinde* threatened to become too much for the authorities, there were in the last resort other methods of remaining master in one's own house. It was part of the logic of Bismarck's system that it's founder did not regard it as final. The nation had not made the Reich and the constitution. These were gifts from the authorities which found technical expression in treaties with 'allied governments'. Gifts could after all be taken back if the nation failed to show proper gratitude.

This was how Bismarck saw the position. The government was not the executive committee of the nation, in essence identical with it, but a power apart which might negotiate with the nation. The authority was the 'allied governments'. On the occasions – rare and only connected with unimportant questions – that Prussia was outvoted in the *Bundesrat* the Chancellor recalled that in fact the Prussian state, ruling over far more people than all other German states together, was the supreme authority in the Reich. But that was not all. Bismarck, when it suited him, even disputed the right of the Reichstag to represent the people against authority. What connection was there, his argument ran, between the productive working people and the party ideologues, the dogmatic theorists, those pompous persons who laid down the law in the Reichstag, the individuals 'whom our sun does not warm and whom our rain does not wet, unless they happen to have gone out without an umbrella'. Monarchistic authority face to face with the people, allied governments face to face with the nation, Prussia face to face with the allied governments, the Reich face to face with the *Reichsfeinde*, the useful people face to face with the useless parties – he was never short of antitheses of this kind which he used as cloaks for his personal power, prepared at any time to exchange one for the other.

Finally there was the antithesis between party and party. Fundamentally he regarded them all as illegitimate, but he needed them to pass budgets and laws, and he ruined them by using them. Because he wanted obedient parties, not independent ones that would negotiate. By playing them off against each other he ruined the two parties, the Conservatives and the National Liberals, which had both on occasion come a very long way to meet him; later he revived them both as weak but amenable followers. These were pyrrhic victories, since they forced him to depend on the parliamentary support of the Centre: he hated the Centre, of course, because he could not deprive it of its independence and the Centre returned his hatred. As for the Social Democrats, he wanted to destroy them altogether.

This was certainly not a healthy, productive system. Nor was it improved by the human dimension which the mind must add to the picture that we have just drawn. Everybody, from the brutal, greedy and cynical personality of the ageing prince-Chancellor, the Prussian ministers and the imperial secretaries of state, the ambassadors, the *Oberpräsidenten*, the attorney-generals, the court-generals and the court clergy to the hack journalists and police spies paid for out of Bismarck's secret funds, was constantly worried about his own position; all of them, anxious for promotion, manoeuvred and intrigued, slandered and flattered. This was the complex, entangled corruption of a personal system of authority which, spreading and becoming more deeply entrenched, lasted for decades.

How we have suffered under this regime. How his [Bismarck's] influence has corrupted his whole school – his subordinates, the political life of Germany. Life in Berlin is almost intolerable if one does not want to be his abject slave. His party, his followers and admirers are fifty times worse than he himself. One wants to utter a cry for liberation and, if it were heard, what a deep sigh of relief there would be. To repair the damage done will take years. If one judges by appearances only Germany is strong, great and united, has an enormous army . . . a prime minister who can give orders to the world, a laurel-crowned monarch and a trade that is trying to outstrip that of all other nations; German influence is active everywhere in the world (even though it arouses little love or confidence). One might think that we have no cause for complaint and ought to be grateful. But if only people knew the price of all this . . .

This was not written by a Social Democrat or a *Reichsfeind*, but by the Crown Princess of Prussia. But we must not ignore the other side of the picture. Bismarck now enjoyed greater prestige in the world than any other German statesman before, or perhaps ever, and he retained it because of his firm though moderate, experienced foreign policy after 1871. He showed that a German victor could show feeling for the dignity of other states and nations, that he could show authority, tact, worldly wisdom and erudition, wit, fantasy and penetrating intelligence. He presented the picture of what is called a great man, not so much because of his achievements as because of his character. The magic which his official papers, speeches and letters exude even today must have been a hundred times stronger during his lifetime. If he degraded German political life he also enhanced it by his existence and bearing. The historian who is above all an aesthete, who believes that the purpose of history culminates in a few Jupiter-like personalities will therefore be an admirer of Bismarck. In the greyness of everyday life a personality like his provides a fascinating light. It is not for us, however, to look at history in such a predominantly aesthetic light. We must ask after the effects of his activity and leave the admiring biographer to enjoy the personality.

Bismarck was wont to defend his rejection of the democratic, parliamentary system with spirit, though using the most contradictory arguments. At times he looked wistfully towards Britain; if only history had arranged things equally well in Germany he too would be in favour of parliamentary government. At others he was scornful about Britain, particularly about Gladstone whom he despised as a vain idealist. At times he rejected the majority principle on the grounds that statesmen must do what duty tells them, without toadying to ignorant, fickle majorities. At the next moment he accused the German parties of being too numerous and of fighting too much among themselves to be able to form a compact majority; if there was one he would be delighted to govern with it, but it did not and could not exist. Then again he used the old Kaiser as an excuse: he himself would be happy to resign and give the deputies Windthorst and Bebel a chance of showing as ministers what they could do; in principle such a change of cabinet was a healthy thing, unfortunately, however, he could never convince His Majesty of its usefulness. Then, at the next opportunity, he praised the monarchical principle; the real Prime Minister in Prussia remained the King who gave his orders which he, Bismarck, like all his colleagues must obey and it was impossible to do without such an authority independent of voters and parties. Then, after his dismissal when the Kaiser really wanted to be his own Chancellor Bismarck changed and called for a strong parliament. All this does not give one the impression of rational, planning conviction. The source of our allegedly theoretical judgements is often a secret will and Bismarck's will was great. He wanted to rule, and in spite of justified complaints about his health, in spite of exhaustion, nervous disorder, sleepless nights filled with hatred and genuine longing for rest, he was unwilling to lay down the burden of Atlas. The reasons which he gave varied, but being a clever man they always somehow made sense.

There is no ideal form of government. The political problem remained unsolved in Germany, but so it did in France, Italy or Spain, not to mention Russia. Provided the inhabitants of a country live together in tolerable peace without tormenting each other too much one does not ask for more. Bismarck was right in saying that Britain in fact owed its parliamentary system to a stroke of good fortune and a masterpiece of history, and that it could not simply be copied. But he did nothing to further Germany's political development. Although opposed to artificial, violent experiment and a believer in letting things take their natural course, in the last resort it was he who made a violent experiment and delayed Germany's natural development. Around 1885 the position of the king-emperor, the position of the Junkers and Bismarck's own position were anachronisms preserved with tricks and veiled force and justified with old legends and new successes. One does not know how things would have developed without them, certainly not ideally either, though probably more naturally and more freely. As long as he was in office the magician who had created the anachronism could mitigate its consequences. During that time there was tolerable order and apparent glory. It is we who come afterwards who know the bitter end. Bismarck's system was not weatherproof in a serious crisis which it was bound sooner or later to cause itself.

Up to 1878 Bismarck ruled with the help of the National Liberals. In spite of constant friction with the party's left wing – the Chancellor called it the 'red' one – the most important reforms necessary for a modern state were accomplished during this period: legal procedure was standardized, a Foreign Office and a *Reichsbank* were set up and a national currency introduced. What, however, gave the period its political character were not so much the sober practical achievements as the so-called *Kulturkampf*, the conflict between the state and the Liberal Party on the one side and the Catholic Church represented by the Centre on the other. This conflict produced much disorder and spiritual confusion, and in the heat generated by it the Centre Party became what it remained for the next fifty years. Today one can only raise one's eyebrows at the famous quarrel. How unnecessary it was is shown by the readiness with which Bismarck broke it off when it suited him. It was not a quarrel between the two Christian confessions; because Prussian Protestantism did not want this quarrel the Prussian Conservatives and Bismarck parted company. Nor was it a quarrel between two religions. Liberalism of the German variety was not a religion or pseudo-religion like the ideologies of the totalitarian states in the twentieth century. Such praiseworthy things as free trade, equality before the law and the right of parliament to determine the budget were no substitute for what the church offered to starving souls. In spite of Pope Pius IX's aggressive proclamation the Catholic Church was not a prehistoric monster impossible for the modern state to live with. Soon there came the time when the Catholic party, without betraying its faith or the interests of its church played a positive role in the state. To that extent the whole conflict made no sense. People like to quarrel, and, if no threatening thunder clouds are visible in the sky, any little cloud will serve as pretence that a storm is approaching. For a time after 1870 Bismarck found in political Catholicism the enemy he needed. And as always happens, one aggressive act provoked another, the attacker found himself attacked and the attitude of his opponent confirmed his original suspicion. In such an atmosphere any understanding soon becomes impossible and the original cause of the quarrel is forgotten. This pattern continues until boredom sets in and both opponents lose their martial ardour. Whereupon everything that for years seemed insoluble suddenly appears soluble.

We can spare the reader the details of the *Kulturkampf* legislation. Some of it took place in the Reich – obligatory civil marriage, prohibition of the Jesuit Order – but most of it took place in Prussia, particularly as Prussia continued to be responsible for religion and education. This legislation served a purpose where it tried to draw a dividing line between state and church. But where it clumsily claimed control of what was the concern of the Church, the education of the clergy, the appointment of priests, and ecclesiastical disciplinary authority, almost nothing has remained, either because the law was repealed after years of grievous confusion or because it was no longer enforced. The church hit back and did not accept anything that was irreconcilable with its innermost nature. There was a time when most of the Prussian bishops were in prison, when thousands of parishes were without priests whose parishioners had to die without spiritual help. At that time Bismarck was the devil incarnate for the German Catholics, and this was not a happy start for the new united Germany. A few years later Pope Leo XIII bestowed his highest order in diamonds on the Chancellor and called him a great, good man.

Historians have assembled a variety of motives which persuaded Bismarck to regard the *Kulturkampf* and its ruthless pursuit as essential. The conflict forged a link between the government and the Liberals. It also fitted in with Bismarck's foreign policy. He believed that the foreign enemies of the Reich were Catholic, French monarchists, unreconciled Habsburg Austrians. Several groups of *Reichsfeinde* within the Reich were also Catholic, the Poles and the Alsatians. By taking the schools in the Polish districts of Prussia away from the priests and handing them over to the state they could be made into agents of Germanization; so that here the struggle against the church coincided with the struggle between nationalities. These considerations were given cohesive force by aggressive political reasoning; that the medieval imperialist demands of the church were intolerable, that in this world the state must be dominant, that kings must not give way to priests and so on – pompous phrases which inflated the affair to large and tragic dimensions.

Equally, rational arguments are advanced to explain the gradual abandonment of the *Kulturkampf* after 1878. By then Bismarck was no longer afraid of a 'Catholic coalition' against Germany; he knew that Austria was bound to the Reich, and that the anti-clerical, republican regime was firmly in control in Paris. At home the alliance with the Liberals had exhausted itself. He gravitated back towards the Conservatives, but as he could not govern with them alone he was bound to welcome the possibility of an arrangement between the Conservatives and the Centre. He particularly needed the votes of the Centre for his economic and financial plans: a protective tariff as a new source of income for the Reich, and perhaps state monopolies. He was also on the point of declaring war to the bitter end on the Social Democrats; and to lead two campaigns simultaneously against the two German mass parties was too much even for Bismarck. All this sounds plausible and there is certainly some truth in it. But it presupposes that the whole conflict was sensible and of this it is impossible to persuade oneself. Such a damaging, poisonous venture could only have been sensible if one could prove that it was inevitable. And how could something have been inevitable that was abandoned so quickly, as though the whole affair had been a misunderstanding, a bad joke?

Two attempts on the life of the old Kaiser in 1878 created the mood which the Chancellor needed to carry out his annihilating blow, long prepared by preliminary skirmishes, against the Social Democrats. The party had of course nothing to do with the senseless assassination attempts and could prove its innocence. In political battles, however, truth usually has a small voice. The National Liberals certainly felt that the proscription of a great party was no way of consolidating the constitutional state, that a liberalism which countenanced exceptional laws and arbitrary police action betrayed itself, and that the methods used against the opponent could sooner or later also be used against their own cause. It was for this very reason that Bismarck wanted the emergency law rather than the less extreme measures which the Liberals would have preferred. A general election created the situation which the ruling class wanted. The Conservatives won and the Liberals lost. Whereupon the latter unreservedly accepted the Anti-Socialist law.

The compromise between Bismarck and the Reichstag was not a genuine one. It would be more accurate to say that it was a compromise between Bismarck and the spirit of the age; that however ready to use force, he could never completely suppress in himself the liberal, humane spirit of the age. A living political movement can only be put down with twentieth-century methods, with concentration camps and mass murders, and in the last resort not even with these; not by gagging the press, by expulsions and minor states of emergency. Therefore the Anti-Socialist law was a failure. It did not proscribe the party but merely suppressed its organizations, newspapers and meetings. This compelled its agitators to use the utmost caution, forced the party to hold its congresses abroad and, while the law was in force, gave about 1,500 of its members a taste of prison. For a constitutional state this was a disgrace; for a repressive, totalitarian state it was not nearly enough. There were judges who took their oath seriously and prison warders who sympathized with their prisoners; when Bebel went to prison the railway guards lined the platform to salute him. It was a typical picture of the bourgeois age: the widely respected, popular deputy who must go to prison, well supplied with books and a canary, and the moustachioed officials doing their duty loyally though they voted Social Democrat, honouring their great friend in the way which the state had taught them. In spite of the obstacles in the way of its propaganda the party continued to grow. It numbered about half a million voters when the law came into force and at least three times as many when it was repealed in 1890. The omnipotent Chancellor still found himself bickering with its members in the Reichstag; and on these occasions they did not fail to remind him jeeringly of his relationship with Lassalle.

The age was essentially a peaceful one both at home and abroad, and the new parties, Socialist and Catholic, could also have developed peacefully. What, above all, provoked the clash was Bismarck's bellicose, irritable and brutal nature. No conflict was ever more futile. The Centre and the Social Democrat outlived the Chancellor and the Reich. The fact that for a long time they could not shake off the psychology of the period of conflict did not harm them as parties; it was the nation and the state that suffered.

In 1879 the imperial government – the governments of the German princes – adopted an economic policy of increased tariffs; partly to give the Reich independent sources of income and partly because industry and agriculture had begun to ask for protection against superior foreign competition. The tariffs were moderate. Bismarck put them through with the help of the Conservatives and the Centre. The National Liberal Party came to grief over the issue as some of its members were free traders and others protectionists. This brought to an end the old alliance between the government and the Liberals. Henceforth the Chancellor worked with uncertain, changing majorities, Centre and Conservatives, Conservatives and Liberals, whichever combination was adequate at the moment. It was the period when he quarrelled ever more bitterly with the Reichstag. He preferred to speak of the past, of the 'conflict' of 1862, of the now almost legendary 'great successes'; unfortunately German unity had not brought what he had hoped for. When a member called out 'shame', he replied: 'Shame is an expression of disgust and of contempt. Do not think, gentlemen, that I do not have these feelings, I am merely too well-bred to express them.' In the eighties this was probably his predominant feeling towards the Reichstag which he nevertheless continued to use as a platform for his remarkable political pronouncements. He had broken up the Liberal Party which could have provided a suitable government; the Centre, on which he had come to depend in consequence, he had turned into an implacable enemy; the Social Democrats he had forced to go underground. What wonder that he felt lonely among all the strange, young faces? His aim, a servile Reichstag, he had failed to achieve. The anger which this aroused in him embittered him and the whole of parliamentary life, as happens at school when the teacher hates his pupils.

The positive achievement of the eighties was the system of social insurance which was a product, a practical, useful left-over, of much more ambitious plans. The intention was to reconcile the workers with the state by giving them something concrete, thus driving a wedge between them and their political leaders. But the Social Democrats were not afraid of the idea; they tried to improve it for the benefit of the workers. They knew what Bismarck shirked knowing, that the Socialist movement was not only a material but also a political and moral one. A few benefits conferred from above could not do away with it. What remained were the concrete achievements: compulsory insurance for accident, sickness and finally for disablement and old age, the costs being borne by the employer and the insured. This venture was satisfactory as far as it went and was later continued and improved in many respects. Britain followed the German example some twenty years later; France and the United States not until the nineteen thirties.

The insurance system was a beginning, though only in one direction. In the other Bismarck was not prepared to give one inch. Nothing was done for healthy workers, nothing to limit the hours of work, to determine minimum wages or to enforce the factory inspection which had long existed on paper. This, he claimed, must be left to nature in order to keep German industry competitive. Surely the workers would not let themselves be told how many hours they should be allowed to work. Insurance yes, but no state intervention in the industrial process itself. Beyond this rigid barrier the old diplomat, who had himself become a manufacturer, was not prepared to go. Even then there was disappointment; even then the new situation was misunderstood. The workers took what the state offered and refused to be grateful.

Finally there was the periodically recurring quarrel over the army. It was part of Bismarck's system, just as the struggle against the new mass parties – and it seems just as superfluous once one imagines the situation without its personal and class distortions. The nation was prepared to give the state what it needed for its defence. Since 1866 it had come to appreciate, too much if anything, the advantages of an army ready for combat. The Reichstag, from the Conservatives to the Progressives, and in a different sense even to the Social Democrats, was willing to spend money on the army. Had it been entrusted with military responsibility the result would not have been an unarmed Germany. But such an arrangement would not have fitted into Bismarck's system. The King of Prussia was king of the army; he wanted to have his regiments as a banker has his money, regardless of the feeling of popular agitators. Bismarck had become Prime Minister during the conflict of 1862 and as Prime Minister twenty-five years later he still remembered what had brought him to power. The way in which he had managed the 'conflict' created the bond of gratitude between him and the old King. From time to time it became necessary to renew the threat and the mood of 1862. Therefore army expenditure must not be allowed to become an item in the budget like any other, to be approved annually. Therefore it was really not desirable to determine once and for all how many regiments there should be in relation to the size of the population, although Bismarck supported the so-called *eternat*. What was ideal for him was the compromise reached in 1874: the *septennat*, the authorization of the military establishment for seven years. This solution ensured that there was certain to be the usual parliamentary crisis every seven years. Every seven years there must somehow be a threat from abroad, urgently necessitating a strengthening of the army. In the winter of 1887, when there were difficulties over a new *septennat*, Bismarck dissolved the Reichstag; he fought the election on the basis of an alleged threat of war with France, against all opponents of a strong seven-year army, and he achieved his objective. The Conservatives, together with the National Liberals, gained a substantial victory at the polls and the new *septennat* was approved.

At that moment it seemed as though the Prime Minister would be master of the situation for a long time to come, more so than he had been since the foundation of the Reich.

4. Diplomacy

After the storms of the sixties a new European equilibrium had evolved. Anyone who wanted to touch it knew'the risk. The longer the peace continued the less advisable it became to disturb it, because the growth of populations and of the armies which they supported, because the advances of science and technology made the 'next war' increasingly into a fantastic, unimaginable affair. The new national states had achieved more or less what they wanted; the old ones had done it long ago and were now inclined gradually to abandon their old dreams of hegemony. An unparalleled prosperity, interrupted only temporarily by slumps, seemed to most people by now more interesting than victory in battles. National glory and power could be had more cheaply in Asia and Africa than on the Rhine. Europe was occupied, shared out, disposed of and very small; easier, more worthwhile objectives beckoned overseas.

However, to explain the long peace only in terms of the natural course of events would mean giving Bismarck less than his due. Between sovereign states there is 'foreign policy', constant lying in wait for each other, challenge and preparations for the worst. This foreign policy is made by men, sometimes well, more often badly. Bismarck made it well. We saw that he failed in guiding Germany's domestic policy, doing more harm in that sphere than good; but he was a great diplomat and there is a connection between his successful diplomacy and his unsuccessful domestic policy. He treated the German parties as though they were states, manoeuvring them to and fro, making alliances and breaking them. Moreover in not wanting democracy in Germany he was motivated by considerations of foreign policy. He suspected that German democracy would embark on a revolutionary, imperialist, pan-German foreign policy the successes and the failures of which would bury the structure of the Prussian state and society. Signs of such a foreign policy had appeared on the horizon in 1848, a year which Bismarck was unable to forget; and even after 1871 it could not be ruled out. Treitschke, a nationalist and a fanatical believer in German unity but no fool, remarked as early as the year in which the Reich was founded upon the danger that in the flush of victory the nation might venture to dream again the imperialist dreams of the Hohenstaufen age. The fact that it did not do so, that victorious Germany kept its sense of proportion and repeatedly employed its concentrated strength to preserve the peace remains the great achievement of Bismarck's old age. Whether it is seen as a senile desire for peace – though Bismarck was not an old man in the seventies, and even as an old man he did not shy away from a fight – as class egoism or as aristocratic indifference to the fate of Germans beyond the frontiers of the Reich, the achievement remains unimpaired. The motives are numerous and can be interpreted as one likes; it is actions and results that count.

Of the various circles of German foreign policy the narrowest fell partly inside the Reich. Part of Poland – Posen and West Prussia – had from of old been Prussian. Part of France – Alsace and Lorraine – had recently become German.

The friendship between Russia and Prussia which for Bismarck was and remained the most appropriate of all German friendships, was based primarily on the fact that in the eighteenth century the two nations had partitioned Poland. Bismarck was no friend of the Poles. Nowhere did the harsh, pessimistic side of his character reveal itself more than in his attitude towards the Poles. It was impossible to worry about the happiness of all nations and races.

> *Wo Eines Platz will, muss das Andere rücken,*
> *Wer nicht vertrieben sein will, muss vertreiben,*
> *Hier herrscht der Kampf und nur die Stärke siegt.**

This is what it said in Schiller's *Wallenstein*, Bismarck's favourite play. It was the Poles' bad luck that they lived between two powerful nations and that they had proved incapable of creating a modern state in the eighteenth century. The rest followed by

* Where one needs space the other must give way. Lest one is driven out one must drive out others. Conflict is the rule and strength alone is victorious.

itself. It was necessary to keep down the Poles whose numbers were increasing dangerously by closing the frontiers, by settling German peasants in Polish areas, and by full-scale Germanization. There must be close, ruthless collaboration with Russia whenever Polish nationalism burst into revolt. War with Russia must be avoided if at all possible, because even a victory over the Tsar could only result in the unwelcome liberation of Russian Poland. The megalomaniacal thought that Germany might conquer both Poland and Russia never occurred to Bismarck. To pursue a policy of peace in the East at the expense of the Poles was all right as long as it worked; it suited Russia and Germany and the peace of Europe. But it involved great guilt, the guilt that comes from the suppression of a self-conscious historic nation as the Poles had ever been. This guilt, however, was nothing new.

In the West the situation was more awkward. At the time Germany could not possibly have found a just solution of the Polish question which depended much more on Russia than on Germany. A wise policy would never have allowed the annexation of Alsace and Lorraine. Bismarck sensed this, but to refuse German Nationalism its heart's desire, Alsace, when he intended to refuse it a number of other things was more than he could do. In addition in 1870 there were the strategic arguments of the generals, and not least his own old inclination to annex and absorb. The result was the *Reichsland* Alsace-Lorraine, a combination of French provinces or parts of provinces which had only the one thing in common, that they did not want to belong to the German Reich. Germany gave them what it could give: an efficient administration, a well-endowed university in Strasbourg, useful and grandiose buildings, and economic prosperity. In the sphere of politics the crass mistakes of the beginning were gradually corrected; very belatedly the *Reichsland* received almost all the rights of a German federal state. Nevertheless the people were never content. The townsmen remained French, the peasants remained Alsatian and nobody became *reichsdeutsch* at heart. Experts assure us that in spite of all German achievements the province was more pro-French just before 1914 than earlier. As such this would only have been an awkward embarrassment for Germany but no tragedy, for there were discontented provinces everywhere in Europe. Things were not ideal in Swedish Norway, in Italian Naples, in Spanish Catalonia and incomparably worse in Russian Finland and in British Ireland. They were not desperate in Alsace-Lorraine. What made the question of this border province into an issue which poisoned world politics was the fact that the French convinced themselves that they could never get over its loss. Of course, the word 'loss' was not pregnant with meaning in the free, civilized Europe of the late nineteenth century. Strasbourg was no further from Paris than before, it was possible to travel in both directions, to publish French newspapers in the 'lost' province and to engage in every form of 'cultural propaganda'; indeed such propaganda flourished. If relations between Germany and France had been sensible the question of which state Alsace-Lorraine belonged to might gradually have ceased to be important. But would there be any 'politics' at all if people behaved sensibly? The *Reichsland* had become a symbol of the enmity between the two nations; a symbol of victory and of defeat. 'You see, we have it', said one side provocatively and 'you see, we do not have it, alas, alas', lamented the other. The French liked to think that with Alsace they had lost a piece of their soul which, wounded, sighed for reunion with the mythical parent body. Poincaré, who later became President of France, tells us in his memoirs that as a young man he looked from his native hills across to lost Lorraine making a solemn vow to regain it one day; otherwise his life would not be worth living. Indignation is an enjoyable sensation and if we cannot be victorious there is some satisfaction derived from being defeated and robbed.

The annexation of Alsace-Lorraine made Germany and France into arch enemies, making any lasting understanding between them impossible. The affair was not worth such a price.

It had been argued that Alsace-Lorraine was more the symbol than the cause of the unhappy relationship. What France could not reconcile itself to were the lost war and the new German hegemony in Europe. It would not have liked its neighbour east of the Rhine better if it had been allowed to keep Alsace-

Lorraine; as in fact there was no basic change of attitude in 1918 when the territory was returned to France. Those were the kind of arguments used to minimize the folly of the annexation. It is impossible to prove such things. The war of 1870 alone made a good-neighbourly relationship between the two nations difficult; the annexation, given human nature, made it impossible. Consequently it became a principle of German foreign policy to keep France isolated while seeking allies in good time, first so that the French would not get them and secondly to be a match in an emergency for any alliance which the French might have managed to form. Of the two purposes the first, the isolation of France, was the more important and could not, of course, be achieved in the long run. As long as there has been diplomacy alliances have provoked counter-alliances.

Bismarck regarded the relationship between the German Reich and Austria-Hungary so to speak as an internal German, not a European one. He had destroyed the German Confederation; yet he was so used to it, was so much a child of Metternich's age that its revival in some form or other always seemed the most natural thing to him. Therefore he wanted an alliance between Austria and Germany, though one which would differ from the Frankfurt Confederation in that Prussia now had the whip hand. It would differ from all *grossdeutsche* imperialist fantasies in that it was not the realization of pan-German nationalism but the alliance of one empire with another; entered into not with Austria's Germans but with the Habsburgs and with whomsoever the Habsburgs chose to put into a responsible position in their empire. That was the idea. The destruction of the Danube monarchy, the union of the Germans of Austria and Bohemia with the Reich would result in a European revolution; Bismarck said that he preferred to go to war against the German Austrians rather than accept such a situation. The equilibrium of Europe depended on the existence of multi-racial Austria-Hungary which now, after all its losses, should remain as it was, reduced but still a great power. It must not be too German – that would have brought it close to the nationalistic, democratic *grossdeutsche* revolution – nor too Slav – that would have alienated it from the German Reich and possibly have led to a dangerous friendship with Russia. In the past there had been only a few European alliances and Bismarck never ceased to fear their revival. There was the coalition between Austria and the western powers against Russia; that could turn against Prussia-Germany and force it into the arms of Russia. There was the Franco-Austro-Russian alliance against Prussia; that too might happen again. There was the danger of a development which so far had never materialized but to which several signs now pointed of a conflict between Austria and Russia alone, a struggle for the Balkans in which Germany would be forced to take sides. Finally there was the memory of Metternich's Holy Alliance, of the league of the three conservatives. To re-establish this under completely different conditions seemed the most desirable alternative to Bismarck.

Hence the League of the Three Emperors of 1873 and 1881, treaties full of conservative, peace-loving sentiments in the style of Metternich. As long as they corresponded to the actual situation there was no danger of large-scale war in Europe. But they never wholly did so and in the end not at all. More explosive forces were at work now than in the period of the classical Romanoff–Hohenzollern friendship; forces which could no longer be suppressed by conservative royal alliances. Bismarck who himself owed his rise to power to the unrest of the age now became a man of peace, the successor of Metternich. But when the young men of yesterday grow old and tired and conservative, new young men appear who look at things differently.

What the Italians and Germans had done in the sixties the Balkan Slavs wanted to do in the seventies and eighties. They wanted to be liberated from the Turkish Empire, to have their own national states. Russia with its decrepit Tsarist regime, menaced from many sides, perturbed by the semi-nationalistic, semi-religious mystical movement of pan-Slavism, did not want to abandon its 'little Slav brothers'. Austria, on the other hand, feared the end of the Turkish Empire, the revolt of the small nations outside and inside its own frontiers, and was afraid that Russia would occupy the peninsula which flanked Austria, not

Russia, and through which Austria's river, the Danube, flowed to the sea. The conflict was an old one. In the eighteenth century it had been kept in suspense by joint partition or plans for partition on the Polish model; in the middle of the nineteenth century because the western powers, not Austria, took it upon themselves to contain Russia on the Black Sea. There came the time when Britain left this problem to Austria and behind Austria there was Germany; this meant the end of the League of the Three Emperors and the creation of the situation of 1914.

Bismarck understood the threat. What words, kind or scornful, could do to reduce it he made them do. He said hundreds of times that the happiness of south Slav sheep rustlers was a matter of complete indifference to him; to Germany the whole of the Near East was not worth the bones of a single Pomeranian grenadier. In one of his last and greatest speeches in the Reichstag in February 1888 he said: 'Bulgaria, the little country between the Danube and the Balkans, is not sufficiently important to plunge Europe from Moscow to the Pyrenees, from the North Sea to Palermo, into a war the outcome of which nobody can foresee; after the war people would not even remember why they had fought.' Wise words, but in the end it happened after all; the fact that the little country concerned was not called Bulgaria but Serbia makes no difference from a philosophical point of view.

For the time being Austria was not alone in its resistance to Russia's imperialist urge to act as liberator. When there was another war between Russia and Turkey in 1877 which led to the establishment of a Russia protectorate over Bulgaria, London adopted an even more threatening attitude than Vienna, and Berlin was for better or for worse obliged to act as mediator. This time the Germans appreciated that with their new power went a new responsibility as well as a danger. Whereas during the Crimean War they had acted the part of a disinterested party, they were now compelled to take the centre of the stage in order to preserve the peace. In 1878 Bismarck presided over the great diplomatic congress of Berlin as the 'honest broker', as he called it, trying to find solutions which were tolerably acceptable to all. Bulgaria, Russia's new protégé, was divided into three parts, one of which was given back to the Turks, the two others were forbidden to unite; Austria was allowed to administer Turkish Bosnia but not for the moment to annex it, etc. etc. These were diplomatic devices which had their impermanent, fatal character written all over them. Nobody was really satisfied, least of all Russia, made to surrender such a large part of its booty.

In the following year Bismarck concluded the defensive alliance with Austria-Hungary, an alliance fatal for the German Reich. He saw himself as 'opting' for Austria between Russia and Austria, a choice into which he was forced by the course of events. Yet although the two monarchies promised to come to each other's assistance, if necessary even against Russia, Austria was not allowed to indulge in any activities in the Balkans which might embroil Germany. The idea was to strengthen Austria against Russia, but also to tie it down and to keep it quiet. No sooner had the agreement been concluded than negotiations with Russia were reopened. The League of the Three Emperors was renewed in 1881 with the result that there were now two alliances, one between Austria and Germany against Russia and one between Germany and Russia and Austria against powers unknown. This was only the first of the diplomatic labyrinths which Bismarck created in the eighties with the aim of keeping hostile powers apart or bringing them together by means of friendly commitments, in order to protect Germany against all possible eventualities. In 1881 there was the German–Austrian–Italian tripartite agreement, an instrument of bewildering complication, whose main purpose was to control the old hostility between Austria and Italy. In 1887 the Austro-Italian agreement was strengthened by a British–Italian–Austrian one designed to preserve the existing order in the Mediterranean and surrounding areas, including the Black Sea. The agreement was aimed against Russia. At the same time Bismarck, who encouraged it and who was an ally of Austria and Italy, worked for a new friendly link between Russia and Germany to take the place of the League of the Three Emperors. The result was the so-called Reinsurance Treaty; another reciprocal promise of neutrality but one which would be invalid in case of a Russian attack on

Austria or a German one on France. It included the explicit recognition of Russia's 'historically acquired' interests on the Balkan peninsula. While this treaty was in force and Bismarck still intended to renew it, he proposed to Britain a defensive alliance against France – to the same Britain which in the Near East had until now been Russia's bitterest enemy against the same France which, as was well known, was about to come to terms with Russia. Nothing came of the German–British agreement. Germany wanted it to be aimed against France and Britain against Russia. Consequently they did not get beyond exchanging expressions of good will.

At no other time before or since have statesmen engaged in political activity like this. To the extent that it was designed to preserve the peace in Europe it was Metternich's policy, but it was not pursued in Metternich's spirit. That spirit no longer existed at the end of the nineteenth century. Although Bismarck tried to preserve the peace he never believed in 'Europe' and despised all talk of European interests as hypocrisy. The Reich which he himself represented was more concentrated than the fragile little Europe whose manifold interests Metternich had cared for. It was not Europe that negotiated at the Berlin Congress but the dynamic, spiteful power-states into which Europe had disintegrated, not without substantial assistance from Bismarck. Now he wanted peace between these states, knowing that the time of restricted wars was past, that Germany could no longer remain neutral in the event of a conflict, and that in a war against Russia it must always bear the main burden without reward or thanks. He said: 'We Germans fear God and nothing else in the world.' Nevertheless fear was the mainspring of his diplomacy after 1871; fear of an outburst of German national energy which he had tamed – he knew the impermanent character of such victories – and fear of coalitions against his own creation, Germany, the great power. That was why he negotiated with all and sundry, why he made promises in all directions, public, semi or quite secret ones, which were rendered ineffective by the fact that the state against which they were aimed soon received and was asked for similar promises. Such assurances were rendered ineffective also because they always referred to 'unprovoked' attacks, and in an emergency it was left to the others to decide who was the attacked and who the attacker. There were no permutations and combinations that were not thought of. In the eighties Bismarck tried to involve France in one of them, notwithstanding the fact that they were all aimed against France. To what extent this staggeringly complex system really served the cause of peace is difficult to say. Some people believed that the great powers would have come to blows thirty years before 1914 but for the old maestro who kept them apart and restored relations between them by his cunning, contortionist policies. Others believe that his network of alliances was really a weak spider's web, which only appeared to be effective because the age was itself an age of peace and economic expansion. The mere fact that he was constantly patching up his work and supplementing treaties or replacing them by others is taken as evidence that they were all fundamentally worthless. Of all these treaties the only one that remained in the end was the first, the Austro-German one which had been the reason for all the others.

5. The Bourgeois Age

When Napoleonic France collapsed in 1870 Thomas Carlyle wrote a letter to *The Times* in which he congratulated himself on being privileged to witness this joyful event: the place of vapouring, vainglorious, gesticulating, quarrelsome, restless and oversensitive France as queen of the Continent would now be taken by noble, patient, deep, pious and solid Germany. A few months later another letter was written which has become equally famous, by the French theologian Ernest Renan to his German colleague David Friedrich Strauss. Renan was prejudiced, he was unhappy about the defeat of France and the loss of Alsace-Lorraine which he regarded as nothing less than a crime against nature, a disturbance of world harmony. But it was not for this reason that he saw the matter in a different light from Carlyle. In the past, he wrote, many nations had won victories and founded empires, the Spaniards, the French and the British. In every case there had been more than political domination; the victors had had something to offer to the world, even to those whom they had conquered, because of their organizing force, their faith, their art or their way of life. The frightening thing about the German victory was that new-Germany only showed force, blank, effective force, without any happy message. Its triumph was nothing but a material one and such triumphs bring no blessing.

Carlyle was older than Renan. In his youth he had written about Schiller, translated *Wilhelm Meister* and corresponded with Goethe. The Germany he knew and loved was the Germany of the classical and romantic writers, the Germany in which small universities and small provincial capitals were rich in intellectual life. That this Germany hardly existed any longer, that it was vanishing, Carlyle did not know. Nations change, but they change slowly and it takes even longer for the world to notice the change and define it. Renan was nearer to the truth than Carlyle, however much his judgement was coloured by the sorrow of defeat.

Dreams come true rarely seem as attractive as they originally did. When the dream of German unity was realized the reality was even less attractive than it had once promised to be because it was granted at an unfortunate time. The late nineteenth century was not anywhere a great, intellectually productive age. France at any rate produced impressionist paintings, the poetry of Verlaine and novels about social conditions, while Russia produced the greatest novels of the century. Germany produced industrial progress, military trumpet blasts and politics. If one looks at the picture from a distance, without examining individual figures, one gains a fatally mixed impression: hard-boiled *Realpolitik* and oppressive piety, ostentatious theatrical poses, self-righteous nationalism combined with internal discord, and finally materialism, overwhelmed by the successes of the natural sciences, but yet prepared suddenly to change into cheap mysticism.

What a difference between Bismarck and a German nationalist of an earlier day, Freiherr vom Stein. The latter lived among ideas and had a high concept of man and the functions of human society; the former despised men and cleverly managed to wend his way between depressing realities, confronting idealists with derision. He had won with these methods, aided by the new material forces, by the railways, by the economic unity of Germany, which already existed, and by the expertise of the army.

Liberalism was no longer what it had been in the forties for it was a liberalism of interests, no longer a humane idea. The path runs downhill from the high-minded poet, Uhland, to the hard-hearted, clever parliamentarian, Johannes Miquel. The national liberal historians, Droysen, Sybel and Treitschke, had all begun as rebels, though rather tame ones. Now their cult of history became the cult of success and they never ceased to sing the praises of Germany's new order. Such critical comments as they made were directed against France, against liberal Britain, against social democracy or against Germany's past. No writer can maintain his standards if he is satisfied with himself and the things around him, be he a supporter of Bismarck, an American, a Communist or anything else. When this happens literature descends to the level of panegyrics. Works like Sybel's *Die Begründung des Deutschen Reiches durch Wilhelm I* (The Foundation of the German Reich by William I) are nothing but one long public address.

State subsidized, representative literature and art was satisfied with itself; it was represented by men like Emanuel Geibel and Paul Heyse, Felix Dahn and Viktor von Scheffel, Karl von Piloty and Anton von Werner. Though they managed to paint some good pictures and to write some fine, even beautiful poems or novels, the bulk of their product was imitation, belated classicism, or false renaissance, lacking an independent style befitting the changing times. The same was true of architecture. Buildings were never more fanciful; railway stations and barracks were built in the shape of Gothic fortresses and industrialists' villas took the form of rococo or renaissance palaces, just as fancy dictated.

We must quickly correct this hasty judgement. True artists are found in all periods. The 'false renaissance' produced such noble work as the poetry of the Swiss, Conrad Ferdinand Meyer, or the portrait-painting of the Bavarian, Franz Lenbach. The Hohenzollerns found in Adolph von Menzel, the painter, a man who glorified them in the most tasteful manner. In Berlin Theodor Fontane wrote novels in which he both criticized and idealized the narrow caste society east of the Elbe through his own deep psychology and worldly wisdom. The aristocracy did not thank him for describing this life with so much insight and even more sympathy than insight in stories of endearing purity of language. The middle classes continued to enjoy Scheffel's *Ekkehard* and Dahn's *Kampf um Rom* (The Struggle for Rome), not *Stechlin* and *Effie Briest*. Fontane died a stranger in his age, doubting at the end whether he had ever served the right cause.

The most popular music, which came from Austria, was that of Johann Strauss; happy music with an endless wealth of melody and rhythm, gay, sweet and sentimental, seemingly beginning to say farewell to the good old days, to imperial Vienna and Austria-Hungary whose best qualities it portrayed magnificently in sound. Fontane who still belonged to the old school, was shocked by these 'music hall' melodies and complained that the *Fledermaus* had been performed a hundred times in Berlin. This was the musical fare which the new cities needed, although soon even it was too clever and subtle; the music halls would shortly produce worse things.

A different, clearer mirror was held up to the bourgeoisie by the Hanoverian, Wilhelm Busch. People derived never-ending pleasure from the works of this apparently gay, infinitely malicious misanthropic humorist. They felt that he saw through them, but in a way they liked. Busch fought with Bismarck against France whose defeat he laughed at viciously; he fought with him against his own loyal Hanoverians whom he ridiculed as 'particularists'; he fought with him against the Catholic Church by never ceasing to satirize in drawings and words priests, crafty Jesuits, alcoholic hermits, hypocritical pilgrims, churchgoers and spinsters. His mocking hatred was directed at the German middle classes, both at the honest little man in the country and at the rich in the towns who lived on the work of others; he derided those who whiled away their time in bored fashion at health resorts and spas, lamenting the moral decline of the age. But that he was capable of disgust, an admirer of Schopenhauer's philosophy, a self-torturing, highly intelligent, compassionate sadist, his readers failed to notice. He expressed his views amusingly in rhymed tales, and, to please everyone, even threw in a happy ending. One can learn more about the mind of the German middle class in the age of Bismarck from Busch than from many sociological theses.

It cannot be said that the great anti-bourgeois organization possessed any big guns in the intellectual sphere. The Social Democratic Party was fighting a political battle and at that time, given the situation, was not and could not be a culturally creative movement. Its philosophy was Marxism. The task of its writers was to adapt this ammunition to the weapons of everyday politics; it was a necessary one given that the party had taken up Marx, but hardly one which could break new intellectual ground for the nation. The intellect must be free; anything that serves the aims of a political party belongs to political history not to the history of ideas. Social protest, divorced from party purposes and doctrines, could certainly bring a new, strong wind into literature; it did so as early as the seventies in Britain and in France, but not until the nineties in Germany.

To the political history but also to the intellectual picture of the age belongs an attempt at influencing the masses which originated in Berlin in 1878 and has since been revived under different names. At first it was called the Christian Socialist Party; its founder was the court chaplain, Adolf Stoecker. This man, an intriguer and a demagogue, had decided that the wind must be taken out of the Social Democrats' sails and that the Protestant Church must also go to the people and offer something to the poor, which the Catholics had long done with success. The King himself must fulfil the 'justified demands' of the workers, throne and altar must form an alliance with socialism which was unavoidable anyway, and so on – ideas faintly reminiscent of the old Bismarck–Lassalle alliance. As the foundation of a party the attempt misfired. The Berlin workers made it known that they would not be satisfied with small benefits or alms proffered from above; they had their own aims, to gain political freedom and subsequently to rule, not to be led to the land of promise by court chaplains. Characteristic of the social democratic spirit, which fundamentally remained the spirit of the enlightened progressive bourgeoisie, was a reply given by the Berlin *Freie Presse* to the Christian Socialists:

At a public meeting, hypocrites and obscurantists have dared to appear before the people, and tried, pretending to love the people, to make the masses abandon their sacred struggle for emancipation. Those who trustingly believe in a personal God and in a devil with horns and a tail think that they can exploit the misery of the poor man, the despair of the factory slave, for the black horde of stylitic priests' lackeys. Never before has the intelligent, hard working and industrious people of Berlin been more insulted.

The workers did not desert the Social Democratic Party. But the element which Stoecker knew how to mobilize and which remained a sinister driving force in German politics was anti-semitism. It was an age-old, evil force which had existed in latent form from Christian, even pre-Christian, times onwards, concealed or under control and almost forgotten, only to break out again into brutal misdeeds. Was the Jew not the typical representative of the liberal economic system? Was he not the rich banker – Mendelssohn, Bleichröder – or even the left-wing liberal member of parliament – Lasker, Bamberber? Was he not the usurer in the countryside, the cattle-trader and moneylender in whose nets the peasant was caught? Was he not also the godless agitator who incited people to false socialism in order to gain more power for his like? Much was wrong with Germany's modern economy and politics and morality; all that was required was to shift the blame from the King and his servants, from the productive capitalist to the Jew on the Stock Exchange, in the pawnshop and the editorial office. Stoecker invented these views or encountered them because such ideas are in the air; others with more brutal minds than he carried them further. An enemy, hatred, a devil, such things liven up politics. Malice lies dormant in all of us and anyone who knows how to exploit it, how to turn it smartly in one direction can hope for an echo. It was one of the sins of the German Conservatives that in order to make their not very popular policy more popular they entered into an alliance with the Jew-baiters. They did this in Stoecker's days, and again, at an even lower level, in the nineties.

In times of established conventions antisemitism could not have flourished. But these were morally barren times. German philosophy, once so creative, lived by studying its own history; pompous or smooth professors occupied the chairs of Fichte and Hegel. Natural science dominated everything, Its superiority was recognized even by those who were not involved with it, by philosophers and historians. Natural science is a vastly important subject but it cannot provide standards of opinion and value. Where those are expected from it false idols appear.

Antisemitism, a much older human aberration, was now offered in the form of phoney science, as the doctrine of the relative value of human races, concocted by a French aristocrat and taken over by the German educational philistines. There were other reasons for its convenient and fascinating attraction. The banner of antisemitism made it possible to unite under a common denominator all feelings of insecurity and dissatisfaction, of pride, fear and hatred. One could be against liberalism – there were liberal Jews. One could be against capitalism – there were Jewish financiers. One could be against socialism – Marx and Lassalle had been Jews. One could be against any form of internationalism – the Jews had been at home in it from of old. One could be against the Austrian monarchy – in Vienna, Prague and Budapest there were many and successful Jews. One could even be against Bismarck – the prince's fortune was looked after by a Jewish banker. Antisemitism therefore had no need to choose a particular enemy at any one time; one could be vaguely against the whole age in so far as this was allegedly represented by Judaism, and one could vaguely want something different and better. The same was true fifty years later when the antisemites threw together capitalism and communism, pacifism and the glorification of war, internationalism and nationalism – an intellectually lazy form of enmity but a powerful one.

Bismarck was not an antisemite, for this he was much too clever, too cultivated and too haughty. He thought nothing of Stoecker's movement and was very annoyed when Prince William became involved with it. Thus the most important antisemites were also critics of Bismarck, for example the Orientalist and political writer, Paul de Lagarde. He was a curious individual, not without depth, who wrote some good poems. But he was a curiosity primarily as a weatherbeaten signpost to wrong roads that were later taken. Lagarde regarded liberalism as un-German and accused Bismarck of having 'kneaded liberalism and despotism into one dough'. He disliked parliamentary government, large-scale industry which made the country dependent on foreign markets and the Jews who served Mammon. Lagarde also disapproved of Bismarck's domestic and foreign policy of the 'little' German Reich. Austria, the whole of Austria, must become part of the Reich, and this, Lagarde prophesied, could not be done without a great war. In addition the Reich must include large parts of Russia, to be settled with healthy German peasants. The whole thing was to be called *Germanien*. In spite of his fantastic notions Lagarde was a good Prussian. *Germanien* would be administered on old Prussian lines, with the King of Prussia as the overlord of the German princes; these, his vassals, would rule over the foreign tribes in the East. The ideas of one such man can later, in favourable circumstances, become an impelling, murderous force.

In a chapter on the age of Bismarck, mention must be made of Richard Wagner, whereas there is no need to mention other German musicians of the period, like Bruckner or Brahms. Wagner was greater than his age but he also belonged wholly to it by virtue of his ambition not only to create beauty but also to assist in changing the moral and even the political foundations of the nation. The period of his last steep rise to German and European fame falls into the seventies.

He had begun as a revolutionary, enthusiastically defending

the right of free man to live according to his own law. The collapse of the Dresden rising of 1849 drove the young conductor into exile. For many years he lived in Switzerland; it was only in 1861 that he was again allowed to settle in Germany. The international elements which were inseparably interwoven in the revolution of 1848 were both present in Wagner. His training was a cosmopolitan musical one, saturated with Italian and French influences. He chose the subject-matter for his operatic poems from many different countries, from Italian and from Celtic sources. He admired Heinrich Heine who inspired his *Flying Dutchman*. His restless life was that of a great European in the nineteenth century, with sojourns in Riga, Paris, Dresden, Zürich and Venice; his warmest admirer and sharpest critic counted him among the phenomena of the French romantic movement. But a man who wanted to be more than a roving adventurer, who wanted to be an artist and an educator of the people needed a nation. A man who had the ambition to conquer Europe with his art could only do this by first conquering his own country. It was in exile that Wagner became a patriot for reasons of ambition, nostalgia, love – for who can separate these emotions. Siegfried, the hero of the tetralogy which he wrote in Switzerland, was a revolutionary but a German revolutionary and a German hero; the gigantic opera of *The Ring* was saturated with elements which came, or were supposed to come, from the Germanic past. In the sixties Wagner became the protégé and favourite of the King of Bavaria to whom he gave political advice. At that time he produced essays such as *Was ist deutsch?* (What is German?) and *Deutsche Politik* (German Politics). In 1871 he composed a victory march in honour of the entry of German troops into Paris which for a long time had been part of his spiritual home. Like the Liberals, like some of those who had fought in 1848 and, after returning home and being pardoned, had become reconciled with Bismarck's Reich, Wagner, at another level, also became reconciled with it. In 1872 he began to build his festival theatre in Bayreuth.

It was intended to be a temple of German art, a centre of the national community. Wagner was a democrat in his way and remained one in theory. In his theatre there were no boxes or circles to represent social differences; as in the amphitheatre of the Greeks and Romans the crowd sat undivided, solemnly at one with what was happening on the stage and in the orchestra. It was not commercial entertainment that was offered here, not an arbitrarily restricted form of art, but all the arts in dramatic oneness, poetry and music and painting and philosophy and religious worship. Such was Wagner's idea. He wanted to achieve for Germany what Sophocles had achieved for Athens; Germany, however, was not Athens. The social reality of Bayreuth was even further away from Wagner's highest aims than was Bismarck's Reich from the dreams of the men of 1848. The whole venture was very costly, particularly as one of Wagner's ambitions was to live in princely style. In order to get money it was necessary to attract the rich who were readily attracted by the novelty of his venture. Oriental potentates and new German millionaires contributed, visited Bayreuth and were entertained by the Wagner family at magnificent garden parties. Bayreuth did not become the centre of a noble community of the people, freed from the curse of gold, as Wagner had hoped. Instead it became the sensational summer meeting place of the European plutocracy. It was certainly a 'national' phenomenon: what was offered here was meant to be German art. Equally national in its way was the capital Berlin, the 'world city', the centre of European politics and finance.

This is no place to speak of the glories of Wagner's music, especially of the greatest and last opera, *Parsifal*, created in the Bayreuth period; it is not for the general historian to do so. Bayreuth must concern us only as a social phenomenon, as a feature of the age of Bismarck. Wagner the writer, who condemned Jewish influence in music, who referred with respect to Paul de Lagarde and in whose *Bayreuther Blätter* real antisemites were given a hearing; Wagner the philosopher, who allowed himself to be convinced by Gobineau's racial theory and promised a regeneration of humanity. Wagner the musician who wanted to create the true community of the people and become its artistic legislator; Wagner the metaphysician whose thought was dominated by the concept of salvation – salvation of the people by the hero, salvation of man by woman, salvation of life by death – and who was at the same time a master of stage management, of the most elaborate theatrical tricks – this Wagner belongs to German history after 1870 and indeed far, far beyond 1870.

6. A Rebel: Friedrich Nietzsche

At the opening of the Bayreuth festival theatre two of Wagner's admirers were present; repelled by so much ostentation both disappeared swiftly, as though panic-stricken. One was the composer's protector and saviour, the King of Bavaria, romantic, solitary, sick, the man who had so deeply regretted Bismarck's foundation of the Reich. The other was the classical philologist Dr Friedrich Nietzsche, professor at the University of Basle, who because of ill health had retired at an early age on a small pension. Of him we must now speak. He was an independent man, not a successful representative of his age but its critic. And there has never been a shrewder critic at any time anywhere.

Nietzsche was the son and grandson of Saxon clergymen, a serious, well-behaved child, a model pupil. As a student he changed from theology to philology and became a professor when he was only twenty-five. After ten years the illness of which he later died and which was probably caused by a syphilitic infection, forced him to stop teaching, Thereafter he had lived as a wandering writer in northern Italy, the south of France and in the Engadine, avoiding Germany. He wrote his most extreme, most explosive works in 1888, the year in which the two emperors died. At the end of the same year he collapsed. It was only of the mentally sick man cared for by his sister that the German public gradually began to take note.

The two masters of his youth were Schopenhauer and Wagner. Schopenhauer he did not know personally. Wagner he knew and admired warmly, but then turned away from, as he did from Schopenhauer. The arguments which he used to criticize these two contain his philosophy, the story of his noble and tortured mind.

To begin with Nietzsche's writings were balanced, moderate and full of good, educational intentions, as in the four meditations which he called 'untimely'. Then his tone became that of a solitary man who knows that he is not being heard: more strident, more virulent, more contemptuous. Balanced essays were replaced by aphorisms, thrown out like orders – a medium which he borrowed from the French writers of the eighteenth century. At the end madness revealed itself, in the biting cleverness of his utterances, as in the precision with which they were made. Nietzsche raised the German language to its greatest heights. No one has written better German, and he also wrote beautiful poems. On occasion he combined prose and verse to create works of unique expressiveness.

Unlike the pure scientist the philosopher not only discovers, he creates, and usually we can forget the creator in the completed work. With Nietzsche this is not so. It is always *he* who speaks, a personality of irritating intensity. Often he says what he does not mean, or means what he does not say, or gives it two or three meanings. He did not create a system like Kant or Hegel. It was impossible for original philosophers to do this in 1880, only uncreative imitators could try. Nietzsche's work is his life which pulsates in his writings. His work was a personal catastrophe which presaged and predicted Europe's general catastrophe. He himself was a catastrophe. Such a person must inevitably have made some irresponsible statements. He prophesied things which he claimed to welcome but at the thought of which he really shuddered.

He prophesied a century of world wars, of revolution and universal turmoil. During it everything false, everything diseased would be stamped out, the weak would be crushed or disappear. Out of it would come a new force, the rule of the strong, of the merciless. Because life was the will to power and the struggle for it, all Christian virtue was merely the deceit of those who were too weak to fight. I do not know to what extent Nietzsche seriously believed this. It is the positive side of his philosophy, since he had to offer something positive, it is also its weakness. Nietzsche, this connoisseur of everything that was delicate and refined, sometimes became a victim of what he hated most: tasteless bombast. As the man himself was full of contradictions so is his work.

Prophesying war and glorifying power as he did, he should have been a supporter of the new Germany; this he was not at all. He loved the old Germany, the Germany of Goethe, not of Bismarck. He thought that the German nation was becoming politically conscious at the expense of its old virtues.

The price of coming to power is even greater; power makes people stupid . . . the Germans – once they were called the nation of thinkers – do they think at all today? The Germans are bored by intellect, politics swallow up all their interest in really intellectual matters. *Deutschland, Deutschland, über alles,* I fear, was the end of German philosophy . . . 'Are there any German philosophers, are there any German poets, are there any good German books?' – I am asked abroad. I blush, but with the bravado which is mine even in desperate circumstances I reply: 'Yes, *Bismarck.*'

Elsewhere he says:

This is the age of the masses, they kowtow to everything 'mass'. This happens also in *politics*. A statesman who raises them a new tower of Babel, some monstrosity of an empire and of power is 'great' to them. What does it matter that those of us who are more careful and reticent for the time being cling to the old belief that it is only a great idea which lends greatness to an action or a cause. Assuming a statesman were to put his nation in a position where it becomes involved in the grand political game for which it is by nature neither fitted nor prepared, so that it must sacrifice its old and more tested qualities for a new and questionable mediocrity; assuming that a statesman condemned his nation to become politically minded generally, though this nation has so far had better things to do and in its heart of hearts cannot rid itself of a cautious distaste for the restlessness, emptiness and noisy petulance of politically minded peoples; assuming that such a statesman whips up the dormant passions and lusts of his people, blames it for its former timidity and wish not to get involved, accuses it of hankering after foreign things and of a secret desire for the infinite, that he makes light of its dearest fancies, warps its conscience and makes it narrow-minded and nationalistic in its tastes – how can a statesman who did all these things, and whom his nation would have to do penance for for all eternity, if it has a future at all, how can such a statesman be called *great*?

The Germans had not even become truly politically conscious; for no great nation had ever given itself to such an extent into the hands of one man. Nietzsche believed in great men, but he detested the only one in Europe at that time, who appeared in cavalry boots before parliament in order to mock at it. In German nationalism Nietzsche saw a betrayal of all Europe's better traditions; a spiteful fusty, philistine atmosphere in which no free spirit could breathe:

One must accept that a nation that suffers or wishes to suffer from national hysteria and political ambition has occasional clouding of the spirit and disturbance of the mind, attacks in which it briefly takes leave of its senses. For example, the Germans of today sometimes have an anti-French phase, then an anti-Polish one, then a Christian-Romantic one, then a Wagnerian one, a Teutonic one, a Prussian one (we only need to look at these poor historians, these Sybels and Treitschkes and their heavily bandaged heads) – and all these other small delusions of the German mind and conscience.

As for the persecution of Jews, Nietzsche's horror of it was almost a physical one; he hated to be in contact with people who made such a filthy pursuit into a philosophy. 'How much mendacity and squalor are needed to raise race questions in today's hotch-potch Europe.' 'Maxim: no social intercourse with anybody involved in the lie of racialism.' Where now were Germans like Goethe, Schopenhauer and Heinrich Heine; the great psychologists, the masters of pure prose, men who recognized and produced work of high quality? It was necessary to look for them in Paris because there were none left in the Reich. Instead there was noisy activity, self-flattery among industrialists and academics, stupid ignorance of the outside world, cringing before the imperial power, before success and before anything with spurs. Nietzsche called himself a 'good European'. When he prophesied wars and pretended to want them – though in reality he did not – he was thinking of wars for Europe, not wars of nationalism. Thus he would not have minded if Napoleon I had triumphed because he regarded him, wrongly, as a fighter for pan-Europe.

I look beyond all these national wars, new 'empires' and whatever else there is in the foreground. What I am concerned with – because I see it coming about slowly and hesitatingly – is a united Europe ... Because of the morbid estrangement which the folly of nationalism has produced and continues to produce among the nations of Europe, because of short-sighted and hasty politicians who come to the top with its help and who do not realize that their policy of disintegration can only be an entr'acte policy – because of all this and many things that cannot possibly be mentioned today, the clearest signs that Europe wants to become one are overlooked or arbitrarily distorted.

Nietzsche never forgave Richard Wagner for betraying his European loyalties, for becoming *reichsdeutsch*. In *Ecce Homo*, his last confession, he described his visit to the Bayreuth festival.

What had happened? – Wagner had been translated into German. The Wagnerian had come to dominate over Wagner. German art! The German maestro! German beer! ... Those of us who know only too well to what sophisticated artists, to what cosmopolitan taste, Wagner's art is addressed, were aghast to find Wagner decked out 'with German virtues' ... I believe I know the Wagnerians ... Here we have the whole range of monstrosities including the antisemite.

He did not forgive Wagner for using his art to woo the masses:

So what's the point of beauty? Why not rather the great, the sublime, the gigantic, those things which move the *masses* ... We know the masses, we know the theatre; the best part of it – all these German youths, horned Siegfrieds and other Wagnerians, need sublime, profound, overwhelming experiences. This is just as logical. 'He who overthrows us is strong; he who raises us up is divine; he who heightens our perceptions is profound.'

In his ironical description of the Wagner public of the eighteen eighties Nietzsche with the hysterical prescience of the prophet seems to sense the spirit of a political mass meeting of 1930.

His criticism of Wagner was exaggerated, attacking all the

things that he had once admired. The writings of this lonely creature became a strident polemic. He condemned Christianity and all religious attitudes, teachings and values which had anything to do with it. He condemned all philosophical or religious thought which sought another, true world behind our real one and which reduced life to a make-believe, a transitory affair. He condemned the Christian virtues of compassion, charity and care for the weak. In politics he condemned the doctrine of equality and brotherhood, democracy, and socialism. But was the new Germany not in fact guided by the principles of *Realpolitik*, taking Christian beliefs less and less seriously? Was it not entirely orientated towards this world, towards science, success, material gain and power? And was not that the very thing with which Nietzsche reproached it? He attacked the romantics, whose intellectual history was diseased, and yet he was dissatisfied with Germany because instead of such types it had strapping generals and factory directors. He attacked 'German profundity' and yet blamed the Germans for no longer producing profound thinkers. What then did he want? Unfortunately he did not know himself. He was not consistent and could not be. What he reproached others with was in him too; otherwise he could not have written so well about it. He was disgusted by the lacunae in the new Germany where morbid artistry had been replaced by glossy, dashing efficiency. He glorified the qualities which he himself did not possess, the ruthless vitality of the renaissance prince, of the Prussian officer, of the 'blond beast', the superman. And because he did not possess them at all he did not write well about them; this remains the embarrassing aspect of his writings. 'Sick cobweb weavers' was what he called the philosophers of the past, but he was himself the sickest of them all; sick with loneliness, an enemy of his age and physically poisoned since adolescence. Nobody suffered as much as this prophet of the joys of power; nobody was in the end as much in need of Christian charity as this enemy of Christianity. Therefore one must never take his doctrine literally. His work is a living process, not a classroom where the pupil is provided with undisputed facts.

His early still moderate criticism of the German system of

education had much to be said for it. He deplored the fact that in the interest of the state technical training and efficiency in middle-class and military caste principles were valued even more highly than a liberal education. Nietzsche was one of the first to speak of *Vermassung*, the proletarianization of civilization, a phrase repeated a thousand times later. What good did it do? To some extent such developments can be directed and made productive by good leadership. They cannot be prevented and mere criticism does not achieve much. Nietzsche refuted not democracy nor socialism. Neither did he refute Christianity as an historical, civilizing force. To believe that for two thousand years Western man has been on the wrong road from which he would soon return to the right one, signified an irrational overestimate of the moment and of oneself. Nietzsche lacked a feeling for moderation even in his sanest period. He was severely punished for it by the use to which his writings were put. He was still alive, or still vegetating, when ladies of the German upper middle class who prided themselves on their advanced ideas carried his *Zarathustra* as their Bible substitute. Then followed a variety of sectarian circles of conceited writers and poets; for them Nietzsche's works were the ladder which they, who stood high above the vulgar mass of the people, used to climb into their prophet's towers. Finally there came a great criminal who seized Germany in the nineteen thirties and who saw himself as Nietzsche's celebrated superman and whose literary advisers drew sedulously from Nietzsche's works. All this would probably have happened without Nietzsche; we must not blame him for it. That he could be associated with it at all is a severe punishment for him. Punishment for the fact that he did not weigh his words and did not ask how they might be interpreted. He knew and despised the human race and he should have reckoned with the public as it is, not with gods.

He solved nothing, He loathed that aspect of the new German character which later found its most repulsive expression in National Socialism and yet he must be connected with it as its culpable precursor: that fact alone indicates how little he solved. Destiny was in him, not solution or truth. If great catastrophes, wars and revolutions solve nothing, neither do personal, intellectual disasters; they are merely warnings, making people conscious of certain things.

Gloomy predictions about the future of man must take the form of warnings because nothing is ever predetermined. Even Nietzsche, an arrogant genius, did not presume to predict the development of the future as something inevitable. That was done in the twentieth century by those who lifted his ideas wholesale He only felt the crisis like a seismograph registers an earthquake and suffered from it without knowing what its form would be; the cries of joy which he uttered over it were like the noises which a frightened child makes in the dark to reassure itself.

As a critic of imperial Germany he was unjust and immoderate, as in almost everything he wrote. Yet he hit the heart of the matter and at the time he was the only one to do so. This explains the solitude which suffocated him. It is a coincidence in German history which deserves reflection that his breakdown occurred in the year that William II ascended to the throne. Nietzsche had long seen through the new ruler's character, without knowing him, regarding him as typical of the new German in general: histrionic, anxious to be approved of, sensation-seeking, empty and boastful. In one of the letters with which Nietzsche inundated his acquaintances during the first days of his madness he said that he had convened a congress of princes in Rome in order to have the young Kaiser arrested; and: that he had just ordered all antisemites to be shot.

Part Eight
The Age of William II (1888–1914)

Henry Adams, an American historian who liked to wander in Europe, reported in 1897 from Paris: 'In my opinion, the centre of readjustment, if readjustment is to be, lies in Germany, not in Russia or with us. For the last generation, since 1865, Germany has been the great disturbing element of the world, and until its expansive force is decidedly exhausted I see neither political nor economic equilibrium possible. Russia can expand without bursting anything. Germany cannot. Russia is in many respects weak and rotten. Germany is immensely strong and concentrated. The struggle is going on with constant German advantage, economically and politically . . .'

Four years later he wrote from St Petersburg: 'Germany, from this point of view, is a powder-magazine. All her neighbours are in terror for fear she will explode, and sooner or later, explode she must.'

Such observations were made frequently and we could quote more of them. Germany at the turn of the century was seen as a new great power wanting to push ahead at top speed but unable to do so without sooner or later 'exploding' and unable to find a genuine, enduring mode of life. If that was true the outbreak of the German world war was only a question of time; and the history of the age of William II must be seen as a stream running irresistibly towards the great cataract.

It has indeed often been seen like this. Not by the German writers who wanted to regard the war of 1914 as a stupid, avoidable accident or as a conspiracy of Germany's enemies, but by those critics, German and otherwise, who were ambitious enough to dig deeper. In their opinion everything was predestined: all the misfortune stemmed from the nature of the Reich as Bismarck created it and as it reached its dazzling zenith under the Kaiser. They then go on to wonder if the Second World War was not a consequence of the First, a new link in the chain of disaster. Were not the men of the age of the Kaiser still in charge in the twenties, although Germany was a republic and there was the semblance of democracy? Was National Socialism not ultimately the realization of the ideas of the pan-Germans, already vociferously at work in 1900? Must Germany's history from the fall of Bismarck to the fall of Hitler not be seen as a continuous story in which one thing followed inexorably upon another, and which certain personalities, for example the pan-German leader, Alfred Hugenberg, witnessed from beginning to end? This too has been done; the period between 1890 and 1945 has been made into a single chapter of history dominated by Germany, in which everything fits and everything was predictable – such an approach is impossible without oversimplification.

Of course nothing happens out of the blue. As things develop their early form becomes increasingly clear in retrospect. This is true of the war of 1914, of National Socialism and also of the Weimar Republic. All three have their roots in the age of William II, but this is not reason enough to describe his reign only as the period in which these things began. It was something in its own right, a period with its own style, its own achievements. Some things which started then unfortunately did not come to fruition or took an unplanned turn. Something altogether different might well have happened.

The historian can never quite forbear to make retrospective prophecies, because he knows the end. But let us humbly remember, when we look at the past, that as far as the future goes the historian can foresee little and that his occasional predictions usually fail to come true.

Let us by all means say 'this is what happened', but not 'this is what was bound to happen'. Let us not claim that the future is determined by the past, that nothing new ever happens. New things do happen in history; to show how they are connected with the past but have their own special character, how they become mixed up with events which nobody could have foreseen, with personal chance and with the actions of individuals – that is the task of the historian.

1. Bismarck's End

The Emperor William I died in March 1888 at the age of ninety-one. His son and successor, Frederick III, was a well-meaning, serious and industrious man who hated Bismarck; a feeling which the Chancellor returned with characteristic violence. His political leanings were towards British liberalism because he was under the influence of his wife, daughter of Queen Victoria, a woman far more intelligent than the average princess. The royal pair had long prepared themselves for their high calling, had studied, planned, drafted manifestoes and waited for the death of the old man who seemed unwilling to die. Bismarck for his part had tried to ward off the danger inherent in the change of monarch by all kinds of safeguards; among them being the forced Reichstag elections of 1887 which had brought him such a welcome victory. All this proved unnecessary in the end. When Frederick arrived in Berlin he was a dying man who could no longer say what he wanted but had to write it down. Soon there were no more orders at all from his sick bed and in June he died, taking his hopes and disappointments with him. Should one call this a fateful event in German history? People say that even as Emperor Frederick could not have done much good. First because, although his views were liberal, he was the slave of class traditions, and secondly because one man could not put right the faults in the social structure of the Prusso-German state, particularly if he was the chief beneficiary of this structure. People say that the fault lay in the institutions, not the men. There is something in this. But if one believes that, because of his character, the Emperor William II did much harm, one must admit that a firmer and wiser character in the same position could have done good.

The democrats and progressives were deeply distressed by Frederick's death. Like their elders in 1840 and 1862 they had put their hopes in the new monarch. The Social Democrats remained unmoved – a change of monarch could not concern them too much – but found dignified, compassionate words for the dead monarch. The conservative parties were glad that he was gone. Bismarck, too, was glad, although he was too well-bred to say so aloud. His son Herbert, who had recently become Secretary of State for Foreign Affairs, was less reticent. The fact that the Emperor's terrible death was the occasion for so much happy relief and so many ugly grins showed that something was wrong. Bismarck had united the state but not the nation.

On the Prussian throne and at the head of the Reich the third generation now succeeded the first. One could say the twentieth century succeeded the eighteenth, because William I, born eleven years after the death of Frederick the Great, had been educated by men of the eighteenth century in a classical, French-orientated and parsimonious spirit. William II, who died in 1941, can be described as a man of the twentieth century. What was left out was the generation of the nineteenth century, faithful to pure liberalism.

The Chancellor, Prince Bismarck, stood between the three generations of Hohenzollern, younger than William I, older than Frederick, and to William II an old man from a legendary past. Because he did not take ideas seriously he could not develop new ideas. He could change his habits, but his thoughts and feelings and ways of life remained unchanged. The two experiences which had done most to shape his political character were the revolution of 1848 and the conflict of 1862. The first he intended to repress with the usual means if it happened to recur; the second had brought him to power and had never ceased to inspire his way of governing.

The old man, now seventy-three, intended to go on running the country. This was natural: power is a drug which very few people have ever managed to give up voluntarily. Bismarck was certainly a patriot who cared for his Prussia and gradually also for his personal creation, the Reich. But he could not imagine that the Reich could thrive without himself as its supreme ruler. His attitude harmed the Reich because it led him to spurn and suppress talent which might have been capable of shouldering the burden after him. This applied even to his family. The only one whom he wished to train as his successor was the untalented ruffian, his son Herbert.

Bismarck thought that he could come to terms with the new monarch. William II had hated his parents who in their turn had been harshly critical of him. He had waited with blatant impatience for his father's death. He believed himself to belong wholly to the old Prussian, conservative tradition, unlike his father with his liberal, pro-British views. As he worshipped his grandfather he would also revere his grandfather's right hand; this indeed he did to the extent that his nature allowed.

What followed has often been told but remains worth telling.

Bismarck was never what is called popular, either with the people or with its representatives. He was not even liked by his closest circle. The old gentleman lived alone among his protégés who feared him, feeling neither sympathy nor loyalty towards him because of his conceit and selfish tyranny.

In the course of 1889 it was said that he was ageing fast, neglecting the affairs of state; it was whispered, too, that all was not well between him and the new ruler. He hardly appeared in the Reichstag; most of the year he spent on his estate Friedrichsruh from where, with a few officials, he thought that he could deal with government business. The election of 1887 had given him an obedient parliament, a majority of Conservatives, Free Conservatives and National Liberals, allied with him and among themselves. But as he neglected parliament and parties this alliance broke up. The right wing of the Conservatives, the Christian Socialists and antisemites, had long been hostile to him because they regarded him as a friend of the Jews, an enemy of the church, a man who prevented the establishment of a strong, national and welfare-minded kingdom. The National Liberals also had unpleasant memories. Their leader, Miquel, noticed that the old flagship was slowly sinking; he was no friend of wrecks.

The enmity or indifference of the parties could not overthrow Bismarck. The Prusso-German system – *his* system – was not made that way. His office depended solely on the confidence of the ruler. William II, on the other hand, had an instinct for what people wanted and did not want. Against the will of the parties, against popular sympathy, the young man would not have dared to take the step which he gradually decided upon in the course of 1889. The crisis – inevitable given the nature of the protagonists – reached its climax over the so-called social question. In this matter the Kaiser was full of goodwill. His attitude was that something needed to be done for the exploited workers, that he was king also of the poorest, that Red revolution must be prevented by sensible concessions and that he would show greater statesmanship than the famous kings who had lost their heads because of their obstinacy. Bismarck regarded this as mumbo-jumbo. To him the social-democrat threat was an issue of power and war which could not be solved by gentleness. The more the people were offered the more they would want. Anyway, the legislation safeguarding the rights of the workers, to which the Kaiser attached so much importance, merely compelled the workers to have something which they did not want because most of them had no wish to have their working hours legally restricted, and so on – arguments which show that Prince Bismarck was indeed ripe for retirement. It is impossible to say how seriously he took them. Partly he was certainly motivated by spiteful obstinacy *vis-à-vis* the popularity-seeking, inexperienced, energetic Kaiser, and partly he was using his old technique of staying in office by invoking the threat of revolution which he, and he alone, could master. But the confident victor of 1862 was curiously unsure now in the winter of 1890 when he tried to re-repeat his trick; he vacillated, talked too much, made plans only to reject them and seemed indeed divorced from the world. On one occasion he was found lying on the sofa in tears; he felt deserted by everybody, a broken man.

The Anti-Socialist Law which had brought Germany into disrepute for twelve years was not renewed by the Reichstag in January 1890. This suited Bismarck because, as he explained to the Kaiser, it was necessary to bring the issue to a head; blood would flow in any case and that would be the moment for a draconic law. William did not take such a bloodthirsty view of the situation. Indeed the future showed that even from the Conservative standpoint, such an attitude was totally unrealistic. Germany in 1890 was much further away from Red revolution as imagined by the frightened bourgeoisie than in 1848. If Bismarck now wanted to use guns against the Social Democrats he lived in a world of hallucinations.

In February the Reichstag elections brought him the worst defeat ever. The parties of his *Kartell* lost more than a third of their seats while the Progressives and the Social Democrats doubled theirs. The enemies of the Bismarckian system now had a clear majority. This was more than just an election episode, it was the collapse of the parliamentary game as played by Bismarck since 1866. The old statesman could not really understand the new constellation. He thought of an alliance of Centre and Conservatives which, to make it numerically workable, would have required the collaboration of such *Reichsfeinde* as the Poles and the Alsatians; he also thought of changing the constitution, of abolishing universal suffrage, of a campaign against social democracy in the turmoil of which constitutional considerations would be silenced. There is no doubt that he was planning *coups*, but they were not thought out; he mentioned them to the Kaiser and then forgot them. He stubbornly sabotaged the imperial projects for the protection of the workers. He wanted to go on being in power, but really in power; it was not in his nature to save his position by adapting himself, by submitting to the young ruler's will.

In the weeks preceding his dismissal – on 18 March 1890 – he must have known that he would not be able to hold his position. His behaviour became more uncompromising, defiant and malicious. But it was the malice of impotence; intrigues and pinpricks were the only weapons with which he could defend himself at the end.

For twenty-five years Bismarck had been Europe's first statesman, at times its arbiter. His personal qualities entitled him to a place among the ranks of the great rulers of the past, Wallenstein, Cromwell and Napoleon. But whereas in comparable crises they did not hesitate to resort to extremes, to civil war and rebellion, all the Prussian Prime Minister could do was obediently to draft his letter of resignation the moment an undeserving young man asked him to do so. The army was loyal to the ruler – thanks to Bismarck's past policy. The Reichstag was impotent – this was Bismarck's fault. In any case the Reichstag hated him. If he had called upon the party leaders for help they would have shrugged their shoulders or laughed at him. He did in fact send for Windthorst, the Centre leader, but Windthorst did not stay long at the Chancellor's house. A Conservative leader, who had also been invited, did not go at all; there was no point in calling on a man who was finished. There remained the masses at whom Bismarck had wished to fire; not in the style of the twentieth century by leading one mass party against another, but in the style of the early nineteenth by setting guards regiments against democrats. Bismarck was the last person on earth to appeal to the people against the King.

Nor was he helped by the personal set-up which he had established over many years. His protégés deserted him or turned against him. The Austrian ambassador in Berlin reported: 'A most repulsive spectacle is offered here by many people who, having until recently kowtowed to Prince Bismarck and to everything connected with his name, now shamelessly dissect his past in order to lay bare insignificant mistakes and minor weaknesses of his.'

A man who despises human beings and treats them accordingly will in the end have similar treatment meted out to him. Of Bismarck's collaborators only one followed him into exile, his son Herbert. All the others were thankful when his successor, General von Caprivi, allowed them to carry on as before.

So he disappeared. The immediate cause does not concern us; it was of a transitory, superficial nature. For a year the causes had multiplied. His last official act was to hand in his resignation which superbly combined dignity, sadness and malice. Parliament received the news with icy silence; there was not a word of farewell or thanks, let alone of disapproval. William II could assure himself that he had acted not only rightly but in accordance with the nation's wishes – if indeed the nation had any wishes in this great matter. The world saw in the apathetic indifference with which the citizens of the Reich watched its founder depart as the revelation of a mean nature. Yet the explanation lies more in Bismarck's history than in the nature of the German people. What reason had social democratic workers, Catholic priests or teachers or peasants or even staunch liberal citizens to strew flowers in his path as he went?

In the years that followed this attitude changed. Bismarck's story is not finished. The name which has taken up so much space in our narrative does not disappear even now. This force of nature found rest only in death. And then not even in death.

He could not believe until the end that, after such achievements, he would finish thus; his anger, his resentment and his thirst for revenge were insatiable. Later, it is true, there was a reconciliation between him and the Kaiser, there were reciprocal visits, tributes and embraces, but nothing really changed. One does not forgive the unforgivable, however much one persuades oneself and others that one is doing so. Bismarck was bad at forgiving all his life.

Moreover, at the age of seventy-five he was still full of energy and not in the least prepared to allow his retirement to be ascribed to health reasons. He had lived for politics for half a century and wanted to go on doing so. Hence his avid study of the press and his contributions to it. He produced hundreds of articles a year, gave interviews and reorganized his staff of journalistic helpers. With a merciless eye he followed the activities of his successors, Caprivi and Hohenlohe, and particularly those of the man who regarded himself as his real successor. Napoleon on St Helena ignored the present and looked only to the past, constructing his legend. Bismarck did the same, with the skill that might be expected of him, particularly by dictating his memoirs. But these continued right up to the present, and he continued to be active in the present. Friedrichsruh became a centre of opposition of which the rulers in Berlin were more afraid than of social democracy and radicalism put together.

The old man made speeches and travelled. He showed himself in places where he had never shown himself before, where he never had been loved and where there had been no reason to love him, in Vienna and in Munich for instance. Now, lo and behold, he was loved there. Now for the first time in his life he was popular. Now the greatness of his past made itself felt, freed from the malice which had so often been inherent in his actions. Now he benefited from the growing discontent caused by William II's personal rule. He played on this discontent, it warmed his lonely, vindictive soul, although he never abandoned the pretence of loyalty: the Kaiser was good but unfortunately his entourage was not. Towards the end of his life Bismarck became a demagogue, almost a democrat. Time and again he said that it was necessary to strengthen the constitution, to increase the influence of parliament which he unfortunately had himself at times unconsciously repressed. But then those had been different times.

Bismarck's great journey through Germany in the summer of 1892 is not the least remarkable event in this eventful life. Monarchs fled in order to avoid receiving the great exile, while mayors and citizens behaved as though the long-awaited hero had arrived. From this period dated the pilgrimages to Friedrichsruh which henceforth never ceased; the special trains from all corners of the Reich, bringing students, rifle clubs and civic deputations. The Prince would dutifully appear on the terrace, looking grey and tired; he would empty an enormous goblet filled with champagne which his visitors had presented to him and rouse himself to make an improvised speech praising the constitution and attacking the government. Then *Deutschland, Deutschland über alles* and the *Wacht am Rhein* were sung and the evening would end with a torchlight procession.

The present author freely admits that he would like to have joined in. The opportunity to see this strange man was something not to be missed, and to admire greatness is not a bad human trait. Nevertheless there was something unreal about the new cult. It came entirely from the Right. The mass parties continued to be anti-Bismarckian; the Reichstag, with a majority of Centre, Progressives and Social Democrats, refused to congratulate him on his eightieth birthday. Those who appealed to Bismarck were dissatisfied with the Court and the government without having any left-wing sympathies; Junker reactionaries as well as middle-class nationalists of a new type to become all too familiar in the future.

'Bismarck would not have allowed this to happen.' 'How differently Bismarck would have behaved.' Those were the kind of phrases used whenever someone disapproved of something done in Berlin. The 'Iron Chancellor' – as he called himself in his articles – would not have estranged Russia from the German Reich, he would not have damaged agriculture by liberal trade agreements, he would have told the Centre and the Social Democrats and all the *Reichsfeinde* to go to the devil; he would have taught the German people manners and also have given it the *Lebensraum* which it needed. Bismarck – the Iron Chancellor, the faithful Eckart of the Germans, the old man in the *Sachsenwald*, Barbarossa, Wotan – became a myth in his lifetime: he also became the political prototype of what was later called 'national opposition', an opposition, which unlike that of the *Reichsfeinde*, had the country's interests very much at heart and was led by a great man. Antisemites, nationalists and pan-Germans who dreamt of a great Germanic Reich climbed on to his band-wagon. Bismarck, the aristocratic, mocking enemy of the people of 1848, the statesman and socialite, the protector of princes, Metternich's late pupil who had founded a conservative *Kleindeutschland* only in order to prevent the establishment of a radical *Grossdeutschland* and who had since carefully preserved the international *status quo* – Bismarck now became a symbol of a pan-German community, controlled internally with an iron hand, which aimed at conquering a limitless horizon. Rising high above Germany's cities the Bismarck towers reminded the people of the man, and of what Germans should be in order to serve his memory. His death changed little; the myth did not die. In comparison with him reality, both imperial and republican, seemed restricted, unsatisfying, fragmentary and squalid. Thus from the first to the last William II and his servants, and after him the rulers of the Weimar Republic, were overshadowed by Bismarck. Until there came a man who regarded himself as far, far greater than Bismarck. Then people began to look for the real politician behind the myth. What had he done wrong, what had he done right? Should one follow in his footsteps or turn in the opposite direction? What lessons could be learnt from him? I believe they still argue about it today.

2. Kaiser and Reich

After 1890 German affairs took a turn for the worse and therefore many historians came to the conclusion that Bismarck's fall was a disaster and the beginning of all Germany's misfortune. But it needs little acumen to show the erroneousness of this view. After all, Bismarck was seventy-five when he was dismissed and eighty-three when he died, long confined to a wheelchair and incapable of work. What difference could it have made at best if he had stayed in office for a few more years? Moreover, we have no reason to assume the best. Germany's affairs did not flourish under Bismarck; the situation deteriorated noticeably in his last years of office and in February 1890 he was at his wits' end. That was why he fell. The personal motives which persuaded the Kaiser to dismiss Bismarck are irrelevant. A wiser ruler could not have acted differently. Bismarck did not disappear too soon, but much too late. The removal of this oppressive anachronism was the most courageous thing that William II ever did. Only he did not understand what he was doing. He was himself a Bismarckian, and particularly on issues over which he quarrelled with Bismarck – social democracy and Germany's eastern policy – he later out-Bismarcked Bismarck. He thought that Bismarck's political edifice was sound and so reliable that it no longer needed the architect; it never occurred to him that it should or could be changed in any way. Only that he himself wanted to take Bismarck's place. Therefore the removal of the aged tyrant remained a purely negative operation, necessary as such but without remedial consequences.

So many unkind things have been written about the Kaiser that one hesitates to add any more. Besides, condemnation of him is condemnation of Germany, of the German aristocracy, the German middle classes, of the whole false development of Germany from 1848 onwards of which he was the culmination. It is also a condemnation of Bismarck who had made of 'His Majesty the King' the 'real Prussian Prime Minister' and with immense efforts had kept him in that impossible position. For all this William was not to blame and he would have had to be a wise man to extricate himself even reasonably well from the affair. An Alsatian Social Democrat rightly said of him: 'He is a product of his environment.' It was no simple environment. In William's soul influences, traditions and dreams struggled with each other; English and Prussian elements, liberalism and absolutism, pacifism and military pageantry, imperial romanticism and the spirit of modern industrialism.

The Germany of the nineties was also the Germany of Gerhart Hauptmann, Richard Dehmel and Max Weber. Yet it was the political Germany and the industrial Germany, Germany as a power-complex, which the young Kaiser represented only too well. The energy, the expansive force, the ostentation, the refusal to recognize danger, the skating on thin ice as though the ground was made of Krupps' steel, all the things that led the American observer to the conclusion that sooner or later there must be an explosion – of those qualities the Kaiser was a brilliant exponent. His flatterers were not wrong when they told him that he was a modern man. What did it matter that those in the know spoke of irresponsibility, even of incipient mental illness; the citizens of Berlin waved their top-hats when he left the palace on horseback and shouted: 'Thank you, thank you'. He gave them what they liked.

He was not a bad man. He wanted to be loved, not to cause suffering. He might allow himself to make bloodthirsty speeches, but bloody action was not at all in his line. He was not given to action of any kind. He was lazy and pleasure-loving. He liked to feast, to travel, to show himself to the people, to lead his guards on horseback into manoeuvres, to exchange toasts with royalty at princely banquets, to sit in the imperial box bedecked like a peacock, smiling graciously at the audience, fondling his moustache. That was how he would have liked to go on to the end of his days; for public life to be an everlasting, golden, military, peaceful spectacle, and he to be at its centre. He was a good actor. Those who came into brief contact with him were charmed by him, not only German professors but American millionaires and even British statesmen, Winston Churchill among them. His intellectual grasp was quick, his memory good and his intelligence above average. He could even show regal dignity; indeed it must be said that the manner in which he spent the long years of exile after his abdication was not lacking in dignity. His sense of humour was devoid of tact ('Tactlessness is masculine' said one of his friends apologetically), his voice was grating and his laugh unpleasant. His glance shifted if one looked at him hard. Those who knew him more intimately realized that there was much amiss, that he was burdened by early family experience, by feelings of both superiority and inferiority, by megalomania and depression. The unhealthy qualities of his character affected those around him; there was something larger than life, effeminate, overheated, sentimental and artificial about his circle. Never until then had there been such an artificial royal style; a combination of Prussian militarism, romantic fantasy, feudal extravagance of dress and an all too modern display of wealth.

This young man, who did not know the world and who was carefully deprived of any opportunity of getting to know it, whose education was that of the Potsdam officers' mess, who had never seriously studied the legal character of his own position was now entrusted, as the expression goes, 'with the fate of the German nation'. This remains the worst that can be said against Bismarck's achievement. If one reads the documents and sees what the Kaiser understood by government, if one sees the

marginal notes which he was in the habit of making on the reports
of his diplomats, one cannot even today, after so many years,
restrain a feeling of pity.

William II knew nothing of the dangers to which Prussia had
almost succumbed in the nineteenth century. He had not witnessed either 1848 or 1862. His memories began with 1870. He
regarded the position which he owed to brilliant manoeuvres
and clever acts of violence as the gift of God, as the natural order
of things. Everything must remain as it was and yet become
better. But Bismarck's misshapen structure was based on success
and new success was needed to preserve it. William sensed this.
The people needed to be offered something to enthuse about; it
must always be Sunday in Germany, with sensational acquisitions, struggles against someone and victories over something.
Such achievements could now be only German, not Prussian;
this meant that they must inevitably change the relationship
between the Reich and Prussia which Bismarck had tried to
stabilize once and for all. Germany, not Prussia, dominated
imagination and reality. Why should Prussia be interested in
Africa or China or the Balkans or Asia Minor or even the
Reichsland Alsace-Lorraine? Or a big navy? These were German
ventures and German spheres of interest, not Prussian ones. The
grandfather had regarded the Reich as a tiresome, modern
affair, as base metal to be kept separate from the gold of the
Prussian crown. The grandson regarded himself primarily as
Emperor. That was also how the world saw him, and the fact
that he was not 'Emperor of Germany' but only president of a
federation of princes, only 'German Emperor' seemed no longer
of any importance. That was how the non-Prussian Germans also
came increasingly to see the situation. The frontiers between the
states became blurred, and although the big federal states preserved their own way of life which in some respects differed
agreeably from that of Prussia, the public affairs of all Germans
were now settled in Berlin and nowhere else. The Kaiser was
regarded as *the* German ruler compared with whom the federal
princes played a vague, insignificant role. The brighter ones
among them knew that William was nothing much to write home

about and the noble princes even occasionally wondered about deposing him; these thoughts, however, did not help them. Their fate was now inexorably tied up with that of the Reich. They sensed that if the Kaiser fell they would share his fate, that the insignificant existence which the Hohenzollern had left them was for better or for worse tied up with that of the Hohenzollern.

The kings of Prussia had ruled their nation of peasants, officials and soldiers reasonably well. To be personally at the head of the German Reich with its tremendous internal pressures and contrasts was another matter. The position of the German Emperor was new and unhistorical. It was closer to Napoleon III's rootless caesarism than to the monarchy of Frederick William III. In those days life at the Prussian court had been frugal and distinguished. Now it was extravagant and eccentric, financed from an inflated Civil List and from secret industrial investments by the royal family and enlivened by visits from European and American financiers, bankers and speculators, who competed in ostentation with the Kaiser. Germany has had only one such emperor. From an historical point of view William is not so much the last King of Prussia as the first of a succession of rulers who in the twentieth century tried to govern Germany and failed.

It would be false, however, to imagine public life under William II as a permanent crisis. Life was pleasant under the Kaiser's personal government. The economic prosperity, while it lasted, benefited the masses as well as the rich. Communal autonomy did admirable things to encourage health and beauty. Foreigners came from distant parts in order to work in the intellectual atmosphere of Berlin, to live in the comfortable, free and hospitable atmosphere of Munich or Dresden. The achievements of the liberal age could be relied upon; if officialdom was rude, it knew its duties and the rights of the citizens. It was this that made William's autocratic gestures seem harmless and ridiculous. Whatever threatening noises he made about 'pessimists' and *Reichsfeinde*, about the social democratic 'red mob', about impressionist painting and naturalistic drama, he could not touch the legal basis of the state, nor did he wish to do so. With a little caution it was possible to print anything; and to be involved in a case of *lèse-majesté* brought the accused more fame and amusement than real suffering. Nobody was ruined because of his public, political, intellectual attitude. No wonder that those years, 1890 to 1914, were later wistfully remembered as the good old days. The only question is why this happy period came to such a bad end.

The German Reich was in fact an enormously strong, concentrated nation-state driven by the motor of powerful industries. In theory it was a loose federation led by Prussia. But fact and theory were never adjusted to each other.

Although Prussia was two-thirds of the Reich it continued to be governed differently. Whereas the King was almost absolute the Kaiser did not even have a delaying veto on the legislation of the Reichstag and the Bundesrat. The Prussian chamber, elected by the three-class system, was conservative; the Reichstag was predominantly liberal or 'leftist'. The Chancellor, as the 'only responsible official of the Reich', had to work with both, yet his mandate did not come from either. It came from the king-emperor, and in the Reichstag he represented the 'allied governments'.

There was no actual Reich government, although during Bismarck's time the Liberals had never ceased to demand one. The Reich departments which gradually grew up were administered by secretaries of state. Some were linked with the Prussian ministries, for example the ministries of the interior and of foreign affairs, and had the same head; others, such as the ministries for the navy and for the colonies, were independent. The secretaries of state were the Chancellor's representatives or delegates, not his colleagues. In practice everybody did what he wanted, particularly those who had minds of their own and enjoyed direct contact with the Kaiser. Bismarck had managed to give the whole irrational machinery a reasonable degree of unity, but after him everything fell apart. His first successor, Caprivi, tried to separate the affairs of Prussia from those of the Reich by giving up the Prussian premiership. It soon emerged, however, that Prussia and the Reich could not be ruled on parallel or opposite lines. Under Hohenlohe, who succeeded Caprivi, the union of the two offices was restored.

The Bundesrat represented the allied governments and Bismarck wanted it to be a kind of Reich government. In fact it rapidly lost in importance. The main initiatives came from Prussia or from the Reich departments; the Bundesrat gave its blessing; criticism was provided by the Reichstag. Although this was part of the general development towards a national unitary state, the Bundesrat could have made something of its position. Bavaria, in particular, as chairman of the diplomatic committee, could have asserted itself instead of simply letting events take their course.

The Reichstag was incomparably more powerful and more alive. It was no longer possible to govern without its support. A Chancellor with whom it repeatedly refused to cooperate in important questions could only resign. Although Bismarck, Caprivi, Bülow and Bethmann were not overthrown by the Reichstag – such a thing was unthinkable – government defeats and anti-government resolutions were directly connected with their fall. The Kaiser could not have dismissed a really popular Chancellor with a solid parliamentary majority behind him, although in fact the Wilhelminian Reich never had such. Nevertheless even the function of the Reichstag was primarily a negative one. With changing majorities it could say yea or nay, it could sell its yea for various concessions, it could reveal corruption and express general feelings of protest. It could debate and sometimes it did so quite impressively. It could not make German policy. Of course, it is said today that legislative assemblies ought not to be able to do this, that governing is a matter for the government and that parliament should only exercise watchful control. This depends on circumstances. The situation is different, for example, if the government is the product of the parliament, if there is an organic connection between the two. Anyway there is no universally satisfactory form of government. Each has its time and its place; at times the *Obrigkeitsstaat* did not do badly. What made the situation awkward was the fact that the Germans no longer had faith in authority but continued to obey it. They lived in the age of democracy and had democratic institutions but these were misshapen and did not fulfil their purpose. Consequently responsibility did not lie clearly anywhere; everywhere there was the semblance of power, divided or hidden power.

Our character is determined partly by the reality in which we live, by the tasks that confront us. The Reichstag had never learnt that power brings responsibility; its members had long been accustomed to arrange things among themselves and with the men who had the royal confidence. They continued to play the old game even when Bismarck's oppressive weight had gone and when the maladjusted distribution of power demanded a strong parliament. The party with the greatest degree of internal integrity and the most powerful organization, soon to become Germany's largest party, that of the Social Democrats, was almost completely excluded from positive tasks, because of the Socialists' own philosophy and because of the authorities' attitude, even after the disappearance of the Anti-Socialist law. The other parties came increasingly to represent certain sectional interests. As though it was not enough that there was an alliance of interests between the Centre and the Catholic Church, the National Liberals and industry, the Conservatives and agriculture, the eighties saw the establishment of big pressure groups – the Central Association of German Industrialists, the Federation of Agriculturalists, the Colonial Society and the German Farmers' Federation – which tried to exert influence through the parties, the Court and by means of direct propaganda. Conflicting economic interests exist wherever men live together. There is no reason why they should not organize themselves, and it is better that they should do so in public than in secret. In Germany after the nineties the clash of economic interests reached degrees of intensity and openness as probably nowhere else but in the United States. The tremendously rapid development of German industry brought considerable friction, and in spite of all patriotic speeches, feeling for the common cause, the mother country, was if anything, less strong than elsewhere.

General von Caprivi had been Bismarck's suggestion as his

successor in Prussia when during the weeks of his final struggle
he thought momentarily of keeping only the offices of Chancellor
and Foreign Minister. The idea was that a non-political
veteran soldier would be the most suitable person to carry out
repressive measures against the Social Democrats. When nothing
came of Bismarck's last plans William II returned to his suggestion,
though for a different purpose. Caprivi was intelligent as
well as stubborn, unprejudiced and incorruptible; of the succession
of German chancellors between 1890 and 1918 he was the
best. He only wanted to do what was right, what would benefit
the whole country and all sections of the community; he wanted
to do this together with anyone who was prepared to help him,
Radicals, members of the Centre, Poles, perhaps even Social
Democrats. But he was innocent in both senses of the word. He
had integrity, but he was politically inexperienced. He counted on
the support of all good men, oblivious of the fact that in politics
only very few people are or can be 'good'. He was not in control
of Prussia-Germany, this labyrinth of crippled democracy and
flourishing byzantinism, dominated by Junkers, industrialists,
soldiers and party politicians.

Caprivi succeeded in putting through the protective labour
legislation over which feelings had run so high during Bismarck's
last days in power: Sunday became a compulsory day of rest,
female and child labour were restricted, minimum periods for
giving notice were fixed and so on. He adopted a conciliatory
attitude towards the Poles by giving up Bismarck's practice of
buying land for Germans in the Polish areas. Together with this
went a liberal foreign policy: rapprochement with Britain and
coolness towards the Tsar. Above all, he tried to increase Germany's
foreign trade, not as a doctrinaire free trader – he was no
doctrinaire – but because he had come to the conclusion that
Germany must export in order to live and that in the long run
there are no exports without imports. Hence his trade agreements
with Austria, Italy, Rumania and finally with Russia. These
brought him into conflict with the Conservatives, or as they
were now called, the Agrarians. Their new militant organization,
the Farmers' Federation, demanded protective tariffs, tax relief

and finally a state grain monopoly and subsidies; at the same time they tried to ingratiate themselves with the small peasants by energetic Jew-baiting.

Max Weber spoke of the 'devastating criticism which the landowners themselves make of the continued existence of their private property by demanding that by means of grain monopolies and an annual subsidy of half a milliard they shall be relieved of the risk, of the responsibility for their property, which are its only justification'. Caprivi, a kindlier and less intelligent man, appealed to the idealism of all citizens:

> ... the more our party life becomes conditioned by economic interests, the more the government must try to preserve an open mind on all matters, in Prussia and the Reich, in order to help them to obtain their rights ... Economic interests are always to some extent based on egoism – it is customary to refer to 'healthy egoism' – whereas the state makes demands on the spirit of sacrifice and the idealism of its citizens.

It was the task of the state to protect all property, industrial as well as agrarian, and it also had an obligation to look after the have-nots ... In the same speech Caprivi uttered a memorable warning against antisemitism:

> What guarantees have the electors who arouse the spirits that the stream which is carrying them along will not in the end join other streams directed against property and public order? I am firmly convinced that the things that are happening are of great importance for Germany at home and abroad and that they contain dangers; I fear that many of those who are opening the floodgates do not suspect whither these things will lead.

At first William II had supported his Chancellor and had firmly refused to be a 'bread profiteer', thus expressing disapproval of the conservative opposition. But he was cowardly and weak. Although he liked to boast that the will of the king must be the supreme law he was incapable of exerting even the modest, real and steady influence which a constitutional monarch, like the British sovereign, still had at that time. He drifted, always giving in to those who knew best how to handle him, and whom he therefore regarded as strong. Having moved away from the Con-

servatives he turned towards them again In 1894 he was back at
the point where he had parted company with Bismarck in 1890,
maintaining that the chief danger threatening the Reich were the
forces of revolution, social democracy, universal suffrage and
so on. The Prussian Prime Minister, Count Eulenburg, enthusiastically shared these imperial fantasies, translating them into
plans for subversion. Caprivi regarded them as nonsense. Having expressed this point of view with characteristic clarity and
dignity he retired and was never publicly mentioned again. His
fall was a lesson: goodwill alone was not enough to straighten
out Bismarck's twisted heritage.

The next man who was allowed to take up this heritage was
Prince Chlodwig Hohenlohe. The choice could have been worse.
Hohenlohe was independent like Caprivi; the latter because he
was poor and proud, the former because he was rich and aristocratic, and because he was not impressed by the Court at Potsdam. Having started as a diplomat of the abortive Germany of
1848, he had gone on to gather parliamentary experience in
Bavaria where he had supported Bismarck's policy. For this he
was later rewarded with high imperial office, culminating in the
governorship in Strasbourg. He had even made good speeches
supporting the Alsatian policy. A Bismarckian in his fashion,
but of a mild variety, entirely without Bismarck's combative
spirit and more prudent politically, small, elegant, cold and tired
– such was the aged aristocrat who now took charge of the affairs
of the Reich. The significance of his appointment, if any significance was intended, could only be that the attempt to please
the left and win over the 'people' had come to an end. The
government would return to Bismarck's static, sober, domestic
policy, though relying primarily on the conservative parties;
once again the *Reichsfeinde* would be cold-shouldered. Only
Hohenlohe, himself a Bavarian Catholic, no longer regarded the
Centre as subversive. He saw it as a party of interests like the
others, whose votes could be bought. The party was all the more
willing to confirm him in this view as the great campaign against
social democracy fell through once more. The Reichstag refused to pass the anti-revolutionary and anti-strike laws which

had been put forward without much conviction; the Kaiser contented himself with verbal thunder – the only weapon for which his nerves were strong enough – against 'men without a fatherland'. The course of foreign policy also at first seemed to indicate a return to Bismarck's policy of domestic graveyard peace: rapprochement with Russia and intrigues against the Poles – in a word, Prussian foreign policy. But not for long.

The semi-dictatorship which Bismarck had exercised in order to preserve the peace, to deprive German development of its momentum, had collapsed in 1890. The verdict was final; it could not be reversed five years later. The energies of the German Reich could no longer be neutralized as in Metternich's day. Something had to be done with them.

3. Weltpolitik

Great states, that is states which under given conditions regard themselves as great, want to be influential beyond their own frontiers. History confirms this a hundred times. Although the individual citizen may be more concerned with his own advancement than with the glory of his country, to the extent that he is involved in the state he wants his state to distinguish itself above others by achievements in government, science, economics and sport.

In the eighteen eighties the states of Europe experienced a period of such expansive, adventurous ambition. This may have had something to do with the fact that the peace which had been established in Europe was such that to disturb it and to expand at the expense of a European neighbour meant taking a terrible risk. It was much cheaper to expand in regions where one needed only to swindle native chieftains but not to fight European mass armies. To that extent imperialism, or more precisely colonialism, could be described as the characteristic of a peaceful, not a militant period. Indeed, the European powers fought no great wars over colonies in the nineteenth and twentieth century; in the end it was always possible to reach agreement on colonial conflicts.

We know today that Europe's last great expansion, the partition of Africa and Asia, was illusory. It was too easy, too quick, too superficial, to establish a lasting claim to great continents; it was the work, not of masses of immigrants but of individual adventurous traders and a few military bureaucrats. At the time, in the rapture of civilizing superiority, the 'Europeanization of the world' was regarded as final.

The German Reich under Bismarck's leadership participated only very late and very half-heartedly in this expansion. Someone who did not believe in Germany's interests on the lower Danube could not possibly seek any in South Africa. Bismarck did not take colonies seriously; that was the reason why he always encouraged France's colonial ambitions. In the end, however, German protectorates were after all established in Africa. Individual shipowners, merchants, explorers and adventurers started the process, and the new Reich did not think that it could refuse them protection. As no private company was capable of retaining its dishonestly acquired territory a small colonial bureaucracy, supported by the army, soon appeared in all areas under German protection. It did its work roughly, though no worse than other colonial nations. But the German colonies cost far more than they brought in and only provided a few thousand Germans with permanent homes. Individual companies and their partners, particularly shipping companies, certainly did well out of the colonial adventure. Yet their wealth did not really come out of the protectorates; it came out of the pockets of the German taxpayer. As the Reichstag regretfully approved the rising expenditure, Centre and Progressive deputies repeatedly voiced the view that the whole venture was best abandoned. Chancellor Caprivi commented despondently: 'In the development of our colonies, which are largely the children of emotion and imagination, sudden changes of attitude towards them are only natural.'

What in the eighties had been the improvisation of individuals, adopted retrospectively by their government, in the nineties became a public philosophy. The tone changed. Theories were advanced according to which the earth was being divided into a few great empires and those who did not participate in the process would soon be of no account. Immeasurable changes were imminent. World powers were replacing the European ones; the European powers must become world powers or lose their independence. Such theories were nurtured by dramatic experiences: the Sino-Japanese war of 1895, the building of the Trans-Siberian railway, the Spanish–American war of 1898 and the sudden emergence of the United States as an imperialist power. What would the future centres of power be? Washington instead of London? Berlin instead of Paris? And then St. Petersburg, Tokyo and perhaps Peking? With what weapons could the world be conquered? What people, what race or combination of peoples should rule the world? Such crazy questions were keenly discussed, the Anglo-Saxons pointing the way. An American, Admiral Mahan, established the new doctrine that sea-power was always decisive. From Britain came the science of geopolitics: to control such and such areas was to rule the world. From Britain also came the new cult of might. At this altar worshipped writers like Kipling, visionary realists, diamond kings and founders of states like Cecil Rhodes. From America the Governor of New York and future President of the United States, Theodore Roosevelt, replied that to act, to display strength, to explore, to conquer, to endure danger and to spread civilization was to give life a noble, masculine meaning. Race mania also entered in. At times it was white men in general, at others the Germanic peoples in particular, who were said to be destined to rule, the Americans, the British and the Germans. Rhodes, the conqueror of South Africa, explicitly held this view.

It found an echo in Germany and there were many variations on the theme. The Kaiser, half English by birth, who admired, hated and loved his mother's country, had Kipling's hymn of praise of power and success above his desk. He devoured the writings of Houston Stewart Chamberlain, German by choice, who proclaimed the superiority of the nordic race and made Christ into a Teuton. Towards Britain also looked the propagandists of the German colonial movement, although their efforts were somewhat crude. The British Empire was the haphazard product of centuries; it had grown up gradually, long before fashionable theory and poetic imagination had seized hold of it. Germany now had both at once, practice and theory, and both very suddenly. 'The aim of colonialism,' wrote one enthusiast, 'is the ruthless and determined enrichment of one's own at the expense of the other, weaker nations.' No Englishman would have said this, or at least he would have done so more pleasantly, less brutally.

International developments may help to explain why the word 'world' was now prefixed complacently to so many German nouns: the world-city Berlin, German world trade, German world-standing; world-politics, world-power. That was what in less than three decades had become of Bismarck's federation of princes, that loose association of peaceful, provincial idylls, Bavaria and Brunswick and Bückeburg. 'The German Reich has become a *Weltreich*,' the Kaiser congratulated himself on the twenty-fifth anniversary of its foundation. 'Thousands of our countrymen live in far-flung corners of the earth. German goods, German knowledge, German industriousness, cross the ocean. German ships carry goods worth thousands of millions. You, gentlemen, have the important duty of helping me to link this greater German Reich firmly to ours at home.'

The Pan-German Union obeyed the imperial call. Although this very curious association of public figures, deputies, writers, scholars and tradespeople never achieved a very large membership – it averaged between ten and twelve thousand – it was influential. Represented in the right-wing and centre parties of the Reichstag, it was led by able politicians – Hugenberg, Hasse and Class – who in their fashion really cared about the German cause. Allied with part of the press and working in close collaboration with related organizations, the Navy League, the *Wehrverein* and the Colonial Society, the Pan-German Union was the ideal vehicle to gather together the political ideas of the age, translate them into German and spread them all over the country: national policy, struggle for national existence, for *Lebensraum*, large-scale politics, world-politics. The aim was to equal the much admired, much hated British enemy; to be at home on all continents proudly as Germans; to establish centres of German power and influence everywhere. To do this in the interest of Germany and also of humanity 'because our German civilization represents the core of human thought and every step taken for Germany therefore belongs to humanity as such . . .'

There was idealistic faith in these pretensions, and although the Pan-German Union had the support of or was later joined by big business, the movement must not be regarded as essentially influenced by private greed. Most of its followers were men whose income was small and who had no hope of increasing it. They wanted to serve a great cause, the German cause. 'We are ready to fall into line when our Kaiser calls . . . but in return we demand a prize that makes the sacrifice worthwhile: to belong to a *Herrenvolk* which takes its share of the world and does not seek to depend on the favour and goodwill of another nation. Germany awake!'

It did not matter to the pan-Germans that the ideas they advanced contradicted each other historically or geographically. They were Bismarckians, but they replaced Bismarck's concept of a 'saturated' Germany by theirs of a people for whose ambition the earth was only just large enough. They thought in racial terms; the regions inhabited by Germans outside Germany, Austria, Switzerland and even Holland, must become part of the Reich so that the state of all Germans would at last come into existence. But they also had imperialist ideas, for they wanted the Germans to rule over foreign nations, particularly over 'such inferior little peoples as the Czechs, the Slovenes and the Slovaks': let them lose 'their useless existence'. In Prussia the pan-Germans supported the traditional anti-Polish policy; on the lower Danube and in Asia Minor they stood for that greater German policy the catchphrases of which Heinrich von Gagern had so temptingly advanced fifty years earlier. In South Africa they wanted a German colonial empire supported by their Teutonic cousins, the Boers, in South America they advocated the energetic union of all German immigrants. Restless, as though bewitched, these people's eyes wandered over the map of the world. Asia, Africa, the Balkans, the Pacific, western Europe – everything suited their purpose as long as territories were acquired, as long as Germany's military and naval power expanded. That they should dream simultaneously of a German Reich in Europe and overseas, this conflict can be explained, if one wishes, in terms of Germany's position. Other European states, Britain, Russia, even France, could found world empires without dominating Europe because they were situated at the periphery of Europe or only partly in Europe. Germany, the country at the centre of Europe, with negligible access to the sea, needed to be secure in Europe, to dominate Europe, before it could become a world power. Unless it controlled Europe its overseas possessions were pure illusion, a fact which became plain during the great crisis. The question simply was whether Germany could be a *Weltreich* at all and what the alternative would have been. The pan-Germans saw only one: the decline of the nation into a weak, dependent power working for foreign nations.

The Union occasionally received money from German Foreign Office funds and then no expenses were spared for its annual conference and its propaganda. In the main, however, it was independent and on this independence rested the influence that it was able to exert through the press, schools and universities, the parties and even through certain sympathetic officials. It created, or helped to create, the intellectual climate in which the ventures of the new *Weltpolitik* were launched and it flourished in this climate. Although the pan-Germans went further than the others, although Emperor and Chancellor were often too cautious, too peace-loving and too pro-British for them, they did no more than to go further, to speak more boldly. The spirit of the age was with them. It was not only the limited number of Union members but the German middle class who thought in imperialist terms in the age of William II and who approved of *Weltpolitik*.

They approved particularly of the creation of a battle fleet. Admiral von Tirpitz, Secretary of State for the Imperial Navy from 1897, was filled with a great love of the sea and genuine passion for his task. Experts believe that he was a great organizer, and if one reads how in a few years with the slenderest means he created the second-strongest navy in the world one is inclined to agree. In addition he knew something about parliamentary tactics, demagogy and publicity; the methods which he used to make his navy popular with the Germans seem truly American. His office had its own news department and he was helped by societies, paid and unpaid propagandists, professors and novelists; the shrewd man even invited Social Democratic deputies to inspect his ships. His posthumous writings impress by their clarity and factual style; they contain no trace of the wild fantasies of the pan-Germans. Tirpitz thought that if all decisions had been left to him Britain could have been reconciled to Germany as a naval power and that a world war could have been avoided; most people who had anything to do with this drama shared his view. But no one man controls the course of events, and political action must be judged not by intentions but by results. What Tirpitz wanted to do with his navy is one thing, what it did in the bustle of 'world politics', of reactions and counter-reactions, is another.

He did not believe in strong coastal protection nor in the cruisers which the Kaiser wanted in order that they might sail the seven seas. He believed in aggressive naval power, in the ability to fight a decisive naval battle, in a battle fleet stationed in home ports.

The navy must become for Germany at sea what its army was on land. The purpose was not to wage war. Tirpitz wanted war even less than the German generals who, while not wanting it, regarded it as more or less inevitable during the long years from 1871 to 1914; Tirpitz thought otherwise. By making Germany a maritime power, by enabling it to enter into alliances, the navy would establish an equilibrium also at sea and thus guarantee the peace – a proud peace, not a peace by the grace of Britain.

Our position in the world was crystal clear [the Admiral complained in retrospect]. Without an industry protected by naval power we ceased to be a great continental power ... Without naval power Germany's status in the world remained that of a mollusc without a shell.

Hitherto Germany had risen to power 'on the broad shoulders of British world trade and British world domination at Britain's pleasure'; while this state of affairs persisted Germany could not be really independent.

. . . only a navy which had alliance value for other Great Powers, that is to say an efficient navy, could give our diplomacy the tool which, if appropriately used, could strengthen our continental power. The aim was perforce the establishment of a constellation of power at sea, which would make injury to and attack on our economic development unlikely and which would transform the deceptive glamour of our *Weltpolitik* into a genuinely independent position in the world.

The navy was intended to be a deterrent, to be used by diplomacy for this purpose. More or less what certain bombs are meant to be today. The aim is always to safeguard the peace, the only problem being that the other side usually sees the matter in a different light. Although one trusts oneself, the others do not trust one; they go by appearances. A German navy appeared in the North Sea; it was confined to the North Sea, and its only visible task was to rival the British navy. British politicians noted these happenings with displeasure. That Tirpitz saw the matter in a different light, that he only wanted to create a power which Britain could not attack without risk – his 'risk concept' – that he only wanted to put Germany into a position of being able to make alliances – such fine points did not alter the facts. Even less could the psychological motives which might have been behind the building of the navy. These motives are described by the word chosen by Tirpitz: *ebenbürtig*, being of equal rank. Germany must have a navy equal to anybody's, it must become everyone's equal by having a navy. The admiral had sailed in Prussian ships as far back as 1870 and had noted then with regret that the British did not take German naval power seriously. The Kaiser had made the same discovery. He looked forward to the glorious day when a German navy could meet the British navy as an equal in joint manoeuvres; when admirals' uniforms and toasts would be exchanged and the royal rulers of the seas would take leave of each other with expressions of chivalrous esteem. A game, but with dangerous toys.

Not only all those who let others think for them but also people with independent minds are subject to the bewitchments of their age. The naval programme was enthusiastically received by most of the middle class; and also by that great scholar, Professor Max Weber. Weber agreed with Tirpitz that power, and yet more power, was needed in order to protect the German economy, and that in the dawning age of world politics this meant power at sea.

Only complete political dishonesty and naïve optimism can fail to recognize that, after a period of peaceful competition, the inevitable urge of all nations with bourgeois societies to expand their trade must now once more lead to a situation in which power alone will have a decisive influence on the extent to which individual nations will share in the economic control of the world, and thus determine the economic prospects of their peoples and of their workers in particular.

The socially minded democrat, which Max Weber claimed to be, surrendered as much to the cult of power as the imperial admiral, as the owners and managers of heavy industry, as the journalists of the newspapers financed by industry, as the clergymen, the teachers of gymnastics and those who spouted forth on the occasion of the Kaiser's birthday.

German industry obviously benefited enormously from ship-building orders; and it vigorously used all its available channels of influence to make the Reichstag adopt the naval programmes.

. . . If the ship-building programme contained in the latest naval bill is carried out as quickly as the German shipyards can deal with it [wrote the President of the Navy League in 1901], many branches of industry will receive new contracts which will enable them not only to keep their heads above water but also to occupy their workers and to re-engage employees who have been dismissed. One of the most important factors, however, that must be mentioned in this connection is that orders for new warships and the resultant stimulus to trade and industry, will produce a rise in the value of the shares concerned, so that many stocks would be saved and the market consolidated.

Nothing could be clearer. It is impossible to say which was the decisive factor, the Kaiser's love for his toy, the admirals' more serious ambitions, the intellectual climate of the moment or the interests of the armour plate manufacturers. It is all part of a whole from which no factor can be singled out. Much talent and work went into the navy, and its construction showed what German technical ability could do. But that unfortunately was all. In politics it did harm. When the crisis came to which it had contributed so much, it was to the despair of its founder, not used at all; neither to protect the German 'world empire' which was lost in no time, nor to fight a decisive battle against Britain. It remained one of the enormous wastages of work and material which nations often allow themselves to be talked into.

Then came the hasty territorial acquisitions which were in keeping with the spirit in which the navy had been built; new protectorates, economic 'spheres of influence', and 'coaling stations'. In 1898 Germany acquired a lease on Kiaochow on the Chinese coast and in the same year it tried to take over the Spanish heritage in the Pacific and to occupy the Philippines; this move was thwarted by the United States. Instead Germany bought a small group of Spanish islands, the Caroline and the Mariana Islands. In 1899 came the acquisition of part of the Samoan islands by a treaty with Britain and North America. Is it worth even mentioning these things? The splendour lasted only fifteen years; it could not endure when it came to the test. Its purpose was to justify the navy which in turn was intended to make these acquisitions necessary. The aged Wilhelm Liebknecht said: 'The crux of the matter is not the aims advanced in public, not that we should have a little more land, but that our disastrous naval policy, the ambitious naval plans, which at present have no basis should be given a basis.' It was an imaginary empire, a toy, not unlike the one that Italy acquired thirty years later. There was a misunderstanding of German as well as of European possibilities, an imitation of the other new 'worldstates' whose foundations were a little, albeit only a little, more solid. There could be no real German independence, even less than French or British independence, which basically did not exist either. It was impossible for Germany, situated at the heart of Europe, to radiate enough power across the seas, across tens

of thousands of miles, to fuse islands, bays and bits of mainland
into an empire. The fear of being 'too late' to share in the partition of the world was not justified either, because this partition
of Africa, China and the Pacific among the European powers,
was illusory.

We realize this in retrospect, having learnt from experience
and been freed from the old spell (perhaps only to succumb to
a new one which will arouse just as much amazement in later
generations?). Nothing that passed through the minds of the
German 'world politicians' at the time was specifically German;
they applied to the German situation an attitude of mind that
existed everywhere. Other countries had long been 'world powers'
and only tried to round off their territory in a suitable way.
Germany was yet to become one of these powers, having started
very late, almost from nothing. Unless it became a 'world
power' it would decline into complete insignificance. 'Vast
areas in various continents will be divided up during the next
decades. The nation which comes away empty-handed from this
share-out will in the following generation cease to be in the ranks
of the great nations which mould the human spirit.' As long as this
view was accepted – expressed here by another eminent scholar,
the historian Hans Delbrück – the conclusion followed. Do we
not today find in space research and all that goes with it the
same feverish urge to be in the lead or at least to join in, lest
'in the following generation we cease to be in the ranks of the
great nations which mould the human spirit'?

What appeared more solid and meaningful on the map was the
German sphere of interest described by the catchphrase 'Baghdad railway'. A railway built with German capital, running
right across the Turkish Empire, linking Mesopotamia and Asia
Minor with the Balkans, with Austria and Germany – Berlin–
Baghdad – and opening up new markets, that was something
grandiose as well as compact and in accordance with the best
dreams of 1848. Moreover, even in an emergency it seemed incomparably more tenable than empires in the Pacific. If Germany's future lay on the high seas, in 'world politics', everywhere, it must lie also, and in particular, in the Middle East.

Germany's mission in the Middle East – there was much mention of this in popular writing and it was dramatically emphasized by imperial gestures. Yet here too reality was different from the enthusiastic vision. 'Our Baghdad railway' was a German or semi-German enterprise only on Turkish territory; Germany controlled neither the railway network nor the trade of the Balkan states. As trade routes, the Danube and the Middle Eastern railway until 1915 remained much less important than the much cheaper sea route, so that Turkey was really one of Germany's overseas trade areas and not a continental one. Moreover, in 1914 German trade with Turkey still took fourth place, coming far behind that of Britain and France. The idea of the closed area, extending from the Rhine to the Danube, the Balkans and Asia Minor, came later, a product of the war. Meanwhile *Weltpolitik* was pursued here, there and everywhere; journalists enthused over the Baghdad railway and over the German colonial empire in Africa in the same breath.

Master of the new policy was Bernhard von Bülow, after 1897 Secretary of State for Foreign Affairs and German Chancellor from 1900 to 1909. He was a man of the world, an experienced diplomat, with polished manners, good nerves, aggressive self-confidence, authority, intelligence, wit and the cold egoism of the courtier. In his diary Geheimrat Holstein, the tyrant of the Ministry of Foreign Affairs, paints the following picture of his rival and subsequent superior:

> Bernhard Bülow is clean-shaven and flabby, with a shifty look, and usually has a smile on his face. Although he has no ideas in store for emergencies he adopts the ideas of others and reproduces them skilfully ... If Bülow wants to set one man against another he says with a charming smile to the one that the other does not like him. The method is simple and almost infallible.

Pleased with himself he wanted to please everybody and thought that there was nothing in politics that could not be arranged. 'As Your Majesty so rightly remarked' used to be the beginning of his lectures to the Kaiser, the gist of which often amounted to the exact opposite of what His Majesty had said. Bülow's aim was to straighten out William's boasts without causing offence, to flatter parliament without healing the serious defects of German constitutional life, to lead Germany through the 'danger zone' into the harbour of a safe position as a world power without antagonizing the senior great powers too much. All this could somehow be done, and, like Tirpitz, Bülow believed to the end of his days that if he had been allowed to have his way he would gradually have solved even the constitutional question.

He solved nothing, however. He only maintained with adroitness a basically untenable state of affairs; his most notable achievement was that he remained Chancellor for nine years. Nobody could fill Bismarck's place. The problem was to change Bismarck's structure and to give the Reich a responsible government which in the twentieth century was bound to be a parliamentary one. Perhaps this problem was now insoluble. At any rate Bülow, who played both the byzantine servant of His Majesty and the jovial man of the people, a gossipy, malicious diplomat, was certainly not the man for the job. How could he have been? How could William II have appointed a man who was equal to the problem? Where could he be found?

Instead of devoting itself to domestic problems popular imagination in the new century increasingly focused on foreign policy which titivated the national nervous system. The same was true to varying degrees of other European nations. Once people had made the mistake of regarding the nation-state as the ultimate human goal and its 'greatness' as an absolute purpose, there was no escape from the wearying game of threats and reconciliations, attempts to expand and withdrawals, of ever-changing speculative combinations; while always on the horizon there was the thing which everyone and no one believed in, war.

As early as the beginning of the nineties the Continent had fallen into two systems of alliance, the German–Austro-Italian and the Franco-Russian. The latter was a reply to the former and was not designed to outlast it. It was a logical consequence of what had happened. Bismarck has been praised for succeeding in keeping Germany's two flanking powers apart and for seeking 'reinsurance' from Russia with a secret treaty in 1887.

Unfortunately Bismarck's incompetent successors had not renewed the treaty, with the result that the 'line to Russia was
broken' and the Tsar was forced to look to Paris. That was the
beginning of all future misfortunes ... This is how Bismarck
and Bülow were pleased to see the situation, and this is how it is
often presented by diplomatic historians even today. There is
not much to support this line of argument. Even in Bismarck's
day Russia and France were moving towards each other. They
were driven in this direction by the Bismarck bloc of the central
powers; alliances, however peacefully meant, always provoke
others, and thus increase the danger they try to avert. If Bismarck
tried to avert this danger by immediately concluding a counter-
alliance, his game could not put matters right; either one entered
into alliances or not. If Germany had a serious alliance it was the
one with Austria-Hungary; no contortions could deceive anyone in the long run about its consequences. Moreover, a piece of
paper such as the Reinsurance Treaty achieved little in the best of
circumstances. Its existence provided no protection against the
real or imagined interests, desires and passions of the Russians;
its disappearance did not prevent German diplomacy from
seeking new contacts with Russia, as it tried to do frequently
between 1890 and 1909. If all those efforts failed in the end, what
reason was there to suppose that the elaborate secret treaty of
1887 would have withstood the test of an emergency? The relationship between the two powers was not determined by treaties
but by interests or issues which diplomats and strategists regarded as vital. Also by passions, by the wanton idea which
many people on both sides had come to hold that a final struggle
between Slavs and Teutons was inevitable. As Germany's industrial and military strength was far superior to Russia's, and as a
German victory over Russia would completely destroy the
balance of power and make Germany master of Europe, Russia
and France inevitably stuck together. This was unavoidable as
long as people thought in terms of equilibrium, states, power and
prestige. Only the Socialists wanted to break this vicious circle
by demanding the brotherhood of all peoples and by taking as
given that the workers of the world were brothers. But their

political influence bore no relation to the magnitude of their promise.

Towards the turn of the century British politicans began to think that the world had become too dangerous to operate in it alone and that they must look for potential allies. France did not seem suitable because of the sharp clash of interests between the two countries in Africa, and Russia, the old enemy in the Near and the Far East, even less so. There remained Germany. At that time the German naval programme was not sufficiently advanced to create feelings of panic in London, and such colonial disagreements as existed between Britain and Germany were harmless compared with the Russo-British conflict. This seemed a great opportunity. German diplomacy under Bülow's leadership eluded the British advances. Bülow never said no and never said yes. He asked more and more questions, he asked for something that Britain did not want to give, that it should become a full member of the Triple Alliance. He allowed the negotiations to fizzle out. Berlin regarded the Anglo-Russian conflict as insoluble and therefore did not believe that it would ever be necessary to choose between the two powers. Germany wanted to be loved by all and feared by all, to be quite independent, a world power. Moreover, it feared that it might be exploited as Britain's continental protection against Russia; a fear that was not unfounded. Although great decisions in life involve danger, there are moments in history when the most dangerous thing to do is to make no decision, and those historians are probably right who say that the British offer, in spite of its vague form, was made at such a moment. The Reich went into splendid isolation at the very moment when Britain changed course for good reasons.

Rejected by Germany Britain made agreements with other powers: in 1901 with Japan, in 1904 with France and in 1907 with Russia The two last agreements were if anything even more modest than what Britain had offered Germany between 1898 and 1901; they were merely settlements of imperialist disputes, in Egypt and Morocco in the case of France, and in Persia in the case of Russia. Yet if any decision was ever taken in the bedevilled affair which ended with the explosion of 1914 it was taken then. Secret Franco-British military agreements followed, not binding but real ones. Frightened by the growth of the German navy which it interpreted as suspicious people were bound to do, shocked by the Kaiser's boasts and the subversive activities of the pan-Germans, incited by the lies and panicking of its yellow press, Britain gradually slipped into the Franco-Russian camp. After 1907 or 1911, there was a Triple Entente as well as a Triple Alliance. Although there was no Triple Entente on paper it existed to the extent that it was effective and would be effective in an emergency. The Triple Alliance did exist on paper, but in reality it was only a dual alliance, since nobody had any illusions about Italy's loyalty to its allies, its sympathies and desires. If one looks beyond state frontiers one is bound to say that at the end of the first decade of the twentieth century Germany had only one remaining ally, the Magyars – an ancient and fateful link.

Everything else had remained in the air; ideas were taken up and dropped again, opportunities were considered until they had passed. Of the continental league between France, Russia and Germany, one of the Kaiser's pet ideas, of the Anglo-German agreement, of the Russo-German one, drawn up in 1905 but not ratified, nothing but disappointment survived. When the haze of proposals and possibilities lifted, when the political landscape became clearly discernible Germany found itself alone at the centre surrounded by hostile peaks.

To ask if this was necessary raises basic questions which cannot be answered definitely but which will always be asked. They concern the purpose or absence of purpose in history. Was there really such a thing as an inevitable duel between Germany and Britain concerned not with specific interests but with the question: can you destroy me or can I destroy you? To put the question differently: was Germany forced into isolation because it could no longer take part in the delicate game of preserving the European equilibrium, because it really wanted, and was forced to want to rule Europe, and through Europe part of the non-European world? Were the diplomats, whose bunglings caused

Germany's isolation, unconsciously doing the inevitable? Or was the whole affair an avoidable piece of stupidity? All one can do is to express views, but one thing is certain: it was not fear of competition that drove Britain into the French camp. German competition certainly hurt British trade, but Germany was itself British industry's best customer and vice versa. Nor were the British politicians so uneducated economically as to believe that the annihilation of a competitor would improve their country's economic situation and that they would do well out of an all-out European war. Nor was there originally any feeling of enmity against the Germans, any conspiracy to 'keep them down'. On the contrary, in the nineteenth century Germany had been definitely popular among the Anglo-Saxons. The unpopular countries were France and Russia, France because it was revolutionary, imperialistic and restless, and Russia because it was exotic, barbarian and despotic. If at first Anglo-Saxon sympathies had gone to romantic, idyllic, slightly backward Germany, once it became known that Germany had changed, they went to the country of science, progress and reliable achievement. It was customary to admire Germany; at the end of the nineteenth century, in the nineteen twenties, and also, I believe, as these words are being written. Only in the last ten or twelve years before 1914 did Germany become unpopular in Britain. The Germans lost the sympathies of the world because they did not believe that they had them and boastfully announced that they could do without them.

They did nothing more wicked than any of the others. It was the fashion to secure a foothold in China – to lease land on the coast and to establish a sphere of influence inland. Russia, France and Britain followed the fashion as much as Germany. The German 'empire in the Pacific' was a childish venture but a harmless one; Britain did not disapprove of it because, depending entirely on Britain's goodwill as it did, it was a pawn for Germany's good behaviour. The building of the Baghdad railway was one of those achievements of economic imperialism that can only be applauded. There was no legal or moral reason why German industry should not be allowed to make itself useful in Turkey, in its own interest and that of other people; indeed, foreign capital also went into the enterprise. On the two occasions, in 1905 and in 1911, that Germany insisted on equal economic opportunities in Morocco, which was gradually becoming a French zone of influence, its methods were more dramatic than strictly necessary; but why should German trade which definitely had more to offer than the French, be excluded from North Africa? Again, the so-called Bosnian crisis of 1908–9, regarded with the impartiality made possible by the passage of time, was not such a wicked German machination. The former Turkish provinces of Bosnia and Hercegovina had for at least thirty years been under the administration of the Habsburg Empire, a state of affairs which derived from the Berlin Congress and which at that time had been confirmed by all the great powers. Their annexation by Austria created no new fact, it only confirmed what had long been known. Furthermore, it was the result of a secret Austro-Russian agreement. If this did not bring the Russians their hoped-for prize – freedom to send warships through the Dardanelles at all times – it was not because of anything the Germans had done but because Britain was not prepared for a change in the agreement concerning the Straits. The fact that the annexation of Bosnia caused such tremendous excitement in Serbia and Russia and even in France, and that as a result for months there was talk of a danger of general war, shows to what extent the European atmosphere had already deteriorated. In the end German diplomacy supported Austria with such threatening firmness that Russia decided to recognize the step. It was Bülow's last political act; he seems to have felt that it was not possible to assert oneself like that indefinitely; at his farewell audience he said to William: 'Do not repeat the Bosnian action.' By this he meant insisting on any issue, important or not, on having Germany's way, on testing Germany's strength. This is what the issue amounted to each time. Materially the Moroccan question was not so important to Germany; it was a case of proving that no serious issue in the world could be decided without the Kaiser. This was the recurring motif, which became more marked as Germany felt itself more isolated.

The results were pyrrhic victories: more or less worthless concessions to Germany in Africa, the resignation of an anti-German
Foreign Minister in Paris and so on, together with the secret
determination on the other side to pay more attention the next
time and to take suitable precautions against being outmanoeuvred. In every case there was something to be said for the German
demands; they were not outrageous. Others asked for more and
were given more. What gain had Germany to compare with the
most recent French acquisitions, Tunis and Morocco? The misfortune of the German situation was that Germany was stronger
and more concentrated than any of its neighbours but that it was
centrally situated and could not expand without destroying the
old order. It did not want war. If Germany had wanted war or
even thought war probable it would have made its pact with
Britain in 1900; it did not do this just because it was afraid of
being forced by Britain into the war against Russia. If Germany
had wanted war against the western powers an excellent opportunity presented itself in 1905 when Russia was completely
paralysed by its defeat in the East and by internal revolution.
But nobody thought of war. Or more precisely there were
thoughts of war, talk of war and of the possibility of war, but
no step was taken towards wicked, daring action at a moment
when it might have promised success. Germany's victories were
diplomatic or sham victories; they proved that Germany had
arrived and must be listened to, even though it had finally
manoeuvred itself into a position of isolation. That was how
matters stood until late July 1914.

The situation was made worse by the personal activities of the
Kaiser who, pleasure-seeking and work-shy though he was, often
reserved to himself the last word on foreign policy, and more
frequently the first and the second; improvised and interfering
words. His speeches, interviews and telegrams were diplomatic
catastrophes. His pronouncements on 'pessimists' and 'jealousy
of foreigners', on shining armour, power, dry powder and cutting
swords made his country feared and unpopular; and they made it
ridiculous. A genuine patriot, Professor Max Weber, wrote in
1906 to his friend Friedrich Naumann:

The degree of contempt which we as a nation by now encounter abroad (in Italy, America, everywhere) – and rightly, which is what matters – because we suffer *that* regime of *that* man, has by now become a factor of first-class 'world political' importance for us. Anyone who reads the foreign press for a few months must notice this. We are being 'isolated' because that man rules us in that way and because we *allow him to do so and make excuses* . . .

The worst was that the Kaiser and his admiral firmly prevented all British attempts to limit the armaments race at sea. 'I cannot and will not allow John Bull to dictate to me the speed of my ship building.' This too was not meant wickedly. The Kaiser was motivated by an antiquated code of honour, by irritable obstinacy and by pleasure in his toy; and Tirpitz by the burning ambition of a man who wanted to make Germany the greatest naval power in the world, although he was perhaps prepared to allow Britain a modest lead. For the British this was not enough.

There are two sides to every conflict and it would be wrong to hold German diplomacy alone responsible for the intrigues and fears that poisoned the European atmosphere in the decade before 1914. Foreign policy is largely irrational and comes up against elements that are also irrational. If it were rational, if there were not always behind it the urge to gamble, determination to have power and deadly fear, it might be possible to find a compromise. Economic competition can be controlled by sensible agreements because it serves the basically sensible aim of making money; the same does not apply to political competition. However, political competition needs several states with more or less the same moral standards. Germany was not wise before 1914. If the others had been wiser they might have pulled themselves, and Germany, out of the vicious circle of competing for power and honour. Only when more than one state tries to expand and to seek glory do expansion and glory become desirable objects. To the French their 'greatness' was as sacrosanct as the Germans' was to them, and they worked for it as vigorously as the Germans but with a little more skill and with greater success. The Russian attempts to increase their power were not one whit better than those of the Germans. They were more brutal, more extreme, and received support from sinister elements which were the result of internal ferment and decay, compared with which Germany's constitutional life seemed sanity itself. They were all alike, the great powers, new and old, the would-be great powers and the little ones, Germany and Russia, Italy and Serbia and Montenegro. They all wanted to inflict diplomatic defeats on their neighbours, to extend their territory under some pretext or other, to protect their protégés, to redeem their unredeemed brothers, to play their national anthems where hitherto they had not been allowed, to raise their flags and introduce their police in new places. They all wanted to enlarge their armies, to improve their guns and to make every conceivable preparation for the war which was bound to come one day.

The opposition was weak. There were good, well-meaning, eloquent pacifists everywhere, in Russia, Europe and America; not least in Germany. But when a Russian Foreign Minister described them as 'Socialists, Jews and hysterical females' he had the support of the middle classes everywhere. When the diplomats tried their hand at pacifism, at the international peace conferences in the Hague in 1899 and 1907, they did not approach the matter seriously but with cynicism or hypocrisy. The Russians set the ball rolling, partly to gain financial advantages from a transitory international limitation of armaments, and partly to put themselves in a position where, if nothing came of the attempt, they could blame other powers for its failure and appear in a noble light themselves. The results of both conferences were as might be expected in the circumstances. A tribunal was set up to which states could submit disputes, although they were under no obligation to do so, and they refused explicitly to do so in cases where their honour was involved. The use of certain cruel weapons was condemned, although when it came to the point nobody paid any attention to this condemnation. Each time the Germans refused even to discuss armaments limitations and thus made a diplomatic mistake. They did what was in everybody's mind, but they did it more honestly, more crudely and with more determination than the others. Germany thought of itself as on the way up, not as having existed and been powerful for a long time like Britain. Permanent limitation of armaments would artificially have fixed the distribution of power on earth as it happened to be at the moment. Nobody really wanted this, least of all the Germans. When a very liberal and critical German historian, Hans Delbrück, was asked many years later why he had not supported the aims of the Hague peace conference he said: 'We omitted to do this on purpose because Germany was still a young nation with a great future and it did not think that such institutions should be allowed to destroy its future opportunities.'

4. *Parliament and Authority*

Foreign policy was determined directly by a few people, the Kaiser and those who had his ear, the Chancellor, the Secretary of State for Foreign Affairs and a few councillors in the Foreign Office. The man who had the greatest influence among these from the period of Bismarck's fall to his own dismissal in 1906 was Geheimrat von Holstein, a scheming individual who shunned the glare of public life. Later it became fashionable to attribute the chief blame for the catastrophe of German foreign policy to this secret tyrant. The present author finds it impossible to convince himself of Holstein's responsibility. German diplomacy was not floating in the air, a weightless object, to be pushed hither and thither by faceless men. The great, real energies of the nation, its economic strength and its spirit, made German diplomacy what it was. It was not the mistakes of individual civil servants that finally led to the isolation of the Reich, neither the end of the Reinsurance Treaty nor the refusal to accept the offer of a British alliance – the two errors for which Herr von Holstein may be held responsible. It was a succession of experiences, of pressures and of reactions at home, a far-reaching, gradual process which prepared Britain to its own surprise for the decision of 1914 which was to be taken again twenty-five years later. The fact that it was taken not once but twice, in spite of all good intentions, shows that it was not an arbitrary decision and that the action did not result from some superficial, false diplomatic moves on the part of Germany.

It is not true that a tyrannical, alien government defied a sensible people, driving it unwillingly along the road to destruction. Such a situation was unknown in the early twentieth century among prosperous, civilized and educated people like the Germans. If Prussian law still allowed the Prussian monarch to present himself as king by the grace of God, and if the Prussian constitution still allowed the aristocracy to have more influence than it should have had, in the opinion of the people, there were many links between rulers and ruled. One can say of William II that he represented with brilliance and accuracy, not *the* spirit but one of the spirits of the nation at that time. If the Reichstag had been made of the right stuff it could in this period have insisted on parliamentary or democratic government. But it had declined in quality; whether this was the fault of Bismarck's system, or of the public spirit, or of the electorate does not matter. It was internally divided, accustomed to look only after the material interests of those from whom it had its mandate and to leave the rest to 'those up there'; it was unaccustomed to use power, still less to reach for it boldly. Conversely one can say that even if the Reichstag had gained complete control there was no guarantee, given its nature, that Germany would have been better governed. A not very distant future would show this.

The chancellors found their majorities where they could. The parties let themselves be paid for their collaboration, if not in the form of legislation then by the gift of offices to their members. As in Bismarck's time, there were in the main two possible combinations, Conservatives and Centre, and Conservatives and Liberals. For the second combination, the left-wing liberals, the *Freisinnige* or Progressives as they were alternately called, were now also needed. With this coalition Bülow governed from 1906 to 1909, trying (but as always in vain) to take a firm stand against the Centre and the Social Democrats. There was a third possibility suggested by thoughtful people: the alliance of all Liberals with the Social Democrats – more or less the combination which in the twenties was called the 'great coalition'. It was hoped that such a combination would encourage parliamentary government and achieve a change in the constitution. In any event it would have been necessary to overcome tremendous obstacles. The affairs of the Reich and those of Prussia were still closely interwoven. In Prussia, however, because membership of the upper house was hereditary and because of the three-class electoral system, the Conservatives enjoyed what amounted to a monopoly of power. Even a politician of Bülow's resourcefulness could not have ruled in Prussia with the Conservatives and in the Reich with the Social Democrats. Anyway he had no intention of doing so although he did not consider it beneath his dignity occasionally to engage the leaders of the right wing of the Socialist Party in gracious conversation.

There was a right wing now because the Social Democratic party was no longer the solid weapon which had been forged by Bismarck's blows. It had developed into a vast, extremely varied organization which needed to make elaborate compromises at its party conferences between personalities, views and trends. 'Revisionism' made its appearance around the turn of the century, in its theoretical form mainly in the writings of Eduard Bernstein. What was revised was the Marxist basis of the party programme. Bernstein believed that it was necessary to admit that there were certain mistakes in Marx's economic and political doctrine and to draw the practical conclusions. It was not true that the living conditions of the workers only deteriorated under capitalism; on the contrary, because of their own efforts they were visibly better off. It was not true that capitalist development destroyed all medium and small-scale enterprises, of which there were as many as before, although partly in different or new spheres of production. It was not true that the rich were becoming fewer and the poor more numerous and increasingly poor, and so on. In short it was not true that the great collapse was inevitably approaching. Consequently it was necessary to abandon the idea of sudden, violent, complete change, of Communist revolution, and to concentrate on profitable practical work within the existing order which would thus gradually be transformed into a Socialist one.

Revisionism did not spread as a theory. The Marxist doctrine was too attractive in its all-embracing, omniscient simplicity. To admit to all the world that it was wrong – which was what revisionism amounted to – and that the German worker in order to help himself had no need of the whole learned accoutrement of Marxist philosophy – was more than the old party leaders could face, particularly as so much was still happening in Germany which seemed to confirm the doctrine of the class struggle. Bebel had become converted to Marxism late in life; he was not the man to change his views in very old age and he was firmly in control of his followers. At the Dresden party congress in 1903 Bernstein's criticism was rejected by the great majority of delegates. But this did not produce real clarity. As the heretics were condemned for something which they had not recommended – Social Democratic participation in the government of the federal states – even the revisionists were able to vote for the resolution which they did not regard as aimed at themselves. What they had tried to do was to reconcile theory with changing practice. The theory remained the same, but the practice fell short of it and could not but fall short of it. The theory was revolutionary; the practice was revisionist, or nothing at all.

How could it have been otherwise, how could a party which had the support of almost one-third of the German electorate be satisfied with the purely negative role of acting as a scarecrow for the bourgeoisie? The tactical situation in the federal states led to electoral alliances, sometimes with the Progressives, sometimes with the Centre. Electoral alliances brought victories and victories obligations. The Social Democrats were called upon to pass the budget, to sit on parliamentary committees and even to pay calls at Court; in the parliamentary committees, in the town councils, they dealt with thousands of necessary and useful matters. It needed a heart of stone to do this work and to remain a doctrinaire supporter of the coming revolution and no more. In the Reich the situation was somewhat different. There were no electoral alliances until 1912 and the mood was more

intransigent. Scheidemann, who was elected a vice-president of
the Reichstag in 1912, caused a storm by refusing to pay the customary call on the Kaiser. Even Bebel, in spite of the rigidity of
his principles, was anxious that the new vice-president should do
his work in a dignified manner. ('Do you have a decent frock
coat?') In the Reichstag also the party had long ago started to
make positive contributions, to examine and criticize individual
budget items. It was the second generation which made a name
for itself in this field, men who had been young during the period
of the Anti-Socialist Law and who had not been completely
moulded by it: Ebert, Scheidemann, Noske and Otto Braun.
Noske, a member of the Reichstag since 1906, later boasted that
he never used the word Marxism in his speeches or articles; that
he was not even a revisionist because the theory which required
revision did not interest him; and that he was interested in practical work, in the army estimates, the naval estimates, the colonies,
everything that concerned him as a conscientious representative
of the people. Although his was and remained an extreme case,
the younger Social Democratic politicians or trade unionists
were more like him than he was like a radical doctrinaire. Bebel
died in 1913. His successor as chairman of the party was Friedrich Ebert, not a revisionist in name but a practical politician who
mediated between the quarrelling factions because in his opinion
the quarrel was not worth the effort. Yet the quarrel was worth
the effort. It would have been better if the party had had the
courage clearly to abandon the antiquated theoretical bases of
its programme. The urgently desirable and obtainable aim, the
democratization of the state and the extension of public welfare,
were one thing. The 'world revolution' was quite another and
not really compatible with the actual situation in Germany. This
was no longer 1847 when such great, vague dreams had har-
monized with the spirit of the age and with a reality as yet in
embryo. It is never good to do one thing and to believe another,
or not even to believe it but to pay lip-service to it with inherited
words. The German Liberals had failed. Tremendous energy
now went into Social Democracy; it united by far the greatest
number of voters and its promise was to put Germany's affairs

in order. Perhaps it could have done this in spite of all obstacles if it had organized itself as the democratic party of social progress. Or would it have followed in the miserable footsteps of the old *Fortschrittspartei*? Was it just because it was a doctrinaire and united anti-bourgeois workers' party that it had drive? Did the same wind that filled its sails also slow down its journey and paralyse its energies? Those are questions for reflection; they cannot be answered.

The Social Democrats had no more to do with the direction of German foreign policy than any other party. They could only influence it indirectly by criticism, by refusing to vote funds and by arousing public opinion. Criticism, however, from such a powerful organization needed in the long run to be constructive, it needed to hint what the party itself would do if it came to power. But again the old Marxian theory was insufficient to provide positive answers to Germany's political problems. What could be gleaned from Marx, and what Lenin did glean from him at the time, was the view that *Weltpolitik* and imperialism must be interpreted in terms of economic interests. The Social Democrats did their best to highlight the propaganda activities of heavy industry, the exaggerated profits which it made from building the navy and the corrupt administration of the colonies. But they did not believe in the inevitability of corruption, imperialism and imperialist clashes that were part of Marx's theory. On the contrary they did their best to pour oil on troubled waters. The same man, August Bebel, who in 1870 had uttered prophetic words against the annexation of Alsace-Lorraine, in 1903 attacked Tirpitz's naval policy and the increasing anglophobia in Germany; in 1911 he attacked the overbearing behaviour of Germany in Morocco. He saw nothing inevitable in all this; he wanted friendship between Britain and Germany, just as liberal financiers, exporters, aristocrats and professors did. He did not play the part of a malicious observer as he should have done as a consistent Marxist in a capitalist society, but tried to warn and to help. A pleasing contradiction, but a contradiction nevertheless. The Social Democrats were patriots – a bourgeois trick according to Marx – and in spite of their criticism of particular military estimates were ready to defend the country. Although they were in close touch with other socialist parties in the West and still clung to the old plan under which an international general strike would immobilize the machinery of war in an emergency, in case of a more serious threat, such as the possibility of a Russian attack, they were prepared to fight; a tradition which could claim to go back to Engels. 'If ever there is a war against Russia,' Bebel said, 'we Socialists shall march to a man.' These were the words of a man whose intellectual roots went back to 1848; but now they were applied to a situation in which Russia had a military alliance with France. In 1913 the Social Democrats in the Reichstag voted for the *Wehropfer,* a wealth tax intended to cover the costs of a further expansion of the army. This was then no longer anything startlingly new; it was the result of an attitude which the party had gradually adopted. Germany was divided in many ways, not simply into Socialists versus the rest. Such a division would have been in accordance with Marxist theory but not with the spirit of the people, nor with social reality.

The Social Democrats therefore in the end did not remain entirely untouched by the wave of imperialism. From a complete rejection of colonialism they moved on to criticize individual aspects of it; this meant that some things should and could have been done better. Indeed, partly because of Social Democratic criticism, there was some improvement in the administration of the German colonies. The 'theory of increasing pauperization' was proved false even there and still more at home. The German worker lived better than he had ever lived. The improvement in living standards was connected with and depended on the successes and profits of German industry. If it was true, as almost everybody believed at the time, that German industry must be as independent as possible of the world market which was always threatened politically and always unstable, that the Reich must protect its raw material supply and export markets, then the representatives of the workers could hardly be completely opposed to 'protectorates' and 'zones of influence'. It was a question of doing things better, and if possible without rattling swords; it was no longer a question of doing nothing. So we see men like Gustav Noske positively welcoming the German colonial empire and Philipp Scheidemann waxing lyrical about the Baghdad railway which he claimed would one day serve to supply the German workers with wheat. There was no longer a complete contrast between the behaviour of the Reich and its German critics. What they demanded was more democracy, not revolution and a new start.

In the late autumn of 1908 it seemed for a few days as if the state was likely to become more democratic very soon. The occasion was a trivial one: one of those remarks by the Kaiser of which he had made several in the last eighteen years. In an interview with a London newspaper William complained of the lack of understanding in Britain towards Germany and of his own difficulties in Germany in trying to achieve better relations between the two nations and so on – mild lapses of taste compared with His Imperial Majesty's past record. Only the psychological moment seems to have been unique. The storm of indignation which broke in Germany was more violent than any Prussian king had experienced since March 1848. The Conservatives participated in it just as much as the Social Democrats. It was said in the press and in parliament that the limit had been reached, that the people's confidence in the monarch was at its nadir, that such irresponsible behaviour must be stopped. The Social Democrats called for action. Said Georg Ledebour:

Genuine ministerial responsibility and the appointment of ministers by parliament is the demand of the hour . . . You, gentlemen, have the opportunity, because of the general discontent of the people, to achieve really democratic parliamentary government, and since you have this opportunity you must use it . . . If only you had the courage at last to acquire the self-confidence of free men.

Very reluctantly Bülow had to choose between the Kaiser and the Reichstag. In the end he chose the Reichstag and admitted that the imperial *faux pas* had been unfortunate and regrettable and that nobody could govern like this; but he assured the Chamber that there would be no repetition. 'It is up to you to

ensure that the misfortune does not become a catastrophe.'
William II lived in cloud-cuckoo-land; he was a braggart, but became distressed and frightened as soon as he came up against
brutal reality. He kept very quiet during the November storm,
disappeared for a while, thought of abdication and left it to
Bülow to extricate himself and his master as best he could.

Soon things returned to normal. During the crisis *Hilfe* (Help),
Friedrich Naumann's paper, had said: 'It is clear that there will
be no decisive constitutional change.' 'Because of the disorga-
nization of our party life most deputies lack the desire for power.
That is the sad experience of this week . . .' Nothing changed
either in the constitution or in the character of the monarch.
Bülow was forced to resign shortly afterwards. He took this step
because his coalition collapsed when the Conservatives refused
to support him over his proposal to make modest death duties
part of a necessary financial reform. The alliance between the
Conservatives and the Progressives broke down as soon as it
was put to the slightest test. It is possible to interpret Bülow's
subsequent resignation as a victory for the parliamentary principle; only it was again a purely negative victory. First of all
there was no majority prepared to support a successor. The Conservatives with their class egoism, condemning Bülow's measures
as left-wing, had refused to work with him; this was not in any
sense a constructive act. Secondly it was not the Reichstag which
overthrew Bülow. What the Reichstag achieved was merely to
make the Chancellor completely dependent on the Kaiser's
whim. William now happily took revenge for what he regarded
as Bülow's treachery in the *Daily Telegraph* affair by dismissing
him. It was like a parody of Bismarck's fall. In both cases the
Reichstag was involved but did not formally decide. In both
cases the event could only have had useful consequences if the
fallen Prime Minister had been succeeded by a parliamentary
government; this did not happen on either occasion. Bülow's
fall, like Bismarck's, merely strengthened the Kaiser's position.
Bismarck's fall strengthened the position of the young Kaiser
who had great illusions and about whom the nation had great
illusions. Bülow's fall strengthened the position of the ageing

Kaiser whom a large section of the nation had long seen for what he was and whose prestige had recently suffered a heavy blow. Consequently Bülow's fall solved nothing whatsoever. For nine years he had defended a shadow of Bismarck's power with a shadow of Bismarck's skill. After him there was only confusion. The fact that the Reichstag parties were for one reason or another in a state of unco-ordinated rebellion against the Bismarck–Hohenzollern order did not give the country a government. It merely paralysed the only one which Germany had and which was precisely of Bismarck–Hohenzollern origin. In fact in 1909 William had the proud feeling that, as in 1890, he was once more 'at the helm'. When Bülow warned him that his successor, Bethmann Hollweg, understood nothing about foreign policy, the Kaiser smiled knowingly: he himself was again going to take charge of foreign policy. For the rest Bethmann Hollweg was the very man to push the deputies back into their mouseholes. The Kaiser intended to assume more personal control over government affairs than before.

Bethmann Hollweg was a bureaucrat who had successfully risen from *Landrat* to Secretary of State for Internal Affairs. He was a worthy, well-meaning man, industrious, sensible and definitely capable in his field, but not much of a diplomat, and certainly no parliamentarian, politician or ruler. He was a pessimist, introspective, unsure of his own gifts, though very conscious of his own virtue, occasionally capable of anger and most convincing on those occasions, at the same time hypersensitive and not entirely innocent of time-serving. That this tall, grey-bearded stranger should now be allowed to present himself to the nation as its only responsible minister implied that German domestic policy had broken down. What could Bethmann do with an old-fashioned, badly arranged state? What could he do with the dissatisfied parliament pulling in all directions? What could he do with the nation which did not know how to use its enormous economic and military strength? What could he do with the rest of the world which had become deeply suspicious and which, in spite of all peace talk, was lining up against the Reich?

Bethmann Hollweg tried several things. He was anxious to come to terms with the Social Democrats whose leaders he invited to fruitless discussions. He played with the idea of a mild electoral reform in Prussia but abandoned the idea when he found himself unable to push it through the Conservative-controlled Lower House. This happened at the same time as the British House of Lords agreed, albeit reluctantly, to a curtailment of its own powers. In Britain this was possible but not in Prussia-Germany; there was no reform in good time, no voluntary resignation. For Alsace-Lorraine Bethmann achieved a constitution which raised the *Reichsland* to approximately the same status as the federal states – undeniable progress. There are reasons to think that if peace had continued the Alsatians might after all gradually become used to being members of the Reich. If peace had continued – the whole German state might gradually have been put in order. But the question to end all questions is why peace did not continue.

The German middle class, as it expressed itself in its press and in the speeches of its members of parliament, was no more peace-loving than its government. The middle of the road course which Bethmann Hollweg steered – if one can call it steering – quickly led him between two fires. For the Social Democrats he was too restless and provocative; for the Right he was too careful. It happened even to Admiral von Tirpitz that the pan-Germans found his attitude too diplomatic. Germany had no genuine, i.e. democratically formed responsible government. But, as things had developed, it was not even possible to demonstrate that a parliamentary government might have been more successful. There were situations from which it was possible to conclude the contrary.

An example of this, a symptom rather than an event of real historical importance, was the 'second Moroccan crisis'. In 1911 France took steps which seemed to foreshadow the establishment of a protectorate in Morocco. In order to protect real or alleged economic interests Germany replied with one of the dramatic gestures which had become so popular in Berlin: a German gunboat appeared in the harbour of Agadir on the western coast of Morocco. This action caused great delight among the German middle classes. 'Western Morocco to be German!' 'Cheers, action!' 'When shall we march?' – those were some of the headlines. Heavy industry took the trial of strength more seriously than had probably been the intention of the German Foreign Office which retreated when Britain issued a strong protest and sided with France. The result was the kind of barter deal which so often ended imperialist conflict. France was allowed to carry off its imaginary booty, Morocco, and in return ceded part of its colony in the Congo to the Reich. Peace, in the balance for months, was saved once more, and a modest gain had been achieved. But in the subsequent Reichstag debate those were in the majority who would willingly have risked everything and who accused the government of 'weakness'. The Chancellor found himself in the curious position of being defended only by the aged Bebel; by a party which he could not use to support his policy. The imperial authority lost its firm grip on the nation; indeed, it had already lost it. This loss of authority, however, did not mean that there were others ready to assume responsibility. It was an absolute loss of authority. Hohenzollern Germany, giving way in turn to conflicting impulses, could not master the country's diverging interests and passions; neither in 1911 nor six years later.

The next Reichstag elections, in 1912, brought a victory for the Social Democrats who became by far the strongest party. Over a third of the electorate voted for them, and in addition a substantial number of votes were cast for the Progressives. This meant that about half the German people were no longer in favour of the policy of sabre-rattling, nor of the propaganda of the pan-Germans, financed out of Foreign Office funds, nor of the armaments race at sea, nor of the Kaiser's bragging, nor of the untenable set-up in Prussia. That was what the election result meant, but it changed nothing. The true strength of the parties was not reflected in the number of seats which they obtained because an antiquated arrangement of constituencies gave the countryside an advantage over the cities. Even a change of constituency boundaries would not have done any good as long as the distribution of power remained as it was; as long as those who had reason to be dissatisfied with the distribution of power did not form a force that could act and was prepared to take over the heritage of power and to manage it better.

In the autumn of 1913 German officers in a small town in Alsace allowed themselves to provoke the inhabitants and as a result a few citizens were illegally imprisoned for one night. Again the occasion was a trivial one, again it gave rise to angry feelings. In the Reichstag Bethmann defended the army with a bad conscience, criticizing it mildly, and mildly also the Alsatians, trying to pour oil on troubled waters, as was his way. He was jeered at and shouted down – 'Aren't you ashamed to talk such rubbish on such a serious issue?' – and finally voted down. With an overwhelming majority – 293 against 54 – the chamber decided that it had no confidence in the Chancellor's handling of the matter. It was a repetition of the *Daily Telegraph* affair, of the vote of no confidence, of the parties' protest which this time was not directed against the Kaiser but against the army which regarded itself as far superior to any civilian. In its unanimity the protest was a very impressive one, but once again it changed nothing. The culpable officers were not seriously brought to book, the Minister of War who had objected to all parliamentary criticism of the army remained in office and the Kaiser, the silly young Crown Prince, the uninspired Chancellor all continued their activities as before. Elections like the one of 1912 and parliamentary resolutions like the one of December 1913 showed that Hohenzollern Germany was in the throes of a domestic crisis. But they allowed no conclusions as to the outcome of the crisis. The present author has several times asked old people how they had imagined the future in 1913, what they had hoped for and what they had expected, but never got a clear answer.

It is true that other nations also had their crises. Britain had suffered a constitutional conflict in 1909–10 and afterwards seen bitter struggles between capital and labour. In Ireland there was the threat of civil war. There was also the suffragette movement, the lunatic intensity of which must be regarded as an expression of the general irritability, of the nervous state of Europe.

France still vividly remembered the great legal battle over Captain Dreyfus, the undeclared civil war which at the turn of the century had split the country in two. The kingdom of Italy had never achieved domestic peace or real parliamentarianism, and had never been able to conquer corruption, disguised dictatorship and anarchy. In Russia Tsarism was in the throes of its last bitter, horrible agony. The Reich seemed a paradise of civilization, freedom and legality compared with its sinister neighbours in the East.

This is not saying everything. If every state was burdened with its unsolved problems Germany's difficulties were of a particular variety. France had long possessed an identity, although parties and ideologies struggled to be in the lead. In Germany there was no real opposition because there was no real government. The conflict between Prussia and the Reich, which was really a social one, was disguised as a clash between political systems which overlapped and at the same time did not overlap. The parties did not acquire an identity by competing for power, not even by opposing. Everybody pursued his own interests; bureaucracy, army, navy and Foreign Office, agrarians, industrialists, artisans, peasants and workers, Centre, Conservatives and Social Democrats. One is almost tempted to say that there was still no nation in the sense in which it existed in the older nation-states. Hence the desperate search for an identity, the nationalistic noises, the fantastic demands and plans of the pan-Germans. Hence also the refusal to recognize that everybody belonged to the same nation, an attitude of mind which characterized the relationship between the parties of the extreme right and left. Yet this nation-state without responsible government, without internal unity, was one of the greatest centres of energy there has ever been. Its population increased annually by almost a million, its industry was surpassed only by that of America and its army was second to none.

5. Creativeness and Impotence

At the end of his book *Die Deutsche Volkswirtschaft im 19. Jahrhundert* (The German Economy in the Nineteenth Century), completed shortly before the First World War, Werner Sombart, one of the most famous economists of the Wilhelminian period, looked at the spiritual life of this admirable industrial state. His findings were pessimistic:

The great ideals which inspired our fathers and grandfathers have faded; the national idea is exhausted after the Reich has been established with a great burst of enthusiasm. What we are offered today as nationalism is a pale second brew which nobody can quite warm up. Empty phrases serve to cover up the spiritual void. The same is true of the great political ideals for which our forefathers died. Some have been realized, some have been shown up to be irrelevant. The younger generation smiles knowingly when it reads about the struggle for political freedom, and celebrations in honour of the great age of enthusiasm turn into ridiculous farces. Yet no new political ideas have emerged ... The nineteenth century ends with an enormous deficit of idealist enthusiasm with which the most recent past in particular was excessively well endowed. As idealistic values disappear material interests naturally come to the fore, and the masses, no longer fettered by ideas, rally round the banner of social class, unless temporary economic interests make them collect in special associations, as the 'agrarians' are doing at the moment; their Farmers' Federation has only developed as a result of the unfavourable market for agricultural goods and will disappear. Yet even this powerful mass organization is the product of a purely utilitarian spirit ... And as one might expect, with the ability to be excited by great ideals, the pleasure of defending great political principles has also disappeared from our public life. An unprincipled, dreary opportunism, an uninspired business mentality has gained control of our political life. Who today still wants to argue hotly about political principles, about the protection of labour, about the right to follow any occupation, about consumer organizations and about free trade? ... It is almost impossible to believe that the nation which a hundred years ago was given its laws by Stein, Hardenberg, Schön and Thaer, the nation in which in the eighteen twenties and eighteen thirties Nebenius, Humboldt and List set the tone, in which fifty years ago the men of the

Paulskirche discussed the fate of the people, in which a generation ago Treitschke and Lassalle thundered on the political horizon, in whose parliaments only a few decades ago Bennigsen, Lasker, Bamberger, Windthorst and Reichensperger crossed swords with Bismarck, that this nation should have reached such a nadir of political life as we witness at present.

There are always people who prefer the good old days to the present. In the nineteen twenties people looked enviously to the high level of German parliamentary life in the age of William II, and in the age of William II they looked with self-critical wistfulness to Bismarck's political struggles and those against Bismarck, whereas the age of Bismarck already seemed intellectually disappointing compared with the promise of 1808 or 1848. Optical illusion contributes to this attitude because from the distance one sees the peaks and not the plateaux. Yet even taking this element of deception into account it is possible to see a decline. Nationalism had become an empty sound, serving only to nurture arrogance and to disguise and promote material enrichment; with corruption flourishing there was a barren clash of interests and, while faith was lacking in spite of all lip-service paid to Christianity, success was worshipped.

Sombart, an admirer of the German middle classes, saw the situation just as his contemporary Heinrich Mann described it with inspired malice in his novel *Der Untertan* and as a generation earlier Nietzsche had done with his strident, solitary comment. The Wilhelminian style was devoid of taste, with its court poets, court painters, and court preachers, its speeches in honour of the Kaiser's birthday and its Sedan celebrations, with its ostentatious buildings, barracks and mock castles. Foreigners also took this view. Let us once again quote Henry Adams who wrote in 1901:

Forty years have added another layer of bad taste to all that went before. It sickens me to think that this is the whole result and all the result of my lifetime. I saw the same thing in Italy, but there the effort has not been so gigantic. Here in Nuremberg I feel it the more because this was one of my first delights in art, way back in '59 . Altogether Germany gives me the sense of hopeless failure . . .

Intellectuals and bureaucrats were worlds apart. Both had their ways of life but neither knew the other. Bogus things appeared side by side with genuine and worthwhile ones. Portraits of field-marshals, vulgar showpieces of the kind that the Kaiser loved could not supplant the powerful paintings of the Impressionists, of Max Liebermann and Slevogt. Gerhart Hauptmann's plays, a mixture of protest, truth and compassion, profound pieces of realism, conquered the free stage, even though the royal theatres were closed to them. The same middle class which relished inferior, light fiction also read Thomas Mann's *Buddenbrooks*, the product of a mature, bourgeois art influenced by Russian, Scandinavian, English and French writers. In close proximity to the Court at Potsdam there were bad poets, epigones of epigones; a long distance away Liliencron and Dehmel and a little later Ricarda Huch and Hugo von Hofmannsthal enriched the eternal store of German poetry with their ideas, with their great verse. It was a brilliant, liberal period for art and artists, for essayists and critics, for experimental writers and even for satirists. Never has a ruler been ridiculed more wittily, more accurately, more gaily and in a more carefree manner than the Kaiser in the Munich *Simplizissimus* and in Frank Wedekind's ballads. The age of William II, as full of cares as any other, in which the middle classes hated the Socialists, in which farmers worried about prices and industrialists about markets, in which there was a succession of diplomatic crises and unceasing talk of coming war, was at the same time a harmless and carefree age. That is how it appears in retrospect; those who lived through it later recalled it nostalgically. The reason for this was the general prosperity and the fact that the foundations of the state, of order and civilization seemed reasonably solid. The intellectuals found the Kaiser's doings too comic or too disgusting to take them very seriously. They were equally indifferent to the efforts of the political parties, uncreative, bureaucratic organizations. If things had worked so far they would somehow continue to work.

The most serious attempt to raise the level of German politics was made by the circle of the Frankfurt parson Friedrich Naumann. Naumann was a member of the Reichstag on several occasions, tried to found a new party or party-like organization, the *Nationalsoziale Verein* (1896 to 1903), and wrote for his own journal, *Hilfe*. All his writings, on social policy, parliamentary policy and foreign policy, on painting and architecture, give the impression of intelligence and kindness, of a courageous, free will to face up to modern problems. Naumann, a Protestant Christian, a Liberal, a Democrat and also a Socialist though certainly a long way from Marxian errors, wanted to see the great Social Democratic Party share at last in political responsibility. He was in favour of Germany's *Weltpolitik*, of its colonial, military and naval policy, all of which he regarded as necessary for the preservation and development of German life. Such was the spirit of the age, in Germany as elsewhere, the influence of which Naumann made no attempt to avoid. Yet he wanted the people to play their part, an aim which in practice could only be realized through parliamentary government. He wanted the Kaiser to become the beloved guardian of a democratic community and Germany to become something better than mere power in the eyes of the rest of the world, and to have something better at home than an antiquated, army-dominated caste system without style, riddled with class enmity and selfish quarrels. Naumann won respect in the country as a whole and in the capital, although one cannot say that he left his mark on history. His effect was not comparable to that produced at the same time by the French Socialist Jean Jaurès who distantly resembled him. The contradictions in Germany were intractable. Naumann's mind could grasp them and produce good ideas on how things should or could develop, but it could not really come to grips with them. The intellectual was impotent in spite of his achievements. He lived apart from the state and was happy with this situation. To him it seemed more important to serve beauty and truth, to explore the beginnings of man's history and the secrets of the soul than to worry about crises in Morocco or Reichstag elections.

Not that the intellectuals altogether ignored society and contemporary problems. 'The hour of the spirit,' says Hegel, 'is essentially now'; if it is alive it must concern itself with questions of the moment. We find the social accusation not only in naturalistic writers like Arno Holz but in artists like Hauptmann and Dehmel who went beyond naturalism. We find historical themes in Thomas Mann's early novels; the decline of the old patriciate in a Hanseatic city, or the melancholy charm of the anachronisms of constitutional monarchy in a small German state. Yet those were only the themes. The purpose was not to produce change but to educate and to mould; it was a game. Those who wanted to produce change or pretended to do so, who criticized society in the style of the French, like Heinrich Mann in his satirical novels about the Wilhelminian age, were regarded as alien in Germany; indeed, it is undeniable that they copied foreign models and felt no great love for their fellow countrymen.

Occasionally the decision to ignore the present, to rise above its vulgarity, its greed and lack of style, became itself a characteristic of the age, as in the case of Stefan George, a most ambitious poet who was determined to write with style, who performed the most complicated and sometimes the most exquisite tricks with the German language. Yet he was outrageously conceited, overbearing, secretive and cliquish. If we look at the *de luxe* editions in which George's poems were published, the elaborate type on hand-made paper, we comment with a smile that this was the taste of the age and that the age had no taste. Some threads lead from George's cult of youth, beauty, aristocracy, authority and cruelty to war, which when it came he at once, anticipating, called the 'First World War'. To want to be better than one's age, to sit in judgement on it with priestly gestures, is to ask ultimately for punishment.

The 'Youth Movement' was better because it wanted to help young people everywhere and did not remain the property of a few proud priests of the arts. Vague in its philosophy it helped by practical means, by teaching men how to live together in harmony, by encouraging them to leave the cities and to return to nature; by protesting against convention, class conceit and philistinism. Basically it was a repetition of what the *Burschenschaften* had done a hundred years before, only that now a much greater need demanded to be satisfied. What the state with its pedantic education and square bashing, what economic life could not give in the age of large-scale industry the young gave themselves: voluntary discipline, games, hiking, camp-fires and traditional songs. Fortunate were those who thereby found a meaning in life. They made the same mistake as the *Burschenschaften* had made: they believed that their activities could change Germany and transfigure the nation into a community. The obstacles in the nation's historical path were much too great to be moved by youthful idealism alone. The trouble with all youth movements is that they fail to keep their promises, however hard they try. German youth did have ideals when it came to nation and state, but given modern society as it was these ideals could only be cultivated by a small, young circle. This led to disappointments and later also to political aberrations. The camp-fires and the traditional songs were replaced by other songs and other fires in 1914. The young Germans, even those who had supported the youth movement, welcomed the war. It satisfied them in a way that bourgeois society in peacetime could not satisfy them. In the last resort most German intellectuals, all those superior, aloof gentlemen, poets, writers and philosophers, also welcomed the war. They were happy that in the hour of common distress they could at last be positive, serve, join in and be people among people. The long separation between the creative mind and authority was followed by a sudden marriage. This, however, was probably based on a misunderstanding. If the modern industrial state did not offer the knights of the quill a suitable arena, war did so even less. How could they, who had ignored politics while there was comparative freedom, direct and give meaning to events that happened under enormous pressure?

6. A Glance at Austria

We have seen how Bismarck created the small nation-state in order to prevent the establishment of the greater one and how he forced the old Habsburg Empire to have its own existence, separate from Germany. The solution looked neat enough on the map, a large part of which – in fact the largest apart from Russia – still showed the Austrian colours; to the West and the North stretched the new German Reich, only a little smaller. But this act of division could not dissolve the historical links, the community of language and culture, of economic and political interests. Two empires, one a German nation-state, the other German by virtue of its origin, its dynasty and its claims although at the same time providing a labyrinthine home for many non-German nations, Slavs, Magyars and Italians – in the age of nationalism such a set-up could hardly provide a lasting solution. It was true that the Germans had contented themselves with a fragmentary nation-state over which they had almost forgotten the dreams of 1848. It was true that they were now concerned with *Weltpolitik* rather than 'greater German' politics and that their energies, economic and political, were directed at the seven seas instead of the Danube valley. Nevertheless Germany and Austria could not let each other go. Even Bismarck admitted this when he entered into the alliance of 1879. The question of whether Austria pulled Germany into the abyss of war or Germany Austria has meaning only in the superficial sphere of diplomacy; and there Austria bears the more direct blame. In every other sense, however, the frontier between the two states was fictitious. The German nation was too involved with itself and with the fate of the nationalities of central and south-east Europe. The Swiss had become a separate nation. But not the Austrians; and given the variety of their groupings within the 'monarchy', in the Tyrol, in the old Archduchy, in Silesia, Bohemia and Moravia, in Carinthia, Styria and in the German-speaking enclaves of Hungary, they could not become one. They might be members of a state, loyal Austrians and loyal subjects of the Emperor Francis Joseph; as a nation they were bound to look beyond their frontiers towards Germany. The concept of the nation had no logical place in the Habsburg Empire.

The German nation realized itself in various political forms, not like the French in a single one. These different forms corresponded to different surroundings, alliances and tensions. In its

Prussian organization the nation could live at peace with Russia, but not in its Austrian one. In its Austrian organization it could live tolerably well with the Poles, but not in its Prussian one. In peacetime such differences were significant, but when it came to a major crisis they disappeared. Then Austria was drawn into the Anglo-German and the Franco-German conflict which did not concern it as 'Austria', just as conversely Prussia-Germany became involved in the Austro-Russian conflict. On those occasions the German nation seemed one, regardless of political frontiers, threatening in all directions and threatened from all directions.

The Habsburg monarchy was a survival of the past, the only great non-national state in the age of nationalism. Once it had had close links with Spain, had ruled Italy and Germany, Burgundy and Belgium. All this was no more; instead its sphere of authority lay along the Danube and in the Balkan peninsula – always the same centre of power, the same capital, the same ruling house. This gave the Austrian state its unity, its real *raison d'être* and because of this it was usually called 'the monarchy'. Yet the political gathering of regions and peoples called Austria was not a haphazard one. Otherwise it would not have lasted so long and its end would not have brought such terrible upheavals, such enduring chaos.

Life in the old Austria during the last decades of the Emperor Francis Joseph must have been agreeable. Here too there was an increase in prosperity, political freedom and legal security; the administration was efficient, if somewhat cumbersome, and there was a mature, still creative civilization. This civilization was predominantly German yet with a quality of its own, still nourished by old cosmopolitan traditions, open to the influences of the South and the South-East; less aggressive than the national culture of the Bismarckian Reich. Then there were the strivings of the smaller nations, Czechs, Poles, Magyars, Croats and South Slavs, for a cultural life of their own. All these influences met in Vienna which was both German and not German, drawing its sap of life from all parts of the monarchy. The ruler of all these peoples was the Emperor, a man from a legendary past, the young master of the counter-revolution of 1848, who had grown old, experienced and pessimistic. People loved him now or at least admired him, his strict way of life, his dignified, dutiful, hard-working existence. He did not make bragging speeches, he did not allow himself glaring lapses of tact but rose summer and winter at five o'clock and worked into the night for the welfare of his peoples, as he saw it. The age of Francis Joseph and of his Vienna was the age of the 'Emperor Waltz' and the 'Tales from the Vienna Woods', of the k. and k. army in south Tyrol, in Galicia and in the Bukovina; of *Hofräte* and commercial councillors, of the Burgtheater and the cafés, of the poems of Hugo von Hofmannsthal, tender, imaginative, noble and profound; of the plays of Arthur Schnitzler and of the pioneering psychology of Sigmund Freud; tears come to the eyes of the old who lived through this period when they see it sentimentally recreated on the screen. Why could it not last? Why should the disaster which so profoundly changed Europe have started here of all places? Why should the Austrian state which had so many sympathetic, tolerant characteristics have become so guilty? Unfortunately there was also much hatred in the old Austria, and Vienna itself, golden Vienna, bred it as a swamp breeds fever germs. The lower classes hated the Jews who were many and wealthy in the capital and their hatred was fanned by demagogues and happily exploited by one of the great parties. The middle classes hated the Social Democrats; the nationalities, Germans and Slavs, hated each other; those who had failed hated those who had been successful. Political problems are human problems. If people had been different the problems of the Habsburg monarchy might have been solved or would not have existed.

After the Austrian defeat of 1866 Francis Joseph had made peace with his Magyar subjects. The result was the *Ausgleich*, a treaty dividing the monarchy into two unequal halves. The one was Hungary, the other all the rest. The monarchy was now called Austria-Hungary. Hungary was an empire in which the Magyars were in the minority compared with the non-Magyar peoples, Rumanians, Croats, Slovaks, Germans and Jews. Here the Magyar aristocracy defended the rule of a nationality and of a class with difficulty and skill. To do this it needed the protection of the Emperor and therefore it finally made its peace with the Habsburg monarchy. But Francis Joseph's complete surrender of Hungary to the Magyar barons, reserving to the Empire only the control of foreign policy and of the army, they owed to the Prussian victory over Austria; indeed their position in Hungary was not unlike that of the Junkers in Prussia. Hence Bismarck's alliance with Hungary which Habsburg Austria joined as a third party. After 1867 the Habsburg monarchy thus depended on two essentially alien powers, on Prussia by which it had been defeated in 1866 – and then pardoned – and on Hungary. This situation was bad for the monarchy. The two allies, the Germans and the Hungarians, prevented Austria from carrying out the reform required for its survival in the twentieth century. Neither Berlin nor Budapest could allow a federation of equal peoples in which Germans and Magyars were in the minority *vis-à-vis* the Slavs.

Whereas in Hungary Rumanian, Slovak and Croat intellectuals were troubled by the rough customs of the ruling nation, people in the Austrian half of the Empire, Germans, Poles, Czechs and Italians, were quite well off. They were in secure possession of all the achievements of the liberal state. They were all represented in parliament, the *Reichsrat*, after the proclamation of universal suffrage in 1907. They controlled the provincial administration, a fact which was of great importance to them because there were thousands of bureaucratic positions to be given away there. Nobody prevented them from fostering their own language and culture in schools, universities and institutes of fine arts. They governed where they were in the majority, the Czechs in Prague, the Germans in northern Bohemia, the Poles in Galicia and the Italians in Trieste. Unfortunately, however, they preferred to quarrel and to hate each other instead of living decently together. For this sickness there was no cure. One sympathizes most with the Italians who were attracted by their new national home, the kingdom of Italy, and who saw no real reason for remaining in the 'monarchy'. The Polish reaction would have been equally natural if there had been a Polish state outside Austria. But there was none and the Poles in Austria were better off than the Poles in Russia. Among the peoples of the monarchy they were in fact one of the most loyal to the Habsburgs. The Germans were divided, pro-Habsburg in the Catholic and rural regions, Vorarlberg, Tyrol and Carinthia; pro-Habsburg but tinged with German ambition in Vienna; in Bohemia and Lower Austria they looked eagerly across the frontiers to Bismarckian Germany. In its milder forms German nationalism wanted to preserve and strengthen the German character of the state as a whole. In its more extreme forms it was ready to abandon the monarchy and to seek union with the Reich – a process in which the rest would anyhow fall under German or Magyar sovereignty. For the Czechs this prospect held no attraction. In the nineteenth century they had developed a national culture, a little artificial, somewhat imitative of the German one, and flavoured with French ingredients, but nevertheless worthy of esteem. Having developed a culture they wanted to have a state, to re-establish the old kingdom of Bohemia as it had existed until the seventeenth century; although this was to happen within the framework of the monarchy the Czechs would be the ruling nation and the Germans a tolerated minority. The Germans had always regarded Bohemia as part of the Empire and could not free themselves from this tradition. The Czechs who wanted to found their own national state there were motivated by a mixture of memories of the medieval kingdom and modern nationalism. The two aims were absolutely contradictory; they were equally awkward and equally unrelated to the realities of the twentieth century.

How deep all this went is difficult to say. The Austrian monarchy was itself a fact of life; a large area in which one could move freely, a vast network of roads and railways across plains and high mountains; its ships sailed on the Danube and it had a harbour at Trieste. There were important economic links and minor ways of life, family connections that went beyond national frontiers, hundreds of thousands of more or less badly paid positions of different kinds, a capital in which all the peoples lived together, an army in which everyone could advance and a church which had close links with the state. Such a structure is solid and cannot be destroyed in a day. Without realizing it most people had come to accept the system. The protests came from dissatisfied intellectuals, from nationalists, from scheming middle-class lawyers who threw inkpots at each other in parliament, drowned each other's speeches with wind instruments like the worst kind of naughty schoolboys and quarrelled over a new school for Slovenes or Ukrainians as though the fate of the world was at stake. At a few minutes' distance from the parliament there was the old Emperor in his palace, conscientious and pessimistic, having witnessed this kind of thing for half a century. The behaviour of the representatives of the people could hardly encourage him to give them more rights than they already had. He would have liked to rule in accordance with the constitution. But because parliament was incapable of making a positive decision ministers ruled with the help of emergency decrees; faceless administrators allowed deputies to rage in the chamber and then arranged small barter deals with the party leaders in some back room. Foreign policy was a thing apart being, as it always had been, in the hands of the Emperor, of the aristocratic professional diplomats and of the generals. In the end foreign policy produced the crisis which internal conflicts alone could not have produced. However, foreign policy and domestic policy shaded into one another in Austria-Hungary.

After the events of 1866 and 1871 the monarchy was Germany's prisoner. Its helplessness increased as Russia's power grew, Britain abandoned its old interests in the Near East and the whole burden of defending south-eastern Europe against the Russians fell on the Austrians. This they could never do without German help. Germany for its part needed Austria because through Austria lay the road to the Balkans and Asia Minor, regions which German imperialism was determined to make its hinterland. After the events of 1904 and 1907 Germany needed Austria also for a worse reason: because it was now Germany's only ally. Not a very strong ally and not a very reliable one, but the only one. This gave Austria's diplomats the opportunity to play a bold game, as the weaker partner indeed often has the upper hand in a partnership. They could not part from Germany but could occasionally draw it into undesirable adventures because now Germany too could no longer part from them. They thought in old concepts, not of nations but of great powers, imperial powers, prestige and diplomatic triumphs. They had never learnt anything else and one could hardly demand it from people of their type. The Russian diplomats thought in similar terms and even the French did not really think in very different ones.

The north of the Balkan peninsula, adjacent to Hungary and Bosnia, was inhabited by the Serbs who in the nineteenth century had gradually won their independence from the Turks, a wild, brave people, a tiny kingdom of peasants, soldiers and police-men. Life in Serbia was barbaric, with palace revolutions and assassinations and there was nothing much to come by there. But the Serb politicians had great plans; they wanted to make their state what it once had been in the Middle Ages. There were Serbs also in Bosnia which was administered by Austria and had in 1908 become Austrian. From a linguistic point of view the Croats and Slovenes who were subjects of the Emperor Francis Joseph could probably also be counted as Serbs. Was there then not something like a great South Slav nation and should all its members not belong to one state? Fundamentally this was nonsense. The history of the Croats differed from that of the Serbs; for a thousand years they had lived in loose community with Hungary and had looked towards the West, towards Rome and Austria. They were Roman Catholics and they had a much more advanced civilization than the Serbs. Yet there was dis-content among the Croats also and dissatisfied intellectuals thought up the idea of a Yugoslav nation. This suited the Serb nationalists who saw that the idea could be exploited to expand Serbia. As Serbia was the only independent South Slav state and had a king, a capital, an army and an administration, it must become the leader of the Yugoslav cause. Serbia as the 'Pied-mont of the Southern Slavs' – this became the popular slogan. Serbia would do for Yugoslavia what Piedmont had done fifty years earlier for Italy. In Vienna and Budapest this comparison stirred disagreeable memories. The imperial diplomats realized that the monarchy was threatened by a danger that needed to be faced: the South Slav movement inside the Austrian provinces and the very lively little kingdom without. As we know Croats, Slovenes and Serbs later achieved their desired unity. In the Yugoslav kingdom the Serbs exercised an iron dictatorship over their beloved brother tribes far exceeding anything ever inflicted on the Croats in old Austria. For their part the Croats, when their hour came, happily slaughtered a few hundred thousand Serbs.

The Austrian Empire believed its existence threatened by South Slav agitation; Russia saw this as a chance to extend its imperialist influence. After all, the Balkan peoples were Slavs and the Russians were also Slavs. It was clearly the duty of the great Slav power to help the little Slav brothers. The Tsar once telegraphed admonishingly to the kings of Serbia and Bulgaria that the 'Slav cause' was at stake. Of course there was nothing in this alleged fellowship. Historically Russia had no business in the Balkans, did not need the Balkans and had enough to do in its vast interior to make the squandering of its energies in Balkan quarrels seem stupid. There was no more a 'Slav cause' than a 'Teutonic' one and the Russians had no more in common with the Serbs than the Germans with the Norwegians or the Boers. But nothing is served by condemning this foolish behaviour in retrospect. If people want to quarrel they will quarrel and any professorial chimera will serve as a pretext.

This was the position in Austria at the end of the first decade of the twentieth century. Tolerable as far as the realities of life went but not at all good as far as politics were concerned. The two spheres did not coincide. The issues of life are concrete and sensible whereas the issues of politics are all too often abstract, imaginary and mad. Internally there were quarrels and intrigues. One old, brash ruling people, the Magyar, did not want to give up its position, and another, the German, no longer knew whether it wanted to remain Austrian or not. There were restless, dissatisfied peoples with desires some of which deserved to be fulfilled, some of which did not, and some of which could not possibly be fulfilled: Ukranians, Czechs, South Slavs and Italians.

Protected by a ceremonial which dated from the Spanish Counter-Reformation there was the Emperor, an aged man upon whose death people expected the internal confusion to reach its climax. There was an army which regarded war, at least a little one, as inevitable, and also as desirable so that the monarchy could once again prove itself. There were irresponsible diplomats, ambitious gentlemen of the old school for whom foreign policy was a chivalrous game, although one which in the last resort did not exclude war. In the South, outside the monarchy, a small state was agitating dangerously and the consequences of its ambition undoubtedly threatened Austria's existence. This small state was 'protected' by Russia which after its bloody defeat by the Japanese in the Far East had 'returned' – as the current political expression went – to the Balkans, because it had to exert its influence and be a nuisance somewhere. Here then, three forms of mischief met, Russian, greater Serb and Magyar-Austrian. Behind Austria there stood Germany sometimes spurring it on, sometimes restraining it, but now no longer able to dissociate itself from Austria.

7. The Permanent Crisis

During the First World War an exchange of letters took place between Chancellors Bülow and Bethmann in which each with the utmost politeness tried to blame the other for the catastrophe. In one of these letters Bethmann spoke of the things which

belong to the more distant past, which through our fault and through no fault of ours led to the great coalition against us, which because of Austria's steady decline and of the ever-growing strength of the Entente brought about an ever more dangerous isolation of Germany's forces. After 1905 in the Moroccan question, then in the Bosnian crisis and again in the Moroccan question these factors compelled us to embark on a policy of maximum risk, a risk which increased with each repetition . . .

Nobody could describe the situation more accurately, except that one cannot quite agree about the compulsion.

Germany had made itself unpopular and feared – not as a result of its economic expansion as such. On the contrary, this brought it into closer touch with Russia, Britain and in particular France. The contacts between the German and French steel industries were never as close as in the years before 1914. Optimists regarded this development as a guarantee for peace. It certainly implied no threat of war. The threat came from politics and economic issues operated only to the extent that industry had a stake in building the German navy. Economic interests bring peoples together, politics divide them. Political activity is competitive and threatening. The question of whether you can kill me or I can kill you arises between all living beings who do not share the same laws and do not trust each other. This question also arose among the European states. In principle it should, of course, no longer have arisen. The states of Europe should have known each other sufficiently, should have been sufficiently of one mind to eliminate the folly of war. It was not the fault of industry and science that they were not. It was the fault of old ideas inherited from the age of chivalry, from the age of Machiavelli. To this were added new follies, rant about the final struggle between Teutons, Slavs and Gauls, about the right of the strong and about the remedial effects of war with which demagogues and misguided military writers tried to incite the masses. At times the Kaiser was influenced by these ideas, however much he liked to play the part of the guardian of peace.

No sooner had Germany, the newest and soon the strongest European power, joined in the political game than it began to frighten its neighbours. It had done nothing to prevent itself being encircled, convinced that it would always remain master of the situation and would not need to choose. After the circle – France, Britain and Russia – had closed Germany had tried several times to break it but had only succeeded in strengthening it. The Reich asserted itself in order to prove that it had arrived and was strong and that nothing could be done against its will. Hence the succession of crises which Bethmann listed in grim retrospect. Invariably almost insignificant issues were at stake, invariably right was not unquestionably on the enemies' side, invariably Germany used methods which involved, to use Bethmann's expression, the 'ultimate risk'. With each incident the risk grew, that is, war became more probable. Because one day the others would no longer allow Germany to assert itself, one day they would refuse outright to give way; then Germany would not be able to withdraw honourably and then there would be war. If the moral standards of others, the French and the Russians, had been higher than those of the Germans then ways and means might have been found to break the vicious circle. But their standards were no higher, they too counted on war. They too were certain that they would win and that after great sacrifices they would reap great benefits. They were happy to see Germany become increasingly isolated and make wrong moves, and they offered no help. Yet they were clever enough to leave to Germany the responsibility for what would happen sooner or later.

Anyone with any insight, soldiers, diplomats, journalists, could not seriously doubt that war would come. It had been expected since 1871 and the longer there was peace the more certain it became that the situation would not continue much longer. Europe had always been at war off and on, almost half the time since the sixteenth century. What reason was there to suppose that this state of affairs would not go on? And yet almost nobody *wanted* war – the exceptions are not worth mentioning. It was spoken of as something that would happen regardless of what anyone did or did not do. There is a truism that war does not come by itself and that one side, if not both, must start it, but people did not see it that way. They expected a situation in which war would become inevitable. They wanted war at some point – at the most favourable moment – but it was also true that they did not want it; they did not know what they wanted and did not have the courage to think clearly.

That much at least was understood, that war, if it *came*, would be different from previous wars, more destructive, more costly in materials and lives. Without having clear ideas about it people occasionally uttered sensible, warning words. Although they regarded war as inevitable and often talked foolishly and irresponsibly, they were afraid of it and were terribly afraid when the oft-invited guest finally knocked at the door. Then at the last moment while attempts were made to keep the door closed because people did not know whether they should open it, or wanted to, the door did in fact open as if of its own accord.

Never had a great European war seemed more probable than in the years before 1914. People knew this; every citizen could know it and yet nobody really believed it. Their reason could have told people that war was close at hand; their powers of imagination failed to make it a living threat. This was because they had long lived in peace and had become used to it, to a solid, international order of things, to banknotes that could be exchanged anywhere for gold, to travel without passport. Was all this suddenly to stop and to make way for an unknown nightmare? The living know they will die but they do not believe it because they have become used to life and only know life. Such, more or less, must have been the mood before 1914.

After Morocco had once again, in 1911, become the object of a 'crisis' from which Germany emerged relatively victorious, the bellicose Balkan nations gained the initiative. Allied they fought a war against Turkey in 1912 in which they showed surprising strength; the booty, the last bits of the moribund Turkish Empire in Europe, had been distributed in advance. It was an old Austrian axiom that the 'monarchy' would not last much longer than Turkey. Both states were supra-national, and violated the principle of the nation-state. If Balkan nationalism triumphed over Turkey it would also triumph over Austria and in Austria. The Austrians therefore regarded the end of the First Balkan War as a defeat. They tried to remove its sting by threatening war in order to prevent Serbia's penetration to the Adriatic. The great powers, assembled in London, agreed. The Serbs were made to give up their part of the Adriatic coastline, Albania, which was turned into an independent little state. This upset the old plan for the distribution of the booty. The result was the Second Balkan War in which the Serbs and the Bulgarians fought for Macedonia and in which the other Balkan nations did not remain idle. Serbia was once more the main victor and appeared on the map almost to have doubled its size. Rumania like Serbia emerged well from the affair; they were the two Balkan states that bordered on Austria-Hungary and hoped to become its heirs.

The Reich was itself a great national state and was not really afraid of Balkan nationalism with which it could probably have come to terms. The Austrians were afraid of it, particularly the Magyars, the Austrian 'master-race'. Although Germany joined in Austria's anti-Serb policy it basically had no interest in that policy. On the other hand Germany did now have considerable interests in Turkey, both economic and political. Here it clashed directly with Russia which, though reluctantly prepared to leave Constantinople to the Turks, did not want to allow any great power to establish itself there. German activities in Turkey were a direct provocation of Russia. Everybody provoked everybody but everybody needed everybody. Concern about the Germans had led Britain to allow the Russians to take northern Persia and no longer to adopt a firm line against them everywhere in Asia. Without the German threat the delicate and unnatural Russo–British agreement would break down. It was probably because the British were concerned about Russian imperialism that they were ready to put up with Germany's position in Asia Minor: in the early summer of 1914 an agreement was sketched out in London permitting the extension of the German Baghdad railway almost up to the Persian Gulf, to Basra. The two nations could probably have reached agreement on such concrete questions, both in the Near East and in Africa. The British Labour Party, the left-wing Liberals and the French Socialists still greatly preferred highly civilized, semi-democratic Germany to Tsarism. There were still thoughtful people in Germany who wanted to come to terms with at least one member of the Entente. Bethmann Hollweg would dearly have liked to reach agreement with Britain on the naval question but was foiled by the Admiralty. Admiral Tirpitz wanted to come to an understanding with Russia, perhaps also with France, but this was impossible because of Turkey and Austria, and because the general staff could not change its plan for war on two fronts. The German Social Democrats disliked Russia, and the idea of war against the western powers seemed mad to them; but Russia was France's ally. Even they, although morally by far the sanest and least affected by the vices of the age, knew no safe way out of the vicious circle. But they were more intelligent than the others and there were moments when they expressed their forebodings in eloquent terms. On the occasion of the second Moroccan crisis, in the last speech on foreign policy of his long and glorious career, Bebel had said:

What has happened between Japan and Russia can be repeated here. It is possible that one day one side will say: things cannot go on like this. It can also say: stop! If we wait any longer we shall suffer, we shall be the weak instead of the strong. Then there will be a catastrophe. Then the tocsin will be sounded in Europe and sixteen to eighteen million men, the flower of different nations, will march against each other, equipped with lethal weapons. But I am convinced that this great march will be followed by the great collapse [laughter] – all right, you have laughed about it before; but it will come, it has only been postponed [great amusement]. It is not our fault that it will come, it is your fault . . . you are pushing things to a head. . . you are undermining your own political and social institutions . . . What will be the result? After this war we shall have mass bankruptcy, mass misery, mass unemployment and great famine [dissent from the right]. Are you denying this? [Intervention from the right: 'After every war things get better'.]

Part Nine
War

Maximilian Harden, a shrewd critic of William II's Reich, even though he may have indulged in some self-advertising histrionics, wrote in May 1914: 'This summer will be fateful'.

Nothing is inevitable until it has happened. Little perception was needed to see that war had been in the air for many years; that every repetition of the 'policy of risk' made the diplomatic game more dangerous, and that if there was no change it would no longer be the diplomats but the lurking military who would take the initiative. But peace too was in the air and until the very end there was a choice. Great conflicts of interest divided the members of the ring which had encircled Germany or with which Germany had encircled itself, and until the end Germany could have broken this ring. This was talked about and thought about. But the ring could not have been broken without the renunciation of great, vague projects for the future, and this would have meant Germany becoming more or less reconciled to the existing order. Some historians think that Germany was fundamentally incapable of making this sacrifice, others find indecision and lack of good leadership a sufficient explanation. At any rate Germany did not opt for renunciation.

We shall tell briefly the story which has often been told in order to have more space for reflections on it.

1. July 1914

Archduke Francis Ferdinand of Austria, the Emperor's nephew and heir to the throne, was an overbearing man but not without an instinct for the realities of the old Empire which he thought he would shortly inherit. He had little sympathy for 'national aspirations' or for 'the people'. His hatred, however, was reserved for the Hungarian ruling class whose arrogance threatened Austria's existence, and he would willingly have given it short shrift. His views on Serbia were more or less those of Bismarck, namely that its plum trees and pigs were not worth the bones of an Austrian soldier. He wanted to humour the Slavs in the Empire, the Croats and the Czechs, by making them the third partner with the other two ruling peoples; in his somewhat brutal, limited mind, however, he had no idea how this would be done. If he held large-scale manoeuvres in Bosnia in June 1914 his ultimate intention was not to provoke the separatist elements there or in neighbouring Serbia. He merely wanted to show the restive natives who was their master; in the same spirit, as a soldier and a prince who was not afraid of his subjects, he paid a quick visit to the capital, Sarajevo. Francis Ferdinand did not return home alive.

His assassins had been trained and equipped on the other side of the frontier, in Belgrade, by men close to the Serb government. In the days following the assassination this fact was not known in Vienna, or could not be proved; it was, however, probable. The King of Serbia himself owed his throne to the brutal assassination of his predecessor, and the same adventurers who in 1904 had had the pro-Austrian royal pair torn to pieces continued to exert the strongest and most sinister influence. Clearly the act of Sarajevo was the work of greater Serb–Yugoslav propaganda, and clearly the government which encouraged this propaganda was at least indirectly responsible. To that extent the Austrians were right; they were right also – if there was any question of right and wrong at all – to demand the strictest investigation of the assassination, the severest penalties and the suppression of Yugoslav agitation.

In all this they would have had the world on their side. The men in Vienna decided to go further; this was their misfortune and the misfortune of us all.

Austria's Foreign Minister, Count Berchthold, an elegant, irresponsible bungler, thought that the moment had come to put an end to the Serb threat once and for all. The Chief of the General Staff, General Conrad, agreed. Lies were needed to win over the hesitant, aged Francis Joseph, who had learnt wisdom from bitter experience, to the policy of the vengeful adventure; he agreed to it on condition that it had the support of his German ally. The German ally supported it and thus everything was decided.

Not only did the Kaiser let it be known that he approved of every, even the very strongest, Austrian measure; he goaded Vienna on. The Chancellor was hardly asked for his opinion. Although the Hohenzollern monarchy had become weaker during the last ten years, William II's position was still such – particularly since Bülow's fall, and particularly because of the lack of responsible, delegated authority in Germany – that in such a serious matter he could decree as he liked.

The German decision swept Hungary along, although the Hungarian Prime Minister, Tisza, saw further than the rest. He was afraid even of victory over Serbia and asked himself what the others did not ask: what should be done with the passionate Slav people once it had been defeated? Austria already had too many Slavs. Moreover, he was not sure of victory, but feared, as he put it in a memorable memorandum, a major European war. Tisza yielded when Germany issued the order.

William did not want the war, or was not sure whether he wanted it; probably he did not ask himself this serious question even alone at night. He regarded war as improbable, only conceding with boastful courage that it might happen. In his view neither France nor Russia was ready and the Tsar in particular was not prepared to come to the rescue of the assassins of princes. But if he were to draw his sword, then better now than later. Lightheartedly we conjure up spirits in whose reality we do not believe. But if to our terrified surprise they appear after all we must pretend to have the courage of our convictions. It is tricky to run away before the eyes of the world if one has struck an attitude.

Germany and Austria therefore again decided to pursue the policy of risk. If anything, they regarded the risk as smaller than in the days of Agadir or the annexation of Bosnia, because this time they were the wronged party in a clear and shocking case. They would carry off a new diplomatic triumph, they would once more prove themselves stronger than the encircling powers. It is untrue to say that such a triumph would have given them or was designed to give them control of Europe. The whole Serb affair was not so momentous. Even if Serbia had accepted the exemplary punishment designed for it by William without resistance and without help from outside, Russia would still have remained Russia and France France and Britain Britain. Given good will on the other side Serbia could have been punished and that would have been the end of the matter. The European balance of power had long been threatened by the concentrated industrial and military might of Germany, the constricted country at the centre of the Continent. This situation lay in the nature of things. The presence of a few Austrian divisions in Belgrade making a nuisance of themselves for a few months, merely to withdraw again in the end, could constitute a threat to the balance of power only in the sterile minds of diplomats.

To be wise after the event is easy. It was not easy to see the situation like this in the poisoned, dazed atmosphere of 1914.

Once the principle had been decided, Vienna proceeded slowly and secretly. Midsummer promised well; great and small departed for their holidays, soldiers went on leave and navies sailed for their summer manoeuvres. The President of the French Republic paid a state visit to St Petersburg. It was better to let this happen in order not to destroy the picture of peaceful normality. Then, almost four weeks after the shots at Sarajevo, the result of Austria's diligence emerged: an ultimatum presented to the Serbs by the Austrian government. Ultimatum was the diplomatic term for a demand the non-acceptance of which meant war. The Austrian demands were stiff and had been drawn up with the express intention of making them unacceptable – because Berchthold and Conrad wanted war against Serbia, the war which would restore the shattered prestige of Austria-Hungary as a great power. Reading the ultimatum today we do not find it all that terrible. This is because we are used to seeing small states ordered about by great ones and because the concept of sovereignty no longer has the inflexibility which it had in those days. Serbia promised to mend its ways and accepted the ultimatum except for one of the main demands: it refused to allow Austrian officials to investigate the past history of the assassination in Serbia. It acted in this way because it was sure of Russian help and because it was incited to resistance by Russia. Thereupon Austria declared war on Serbia hastily, imperturbably, in order, as Berchthold put it, to present Europe with a *fait accompli*.

Now Russia intervened. The self-appointed guardian of all the Slavs could not accept the violation of a small, brave people by a great power, or whatever the phrases were that flowed from the pens of monarchs and ministers. Unless Austria immediately gave up its war against Serbia, Russia would mobilize. At first this mobilization was aimed only at Austria and involved only part of Russia's military force. Then, however, Russia decided after all on complete mobilization because a partial mobilization would ruinously confuse the general plan of campaign. Therefore there was full scale mobilization, against Germany as well. After all, was Germany not the mainstay of the alliance of the Central Powers? Without encouragement from Germany Austria's self-assertion was inexplicable. It was true that Germany had encouraged Austria in every way. Now that the ultimatum and declaration of war had been issued, now that shrill warnings disturbed summery Europe and that improbable and terrible events suddenly seemed close at hand, Berlin ceased to give further encouragement. Bethmann Hollweg sent restraining, even imploring, telegrams to Vienna. But they were neutralized by a very different kind of advice which the Prussian Chief of the General Staff, von Moltke telegraphed to Austria: they must immediately place their whole army on a war footing. 'What a joke!' said Berchthold. 'Who's in charge in Berlin?' This was it. In Berlin many different authorities had long been issuing parallel or contradictory orders. But when war was heralded the war machine, perfected over decades, and its chief engineers, the generals, took over command. What the civilians did was, whether they knew it or not, mere sham activity. They continued to try. London made three proposals for a settlement; to hold a conference of the great powers as during the Balkan war; to bring the Austro–Serb conflict before the International Court at The Hague; and to initiate direct negotiations between Vienna and St Petersburg. The last proposal at least was not rejected by Berlin. But before it could be put into practice Nicholas II ordered the mobilization of the whole Russian army; and before the completion of this process, which required weeks or months, the German military leaders decided to strike. Of what avail was it that William and Nicholas exchanged brotherly telegrams imploring one another to be reconciled just this once more, for the last time, to give way and to save the peace? The machines of war were stronger than the fear and premonition that now belatedly seized the rulers. On 1 August, in the words of the chivalrous German ambassador, 'the Kaiser, my noble master, [has accepted] the Russian challenge in the name of the Reich'.

The rest was like the unfolding of a familiar process. France had been Russia's ally for a quarter of a century. German strategy envisaged an all-out attack on Paris through Belgium and northern France; it was essential to defeat France before Russia could deploy its full strength. Then, secure in the West, Germany could turn against the East. But France would not remain neutral, moreover it must not remain neutral, because Germany could not allow an undefeated enemy or dubious neutral to rule in the West. What German diplomacy proposed to demand in Paris in case of need, the surrender of the French frontier fortifications as a pledge of good behaviour, was tantamount to forcing France to go to war. But the occasion did not arise. The answer which Paris gave to the first of the German questions was such that no further banter was needed. On 2 August Germany declared war on France, a tactical mistake but unimportant for the seekers after truth. Even without the German initiative France would have gone to war.

There had been no great European war in modern times in which Britain had not taken part, and there could not be according to the time honoured rules of British policy. Britain would dearly have liked to prevent the war, but if this was impossible then it must sooner or later join in to see that the struggle ended in the right way. In this instance it was necessary to intervene fairly soon because the war would be a quick one in which the first weeks would be decisive. Moreover, the British general staff had long ago entered into various agreements with the French which, though not binding, were more committing than the nation knew. In other circumstances Britain would have found it very difficult to enter the war. Cabinet, parliament and electorate were predominantly pacifist and would not readily have recognized the semi-obligations into which Sir Edward Grey, the Foreign Secretary, had secretly entered. What made the desired end possible all at once was the German invasion of Belgium, or more accurately Belgian resistance. If Belgium had crumbled under the weight of Germany's crushing force with a mere protest, the indignation of the British could not have been translated into such prompt action. But Belgium hit back and addressed heart-rending cries of help to the powers which had guaranteed its neutrality in 1839. Britain now had a good reason for going to war.

On one side there were Germany and Austria; on the other Russia, France and Britain. Russia was there because of Serbia, Britain because of Belgium, and France, according to the official formula, to do 'what its interests demanded'. Austria was there to score its small, local, silly triumph in the Balkans, and Germany to win the war. It attacked not to conquer a particular thing but to win; once war was almost certain Germany had to make quite certain of it by attacking quickly because by this method, and this method alone, could its military plan be successfully executed. Bethmann-Hollweg openly admitted this motive to the Reichstag. 'Should we,' he asked, 'have continued to wait until the powers wedging us in chose the moment to attack? To expose Germany to this danger would have been a crime.' Europe was so civilized in those days and Bethmann Hollweg was so honest that he admitted the wrong done to Belgium in unequivocal terms.

Our troops have occupied Luxembourg and perhaps already Belgian territory. This is contrary to international law ... We shall undo the wrong that we are doing as soon as our military objective has been achieved. Someone who is threatened, as we are, and fights for his all can think only of how to cut his way through.

The minutes of the proceedings record 'tremendous emotion, stormy and prolonged applause' after these words.

2. The War Guilt Question

Ex-Chancellor Bülow, who hung about jobless in Berlin in the days following the outbreak of war provides us in his memoirs with a vivid picture of the responsible men as he found them. He saw the Kaiser, looking 'pallid, frightened, I might almost say, desperate,' with flickering eyes 'excited and yet exhausted'. He saw the 'incredibly helpless and sad expression' in the eyes of the Chancellor and asked him: 'How on earth do you think this happened?' 'Bethmann raised his long arms to heaven and said in a dull voice: "Heaven knows".' Nothing could describe the situation more accurately. The men who to the world appeared as the ruthless authors of the war did not know what had happened to them.

They were sincere when they said that they had not wanted it. They had thought that all might end well once more and although they had been conscious of the danger that things might end badly they had not really taken it seriously and fully into account. They had asked nobody for advice – not the political party leaders, not the experienced diplomats whom Germany possessed, not the travelled businessmen such as Albert Ballin or Rathenau, not the great political theorists, Hans Delbrück or Max Weber. Monarch, Chancellor, Secretary of State, Under-Secretary of

State and a few ambassadors had acted secretly, as they pleased, from the first day of the crisis, until the moment when the heavy hand of the general staff descended on the helm of the ship of state. They ought to have restrained Austria and they could of course have done so. Instead they encouraged Austria, allowed it to do what it wanted, sabotaged the British mediation proposals and only started to warn Vienna when it was too late. The Kaiser was his own master, but only too quickly became the prisoner of the decisions which he had irresponsibly taken in the first moments. When the reaction of the others was different from what he had expected, when the improbable became probable, when one nation anticipated the military decisions of the other and the weight of the military machinery began to crush the increasingly feeble efforts of the diplomats, the Kaiser lacked the strength or the courage to turn back. He was secretly convinced, as were all the others, that what everyone feared must happen sooner or later and that it might just as well happen now. There is ample evidence to suggest that he was unhappy, had terrible premonitions about the outcome, and did not think that Germany was taking the initiative. In fact Germany had surrendered the initiative early on. Thereafter its only activity had been to refuse to moderate or to undo what it had partly brought about, while all round reactions occurred which the Germans in turn regarded as initiatives. This explains their feeling that they had been attacked and that they had done nothing positive to start the war.

The theory which equates mobilization with war may seem strange to us today when the great powers are permanently mobilized. In 1914 this was not, however, a specifically German view; Russian and French strategists had also secretly accepted it. But they were not anxious to have it publicly sanctioned because the Russian mobilization needed time and should take place undisturbed. It was the object of German strategy to prevent the enemy from enjoying this period of 'war in peacetime'; so Germany, and Germany alone, thought that it must translate the equation of mobilization with war into reality as quickly as possible. For the others whose strategy was not based on speed the situation was different. They saw in Germany's hasty declaration of war on Russia an attack, if a preventive one. Bethmann Hollweg with his question 'should we have waited until the others attacked?' himself admitted the preventive nature of Germany's action. The poor man never got over the qualms of conscience which the affair caused him. History has disproved the military argument on which Germany based its hasty action. The plan miscarried; France was never eliminated. Nevertheless the German army finally managed to get the better of Russia – an illustration of the old truth that politics should not be based on the uncertain calculations of the military. In this instance William II was cleverer politically than his generals. He would dearly have liked to reverse course at the last moment and to turn the whole of Germany's military strength against the East, provided Britain would guarantee the neutrality of France. But Britain did not do so and the German general staff insisted on carrying out its own plan.

Could there have been a compromise between Austria and Serbia? For the moment, yes. If Count Berchthold had been a little more restrained, if he had not actually wanted war against Serbia, which, as we know, he did, he would have been sure of diplomatic success. What would have happened if the Serb government had accepted the Austrian ultimatum in all its points? Not much. Such an acceptance would have made it absolutely impossible for the Austrians to go to war; whereupon a few Austrian officials sent to Serbia to investigate the assassination would have presented a spectacle of helplessness. The excuse that such a visit was incompatible with the Serb constitution can hardly be taken seriously; things which were still less in accordance with the constitution happened in Serbia. The Austrian Cabinet wanted its little war against Serbia in order to strengthen the position of the Habsburg monarchy, and was prepared to accept the risk of a great war. The readiness of the Serbs to play the Austrian game instead of withdrawing from it by making what in substance was an insignificant sacrifice shows that they too accepted the war, not the little one but the great one which alone could bring them salvation and gain. They considered political unification with national groups with which they later lived in not very happy union sufficient reward for a Russo–Austro–German–French war. They acted as they did because they were sure of Russian help.

If the chain of cause and effect was strongest at the places of origin of the crisis, that is in Vienna and Belgrade, the responsibility did not diminish in proportion to the distance from the immediate scene of action. In spite of all frivolity, narrow-mindedness and orthodoxy, the Austrian diplomats could claim that in the last resort the existence of something was at stake without which they could not imagine either the world or themselves, the Danubian monarchy. Official Russia had nothing comparable to risk. What for the Austrian state were questions of life and death were for the Russians marginal matters, questions of prestige, and fictitious aims. Even if the whole of Serbia had temporarily been occupied by the Austrians Russia's safety would not have been threatened. It is said that Russia had a sensible reason for being interested in Serb independence; it did not want the Germans in Constantinople, it wanted buffer states between the German powers and the Straits. But in the reaction of Russian nationalism against Austria there was more hysteria, more drivel about 'Slav brotherhood', more hankering after war than sound commonsense. The fictitious character of the Russian 'friendships' in the Balkan peninsula is illustrated by the example of Bulgaria, for whose foundation, existence and expansion Russia had struggled in Bismarck's time, only to discover very soon in Bulgaria its Balkan enemy and to embrace Serbia instead. Only for deluded and frightened politicians would such friendships have been worth a war.

France's attitude was one of icy correctness. The French did not oppose the British attempts at mediation, neither did they do anything to stop the hasty Russian mobilization which it is said they regretted. They preferred war to a diplomatic defeat and did nothing to minimize such a defeat in time, in order to make it acceptable. Their main concern was to be the attacked, the innocent in this war. With the best will in the world one cannot say that they displayed much imagination, passion or human greatness in preventing it.

Britain's position was different. There alone the seriousness with which people took the crisis corresponded more or less to the seriousness of the situation, there alone people knew more or less what was at stake. Later it became fashionable to say that Sir Edward Grey, the Foreign Secretary, could have prevented the war if he had made a timely and determined stand and had frightened Germany off; but it must be remembered that, given the British mentality and the British constitution, he could not make an early stand. Moreover, he must have feared that an open promise of help would tempt Russia and France to adopt an even more intransigent attitude. He could no longer do the right thing in the poisoned situation of that summer; error and danger lurked whichever way he turned. At least he tried desperately.

Nobody knew what anybody else would do. This was the basis of the risk, of the bluff, the sportsmanship of the affair; this has always been the basis of the game of politics. Even in a game of chess the players have to keep their plans secret. The fact that nations and states are not pawns to be played with is in conflict with the character of the sovereign state and the conventions of a so-called foreign policy itself; efforts are being made to do away with them in our day, so far without success. We know at any rate that merely to announce what one is going to do is not enough to solve problems of foreign policy and to prevent wars. In the light of the experiences of 1914 it has become fashionable since the thirties to list, frequently and loudly, all the issues on which one is going to go to war. This did not help in 1939 and probably does not help much today. During the war the most fantastic war aims were put forward in Germany, occasionally by the government or its officials, more often by politically irresponsible groups, associations, writers or generals. The provisions of the Treaty of Brest-Litovsk were also fantastic. It is easy to conclude that there must be a connection between war aims and the cause of the war. It is sensible if one has an aim to use those means, and only those, that are likely to lead to its realization; the aim becomes the reason for the means. In order to make the conclusion convincing it is necessary only to prove that expansionist aims – if not always identical with those thought up during the war – had been in the air in Germany before the war.

To say, however, that there was a 'connection' is not saying anything very definite. Nobody denies that the German feeling of not being 'satisfied' existed even before 1914, that it was strong and helped to create the atmosphere, the expectation of war and the preparedness for it. But it is not possible therefore to jump to conclusions as to the real cause of the war. If it were, the same yardstick could be applied to others who also had aims, less extreme aims perhaps but more precise aims that were clearly circumscribed by geography and history and so had greater weight. France had designs on Alsace-Lorraine, and Russia on Constantinople, which it was in fact promised in the secret treaties of 1916 and which had been a notorious Russian objective long before 1916. If war aims are proof of war guilt then all were guilty to a greater or lesser degree and it only remains to ask in whose favour the difference of degree operated. While the Russians knew what they wanted the Germans did not; at one time they wanted only a little, at another a great deal; they set their sights high in one place and low in another, and vice versa, and for four years they argued passionately about their war aims. In what other country was there a 'war aims discussion' of the kind that went on in Germany?

Historians make the point that the others also had aims, but that they were marginal aims that could have been achieved without war. Germany being centrally situated – 'hemmed in' as Bethmann Hollweg put it – could not realize its imperial dreams without breaking out or 'exploding', without making itself master of the Continent. People had long prophesied Germany's impending explosion. Such prophecies help to explain how a world war became possible, they do not represent a chain of cause and effect.

In the whole German–Austrian dialogue of July 1914, in the telegrams, the protocols, the top secret documents, there was no mention of Germany's imperial aims. There were references to the need to put an end to the intolerable conditions on Austria's southern frontiers, to the necessity of supporting the country's wavering ally because it had no other. It was said that if there must be a war it had better happen now rather than later. Very rarely, in the most intimate discussions, there were hints that, if all were to end well, the ring round Germany, the Franco–Russian alliance, would be broken. Then, when Russia started, at first in secret, to prepare for action, there was mention of the threat of an undisturbed Russian mobilization occurring in peacetime. And this fear pure and simple overwhelmed everything and decided everything. There was not a word about imperialist aims. Of course, it is possible to argue that these people kept their innermost thoughts to themselves. But they did not. William II never made more incredible off-the-cuff statements than in July 1914. If the idea that Germany needed the war because it wanted to conquer something or other had crossed his mind he would have been the last person not to write it down; during the war, in fact, he did not hesitate to put down on paper or to voice the most ridiculous ideas on those lines; but not during the crisis. When he realized that the peace was lost the Kaiser poured all his sorrow and fury into the remark that if Germany must bleed to death Britain should at least be deprived of India. This is not the language of a conqueror.

No other historical question has been so thoroughly examined as the question of the responsibility for the war of 1914. In Germany there was a journal called *Die Kriegsschuldfrage* (The War Guilt Question) and there were university chairs whose holders concerned themselves with almost nothing else. The reason lies largely in the tactlessness of the victorious Allies who, boldly anticipating the findings of scholars, prejudged their own case by including in the peace treaty a reference to Germany's sole guilt for the war. On this paragraph they based their demand for reparations; therefore in order to destroy the whole moral and legal foundation of the Versailles Treaty German historians only had to refute the theory that Germany alone was responsible for the war. Hence the fervour with which scholars on both sides devoted themselves to unscholarly ends. Now at last the actors of the drama of 1914 are all dead and the young volunteers of those days are old men. Now that this bloody story has moved sufficiently far into the background and is overshadowed by more recent and even more wicked misdeeds, it has become possible to describe it, without scholars having to quarrel over it – to describe it as it really was, with its guilt and partial guilt, with its human inadequacy everywhere.

3. Moods

All thought they were being attacked, kings, diplomats and nations. Logically this was not correct; if all are attacked nobody attacks and nobody is attacked. Reality, however, does not aspire to be logical. In fact Russia thought itself attacked by the Austrian action against Serbia, and Germany by the Russian mobilization; to some extent the conflagration was self-igniting and as a result everybody accused someone else and everybody saw himself as the victim. But at the same time they were all happy to be attacked. There was jubilation in Europe in the early days of August 1914, as well as aggressive fury and aggressive enthusiasm. The feeling differed in intensity from country to country; in France it was probably somewhat less strong than in Germany, where it was a little stronger than in Britain. But it existed also in Britain. Even in London the masses thronged the streets clamouring for war while the Cabinet made its last feeble peace gestures. For years the peoples of Europe had been set against each other and deceived by politicians and journalists. Yet it would be wrong to say that at this moment in their heart of hearts they wanted to preserve the peace. The war would be short and glorious, an exciting, liberating adventure. God would be on everybody's side and everybody would win.

This mood was particularly prevalent in Germany because the Germans had after all been the first to attack. They had acted with lightning speed before the enemy could tighten his net. They had been attacked, they were innocent and yet they had been the first to unsheathe their swords. Could there be a nobler combination? And then there was the feeling that at last there was action, that at last the plans prepared over many years were being put to the test. That the boredom of everyday life was being interrupted by an adventurous holiday which allowed the little man, the employee, the young teacher, not only to leave his job but to be a hero into the bargain. That there was a fatherland again, one that was in great danger and for which men were allowed to risk their lives instead of remaining eternally shut up in the prison of their own insignificant designs. That at last there was a nation again instead of parties and classes, instead of futile quarrels. Soon flags and gun salutes proclaimed the first victories. How wonderful to take part in all this as a soldier or at least as a patriot in civilian clothing; how sad to be excluded. Such was the mood in August 1914. Even the most level-headed, the most intelligent people were affected by it. Professor Max Weber, the severe, melancholy realist whom we have already met, wrote about 'this great and wonderful war', how splendid it was to be there to see it, how very sad not to be allowed to fight because of his age. Philosophers, aesthetes and aristocratic poets who had always kept aloof suddenly felt in touch with the people and were happy because of it. The long years of division between the state and the intellectuals, the years of satirical comment, were forgotten. They volunteered for military service, they wanted to fight with the rifle or the pen; in crude manifestoes and elegant essays, in bad or good poems they praised the awakening of the nation.

By nature man oscillates between egoism and the desire to destroy himself for a great cause. The peaceful years of William II's reign had made too few demands on the general desire to serve the community. Now it was satisfied by the war which seemed to need everybody. Hence the general feeling of happiness.

A few kept aloof from the start, half-Germans or writers who in character had become half-Germans. They gradually increased in number because the feeling of happiness was deceptive. The desire to serve the community is praise-worthy but a state of intoxicated enthusiasm cannot satisfy it in the long run. In August 1914 war showed its most attractive and most deceptive side, but not for long.

Of the political parties the extreme right had fanned the crisis to the best of its ability. The groups which had always regarded German policy under William II as 'too half-hearted' now spurred on the weak monarch; we shall meet them again during the war years. The Social Democrats kept their heads. For many years they had prepared themselves for the hour of danger, had protested at interparliamentary congresses against the armaments race and imperialism, and had agreed with their French colleagues on joint action to prevent war before it happened and to stop it if it should come. Now they condemned the Austrian ultimatum in words which still ring true today. They organized meetings in Berlin designed to counter-balance the frenzy of the war enthusiasts, the pan-German professors, Father Jahn's gymnasts and the bearded veterans of 1870. So far so good. But then came the news of the Russian mobilization which even to the Social Democrats seemed equal to an attack. They too were Germans and good patriots and their dearly won liberties too would be in danger if the Tsar's despotism triumphed over Germany. They were not responsible for the mistakes of either the distant or the recent past for they had protested against them while there was time. Now, on 31 July, they sent one of their number, Hermann Müller, to Paris to establish contact with their French colleagues as arranged. The French told him that their own situation was quite different from that of the Germans, that they had not been deceived by their government, that they could exert legitimate pressure on the actions of their republic and that as France was being attacked by Germany they must stand by their threatened country. It was for the German workers to protest against the war crime of their own state. Müller replied that the danger did not come from Berlin but from St Petersburg, and that the German workers must resist that threat. He just managed to get out of France; his report to the Berlin party executive was not an encouraging one.

The German Reichstag had nothing to do with the declaration of war which was a matter for the Kaiser and his advisers alone. But it had to approve the expenditure, the credits required to fight the war. This was where it could express approval or disapproval of the situation and its attendant demands. After passionate discussions the Social Democrats decided to vote for the credits. The minority, fourteen members who thought differently to the end, submitted to party discipline. As a reward a representative of the Social Democrats was allowed to speak after the Chancellor's statement:

... The Social Democrats have fought this fateful development with all their strength; they have worked until the final hour to preserve peace by organizing powerful demonstrations in all countries, particularly in close understanding with their French comrades. Their efforts have been in vain. Now we face the iron fact of war. We are threatened by the horror of enemy invasion ... Much, if not all, will be at stake for our people and its future freedom if Russian despotism, stained by the blood of the best of its own people, is victorious ...

To defend one's country, one's civilization, was in accordance with the ideas of the Socialist International; a war of conquest, however, was not. Peace must be made as soon as Germany's opponents were prepared to do so and it must be a peace of friendship and justice likely to last.

Bethmann Hollweg, who had long been anxious to establish contact with the Social Democrats, was delighted by their attitude. The Conservatives were less delighted about the positive and leading role which their left-wing opponents seemed to assume. 'The golden opportunity which we have provided for the Social Democrats to take a position which they would probably have had to adopt anyway may later bring them great advantages', said the Chairman of the parliamentary Conservative Party, Count Westarp. This was one of the paradoxes in which modern history is so rich. The war, to the extent that it was a German undertaking, resulted from the distorted, tense class situation. For the rulers, probably subconsciously rather than consciously, the purpose of the war was to preserve this situation. But this purpose the war could never achieve. The war of the masses could not be fought unless the masses and their party, the Social Democrats, co-operated and worked with the government; the war thus brought about the situation that it was meant to prevent. On the other hand the Social Democrats did not join the government on their own terms. They could not mould it to their image. What now gave the state its identity was not the Kaiser and the Junkers nor democracy and socialism, but the war itself, and it did so increasingly in the years to come. Bethmann succeeded in arranging a truce between the parties. Domestic conflicts would be postponed until the external threat had been overcome.

Critics later charged the German Social Democrats with treason for their decision of August 1914. This is easily done in retrospect. At the time even the future Communist, Karl Liebknecht, voted for war credits; reluctantly, but he did. That was the position, in Germany as in France. The war could have been prevented by diplomacy and we have seen that German diplomacy was about the worst possible. It was the fault of German history and of all those who shared in it that a few bunglers had been allowed to determine German foreign policy. It was no longer possible to withstand the storm of August 1914. It swept through the whole nation, and the German workers who voted Socialist were a part of the nation and of the state, to a far greater degree than Marxist theory would allow. This fact now became clear. Happiness unites men. If the war was a disaster, at first it was one that brought happiness to all those who were affected by it. The trouble came later, and it was only later that parties and classes once more turned against each other.

About the same is true of the German states, the members of the Bismarckian Federal Empire – with the difference that the states were much weaker than parties and classes. Foreign policy had long been the responsibility of the Reich and not of Prussia. The Reich, not Prussia, had become Russia's enemy. What business had Prussia in Constantinople, what interests had Prussia in Serbia? Nothing would please a convinced federalist more than to be able to say that Prussia had dragged southern Germany into the First World War. But that is not true. The whole of Germany flung itself into the war; the mood was as bellicose in Munich as in Berlin. The dynasties and governments of the states were compelled to take part as they had been compelled in 1870 and 1813; after all they too were German. What they thought in private, how an intelligent man like Prince Rupprecht of Bavaria felt, is difficult to say. He could prevent nothing; all he could do later as commander of an army group was to utter impotent warnings about the degeneration of the war. The German dynasties, William II apart, bear no blame for the First World War. It was not in their interest because its consequences were bound in one way or another to be revolutionary. It was a German, a 'greater' German war, not one that was in the interest of Bavaria or Baden. If they are to blame it is because they did not try to correct Berlin's foreign policy in time, as Bavaria, for example, could have done with a little energy and wisdom. Political theorists regard federalism and parliamentary government as irreconcilable. In the fateful question of German foreign policy both had failed, the national parliament and the federal states. Now they both had to follow the lead of the forces that for the moment alone remained, the military leaders and the people.

Germany's young men marched off to the field of battle, conscripts and volunteers, pure in heart, as it was said. Strictly speaking this is a somewhat romantic description of the situation because they travelled by train, but pure in heart they certainly were. They did not know that politics had not been pure and preferred not to know it even later when scholars proved it to them. Their own experience led them to a different conclusion. They marched, as it was further said, 'against a world of enemies'. But why had a world of enemies descended on Germany? And why Germany? An American student on holiday in the country that he admired, who was caught in the storm of the last crisis, wrote to his mother on 28 July from Dresden:

Last night the streets were filled by masses of people singing patriotic songs until two o'clock in the morning and shouting 'long live Austria', which had just declared war on Serbia. The situation looks very critical and I am afraid these warlike Germans may start a conflict that will become the most terrible war the world has ever seen. [He went on:] The threat of war ... drives the whole world mad. I became very thoughtful when I heard masses of young people march through the streets long past midnight singing *Die Wacht am Rhein*. Their activities

will give the statesmen ... a good excuse for their own folly, because
they can say that they were forced into it by the enthusiasm of the
masses ...

In August, on his way home, he wrote: 'The clockwork of
Europe has come to a complete stop, and the civilization that I
used to admire so much is so clearly tearing itself to pieces that
I can no longer bear to think of Europe ...'

4. Frustrated Plans

Europe was strong in those days. Although it had finally lost its
nerve over all the diplomatic crises and gone to war, it was healthy
enough to fight the war as no war had ever been fought since there
were men on earth. All the capital accumulated by the richest
continent in a hundred peaceful years of unparalleled industrial
progress, all the knowledge, all the assembled strength and
courage and exuberance were now devoted to one purpose. All
countries believed that they were the victims of attack, but all
attacked. All general staffs – German, French, Austrian and
Russian – had long prepared and nurtured grand offensive plans
which they now put into action. The German plan was as simple
as it was daring. It envisaged two offensives, a sham one from
Lorraine, meant to draw off the enemy, and a real one through
Belgium and northern France. This would outflank Paris and,
turning eastwards west of Paris, encircle the French armies. The
French plan fitted in well with this scheme because its highlight
was an offensive against Alsace-Lorraine, continuing, if possible,
across the Rhine. The Austrians intended to advance from
Galicia against the Russian armies in Poland, whereas the
Russians had their eye on the Austrian front in Galicia. After six
weeks nothing was left of any of these plans and elaborate
stratagems. It is said that the German plan was watered down and
badly executed, that the Chief of the German General Staff, von
Moltke, fatally weakened the right wing on which everything

depended while strengthening the left wing unnecessarily; that at the last moment he transferred to East Prussia two army corps needed in the West. Whether the outcome would have been different without these mistakes is for the military experts to decide. Wars have almost never gone according to plan; sooner or later they have developed in a way not foreseen by the strategists on either side.

The failure of the French offensive in the South was the first indication of the fact that in this war defence was stronger than attack. The French troops were hastily withdrawn and reorganized for the defence of Paris. To start with the German offensive in the North was successful and Belgium and northern France were occupied; but then confusion began. Some German armies were too far forward, others too far back; there was a lack of contact between headquarters and the commanders in the field, there were gaps between the moving armies. The Germans improvised; they tried to encircle the enemy more narrowly than originally planned. Then the French mounted a concentrated counter-offensive and the Germans withdrew. Not in a panic, not ceding much ground, from one small river, the Marne, to the next, the Aisne. 'The enemy is not pursuing anywhere,' announced the German High Command communiqué of 10 September. 'The spoils of the battle so far amount to fifty guns and several thousand prisoners.' This was a polite way of telling the German people that the great plan had failed. The high Command maintained the same polite tradition for the next four years.

In October and November the Germans tried to reach the Channel ports in order to cut France off from Britain. This move also went well up to a certain point and then came to a standstill.

From then on, November 1914 to March 1918, nothing much happened on the Western front. Only offensives and counter-offensives in the places where the enemy was strongest; slaughter with ever more effective means of mass extermination. But the front never moved more than about six miles.

If things did not go according to plan in the West, they did not go according to plan in the East either; but there because the Germans were triumphant. Two Russian armies which, in order to relieve France, had tried a premature, badly prepared invasion of East Prussia were attacked so successfully in the last days of August that nothing remained of them. The defeat was not yet decisive; the main Russian force was still to come. But it was very important for German morale and the name 'Battle of Tannenberg', alluding to a German defeat of long ago in the struggle against the Slavs, was well chosen. This time it was the Germans who had humiliated the Slavs at Tannenberg in a way that they would never forget. This was the first occasion on which enormous numbers were mentioned, 100,000, 250,000 enemy soldiers killed or taken prisoner; old and young were shown pictures of dead or drowning, headless or limbless Russians being blown sky high. The public attitude hardened quickly; perfectly civilized people liked to read about the fronts where life was anything but civilized. There appeared before the Germans the two faces that were to look down on them for the next four years; one with an enormous moustache, old, square, good natured, dignified and sly, the other elongated by a heavy chin, hard, angular and surly: Hindenburg, the general commanding in East Prussia, and Ludendorff, his chief of staff. It soon became public knowledge that Ludendorff was the master mind, the real victor of Tannenberg; but this did not affect the new myth. They belonged together like Blücher and Gneisenau, like William I and Bismarck, and where the confident authority of the old man and the ability of the other were combined all must end well. They became the heirs of the 'success myth' which had been waiting for a new incarnation since the fall of Bismarck and the decline of William II. Soon it was no longer the Kaiser to whom people looked for leadership and salvation nor the new chief of staff of the army, Falkenhayn, but Hindenburg and Ludendorff. In spite of the victories in the East, in August and December, the war developed into something that no one had foreseen. There was too much reserve strength on both sides, in the form of industry, human beings and combative spirit. Both sides threw quantities into the battle the like of which in sheer destructive force had never been seen before. If this had been more or less expected, the completely unexpected factor was that defence proved stronger than attack. Not in the East where the Russians had already lost irreplaceable reserves of arms and munitions, and where the Germans could count on the superiority of their industry, but in the West. The defensive positions, mine-fields, wire entanglements and trenches, covered by artillery, which started as improvisations and were later developed with the utmost thoroughness, were stronger at this historical moment than the strategy of attack which was based on the experiences of the preceding century. But the spring and autumn attacks con-tinued. So far neither the French and the British nor the Germans had any doubt that the decisive action must be taken in the West. That had been the original plan and it was preserved although it was plain for all to see that it had failed, and although no one had any clear idea of how such action could still be taken.

Hence the tentative search for other possibilities, for new theatres of war and new ways of fighting. Hence the wooing of uncommitted states, the attempt to lure neutrals into the war, as a morphine addict tries to make others share his vice. The Entente succeeded in grabbing Italy in the spring of 1915, the Germans Bulgaria in the following autumn and the Entente Rumania in the summer of 1916. The newcomers were promised loot and they chose the side that could promise the most, provided it promised victory; in the autumn of 1915 the Bulgarians apparently regarded a German victory as probable. Hence also the cruel perfection of economic warfare. The British strengthened their blockade of German ports, allowing the neutrals to import only what they needed for themselves and pursuing a system of control and confiscation on the high seas hitherto unknown to international law. If the law did not allow them to behave in this way their superior navy did. The German navy, which had done so much to poison Anglo-German relations, stayed idle in port; Tirpitz, its creator, at imperial headquarters felt the most useless, unhappy person in the world. 'My position here is permanently unpleasant because I am really superfluous . . . I now think that it [the navy] will not fire a shot and my life's work will have been wasted.' The Kaiser let it be known that the navy was of some use because it defended the north German coastline. The Germans were left with the submarine and the torpedoing of enemy ships.

Soon this weapon was used against passenger ships suspected of carrying war material from the United States to Britain; the war was not a year old when the sinking of the British liner *Lusitania* and the drowning of 1,200 civilians caused indignation both among Germany's enemies and the neutrals. 'It is very curious how we have become the most unpopular nation on earth,' wrote Tirpitz as early as the autumn. Crimes like the sinking of the *Lusitania* made it all too easy for enemy propaganda to make this statement come true. Looked at from a distance, it is debatable whether they were worse than the blockade designed gradually to strangle life in Germany; at any rate they were incomparably more terrible for the nerves of a world that had not quite forgotten the habits of peace. The adversaries led each other on. Each was convinced that the other was a barbarian, his country's mortal enemy, motivated by a mad destructive urge; in dealing with the opponent it was therefore necessary to use means that would be understood, and if it was impossible to retaliate with the same weapon similar and if possible even fiercer ones must be used. Of course, everybody claimed to be acting under duress.

What then was the point of this terrible war that nobody wanted, that in cruelty transcended anything that man had so far known; this war with its minefields and its corpses, its flame-throwers and wire entanglements in which the wounded died a slow death, its hunger blockade and counter-blockade? How should the war be brought to an end? What were its aims, what purpose did it serve? Did it serve any purpose at all? These questions were discussed, thought about and quarrelled over from the late autumn of 1914 onwards.

5. *War Aims and Domestic Friction*

The theory of the western powers was simple. They had been attacked by the most ruthless military despotism that had ever been. They proved their point by reference to the history of the immediate pre-war years, ignoring anything discreditable to them; to speeches by William II and to gleanings from German literature, Nietzsche, Treitschke and pan-German zealots. They were not worried by the fact that they had gathered together a curious assortment; war propaganda is prepared for tough stomachs. Their objective was to break German militarism and everything else was of secondary importance. Prusso-German policy had not taken a despotic turn only yesterday, it had always been monolithic; therefore the occasion must be used also to redress past wrongs: France must regain Alsace-Lorraine. It was even possible to justify the enormous promises made at Austria's expense to Italy in order to entice it into the war; after all Italy would only be given things to which it had an historical, national, geographical or other claim. Other, more secret, agreements fitted less well into the beautiful picture; for example, Constantinople's being promised to Russia, or indeed the fact of the alliance with Tsarism which even the most brazen propaganda could not pass off as democratic. The argument there was that Russia was a special case, a military not a moral ally; that the war was nevertheless a war between peace-loving, Western democracy and Teutonic barbarism.

This line of argument was effective. It was believed in varying degrees even by those who invented it and spread it assiduously in the neutral world. The task of the Allied propaganda was made easier by the fact that German troops were everywhere in occupation of foreign territory and behaved as troops have always behaved on enemy territory. The U-boat war also helped. Given the British line peace negotiations became very difficult. How was it possible to make peace with an enemy who was a 'hun', a criminal unique in the annals of humanity? As the war became more vicious the propaganda which provided its intellectual foundations also became more vicious and peace became proportionately more difficult.

If this was the generally accepted view of the situation in Britain and France, a view which also became increasingly popular in the United States, there was no such common line of thought in Germany. Here everything, the origin of the war, the means with which it should be fought, its aims abroad and its effects at home, was judged on the basis of party loyalty, personal sympathy, desire and caprice.

The Allies had only one enemy, Germany (the fact that Austria had actually started the affair was quickly forgotten). The question which the Germans were soon asking themselves was who was their chief enemy. Hardly France; only for the older generation who remembered 1870. Russia? That was the view of the German left, of all those whose thinking was inspired by the tradition of 1848, who saw despotic Russia as the enemy of a progressive, democratic 'greater' Germany. Or Britain? That was soon the most widely and ardently held belief. The belief of the pan-Germans, of the navy, of the patriotic professors, of the right in general, and then, under the impression of the blockade, probably also the mass of the people. The war, which the Germans had imagined as a continental war in the style of Moltke, was transformed by Britain into a world war; it deprived the German victories on land of their importance by isolating them. Britain brought into play the full strength of its national character, the whole force of its world-wide organizations and connections, of its dominions overseas; it was the bridge to America, and the channel through which all essential war material reached Germany's enemies in an uninterrupted stream. France and Russia had both been defeated more than once in modern times and had adapted themselves to defeat; Britain never. That was its glory, and its efforts were correspondingly great. Seen from that angle Britain was the fiercest of Germany's enemies. As Germany had nothing that Britain could want and as even the pan-Germans did not intend to make conquests at Britain's expense, it followed that the struggle between Britain and Germany was one of life and death. It was not a question of this or that possession but of survival. As the Germans saw it Britain envied Germany its new splendour, its industry, its trade, its power in Europe and over Europe; there were pre-war quotations from the British press to prove the point. Quietly, busily Britain had spun the poisonous web of the coalition; with unctuous words *Lügen-Grey* (liar Grey) had drawn it tight at the opportune moment.

> *Was schiert uns Russe and Franzos*
> *Schuss wider Schuss und Stoss wider Stoss*
> *Wir kämpfen den Kampf mit Bronze und Stahl*
> *Und schliessen Frieden irgend einmal.*
> *Dich werden wir hassen mit langem Hass*
> *Und werden nicht lassen von unserem Hass,*
> *Hass zu Wasser und Hass zu Land,*
> *Hass des Hauptes und Hass der Hand,*
> *Hass der Hämmer und Hass der Kronen,*
> *Drosselnder Hass von siebzig Millionen.*
> *Sie lieben vereint, sie hassen vereint,*
> *Sie haben alle nur einen Feind:* ENGLAND!*

The Germans deduced non-existing causes and motives from what was now an overwhelming fact. In the war Britain certainly seemed the toughest, most self-assured and most dangerous enemy. It had succumbed to the fascination of war just as much as every other country. It was less clever, less reasonable than the Germans assumed. For the sake of victory it forgot the more permanent Russian danger over the ephemeral German one; it used all its energy to help Russia to defeat the Germans, an endeavour which, if successful, was bound to cause the most terrible disturbance of the European balance of power; it even offered the Russians as a gift the very Constantinople which for centuries it had consistently tried to keep from Russia's grasp. Let Russia control the Straits, let it break into central Europe and into the Mediterranean, provided it helped the western powers to win. This was war mentality. In wartime it is not political sense that rules, but war – the generals or civilians who know how to wage it.

---

*What do we care about Russians and Frenchies; we repay shot with shot and blow with blow. We fight with bronze and with steel, and some day we shall make peace. But you we shall hate with lasting hatred and we shall not relent; hatred on the seas and hatred on land, hatred of the mind and hatred of the hand, hatred of the hammer and hatred of the crowns, strangling hatred of seventy millions. United in love and united in hatred they have only one enemy: England.

The war had no meaning. For something that has meaning war is not necessary. But once war is there people find a meaning for it; they cannot believe that all their sacrifices are meaningless. The leaders look for a meaning in order to fill the people with enthusiasm and to keep down despondency and indifference. The meaning of the German war therefore was to measure Germany against Britain, to punish Britain for jealously having wanted to destroy Germany's greatness. Those poor people everywhere – how they allowed themselves to be fooled, how they fooled themselves. How courageously, how patiently they bore the consequences; what sorrow, what immeasurable misery they suffered.

The Germans clung from the start to the view that the war was a defensive war, even if many of them were delighted to have been attacked. Soon, however, people began to say that defence alone was not enough, that moreover Germany was winning and that it was necessary to have positive aims, directed towards protection and territorial gain. The soil, the argument ran, on which German blood had been shed must remain German, for such great sacrifices must not have been in vain. Germany's enemies, who were making equally terrible sacrifices and also regarded themselves as having been attacked, had similar notions; as everybody intended to compensate himself at the expense of the other and to make sure that he would be safe in future a return to peace was made even more difficult.

The German government, which had stumbled into the war like all the rest, had at first no war aims and did not regard their public discussion as desirable. 'We had been attacked,' commented Bethmann Hollweg. 'Provided we stood our ground we were bound to win the war.' This was not the view of the 'war aims movement' led by the pan-Germans. In pamphlets, privately circulated at first but later published, at conferences and in committees 'for a German peace', this powerful group set about with its customary energy to prepare worthwhile war aims. It had the support of individual industrialists like Hugo Stinnes, Alfred Hugenberg and Emil Kirdorf, as well as of most of the big pressure groups: the Central Association of German Industrialists, the Farmers' Federation, the German Countrymen's Federation and the Association of the German Middle Classes. The appetite of these groups, stimulated by pan-German theorists, was considerable. To protect itself against Britain Germany must keep Belgium, as well as the French coast as far as the mouth of the Somme. Hugo Stinnes also demanded Normandy because of its ore deposits. Germany must settle its account with France by taking the belt of fortifications from Verdun to Belfort, and Toulon must become a German port. The possessions of France and Belgium in Africa must also fall to Germany. In the East Germany would keep the Baltic provinces and parts of Russian Poland. There was some disagreement on details, for example should these territories be taken over 'free from people', as the new expression went, or should the existing inhabitants be allowed to stay as German subjects, though not with equal rights. The aim was clear: 'autonomy', 'immortality for the German Reich which sufficient unto itself and independent from outside interference, will thus become truly free'. Strategic safeguards, economic safeguards, space and work for all Germans – the word *Lebensraum* had not yet become popular, but that was the idea.

The Prussian Conservatives did not associate themselves completely with such programmes, either because they were still genuine Prussians or because they were a little more experienced in political matters. In a letter to the chairman of the parliamentary party, von Heydebrand, von Westarp said that he had not been able to hold out longer against the pressure from the pan-Germans and the industrialists but that he was not very happy about giving way; 'we have gone pretty far in the East and also in the West'. Heydebrand spoke openly of the 'utopias and undiluted drivel' of the pan-Germans. But even Conservatives believed in the principle of a 'German peace' and of annexations.

The majority of politically conscious Germans shared this attitude. The leader of the National Liberal Party, Gustav Stresemann, and the very influential Centre member, Matthias Erzberger, advanced war aims not substantially different from those of the pan-Germans. Even such a severe critic of the war aims movement as the historian Hans Delbrück, a liberal and moderate man, did not deny the need for positive aims.

In Germany the position is different. We are the victors ... The whole German nation feels that we, first hemmed in and then attacked by a coalition partly envious and partly vindictive, can and must use our victory to secure our political future and to put our national future on so solid a basis that we shall remain at least equal in standing to the other great peoples of the world.

The aims had not led to the war but the war, once there, led to the aims. If the determination of the French to regain Alsace in no way proved their responsibility for the war, the same was true of the German aims; they too were a product of a war the like of which had never been experienced before. Yet a comparison of the aims of the two groups reveals something about the situation in which their countries found themselves. Even the most extravagant desires of the western allies were negative, amounting to a permanent weakening of Germany. Only Russia lusted after a big prize, Constantinople, the domination of the Balkans and of the peoples of Austria-Hungary. Only the Russian fanatics wanted, like the German fanatics, substantially to change the position of their country in the world; the Germans, however, had relatively speaking the more sweeping plans. Although even the most extreme among them did not want Germany to dominate the world, their aim was to achieve strategic and economic parity with the greatest powers. They did not want to found *the* universal empire but *one* such empire; they wanted to make themselves independent of Europe within its own narrow confines, to rule Europe and yet to remain a nation-state.

Among liberal professors it was fashionable to demand the acquisition of more favourable frontiers, while at the same time claiming that Germany was fighting for the freedom of all peoples, and to toss back at the Anglo-Saxons the accusation of wanting to dominate the world – so much so that the President of the United States, Woodrow Wilson, could comment ironically that as the two adversaries seemed to be fighting for the same aim it ought to be possible to find a basis for negotiation. Only German Social Democrats believed from the first day of the war to the last in the idea of peace without conquests, thus proving once again how superior their political education was to that of the middle classes. For them the war was a defensive war, and in spite of all victories, in spite of the vast territories which German armies occupied in Russia and in Poland, in the Balkans and in Belgium and France, they never wanted it to become anything else. The ablest advocate of this view became the deputy Philipp Scheidemann; no genius, to judge from his writings, but a man who enjoyed life, sensible and ebullient, who courageously tried to stem the tide of annexationism. A 'Scheidemann peace', his supporters called what he stood for; a 'feeble peace', a 'peace of renunciation' was what his opponents called it.

It is difficult to have sensible aims in the midst of an orgy of senselessness. To return to the pre-1914 situation, to the *status quo ante*, was to admit that the whole war was nonsense, an admission which none of the adversaries had the courage to make. As the war had started – that was the general feeling – it must be fought out; it was impossible to behave any longer as though nothing had happened. Even a 'peace without victors or vanquished', a return to normality, threatened to lead to anything but normal conditions. What would the peoples, the masses, do if they suddenly saw the whole enormous war effort as a cruel piece of foolery? How would the monarchy fare, and the long postponed reform of the constitution? And how would the whole affair be paid for? In Britain, where it was paid for largely from taxes, people believed that the war was making them poor, which it was. The German government on the other hand preferred the system of war loans, thus preserving the beautiful illusion that the cost of all this folly could later be paid back with interest. If this meant anything at all it meant that the vanquished would pay; in fact there was frequent reference to indemnity payments in the peace programme of the German patriots. 'The instigators of this war deserve to bear the leaden burden of milliards; let them – not us – carry it through the years.' But if there were no vanquished? It was a grey workaday that Germany was heading towards after such a long, fantastic holiday; burdened with problems each of which might well frighten the bravest. It was easier to go on, to win more battles and to risk ever more, since so much had been risked already.

It was like this everywhere; both sides really shied away from a negotiated peace, though neither was willing to admit it. This attitude was even more marked in Germany than elsewhere because Germany had thrown itself more deeply into the war than the western powers, because it was dominated even more completely by its evil geniuses.

Between the pan-Germans and the Social Democrats, between a 'German' and a 'Scheidemann peace', stood the official Reich, Kaiser and Chancellor. William II's star, long on the wane, faded quickly during the war years, giving way to the new twin suns of Hindenburg–Ludendorff. The old braggart had neither the ability nor the nerve to do what now needed doing. News of victory could still raise his spirits but on the whole he was inclined to depression and, if he had to take decisions, towards moderation; he was sufficiently far-sighted to recognize the consequences of the lost battle of the Marne. He snubbed the supporters of the war aims movement who tried to win him over. The man whom the world still regarded as the German leader, whom Allied propaganda pilloried as the bloodthirsty King of the Huns, as the 'beast of Berlin', was cowed and sad. Events and people had become too much for him. So long as the Kaiser had anything to say at all, until 1917, he protected his Chancellor.

Bethmann Hollweg tried to please everybody. He regarded himself as having everybody's confidence, particularly since party conflict had stopped as a consequence of the political truce. His policy, he later explained, could only be a 'diagonal' between the extremes. To draw a diagonal between the 'German' and the 'Scheidemann peace' was a difficult task. The holder of Bismarck's office was expected to be closer to the right than to the left. In fact, over the major questions of war and policy Bethmann was now closer to the left and tried sincerely to maintain fruitful contact with the Social Democrats. He neither supported nor disavowed the war aims movement. His criticism was always mild, his approval always cautious. He hoped for accommodation with Britain, for accommodation with the Tsar, for a revolution in Russia. He hated the war, the causes of which he did not understand; he always hoped, did little, and never chose between the possibilities, anxious to keep all doors open. Occasionally he boasted to please the Right: 'We went to war to defend ourselves. Meanwhile, however, the situation has changed. History has advanced with firm step; there is no turning back ...' Then again defence and nothing but defence, agreement and nothing but agreement were his objectives. Bethmann Hollweg, who tried to please everybody, pleased nobody; by some he was regarded as a defeatist, by others as an agitator, a situation in which he had found himself even before the war. This spelt the poor man's downfall; yet after him the situation did not improve; on the contrary.

In the democratic countries of the West strategic questions were decided by those whose job it was to decide them, ministers and generals. Germany had the reputation of having an autocratic government, yet less authority emanated from the crumbling semi-absolutism of the Hohenzollern than from any tolerably functioning parliament. Matters that ought to have been dealt with in secret by those who ran the war became the playthings of demagogues. The main subject of dispute was the submarine, how to use this new weapon. It was employed cautiously after neutral America had made threatening protests against its indiscriminate use; Bethmann Hollweg had no desire for new enemies, least of all for the enmity of the United States. The Admiralty led by Tirpitz, the vigorous Minister for the Navy, was incensed by Bethmann's caution, as were the circles which gave their support to the war aims movement, industrialists, professors, politicians and pan-German intriguers. America, they argued, was anyway Germany's enemy because it supplied the Entente with all its war requirements; even as a party to the war it could not do more. In the submarine Germany had the weapon with which to force Britain to its knees, provided it was ruthlessly employed and that every ship, neutral or hostile, trying to approach the enemy's coasts was sent to the bottom of the sea without warning. 'Unrestricted submarine warfare' became the catchphrase. The majority of the Reichstag, from the right to the Centre, believed in it; and the man in the street, the housewife who queued for skimmed milk and sugar beet jam, also hoped that it might help.

They believed what the military experts and the demagogues told them. The war which was becoming increasingly oppressive must end some day. And if the submarine weapon, used properly, could end it, why not use it? Why not get even with Britain for what its hunger blockade was doing to the Germans and give it a taste of its own medicine? Because of some false humanitarianism? Or perhaps because the Kaiser was half British? Or because the Chancellor kept his money in the Bank of England? Those were the arguments. The attack gained momentum and grew into a storm that fitted ill with the concept of an authoritarian system.

For two years Bethmann resisted. He knew that the claims of the submarine enthusiasts were exaggerated; he also sensed the moral importance of the issue. 'If Germany resorts to such methods,' he said, 'the whole world will kill it like a mad dog . . .' Admiral Tirpitz resigned over the conflict, a belated, fruitless triumph of the civil authority.

A third issue which continued to occupy interested groups, if not the people, was the constitutional question, the so-called 'reorientation'. The supporters of the 'Scheidemann peace' who were opposed to unrestricted submarine war, wanted the reorientation. The others did not.

There is a connection between modern war and democracy because it is the masses, the workers, who must fight it in the army and in the factories, and if they do not collaborate the war cannot be continued. In Germany it had begun as the Kaiser's war; but before it had started seriously the masses had made their presence known. It was impossible to arouse their enthusiasm and their hatred, to appeal to their reason, their patience and their courage, to demand countless sacrifices from them, only to send them packing in the end. Even supporters of the old system thought that the war would lead to a strengthening of democracy.

The war [wrote General Wilhelm Groener, one of Germany's ablest officers] is the biggest democratic wave that has ever swept across the planet. It will knock over whosoever tries to stem it; one must steer with it. Consequently the choice of helmsman and course must be such that we are carried along on this wave and reach port even if the war ends badly.

Even Admiral Tirpitz saw this: 'The existing caste and class system is finished. Victory or defeat, we shall have pure democracy.' However, from such a general appreciation of the situation to an actual change was a big step.

As before, Prussia was ruled by the Conservatives who controlled the administration because of inherited privileges and the chamber because of the three-class electoral system. As before, there was no central government and the Chancellor was responsible only to the monarch. Conditions forced him to keep in close touch with the parties in the Reichstag, and this was in conformity with Bethmann Hollweg's wishes; but the Chancellor was not parliament's man nor did he have to carry out its decisions, if any were taken. The third and strongest power which gradually emerged from the war had not been provided for by Bismarck's constitution; it was the army leadership, the High Command as it was now called. It was in constant conflict with the leader of the Reich, the Chancellor: over the submarine war, over the future of Poland, over war aims in general, over peace offers, over all great policy issues. The Chancellor was in a weak position, particularly because he did not have a strong parliament behind him and was prevented by the nature of the constitution from referring to the Reichstag as his authority. A weak, almost forgotten and despised Kaiser was constitutionally his only support. This was not a fault on paper only but a fault in the actual structure of the state. As a result the political parties, particularly the Social Democrats, were involved in everything and forced to take part in everything, without being able to control the system; responsibility lay everywhere but nowhere unequivocally. Hence the two demands of the Social Democrats: a parliamentary government for the Reich to be formed by the majority parties, and the abolition of the three-class electoral system in Prussia.

Bethmann admitted the justification of both demands with characteristic procrastinating lack of precision, not wanting to offend their opponents. Reforms, he conceded, were necessary, particularly in Prussia; it was better though to leave them until after the war; now there was enough to do against the common enemy and the party truce must not be broken. But the truce had long been broken. It had been intended for the six-week war in France and the six-month war in Russia, not for a four-year war. It was broken by the clash over strategy, war aims and reorientation. It was broken by the growing misery of everyday life, by the hunger of the poor and the affluence of the rich. After a year nothing much remained of the noble, unifying, exhilarating experience of August 1914.

6. Changes

What was important? Was it party policy, economic issues, the war experience of the masses in the trenches? Or was it the war as endured by a few thoughtful, philosophizing soldier poets? Was it the worker's wife, the woman tram conductor, the peasant's wife who looked after her farm? Was war literature important, the subtle arguments which eminent writers used to invent their own war, contrasting German and Western civilization? Was it important that the Social Democratic Party finally split under the pressure of the war and that those who in 1914 had voted reluctantly for war credits formed themselves into the Independent Social Democratic Party? That Bethmann Hollweg manoeuvred with decreasing success between right and left? Most important probably was the way in which the war gradually transformed Germany's face and character. But this change is more easily described in a novel than in an historical account. The creative writer has the advantage of not claiming to give a complete picture but merely a view, an interpretation. Unless the historian jumps from one topic to another, he is accused of presenting a one-sided picture. If he does jump about, he may well provide a series of individual impressions instead of a picture.

Let us for a moment consider Germany's economic development. The war economy became a controlled economy because Germany and Austria were now largely dependent on themselves and it was therefore necessary to plan production and allocate the product carefully. Nobody had foreseen this. The German general staff had planned the military campaign; nobody had planned the economic one. There were not even any grain reserves. When the situation became critical it was necessary to improvise. The result was an economic system the like of which had never existed in modern times, not the product of socialist theory but a military necessity.

A War Raw Materials Department had been established as long ago as August 1914 under the direction of the industrialist, Walther Rathenau; its purpose was to ensure the production, synthetic or otherwise, conservation and rational distribution of essential raw materials. What Rathenau suggested and set afoot within a few months provided Germany with the material resources to fight a four-year war; even in November 1918 Germany had not come to the end of its raw material reserves. Rathenau was able to write in October 1914:

Metals are subject to control, as are chemicals and textiles if based on wool and jute, and a great number of other products – leather, rubber, linen, cotton – will shortly be controlled. The most vulnerable item was saltpetre which forms the basis of all our explosives, supplies of which would have irretrievably run out in the first half of next year without intervention. I have initiated the construction of big saltpetre factories to be built by private enterprise with state subsidies ... It is the campaign for materials which we have organized in these seven weeks at the Ministry of War.

Rathenau believed that the central authority set up by him, with its subordinate organizations covering individual branches of production would continue to exist in some form after the war. Himself one of Germany's big capitalists he thought that the day of unrestricted capitalism was over; that it had been over before the war, and that the war was revealing and hastening what was in the air. Planning was in the air, efforts to promote the welfare of all, the concept of the state which made productive use of milliards instead of a few millions. 'The state can act,' Bismarck had written but he had not kept his promise. Now the state was forced to act. Rathenau believed that henceforth it would always need to act, that it would become the biggest employer, the planner and guardian of national production.

What he had done in one stroke for industry was done later piecemeal for food supplies and the needs of the civilian population. First the authorities established maximum prices, then national buying organizations were set up and finally came requisitioning, distribution centres and rationing. First to be rationed was bread, followed by meat and finally by almost everything. A complicated machinery for distribution and control was set up, starting at local government level, continuing at regional and state level and culminating in the central authority in Berlin. A system demanded by the consumers, the big cities, the trade unions and the Social Democrats and which could never be sufficiently strict or sufficiently fair for them. Even the Conservatives agreed that it was a necessary system. But human nature cannot be changed and appeals to patriotism and unselfishness in economic matters are usually fruitless. Farmers became less enthusiastic producers as the state interfered with their activities, as it told them how much to produce, what to feed and at what price to sell, leaving them only inadequate quantities for their own needs and, if they failed to make satisfactory deliveries, even putting the army on them. Goods went wherever they fetched the highest price; if not on the open market then on the black one. Country dwellers lived better than town dwellers, and the rich lived very, very much better than the poor. Shop windows were empty or decorated with unprepossessing dummies. People queued for ever shorter rations; there was one egg a fortnight per person. The German's average weight went down by a fifth and the number of those who died of diseases caused by undernourishment approached the million mark. Yet in quiet back parlours the army contractor's wife found what her heart desired: coffee, geese and butter, wine from France, and chocolate from Budapest. What then remained of the community spirit, of the thrilling summer experience?

The value of money fell and two forms of currency appeared: one which was spent without much thought with the ration points which were the really important thing, and the other used, according to very different calculations, for black market transactions. There was too much money in circulation. The Reich went off the gold standard in the first days of the war and printed as much money as was needed to pay for the war, three or four milliards a month. The money went into the economy and the government's intention was to pump it out again by voluntary war loans. The loans, apart from being themselves a promise of future riches, did not achieve this aim. The money in circulation increased while the quantity of goods available declined; prices rose and would have been higher still if there had not been two markets, an officially controlled one and a black one. Money flowed into the pockets of industrialists who had never been so well-off as far as profits, orders and assured sales were concerned. Money flowed into the pockets of the farmers, of the middlemen, of the black marketeers, of all the twilight figures who in normal times live precariously in the shadows. Factory workers – 'heavy workers' as they were called because they received bigger rations – were also comparatively well paid as they were in great demand. The losers were employees with fixed salaries, pensioners, war widows and the old middle class which had been unable to adapt itself to the new, greedy atmosphere. War is known to strengthen the strong and to weaken the weak, those who are already on their way down. The strong were those who were capable and who could be made use of, but they were also vulgar, ruthless and shameless. A new wealth appeared, a style that laid it on thick. The Bavarian Crown Prince wrote:

> Heavy industry sets the tone in Germany . . . they all dance round the golden calf. Like a cankerous poison mammonism had spread from Berlin and produced a terrible lowering of intellectual standards. Business and pleasure were the only topics of discussion (at least in Berlin). Ruthlessly exploiting the distress created by the war the businessmen of Berlin have managed, by establishing a great variety of central offices in Berlin, to bring the whole economy under their control.

Old, distinguished wealth is bearable. But what is more disgusting than vulgar new riches in the midst of misery?

The state governments became mere executive organs; the power rested with the High Command, with the central authorities in Berlin. Three years of war accomplished what thirty years of peace had been unable to do. The general enthusiasm and, after it had ceased, the strict coercion to which all citizens of the Reich were subject made Germany into a unitary state in practice. But there was no rejoicing. In the South, particularly in Bavaria, the feeling spread that the states had been drawn into the war by the Reich, by Prussia, and that but for the commissars coming from Berlin to requisition cattle and grain there would be enough food. A new particularism of discontent developed. Because it was based on resentment the dynasties could not benefit from it. On the contrary, it was directed against them as well because they had failed to save their states from the clutches of Prussia and had simply become vassals of Berlin. In 1914 the princes had weakly followed the mood of their peoples, the mood of the nation. Now that the mood had passed they were blamed.

The ordinary people hated the 'war profiteers' and there was an estrangement between town and country, between North and South, between soldiers and civilians. It was impossible to explain to those at home what it was like at the front. While the workers earned tolerably well, and farmers, manufacturers and profiteers extremely well, the men who risked their skins for their country earned only honour and medals. To remedy this situation the High Command transformed the workers into soldiers by declaring all Germans from seventeen to sixty liable for military and civilian service. This was the ideal of General Ludendorff who in his fashion was a democrat or at least a leveller, a fanatical believer in national unity. Let those at home bear the same burdens as those at the front and for the same reward. Such a policy would have hit the workers, but hardly the war profiteers. Reichstag and trade unions resisted and the result was a compromise: an auxiliary service law under which all those not already engaged in war work could be called up and under which changes of employment were subject to certain controls. The law was not very successful. The Conservatives blamed the class egoism of the trade unions; so many safeguards against sweated labour and compulsory employment had been built into the law that nothing remained of its great intention.

The fact, however, was that in a situation where there was no genuine community spirit, where such a spirit had only seemed to exist for a few delirious months, then given way to cold conflict of interest – that in such a climate the workers could not afford to let patriotism take precedence over the economic struggle for existence. The economically strong section of the community who could more easily have done so should have set an example, but did not. General Groener, for example, who as head of the *Kriegsamt* not only succeeded in raising armaments production but also knew how to get on with the trade unions and who recommended a cut in excessive industrial profits, could not keep his position and was sent back to the front. He was told why: 'I knew that for months there had been an intrigue against me. It originated from a small but powerful clique, from the Rhenish Westphalian industry . . .' While industrialists were pursuing political ends in this way it was not surprising that the workers had no real confidence in the party truce. In the spring of 1917 there were serious strikes which the trade unions did not want but in which they were forced to take part in order to retain control of them; the strikes were caused by hunger, although they were not entirely free from political motives. The unrest grew and was exploited and fomented by agitators. This situation placed the trade unions and the Social Democratic Party in a dilemma. Although they were loyally prepared to defend their country they could not remain idle when their new enemies, the Independent Socialists, turned against them the most popular slogans about war profiteers and people who prolonged the war. They were forced to take part, trying to observe moderation.

The Germany of 1917 was an exhausted, irritable country. News of victory still came from the fronts, if not from the West from the East, the South-East and the South. The war still seemed like a world-wide adventure whose results and successes could not and must not be reversed. But the heart that was meant to animate the enormous burden of conquered territory became ever more tired.

What about the soldiers? They were as patient as the people at home, probably more so. The soldier's scope for independent action is after all more limited than that of the civilian. He is given orders, he is looked after, he is involved with others, there is no choice. Moreover, the spirit of comradeship is strong, the concept of honour binding. The soldiers proved themselves where they had to and to the end they were able to satisfy the urge that lies dormant in every man for bravery, for leadership in miniature, for samaritan service and for chivalry. Work at home offered no such compensations and the army was thus more loyal in its support of the war than the civilians.

But William II's model army was gone. So was the army of young volunteers who had assaulted the enemy positions singing the *Deutschlandlied*. There was no more waving of flags, there were no more cavalry charges. The old soldiers' songs remained and there were perhaps a few new ones, but the patriotic poets with their bristling moustaches and their sadistic verses about the war had grown silent. The army, less glamorous and more bourgeois, had long become used to its work. It is difficult to say how life in the mud of the trenches, with periodic surges of deadly fire, affected people's souls. Most of them returned home to become good citizens as before, remembering only occasionally and then not unwillingly the years at the front. Some never recovered from the experience.

7. Chronology

In 1915 the Germans conquered Poland. They could probably have defeated Russia there and then but were prevented from doing so by their cautious strategy. Great successes were achieved but no decisions. The French and British offensives in the West caused slaughter without change. Italy's entry into the war forced Austria to transfer divisions from the eastern front to the South. Italy did not accomplish much. In the autumn Bulgaria joined the Central Powers. A German–Austrian–Bulgarian campaign against Serbia led to the occupation of Serbia and the establishment of overland communications with Turkey. Germany, it was said, ruled from the North Sea to the Tigris. The Allies maintained their positions in Salonika and the British gradually pushed from Egypt into Palestine, Syria and Mesopotamia.

In 1916 the German leaders still sought a decision in the West. Because they could not get at Britain they decided to break Britain's continental sword, France. The idea was to force the French army to exhaust itself by attacking the strongest French position and to make the enemy use his remaining reserves. Hence the battle of Verdun of which Hindenburg later said that 1916 was 'frittered away bloodily'. In order to relieve the western front the Russians launched a last major attack on Galicia, proved superior to the Austrians but were finally repulsed by the Germans. After that they were finished, ruined by their poverty of material and their victory was turned into a defeat amounting almost to a collapse. In the summer the Chief of the General Staff, Falkenhayn, was replaced by Hindenburg with Erich Ludendorff in command under him as 'first quartermaster general'. This step in reality made Ludendorff into the generalissimo, the planner of war and peace. In other countries the crisis brought to the top the most ruthless, most imaginative politicians, Lloyd George in Britain and a year later Clemenceau in France. In Germany it was the general who assumed the burden; misguided by his own powerful, arrogant and selfish nature, but also misled and in a way coerced by the civilians who cringed before him. It is logical that when war penetrates and dominates everything, when it is 'total' war, the general must rule. Ludendorff's position and character indicated more clearly than anything else that the adventure had degenerated into something quite new and unbelievable. Ludendorff's position was no longer that of the elder Moltke, a man of very different character, noble, discreet and humane. Ludendorff was a tremendous worker, an expert on the new weapons, a man whose head was full of figures and names but who was irritable and brutal and in the subtleties of life as inexperienced as a child. At the same time he was cunning and fully aware of his and the old Field-Marshal's mythical fame which he used to blackmail the monarch. Ludendorff knew only two possible ends to the war, total victory or total defeat. What purpose total victory would serve was no concern of his. Defeat he called 'annihilation' again without envisaging what form this annihilation would take and what would come after it. His appointment marked the beginning of a game which appears to have appealed to the German character in the first half of the twentieth century, seeing that it was played again twenty-five years after Ludendorff: 'victory or annihilation', 'all or nothing'.

Ludendorff reorganized the western front, withdrew the armies to a new and elaborately prepared line of defence and pushed through a programme to raise armaments production. In the winter the Germans conquered Rumania which, under the influence of the latest Russian offensive, had allowed itself to be tempted into the war to gain territory from Hungary. This victory represented another expansion of the central fortress, of the big prison that was being defended by Germany; all the same it remained a prison. Around it lay the wide world, the seas which Britain's fleet controlled, the continents from which Britain drew new strength. In November 1916 General Ludendorff suddenly asked a Conservative deputy as though he could answer the question: 'How on earth is this going to end?'

In December 1916 Germany offered to start peace negotiations. The Kaiser was sincere about the offer; he longed for the good old days and had come to regard the war with profound dismay. On the basis of the latest successful campaign in the Balkans Germany thought that it could risk the offer. Unfortunately the wording 'put too much emphasis on the victory note' – as Bethmann put it – instead of making concrete proposals such as the evacuation of Belgium, which the Germans did not want to mention, first because they did not really want to give up Belgium and secondly because any public renunciation might have weakened the morale of the army. As a result the peace offer became worthless, almost as worthless as the one that the German Reich made and repeated in a subsequent war. Further still it ruined President Wilson's efforts to mediate. Nevertheless the Germans must not be given the sole blame for the failure of this peace move. The Allies felt temporarily at a disadvantage, although in principle and in the long run they regarded themselves as stronger than the Germans; given their position they were not anxious to negotiate. They believed even more strongly than the Germans that right was on their side, and the hearts of their leaders whose position depended on the war were even more hardened than those of their German counterparts. None of the parties to the struggle could admit that the war was nonsense; each had to blame the other for it, as Germany did in its peace offer. The Allies indignantly returned the compliment. This deplorable quarrel was by itself enough to prevent the opening of honest negotiations between equals.

Thereupon, in January 1917, the Germans decided on unrestricted submarine warfare. It was the first fateful decision which General Ludendorff forced on the Kaiser and the Chancellor. The High Command ordered the submarine war, which it needed because it wanted to finish the war by the summer if only because of the vacillation of Germany's allies; and the submarine war could finish it. The Admiralty produced calculations to prove this claim. The effect of America's entry into the war, thought Admiral Capelle, Tirpitz's successor, would anyway 'be nil'. Before the United States could assemble an army, within six months, starving Britain would be begging for peace. That was the view not only of the army and the navy but also of the great majority of the Reichstag. The parties had long expressed themselves in favour of unrestricted submarine warfare or at least, as in the case of the Centre, had gladly left the decision to the army leaders who were worshipped as gods. What Hindenburg and Ludendorff wanted was right. That was also more or less what the man in the street thought. He no longer trusted anybody, not the calculating, complaining Chancellor, nor the subdued braggart of yesterday, the Kaiser, nor his princes and their ministers, nor his deputies; they had all become insignificant figures. But he trusted Hindenburg and Ludendorff. Hindenburg and Ludendorff knew this. They knew that they had the people behind them when they asked the Kaiser for something that he was unwilling to give, and they knew that William II was no longer strong enough to treat them as he had treated Bismarck. It had been Bethmann himself who had induced the Kaiser to change the supreme command. Since then the importance of the army leaders had increased relatively to that of the politicians. Therefore it cannot be said that Ludendorff led a reluctant nation into the new war at sea. The authority of the victors of Tannenberg was very popular; their aims coincided with the desires of the masses. The party leaders too were one with the people, they too stumbled along, seduced by the promises of the Admiralty, weakened by hunger and impatience, stupefied by cheap arguments about the cruellest weapon being the kindest, about might always coming before right, about success being everything and so on. The Social Democrats issued warnings as usual. The Chancellor hesitated as usual and stated his doubts merely to agree with a heavy heart that this 'last card' must be played.

When unrestricted U-boat warfare was proclaimed the United States broke off diplomatic relations, and, after several American ships had been sunk, declared war on Germany. America had wanted to remain neutral but it had been attacked, its most sacred right had been violated; now it must help to destroy German military despotism. This was the official thesis. It did not contain the whole truth. America had long been closer to the Allies than to the Central Powers and it had not remained unaffected by Britain's clever propaganda. Nor had Washington remained unaffected by realistic political arguments: a Europe dominated by Germany would upset the balance of power in the world; America itself must then become an armed camp; therefore it was better to come to Britain's rescue in time so that it might emerge unscathed from the affair. Such arguments, however, could not be uttered aloud or even admitted frankly in private because the American tradition despised the tricks of European diplomacy and did not want to have anything to do with power politics. America was not prepared to fight for the European balance of power, only for right and for the highest aims: justice, democracy, freedom of the peoples and so on. From the beginning President Wilson had been in favour of a new kind of peace and had tried to bring it about while he was neutral – a peace without victors and vanquished, with justice for all – since he believed that defeated nations provided the seeds for a new war. This view the President continued to hold. He realized that he would have to be very careful and to act very wisely in order to prevent the tremendous American weight from suddenly sending the German side of the scales high into the air. Otherwise someone would after all be defeated and the aim of a just peace without hatred or revenge would be missed.

There was no mention of this in March 1917. Neither the Germans nor the Allies fully understood the immense importance of the American decision, this return of America to Europe. More than a year passed before the first American divisions could be sent across the Atlantic. Meanwhile the submarine war seemed to be achieving what the German leaders had promised; not a day passed without some news with the words 'sunk without trace' to cheer tired spirits. How long could Britain stand the loss of millions of tons of shipping and of the valuable cargoes carried in the ships? The German Admiralty gave itself and the enemy six months. Several things happened during those six months; signs appeared on the horizon indicating that the end was near.

There was the Russian revolution. Though moderate, bourgeois-liberal, even aristocratic at first, it opened opportunities for a Russian defection from the Great Alliance. The leaders wanted to intensify the war effort but among the exhausted soldiers, among the peasants and workers a different attitude of mind prevailed; there were parties which were permeated by this attitude of mind or hoped to use it in order to obtain power. The German army leaders knew this and decided to lend a helping hand. Ulianov-Lenin, the leader of the radical Russian majority Socialists (the Bolsheviks), was taken in a sealed railway carriage from Switzerland through Germany to Scandinavia from where he could set out for St Petersburg. There his friends received him as the herald of the true revolution and of peace, and his enemies as a German agent For the moment he was both.

The collapse of the Tsarist regime gave political life in Germany new stimulus. If this could happen in Russia in the middle of the war, all sorts of things could happen in Germany. The moment for great changes seemed to be at hand, be it to prevent or to encourage a development like the Russian one. To the left of the Independent Socialists there appeared the Spartacists who tried to bring together the radicals with Leninist leanings. The Independent Socialists and even the majority Social Democrats were driven to activity in order not to be overshadowed by their rivals. Hence their cautious participation in the strikes; hence also the renewed flare-up of the 'reorientation' issue. The question of the Prussian franchise was declared to be a German question and a committee appointed to prepare its solution. The Kaiser for his part condescended to promise that henceforth his brave people must be called upon even more readily than before to participate in shaping their own destiny; and that therefore the class franchise was no longer suitable. Well-meaning, belated, vague promises such as Bethmann Hollweg liked to make. The Conservatives continued to be irreconcilably opposed to any reform; they seriously maintained that it was better to adapt the national franchise to that of Prussia than the other way round.

In the summer of 1917 the political crisis came to a head. Relations deteriorated between the powerful, brutal, politically blind army leadership, that is to say Ludendorff, and the clear-sighted, weak, melancholy leadership of the Reich, that is to say Bethmann. Relations also deteriorated between parliament and Bethmann. For the Right, for the Conservatives and the National Liberals, he was insufficiently in sympathy with the army leaders, with 'positive war aims'; for the Left, the Centre, the left-wing Liberals and the Social Democrats he was not sufficiently – not definitely enough – out of sympathy with these aims. Everybody called for new leadership. The General wanted leaders who would do what he said because he considered himself capable of dealing with the political issues, and the pan-Germans did not see why Field-Marshal Hindenburg should not be made Chancellor as there was no longer any distinction between political and military leadership. The left-wing parties wanted a strong government, one that could negotiate, make peace and be in close contact with them.

Ludendorff knew that the war 'could no longer be decided purely in the military sphere'. He therefore thought it even more essential that Germany should assert itself politically. The leaders of the mass parties, in particular Matthias Erzberger, the most industrious and influential member of the Centre group in parliament, came to a different conclusion. Erzberger had become convinced that the submarine war had not brought the promised result. This was pretty obvious because Britain was supposed to have been crushed by the summer and Britain was not crushed. There was more unrest, more gloom among the people than ever before, and more questions were asked. There were limits to the country's patience, to its courage, to its blind acceptance of what the authorities did. Erzberger proposed a Reichstag peace resolution'. He argued that Germany must abandon the war-aim fantasies of the years 1915 and 1916 and return to the pure mood of the summer of 1914, stating publicly that it had never sought anything but a peace of reconciliation; 'enforced territorial surrender' or 'political, economic and financial rape' were incompatible with such an attitude.

The proposal caused a storm. Ludendorff asked to be relieved of his duties on the grounds that he could no longer work with the chancellor – an act of insubordination which alone would have sufficed to seal Bethmann's fate, because William II, whatever gestures of authority he still reserved to himself, in the end had to do what Hindenburg and Ludendorff demanded. The Conservatives and National Liberals criticized the Chancellor for defeatism while the Centre criticized him for being compromised by the past course of events. Thereupon, after the view of the parliamentary party groups had expressly been sought, Bethmann Hollweg was dismissed.

His departure solved nothing. It was as ambiguous in its significance as Bismarck's fall or Bülow's fall had been. Who had overthrown Bethmann? The army leaders or the parties? And if it was the parties was it those that identified themselves with the army leaders or those who wanted an 'Erzberger peace'? Was Bethmann's fall a victory for the parliamentary principle or for its exact opposite, military dictatorship? Germany's affairs were so confused that it was impossible to give a clear answer to these questions. Two dissimilar birds, parliamentarism and military dictatorship, wanted to emerge simultaneously from the bursting egg of the old regime.

Thus the colourless, well-meaning, weak Bethmann disappeared. Perhaps his heir provides a clue to the significance of his disappearance. It was not the aged Prince Bülow who would have liked to become Chancellor; still less was it a parliamentarian, a party leader. Ludendorff chose the man: an honest civil servant who understood as little about politics as the general himself and who was almost unknown to the Reichstag. This meant that with Bethmann's fall Ludendorff's power reached its zenith. Chancellor Michaelis was Ludendorff's creature.

Meanwhile a Reichstag majority, consisting of the Centre, the left-wing Liberals and the Social Democrats, passed Erzberger's peace resolution. It was a different majority from the one that had overthrown Bethmann. Michaelis encouraged it, expressing approval of the resolution 'as he interpreted it'. As he was close to the pan-Germans it is probably justifiable to suspect his interpretation of being somewhat broadminded. Michaelis sabotaged the Vatican's peace mediation which, with Britain and France both tired of the war, had more chance of success than Wilson's attempt of the previous winter. He did not want to give the required undertaking about Belgium's free future. He talked politely round the issue while making the Reichstag believe that he had promised the complete restoration of Belgium. The government stalled and prevaricated. The masses believed that Germany was fighting only to defend itself; this was the only argument which could still convince them of the need to 'hold out'. Yet at the same time there was the reluctance to give up Germany's conquests, the desire to preserve their ill-gotten gains on the grounds that those conquests constituted pawns needed for negotiation. The pan-Germans were more honest.

Germany's internal political development also continued to be ambiguous. There was a trend towards military dictatorship as the only power capable of somehow administering the vast beleaguered fortress, of preserving a part of a crumbling society. But there was also a trend towards parliamentary government, towards democracy. There could be no Chancellor who did not get on with Ludendorff but neither could there be one who was not at least tolerated by the Reichstag, as Michaelis was to learn. The episode of his Chancellorship came to an end after only three months because the left in the Reichstag refused to give him the confidence he did not deserve.

It was the 'peace resolution' parties who forced him to resign and who told the Kaiser that before appointing a successor he should consult the parliamentary parties. From the point of view of constitutional law this was an interesting step. Since the summer there had existed in the Reichstag a proper coalition of the 'left' majority which now claimed to be entitled to have a say in the formation of the government: the 'inter-parliamentary party' committee, composed of the Centre, the Liberals and the Social Democrats. On occasion the National Liberals also formed part of it. To some extent the committee anticipated developments which happened under the Republic; and in the meantime it was a private discussion club, which called meetings when there was something to discuss – which in fact happened continuously.

Did the new Chancellor, Count Hertling, have the confidence of this majority? He behaved as though he did and could do so because he was a parliamentarian of long standing, Bavarian Prime Minister for many years, a pillar of the Centre Party. Thirty years earlier when he had said that Bismarck was irreplaceable Ludwig Windthorst had replied: 'Anybody can do that job, you can do it.' Now, as an old man, he had to show whether he could do it; in a situation which Bismarck would never, never have allowed to arise. The coalition too behaved as though it was satisfied with the choice of Hertling; the Chancellor was given as Secretaries of State two proper party representatives who were, however, forced – in accordance with the Bismarck constitution – to resign their seats. Unfortunately neither understood much about the use of power. Hertling himself, who perhaps knew enough about it in the context of the Bavarian idyll, senile, disliked in Berlin as a Bavarian, and distrustful of the 'reorientation', was the last to lead the majority, to shape political decisions with its help and to implement them. He tried, like Bethmann, to be on good terms with all parties and allowed Ludendorff to play the strong man. The progress which his government was supposed to represent was thus once more merely a semblance of progress; at a moment when only the strongest, most determined *political* leadership could have brought help.

As a climber who has lost his way clings to a sheer face near the summit, unable to go any higher but reluctant to come down since the descent too is perilous and must render vain all his past striving, Germany in 1917 could neither make peace nor win. It could not make peace because it regarded itself as the victor and on the map it did indeed look like the victor, given all the states it had conquered, given the vast areas it had occupied. This factor combined with the enemies' venomous propaganda prevented Germany from finding the right tone of wisdom and humility. Yet it could not achieve a decisive victory. The enemy front in the West was impenetrable, American help flowed more freely than ever and American naval strategy had succeeded in dealing a decisive blow to Germany's submarines, namely the mine barrier between Scotland and Norway which made it almost impossible for the Germans to get out to sea. Training in camps on the other side of the Atlantic there was the vigorous, adventure-seeking young nation, pampered by peace, and divisions were being formed for the purpose of ending the war in Europe. This would take time, but less time than Germany's military pedants assumed. Everybody knew that time was working faster and faster against Germany. The moment might come when it would be too late to do the right thing. With a clever German leadership this would probably still have been possible in the summer of 1917. Perhaps even in the following winter. But time passed and it became more and more difficult to make peace. Woe betide the people that entrusts its fate to a man who understands only war.

In fact Germany's great adventure reached its climax in the fourth year of war. The dance became wilder and wilder as the end approached.

In September 1917 the *Vaterlandspartei* (Fatherland Party) was formed with the intention of being a party above the parties, a national movement to save the country from a soft peace. It was the most ambitious achievement of the pan-Germans who succeeded in persuading Tirpitz to become the party's leader. This was something new in Prussia: a retired admiral becoming a public speaker and perorating at the top of his voice against parliament, indeed even against his own government.

> We know that the existence of our nation and its position in the world is at stake. Unlike Britain the German people is not concerned only with business. Britain, the instigator and persistent fomenter of this conflagration, is in desperate straits. At sea and on land we are the victor . . . We do not want the kind of peace which will mean that we shall starve. In order to achieve an early peace we must obey Hindenburg's command and keep our heads. If we put up willingly with misery and privation the Germans will have the kind of peace that Hindenburg wants and under the terms of which the nation's immense sacrifices and efforts will be rewarded. Any other kind of peace means a crippling blow to our future development . . .

Reward or ruin – the *Vaterlandspartei* saw no third choice. If it called Hindenburg and Ludendorff as its witnesses it did so more or less rightly.

Events in the East seemed to confirm its hopes. In November Lenin seized power in St Petersburg; he published the secret agreement between the Tsarist government and the Western allies and offered the world a peace which 'guarantees to every nation freedom of economic and cultural development'; a 'people's peace', an 'honourable peace of agreement'. His captivatingly simple proposal was designed to discredit governments in the eyes of their peoples, to force the latter to declare themselves and to prepare the revolt of the masses. The Western powers, to whom Lenin was nothing but a traitor, refused to recognize his government of people's commissars, of workers' and peasants' councils. President Wilson hastily produced a peace programme intended to compete with Lenin's; the idea was to deprive the Bolsheviks of the opportunity of presenting themselves as the only people concerned with a just peace. Wilson's plan took over several of Lenin's ideas, particularly that of the right of nations to decide their own fate, the right of self-determination. But Wilson's Fourteen Points were much more precise than Lenin's proposal and anyone who studied them – which Ludendorff never considered worth the effort – must have recognized that by accepting them Germany would lose something and gain nothing. It would lose Alsace-Lorraine to France and naturally it would lose Belgium; it might also have to cede its predominantly Polish regions to a new Polish national state. The fate of the Austrian monarchy remained uncertain because Wilson, although he did not insist on its dissolution, demanded 'autonomy' for its peoples, a proposal which could be understood in various ways. All peace programmes are open to interpretation and how they are interpreted depends on the strength of the negotiator's position. If at that moment Germany had accepted Wilson's Fourteen Points as a basis for negotiation it might have lost rather than gained but it would still have presented the appearance of a great and terrible power and it could have insisted on decisions favourable to itself on several issues. Germany, however, did not consider itself ripe for a peace of renunciation, less than ever now that Russia was finished. It decided to accept Lenin's proposal and to interpret it in terms of the relative strength of the two countries. Undefeated in the West and victorious in the East, exhausted and hungry but with immense possibilities before it, Germany met the Bolsheviks at the round table in Brest-Litovsk.

8. The Last Year

Lenin thought in international terms; he lived in the service of world revolution. For this he regarded Germany, not Russia, as the most important country, so much so that he was prepared to sacrifice Russia in order to produce revolution in Germany. On the other hand the new masters of Russia or St Petersburg were as imperialistic as the old ones; there was no clear-cut frontier between old Russian and revolutionary power. The Bolsheviks conceded to the non-Russian peoples of the Tsarist empire, even to the Ukrainians, the right to determine their own fate. The ruling, exploiting classes apart, peoples could be nothing but socialist; it was the Bolshevik Party alone that led to socialism. Therefore, it left 'to themselves', all these countries would rejoin Russia and Russia's imperialist interests would be upheld.

The Germans saw the situation differently. They had military control of Poland and parts of the Baltic provinces; they could, if they wanted, also gain military control of the rest, Finland and the Ukraine, because Russian resistance had collapsed. The State Secretary for Foreign Affairs, von Kühlmann, maintained that those regions had already exercised their right of self-determination and had broken away from Russia; that they had provisional governments or committees with which the victorious Germans and their allies could come to terms without further Russian intervention. Over this point, the meaning of the principle of national self-determination and its correct application, the chief Russian negotiator, Leon Trotsky, and his German counterpart fought sharp verbal duels which seem to have been enjoyed by both these super-clever men. The German position was probably not more dishonest than the Russian one because 'national self-determination' is a doubtful matter and, given the chaos of the disintegrating Tsarist empire, of nations fighting each other, of national splinter groups, parties, classes and murder-gangs, it was bound to be complete mumbo-jumbo. But the German diplomats allowed themselves to be outplayed by the Communists. They gave no guarantees that free plebiscites would later be held in the Baltic provinces; thereby allowing Trotsky who demanded them to appear as the champion of justice without making any sacrifice. Germany had military strength behind it; the German negotiator and even more the German general, Max Hoffmann, did not fail to use this strongest of all arguments when the subtler ones were foiled by Trotsky's brilliant impudence. It was not superiority of principle but of strength which put an end to these grotesque, grotesquely drawn out, negotiations. When the German armies continued their advance into the Baltic Provinces, expelled the Bolsheviks without much effort and reached Lake Peipus, Lenin gave way – without having read the peace treaty which he authorized to be signed in March. He regarded it as unimportant because the world revolution would tear up all political maps.

For the Germans too the peace of Brest-Litovsk and everything connected with it could only be a provisional arrangement. The chaos in eastern Europe could not be mastered as long as the war in the West continued. The German rulers were all the further from mastering it because they could not agree on their aims, either among themselves or with their allies.

Among the Conservatives the annexationist view which demanded the greatest possible, most direct territorial gain at Russia's expense clashed with the other view which held that the Russian Empire must not be shaken to its foundations and which regarded a restoration of the old German–Russian friendship as desirable in the long run; in that case Germany could not deprive Russia of such vital regions as Estonia and Latvia. Could these countries, people wondered, with their thin German upper crust, really be passed off as German? Could they exist as independent states? What form should their dependence on Germany take? Was it right to combine the principle of national self-determination with annexationist practice? Was the principle as such right? In what form should it be applied to Poland? In 1916 Germany had proclaimed a Polish kingdom, hoping to arouse Poland's active sympathies even in the military sphere; but these hopes had not materialized. The Poles mistrusted the German liberator who for so long had been one of their oppressors, and it was their way to demand more than they were entitled to. Their dream of reestablishing the old Polish Empire between the Baltic and the Black Sea was irreconcilable with the actual situation in these areas. But in that case what should be done with Poland? Should a wide strip of Russian Poland be incorporated into Germany as Ludendorff demanded, producing the only argument he knew, the military one? Should the rest, a mutilated kingdom, be made part of Austria, as the Habsburg diplomats wished? Or should it later be returned to Russia? These questions were discussed to the bitter end. The chaotic condition of eastern Europe did not permit any uniform plan - except of the most brutally destructive kind ignoring the confusion of life. In the winter of 1918 Germany lacked the will to pursue such a course of action. Although a taste of power and the spectacle of Russian disintegration had excited the imagination of the Germans, they had political and humanitarian scruples, needed to consider their allies and held diverse views.

'Even the so-called Eastern peace,' wrote General Groener, 'is a highly problematical affair; here too the war continues, only in a different form.' The Germans had to police the regions detached from Russia by the treaty; such material help as they hoped to find there, Ukrainian wheat and Caucasian oil, their troops had to fetch. Consequently it was not possible to transfer as many units as had been hoped from the East to the Western front, only about a million men. The others remained where they were, in fact they moved much deeper into former Russian territory. While on the Black Sea and in the Caucasus dazzling prospects opened up before the greedy eyes of the German upper classes, soldiers, economists and journalists, this encounter with things Russian also presented a threat to the existing order. Tsarism had kept the two empires strictly apart. Now Germany was tempted in two ways by Russia: enticed to conquest, exploitation and domination, and confused by the steaming vapours of the revolution, which, as Trotsky's piercing voice proclaimed, was the beginning of a new epoch in world history. Many German soldiers believed this, thought about what they heard in Russia and finally brought it home.

Meanwhile the Western powers saw the peace of Brest-Litovsk as further, latest and final proof of the brutality of German war aims and raised loud cries of indignation. Their Russian brothers had been robbed of an area about the size of Austria-Hungary and Turkey put together, with fifty-six million inhabitants, with seventy-nine per cent of their iron and eighty-nine per cent of their coal production. Such behaviour was unbelievable. How could one negotiate with a power that used its defeated enemy thus? Did this behaviour not show all too clearly what Germany intended to do to France and Britain? The treaty of Brest-Litovsk did not improve Germany's standing in the world and did not make it easier to find a basis for negotiations.

Germany was happy to have got rid of one of its major enemies and to hope for a supply of food from the Ukraine. In fact, however, not much arrived. Even the parties which had supported the peace resolution of the previous summer voted in favour of the treaty – at least the majority Social Democrats did not vote against it.

As for finding a basis for negotiation, the man whose will counted most in Germany whenever it came to a serious decision was not interested in negotiations. In General Ludendorff's view war was decided on the battlefield. That was how it had been decided in the East and that was how it could also be decided in the West where Germany, thanks to the divisions transferred from the East, was now for the first time since 1914 numerically superior to the enemy. Now Germany could do what it had wanted to do almost four years earlier: break the enemy's determination to fight, divide the Allies, throw the one into the sea and seize the other's capital. Then would be the time to make peace, a peace that was worth the fight. Once more Kaiser and Chancellor, politicians and people believed Ludendorff. He had promised Britain's capitulation after six months of submarine warfare; it did not happen. He had said that America's intervention was not worth mentioning and had described American troop transports as fair game for German torpedoes; no transport had been sunk and American divisions had begun to arrive in large numbers. Such errors could not diminish the strength of Hindenburg's and Ludendorff's position; their decisions carried the weight of natural laws in Berlin. If it was no longer possible to trust the two commanders, whom was it possible to trust, what was there still to hope for? William II ordered what Ludendorff dictated: all or nothing. 'And what happens if the offensive misfires?' Prince Max von Baden asked Ludendorff who replied magnanimously: 'Then Germany must perish.'

The storm broke on 21 March 1918: three-quarters of a million men and six thousand guns on a front of forty miles. Gains were made, in territory, material and prisoners. At the end of March Berlin was more confident of victory than at any time since September 1914. 'To have seen this . . . is to have seen world domination,' commented a young officer attached to the German Foreign Office Hindenburg spoke more forcefully than ever of the price the enemy would have to pay for this last bloody sacrifice of the Germans; and was decorated with the *Eiserne Kreuz mit goldenen Stahlen* (Iron Cross with Golden Rays). At the same time the intelligent Bavarian commander, Prince Rupprecht, wrote in his diary: 'We have now lost the war.' The offensive, regardless of all glorious horrors, had not achieved any of its aims.

The Germans decided to try once more. They tried on the French front what had failed on the British; they did so with less material, with more exhausted soldiers. A new offensive took place at the end of May with Paris as its aim; there were fresh successes and then again the advance came to a halt and again the battle was broken off. Even now Germany did not draw the political conclusions. The State Secretary for Foreign Affairs who tried to draw them and who spoke in the Reichstag of the fruit-lessness of mere military victories, of the need for new political methods, was dismissed at Ludendorff's behest.

The last break-through was attempted in July on the Marne and broken off on the 17th. The initiative passed to the enemy. On 8 August he took it with complete success. On 14 August Luden-dorff informed the Kaiser that Germany could no longer hope 'to break the martial will of our enemies by military action'. The realization came late and its formulation was cautious; a pithy final word by Hindenburg weakened it further. Yet it might have been enough to initiate at last the 'new methods' that pride and greed and delusion had obstructed for four years. These methods required a new government and it must be said in Ludendorff's favour that he would probably have offered no opposition to such a government. He gave no order, he vetoed nothing, he merely passed on the responsibility to those to whom he had hitherto given orders. But they were used to his orders and did nothing unless they were told to do so by him. They only meditated and moaned and waited, unable to understand that they, the victors even yesterday and for four years, were suddenly the vanquished. Therefore no political action was taken for six weeks after 14 August. The party leaders in Berlin, confident of victory even in the early summer, had scarcely begun to worry.

During those six weeks the military situation deteriorated very rapidly. Germany's allies, who a few months earlier had quarrelled over bits of Russian or Rumanian booty, deserted and surrendered unconditionally to the enemy. The first was Bulgaria. In the middle of September the Austrian government tried to use the small remains of its authority to obtain a separate peace. The Turkish front collapsed and the Austrians in Italy began to give way; the Germans in the West held out but under the signs of a mercilessly growing threat. What was to happen? The parliamentary leaders of the Centre, the left-wing Liberals, the Social Democrats and even the National Liberals, until recently very annexation-minded, agreed on the need for action, discussed and criticized; but they did not draw up a programme, they did not rush to seize the power which they had never been allowed to exercise and which they had no desire whatsoever to exercise for the first time in such gloomy circumstances. Even now they expected the decisive action to be taken by the Kaiser in his headquarters.

Finally it was taken. On 30 September a decree of William II announced that the people should 'participate more effectively than before in determining the fate of their country'; 'men enjoying the confidence of the people' should 'share extensively in the rights and duties of government'. Hertling, who could certainly not pretend to this qualification, resigned. The imperial decree granted what thousands of serious and informed Germans, deprived by a false system of all practical influence, had vainly demanded for years, parliamentary monarchy, a greater degree of democracy.

Unfortunately, however, the decision was very closely linked with another, taken on the previous day, namely to ask the enemy for an armistice, immediately, without delay or with no more than twenty-four hours' delay. During the armistice peace negotiations could be started. What General Ludendorff was now primarily concerned with was the armistice itself. To request it was to be the first task of the new government which 'enjoyed the confidence of the people'.

The head of the new government was a south German aristocrat, the heir to the throne of Baden, Prince Max. Not that he had been proposed by the Reichstag majority; even now the suggestion came from the Emperor, but the Prince had long been known to the deputies and they accepted him because in the circumstances he seemed the best mediator between the old and the new powers, perhaps also between Germany and the enemy. This view was not unjustified. Prince Max had made a name for himself by politically intelligent and highly moral speeches. His programme was good: to enter into discussions with the enemy while Germany still occupied a threatening position, and to influence the Anglo-Saxon mentality by clever concessions, particularly regarding the restoration of Belgium; political offensives which, carried out before the military ones, might yield success. Germany had not listened to Prince Max, either in March when the moment for such a policy would have been opportune, or in August. Now it was late; what could concessions made after a series of defeats achieve? Prince Max came to Berlin with the idea that Germany could no longer win but that it could still make victory difficult for the enemy; on this he hoped to build a policy that would lead to a peace with limited losses, not to capitulation. He had not yet taken office when he learnt for what task he had been selected. He protested and asked that Germany should hold out for at least another month. Repeating 'I want to save my army,' Ludendorff insisted on the request for an immediate armistice. Prince Max gave way, despair in his heart. The policy that he had hoped to pursue was lost for ever.

Ludendorff failed to understand this point. He did not see the political significance of the armistice which he was demanding. He really believed that during this time he could safely withdraw his exhausted army, together with all its belongings, from France and Belgium and strengthen it for new action, so that if the peace negotiations failed to take an acceptable course the Germans could fight with fresh forces. So easily did he think that he could suddenly extricate himself from an affair which he had until now pursued with such deadly seriousness. The members of the Entente saw the matter in a different light. They knew that at last they were superior to the enemy and that the enemy regarded himself as lost without a truce. Why on earth should they agree to a truce unless it was one that would make it impossible for him to resume the struggle? Why should they now renounce the phantasm of complete victory for which they had suffered such agony for four years? The war was no longer a chivalrous game, every advantage counted.

That was also the impression gained by the German party leaders when a major from headquarters tersely explained the situation to them. 'Each twenty-four hours can bring about a deterioration of the situation and allow the enemy to recognize our fundamental weakness.' An urgent request for an armistice made this point even clearer of course. The Conservative, von Heydebrand, expostulated: 'We have been lied to and deceived' – by Ludendorff's confidence in victory. The Social Democrat, Ebert, was white as a sheet, the National Liberal, Stresemann, for long Ludendorff's ally, struggled for breath. But it was a German general who wrote: 'We must blame our own folly and presumption. For many years I was worried that Ludendorff might overstretch the bow of our strength.'

Just as the army leaders had never paid any attention to the psychology of the enemy, they now gave no thought to the effect which their armistice offer must have on the German masses. Only a few months earlier Germany had been living under the intoxication of the profitable Russian peace, under the spell of promises and hopes. These alone had made the rigours of daily life bearable. Now suddenly everything had been in vain. Now it emerged that Germany had been misled by its leaders, by the Kaiser, the princes, the ministers and the generals; that only those men had been right who had warned their countrymen, particularly those who had been imprisoned for subversive activity like Karl Liebknecht. Was there any point in continuing to fight? Was there any point in continuing to starve? A policy of the kind planned by Max von Baden might have kept up national morale for a while. After the armistice offer there was no chance of holding on. Discouragement and dissolution at home henceforth influenced events abroad. People who complained about this effect asked for more than it is possible to demand from even the most patient nations.

Prince Max's cabinet included representatives of the parties which in the previous year had pushed through the Peace Resolution, Centre, Progressives and Social Democrats. Although the Social Democratic leaders were reluctant at that late hour to compromise themselves with such a problematic future they thought that they owed it to their country. Half in opposition and half in office the Social Democrats tried to explain events to their voters and to keep changes yet to come under control. They had no interest in the overthrow of the monarchy; given their programme they should have wished for it, but in practice they did not. On the other hand they needed to keep in close touch with the masses; otherwise, as Ebert put it, 'the whole lot will desert us for the Independents'. They worked under heavy pressure. The example and propaganda of the Russian Bolsheviks strengthened the mood created by the armistice offer. The Independent Socialists themselves were not sure of their case; i t was contested by Lenin's German supporters. How in such circumstances was it possible to build anything solid. The constitutional change pushed through in October in order to make the German Reich into a parliamentary monarchy on British lines resembled the emergency baptism of a weakly infant.

Prince Max had been forced to ask the President of the United States for an armistice. Wilson, a profound student of politics, asked further questions: how was the offer to be understood? Would his, the President's famous peace programme, be honestly accepted? Was he dealing with the autocrats who had hitherto ruled Germany in such irresponsible fashion, or with genuine representatives of the people? If it was with the latter what guarantees could he be given that the King of Prussia would not deprive them again of the authority which he had hypocritically granted them, and so on – self-righteous, pedantic questions, based on a study of German conditions which the professor had made many years before. These comings and goings took time. The Germans replied as positively, as clearly and with as much dignity as they could; they even agreed to give up the submarine war. In the end Wilson came out with the most important point; that the armistice conditions would be such as to prevent Germany from reopening hostilities. This lay in the cruel logic of things. What the President-professor did not notice was that this very logic decisively weakened his own position *vis-à-vis* his allies. Wilson wanted a 'just' peace, whatever he imagined that to be. The French and the British did not believe in the new transatlantic gospel. They had regretfully accepted it as long as they needed America against their mighty enemy; once Germany was crushed they had no more need of Wilson.

During this exchange of notes Ludendorff was dismissed. The general played a nasty game. Weeks after having precipitated the German capitulation he suddenly changed his tune, thundered against the consequences of his own action and against Germany's prostration before Wilson and spoke of fighting to the last man.

Those were words [Prince Max von Baden commented in his memoirs] which might have become a commander who had remained firm on 29 September in the face of a disheartened government, but not General Ludendorff who had forced a government determined on national defence to hoist the white flag ... I cannot deny that I began to suspect that General Ludendorff was less concerned to change our decision than to demonstrate against it.

The demonstration – the lie – later served him and all his supporters well.

In his third note Wilson urged the German nation to get rid of all its princes; then it might hope for a better negotiating position. The proposition was expressed in guarded terms but it was there, and that is how it was understood by the world and by Germany. The fact that William II had been powerless for years was of no help. To the Anglo-Saxon world he was the great criminal, and since Germany's chance of peace depended on the Anglo-Saxons, to many Germans he was a tiresome obstacle. The idea got about, it was even discussed in the bourgeois press, that the Kaiser must disappear in order to give Germany a tolerable peace. In order to keep the support of the masses the Social Democrats listened to these voices and took part in making Germany radical, a development which they basically disliked. Prince Max tried to persuade the Kaiser to make a 'grand gesture', to abdicate voluntarily, in the hope that it might save the German dynasties; but in vain.

William seemed determined to compress all the follies of his life into ultimate humiliation. Blind to what was happening in the country and to his own guilt he determined to march on Berlin at the head of reliable troops and to reconquer his throne; if necessary the capital must be reduced to rubble. There was nothing to be done with the man.

On 6 November the German armistice delegation, headed by Matthias Erzberger, set out for enemy headquarters. Peoples and leaders of the Entente powers wallowed in the sad, dirty illusion of victory.

9. Gloomy End, Gloomy Beginning

What held good for the party leaders – 'we have been lied to and deceived' – also held good for the mass of the German people, and for them more than for the leaders who could and should have known what was happening. The politicians had deceived themselves; the masses had been deceived. When they realized this fact there was no hope of holding on. The war, which for four years had been fought as an aggressive war with victory as its goal, could not now be fought as a defensive war; the war of the High Command could not be made into a people's war; the people had long ago exhausted themselves providing material for the mass army.

The feeble revolution from above, the move in October towards parliamentary government, was followed in the first days of November by a feeble revolution from below, a military strike. It began in the navy at Kiel, with a refusal of the sailors to obey orders, with a strike of the workers; spreading quickly to other ports, to Hamburg, Bremen and Lübeck, and then to various cities in the Reich, to Munich, Cologne and Brunswick, it eventually caught on almost everywhere and finally reached Berlin; there were red flags, open-air meetings and processions, shooting and much driving about. The Social Democrats wanted to save constitutional continuity – monarchy in one form or another. When the revolutionary movement gained the upper hand they had no choice but to approve of it. In Berlin on 9 November Philipp Scheidemann, from a window of the Reichstag building, proclaimed the republic, two hours before Karl Liebknecht, outside of the palace, proclaimed the socialist republic in the Russian sense. The Social Democrats merely got there first, recognizing the republic from sheer necessity. 'The German people,' added Scheidemann, 'has been victorious all along the line.' But what a late, miserable, hungry victory of the vanquished.

The princes renounced their thrones and disappeared. William went to Holland – he sent an act of abdication later. In Berlin Max von Baden appointed the Chairman of the Social Democratic party, Ebert, as Chancellor. The next day Ebert formed a provisional government consisting of six Socialists, three of the old party and three Independents. He had them elected by a plenary committee of the Berlin workers' and soldiers' councils, so that the Prussian capital, or what passed itself off as its representatives, appeared to be acting for the whole of Germany. But this was only a temporary expedient until a broader foundation of democratic legality could be found. Ebert planned that it should be provided by a German national assembly.

And the Supreme Command? The men round the aged Field-Marshal assessed the situation quickly and accurately. The monarchy could not be saved but order could; an orderly retreat of the armies across the Rhine; order generally, without which they could not imagine the world. Let there be no Russian conditions, no decline into Bolshevik chaos which would be followed by the occupation of the whole of Germany by the Entente. The generals, once they had let their Kaiser go, had to make common cause with the new rulers in Berlin, who – why not admit it – were decent, sensible men with whom they had been on reasonably good terms during the war. During the night of 9 to 10 November, Ebert had a memorable telephone conversation with General Groener, Ludendorff's successor. The following morning Groener noted in his diary: 'The Supreme Command puts itself at the government's disposal.'

Friedrich Ebert, less than fifty at the time, was one of the ablest Social Democratic politicians. He had begun to work for the party under Bismarck's Anti-Socialist Law and had passed through the classical career: artisan, trade unionist, journalist, member of parliament and finally party chairman. His energy, tact, natural dignity, sound common sense, authority and experience were undisputed. He was a man of the golden mean, of practical work, not given to theoretical hair-splitting. He believed in socialism yet he did not worry too much about the exact meaning of this venerable term. More firmly, more clearly he believed in democracy. The people must let itself be ruled by men of its choice at the local, state and national level and must control them through its assemblies. Such a system would inevitably bring the Social Democrats to power and they would inevitably do what was good for the German worker and the country; they would not interfere with other parties or social classes. Logically this development would occur within the framework of a republic but it could also happen within the framework of a monarchy which Ebert seemed quite prepared to accept in the autumn of 1918. There was no conflict between loyalty to the party and patriotism. Ebert had led the party in the defensive war, as he saw it, and in spite of the Independent Socialists had kept the majority of the party on the road taken in August 1914. The decision of September 1918 to send his Social Democrats into Prince Max's cabinet was in line with this attitude. He knew then what Ludendorff would shortly force the new government to do. He placed his country above his party and his party, in spite of everything and once again, at such a desperate hour at the service of the country. One thing he did not know: how wicked people can be, how shamelessly the German Conservatives would later reward him for his loyal service. Later? They were busily at work even then.

However much Friedrich Ebert believed in democracy his instinct, the instinct of a German master craftsman, needed a solid system. He profoundly detested all disintegration, collapse of authority, disobedience, rabble rousing speeches, hysterical gestures, robbery and murder. Such things he regarded as un-

German and intolerable. This means that he was no revolutionary because revolutions are characterized by such manifestations, as recent events in Russia had again shown. The fact that Ebert, as Chairman of the Council of People's Commissioners, felt responsible for Germany's fate was bound to strengthen his anti-revolutionary instinct. What would happen if law and order collapsed, if the troops, three million men from the West alone, returned home as leaderless gangs and found no work? If the Reich disintegrated into a few dozen separately governed, experimental, mad republics with all sorts of titles while the mighty victor lay in wait west of the Rhine? What would happen if the transport system, if food and coal supplies, collapsed? Germany was not Russia, it was a highly delicate, complex, vulnerable organism. Woe to him who injured it. Law and order must be preserved at all cost. This did not mean abandoning the new democracy; on the contrary, in Ebert's view it was the first prerequisite for its existence. Of more or less the same opinion were the men closest to him in the new government committees of the Reich and of Prussia: Noske, H. Müller, Otto Braun, W. Heine and K. Severing – former workers, artisans and employees who had risen from the party ranks, experienced local politicians and administrators, firm and uncomplicated souls concerned with practical matters, and, much more than they realized, products of national German education of the age of Bismarck.

The Supreme Command made its pact with Ebert and his friends on 10 November. 'It can be announced,' Hindenburg telegraphed to the army commanders, 'that the Supreme Command wants to collaborate with Chancellor Ebert, the former leader of the moderate Social Democratic Party in order to prevent the spread of terrorist Bolshevism in Germany.' Generals and Social Democrats had this in common that they were both greatly concerned with law and order.

The middle classes were pleased. Industrialists, senior civil servants, members of the 'war aims movement' and of the Conservative and National Liberal parties felt impotent; for the moment they pretended to be dead, they were unavailable. At the time they would certainly have adapted themselves to a democratic social order provided it guaranteed them just a fraction of the old amenities of life.

However, it never happens in times of crisis that one idea of how to grapple with the situation, like Ebert's, can assert itself without opposition and be carried out as neatly and fairly as intended. Other people have other ideas and what comes out of the clash of views no one has wanted. For the moment the generals wanted more or less the same as Ebert, whereas the extreme left wanted something different. It believed that the revolution must be pushed further and, as the Russian example had shown, that it could be pushed further, as far as communism. As Lenin followed Kerensky, Karl Liebknecht must follow Ebert.

There were gradations between Ebert and the extreme left of the Spartacists: left-wing majority Socialists who wanted to start by nationalizing the mines, right-wing Independent Socialists who were satisfied with parliamentary democracy, left-wing Independent Socialists who wanted to replace parliament by workers', soldiers' and peasants' councils without necessarily wanting dictatorship in the Leninist style, and so on. But these nuances within the three Socialist parties had no conciliatory effect, they merely increased the confusion. There was a difference between the situation in the capital and in the Reich, particularly in Bavaria, where under the imaginative leadership of an Independent Socialist, Eisner, the political unity of the whole left seemed momentarily assured. Berlin was the most radical spot. Here people talked loudest of a 'second revolution'; honest, free and courageous men like the Socialist hotspur Ledebour; subtle and bitter theorists like Rosa Luxemburg; fanatics obsessed by the cause as well as by awareness of their own mission like Karl Liebknecht; serious people and adventurers, demagogues and those spellbound by them. Ebert and Scheidemann, it was said, had betrayed the revolution to the middle classes. Public buildings and newspaper offices were occupied, there were demonstrations and illegal, threatening gestures. Was there, Ledebour argued, any legality left anywhere? Did not the people's commissioners themselves owe their mandate to an illegal movement? Had not everything been illegal after 9 November and was not therefore the people's first and foremost duty to have a complete revolution?

Ebert and his friends disliked these arguments. They believed that they were doing good work for the people. The eight-hour day, long an aim of the trade unions, was introduced everywhere in the Reich, a system of unemployment benefits was established, the demobilized were given back their jobs wherever possible and wage agreements between trade unions and employers were made legally binding for the industry concerned. In future all political representatives were to be elected in a universal, equal and secret ballot by all men and women over the age of twenty. Were these not useful reforms, social and democratic innovations? Were they not carried out in difficult and dangerous circumstances, while the government was committed to fulfil those terrible armistice conditions, to bring the troops across the Rhine and disband them and to deliver locomotives, goods trucks, machinery, cattle, ships and gold to the enemy? In such a situation Germany did not want a second revolution, in fact it did not want one in any situation; indeed it had not wanted the form of its first revolution but only its objective, a greater degree of democracy. This was how Ebert and Noske saw the situation – that was how Liebknecht and Ledebour saw it.

The result was clashes. But the government had no military power. That was controlled by the army; indeed not even by the old army because some units proved unreliable and useless in the struggle against internal enemies. It became necessary to form detachments of keen volunteers from among the old army – the *Freikorps*. They were headed by politically conscious leaders, men who despised discussion and who believed in the sword that cuts the knot. They were used against the Spartacists or, as they had recently started to call themselves, the Communists – in January in Berlin, then in Saxony, Thuringia and Munich. Though nominally they were all, or almost all, under the control of the People's Commissioner, Noske, they were in reality dominated by their own spirit, which was not the spirit of true soldiers but of adventuring mercenaries. The Social Democrats failed to form their own units or to make use of those that developed in spite of them.

Nobody was in control of the German, the central or east European situations. Neither the victors in Paris, nor the defeated Germans, nor the defeated victor in the East. Lenin had worked out everything, had planned all the revolutionary operations, yet he too failed to get what he wanted. The revolution in Russia was to be only a means of unleashing revolution in Europe, particularly in Germany. Yet the very spectacle that Russia offered compromised European Communism from the start, once and for all. All that Lenin's friends and agents in Germany accomplished was to split the country in three, to weaken the cause of democracy, to strengthen their enemies and to drive their supporters into a blind alley of fatal double conflict.

Hence the rapid worsening of the atmosphere, the assassinations, the instances of persons 'shot while trying to escape', the crowded prisons. The Communists also murdered, the raving mob also committed acts of horrible lynch justice. But when it comes to figures the White terror was the worse one. Worst of all was the fact that the Social Democratic rulers were connected with it, without controlling its perpetrators. They were extremely angry about the assassination of Karl Liebknecht and Rosa Luxemburg by the *Freikorps*, yet helplessly allowed the cynically mild sentence on the murderers to stand, just as four months later they regretted the mass executions in Munich without stopping them. The use of force was inevitable in the situation of this gloomy winter and spring; the Communists who looked up to Lenin as their model could hardly complain about it. The misfortune was that it was not the force of democratic authority but of rough mercenaries who had no connections with the new republic that was used against them. Consequently the democratic government soon found itself placed in a false light and in a false position of authority. The rulers had not wanted this, they had not foreseen it; and they were quite right when they later accused the Communists of having caused the chaos. Yet if they had mastered it themselves with their own resources, they and what was dear to them would have emerged unscathed; instead the history of the first German republic began with mean and brutal deeds.

What a burden the Social Democrats carried on their shoulders, what conflict there was in the minds of these men who were fitted for practical work but far less for resolving intellectual contradictions. They had done everything humanly possible to prevent the revolution; but they had called themselves revolutionaries in the past and the men whose revolutionary efforts they now helped to suppress had risen from their own ranks. They put down the Red revolution together with the generals, with the right; but as at moments and perforce they took part in the revolution, in order to bring it under control, and as they were connected with it by old theories and names, the generals and the right later accused them of having made the revolution while the radical left accused them of having betrayed it. They seemed to be in league with their enemies in order to fight themselves, the socialism which they pretended to represent. From this maze of contradictions there was only one way out: to be strong oneself and to act. Strong men could afford contradictions; those that could not be resolved by reflection would disappear in the face of successful, creative action. Would the Social Democrats in spite of everything be strong and act?

National elections to a constituent assembly were held on 19 January and the assembly met in Weimar at the beginning of February. The town of Goethe and Schiller was chosen in preference to turbulent Berlin or the city of the *Paulskirche*. It was a well meant gesture. The Social Democrats were by far the strongest group, the Independent Socialists a very small one. The old Conservative Party which now called itself the *Deutschnationale Partei* – the only party whose programme professed loyalty to the monarchy – also had only a small following. The nation seemed to have decided by its vote to have neither a Hohenzollern monarchy nor a Soviet republic. Was Ebert right then to trust the people, to despise the extremists and to observe the rules of the democratic game?

10. Reflection

The stream flows on. It is the observer who must stop now and again, and the period with which we are dealing invites us to pause. The recent past misunderstood and terrible; people's minds confused, and disappointment, hatred, malice and tiredness mingled with vague hopes; legal and moral concepts unsettled, the economy in a state of chaos and the national frontiers uncertain; with misery on all sides there were seemingly also great opportunities the realization of which needed creative daring. 1919 was a fateful year. It was up to Germany to come to terms with its recent past, with the start, the direction and the end of the war, and to reform its state and society accordingly; it was up to Europe to end the war by making the right kind of peace.

In fact Germany could not come to terms with its recent past. Those who were most to blame were of least help. Tirpitz and Ludendorff published their memoirs in the early summer of 1919, works full of bitterness against everything and everybody except themselves. They had always done everything right and everything would have come out right in the end if only people had listened to them. What egoism, what unshakeable self-righteousness after such a fall! Surely there are moments of self-examination, moments in which one must try to rise above oneself and to be fair? Nothing like that occurred in the minds of the rulers of yesterday. They, who should have been glad not to be in the dock, accused God and the world, Britain, Russia, Wilson, the Social Democrats and the German people. They ignored, obliterated, distorted and denied whatever did not fit in with their self-praise.

Hindenburg, too, succeeded in bringing his fame through all post-war confusion into the republican epoch. The supreme commander of the German army was absent when the bitterest decisions on war and peace were made; on those occasions he left the room and let others stick their necks out. Later he expressed disapproving approval; he was a living symbol of the old, unconquered glory. His railway carriage was smothered in flowers when he returned to his native Hanover in the summer of 1919.

In the autumn he appeared before the commission appointed by the Constituent Assembly to examine the conduct of the war and the collapse, and announced tersely that the German army had been stabbed in the back. Many people puzzled by the defeat were relieved to hear this. It was the idea which a German general, Schulenburg, had voiced as early as 9 November 1918: 'Our men will claim in any case that they were stabbed in the back by their comrades-at-arms, the navy, together with Jewish war profiteers and shirkers . . .' Max Weber on the other hand wrote:

> The cheap judgements now made by the supporters of the unsuccessful gamblers' party – of course – are contemptible, unfair and unkind. More than four years of hunger, and in particular more than four years of camphor and morphine injections to keep up emotions – no nation has endured anything like it.

This was a momentous, intentional or unintentional misunderstanding to which even decent, chivalrous officers succumbed. They believed that by their attitude the people at home had caused the defeat, whereas the events of November were only a reaction to the defeat that had long ago been certain and was suddenly admitted.

To understand the defeat after all the victories and achievements was difficult. It was difficult in wartime to find the right perspective: to honour the sacrifice, not to heap undignified insults on one's country, one's nation and oneself and yet to produce the criticism without which any new beginning was impossible. It was difficult to be moderately clear even about the so-called war guilt question. As the Entente inserted a paragraph about Germany's 'sole responsibility' for the war into the peace treaty – a stupid, senseless assertion inspired by rage, suffering and arrogance – so all the efforts of German scholarship were to be directed towards proving that the Germans were not the only guilty party, that they were not guilty at all, that all the others were but not the Germans.

Why did Germany not make peace at the right moment? Over this question too there was much confusion. After all, Germany had offered peace in 1916 and accepted the Russian offer in 1917 whereas the Entente had never offered anything and had rejected everything. That was true. However, the realization that Germany as the strategic attacker, as the victor who had penetrated far into enemy territory, should not just have offered peace, but a peace clearly renouncing all gain, that such a detailed and honest offer alone might have had a chance of success, that even the enemy could not have refused it – this realization presupposed a considerable desire for truth. A desire which the Germans rarely have. They believe what pleases them, what satisfies their pride and their hatred; that is their truth. Those Germans, on the other hand, who proclaimed their country's guilt often did so in such a brash and gloating manner that they irritated the public without convincing it. It was no achievement as such to say and write that the war had been madness. Every soldier had achieved more than that. What mattered was who said it and how. The memory of the collapse, of the great victory that suddenly turned into the greatest defeat, confused the nation and was misused by bad men for their own ends then and many years later.

The princes went. Hohenzollern and Wittelsbachs, Wettiner and Guelfs and Zähringer, the dynasties which for a thousand years had shared or decided, as they did in 1848, the fate of Germany – within two days they all vanished. What an unprecedented event this would have been in less unprecedented times. Now it seemed to make little difference. They were not hated, the princes of Württemberg, Baden and Hesse, and there was no reason to hate them. They were sent packing because there was a revolution and this was what happened in revolutions. No hand was raised on their behalf; royal ministers shortly applied for and were given office under the Republic. Something that died so easily could not have had any vitality. We know how weak and harmless the German monarchies had long become; at first all the others and in the end, during the war, even the Hohenzollern. It is possible to think that it might have been better to keep them. While they could not achieve much nor prevent much, they were at least centres of tradition and style. Perhaps they would later have acted as a restraining element – with a king in Munich or Stuttgart it is difficult to imagine a victory for National Socialism. However, these are speculations. One can also argue that the victory of National Socialism everywhere in Germany fifteen years later shows how profoundly the Wilhelminian era, the war and the post-war period, the inflation and finally the economic crisis, had changed the character of the nation and how very tenuous had become the links with the past which the dynasties represented. We must deal with the facts and try to understand them as best we can and not speculate about what might have been for a while longer. Let us then take farewell of the names which played so important a role in the first part of our story; let us watch the noble lords retire to their properties from which they occasionally emerged for a military reunion or the unveiling of a statue, before they died one by one.

To the extent that the revolution hit the Kaiser and the princes, and almost no one but them, it hit a phantom. The princes had not caused the war and they had certainly not led it; after 1866 they had no power. They were innocent; the guilty – if it is possible to attribute guilt to a particular class of human beings – were very different people: the industrialists, the members of the Farmers' Federation, of the War Aims Movement, the hack writers and politicians. They had no qualms about throwing the princes overboard, harmless ballast which they did not care about, provided more important things remained safely stored in the hold of the ship. People believed that something had been achieved just by the establishment of the 'Republic' – as though they were still living in the middle of the nineteenth century when the fall of the monarchy might in fact have had creative significance. 'The German Reich is a Republic', said the first sentence of the new constitution. Unfortunately this did not signify much.

Germany was not fortunate in matters of politics. How could it be so now, in such sombre circumstances, when it had not been fortunate in recent years, when all its efforts and heroic deeds had come to nought because of bad policy. There was no sense behind the November revolution just as there is no sense behind the nervous breakdown of an individual. If it was supposed to achieve what did in fact come about, a parliamentary, federalist republic, there was no need to do more than to carry the October reforms a little further. Constitutional monarchy has many advantages over a republic and hardly any disadvantages. The revolution would have made sense if it had developed along the lines envisaged by Liebknecht who wanted to give it a Russian, Communist purpose. But could Germany have benefited in any way from the Russian system? To what new absurdity, what new agony would that have led? There is no reason to regret that this development did not come about. One may regret the nervous breakdown, although the patient was not responsible for it. The preventive treatment which would have been advisable was refused by the rulers, a peace offer at the right moment and at the end also the Kaiser's resignation at the right moment.

The disappearance of the dynasties might have meant the dis appearance of the system which had been of dynastic origin and character, the system of the federal states. But they did not disappear. Kingdoms and grand duchies remained, they only changed their names, calling themselves free states, peoples' states and so on. The administrative machinery, the ministers and the parliaments remained. Even Prussia remained, Hohenzollern-Prussia, the artificial kingdom that had long ago lost its historical identity and had become part of Germany; it continued without the Hohenzollern, and did so within the accidental frontiers that Bismarck had given it. None of the annexations of 1815, the Rhineland and the Province of Saxony, or of 1866, Hanover, Kassel and Frankfurt, were renounced. There was some attempt to do so, but it did not succeed, just as no attempt at a rational reorganization of the Reich succeeded. The past had done its work well and the present was uncreative. The princely edifices remained although they were no longer occupied by princes; political bureaucrats reluctantly replaced the noble masters. A revolution, however modest, always contains a variety of elements. A German republic, one and indivisible, would have been in the style of the French revolution, in accordance with the ideas of the extremists of 1848 and with Lassalle's ideas. But let us not forget that even the older Socialists were divided about what form the German state should take, and that Bebel and Wilhelm Liebknecht began as 'greater' German federalists. Now *one* driving force of the revolution was directed against the Prussianized Reich, against 'the centralism of Berlin' which fed on war and became the hated force behind the war. On this point the Bavarian Socialists agreed with the Bavarian Conservatives. Even before the end of 1918 it was certain that the federal states would remain, whether their existence was historically logical or not.

Yet how could they remain after the disappearance of the other great age-old obstacle over which the German revolution in 1849 had come to grief? When the most splendid dynasty, the one most encumbered with blessings and curses, the House of Habsburg, had disappeared with the other German dynasties? Austria-Hungary was in a state of total disintegration, a fate which had threatened the Habsburg Empire for seventy years. If Czechs and Slovaks, Croats and Slovenes, Rumanians and Magyars were allowed or compelled to establish national states and statelets, what alternative did the German Austrians have except to do what they would have done in 1848 but for the existence of the monarchy, that is become part of a German Reich. The *grossdeutsche* parties, Social Democrats and Catholics, were now in charge everywhere. The colours of 1848, black, red, gold, reappeared. There was no king of Prussia, no Windisch-Graetz or Schwarzenberg to veto the natural course of events. Could the loser, Germany, then be the winner after all? West of the Russian frontier the Germans were the strongest nation in Europe in terms of energy and numbers. If the principle of the national state had been seriously applied, as Paris and Washington intended, national frontiers would have been drawn everywhere to accord with linguistic frontiers; and Germany, enriched by large Alpine and Danube regions and probably also by northern Bohemia, could have got over the loss of Posen and Alsace-Lorraine. Its new constitution envisaged the unification of German Austria and the Reich, and the two governments in Vienna and Berlin prepared to put this into effect.

But that was not how the victors saw the situation. They were certainly not prepared to see their painfully achieved triumph provide the enemy with more spoils than themselves, so that he would appear stronger and bigger on the map and become a threat to the independence of their new friends in the East and South-East. It was not possible to apply a concept like national self-determination all that consistently. It was applicable where it could be used against Germany but if its effect was overwhelmingly in Germany's favour it must not be applied. The Austrians were told that they must not unite with Germany. It remains to be asked whether a prohibition of this kind has any value. Short-term, diplomatic decisions can only have lasting validity if they coincide with what is really wanted, and what was really wanted needed yet to be discovered. The fact was that the dissolution of Habsburg Austria helped the Germans politically. Did they still want a complete nation-state as the men of 1848 had done? Could they still give it the purpose that those men had wanted to give it? If so the veto of an ephemeral constellation of powers would hardly keep this from happening.

Great victories and great defeats prove and achieve little and Kipling is surely right when he describes them as impostors:

> If you can meet with triumph and disaster
> And treat those two impostors just the same . . .

Either they record what was anyway about to happen, like the decline of the Spanish empire since the seventeenth century; then they are merely signs and not decisive in themselves. Or they state the relative position of power at a given moment. In that case the decisions and actions taken as a result will not outlast this situation even momentarily. The rulers of France, Clemenceau and Marshal Foch, knew this. They knew that in spite of all glorious achievements it had been America and not France which had conquered Germany. They also knew that Germany had conquered Russia and that without the Russian contribution the West as a whole could not have won. They knew that the position of November 1918 could be maintained only as long as America was involved and active in Europe – an uncertain factor. Hence their pathetic attempt to transform the ephemeral situation into a permanent one by various tricks and additional safeguards which could also be only ephemeral. It was impossible for any treaty system, however much devoted malice had gone into its preparation, to create a solid order from the chaos of the disintegrated empires. So far the right of the stronger had always prevailed and in a confused situation it was bound to prevail even more than in the days of wise old diplomats and monarchical solidarity.

The Peace of Brest-Litovsk has been called the forgotten peace but the Germans have not forgotten it. They know that they defeated Russia and sometimes they look upon this proudly as the real, if unrewarded European achievement of the war. 'We warded off something . . . *much* worse – the Russian knout. This achievement we retain,' wrote Max Weber. It probably really was a European achievement. It is Europe's self destructive problem that those who protected it in the East against an anti-European power were made to lay down their swords not once but twice by a West European coalition allied with Russia; and that, given the German's behaviour, the alternatives with which they presented the West, this suicidal act was almost inevitable. Europe wanted to become neither German nor Russian. The German danger seemed nearer, more direct and therefore the West blindly accepted the other until finally all Europe combined could no longer counter-balance the weight of Russia. This strategy was not apparent in 1918 because both giants had been defeated, Russia because of the exertions of Germany and Germany because of those of the West. But such a paradoxical ending is rare in history and it could not be final. To quote Max Weber once more:

American's domination of the world was as inevitable as Rome's after the Punic War. Let us hope that there will be no change and that it will not be shared with Russia. *This* for me remains the aim of our future world policy, because the Russian danger has been exorcized only for the moment, not forever.

Naturally the peace-makers in Paris knew that Lenin's Russia was the enemy of their Europe. They themselves made feeble, unsuitable efforts to crush Bolshevism. At moments they did not prevent German *Freikorps* in the Baltic from fighting the Communists, under the formal control of the new Estonian and Latvian states. But when it came to serious decisions the French were more afraid of Germany than of Russia. They preferred to find support against Russia among their new allies in the East, Poland, Czechoslovakia and Rumania, hastily created states that had yet to prove themselves.

Would it have been possible for Germany to make common cause with the other defeated and outlawed nation, for example against Poland? This idea too appeared at once as it was bound to; in foreign policy there are only a few elementary alternatives which always reappear in different forms. But the Russian possibility was not a feasible one at that moment. Both nations were too weak, and the Russians were in the throes of the most terrible civil war; the alliance of two sick nations cannot produce anything healthy. Moreover it would have meant an alliance not merely between states but between social forms and ideas, and Germany would have had to throw itself into the arms of Communism. This step it could not and did not wish to take. Even if it had wanted to take it the Western victors would not have allowed it. 'If the men (the Communists) in Berlin should get the upper hand in spite of everything the Entente will occupy Berlin. The prospect is not a pleasant one but it is a re-insurance,' General Max Hoffmann wrote. Germany thus remained dependent on itself, alone and cut off. The victors gave it no advice, being too arrogant and too malicious to do so. Germany and its allies had to fend for themselves, humiliated and in misery. The past did not help even though the old, pre-Bismarckian past was still there and honest men tried to link up with it. The official writings of Bismarck's opponents, of the men of 1848 and even of 1870, were republished: back to Freiherr vom Stein, to Ludwig Uhland and Konstantin Frantz. The illustrious dead who had not been able to do much in their lifetime could do even less in these strange times. Between them and the present lay the obstacle of the Bismarckian Reich and the terrible dream of the four-year war. Those who wanted to perpetuate the nature of the Kaiser's Reich without the Kaiser, industrialists and landowners, professors, judges and bureaucrats, were very strong politically and economically. A society like the German one, highly civilized and integrated, consisting not of two classes, as Marx imagined, but of hundreds, cannot be transformed by an act of revolutionary theory; it changes gradually under the pressure of new facts, but it cannot be changed by voluntary decision. That was the position of the Conservatives, and without intending to do so the Social Democrats worked towards the same end. Although they wanted social democracy they also, and above all, wanted order without which, they believed, the highly complex supply system would collapse and give way to famine and civil war; they wanted to keep the Reich together and show that they could rule. This attitude and the fact that they rejected any complete change inspired by theory – socialization or confiscation, overthrow of the old bureaucracy, 'councils' instead of parliaments – had the effect of making the activities of the groups on their left even noisier and more confusing. There was little to distinguish the extreme 'Right' from the extreme 'Left'; imaginative ex-officers, adventurers, estranged from civilian life, enemies of the bourgeois Reich and of bourgeois democracy, dreamt of a new national community that would fight for the interests of the country, mastering matter without being materialistic. Such ideas were in the air and could be expressed in attractive terms but their supporters were certain to be disillusioned because reality cannot be shaped by fanciful doctrines. Practice and fantasy part company. Whereas the practical men regarded all great hopes as utopian the idealists overestimated Germany's possibilities at such a difficult moment, and they demanded too much; as a result they intensified the nation's internal division and self-alienation.

In the spring of 1919 two assemblies deliberated in Europe. The one, in Paris, was meant to give the world peace, the other, in Weimar, was meant to transform Germany into a republic on the Western model. 'A new order which is the product of this terrible defeat and violation is unlikely to take roots,' wrote Max Weber.

Part Ten
Weimar

In the turmoil of events in the twentieth century no nation is
master of its destiny. All contribute to the general world climate
but none determines it. Over the last years Germany had done
more than any other nation to shape events. During the four-
year war it had divided the world into two parts, a small one
which it ruled and a very much larger one against which it fought.
The strain on its resources was tremendous; it was possible to
bear because the Germans were the strongest nation in Europe,
and Europe continued to be regarded as the most important
continent and the centre of the world.

For four years Germany fought and defied the five continents of the
world by land and sea and air. The German armies upheld her tottering
confederates, intervened in every theatre of war with success, stood
everywhere on conquered territory and inflicted on their enemies more
than twice the bloodshed they suffered themselves. To break their
strength and science and to curb their fury it was necessary to bring all
the greatest nations of mankind into the field against them. Overwhelming populations, unlimited resources, measureless sacrifice,
the sea blockade, could not prevail for fifty months. Small states were
trampled down in the struggle; a mighty empire was battered into un-
recognizable fragments; and nearly twenty million men perished or
shed their blood before the sword was wrested from that terrible hand.
Surely, Germans, for history it is enough! [Winston Churchill]

The nation which had done these deeds now faced the problem
of returning to everyday life, of coming to terms with itself and
the world; of continuing old habits and yet making a new start;
of striking a new balance between classes and parties and giving
order and meaning to the cramped existence of sixty-five million

people. Above all, and this had long been their most difficult problem, the Germans had to *live*; to live within reduced frontiers, deprived of the fruits of years of work. They had lost their capital abroad, their colonies, their trade connections and their merchant fleet; at home nothing remained but the grey residue of four years of highly unproductive bedevilment. 'We start again from the very beginning, as we did after 1648 and 1807. This is what it amounts to. Only that today we live faster, work faster and show more initiative,' wrote Max Weber.

There are certain moments of intoxication, of crisis and universal confusion in which the individual is gripped by political passion, in which public affairs seem more important to him than his own. Such a moment occurred in August 1914 and perhaps in November 1918. Normally, however, the citizen notices politics no more than the healthy man notices his body; he knows that he has it but he pays no attention to it; it works automatically. Most Germans wanted to return to a normal existence, to work and to eat. But how they would work and eat and be housed, how their children would grow up, how the old would live and die, depended only in part on them; it depended on German politics and world politics. Then there were restless spirits whose main purpose in life was not their own advancement but to see the state make their noble or foolish dreams come true. There are always such people. In quiet times they remain restrained and unheard; in unquiet times they find scope. The times to come were unquiet and could but be so. The war had destroyed or weakened old systems; it had not created new ones.

1. Two Basic Documents

Henceforth Germany was to live under two basic laws. The Treaty of Versailles governed its relationship with its former enemies, with the outside world. The Weimar Constitution gave new form to its domestic conflicts and endeavours.

The peace treaty was a misfortune, only explained – there is no question of excusing it – by the fact that misfortune usually leads to new misfortune, that the men who had directed the war, and directed it in the way they had, could not now transform themselves into men of peace. Wilson, the American, wanted to break the chain of evil and to establish justice wherever there had been injustice. This he failed to do. Justice could only have been established if all states, nations and people concerned had been just. As long as they were not – and there was no reason to suppose that they would be at this bleak, grim, vindictive moment of history – there could at best be practical solutions, careful compromises between power and power, between the wishes of the weak and the hard facts that had become history; there could be no 'justice'.

The American professor who wanted to cure the world with a panacea brewed up in the tidy laboratory of his mind fell out with his European partners – particularly with the most pessimistic among them, the French Prime Minister, Clemenceau. Wilson stood for naïve, young, powerful America for whom the war had been fun. Clemenceau stood for exhausted, tragic France. The old man who could forget neither 1918 nor 1871 (when he was thirty), had only one thought: to preserve for France by means of hundreds of cunning tricks the position gained by such terrible sacrifices but untenable in the long run without the help of its allies.

The product of this clash of attitudes was repulsive: a close-knit mesh of regulations, intending to be 'just' and unquestionably so in many details, but allowing injustice inspired by malice, hatred and the intoxication with victory to slip in wherever possible; so much so that the whole, in spite of individual examples of justice, seemed an enormous instrument for the suppression, exploitation and permanent humiliation of Germany. Whatever wrong Prussia-Germany had done in the 150 years was to be redressed: the Polish partition of 1772 – the new Polish state was given Posen and West Prussia, so that East Prussia was once more separated from the main body of Germany; the annexation of Schleswig-Holstein – there was to be a plebiscite in north Schleswig to enable those who so wished to join Denmark;

naturally Alsace-Lorraine was to be given back to France and there were to be other, smaller, clumsier frontier rectifications. There were to be plebiscites in any place where there was a possible majority that might not want to remain in Germany, such as in Upper Silesia, in parts of East Prussia. Yet plebiscites were not allowed in countries that did not belong to Germany and the majority of whose inhabitants now probably wanted to join Germany, such as in Austria, in northern Bohemia. The new concept of legality – that a people must determine its own fate – was applied where it could harm Germany, not elsewhere; in the same manner as the Germans had applied it at Brest-Litovsk against the Russians. The Allies were happy to let the Brest-Litovsk settlements stand, in so far as any control of the chaos in the East was possible. They welcomed the fact that Germany had weakened Russia by the application of 'just' principles and they were glad to weaken Germany by applying the same principles. The rest was a scuffle among the new or Successor States which tried to expand as much as possible at the expense of Germany, Russia and each other, using historical, statistical, economic, national or linguistic arguments or just the right of the stronger. What became clear in the process was that 'justice' was unobtainable even if there was no powerful unjust force to prevent its establishment. The three unjust giants, Russia, Germany and the Habsburgs, had been defeated; yet the Poles and the Lithuanians, the Czechs and the Poles and the Slovaks, the Hungarians and the Rumanians, the Yugoslavs and the Italians were still incapable of ensuring that justice was done among themselves. Lloyd George said angrily to the Polish negotiator in Paris:

We, the French, the British, the Italians and the Americans, fought for the freedom of the small nations, which you had not the slightest hope of obtaining without us. You know that I myself belong to a small nation and it hurts me bitterly to see all of you, before you have even crawled into the light of freedom, want to oppress nations or parts of nations that do not belong to you. You are more imperialistic than Britain and France.

By drawing political frontiers for Germany based on the result of doubtful plebiscites a dangerous precedent was established.

Nobody, however, imagined that Germany could one day use this principle for its own ends; or asked what might become of central and eastern Europe then. For the moment Germany lost a tenth of its population – of which about half spoke German – an eighth of its territory, the major part of its iron ore and a substantial part of its coal – immense assets whose value was not calculated because their loss was intended only to redress old wrongs. The same applied to the colonies; they were taken from Germany not because it had been defeated but because it had by its barbaric behaviour proved unworthy of possessing colonies. On the same grounds the victors did not annex Germany's colonies outright but had their administration and exploitation transferred to them by the new League of Nations. These were self-righteous, greedy and short-sighted tricks; dissimulations that one does not like to remember and that would best be forgotten were it not for the fact that otherwise the rest of the story becomes incomprehensible. These deceptions hung like a millstone round the neck of the new German republic and oppressed the future of Europe as the great war itself, had it been terminated with a modicum of sense, could not have done. Mutilated Germany, further condemned to various immediate deliveries – locomotives, ships, cables – from its war-ruined stocks, was called upon to bear the blame for all the damage which the war – its war of aggression – had inflicted on the allied nations. No one knew the amount involved or over what period it was to be paid. Only this much was clear: the sums at stake could be increased arbitrarily, depending on what was included in the losses of states and civilian populations, and surpassed all imagination.

We have learnt something since then and such an iniquitous folly as 'reparations' was not repeated at a later period which also had its follies. We know today that the wars of this century are bad for everybody and that the victor cannot undo the damage done to him by doubling or increasing a hundredfold that done to the defeated enemy. If he tries to do this he multiplies the damage done to himself. Victory is an illusion. The Paris peace-makers did not know this, and if we criticize them for it we should remember that influential Germans were equally ignorant and had intended to mete out to the Entente the treatment that Germany was experiencing. Let us not linger over examples of the blindness of statesmen and experts who here revealed themselves in all their human frailty. Let us only say that the principle of reparations as applied by the Treaty of Versailles created thirteen years of chaos and folly and that it could not do otherwise. Europe was much too densely populated, too small and too poor to be divided into two parts, one that paid and one that was paid for. This did not mean that Germany should not have made an honest contribution towards rebuilding the ruined French and Belgian territories. It could and should have done so; and it was ready to do so.

An American journalist reporting the Paris negotiations wrote: 'We are going to have a League of Nations, weak, wrong, capable of great abuse; and we shall get a peace also, full of dynamite which will burst into war.' About the peacemakers he said:

The rulers of the world have sat here with the problem of human living before them, laid out on their table by the tragedy of war. That should have opened their minds and hearts to tackle the job in some new, big way. They wanted to. There was good-will here. But their old bad habits of mind, their fixed attention upon things they do not really want, their age, their education – these have made it impossible for them to do their work.

Not only the diplomats but also the nations were to blame for the bad treaty: 'Only I see very clear here how it is not merely a class division, but an issue which divides every human heart against itself. Every little peasant and working man wants both his revenge upon the foe, his share of the recompense for injury done *and* no more wars.' These were two conflicting wishes, the one cancelling out the other. In fact what the peacemakers in Paris had promised to do was neither new nor unprecedentedly just, but old and bad: 'Consciously or not they are all working, fidgeting and intriguing to get back to the point where they stood before the war . . . But the world cannot reverse gear; it cannot. It can fall or decline, like Greece or Rome, but it can never reverse gear.' The journalist, Lincoln Steffens, an intelligent critic was as disappointed by the attitude of the Germans as by the peace treaty; but more about that later.

It is an old truth that one should place least trust in one's own right, in one's own power and its duration when one is on top; then is the moment for humility, the moment to doubt of one's own merit. There is always something in victory to be ashamed of. The guilt of the peacemakers of 1919 lies in the moralistic superiority with which they treated the defeated enemy; having all sinned heavily themselves during the war, albeit with differences of degree; and being all about to sin heavily again. They had a right to impose this or that condition on the vanquished, but not to decree that he alone was responsible for the war, thereby anticipating historical research. Nor should they have founded a League of Nations in which they did not believe and for the realization of which they were not prepared to make sacrifices or great moral efforts; as a result they sullied and spoilt the whole idea for a long time to come. It is bad to reach for the sublime with an impure heart.

The German government signed the treaty. The paragraph on war guilt and reparations, the limitation of the German army and navy to the size of those of a small state, the occupation of the Rhineland for fifteen years or more, the separation from the Saar whose mines France would exploit – everything was accepted. But not approved. The Germans signed under protest because they had no choice. They called the treaty a 'dictation' which indeed it was; because genuine negotiations had taken place only between the victors, not between victors and vanquished. Such a treaty does not last longer than the political situation on which it is based. The vanquished observes it only as long as he is defeated and weaker than the others. He has no moral obligation to observe it. And, given the world, and the way in which the balance of power is eventually redressed, it was unlikely that the Versailles treaty would last long. The only question was how it would be revised. This depended on both sides, on Germany and the Western powers.

Indignation in Germany was fanned by the belief of the Germans that they had been deceived; they had surrendered believing in Wilson's just peace programme, but the peace which they had been given, although bearing some relation to the Fourteen Points fell short of them in spirit, as a whole. What the Germans could not and did not wish to understand was simply that when Germany requested an armistice in October 1918 for moral and military reasons it no longer had any claim to Wilson's programme. It ought to have accepted the 'just peace' while it could still do wrong or abstain from doing wrong; while it was still a power. After Ludendorff's sudden 'we are lost' it was no longer a power and its appeals to Wilson's noble principles sounded hollow and morally false. The good-natured, stupid German Michael had surrendered voluntarily because he believed in the American gospel when he could have fought on and won – that was what the rabble-rousers now told the Germans. If it was untrue the truth was complicated and unpleasant. Why worry too much about it?

Those whose indignation was loudest were those who were most to blame; who for four years had contemptuously rejected a moderate peace; who had been determined to impose on the enemy conditions at least as brutal as the Treaty of Versailles, and who then suddenly and at the worst moment had cried 'we are lost'. They directed their false anger not so much against the outside world as against part of their own people. Against the left, politically speaking. Against the parliamentarians who for years had preached restraint and who had been called upon too late to assume responsibility; who had not wanted capitulation in October 1918, the men of the Social Democratic Party, of the Centre. They were now presented as the real criminals. Had they not assumed power or the semblance of power at the very moment of military catastrophe? Were they not spiritual brothers of the Entente, these democrats, these supporters of the parliamentary system and of the new American gospel which had proved such a terrible failure? Had they not signed the treaty in spite of the protest of the Conservatives, or as they now called themselves the *Deutschnationalen*? It was easy to forget that the Supreme Command had advised or ordered the treaty to be signed, particularly as Hindenburg had happened to be out of the room when the

Chief of Staff, Groener, stated the army's views for the last time. Those who bore the greatest guilt pretended to be innocent. Those who were innocent or much less guilty appeared as the creators and as true, typical representatives of the Versailles system.

The peace treaty affected Germany in two ways. It created a distorted, unnatural relationship between Germany and the world, its neighbours to the West and the East; and it divided the nation because one group of politicians and their supporters quickly found themselves insidiously being made to shoulder the responsibility for every misfortune. They protested, but not very vigorously nor very successfully.

The second basic document, the Weimar Constitution, was not dictated but freely drafted by German hands. On paper it looked as good as the treaty looked bad. But constitutions, like peace treaties, only in real life become what they are. What is put down on paper at the beginning will influence future events without determining them.

Hugo Preuss, the author of the first draft, wanted to create something homogeneous and to move firmly away from the recent Bismarck–Hohenzollern past. He wanted the German nation to be a living organism which ordered its state as it wished, without mumbo-jumbo about 'allied governments', divided sovereignty or sum of sovereignties. It was essential to break up the old authoritarian kingdom of Prussia into its component parts. Let the other federal states, or at least the large ones, continue to exist if they must, though no longer as 'states' but as self-governing units completely under the control of the Reich. There was to be one country, one government, one people – and the people were to be called upon to decide by direct vote whenever their various representative organs, Reichstag, House of States and President, failed to agree. This went as far as only the most extreme unitarians had gone seventy years earlier, in the *Pauls-kirche*. Hugo Preuss believed in the German people and in the good judgement of the majority.

As it happened his wine was somewhat watered down. Prussia remained Prussia. The federal states – the *Länder* – continued to take part in legislation through the *Reichsrat* and retained all rights and duties not explicitly transferred to the central government. Those reserved to the Reich were, however, the decisive ones, as they had in practice become in the days of the Kaiser and Ludendorff. The head of state, the Reich President, was to be elected by the whole nation. It was a strange choice of title – 'Reich' and 'President' went oddly together. The President appointed the head of the central government, the Chancellor, and, on the Chancellor's advice, the Reich Ministers. These had to resign if the Reichstag ceased to have confidence in them, unless the President chose to dissolve the Reichstag and let the people decide through new elections. The President could also submit to the electorate any proposed piece of legislation on which he and the Reichstag disagreed; whereas conversely the electorate could submit proposals to the Reichstag through a *Volksbegehren* (popular request) and in case of opposition by the Reichstag carry them out after a referendum. Every man and woman over twenty in the Reich and in the *Länder* had the vote. The voter was a free, responsible citizen, aware of his or her duties. A number of 'basic rights and basic duties of Germans' conferred upon them the benefits which the liberal states of the West had acquired in the course of centuries: equality before the law, the protection of private property, the ownership of which carried with it certain moral obligations, freedom of assembly, the right to petition, and so on. In the event of 'serious disturbance of or threat to public safety and order' the President could intervene on his own initiative, 'if necessary with the aid of the armed forces'. This was obvious; it hardly needed to be embodied in the constitution. It was equally obvious that the Reichstag had the right to repeal such improvised emergency measures at any time.

The constitution was well thought-out all in all, a belated realization of the dream which the men of the *Paulskirche* had hardly dared to dream. It could not completely do away with what Bismarck had created, any more than Bismarck had been able to do away completely with what had been thought up in the *Paulskirche* or practised by Metternich's *Bund*. This was no disaster, it was natural. A nation can never begin from the very beginning, whereas it can learn from others, and indeed there were echoes of

American, Swiss and French tradition in the Weimar Constitution. The assumption was that in Germany's recent history it had been the authoritarian state that had failed, not the people; therefore the authoritarian state must be done away with completely and the people must be given complete power. The constitution placed absolute confidence in the people. It wanted to establish what Bismarck had tolerated to a limited degree and prevented to a large degree: government of the people by the people, the identity of state and nation. The majority was right and must decide. There must be no government without a majority in the Reichstag; no Reichstag majority without a majority in the nation; direct decision by the nation whenever President and Reichstag or Reichstag and people disagreed. No division of authority as in America but unrestricted parliamentarianism as in France, with a strong admixture of direct democracy as practised in the Swiss Confederation and its cantons. But then the Swiss had a very ancient, gradually evolved democracy and they were agreed on the basic ideas of their communal existence.

The Weimar Constitution presupposed that the Germans were agreed on the basic concepts of their communal existence. That they respected each other and were prepared to live together. It was possible to have differences of interest and opinion, they existed everywhere and could be dealt with. But the nation needed to be reasonably at peace with itself and with the rest of the world. If it was not no constitution could help it; such a magnanimously democratic constitution basing everything on the unanimity and sagacity of the people governing itself probably even less than a provisional exploratory arrangement. The old authoritarian state was dead, after a gradual decline and a belated collapse. Henceforth the nation would be its own authority and there was no other. Could it do this in the condition in which it had been left by the authoritarian state? If not, where would it derive its authority from?

2. Unrest, Followed by Apparent Consolidation

We went to school in those days, we were given homework, marks and punishments as though everything was normal. But now and then schools were closed because of 'disorders' or shortage of coal, and now and then a minister was murdered and the school-boys rushed out into the streets and cheered. People worked and, if they could afford it, spent their holidays by the seaside, enjoying themselves in their accustomed ways and in new ones; there was the cinema which had just become a mass medium, jazz which came from America, and presently the wireless. Social life goes on whether there is war or peace, whether it is the Emperor who rules or this or that party, whether bread is paid for with pennies or with milliard notes. Social life does not allow itself to be defeated by revolution. Moreover, there was no real revolution in Germany between 1919 and 1924; only embarrassment and helplessness which a number of individuals and groups made clumsy attempts to exploit.

In modern times the German nation has oscillated repeatedly between exaggerated centralization and the reverse, disintegration into individual units. The war had gripped the country in the iron vice of extreme centralization. Now, more than at any time since 1866, the regions asserted themselves. The central authority was new, inexperienced and weak, and dangers threatened from all sides; each man had to fend for himself as best he could.

The territory west of the Rhine was occupied by the French, the Belgians and the British; outside the officers' quarters hungry children and the unemployed waited for scraps from well-stocked kitchens. A few adventurers tried to separate the region completely from Germany thereby belatedly fulfilling Clemenceau's wish; a folly which, in spite of everything, went completely against the instincts of the people and ended accordingly. In Upper Silesia the Poles wanted to take by force what the peace treaty promised them only after a plebiscite. The Germans resisted; troops, *Freikorps* and units established in a spirit of self-projection fought a miniature war of considerable violence. When the plebiscite had finally taken place the League of Nations carefully arranged for a dividing line to be drawn through this rich country: places where the Germans were in the majority went to Germany, the others to Poland. Undoubtedly the arrangement was just. Who bothered about the fact that the province which was an economic whole and had been an integral part of Germany for centuries could not be divided in this manner?

There were outbursts in support of the extreme left in Saxony, Thuringia and the Ruhr revealing much hatred, poverty, suspicion and utopian hope. The unorganized Red terror was followed, as so often, by organized White terror; after murder by furious mobs came counter-murder by the army and the *Freikorps*. The result was order, but not a free, noble order as envisaged by the Weimar Constitution, not one from which people could derive pleasure. Germany had lost its natural, domestic peace.

The *Land* of the extreme right was Bavaria, if by 'right' is meant reaction against the events of 1918 and 1919, determination to preserve the old order. Yet even here this determination was not clear and uniform because it was both nationalist and particularist. The Bavarian middle class wanted a state placed farther apart from the rest of Germany than before; at the same time it wanted to be more German than the rest, than 'left-wing' Germany, and to protest more strongly than anyone against the Versailles treaty. Munich thus became the centre both of Bavarian opposition and of an all-German conspiracy against Berlin democracy. These were conflicting passions, but then it is not the nature of political passion to indulge in critical self-analysis. There was talk in Bavaria of separation from the Reich – and at one moment this almost came about – partly because its inhabitants wanted to be Bavarians only and partly because they wanted to restore the old, better and true Empire. Then there were new politicians in Munich who were hatching something very different from mere restoration.

Berlin was supposed to hold together this divided, threatened and deeply dissatisfied nation; it was the seat of the President, of the government, of the new parliament, of the various party headquarters, of the Army High Command; inhabited by masses of human beings it was an enormous centre of energy, living wholly in the present, bustling with activity, now almost without history, predominantly ugly and predominantly sad. Big cities have not proved a source of happiness in our age and of Europe's big cities Berlin less than others.

There were new regional divisions and old class contrasts. The German workers, by far the most numerous section of the employed population, had their republic, intended to be a socially just one, and often found themselves represented in the national, provincial and local governing bodies by men of their choice. Nevertheless they did not quite know whether the state was theirs. The majority wanted to think so, that majority which continued imperturbably to support the Social Democratic Party. A varying minority, small at times, at others almost becoming the majority, did not think so; it supported the Independent Socialists and after their dissolution the Communists. Although in form the Weimar state was democratic, in fact it was not socialist; this great, vague promise remained unfulfilled. In reality people did not live even as well as before 1914. Germany was poor; the employers, experts in their field, but hard, narrow-minded men who all stemmed from the Wilhelminian era, could not imagine a free, dignified relationship between labour and capital. They thought in terms of social power and authority, not of a society of equals; not of production for a flourishing domestic market in which the most numerous wage-earning group was given the biggest share. Besides the factory workers there were the white-collar workers, a section of the population which began to attract the attention of sociologists. It, too, was very numerous and poor, but difficult to organize because incomes varied greatly and its aims and values were uncertain. The white-collar workers lacked the firm tradition which the factory workers had struggled to achieve, and they were more susceptible to untried ideas and slogans. Then there was the bourgeoisie, still tied to its possessions, continuing to follow academic, bureaucratic and technical careers and still very much inclined to regard itself as the most important class in the state. The economic chaos of the post-war years, the growing inflation brought with it a profound change. Those who were strong, clever and active became stronger, the others poorer. New wealth appeared and the old, modest prosperity vanished. Confused and embittered old people occupied one or two rooms of their splendid houses of yesteryear, compelled to let the rest. It was a cruel world that gave those who worked hard and monotonously only the bare necessities of life, that drove the aged, the disorientated into misery and allowed the cunning, the clever operators, the go-getters to rise to opulent prosperity. The rural population frequently felt itself to be better off than the townspeople because its possessions retained their value and because during and after the war people depended heavily on its products. The farming population, from farm labourers to landowners, could never belong to any particular class; those who earned their living from the land stretched from the proletariat to the upper middle class and the aristocracy. The nobility continued to exist, although their titles were now regarded as part of their names and not as a rank. The south and west German aristocracy lived as before, only without positions at Court; the Prussian aristocracy had lost more, its inherited right to the senior positions in the administration and the army. It accepted this situation because it was forced to but it did not like the Republic and had no reason to like it. The Republic, correct in matters of private property, did not touch the possessions of the aristocracy, any more than it touched those of the owners of coal mines and foundries. The great industrialists were very strong economically and therefore dangerous. The East Elbian landowners were economically weak and threatened – and therefore no less dangerous when given an opportunity. We are speaking of the class as a whole and do so with the prudence required in using a collective noun of this kind. There were civilized and decent men among the Junkers, then and later.

What has just been described was not new. The classes of the Republic were those of the Wilhelminian Empire as shaped by the war. The revolution changed the political system, not society. Let us not hold this against democracy; the extermination of entire classes, as carried out in Russia, was an unnatural affair, totally abhorrent to the European spirit. What was new was that there was no longer a big Prussian army but a German *Reichswehr* of only 100,000 men. This made most generals,. most officers, redundant; they had to find civilian occupations, to cherish the past in an alien present, representatives of a spirit that was no longer wanted. No wonder that they too did not love the Republic. The old professional officers at least were cared for; they received their pensions. Not so the members of the *Freikorps*. Their home, occupation and meagre source of income was the association to which they belonged; after its dissolution they faced ruin in the cold, impoverished world of German industry which had no use for their type. It was not only love of adventure that kept these men with the colours, not only class-hatred, which was absent in most of them because their origins were not far removed from those of the workers; and only a few of their leaders, of the inveterate bohemians, were motivated by vague authoritarian ideas, by the wish to destroy democracy, to set up a differently constructed state. It was fear of the misery of civilian life that kept the rest of the *Freikorps* together and made them a problem for the state and even the new army.

The new army gradually grew out of the old one. It might be said that it was the old one as it had been before the call-up of millions of reservists in 1914 transformed it into a nation in arms. The senior officers, the real creators of the new army, came from the old general staff, if not from Ludendorff's Supreme Command; they were able men, military technicians, who had proved them- selves in war. They disliked reckless adventurers, undisciplined mercenaries of the type which, to their disgust, had appeared in the *Freikorps*; they were not political visionaries. But neither were they friends of what was going on now. They regarded the Republic as a provisional arrangement, dictated by the enemy, with which they must go along for a while; then they would see. One of these men was the head of the 'army office', General Hans von Seeckt, a good commander and a fine stylist; cool and daring, cultivated, clever up to a point, but in the last resort politically ignorant – he regarded a future war between Britain and France as a certainty – arrogant and profoundly insolent in dealing with the new democratic politicians. Loyalty he felt only for his King and when he spoke of the abdication of William II tears would appear behind the monocle which controlled his immobile face. Loyalty is a good quality, but if there was to be a republic a man like Seeckt should never have been its general. He despised his new employers to such an extent that he did not even bother to make his hostility clear, so that they might know with whom they were dealing. They did not deserve even that much in his view, those men whose authority derived solely from the perfidy of November 1918. He was prepared to have dealings with them, even to help them, and he did nothing against them to begin with because he was too intelligent; but he was never one of them, although appointed and paid by this government. When it was threatened by the extreme right, by the *Freikorps*, by parts of the army itself, a malicious, sphinx-like smile crossed von Seeckt's stony face. '*Reichswehr* does not shoot at *Reichswehr*', the oracle pronounced, or 'the army is behind *me*,' a remark which failed to make it clear where the oracle itself stood. Did von Seeckt know where he stood or did he only pretend to know? It was regrettable that men with Seeckt's attitude should have had to shape the new army. Good policy could lessen the effect of this situation but it could not eliminate it. An army does not grow out of nothing. Prussia-Germany had only *one* military past; if the Weimar Republic was to have an army at all it was impossible to spirit away the past. The situation was different in Russia where something new had indeed emerged from the terrible civil war. But when Germany decided against Communism in January 1919 – and how could it do otherwise? – it also decided against the 'Red Army'. Anyway we know that even the Red Army, even the armies of the French Revolution, were not quite as new as they sometimes seemed.

Mediator between the Army and the democratic Republic was meant to be the Minister of National Defence, Gustav Noske. He has been bitterly criticized by the German left and he is one of those people about whom the author is compelled to declare himself. Noske was not a subtle thinker. But he was a forceful, practical man and his heart was in the right place. It was almost a miracle that this 'Red' who never hid his social and democratic convictions really won the admiration of the Army, both of men and officers. He may have made mistakes but the Republic had no better man to control the general staff, having once made a pact with that body. Therefore it would have been wiser to let Noske continue what he had begun. But his career came to an early and abrupt end.

The social classes were old and the leadership of the army was old; equally old were the political parties which were now called upon not just to exert some control over the government but actually to form it. Some of them changed their names, hastily adding the prefix 'people's', so that the Conservatives were now called *Deutschnationale Volkspartei* (German National People's Party), the National Liberals *Deutsche Volkspartei* (German People's Party) and the Bavarian wing of the Centre *Bayerische Volkspartei* (Bavarian People's Party). The Progressives or left-wing Liberals called themselves 'Democrats'. The Social Democrats and the Centre kept their old names; they, who had been Bismarck's opposition parties, had no reason to pretend a change of character. But they too were parties of the age of Bismarck and their leaders had received their political baptism of fire in the later years of Bismarck's rule. Only on the extreme right and left was there anything new: on the left there were the Independent Socialists who quickly split, their moderate wing rejoining the majority party, while the radical one joined the Communist sect, thus for the first time establishing a Communist mass party. To the right there was a variety of curious nationalistic or 'folkish' groups whose aim was not restoration like that of the Conservatives but the fulfilment of age-old or very new, strange, wild dreams of Reich and race. This was something new, the monstrous product of the age, of the war and of the post-war period. One cannot say that the Communists were the logical heirs of the old Social Democrats. They modelled themselves on the Russian example which itself was new and conditioned by the terrible experience of the war and by the ideas of one man, Lenin. Russia was their fate, then and later and to the present day. These two, the Communists and the nationalists, were the new pieces on the board, awkward pieces which the players would have liked to ignore.

Genuine revolutions, we have said, are nothing to be admired and they ought not to be made into a philosophy, into a supreme purpose. They interrupt historical continuity, they divide the country into hostile camps and create struggle and misery. The damage which they do cannot be undone for centuries. If on the other hand a revolution merely upsets the country's political structure, leaving its social structure unchanged, the new building will stand on shaky foundations; in that case it is better to allow the old system to survive, changing it only a little, carefully, as Max von Baden had tried to do in October 1918. He had tried to do it together with the Social Democrats. The significant fact, however, was that nobody had *made* the events of November, least of all those who reluctantly assumed the leadership. There had been a collapse, unforeseen and undesired, not a creatively directed revolution. Consequently the whole administrative and intellectual structure of the Wilhelminian Empire was preserved: bureaucracy, judiciary, universities, churches, economic system and general staff. Consequently the politicians were weak; they worked with bureaucrats, judges and teachers who continued to follow their professions without believing in the Republic. Consequently those who believed in a genuine revolution, that is to say one which changed the structure of society, were not at all satisfied with what had been achieved; they wanted to overthrow it from the left, after Lenin's example. Consequently the supporters of the old order possessed at least two attractive arguments in favour of a counter-blow from the right: the new democratic authority had feet of clay; and it allegedly offered no guarantees against the Communist or anarchist threat.

The first man who tried in March 1920 to translate such arguments into action was an old Prussian bureaucrat by name of Kapp. He used a *Freikorps* stationed near Berlin whose members were afraid of being disbanded and were ready for any adventure. Kapp managed to occupy the capital, to force the central government to withdraw hastily to southern Germany and to act as Chancellor for a few days. It was during those days that General von Seeckt took up an ironic, neutral position: time would show how far Kapp got. This time he did not get far. A *coup d'état* needed more careful preparation. The people did not join in, neither did the civil service; above all not the workers. A general strike, ordered by the trade unions and energetically applied, forced the dictator to resign after four days and President Ebert was able to return to Berlin.

This was an unpleasant episode. Few people had lifted a finger for the four-day dictator, but it was an open secret that he spoke for many Germans when he fulminated against the weakness of parliamentary government. The parties of the right disapproved if anything of his methods, not of his aim; the army did not disapprove even of his methods. Parliamentary democracy presupposed agreement on basic principles. What could have been known before had now become clear: there was no such agreement. A substantial minority regarded the existing system as temporary and did not accept it heart and soul. To this minority belonged the Army whose task it was to protect the new system.

The anger which the Social Democrats felt about their Minister of National Defence was understandable. He had not achieved what he had promised, he had not made the Army into a reliable instrument of the Republic. Had he learnt from his defeat? Would his successor do better? When no Social Democratic successor could be found a member of the 'bourgeois' parties took over the post which he kept for many years, allowing the generals to do as they pleased. Only after Noske's fall did von Seeckt make himself 'Chief of the Army Command', only then did he seriously begin to transform the Army into a state within the state, pretending to be Prussian but in reality not Prussian at all; the old Prussian army had been loyal to the state whereas Seeckt's *Reichswehr* regarded the Republic as 'alien' and wished to have as little contact with it as possible. The *Reichswehr* was supposed to be an élite army, neat and compact, a powerful weapon; the men were carefully selected so that, discreetly, there were no Socialists among them; the officers stuck together, an arrogant order, convinced that they knew best, even if they were unclear about what they knew. The democratic forces allowed this to happen. They were used to being in opposition to the

Army since 1848, since Roon and Bismarck; as they had been unable to imbue the Army with their spirit in a year and a half, as Noske's brief attempt to reconcile Army and people, the Prussian tradition and Socialism had failed – the democratic forces found themselves once again in opposition to the Army. Although they occasionally tried to create obstacles they no longer attempted to make the Army their own. It is possible to find a psychological explanation for their behaviour – as for most foolish acts.

The Social Democratic Party soon found itself in opposition also on national policy. At the elections to the first regular Reichstag which took place soon after the Kapp *putsch* it lost almost half its voters, partly to the more radical Independent Socialists and partly to the Moderates and the right which scored a tremendous gain. Thereupon the Social Democrats left the government which was reconstituted on a purely bourgeois basis, with the inclusion of the *Deutsche Volkspartei* which at that time was anti-republican in character. The process might have seemed like a routine event of democratic politics; yet it was a very important occasion for a democracy as insecure as the German one. Because basically the Social Democrats were the only great republican and democratic party in the state. They had been in opposition for half a century and in power for a year and a half. They had not consolidated their authority by dictatorial methods at the time when almost half the nation had given them a vote of confidence, and they had rejected the example of Lenin who had established a party dictatorship on a much narrower basis. From the beginning they had shared the power with the smaller parties which supported the Republic and had arranged the constitution so that any party which won over the majority of the electorate was entitled to govern. These were honourable and good rules; but they were good only if everybody played the game, if everybody believed in them. During the eighteen months of their administration the Social Democrats had wanted to lay the foundations of a democratic welfare society but exhausted themselves struggling to preserve order; and their achievement had quite evidently disappointed the masses. Therefore they now stood down and found themselves in opposition to the state which was their own creation and in which they alone believed; because the followers of the Catholic Centre believed this or that, they were not particularly concerned with political forms, and the bourgeois 'Democrats' soon became an insignificant group. The Social Democrats, loyal to the rules of the parliamentary game, entrusted the Republic to those who disliked it, first to its lukewarm friends and then, more than once, to its avowed enemies. Ebert, the Social Democratic President elected by the National Assembly, remained in office, but it was his duty to be above the parties and he wore himself out mediating between false friends and enemies, rejecting calumnies that rose up against him from the morass of a poisoned, hate-ridden public life.

On several occasions the Social Democrats rejoined the government, in 1921, 1923 and 1928. Once more, in 1928, they provided the Chancellor. But these were governments that did not give them a decisive influence, much less a 'monopoly of power'; in which they were forced to reach a *modus vivendi* with avowed enemies, with the *Deutsche Volkspartei* which advocated a conservative economic policy. The German Republic, in so far as it was meant to be a social democratic one, had come to an end by 1920. If it was meant to be what henceforth was the most it could be, then it would indeed have been better to retain the monarchy. This was why Ebert, who knew his Germany, had wanted to save the monarchy in November 1918.

But the Republic was still the 'Reich' with its federalist structure; the federal states continued to exist. And now something strange happened: the Social Democrats who had been unable to control the whole, the three-thirds of the Reich, came to control two-thirds, the great federal state of Prussia; and on several occasions also other *Länder*, Hesse, Saxony, Thuringia, not to mention countless municipalities. Above all, however, they controlled Prussia; sometimes within the framework of the so-called 'Big Coalition' which ranged from them to the *Deutsche Volkspartei* but usually in alliance only with the two other republican parties, the Centre and the 'Democrats'. Here their ablest politicians were allowed to show what they were capable of, the

Prime Minister, Braun, and the Minister of the Interior, Severing. They were very capable and they accomplished a great deal. Creative municipal government, better schools, the encouragement of popular education, the establishment of an administration, of a police force intended to be republican – these were no small achievements. In contrast to the all too frequent changes at the national level there was stability, peace and a simple dignity of public behaviour to which Otto Braun tried to give a traditionally Prussian as well as a democratic character. Nevertheless this Social Democratic Prussia was fundamentally an illusion, because Prussia had long ceased to be a real state. Two-thirds could not go a separate way from the rest of Germany; Germany's fate was Prussia's fate, not the other way round. It was more possible for Bavaria which was only one-tenth of Germany, and a long way away, to live without, or at odds with, the rest of the country; Prussia whose provincial capital was the capital of the Reich could do this less than any *Land*. The vital laws were made in the Reich. Prussia administered, the Reich made policy, and it was the policy, not the administration, which decided the country's fate. For the moment the easy, satisfying solution was to withdraw from the Reich and to concentrate on Prussia; Prussia had many livings to distribute. But the problem of *power* could not be solved by this limitation to mere administrative arts; it could only be concealed and confused.

Divided and alienated from itself, led by weak or reluctant politicians, the nation was confronted by problems the hopeless confusion of which would have daunted a Bismarck. The European civil war which had begun in 1914 continued in the cold peace. As the German industrialists wanted to base their own power on the economic and political weakness of the workers, so France thought that it could live at odds with Germany, an inflexible, isolated entity growing more prosperous as Germany grew poorer and weaker. There was little wisdom in Germany then and it could not assert itself. But even if it had been able to assert itself at home and if it had had the wisdom of a god it could not have prevailed against the malice and passion of the outside world.

The main issue was that of so-called reparations. There were several reasons why Germany should continue to pay them, although it had already made tremendous sacrifices immediately after the war. It had, allegedly, caused the war. But this assertion could not be proved; the Germans did not believe this, it did not agree with their own experience and it was possible to demonstrate scientifically that this was by no means the whole truth. Secondly Germany had done more damage to the enemy than the other way round; villages had been reduced to ashes, mines flooded and orchards cut down. There was no denying this and if handled intelligently and humanely the argument could have provided the basis for German reparations. But this was not what the Allies did. On the contrary, Germany's proposals for a reconstruction of destroyed regions by German labour and material were coldly received in Paris. Not the French people but a few all too influential Frenchmen were less concerned with material help than with weakening German productivity. And that was the third and real reason why Germany was to pay reparations; it had lost the war and this temporary defeat was to be perpetuated. Because only someone who is permanently at a disadvantage does what he does not want to do; he must be forced to do it, not once but again and again. His defeat must be kept alive and demonstrated anew. After earlier wars the situation had been different. The vanquished had given at once all that had been asked of him and then the two sides had called it a day. This happened as late as 1871 when France was forced to make a large contribution but one within its means, which it managed to pay in a short space of time. With the best will in the world the Germans could not have made such an effort; their whole country was hardly worth more than the ridiculous sums demanded from it, which it was to pay in the course of the century. This fact made the affair so unending, so sad, so disgusting and gained popularity for politicians who thundered against the 'infamous treaty' and against the 'tribute'. Not only did the Germans wish not to pay, either excessive or reasonable sums; they had the feeling that there was no reason to pay because they had not really lost the war, only seemingly, because they had been betrayed.

Hence the many international conferences at which German payments proposals were defeated by Allied demands; hence the enemy's ultimata, the occupation of west German towns as 'pledges' and the resignation of impotent, perplexed German governments. Hence the oscillation of German policy between sabotage of the payments and so-called 'fulfilment' – fulfilment to the limit of the possible in order to make the enemy listen to reason and be ready to talk. Unfortunately the enemy did not listen to reason. He did not trust Germany, had little reason to do so, given the chaotic state of the country, and preferred to harm it wherever he could. Whereas resistance to reparations brought new reprisals 'fulfilment' was not rewarded with a reduction of the sentence. How could people live decently together in such circumstances? How could Europe maintain its place in the world if its member states, its most important citizens, behaved so foolishly to each other? There is no need to go into the details of these conferences, the demands and changes of government. Nothing good or lasting emerged from them; it is better to forget them and not to know the names of those concerned. But it is self-evident that these happenings greatly harmed the German Republic in the eyes of the Germans themselves. They did not reflect about causes, possible and impossible courses of action, merit and guilt. They only saw that things went badly.

Connected with the evil of reparations was the inflation. The German government was compelled to buy the foreign currency which it paid to the enemy with its own which was thrown on to the market in ever greater quantities and continued to depreciate. Long ago, during the war, the government had been accustomed to balance its expenditure by printing more money instead of raising taxes; this art now became a frantically practised vice. At the beginning of 1922 the mark was still worth about a fiftieth of its pre-war value; one year later not even a ten-thousandth. The new leaders maintained they knew nothing about the secrets of money and allowed themselves to be impressed by financial experts and greedy industrialists. For the moment these men were not interested in saving the mark; they were interested in its collapse and, if the process was occasionally arrested, if it happened too slowly, they took care to hasten it by throwing large sums of German money on to the market. From patriotic motives if one likes, because the complete ruin of the German currency would put an end to reparations payments. But they probably also had less noble motives. Money is printed paper and when paper loses its value no real assets are lost. They merely change hands. The rich become richer and the poor poorer. Those Germans who only possessed paper, the paper claim to real assets, pensioners, small savers and particularly those who were paid in paper, workers, white-collar workers and civil servants, were the ones who lost; those who owned land, factories or mines were the ones who gained. The employers determined a few days before pay-day what wages to pay, which by then had lost half their value. They took up loans in money which was still worth something and paid them back in worthless paper. Those who were economically strong bought up the weak; German heavy industry, which even before 1914 had been concentrated in fewer hands than any other in the world, was reduced to a few empires. One of these – that of Hugo Stinnes – assumed dimensions the like of which had never been seen before, not even in America, growing as the mark depreciated. Goods were produced cheaply and cheap goods were brought on to the world market. This meant that there was no shortage of work and that there was even a certain hectic gaiety. Those who knew how to speculate, to buy and sell at the right moment, were able to live well and spent their easily made profits freely. Shop windows glittered and turnover was high; new American dances were tried out in crowded places of entertainment while politicians drivelled contentedly about misery and lost honour. Meanwhile most people suffered real misery, the old, the pensioners, those who did not know how to speculate and all those who worked for a wage and owned nothing. A few years previously the German worker had won the eight-hour day and wages agreements. What use were they to him now? This 'inflation', one must emphasize even today, was one of the instruments which industry used to regain the position which it had lost for a short time after 1918.

It is possible that most of the men involved were not fully aware of the effects of their actions. One must not overestimate the extent to which such things are planned. The effects were clear, the motives were not. Least of all to the great mass of those who had been robbed. How could they understand what was happening if even Walther Rathenau did not understand it; how could they see through the mysterious forces by which money became trash in their hands and trash became gold in the hands of a lucky few? They only felt that once again they were being deceived, as during the war; something unprecedented was happening to them, and the central government, which took no counter-measures, did not understand its business. Therefore the Republic was no good. Whether those who governed the country really were republicans and whether, even though they were in the government, they really had the power to restrain the tycoons of industry and finance, was a problem for scholars, not for the man in the street. The depreciation of the German currency in effect produced a second revolution after the one of the war and the post-war period, and again a predominantly destructive one. Whole sections of the population were expropriated and an age-old confidence was destroyed and replaced by fear and cynicism; what could still be relied upon, who could be trusted if such things were possible? The day of reckoning will come sooner or later if too much is expected from people.

The Western Powers, France in particular, never ceased to prove to the Germans that they had lost the war and had been humiliated. The Germans replied by depreciating their currency. Were there other, more conventional, diplomatic, methods of detaching the country from the West and of making it capable of political action again? Western Europe was not Germany's only possible partner, there was another in the East, the old mysterious friend-enemy of Brest-Litovsk. If Germany was the loser of 1918 and almost outside the law of society the same applied to an even greater extent to Russia. Inside Germany the Communists did their best to help the forces of reaction; each time that the army or the *Freikorps* put down a Communist rising, in 1919, 1920 and 1923, democracy became weaker and its enemies on the right stronger. Might then the Russian state not render the German state a service although in a completely different way? Might they not make common cause against the West or possibly against Poland? All kinds of things were written and said on this subject during those confused years and something also materialized, although not very much.

The Treaty of Rapallo was concluded in April 1922 between Germany and Russia. It put relations between the two countries on a normal footing, envisaged the mutual abandonment of a number of claims which would anyway never have been fulfilled, and promised trade based on preferences. In normal times the treaty would have been something normal. These times, however, were different. The fact that the two great criminals suddenly agreed caused terrified consternation in the West. Might the harmless treaty not be a cover for extensive conspiracies?

The German Foreign Minister, Walther Rathenau, was a definitely western-orientated man; to him not to reject the proffered Russian support was nothing but a matter of traditional diplomacy designed to restore the balance of power. Given the way in which the West was treating Germany there was no reason to give up anything for the sake of the West. General von Seeckt went further and thought that Germany in alliance with Russia should finish off the Polish state; the Bolsheviks had already changed their coat; there lay the way to new German power. These were crude dreams, childishly simple like all projects involving power politics, and characteristic of Germany's ever dangerous, ever seductive situations between East and West. The two armies established secret contacts; shells were produced in Russia for the use of the Germans and German officers were allowed to use Russian territory to train with weapons forbidden to the Republic under the terms of the Treaty of Versailles: with tanks, aeroplanes and submarines. Cunning Russians inquired if the cause of poor, exploited Germany was not fundamentally the socialist one, if German nationalism could not leave its alien capitalist ally to make common cause with the Communists against French and American imperialism? Might 'national Bolshevism' not be the combination of the future? There were Germans who were attracted by such sophisticated ideas, searching, daring spirits not satisfied with anything real in the world, with existing polarities. Yet one must not overestimate the importance of such writings and talk. One must not overestimate the ideas of this age so rich in fruitless acts of violence and so poor in lasting creative achievement, this age in which the most outrageous things seemed possible, and which then, thanks to American loans and Stresemann's diplomacy, quickly culminated in a sobering return to normal conditions.

Fruitless acts of violence – they too must be mentioned because they belong only too much to those years, being the result of internal division, of cruel, stupid hatred, of blustering ignorance. The anarchists in their day had thrown bombs because in an established, secure society they had found no other way of making their self-destructive protest. Now the representatives of a new, weak regime which almost collapsed under the burden of its task, were murdered, and the murderers did not even need to feel that they were risking their lives; somehow they would be allowed to escape. Indeed several of them, though not all managed to do so. They came from the extreme right, desperate members of the *Freikorps*, immature young men who wanted to ape their elders. They murdered the Minister of Finance, Erzberger, the Centre member who in 1918 on Hindenburg's orders had signed the armistice, and a year later they murdered the Foreign Minister, Walther Rathenau. They fired their sub-machine guns, threw their hand grenades and raced off. Part of the nation was genuinely revolted, particularly the Social Democrat workers, those very men whom people despised on account of their 'materialism' and lack of Christianity. But another, substantial part of the nation was not at all revolted, shrugged its shoulders, smiled secretly and rejoiced openly. There were upper-middle-class ladies, good Christians one must suppose, who were delighted by the news of Rathenau's murder. Was he not a democrat, a politician who wanted to 'fulfil' the peace treaty, and a Jew to boot? That was so; the fact that he was also an ardent patriot and one of the very few creative statesmen of the period, that his great planning achievement alone had enabled German industry to provide the material necessary for the war, was forgotten in the general campaign against him; it did not penetrate into men's brutish, poisoned minds.

One hesitates to record such things; the historian should understand and help to reconcile not revive old discords. But they must be recorded because they were harbingers of worse to come. What could one expect from citizens who allowed cowardly acts of murder of noble political opponents, who even rejoiced in them? *Anything* might happen to such citizens.

The height of thoughtless, active folly in domestic as well as in foreign policy was reached in 1923. At times it almost seemed then as though Europe was about to come to terms on the basis of common conservative or anti-revolutionary interests. In Italy the post-war party of the Fascists was in power, brutal, boastful and shallow but not devoid of a certain external glamour and clearly making common cause with the old feudal and capitalist forces. Britain was governed by the Conservatives and France by the harsh, narrow-minded, virtuous man of 1914, Raymond Poincaré. Even Russia understood that the age of European revolution had ended for the moment; hence Lenin's new policy of waiting, of treaties with non-Communist states, of return to private enterprise at home. The German government too was definitely conservative, almost anti-revolutionary in character, in very close touch with the Rhenish industrialists and the old-cum-new Army. The main occupation of the Chancellor, Cuno, was to be Director-General of the Hamburg-America Shipping Company. 'Your fate, Germany, is made by industries, banks and shipping companies,' mocked one of the Berlin left-wing writers in bitter but almost accurate doggerel. Perhaps the sympathies of the industrialists could achieve what the idealistic speakers of the left had failed to accomplish, namely tolerable international understanding? There had been much talk about this in the last months of 1922; Hugo Stinnes in particular, the greedy builder of the most motley, fantastically far-flung industrial empire of all times, worked or planned towards this end. Germany would regain its sovereignty by paying, delivering and working on French and Belgian soil; German workers could work more without extra pay to achieve this. At last again completely master in his own house, as in the good old days before 1914, the German industrialist would come to terms with his western partners.

But state interests and national passions have always been stronger in Europe than personal or material links between private industry in different countries. If a hundred years previously the conservative fellowship of the monarchies had proved an illusion, incapable in the long run of forming the basis of a common policy, big capital also demonstrated repeatedly that it could not create an international system. The industrialists were themselves nationalists; they either expected their own state to eliminate foreign competition and to provide them with profits from abroad, or, blinded by pride and nationalism they lost sight of their own rational interests. Raymond Poincaré was the great advocate of the French steel industry, but this did not make him a friend of the Germans, on the contrary. He was dominated by patriotism as it was called; by the passionate desire to keep before men's eyes the pathetic phantom of French victory, to strengthen and make it secure for ever. Nothing came of the Stinnes Plan. Instead German industrialists came to know the inside of French prisons.

It began when Poincaré on a legal pretext sent the French army into the heart of the German industrial region, the Ruhr. Germany was behindhand with deliveries of coal and wood. The French decided to fetch what they had not been given voluntarily. They would show Germany once more that it had been defeated for ever. Perhaps on the same occasion they might somehow separate the occupied region from Germany, thereby weakening Germany and strengthening France. These were foolish ideas, wilful and dogmatic gestures resulting from barren political aims inherited from the seventeenth century and now pursued by pedants belonging to the pre-war and war period. This was the European civil war of 1914 being fought nine years later in its most pointless, most provincial aspect, namely that of Franco-German enmity. As if the world, Europe and Germany and France, had had no other worries in those days. Berlin sought to arouse the nation to react with impressive unity: by passive resistance, strikes, a total refusal to collaborate with the occupying force and the interruption of all reparation payments. A united front was the slogan almost as in 1914; and again, as in 1914, the Social Democrats participated without determining policy. But the nation was too weak, economically, politically and morally, to maintain a united front for long. The miners' strike in the Ruhr was not complete, unlike the separation of the Ruhr from the rest of Germany, which was France's answer to passive resistance; it was the people, not the foreign soldiers, who paid and suffered. Acts of sabotage, the blowing up of bridges organized by trusted *Freikorps* members, led only to the usual reprisals. Food supplies failed and the families of the workers and clerks, who even in good times had only just enough, began to starve. As the state was cut off from its chief industrial centres and from the income derived from industry, as it had to give financial help to the unemployed population of these regions which were its richest, the German currency collapsed completely; if in January the gold mark was worth a few thousand paper marks, in the summer it cost millions, then milliards and finally billions, to buy. A comic, incredible, mad state of affairs. But for the great mass of the people who exchanged their labour for a wage or a salary it was an affliction and an agony; the situation now became disquieting even for the small minority who understood and controlled it and who had so far suffered no disadvantage from it. Such a complex, vulnerable organism as the German one cannot live in chaos. The ones who benefited were the Communists. By mid-summer the right, the industrialists and the financiers, understood this fact and by their parliamentary action the Social Democrats too made it clear that passive resistance was no longer possible. The front pages of the illustrated journals showed the portrait of a new Chancellor, Gustav Stresemann.

What happened now was like a repetition of the events of the late autumn of 1918. As Max von Baden had to declare himself prepared to accept the armistice, Stresemann declared himself ready to negotiate, to pay. As then the Social Democrats had been called upon to form a government they now rejoined the cabinet of Stresemann, ex-National Liberal; always ready in the hour of the greatest need to shoulder the burden of responsibility, always kicked out as soon as the middle class and the Army believed that they no longer needed them. In the summer of 1923 as in 1918 defeat led to parliamentary government and then to republicanism; one is tempted to say that the Republic was founded anew in 1923. Stresemann professed loyalty to it and to the constitution, and did so with sincerity whereas his predecessors had only regarded it as a provisional evil. Once more Germany made peace with the outside world and with the Republic at home. But this very fact, the coincidence of the defeat abroad and the victory of the republican principle at home, in 1923 as in 1918, explains why the Weimar Republic never came to be more securely based. The Germans were republican only when they gave in to an obstinate enemy. How, in such circumstances, could the country love and respect the republican symbols?

As in 1918 and 1919, in the autumn of 1923 the new Republic faced various forms of opposition from the left and the right. Now as then there were groups which had hoped for a different development and which urged that the harvest of chaos be reaped before the chaos was cleared up. The federalist structure of the Reich seemed to them to provide an opportunity. Berlin was one thing, the system of the *Bundesländer* another.

In central Germany, Saxony and Thuringia, the Communists had formed an alliance with their former enemies, the Social Democrats, a move in line with Lenin's new policy of postponing indefinitely the revolutionary message. The governments which emerged from this alliance kept within the framework of republican legality; their achievements were pitiable. Communists in 'power', be it merely the feeblest semblance of power, was something which the Reich of Stresemann and General von Seeckt could never allow. Particularly because in Munich there was a powerful concentration of the extreme right, thirsting for action and in charge of government affairs. Here the situation was confused but explosive. The government was Bavarian-particularist in the good old sense and close to the deposed royal house. It was close also – because people often are unclear about what they really want – to a number of un-Bavarian groups and cliques, homeless adventurers sailing under the nationalistic flag, demagogues, *Freikorps* leaders and retired Prussian generals. Erich Ludendorff himself had taken up residence in the Bavarian capital from whence he poured out his confused ideas in pamphlets and speeches. The Munich government was both Bavarian and a rival German government. It believed that it represented the whole, true Germany, unlike the traitorous gutter democracy of Berlin. A wild, young rabble-rouser, the product of the stifling pre-war and wartime years in Austria, an agitator of monstrous pathological energy was the man who called loudest to battle. He wanted to push the people of Munich into action against central Germany and against Berlin. The party which he had set up for himself was called National Socialist.

But Stresemann, the Minister of National Defence, Gessler, and the commander-in-chief of the Army, von Seeckt, rooted nationalists, did not want the success of such undisciplined, complex efforts. A race developed between Berlin and Munich to see who would be first to restore order and to slay the Communist dragon. Berlin struck; Seeckt, with the authority of the Reich government, removed the Communist governments in central Germany without much trouble. This was not legal; but then much that had been done since January 1919 had not been foreseen by the pious fathers of the constitution. At the same time serious efforts were made to reform the currency and to banish the spectre of inflation. The Hitler *putsch* was an epilogue, not a main event, in this incredibly confused and miserable story. In November the young madman attempted what might have been successful a few months earlier. He thought that he could rouse his past supporters, officials, monarchists and leaders of the Bavarian *Reichswehr* division to action by putting a pistol to their heads. But they ran away as soon as they were no longer threatened by his pistol. In the end, they decided that they had more in common with Seeckt and Gessler than with the hysterical agitator who had been their bedfellow. Ludendorff and Hitler found themselves alone with a handful of personal supporters whom the police put down with one salvo. A few days later Seeckt proscribed Hitler's party on the strength of the authority conferred upon him by the central government. There was only one man the general once remarked, who could organize a successful putsch in Germany, namely himself, and he would not do it.

The old currency was called in and a new one issued which corresponded to the pre-war currency; 1,000 milliard Reichsmark could be exchanged for one *Rentemark* and later for one gold mark. A task for financial experts, manageable at any time provided rulers with authority and clear ideas gave the necessary order. This was not as obvious in the first third of the century as it is today; therefore the creators of the sound currency, particularly the President of the Reichsbank, Schacht, were admired like successful conjurers. All these men did was to adopt a few classic measures which, had it been so desired, could have been adopted years before: rigid control of the printing of banknotes, various forms of saving and a reorganization of the system of taxes and tariffs. The nation had always been willing to work, it had merely been badly governed. Now it went to work, at first for miserable wages but at least for reliable ones. As wages rose and people could begin to hope for a few of the good things of life they became reasonably contented. They longed for normal conditions, for the end of the charade that had lasted ten years, a longing which seemed to be coming there. It coincided with similar moods outside Germany. In France Poincaré gave way to a government of good democrats, in London Labour assumed office for the first time, men who seriously believed in the ideal of understanding among nations. At the same time America decided to return to the European arena from which since Wilson's collapse and the 1920 elections it had kept away with the contemptuous pride of good fortune. It did not return in a political sense – the last thing that Washington wanted even now was to have anything to do with European diplomacy – but in an economic one. On the German payments to the Western Powers depended the latter's payments to America; the restoration of Germany's economic health enabled the European market to take America's products, and allowed the recovery of the world economy generally. That much at least Washington now recognized.

After 1924 there was universal readiness to do what with a little self-criticism and foresight could have been done five years earlier: to make peace. Under American guidance a plan for reparations payments was prepared, which, though still unwise in principle, still an economic and moral burden, was bearable compared with the frenzy of previous years. The French and the Belgians left the Ruhr and a year later there followed the concoction of a curiously complicated treaty system the general purpose of which was to ensure the safety of France and Belgium against Germany, but also that of Germany against France – no repetition of the occupation of the Ruhr – and thus to calm men's minds. Britain and Italy acted as guarantors, agreeing at all times to come to the assistance of the attacked, regardless which side it was. An alliance of all with all against all – such was roughly speaking the Treaty of Locarno of 1925. Such artificial contrivances do not last when it comes to a serious quarrel. Providing, however, no quarrel occurs because none of the participants wants one, diplomatic mumbo-jumbo can at least express this desire, and by doing so strengthen it a little on both sides and project it into an uncertain future. Locarno helped the Germans because retrospectively it gave the dictated treaty of Versailles the semblance of a voluntary act. This was not much but it was useful for the moment. A year later, in 1926, Germany joined the League of Nations, with a seat and a vote in its Council. This event too was of little real importance because the League of Nations was useless; it could do nothing important and merely provided a forum where the spokesmen of the powers met periodically. But this event also had at least symbolic significance. In theory, from which reality was all too far removed, the League was a universe of all the civilized states of the world; by its election the Reich was given confirmation that it was one of these.

The man who led the process of normalization, of restoring Germany to the Western community of states, must not remain unmentioned. Stresemann, first Chancellor and then for six years Foreign Minister of the Republic, was an experienced parliamentarian, by profession legal adviser to industry, a National Liberal in politics. During the war he had belonged to the most vocal supporters of the War Aims Movement and had been one of Ludendorff's private informants. Nevertheless he was highly intelligent; even intelligent people go wrong in times when all sense of proportion is lost. In the post-war period Stresemann wanted to find a way back to moderation. He was capable of development at an age when most people become set in their ways. His portrait shows the ugly but intelligent face of a man who could think and suffer and who late in life discovered in himself aspirations with which he had been unfamiliar in his youth: to achieve peace between nations as between classes. Of course he was by nature a monarchist, but as nothing could be done with the Hohenzollern he accepted the republican form of government. Of course he hoped that Germany would be powerful again and regain at least part of what it had lost in 1919, if not in the West at any rate in the East. Let us not critize him for this. No German had any reason to worship the Treaty of Versailles as an eternal decree and Stresemann was a patriot; cunning as well as romantic, an old hand at party affairs, he dreamt of the Reich's past glory. That such a man should now support the League of Nations, that in political matters he should be willing to work with the Social Democrats and in economic matters with the trade unions and not against them, was creditable. As regards the hoped-for revision of the eastern frontiers everything depended on the method. Stresemann was too intelligent to think of anything but peaceful methods.

The Stresemann years – 1924 to 1929 – were years of economic productivity and cultural flowering. Years, it seemed, of domestic consolidation. Was it not a sign of the Republic's growing strength that there were no more murders and *coups*? That even the Conservatives, the *Deutschnationalen*, repeatedly joined the government, whereas the parties of the extreme right and left made no further progress? That Bavaria, up to 1924 the stronghold of the counter-revolution, gradually reconciled itself to the new conditions and developed a sensible equilibrium? That Socialists and Liberals, employers and trade union leaders met for peaceful negotiations? There was no reason why this should not have gone on except . . . yes, except. The first Republic came to grief over the economic crisis of 1930 and it is impossible to say with certainty that it would have come to grief otherwise. One cannot say that the normality of the years 1924 to 1929 was an illusion and had no genuine chance of lasting. One can only say that the equilibrium of those years was always threatened from within and that the sources of danger are more apparent in retrospect than they could be at the time. A man may survive a serious illness, but when it comes to the last crisis his previous medical history will count; the weakened organism cannot support what a stronger one might have supported. The Weimar Republic somehow survived the melancholy facts of its origin, the Treaty of Versailles, the limited, but ugly, civil wars of the first years, the occupation of the Ruhr, the inflation, the blind fury of the Communists, the arrogant indifference of the Army, the sullen refractoriness of the upper classes, bureaucracy, judiciary and universities – and to its own surprise it even experienced a period of reasonable health. But the arrival of the second economic crisis and the unleashing of all the furies of demagogy – that was the last straw.

3. Achievements

The Germans frequently took the position that there was a universal conspiracy against them, that they were not allowed to get on their feet again. It was not surprising that a concentration of power as the Reich had been for fifty years at the heart of Europe, should cause disquiet; the crimes committed by Germany during the war remained unforgotten. Until 1924 it was unquestionably the aim of France's policy to weaken its terrible neighbour whenever the letter of the Versailles treaty offered an opportunity. Britain and America pursued this policy only half-heartedly or not at all. After 1924 there was an increasing tendency to admire Germany and, stimulated by admiration and by business and political interests, to help it. The American business world in particular developed marked sympathies for the European people in whom they found it easiest to recognize related efforts and abilities; just as the American Army immediately after the war had been more enthusiastic about Field-Marshal von Hindenburg than about Marshal Foch. The Germans were not much interested in these foreign sympathies. They had enormous respect for themselves, reaffirmed by the achievement of the recovery after 1924, and little respect for the achievements of other nations. The Germans believed that what they had accomplished had been done not with but in spite of the world. The advances in German science and technology seemed national triumphs, victories over the rest of the world. In fact the rest of the world did not put any serious obstacle in the way of Germany's recovery during the Stresemann years. It helped more than it hindered.

Nevertheless Germany's economic achievements after 1924 were considerable. We need not ask here whether they were greater than those of the British or the Japanese. The greatest achievement of all such industrialized nations living in large numbers in a confined space has always been that they lived at all, that they multiplied and that their standards of living gradually rose. In the political sphere there were quarrels and disagreements, but not in the world which supported the political structure and in which coal was mined, steel forged, new patents studied, and houses, streets and ships built.

Germany, Max Weber had written in 1918, would have to start again as after the Thirty Years War, only that now everything happened more quickly. This it did. Although immediately after the war the income of the nation had fallen to about half the pre-war level, ten years later it was back to where it had been, or even higher. All the worn-out, antiquated equipment, all the things handed over after the war were replaced. Germany had the most modern merchant fleet, the fastest railways and an adequate system of roads. In matters of high politics the state behaved as though it was stumbling from one crisis to another, and it was to these that the banner headlines of the newspapers referred. But the administration was good, the workers worked well, the inventors, engineers and technicians were good. Industrial planning was magnificent and effective.

Experts question whether it was wise. What was accomplished after 1924 was a tremendous rationalization, an increase in productivity through mechanization which went hand in hand with further concentration of economic power, this time within particular industries. The *IG Farbenindustrie A.G.* controlled almost the whole of the country's chemical and pharmaceutical industry and the *Vereinigten Stahlwerke* about two-fifths of its iron and steel production; similar mammoth formations existed for the electrical industry, the production of cement, rubber, artificial silk and so on. The rest was done as in the days of old by a variety of cartels – to protect prices, to standardize, to plan production – which had also grown in number since before the war. Concentrated in this manner, and organized in a *Reichsverband*, industry was even more powerful *vis-à-vis* the state than in the Hohenzollern period; it negotiated as an equal and was at the same time part of the power of the state, particularly when the propertied middle classes provided the government as was almost always the case between 1924 and 1928. One cannot accuse the German industrialists of not taking their job seriously. In a certain sense they regarded themselves as responsible for the nation and for their own workers, as implied by the German word *Arbeitgeber* – one who gives work – for employer, which has no equivalent in English or in French. They wanted to give work, but on the terms of those who had a full picture of the situation and who bore the responsibility. The trade unions as equal negotiating partners, the eight-hour day and legally binding wage agreements, the right of the state to act as arbitrator – all this had been accepted immediately after the war; it was weakened and undermined whenever the economic or the political conditions offered an opportunity. Above all the German industrialists did not realize that the buying power of their own workers could, and in the long run must, constitute the most important market. Even the American industrialists only came to appreciate this in the twenties and not fully then; and America was in a far better position to try out the new theory because it had a shortage of manpower, labour was expensive and there was no shortage of raw materials, which Germany had to import in exchange for finished goods. German industry worked for the state and for the export market, not for the gradually rising standard of living of the masses. The director of the coal mine did not like to see his foreman own a motor car – it was not befitting for a member of the upper working class. It was even less befitting for the ordinary worker to have a decent home, a motor bicycle and a refrigerator. As long as he could work and live, and on top of it was insured against accident, sickness and old age, the employers considered that they had done their duty towards him.

The state for its part recognized its general social responsibility and tried to behave accordingly at the three levels of nation, *Land* and commune. This was done in direct continuation of old authoritarian traditions revived under Bismarck, which had reached a new peak during the war. It was customary, it was natural that the state should be responsible for education, that it was the guardian of morals, the central agent of scientific research, that it commissioned and promoted the arts and above all that it guaranteed the bare existence of its citizens. Here, too, foreign capital provided dangerous help. Mayors and finance ministers rushed to America to raise loans for useful or at least 'promotional' purposes: agricultural improvement, canal and road construction, settlement projects, exhibitions, parks, swimming pools and youth hostels. This was constructive and enhanced the amenities of civic life. If the state interferes so much in the life of the individual, directing him, confiscating from him and supervising him, it must at least give him something in return. The Weimar Republic did this for as long as it could. Before the war Germany's cities had been examples of creative administration to the whole world; they were so once more in the Weimar period.

To put it briefly, during the Weimar Republic as well the state fulfilled its functions adequately, and in the twenties these were extended into assuming sole responsibility for economic and cultural matters. Not all the credit must go to the 'Republic'. The walls of the state were the same although a few towers and turrets had been removed. The national and provincial bureaucracies functioned as before, and as before they trained their successors. A new spirit tried to assert itself in places where the parties of the left or the left-centre were in charge, particularly in Prussia and in some of the most important cities. A republican police was intended to be the citizen's reliable, polite servant instead of grimly representing authority. In the schools a relationship established on confidence and free co-operation between teachers and pupils was meant to replace the old discipline based on authority and fear. The newest universities, Frankfurt, Hamburg and Cologne, had the unwritten task of liberalizing the academic spirit; *Volkshochschulen* offered ways to education and knowledge to the many to whom the universities were closed. These were well-meant efforts and they were not unsuccessful. But the matter which the new spirit was intended to penetrate was tough and those who represented this spirit sometimes lacked tact and sometimes the necessary character. A few faculties collected the progressive, 'left-wing' intellectuals; the majority looked back-wards to the imperial past and regarded the present with super-cilious resentment. The professors could hardly have said what they really wanted, they only knew that they did not like what was there. The Republic was so tolerant and so good-natured about preserving freedom of teaching and research that these gentlemen were able to express without risk their contempt for the state which employed them. But then the state was divided, at odds with itself, without much faith in its own cause and often in alliance with its enemies.

There are tensions and differences in every community; there would be no life if there were not. In Britain too there were many conflicts of interest and class, regional differences, determination to have new things and longing for the good things of the past. But in Britain these conflicts occurred in a nation fundamentally united. Of the absence in Germany of this underlying identity Berlin was an example.

The capital was confident that it was now really the head of the nation, and in some sense this was its greatest time. Munich, Stuttgart and Dresden lost by the disappearance of the monarchy, but not Berlin. The Hohenzollern had long been at enmity with the great democratic city and had contributed chiefly horrors and stupidities to its cultural flowering. What had been the opposition under the Kaiser now came to the fore and formed a more or less official republican intelligentsia, in literature, pictorial art, theatre and film. People were eager to experiment; progressive citizens of the West, Frenchmen, Britons and Americans flocked to take pleasure in the new German artistic and social life. The city of the Hohenzollern as Europe's most free-thinking, most active cultural centre was something new. Growing with the ever-growing political, industrial and financial bureaucracies, with the functions of the central government whose importance increased relative to that of the *Länder*, as the focal point of the business world as well as of the idle rich, Berlin could afford to represent the nation. It gave the nation's energies, particularly its intellectual and cultural ones, a single focus. Germany of the Weimar Republic had, really for the first time in history, something like a single capital. One ought to speak of the Berlin, not of the Weimar Republic.

But the capital was not popular, partly because the old Germany, the federalist Germany of the *Länder* and provinces, did not really want a capital of this kind. The inhabitants of Munich and Hamburg, the Junkers in East Prussia and the peasants in the Black Forest regarded Berlin as the meeting point of every alien and repulsive tendency. It was the capital of the Republic, it owed its new character to the war and to the Republic, and its population was predominantly republican and democratic, social-democratic with a strong Communist admixture. The part of Germany that was not republican was therefore against Berlin; just as to a much more dangerous degree conservative Austria had long fallen out with its capital, Vienna. The great pulsating city had no links with the German past; it resembled Chicago more than the small, elegant provincial capital which it had once been. It was here that by far the strongest concentration of the changing German character was found. The Germany that was at odds with itself, that hated its own present, did not get on with Berlin; it liked to think of its capital as a morass of corruption, a Babel of every sin. Other German cities had also grown but they had managed to preserve something of their old style. Berlin lived entirely in the present, it was Germany's America; indeed, it was receptive to American influences and in its press, its entertainments and its advertising methods it was more American than its model. Germany had always looked to authority and there was still a remnant of the old authority in the *Länder*. The Berlin of the Berlin age was without authority. It flattered the masses who thronged the main streets on Saturday nights in search of dreary pleasures, snatching up special editions of the gutter press. It flattered the minorities by experiments of all kinds, valuable ones and worthless ones that were snobbish and lurid, pretending to be new and progressive.

By its very existence Berlin raised the question of how an undisciplined society, estranged from its own past, should live. We all have base instincts only too easily exploited for business or political profit. The time was to come when the stimulation of sensationalism and hate would overcome all counter elements, destroy the old system and on its ruins establish an authority which, while originating with the masses, loathed humanity. Of all the great scholars who in the twenties had concerned themselves with the problems of society, not one had predicted this.

4. The Intellectuals

The spirit of a great nation has many facets. There is the difference of spheres: the great institutions, churches, universities and parties; individuals who speak to the multitude and express the ideas of the multitude; individuals who only speak to a few but who because of their spiritual strength are as real and as representative of their age as the authors of best-sellers. There is the difference of generations which, although living together for the moment, belong to distinct ages. There is the difference between personal opinions, attitudes and characters. However many-sided and versatile the individual personality may be one cannot deal with an historical epoch without describing it 'spirit'.

We know the spirit of the Weimar Constitution. It was unitary and democratic, modified but not denied by the federalist heritage. In so far as the idea of a united nation which gives itself a constitution was first realized by the French Revolution it must be said that the official philosophy of the German Republic came close to the French tradition. But only a few people believed in it – among the parties really only the Progressives or, as they were now called, the Democrats, a group which had the support of the remains of the liberal propertied classes, whose voice was heard in a few newspapers with a large circulation, but which had only a small following among the electorate. It represented the comfortable spirit of progress without force and without excessive cost to the propertied classes: humanization of justice, constitutional reform in favour of a unitary state, international understanding, particularly between Germany and France, and indifference in religious questions. These were radical bourgeois ideals from the last century. They were advocated in more extreme and more critical form than was done by the party by a few writers who, after long years of ironic opposition to the Hohenzollern Empire, now became the semi-official spokesmen of the Republic, like Heinrich Mann. As a critic of the Wilhelminian age and of the middle classes, the author of *Der Untertan* – the Kaiser's subject, whom he dissected – achieved great things. As a constructive educator he was less successful. Basically he was a romantic who only pretended to be a man of the masses, who avoided unpleasant truths and in a brittle style offered a strongly idealized France as a model. When it came to accusation there were flashes of noble anger and truth in his illusions. Although he was not entirely devoid of intuitive insight he only played at politics; he did not influence political affairs through literature as did his French models; politics itself and society he saw as something artificial and grotesque, invented by writers, the corruption and wickedness of which secretly amused him. The Republic – not the Reich but its Prussian *alter ego* – turned him into an official speaker, a President of the Academy. If this was a gesture of affirmation it was also a symbol of internal inconsistencies. The Berlin of 1930 was not the Paris of 1890; 'Weimar' was not the Third Republic;

Heinrich Mann, the satirist, and aesthete who enjoyed pomp and splendour, was neither the Victor Hugo nor the Zola who it was his playful ambition to be.

More solid, within the Weimar framework, was the position of other, great writers who had started their careers in the Wilhelminian period. Life is long while historical or political epochs are short. As Victor Hugo was active from the Bourbon restoration until far into the Third Republic Gerhart Hauptmann lived through the period of William II from beginning to end and then through the Republic and then through yet another period and somehow found a place in all of them. Under the Hohenzollern he had been in opposition, now he was the king of literature. It must be said that the imposing figure of this playwright was much closer to the people than that of the Frenchifying novelist who instructed the Germans while detesting them. Hauptmann made his countrymen feel at home because he was basically unpolitical, a poet who concentrated on feelings and forms and not on clear thinking. The misery of the poor and downtrodden had awakened his compassion, sometimes in his historical plays even the unfortunate fate of the nation. Now he was old and he had done his best work; but he was happy to be the poet prince of the Republic and to show his majestic head on official occasions. When the end of the Republic approached he was silent; when it ceased to exist he managed without it and lived on reasonable terms with its assassins.

Hauptmann's rival monarch was Thomas Mann – a much more complicated case of predominance in the realm of the German spirit. Whereas the playwright avoided thought Thomas Mann thought too much and if he had not been so determined to be creative he would have run aground in the cataract of intellectual problems. He too had his roots in the pre-republican period. He began his long career as a writer in the year of Bismarck's death, as an urban patrician, a poet of beauty, a metaphysician to whom social questions were of little importance. His first novel, *Buddenbrooks*, was later seen as a piece of critical social history, as the story of the decline of the old, genuine bourgeoisie, and it is true that this was in it, although the author himself was hardly aware of it; at the time he was interested in very different things. After twenty-five years of purely artistic, purely intellectual activity, he opened his eyes to politics, suddenly and wide, at the beginning of the war. The result was as profound and rich as it was complicated and clumsy, as German as anything could be. Although he became a political writer Thomas Mann did not want to abandon his past which he regarded as the German past; his past of music, nobility, reverie and love of death. His view now was that German politics must be non-political and that the war was fought for German culture against the politically minded, democratized civilization of the West. If this noble, highly intelligent, honest muddle had any practical meaning it amounted to a defence of the German authoritarian state, long shaken to its very foundations. His *Betrachtungen eines Unpolitischen* (Reflections of a non-political person) was in fact aimed directly against the adulation of democratic France, indulged in by his brother Heinrich. At the same time he hinted more than once that in him too were the things that he was fighting, and that his cause was anyway a lost one. A few years later he professed his loyalty to the Republic. But just as he had invented a meaning for the war which had little relation to reality, his intellectual justification of the Republic was well invented, garnered from old German poetry; it was literature, not reality. The party bureaucracies whether to the left or to the right could do nothing with such ideas. The young student generation at whom Thomas Mann's address *Von deutscher Republik* (Concerning the German Republic) was mainly directed was also romantic and unfamiliar with political reality; but it was hostile to democracy, whether intellectually based on German classicism and romanticism or the mundane actually existing variety. Talking or listening the writer and his people were always at cross purposes. Thomas Mann was a more profound thinker than his brother Heinrich, who ceased to follow through an idea when it suited him whereas Thomas Mann went on pursuing the idea and did not shrink even from the most painful truth. He was blessed and burdened with concern for mankind and when he doubted the truth he did so for love of the truth. What the two brothers had in common was that however much they felt committed to intervene in politics for the sake of clarification they worked only with the products of their own minds and barely came to grips with reality. How basically un-suited Thomas Mann was to take decisions was revealed by his great novel *Der Zauberberg* (The Magic Mountain), a delicately carved puppet-theatre for the display of intellectual and historical possibilities, a stage on which everything was discussed and nothing decided. There was the intellectual fanatic who predicted terror and the totalitarian state; there was the amiable progressive and the liberal optimist, the psychoanalyst who talks cleverly and voluptuously of the relationship between the diseases of the body and the mind; there was also the German officer who is silent, does his duty and dies. The author liked them all to varying degrees and moved freely among them, above them; he was con-cerned with vivid description, with perfect expression, not with decisions. Published at the right moment *Der Zauberberg* became the representative novel of the Stresemann years, a work which provided stimulus and first-class entertainment but did not tell people what to think and why. In practice, in spite of conflicting emotions, its author supported the Progressives and frequently spoke up for social justice and a levelling of classes, for Franco-German understanding and pan-Europe. Noble prospects, the realization of which was to give him the peace to follow his real, non-political interests. In the end, when the extreme right mounted its great attack on the Republic, he became a fighter. His 'yes' had always been half-hearted, qualified by criticism and self-criticism. His 'no' was clear and strong. The great bourgeois set the bourgeoisie a personal example which it could and should have followed. In the end it did so a quarter of a century too late. And this remains the renown of Thomas Mann, the politician; he witnessed in the last years of his life the beginnings of what he had advised and had seen coming, Franco-German understanding, the unification of Europe, social democracy, the reconciliation of the bourgeoisie and Marxism. Should one say that he was wrong because it came later than he had hoped and because, before it happened, noxious ideas of the eighteen nineties, noxious energies of 1919 and the despair of the economic crisis of 1930 led to the set-back of the wretched Nazi adventure? Should one not say instead that he was right even then and that it was history not he that was wrong?

If Gerhart Hauptmann and the Mann brothers allowed their fame to be used to further the cause of democracy, other great writers who survived into the Weimar period kept aloof. Hermann Hesse continued to send poems and melancholy novels from Switzerland. He gained new friends with them among German youth but he was indifferent to the German Reich; a stranger in his time, welcomed by other strangers living in a noisy, hectic present at odds with themselves. Ricarda Huch was another who did not fit into the age, who looked longingly towards Germany's distant past – which she conjured up so well in her historical studies – even though the state invited her to sit on its academic councils and tried to make a public figure of her. In Vienna Hugo von Hofmannsthal wove his librettos, his tales from the eighteenth century, his noble intellectual and philological investigations. 'What shall we Austrian writers do now?' the poet had been asked after the dissolution of old Austria, and he had replied: 'Die.' Nevertheless he survived the monarchy by ten years and even tried, as there was no more Habsburg Empire, to speak as a German to the whole of Germany. When he did so, however, he did not do it for the Republic. What connection was there between wage struggles and party coalitions and the realm of beauty and anxiety to which this hypersensitive aristocrat belonged? These are noble names to which others could be added if we were primarily concerned with intellectual or literary history.

We have said that of the political parties of the Reich only the Democrats, who were numerically insignificant, were loyal to the spirit of the constitution. In practice the Social Democrats, they above all, were also loyal to it. Their theoretical position, however, remained obscure. Although in fact they had left the Communist Manifesto a long way behind they had never openly rejected it. The old party members, the Crispins and Scheidemanns, still sported the slouch hat and beard of the Marxists of the previous century. Spokesmen of the intellectual wing, the Breitscheidts and Hilferdings, continued to use Marxian jargon and ideas in their speeches. But for Marx the 'bourgeois' republic had at best always been only a curtain-raiser, a springboard to other things. What then was the Weimar Republic? Was it the state of the people, of the workers? If not, was the real thing, the socialist revolution, yet to come? Enmeshed in old theory and new practical necessities the Weimar Social Democrats never gave a clear answer to this question. They spoke of the bourgeois republic from which for the time being the best had to be 'got' for the workers. This meant that the second, proletarian revolution was yet to come. But at the same time they governed and were called upon to defend the existing system in Berlin, in the great *Bundesland* Prussia, and they were by virtue of their official position as well as their attitude as a party, at war with the Communists who were trying to be serious about the second revolution. It was an awkward conflict. The less Marxist doctrine was suited to reality and to their own activities, the more tenaciously the Social Democratic leaders clung to it, feeling that with 'scientific socialism' they were surrendering the ground on which they stood. As though there was not an abundance of new tasks unforeseen by a hundred-year-old 'science', as though new minds and fresh blood were not needed to tackle those tasks. But little fresh blood was forthcoming. The rigidity of the Social Democratic Party prevented the intellectually homeless young generation from joining it and the young workers too began to be bored by the eternal repetition of the same theories. Among the younger generation, those who had fought in the war, there were men who tried very hard to break the deadlock. They believed that it was necessary to get away from the theory of the class struggle for which, however much it existed as far as the employers were concerned, there was no need to find philosophical justification. They believed that it was important to put the half-truths of historical materialism in their right place and to make room beside them for faith, freedom, willpower and love. Let people not wait for the Day of Judgement of the revolution; let them accomplish what could be accomplished here and now and send Marxism to the devil. The Prussian ministers, Braun and Severing, practical men and good patriots, ought to have been close to this group, but they had little time and inclination to worry about philosophy. In practice it never made much headway.

All the theoretical debates [Julius Leber wrote looking back] went round and round in circles and never came near the real problems. It was as with a ship at anchor which turns and twists with the wind and the current in this direction and that, though always only in a circle determined by the length of the anchor chain; so all social democratic political ideas and considerations were held tight by the anchor of out-dated Marxist concepts . . .

For others the Party was not Marxist and revolutionary enough. By adapting itself to the bourgeois republic it had betrayed the great cause. These accusations, familiar to the Communists, were also made by men free from Communist Party discipline and limitation, by uncommitted left-wing writers. There were many of them in Berlin and some very talented ones among them. The penetrating malice with which Kurt Tucholsky ridiculed the Republic, its lameness and falsity, is distantly reminiscent of Heinrich Heine. He had some of the great poet's wit and spleen but unfortunately only little of his love. Radical literature was free to criticize, ridicule and unmask and in this way acquired a facile superiority which however proved nothing about the quality of its own character. It was used to its trade from the days of the Kaiser and continued to pursue it under the Republic which also offered no lack of targets for derision. Did these literary activities do good? Perhaps they did when the protest came from a genuine poetic genius like Bertolt Brecht. Great poems always do good, always put something in order, always calm the soul. But even in Brecht's poetry and plays there was plenty of provocative impudence and irresponsibility. Although this uncommitted left made merciless fun of the Republic and although it had nothing to do with Social Democracy the right nevertheless regarded it as a typical expression of the 'System': 'asphalt literature', 'corrosive Jewish intelligence' or whatever the current expressions were. Radical literature was not part of the Republic but of the republican age in which alone it could find such vocal expression in the press and the theatre. It harmed the Republic in two ways: by a merciless revelation of its weaknesses and because it was nevertheless regarded as a valid expression of the republican spirit. As though this was something purely negative, best represented by humorists who ridiculed their country and even their own cause.

An intellectual ally of the Republic of almost equally doubtful value were the progressive social sciences as taught at some universities. Their advocates followed in the footsteps of Max Weber who had demanded the absence of value judgements or pure factualness of sociology, but they lacked his stature. They also followed in the footsteps of Marx, refining his methods while preserving his basic theories, particularly the one which says that all social and moral ideas are determined by environment. In plain language, ideas and values had no truth; it was necessary to show what interests were hidden behind them, where they came from and why they were doomed to disappear. While this method gave the teacher an opportunity of showing how clever he was, it did not offer the pupil much. How could one help to overcome the much discussed 'spiritual crisis' if all spiritual values were seen as transitory social phenomena? Small wonder that the pupils ran away from their teachers; and that when the last, real crisis came this sociology was left open-mouthed, unable even to understand what was happening, let alone to become a stronghold of resistance. How much more helpful were the old centres of faith and tradition, the Christian churches.

At the same time, a far cry from the 'sociology of knowledge', the 'theory of ideology', the 'analysis of crises' or whatever these efforts were called, there appeared at the universities a new philosophy: Existentialism. It too was typical of the age and highly conscious of it, but not in the sense that it concerned itself with the latest products of history: the republic, democracy, the economy and society. This it did not do at all. If it referred to the state, civilization, society and economic matters at all it was only to demonstrate to the individual that in this, the public sphere, he could not find the meaning of life. The public sphere – that was concern for the welfare of the masses, state or party, bureaucracy, shallow, dishonest demagogy, superficial entertainment, sensationalism and empty talk. History had created these things, they had to be there and could not be altered. But this was not where happiness, support or comfort could be found. The world had lost its gods; people no longer believed the philosophers who had sought God in history, in the state. The individual who wanted to fulfil his life must do so together with other individuals, freely, on the strength of his own daring, in alliance with other individuals. Such ideas came pretty close to a philosophy of despair, although the two most important representatives of the new school only wanted to show the abyss of loneliness and ruin, not to fill it with victims. The one, Karl Jaspers, was a serious, learned man, a true pupil of Kant; he gave his pupils no positive philosophy but taught them useful distinctions between knowledge and faith, between necessity and freedom, between historical and eternal values. The other, Martin Heidegger, was perhaps the more poetic, but he juggled with words; his philosophy was a mixture of profound thoughts and spiritual deception. Both men drew large crowds when they lectured and gave the young something which they had not had since Hegel's death, a philosophy which meant something to them. For this one can be grateful to them. Their attitude to contemporary politics was one of indifference or hostility; indeed, ambition made Heidegger show up very badly in the period that followed.

The historians wanted to be the nation's advisers in political matters, but their ways remained unchanged. Most of them were first or second generation pupils of the old National Liberal glorifiers of Prussia and Bismarck, but without Droysen's intellect or Treitschke's fire. With praiseworthy scientific technique and only slightly clouded objectivity they tried to prove over and over again that France was responsible for the war of 1870 and that Germany was not responsible for the war of 1914; or that even if it bore a small share of guilt, it was clumsiness that it had been guilty of, never of ill will. Some criticized William II, some the Chancellor, Bülow, others attributed all German errors to Bismarck's fall; they never considered whether something had not been fundamentally wrong in a state in whose history the dismissal of one old man could be such a momentous event. The Weimar Republic they regarded as something that had not yet been and perhaps – probably – never would be justified by history. On the other hand they regarded the dissolution of the Habsburg monarchy as historically legitimate. Had not the young Bismarck already likened Prussia to a trim frigate and Austria to a worm-eaten old man-of-war? Was not the end of the Habsburg monarchy a fulfilment of earlier national dreams, was not the Weimar Republic an heir, albeit unworthy, of Prussia-Germany? The successors of the *Kleindeutsche* were delighted that the Danube monarchy had disappeared. The conflict between 'greater' and 'little' Germany had thus become resolved in favour of the *Kleindeutsche*. Now it was up to German Austria to join the Reich and to Vienna to take its laws from Berlin, not vice versa. In spite of notable individual achievements the German historians had learned little and forgotten little since 1914. They continued to be enmeshed in the ideas of the national state and regarded Germany as at least as important as the whole of the rest of the world. They did not produce much fertile national self-criticism.

Of a different nature was the intellectual obstacle which in the last year of the war was thrown by a solitary individual into the stagnant stream of German historical thought where it now lay dividing the waters. I mean Oswald Spengler's *Untergang des Abendlandes* (Decline of the West) and the later lesser works of this powerful and strange man. The *Untergang* belongs to the Weimar period as much as the *Zauberberg* and even more so, because it appeared at the very beginning and at the very beginning repudiated the republican attempt with impressive arguments. If Spengler was right the democrats were wrong and what was in store for the Germans was anything but parliamentary government, civic freedom and eternal peace. Spengler was as German as Thomas Mann but in a very different way. He did not belong to the category of searching, gentle and retiring beings. He knew what was what, once and for all, as Karl Marx before him. With tremendous ambition, with great literary determination he set out to acquire universal knowledge and to conquer the public with it. 'In this book,' he began, 'an attempt is made for the first time to predetermine history.'

Hegel, a hundred years earlier, had not done this. He had only wanted to understand the past and the present that was congealed past; wisely he had not said a word about the future. Spengler, like Hegel, was aware of living at the end of an historical epoch, and he was stimulated by the war as Hegel had been by Napoleon's appearance. Like Hegel he wanted to understand fully what was wrong with his age. This is a temptation for philosophers, particularly for German ones, in times of crisis. However, a comparison of the works of the two men shows how much the German mind had lost in sensitivity and depth in the course of a hundred years. Whereas Hegel's philosophy is steeped in Greek and Christian tradition, in humanism and idealism, in faith in right and eternal truth, Spengler's is crude. What was dangerous in Hegel, the glorification of war, the worship of power and success, Spengler took over. He had no use for Hegel's belief in humanity, for the delicacies and beauties and perverted piety of the dialectic. Man, in Hegel, never freed himself from nature; his task was to come to terms with himself on the basis of the natural, to become mind, to kindle the smouldering divine spark within himself into fire. For Spengler man was and remained a predatory animal, distinguished from others mainly because he had a 'prehensile hand'; and ideas about humanity, right and truth were feeble democratic jokes. The experience of the war had shown that man could become an animal and worse. Others too had noticed this and thought about it, like Sigmund Freud, the psychologist. He taught that primitive man had been a murderer, that we were descended from a 'race of murderers' and that in spite of all civilization the old murderous desire lived on suppressed in us, and would break out if given a chance; that peace and order and civilization had been dearly won, were always threatened and were and remained achievements to be defended by liberal learning. Spengler agreed about the thirst for blood but not with what Freud had to say about the defence and preservation of an existence fit for human beings.

His basic idea can be expressed in a few sentences. 'Cultures', he claimed, appear and vanish like organic beings. As had happened to other 'cultures' the European-American now faced extinction. Before its death, however, a number of interesting things could be expected. Every 'culture' as it approached its end passed through the phase of 'civilization': technical advance, concentration of the masses in vast cities, rule of money. In politics the corresponding phase was democracy; a cunning invention of the capitalists designed to disguise their rule, to allow them to incite or suppress the masses as required. There was talk of equality and freedom, of humanitarianism, of eternal peace and of other such empty ideals, while at the same time the higher achievements of art, music, poetry, philosophy and religious belief were unavoidably lost. 'As far as religion goes the West is finished.' But this, according to Spengler, was not yet the end. A new race confronted the democrats and plutocrats: the real, brutal captains of industry, army and state, the caesars of the future. They were not concerned with wealth and pleasure, but with the development of power for noble, merciless purposes. Dictators would appear of whom Napoleon, Bismarck and Ludendorff had given only a mild foretaste. There would be wars compared with which the one just finished would seem child's play; the humanitarian phrasemongers, the aesthetic weaklings, would vanish in this storm, a prospect which gave no cause for regret. Blood would battle with gold and blood would win. And then what? That was the end. Nothing would come after the great wars and victories and the brainless but noble and iron regimes of the dictators. The Europeans would sink back into the existence of uncivilized fellahs and Berlin and London would look like Nineveh.

Not a pleasant prospect really. Spengler, however, forbade us to lament; only miserable creatures lamented the inevitable, whereas the brave màn resigned himself in a manly way. He died, 'impressively', not in an ugly, wretched manner, and the decline of the West was to be impressive. This challenge appealed to a large section of the public, old and young. What they read gave meaning to their own experiences, and while they were reading dictators of the type foreseen by Spengler appeared on the horizon, Lenin in Russia and then Mussolini in Italy. People were not interested in the end which he predicted; that was still a long way off. What made Oswald Spengler into a central intellectual figure was his description of the present and the immediate future.

Others, too, rejected the Republic. But he rejected it in a different way, by placing himself outside its conflicts and adopting a position which was incomprehensible in terms of the clash of parliamentary parties. He was against the monarchy, against any attempt to restore it; against capitalism, against the Democrats, the Socialists, the Communists and whatever offered itself to the electorate. All this was equally out of date, it all belonged to the 'democratic' phase, even though there was the pretence to the public that struggles went on. The hard times to come would do away with all this. There would be a new socialism reconciled with a soldiery and a new, strong economic leadership, not 'capitalist' but headed by experts devoted to the service of the community. Everyone would be servant, worker and soldier, and a few would be both master and servant. On paper this sounded quite attractive. 'Blood for gold', was what Spengler taught, and 'work for moneybags, blood for gold' was what the National Socialists sang later. However, the prophet was not happy when the German Caesar appeared in the thirties and started to make the Reich of the worker-soldier a reality, to establish 'Prussian socialism'. He had imagined something more elegant.

By praising old Prussia but criticizing the monarchy, by ridiculing the ideal of progress, by glorifying war but claiming to be a socialist, by completely overthrowing conventional ways of thinking in politics Spengler became the co-founder of an intellectual movement which the present writer cannot ignore, however confused it was and however little came of it in the end. It was called the 'Conservative Revolution'. A strange combination of words, indicating that its supporters rejected not certain aspects of the Republic but the whole of it, and the whole present; they regarded 'Right' as outmoded as 'Left' and wanted to ask completely new questions and offer completely new ideals. This they all had in common, however much their views differed otherwise. They were unsuited to become a numerically important organization if only because their aims depended too much on their individual character, talent, experience, dreams and arrogance. Their qualities lent themselves to the formation of small groups, the foundation of periodicals, the writing of poems and essays, but not the establishment of parties. They disliked the face of European democracy; the League of Nations with its impotent hypocrisy; the Reichstag with its intrigues and jobbery; the well-fed parliamentarian in his top hat and pin-stripe trousers. They wanted a new Reich without party squabbles, a Reich of the young and of masculine virtues, a great, proud gathering around a camp-fire instead of the capital Berlin. They expected much more from the modern state than it can give at the best of times.

Some of them had their roots in the pre-war youth movement. But their aims, their longings went beyond those of the *Wandervögel* and the scouts. Others were a product of the war and had, as the phrase went, been formed by the experience of fighting in the front line. Ernst Jünger was the most important spokesman of this group, a brave soldier and a great stylist, a philosopher, an aesthete and an adventurer. We cannot know and he probably did not know himself, what he wanted, what he feared with compassionate sensitivity and what he only pretended to want. The doubts which tortured his fine mind he hid behind the mask of the inflexible writer-officer who gives his reader orders; and what orders! He demanded a revolution, of which the youth of 1918 had in his view been cheated, not a left-wing or a right-wing one but just a 'revolution' and a thorough one. From it would emerge the 'Reich of the worker', of the hard, unintellectual, dreamless machine-man who is ruled and who rules himself and everything. This would be the new aristocrat, whether he dug coal or flew an aeroplane. Domination of the world would be determined by a 'series of wars', of 'battles of material'; in the end the earth would become a landscape of factories, a planned world dominated by a new, merciless class of knights. Away with the things that still linked Germany with a vanished past. Away with the museum pieces, with humanist education, away with babbling fountains in old market squares, with effeminate, anachronistic irritations. Everything in its time. There would be no place in the emergent totalitarian state for writers and dreamers, for romanticism about lime trees in village squares and postillions' horns, for bohemians, for discussion, nor, of course, for democratic mumbo-jumbo. There were very many things for which there would be no place. An understanding of what really lay ahead was mixed up in Jünger with extravagant style, with aestheticism. But he appealed to many clever young people.

It turned against itself, this 'Conservative Revolution', and one's head reels in dealing with it. The idea of a 'workers' state' was common to many of its representatives, although they did not all go as far as Jünger. This hyper-modern view ignored the past and was attracted by an absence of emotion, by hardness and brittleness. Yet at the same time the conservative revolutionaries were romantics and enthusiastic lovers of the past, a conflict also experienced by Jünger and one which he could not disguise. After all, they or their predecessors had rediscovered the beautiful old songs, had lived like the wandering scholars of the Middle Ages, had set out to journey to old towns and foreign countries. They nursed their community ideal with medieval words and concepts: estates versus classes, guilds versus mere associations of interest and so on. Even the idea of the empire came from the Middle Ages and there was mention of the old Hohenstaufen glory. Their ideal of brotherhood and adventure was inimical to the modern world, to its business sense, its atomization, its vulgar entertainments. Intellectual life, however, is always full of contradiction and it is vain to ask the young in particular to follow a single system of consistent concepts. We remember how many forms the aspirations of the *Burschenschaft* had taken a hundred years earlier, how it too wanted both to return to the good old days and to progress to something new, how it hated the French Revolution and accepted some of its ideas. It must be said, though, that the young and not so young men of the Conservative Revolution permitted themselves an unusual confusion of aims. Sometimes they helped themselves by hinting that ideas, of which there was an abundance in Germany, were less important than character, activity and life – in this they could hardly go wrong. They were a living symbol of the age and some of their proposals and actions were good. They did nothing, however, to clarify the prevailing confusion of thought and had no intention of doing so. They did not join in the game because they disliked the state of public affairs; they were content to upset the rules, to muddle up the pieces. Their contribution was to protest against state and society as they were.

The Conservative Revolution had the support of university students and even professors; of young army officers, and veterans' organizations. Occasionally an average Conservative of the old type tried to woo it and to speak its language, as for example Franz von Papen. Occasionally the movement tried to form an alliance with a political party, with splinter groups of the extreme right, with the Communists. This rarely worked. There came the time when it was much talked about because people needed help and advice and, just because the parties seemed to have failed, they sought to find it with those who had turned against the old party system at an early stage. This was the time of the great economic crisis. Thereafter the Conservative Revolution disappeared rapidly. It was absorbed and ruined by the real, anything but 'conservative', revolution which now began in earnest.

5 From Stresemann to Brüning

If it is possible to describe the happenings of 1918 and 1919 as a decision then Germany had decided on democracy at a time when parliamentary government began to be ailing even in its classic homes. 1919 was the great hour of democracy but it was not a happy hour. President Wilson's democratic foreign policy collapsed and of the numerous states and statelets which owed their existence to him many were incapable of surviving, let alone of establishing democracy.

The great party of the masses, the Social Democrats, had decided that Germany must be a democracy. The people must govern themselves, the majority must decide, regardless of *what* the majority decided, regardless of whether a viable majority could be found. This attitude was courageous and from a demo-cratic point of view consistent. It was optimistic, assuming as it did that a sensible, constructive majority would be found. It was also an easy way out because it transferred responsibility from the leaders to the 'people'. The people was a chaos of conflicting hopes and fears. Chaos does not resolve itself on its own; what is needed are ideas and determination and not just a well-prepared constitution. The leaders of the Social Democratic Party replaced determination to govern by determination to keep order and by considerable, affecting integrity.

To keep order they did not lack excellent administrators but they lacked the means of coercion. Instead of creating these they borrowed them from the old army. It was the old army which kept the Reich together in 1919, 1920 and again in 1923, behaving brutally towards the extreme left but indulgently towards the extreme right. From the old army emerged the *Reichswehr* which under its chief, von Seeckt, was built up into an élite army – calling itself thus – designed to be above party struggles and to be politically neutral. But as the party struggles were not concerned with internal republican conflicts but with whether there should or should not be a republic, the alleged neutrality of the *Reichswehr* signified coolness towards the Republic and all its institutions. It served, the argument went, people and state, not the transitory government of the moment. Above all it must continue to be an effective instrument in the hands of its commander; the rest remained to be seen.

The way in which the Social Democrats governed disappointed the electorate and as the Socialists' mandate was derived, according to correct democratic principle, from the electorate, they lost it as early as 1920. Henceforth the Reich was ruled by 'bourgeois' governments, that is to say by people whose attitude towards the institutions represented and administered by them was one of doubt, if not open disbelief. Nevertheless the Social Democrats did not become a strong oppositional party. For the moment no one doubted the basic principle of democracy, that the majority must govern, that a majority in the Reichstag and therefore indirectly a majority of the nation was needed to pass any law. Majorities without or against the Social Democrats were, however, difficult or impossible to find, particularly as the extremist parties could not be fitted into any majority. In this situation the Social Democrats helped themselves, or rather the state, by the principle of 'toleration'. They voted with the 'bourgeois' government which they were not allowed or did not want to join; for example they supported Chancellors Cuno and Stresemann in 1923 and Luther in 1926. In 1923 they voted for an Enabling Law allowing Chancellors Stresemann and Marx, or rather their Ministers of Economics and Finance who came from industry, to take those measures made necessary by the currency reform which dealt a particularly harsh blow to the lower middle classes, the workers, white-collar workers and civil servants. Most of the time the Social Democrats of the Weimar period were therefore both in opposition and not in opposition, because without their passive help it was impossible to 'govern' the Republic at all.

The situation was further complicated by Prussia. The fact that the Prussian state existed at all, that two-thirds of the Reich was still called Prussia and that its administration was based on different political principles, was one of the typical paradoxes of the Weimar period. Prussia had long ceased to be a genuine state; it was much less of one than Bavaria or Württemberg because it was too big, too much part of the Reich which it had created. Under the Kaiser its continued existence had served the dynasty, the Army and the ruling classes. Now it continued to exist because of the sheer weight of its past, because in 1919 Germany had been too exhausted and too lazy to invent anything better. Since it existed and since the election results remained somewhat more favourable here, the Social Democrats thought that they could do in Prussia what they did not do in the Reich; they wanted to make the old kingdom into a model democratic state. This was not easy. The legislation that counted was made in the Reich; taxes, tariffs, labour laws, social insurance and of course foreign policy and the army were all matters for the Reich. Otto Braun, for many years Prime Minister of Prussia, makes it clear in his memoirs how completely the Reich – government, Central Bank and Army – usually spoilt his best plans. Even in Prussia the Social Democrats could not govern alone. They worked together with the Centre. A combination of the three opposition parties of the Bismarck period, Social Democrats, Centre and left-wing Liberals, was nothing abnormal as such; in fact it was even tried in the Reich, though not for long, to be succeeded by the 'bourgeois bloc'. In fact the party which decided the fate of the Weimar Republic was the Centre. It was possible at a pinch to get along without the Social Democrats, but not without the Centre. The party was a microcosm of German society, superbly organized, firmly held together by religion; industrialists and trade unions, small farmers and landowners, city dwellers and backwoodsmen were all represented in the Centre. There was some justification for the party's name and the words of its founder, Windthorst, *Extra Centrum Nulla Salus*, were never truer than during the period of the First German Republic. The party could turn either to the right or to the left; it had experienced politicians at its disposal for every course and the occasional Centre politician also found it possible to be friendly with both sides. In the divided German multi-party state, unable to produce either a genuine majority or a genuine opposition, the Centre was useful as long as it could be. In the Prussian two-thirds of the Reich the Centre governed with the Socialists. In the three-thirds, in the Reich itself, it governed with the anti-Socialists of the *Deutsche Volkspartei* and at times even with the monarchists, the *Deutschnationalen*. The three-thirds were much more powerful than the two-thirds, much more important. The Reich had no need to make allowances for Prussia whereas Prussia needed to make allowances for the Reich if the Prussian coalition government was to survive. Prussia's government was much steadier than that of the Reich. It had adroitness and dignity and where it could act at all it acted with energy. Nevertheless, what Braun and Severing had built up in Prussia was only the semblance of power. The political 'neutrality' of the Army, the delicate co-existence of the Reich and Prussia, the toleration of bourgeois bloc governments by the Social Democrats, the inexhaustible adaptability of the Centre – these roughly were the political factors which determined the good years of the Weimar Republic, from 1924 to 1928 and beyond.

German policy during these years was given meaning by the Foreign Minister of all the bourgeois bloc governments, the right-wing coalitions and the 'Big Coalitions', Gustav Stresemann. The Social Democrats supported his diplomacy by tolerating the 'bourgeois bloc' cabinets. It was the diplomacy of agreement, of slow, peaceful, determined regaining of German sovereignty. As we have already seen it was successful. Its achievements were 'Locarno', Germany's entry into the League of Nations, the disappearance of the Allied Commission supposed to supervise German disarmament, and the beginning of the evacuation of the occupied territories west of the Rhine. Nor would foreign credit have been so readily available without the confidence which Stresemann gained for himself and those who had entrusted him with his mission. Yet by what efforts. He was not old then and might well be alive now had his life lasted the normal span. If he looked ailing and died young, it was because of the torture of his work; the unyieldingness of the material with which he struggled, the lack of understanding and malice of many of his countrymen. He received no thanks for any of his achievements and he was blamed for everything that he had failed to achieve. The businessman from the Wilhelminian age, Ludendorff's friend who had become reconciled to the Republic and to the workers' position in the Republic, was hated and reviled almost as much as Walther Rathenau. Because he was a good parliamentarian and tried to keep coalition governments together by compromise, he was regarded as corrupt. Because he fought to give Germany the same rights as were enjoyed by the other states in Europe but not to give it superiority, the extreme right regarded him as a traitor.

The good period of the Weimar Republic was thus, on closer inspection, not so good after all. Nor was it felt as such. The newspapers wrote about crises, disgraceful incidents and emergencies as though they were everyday occurrences. The governments, which under the constitution needed a majority in the Reichstag, fell frequently only to return in a slightly changed guise. The people gained the impression that a government term of office lasted no longer than the time taken to form it, and found the whole proceedings undignified. There was much excitement about minor issues: should German consulates in foreign ports fly the old black-white-red merchant flag or the black-red-gold flag of the Republic? Should a grandson of William II be allowed to take part in Army manoeuvres? Silly issues which all arose from the same vexatious fact, that Germany had had a revolution which was no revolution, that allegedly there was a new state but that people had been unable or unwilling to let go of the old one.

To the restlessness, the feeling of impermanence which the right did its best to whip up into the feeling that the situation was unbearable, Germany's eastern frontiers made their contribution. The relationship between Germany and the new Polish state could not be good. Poland had been created at the expense of Germany, as Prussia had been at the expense of Poland. The fact that Polish territory separated East Prussia from the rest of Germany would not in itself have been a tragedy if the two nations had understood and respected each other; but as they did not, as on the contrary they eagerly seized every possible cause for offence, the 'corridor', the isolation of East Prussia and the artificial existence of the Free City of Danzig were felt by Germans as a dishonour. At Locarno Stresemann had recognized the western frontiers as fixed; in the East no German Foreign Minister could have dared to do this. The Germans felt superior to the small Slav nations in a very different sense from that in which they felt superior to the French. It seemed normal to them that Poles lived under Prussian rule because the strong expands at the expense of the weak; but that hundreds of thousands of Germans were now compelled to live in Poland seemed historically wrong and intolerable. The situation in the other hastily founded new state, Czechoslovakia, was similar. Here too, Germans lived as a so-called national minority, protected by written laws and the League of Nations, but molested whenever an opportunity offered itself without open violation of the law. Czechoslovakia unlike Poland was not ruled by soldiers but by philosophical rhetoricians; its administration, based on Habsburg foundations, was better. But the same mutual, arrogant dislike separated Germans and Czechs, the latter regarding themselves as morally superior and the former as basically stronger, as having the justification of history behind them. Was it not their victory over Russia which alone had made possible the whole new system of the East? A pretentious Victory Square in Prague now recalled the fact that the Czechs had been manoeuvred into the victors' camp at the right moment; as though they, and not two-thirds of the inhabited world, had forced Germany to capitulate. Both Poland and Czechoslovakia had a military alliance of obvious significance with France.

Then there was Austria. This too seemed fundamentally an unsolved question to the Germans. And again we must admit that to some extent they were justified. How could one forget that the Austrians in 1919 had wanted, but not been allowed, to join the Reich. What was this Austrian state, the like of which there had never been before? It called itself 'German-Austria' and it had been formed by drawing arbitrary frontiers around one-tenth of the old monarchy in which German was spoken. The action did not create a genuine state, certainly not a national one, because there was no Austrian nation. This area contained the old capital of south-eastern Europe, the focal point of so many arterial roads which were now severed by customs barriers, the stronghold of a glorious past recalled by desolate palaces and museums. Under the last Habsburgs Vienna had become a very big city, and it had been left only a very narrow strip of hinterland. Poor, lovely Austria, sunk so low because of foreign folly and its own. The countryside was predominantly agricultural, Catholic and conservative, the big city was predominantly socialist. Hence there was an unhealthy tension between town and country. Poverty went deeper than in the Reich; in Germany people were well-off compared with Austria. Nevertheless, in the late twenties there was no longer the same unanimity on the question of the *Anschluss* as in 1919. Austria's two main parties, the Socialists and the Christian Socialists, the Clericals, disliked the development in the Reich; the desire to become part of and fit into the Reich cooled off. After all, there were other possibilities. In the way of the restoration of the old unity of the Danube region in a more modern form there stood the ineradicable fear and dislike of all the peoples and groups and individuals who had benefited or thought that they had benefited from the dissolution of the Habsburg Empire. In Prague people were more afraid of the spirit of the Habsburgs than of the living might of the Germans. A military alliance of Austria's three inflated successors, Czechoslovakia, Yugoslavia and Rumania, was directed mainly against Hungary and the Habsburg past, and only in the second place against the German Reich. Wherever Vienna turned it failed to find good neighbours. Germany looked at the problem simply without worrying about Austria's internal development. Austria was German, it had wanted to be German in 1919 and German it must sooner or later become.

This was one of the basic problems of the Weimar Republic, the child of defeat. Bismarck's German state had never embraced the whole nation; not the Habsburg Germans, nor the Germans who were the masters in Russia's Baltic provinces. As long as Germany was strong and on good terms with its two neighbours there was no need for serious concern; the Germans in Austria were well-off, and the Germans under the Tsar were tolerably well-off, though even before 1914 decreasingly so. The triumph of nationalism in the East coincided with the German defeat; the Reich no longer had power and prestige to protect the Germans abroad as before. Consequently the fragmentary character of the Reich of 1871 now showed up much more clearly than before. It had always been known that Bismarck's Germany was not 'greater' Germany, although the fact was not taken too tragically in the period of Hohenzollern splendour. The dissolution of the Habsburg Empire to the advantage of the Slavs invalidated the compromise of 1870 for the Germans also, raised old questions anew, reopened old wounds and gave the words 'greater German' a revolutionary meaning which they had not had in 1848.

Let us return to the course of events. During the war Field-Marshal von Hindenburg had once remarked that there was nothing wrong with Kaiser and Reich, but that he was too old for them and that for him the Kaiser was still above all the King of Prussia. These were understandable views in a man who had witnessed Bismarck's career almost from the beginning, who had been present at Sadowa in 1866 and at the proclamation of the Emperor in the Hall of Mirrors at Versailles in 1871. Yet a man who considered himself too old for the Wilhelminian Empire was hardly young enough for the Republic. A dignified retirement in

Hanover, an occasional 'Tannenberg celebration', a reunion with old comrades, a letter from the banished Majesty – that should have been enough for the old man who, though hale and hearty, no longer understood the age in which he lived.

It happened differently. The Weimar Constitution provided for the election of the President by the people, by all men and women entitled to vote. The first President, Ebert, had not been elected under this procedure, but had been appointed by the National Assembly. After his death in the spring of 1925 it became necessary to hold an election. The united right chose Hindenburg as its candidate and Admiral von Tirpitz persuaded him to accept the honour – two veterans of 1870. Hindenburg was elected, although by a narrow majority. Had the Communists not put up a third candidate, the 'popular bloc', represented by a mild Centre republican, would have triumphed over Hindenburg's 'Reich bloc'. In order to harm the Republic, even if it did not help themselves, the Communists, abysmally deluded and malicious, led the imperial marshal into the presidential palace. There he was: what did this signify?

At first it signified nothing precise. Hindenburg had received the votes of all right-wing opponents of the Republic, of the followers of Bismarck and Ludendorff, of the pan-Germans, of the members of the *Vaterlandspartei*, and also of the 'particularists'; of everybody, to call them by their new names, from the National Socialists to the Bavarian People's Party. But the very fact that Hindenburg had the support of relatively moderate groups made it more difficult to find a precise significance in his election. The old soldier fought the electoral campaign in an honest and restrained manner. He let it be known that although he was of course a monarchist he was too old to hope for a restoration and would be a just President and guardian of the constitution. His views on the constitution coincided more or less with those of his King, William I, sixty years previously: he preferred not to ask whether constitutions were good or bad; as they existed, it was necessary to uphold them. This was Hindenburg's intention, regardless of what went on in Tirpitz's more intelligent and more wicked mind when he persuaded the old man to become a candidate. Let those who came after him see how they managed.

For years things went fairly well. Hindenburg carried out his functions in a dignified manner, and although somewhat parsimonious he did his duty, went hunting, took salutes as he had done for half a century, and now and again even addressed a word to a Social Democrat. He thought that some of them, Otto Braun, Hermann Müller and others, were really quite decent. The pity was that they were *Sozis*, that they had not remained what they ought to be: hard-working foremen, upright sergeant-majors or farm managers or compositors. But the age being what it was adaptation was called for. Hindenburg had no intention of doing anything against the spirit of the age. Phlegmatic, slow, limited by the ideas of his class, he was by no means unintelligent, and more flexible than his big, immobile face might have led one to believe. Had he not advised his Emperor to flee in 1918 and had he not had himself made commander-in-chief by a revolutionary act? Although the memory of his behaviour continued to haunt him, although he never got over it, he had done it. Similarly he had recommended the signing of the peace treaty in 1919; also with regrets and also without making it clear that this was what he advised. People wanted it that way, they wanted the 'Hindenburg myth' Hindenburg had enough instinct and vanity to adapt his behaviour accordingly. He gave them what they wanted. Now, under the Republic, they wanted someone who stood head and shoulders above the morass of party squabbles, who intervened firmly, paternally, if somewhat contemptuously, when the birth pangs of a new government went on too disgracefully long – the 'faithful Eckart of the German people', a symbol of the non-political, the incorruptible in an age of politics and idle talk.

In reality Hindenburg was not quite as incorruptible as all that. However, let us overlook such minor flaws. What mattered was that this was how people saw him and that in some respects he was like this; if only all else had been well this might have been enough.

The effect of Hindenburg's presence in Berlin was contradictory. On the one hand he harmed the Republic, as Tirpitz and the

Communists had intended that he should. Everybody knew that Hindenburg was no republican; he offered the people a point of integration which lay, so to speak, outside the Republic. On the other hand he was the President of the Reich. If Hindenburg invoked the constitution, if his residence flew the black-red-gold flag, respect for these things went up a little. Whatever one thought about the Republic its highest office was now held by a true German, by the universally venerated Field-Marshal, and this reflected beneficially on other republican offices. Particularly as he was not to be trifled with when it came to an oath to the constitution. The old gentleman no longer attended officers' reunions at which the Kaiser's health was drunk, however bitter it was for him to stay away. He was correct in his dealings with the left-wing government in Prussia. And when the Social Democrats emerged once more as the strongest party at the Reichstag elections in the early summer of 1928 he did not hesitate to offer the chancellorship to the chairman of their parliamentary party, Hermann Müller, who accepted the office.

This was a normal process. The party 'recuperated' in opposition and when it had recuperated sufficiently it occasionally rejoined the government. Not in order to embark on great economic and social changes; this seemed particularly uncalled for at the moment as the defeat of the right had indicated that in general the country was tolerably satisfied with conditions, that is to say with the economic boom. The Social Democrats aimed at carrying out the routine duties of government in a dignified manner and, where possible, at 'getting something out of it' for the workers. They could not do much because for a majority in the Reichstag the so-called 'Big Coalition' was necessary, and this, in addition to the Socialists, consisted of representatives of the arch-capitalist *Deutsche Volkspartei*. Trade unions and big business were reluctantly compelled to govern together, as in 1923 when Stresemann first held the office of Chancellor and for the last time when he was Foreign Minister. The Ministry of Defence was entrusted to the upright man whom we remember from 1918, the general from Württemberg, Wilhelm Groener.

The story of this last parliamentary coalition is pitiful. It suffered the fate of people who set out on an outing in fine weather but are overtaken by threatening clouds. They go on because they have started, but hope diminishes and the general mood becomes increasingly subdued until finally the storm breaks and they all scatter.

The parties bargained and bartered as usual, and as usual the Social Democrats were the losers. During the election campaign they had heatedly opposed the building of the small navy allowed under the peace treaty but so far not embarked upon; they argued that the money was better spent on feeding hungry school children. Under pressure from the Army the government now decided to make a start with an armoured cruiser. The Chancellor gave in to the coalition partners; his party did not, with the result that as a deputy he voted against the bill introduced by him as head of the government. The bill was pushed through by the votes of the right. A petty operation, but one worth mentioning. General disarmament had ,always been promised and never carried out; while its neighbours kept navies Germany had good reason to do the same. If the idea was that Germany should not have any warships at all then there was no point in having an army. Yet such fundamental questions were never decided, they were only toyed with from instance to instance. The fact that the Chancellor voted for the navy while his party voted against it merely produced the situation with which we have long become familiar; when the Socialists 'governed' they were at the same time in opposition, just as in opposition they often supported the government. The result was disappointment and confusion among their followers, survived by the party only because it could make any demand – or almost any – on the loyalty of its supporters.

Unpleasant though it was the dispute over the cruiser was quickly overshadowed by more serious problems. They came from the economic sector. Henceforth all the conflicts which Germany had permitted itself in the days of tolerable prosperity – black-red-gold versus black-white-red, religious school versus nondenominational school, army budgets, constitutional reform and whatever else – seemed like a child's game.

There had been signs even in 1928 that the economic boom was coming to an end. Foreign capital was becoming scarce. The number of unemployed rose and with it the financial burden of unemployment benefits; tax receipts fell. Lock-outs and wage disputes occurred in the iron and steel industry which once more after long and difficult negotiations were settled with the state acting as mediator. The employers began seriously to attack the whole system of 'political wages', of arbitration and collective, state-protected wage agreements; on the grounds that all this had caused the beginning decline and was economically irresponsible. Inevitably the clash between capital and trade unions also made itself felt within the government. The idea of the Weimar Republic, to the extent that it had one, was compromise, peace between classes, not class struggle to the bitter end. It had never mastered the great economic powers which were as powerful as in the Kaiser's day. On the other hand the state now took a much more active interest in economic matters. It had promised the worker the eight-hour day; it guaranteed him a wage designed to give him and his family a decent existence; it helped him in the distress of unemployment. The co-existence of a powerful, effectively organized private sector and a state which intervened politically in economic matters was possible only while both parties were anxious to be on good terms and while business was satisfactory. In the long run there could, therefore, be no successful co-existence. Business was no longer satisfactory and most of the big industrialists were not prepared to be conciliatory. They were uncompromising men from the Wilhelminian age, if not like Emil Kirdorf from the age of Bismarck. Their desire, only temporarily repressed, had always been to do away with the whole of the Republic's hated labour legislation. These were economic questions as much as political ones. It was impossible to separate the two spheres; to that extent Marx was correct. If the industrialists now took the offensive it was not so much that they were driven to do so by their own economic difficulties as because growing unemployment weakened the position of the trade unions; there was the hope of weakening the weak still further. Nevertheless the employers saw themselves as good patriots. Did they not bear the heavy responsibility of feeding the German workers? Did they not have a right to do this in their way instead of being interfered with by trade union agitators, parliamentary nitwits and camouflaged Communists? Their interests were those of the German economy, of the nation as a whole. This was roughly how they saw the situation.

Foreign policy also entered. The Reich was still burdened by reparation payments. Although these did not play the decisive role attributed to them by right-wing agitators – what Germany received in credits from abroad was more than what it paid out in the form of reparations – they represented a disturbing factor and an economic absurdity. The more difficult foreign credit became to obtain, the less industry was inclined to continue to pay reparations, or even to pursue Stresemann's policy of international understanding. With the policy of social compromise at home went a peaceful foreign policy. With the policy of class struggle, of class rule at home went an aggressive foreign policy which was sooner or later bound to lead to a bigger army and to increased armaments orders. Industry – that is to say its most powerful sector, the Rhenish-Westphalian industrialists – now turned its back on the policy which its most liberal representative, Stresemann, had been allowed to pursue for five years.

In the early summer of 1929 an agreement or plan for the settlement of reparation payments was reached which, compared with the earlier one, envisaged some easing of the burden. It was intended to cover a period of sixty years – apparently the great financiers and learned experts who prepared it really believed this. In practice it brought advantages; the victorious powers agreed to lift all controls to which German financial activities had hitherto been subject. Nevertheless the plan stimulated nationalist demagogy; the enslavement of German children and children's children for two generations was a rewarding theme. A few months later, at the beginning of October, Gustav Stresemann died after a stroke.

This was a loss of the kind which the Republic could least afford at this moment. Like no one else Stresemann had kept parliament together, had personally made possible the compromise between labour and capital, and by his diplomacy had given meaning to

Germany's existence as a state among states. Recently historians have proved on the basis of documents that Stresemann was not a consistent pacifist, not an internationalist and that he did not faithfully carry out the conditions of the Versailles treaty. How could he, given his origins and past? Why should he, as long as the world was as it was? He knew about Germany's secret rearmament; he knew about the gradual increase in the size of the Army. How could it not have been his wish to see Germany strong again, to set aside the consequences of defeat? Did not all Frenchmen, even the Socialists, want to see their France strong, and all Britons their Britain? A human being is many things at once, but what he develops into is more important than what he was at the beginning and can never cast off completely. In judging a statesman the effect of his activities in general counts for more than his secret intrigues. Stresemann had created the only powerful symbol of the Republic, as striving for honourable social and international peace. The German industrialist and imperialist had become a citizen of the world and yet he had remained the most German of Germans. His last wish was to have *Am Brunnen vor dem Tore* (By the Fountain at the Gate) played at his graveside.

Ten days later New York experienced a collapse in stock prices the like of which had not been seen since the eighteenth century. This was the terrible end of the world boom, the beginning of a crisis which one by one affected every state not living in complete isolation. Germany was the country most liable to be affected by a crisis. Markets shrank, short-term credits were withdrawn, new ones were unobtainable, and so the basis of German prosperity vanished; its over-concentrated, over-rationalized industry no longer knew where to turn. Factories reduced output or closed down, the number of unemployed rose and so did the sums paid by the Reich insurance organization, tax receipts fell, there was a government deficit – all this being part of one and the same process which, once it had begun, was self-generating; as it went on the clash between the parties which represented the great economic interests became fiercer. The blanket could no longer be stretched to cover the unequal bedfellows; one of them had to clear out. In the spring of 1930 Stresemann's Big Coalition collapsed over the question of whether unemployment benefits should be reduced or kept up by raising contributions. The Weimar Republic had always needed the centre parties for effective government because the extremist groups were unwilling to make a positive contribution. But the moderate parties themselves were split by the old, classical conflict between capital and labour, and pressure was constantly brought to bear on them by extremists on both sides. The split down the middle now became too deep; even the skill of a Stresemann, one may assume, could not have prevented the break-up for long.

It was the chief of the political department of the Army, General von Schleicher, who proposed the new Chancellor to President von Hindenburg. Schleicher dabbled in politics like other generals before him, but without worrying much about theory. He was a man of personal contacts, of drawing-room chats and secret intrigues; when he was in charge of the political interests of the Army he built up an extensive propaganda and defence apparatus. The Minister of National Defence, Groener, the better man, although less subtle, trusted him blindly. Hindenburg too, dependent on advisers as he was throughout his life, listened readily to the elegant, clever, good-tempered, pleasure-loving officer. Herr von Schleicher was primarily interested in increasing the size and strength of the Army. As a general, aristocrat and friend of big business he had no liking for the parliamentary republic, least of all for the Social Democrats; as everything was so difficult now, and as the Reichstag majority had once more vanished into thin air, he thought that the moment for other methods had come. These ideas coincided with wishes which had always been self-evident to Hindenburg but for which he had not been able to gain much support while Stresemann was in charge. In fact many people, even among bourgeois moderates, shared these ideas. They felt that the coalition governments whose members were no more than the postmen of their squabbling parties had proved a failure. The threatened country needed someone with firm authority who would work together with parliament without depending on it in every respect. One of the people whose thoughts ran along these lines was Heinrich Brüning, recently made chairman of the parliamentary Centre party, and it was he whom Hindenburg, not without Schleicher's influence, appointed Chancellor with the admonition that in forming his cabinet he should take no account of party allegiances.

Schleicher and Brüning – no allies could have been more dissimilar: the jovial schemer and social lion and the scholarly Catholic with the soul of a monk and a soldier. Brüning was the very curious case – anywhere, but particularly in Weimar Germany – of a politician who represented no class, group or material interests. He was patriotism, scholarship, self-control and selfless virtue incarnate. Of course, pure virtue does not exist in man, certainly not in political man, and the psychologist whom we do not wish to emulate here will speculate on the sympathies, sorrows and longings hidden behind the irreproachable façade of the new Chancellor. What soon became apparent was his weakness for anything military, anything Prussian: matters fundamentally alien to him (for what connection was there between the Westphalian middle class and 'Prussia'?); particularly for the old man in the presidential palace. Above all he wished to 'serve' Hindenburg, to derive his authority from the President's confidence; just as Bismarck's position had depended on the confidence of William I. The difference, however, was that the year was no longer 1862 and that the return to a king-and-chancellor relationship, long since refuted by history as a basis of authority, could not be a genuine repetition. Hindenburg was a substitute monarch, his authority was not based on deep-rooted, supra-personal tradition. The king, as long as people believed in kingship, had no need to pretend to be more than he was. With Hindenburg it was necessary to persuade people that he was something which the poor old man could never be. Although the new king-and-chancellor loyalty lasted barely two years instead of a quarter of a century there was something curious in this subconscious attempt in a crisis to return to an antiquated form of German constitutional life.

Technically the Chancellor depended on the confidence of the Reichstag majority, his appointment by the President being intended to represent a mere formality. How then could 'presidential government' be combined with the letter and spirit of the constitution? For a long time admirers of dictatorship among German constitutional lawyers had been devoting their attention to Paragraph 48 of the constitution. We know its limited meaning and purpose. It provided the legal basis for measures 'to restore public safety and order', for police action. It certainly was not designed to enable the President to govern without the Reichstag, as was made clear by the Reichstag's right to revoke any order made under Paragraph 48. So much for the wording and the meaning. However, there was no shortage in Germany of learned sophists, of skilled interpreters who argued that a constitution needed living beings to expound it by relating the test to the demands of the present, to the actual situation – or else manage without the text. A piece of paper, Metternich had written a hundred years earlier, did not make a constitution; only time did. It was true that the Weimar Constitution had not had much time to become a genuine constitution nor had it been fortunate. What could be done with a Fundamental Law in which half the population did not believe; what could not be done with it if it were to be interpreted? Be that as it may it was Brüning's considered intention to govern with parliament if parliament was ready to co-operate – if it obeyed, would have been the phrase in the good old days – or else to govern without it on the basis of Paragraph 48. It was necessary to have the courage to take unpopular steps, particularly in the economic sphere. Had Germany not lived on illusions since 1914; even after the currency reform of 1923 which for a moment had shown what cold reality was like had it not avoided the truth by exaggerated borrowing? Brüning was not hostile to any particular class, least of all to the workers; he had himself been active for the Christian trade unions. But he was a fervent, ascetic believer in scientific economic practice. It was essential to restore order, to balance the budget, to put the finances of the Reich, the *Länder* and local government on a sound footing. If this was impossible without reducing social benefits then they must be reduced, taxes must be raised and imports cut. Wages would follow suit, and then also prices. Once the weeds had been killed by deflation the productive plants would grow again unobstructed. This was logical as well as traditional; most economic theorists and practicians supported the virtuous, gentle and determined head of the government. Of those who had learnt to think differently, of John Maynard Keynes for example, Brüning had hardly heard. Were there not limits to what could be expected of even the most patient people? Would the living flesh not one day rebel against the operation, painful and never-ending, that was being performed on it? He asked no questions, his only concern was that the operation should be scientifically correct.

Dr Brüning pushed his first batch of reforms through the Reichstag with the help of the Conservatives. But not the second. It was brought in under Paragraph 48 in the form of a presidential 'emergency decree'. When the Reichstag declared the decree null and void President and Chancellor dissolved the Reichstag, realizing all too well, however, that the forthcoming election would be an unusual one.

6. Crisis and Disintegration of the Weimar Republic

For years Germany had been haunted by a political party which was old, but which thanks to conditions now acquired new energy and which spread with a virulence unparalleled in the history of modern democracy. It was the National Socialist Party.

As early as 1923 its demagogic rabble-rousing leader had represented a dangerous force in Bavaria and had been able to establish connections with like-minded north Germans. Then he had briefly vanished to serve a mild prison sentence; and having been set free he could at first do no more than keep his little band of loyal supporters together. The comic details of the beer-hall *Putsch* had not served his cause in the long run, nor did the gradually growing contentment of the Stresemann years. Whereas in the Reichstag of 1924 the 'Nazis' had had thirty-two members, in the Reichstag of 1928 they mustered only twelve. Instead of being taken seriously they were regarded as part of the 'lunatic fringe'. And that is how things would probably have remained but for the economic crisis. Hitler was as good a speaker in 1928, as much a man consumed by determination to conquer, to have power and success, as two years later. Some who listened to him in the Bavarian capital – inspecting as it were a grotesque curiosity – felt his fascination and went home momentarily confused and thoughtful. Yet Hitler made no progress as long as things were going tolerably well in Germany. But now they no longer went at all well; the number of unemployed does not give a complete picture of the catastrophe. Almost everybody was affected by the contraction of the economy: peasants whose products no longer brought them an adequate income, white-collar workers who had cause to fear dismissal, innkeepers who were compelled to stand in the street to attract a few customers, students who were in no hurry to finish their hungry period of training, because they were afraid of what came after, craftsmen, traders – everybody.

The Nazi Party had the advantage that it was in no way involved with what had happened in Germany since 1919. All other bourgeois parties, even the Conservatives, the *Deutschnationalen*, had at some time or other been in the government and had voted with the government and compromised themselves. Not so the Nazis. For ten years they had accused, hated, scorned, cursed and nothing else. They could attack without having to defend themselves with a single word. What had happened to the things which the other parties, the right as much as the left, had promised for ten years? Where was the welfare republic of the left or its defeated capitalism? Where the flourishing industry and agriculture of the right? By its fruits the 'System' would be known, and part of the System were all those who did not support the leader of the National Socialist German Workers' Party. He alone had warned the nation, he alone had predicted what was now happening, and had explained the causes: the crime of November 1918, international Marxism and its alliance with international capitalism, corrupt party rule, the folly of reparations, the diabolical intentions of the Jews. 'Nation, open your eyes, recognize the

fraud ... Defeat the traitors. Send the bankrupts to the devil ...'
This stuff was effective, it left his opponents breathless. After all
it was correct that they and not the Nazis had governed the Republic and it was correct that the situation was critical. Yet the
reasons were not those which the rabble-rouser rushing by plane
from meeting to meeting, drummed into his supporters. The
economic crisis had little to do with reparations, with the foolish
Young Plan. It affected also the rich, victorious countries;
America first and foremost; then gradually Britain and finally
France. But the desperate German electorate was not interested
in France, Britain and America. It was not interested in the expert
and serious approach of Brüning's government programmes.
Here was a man who explained things more simply, who brought
life into the stagnant air of German politics. In the audacity of
his attacks, in the boldness of his self-praise, in the captivating,
ingratiating cunning of his arguments, in hatred and ridicule,
even in the physical intensity of his screams and tears he had no
equal anywhere. People compared what he said with the long
chain of their own bitter experiences – war, defeat, inflation,
economic crisis – and found it worth listening to.

It was normal for the opposition to put all the blame for the
crisis on the government. This was part of the rules of the democratic game, a tough game all the world over in which fairness
never plays much part. In America too the ruling Republicans
were blamed for the economic chaos; and as a result the Democrats won the next election. In America, however, and even more
in Britain, people were agreed on the basic concepts of political
life. Hatred was not the main motivating element in politics, the
game was not played with deadly seriousness; it remained hedged
in by old constitutional traditions. In Germany the storm now
turned against the Republic itself, against the whole 'System'
and all who had been part of it; as a result the *Deutschnationalen*
who had occasionally been part of it now quickly severed all
connections with it and imitated the Nazis. The Communists
were able to do the same; they too had never been part of it,
they too stood outside the republican arena. The number of their
supporters rose also, but they were not nearly as well led as the

National Socialists; their success was limited by their notorious subservience to Russia and the exclusive rigidity of their doctrines. The rootless German citizen did not want to be counted among the 'proletarians' to whom alone the Communist doctrine was tailored. The tune of the extreme right appealed more to his hates, his ambitions.

The Nazis provided a remarkable number of able and distinct propagandists. One played the part of the conservative, the much decorated officer, the corpulent would-be aristocrat. Another acted the solid working man anxious to voice the decent instincts of the German workers deceived by Marxism. A third specialized in arousing the age-old, wicked instinct of anti-semitism, latent in all European peoples. Yet another could do whatever he chose; he was the vulgar and malicious, the outstanding and impudent intellect of the Party. One thing they all had in common: they were demagogues of a kind which Germany had never seen before. What well-bred, learned, harmless men by comparison were the founders of socialism, Bebel and Lieb-knecht; what an aristocratic philosopher the great orator, Ferdinand Lassalle. As for the Social Democratic leaders now having to withstand the storm, Braun and Müller and Severing, what decent politicians were they compared with this nihilist gang! The Nazi leaders made their entry into crowded meetings with their energy untapped, with an unshakeable presence of mind, tireless students of what they themselves called 'modern mass psychology', unscrupulous, malicious, arrogant and convinced that they would be victorious; a feeling which was strengthened by the growing misery. Deafening martial music prepared the way for them; flags and banners, shouts of jubilation and of hatred completed the feeling of oneness between speakers and audiences. At the same time a distance was always kept between them and the man whom they called the *Führer*. He knew how to preserve his authority. They spoke for him, he did not speak for them but only for himself.

It is difficult to understand the mind of an individual completely; it has levels which it does not itself know and changes as long as it lives. The demagogue of 1930 was not yet the insane commander and executioner-in-chief of 1944. Of course he already had in mind the goal which we have come to know in retrospect and in the last years and days of his life he achieved his most cherished, secret dream; only then did he show completely what he was. But that is not how we must describe him in 1930. He did not know either himself or the world so well as fifteen years later, nor did the world know him so well; the reality of this catastrophe had not yet been unfolded. He played various roles, sometimes that of the future conqueror, sometimes that of the man of moderation and common sense. One did not know what was hidden behind these façades, what was hypocrisy and what was genuine; probably he did not know himself because in order to make others believe he needed to believe himself at the time, even when he lied. The masses who succumbed to his fascination were anyway lost to reason and stopped thinking. While those who did not succumb were disgusted by the fraud of the whole thing rather than really conscious of the danger of the man. They regarded him as a lunatic, which he was, and his success as a spook soon to vanish. It never entered their heads that such a lunatic would make world history, first gain control of a great people, then with this people conquer Europe, and so reveal our civilization in all its weakness. He knew this, and the more they underestimated him, the more furious became his determination to make them suffer for it, and to show them who was the master.

Much was, or could have been known, about him even then. He came from the twilight of the decaying Habsburg monarchy. There he had imbibed hatred of the Slavs and antisemitism, poisons which took a much more deadly form in the frontier regions, in racially mixed areas and in Vienna than among the Germans of the Reich. Casual labourer, lodger in men's hostels, artist whom no art school was prepared to accept, day dreamer, riffraff of the lowest order, such was his life at that time; lonely but inquisitive, full of resentment against state and society which had conspired to prevent his rise. From Vienna he went to the Reich, to Munich, and from Munich into the war of which he tells us that it came to him as a deliverance and as a wonderful experience. He seems to have been a good soldier, one of millions, although disliked because of his arrogance and ambition. He returned from the war convinced that Germany could have won with better leaders, that it had been betrayed by Socialists and Jews and that next time he must do things better. The question was mainly one of propaganda. One must speak to one's people as the enemies, Lloyd George and Clemenceau, had spoken to their people. This he could do, this he would learn. Demobilized, but still living in barracks, he became involved in the murky goings-on of post-war politics in Munich. This was the scene: the Army in a state of disintegration, *Freikorps* and *Reichswehr*, the destruction of the *Räterepublik*, the Bavarian Soviet republic, spies and informers, and murder. He was allowed to address the soldiers as a national teacher and in the process he discovered his oratorical gifts. Having accidentally joined a small group of conspirators, the National Socialist Workers' Party, he soon became its master. Now began his first rapid rise with which we are familiar. After three years the down-at-heel Viennese painter was, or seemed, a key figure in Bavarian politics. Neither the *Putsch*, nor the trial which followed, could destroy his new glory. The grotesqueness of the unsuccessful venture disappeared behind the boldness and self-assurance of his defence; his erstwhile allies, who bore witness against him, cut a much worse figure than he. The judges were on his side; they too were nationalists, although the accused was a little too wild for them. Treated honourably and given a mild sentence he was able to rest in comfortable detention. There he dictated his book *Mein Kampf*.

The title was apt. In its thousand pages many things were mentioned, war and foreign policy, economic and social matters, Marxism, Judaism, trade unions, school education, art, propaganda and much else; but always also the author himself. Everything referred to him; there were these two things, A.H. and the world, and the tension between them which must be resolved. Among all the individuals who in recent times have intervened in the course of history he was the most egocentric. How otherwise could he have made his name into a greeting? It is hard to believe that he dared to do it, and that people accepted it. Yet both things happened; a sign of the tremendous egoism which burst from within him, with which he dominated people. It has subsequently been said of *Mein Kampf* that it was merely a cover-up and that what was said in it was much more harmless than the man really was. The present author cannot agree with this view. The book was honest; it went as far as its author had himself then got. He believed that the world was always at war and that in war everything was allowed; that superior nations had the right to expand at the expense of inferior ones; that in Russia especially the space must be found which Germany needed for its existence, and that the Germans, if they wished to do so, could rule the whole world – all these absurdities, interspersed with quarter-truths and cunning observations, were there black on white. Nor did Hitler disguise his contempt for the 'masses'. He likened them to a woman attracted by brutality and danger, and he claimed that nothing was too barefaced, too simple for them and that everything needed to be repeated over and over again. He candidly revealed such views and tricks; his opponents did not take them seriously because they did not want to take the man himself seriously, but there it was written down. This was the most curious thing of all: the Nazis announced what they were doing and what they planned to do later. They proposed to use democratic institutions to overthrow democracy and to do this the democratic state would pay them as deputies. The thought was screamingly funny but if democracy was so stupid why not use it? Once they had gained power by democratic means they would never, never surrender it again. So sure were they of the blindness and helplessness of their opponents that they could say such things and have their fun. They were themselves men of the masses in the worst sense of the word. They both despised the masses and were able to win over a large part of those whom they despised and to arouse their enthusiastic support.

On this was based their confidence in victory. Once, in 1923, Hitler had tried to take the state at the point of the bayonet with a small minority. He had been foiled by the lawful authorities and by the Army which supported the authorities. He would not repeat the attempt. He would outmanoeuvre the Army and 'come to power legally', as the expression went, and for this he needed the votes of the masses. He proposed to use the existing, constitutional government to do away with the constitution and to gain absolute power. Mussolini had shown the road in Italy, and so in a different way had Lenin. Hitler wanted to take the same road and he was honest, obsessed and impudent enough to broadcast his ideas to all and sundry. And while people still thought that this wild man did not really mean what he said, events gave him no cause not to mean it. When the votes were counted in September 1930 it appeared that the supporters of the National Socialists had increased tenfold. From being a crazy splinter group they had become the second-largest parliamentary party. Was there any reason why they should not soon be the largest?

The new Reichstag was scarcely capable of doing the things which a parliament is supposed to do, of positive investigation and decision. Debate was no longer possible with the inflated Nazis on the right and the Communists, also much more numerous, on the left. The right left the chamber when the left spoke; if it stayed it was to produce scenes of shameful confusion. Yet Heinrich Brüning could govern with this Reichstag, and in some sense better than with its predecessor, just because it was weaker and paralysed itself. There was still a majority of moderates, the majority of the old Big Coalition. It was no longer capable of making a positive contribution, which the circle around Hindenburg did not want it to make anyway. But it could tolerate and in retrospect approve the action which Brüning took under Paragraph 48, by refusing to revoke the President's emergency decrees; this happened regularly in the time ahead, and with a reliable, if modest majority. The pillars of this 'toleration policy', as it was called, were the Social Democrats. They now had to swallow things which were much harder for their workers to take than those over which they had broken up the last parliamentary coalition in the spring. They did it because to them Brüning's government seemed the lesser evil compared with a Hitler government; it was generally assumed that after the fall of the coalition of the moderates the much more dynamic right would come to power. If the Reichstag did not obey Hindenburg could dissolve it again and entrust a still further inflated Nazi Party with the formation of a government. To prevent this from happening the Social Democrats returned to the 'toleration', practised from 1923 to 1925, and to passive co-operation in the hope that the storm would blow over, that the Nazi avalanche would break up as quickly as it had grown. In fact there was a return to the semi-parliamentary government of the early Bismarck period. A Chancellor dependent on the confidence of the monarch made the laws, raised taxes and tariffs, reduced wages and salaries, and allowed parliament to comment on his actions; confidential preliminary discussions still allowed some influence to be exerted on the government programme. This was how the country was governed for eighteen months after September 1930. The arrangement worked as long as the President was prepared at any time to exercise in Brüning's favour his two rights, that of issuing emergency decrees and that of dissolving parliament. The system by which Germany was governed depended on the pleasure of the President.

Hindenburg thus found himself burdened with a responsibility undreamt of by him five years earlier. There is no doubt that the old man, eighty-three, eighty-four, eighty-five as he then was, suffered under it; the questions which he was made to decide confused and frightened him. The situation was not of his making. If, in the times to come he made serious mistakes, the fault lies not so much with the old man elevated to a greatness which he never possessed but with German history and the nation as it then was. Yet there is no doubt either that his new-found indispensability and the role of sacred monarch flattered the Field-Marshal's vanity, and that the position of power in which he found himself brought agreeable compensations. Like a man who suddenly discovers that he can conjure, Hindenburg discovered that he could give any order. This was bad for the character of the *Alte Herr*. Old monarchs – history provides examples – become selfish, obstinate and faithless. Hindenburg's preparation for the monarchy had come very late and had been inadequate.

Inevitably his advisers influenced him. All his life he had never decided without listening carefully to the advice of his collaborators and had always acted on that advice. Only that now there was no longer an able and powerful man like Ludendorff at his side. Instead there were his official political advisers, particularly the Chancellor and the Minister of Defence. Then there were also the less official, the more intimate ones, the Secretary of State for the President's Office, a cunning old fox who had served Ebert, and General von Schleicher. These two there were joined by the President's son who described himself as his 'adjutant'. These are names which are of no account and which do not deserve mention in a history of Germany. Momentarily, however, their bearers were able to play a decisive role because the President listened to them. Germany had reached a state where the men who had the President's ear could make and overthrow governments. They could even appoint a certain last government only to discover to their painful surprise they could no longer overthrow it. For the moment people still swore by the constitution the first paragraph of which said that the authority of the state derived from the people. But the people had not known how to use its 'authority'. The irresponsible camarilla around Hindenburg was more powerful now than the camarilla around William II had ever been.

It was enlarged by Hindenburg's East Prussian landowning neighbours. One of them, an aged, cynical Junker from the last century, had had the clever idea of buying back with the help of the Rhenish industrialists, the Hindenburgs' lost family estate and of giving it to the President on the occasion of his eightieth birthday. As a result Hindenburg himself had become an east-Elbian landowner and now lived part of the year among men of his ilk. He learned to share their worries, to approve of their greedy demands on the state; he got back into the social atmosphere to which he belonged by birth but from which his career had temporarily taken him. Here people talked in the old way, so familiar to him. Hindenburg listened and enjoyed himself. He discarded the new ideas which he had painfully acquired in the course of the years, that the Reichstag was something better than a 'drivel shop' and that democracy, parties and trade unions, were part of modern life; he could afford to do this all the more because the party system really had failed. Does this mean that the old man was only now showing his true face? Probably not. Since 1925 he had tried to make a success of the Republic, although to do so had been against his deepest beliefs, and he had played the game according to the rules. He had allowed Stresemann to govern. What was there now, the economic crisis, the Nazis, the Communists, the whole confusion and paralysis of German policy, was not of his making. But given the situation as it was, the easiest solution was to return to his old ways of thought which recent experience seemed to endorse. It was impossible to do without firm authority, independent of party comings and goings. What if in the process his landowning neighbours benefited a little by the reduction of freight charges, the cancellation of debts, and more openly by substantial gifts of cash? More influential than was good for them, the men around Hindenburg slipped into real corruption without being aware of it.

They both welcomed and feared the Nazis. They were afraid of them because they were rabble rousers who even claimed to be socialists. They welcomed them because they were the force which could be used temporarily to check the Social Democrats in order perhaps to do away with them completely later. As late as 1932 Schleicher could write that if the Nazis were not the best of companions he was happy that they constituted a counterweight. 'If they did not exist one would have to invent them.' The Social Democrats had done no harm whatsoever to the Army, to the Junkers or to the rich, not even in their most powerful period. Now they had anyway been deprived of their power, by the Nazis and by the economic crisis. What trumps were left to trade unions with half their members out of work? What kind of a weapon was a general strike with four, five or six million unemployed? The great party which after 1914 had so often saved the state had become self-effacing and helpless. The would-be wise men around Hindenburg did not see that in the interest of the state the Social Democratic Party itself now deserved help. They saw the opportunity of making life difficult for those tiresome 'Marxists', those 'proletarians'; all that was needed to do this was to catch the Nazi movement, to 'tame' it and to use it for higher purposes. The wild men were after all on the right side, even if they went a little too far; they had the 'national' interest at heart, they were in favour of a strong Germany and, offered the bait of limited collaboration, they would certainly not place any obstacles in the way of expanding the armed forces.

We have anticipated events. Although the moods and motives just described had always existed in latent form, their full force only came to be felt in the spring of 1932. For the time being Hindenburg loyally supported Brüning and lent his name to all the grim emergency measures prepared by the Chancellor 'for the redress of financial, economic and social emergencies'; economy measures to reduce the costs of production, to reduce wages and prices, to support agriculture, particularly that of East Prussia, particularly that of the big estates. These were severe measures, felt more painfully by the people than anything decreed 'from above' since the war: student teachers without jobs, unemployed workers with reduced benefits and finally with none at all. Of what avail was it that these measures were 'scientifically' correct and, in their terrible unpopularity, dictated by great courage? Of what avail was it that the operation was correct if the patient died on the operating table? The more Brüning cut away from the body of the German economy so that it might fit under the shrunken coverlet, the shorter the coverlet became. Unfortunately, the Chancellor's courageous but bleak announcements said, the hopes of a general economic recovery had once more failed to materialize; new sacrifices were therefore needed as everybody must understand. People, however, did not understand. They only saw that the number of unemployed and the number of suicides continued to rise; the papers brought tales of fathers killing their families because they could no longer bear their children's misery. The government was accused of 'decreeing distress'; this was the only immediately tangible result of the emergency regulations. There were still quite a few people who lived well. They did not disguise the fact that they were having a good time, whereas the poor suffered in secret, although their misery grew. In 1932 Germany produced scarcely more than half of what it had produced in 1929. This was Brüning's misfortune and that of the half-republian half-monarchist, moderately-democratic constitutional state which was his goal.

His historical guilt is great; this is particularly sad because personally he was completely innocent. In his favour one might say that he was short of good advisers, that the President of the *Reichsbank*, Luther, in particular proffered no advice except the lethal proposal to fight deflation by superdeflation. The world of high finance shared this point of view, taking as its yardstick the family budget: if times became hard it was necessary to save and the harder they became the greater became the need to save. There were exceptions, a few professors, a few journalists who understood the function of money and the reasons for its collapse. They were regarded as lunatics, in the Reichstag – particularly by the parties in office – and outside. Yet it has not been proved that if the Chancellor had reversed course and submitted an imaginative plan for the creation of money, for finding work and raising prices he could not have had his way. His authority was considerable; it exceeded that of the Reich President who protected him and who signed his 'emergency decrees' with growing doubts. Finally one must not forget that the class which was close to Hindenburg, the farmers east of the Elbe, belonged to the section of the population which was hardest hit. The Junkers could not be so blind as not to suspect what was wrong; why their produce, potatoes and butter and meat, could not be sold for a third of the old price while a third of the nation was starving. Although their own theorists could not offer a programme it is unlikely that they would have rejected the saving expedient if the government had thought of it. Dr Brüning did not think of it. In brave, reserved solitude, imperturbable, without advice from the Conservatives, without advice either from leftist intellectuals who saw the whole crisis as nothing but a perfidious conspiracy designed to get higher profits, he continued to follow the same road.

This was the good fortune of the National Socialists. The intensity of their propaganda war alone would not have given them success; it was the misery and the fear of misery which drove people into their arms. Being fully aware of this they even exaggerated the situation which was bad enough, and joyfully predicted ten millions or more unemployed for the coming winter. They made the situation worse still. The so-called world crisis did not have one but a number of very different causes which came together in very different ways from 1929 to 1933. Some of them could be expressed in terms purely of economic theory while others were of a political nature: the after-effects of the last war, fear of a new war, the furtive struggle for power among European states. There were also causes of a domestic nature. In Germany civil war had threatened since 1930; this was not a climate in which the economy could flourish. Although the threat came primarily from the National Socialists it drove people to join their ranks because they felt that the situation had become unbearable, that the nation must be united under a strong hand. Hitler himself was largely responsible for the disease which people asked him to cure. Here was a man who claimed to love his people – there is no reason to doubt Hitler's assertion that he thought much about Germany and worried about its fate – and who was nevertheless delighted that this people suffered because as a result he was given an opportunity to become its master.

All the major parties by this time had their own 'strong arm' squads; the Communists the *Rote Frontkämpfer*, the Social Democrats the *Reichsbanner Schwarz-Rot-Gold*, while the *Deutschnationalen* had formed an alliance with the ex-soldiers' organization, the *Stahlhelm*. By far the most militant group, however, were the *Sturmabteilungen* – SA for short – of the Nazi Party, an army organized to fight a civil war. Much of the youth gathered together there was good-natured at heart: young men out of work who had wasted their days in public parks until the Party took charge of them, issued them with brown shirts and food and gave their lives some self-respect and meaning. Because the state, the thrifty, unimaginative, wretched state failed to do this, the Party could catch them. Yet even harmless youths cease to be harmless when the brutal instincts latent in man are flattered; insolence, sadism and bloodthirstiness were given free rein in the SA. The Communist counter-organization replied in kind wherever it could. A wave of murder swept the country; there was no election which did not cost dozens of lives. On the posters announcing his arrival, a National Socialist speaker proudly had himself introduced as murderer so and so.

Heinrich Brüning overlooked these things as best he could. He never abandoned the hope which was the hope of his employers: of coming to terms with the big, unruly party on the extreme right, of turning it into something constructive and somehow incorporating it into his system. Meanwhile he had set himself two aims: to put the German economy in order and to restore Germany's position of equality among the nations of the world; to achieve the cancellation of reparations and to obtain for Germany the right to rearm, or else to insist that the others disarm. Once these justified demands of German nationalism had been achieved, he thought, tension would decrease and the domestic crisis could be mastered; a thorough constitutional reform would then ensure that there could be no repetition of the crisis. These aims he pursued with a perseverance, with a control of his noble and suffering soul which one can admire; like the knight in Dürer's engraving who rides on bravely in spite of the gruesome figures following on behind and who already sees his native castle in the distance. Brüning thought that he could see the castle, he wanted to reach it, but the road became increasingly bleak and horse and rider increasingly weak.

The world – *das Ausland*, as the Germans say – did not give Brüning much help. The world was no wiser than Germany. It never occurred to the other powers that it was in the interest of Europe's future to help him even at a price. In the spring of 1931 the German Reich and Austria set up a customs union; there were sensible economic reasons behind this step, but also political ones. It would at last have been a success for Brüning's national policy, a decision taken by Germans acting independently, a step towards the fulfilment of the 'greater German' aim which Hitler, the Austrian, also claimed to be pursuing, taken not by the wild man, but decently and freely. France raised objections. The *Zollverein* had been the beginning of Germany's unification; therefore it followed that this new customs union was the beginning of 'greater German' unification. This was contrary to the peace treaty which committed Austria to an everlastingly independent existence. The matter came before the International Court of Justice in The Hague which gave its verdict in favour of the French. The step which should have brought Brüning's sensible dictatorship of Moderates the strength it so acutely needed, ended in a shameful defeat.

Slowly, fearfully slowly, Germany approached also the goal of military 'equality'. The French did not trust Germany, and the spectacle which it now offered was indeed likely to arouse suspicion. What they did not understand was the connection between their own uncreative, rigid attitude and the chaos of German political life. Later the Western powers made to the villain all the concessions which they had refused Brüning; those and hundreds more.

The only generous gesture in these terrible times came from America. The President of the United States, Herbert Hoover, suggested in the summer of 1931 a moratorium of reparations as well as of the payments of the Western powers to America. It was probable that once interrupted payments would not start up again, but superstitious prejudice still prevented this fact from being voiced. Max Weber's description of political activity as 'dogged boring through thick boards' has never been so true as of the career of the last statesman of the Weimar Republic.

It is impossible to single out all the elements, poisonous or healthy, that fed the Nazi movement. There was the feeling that the Weimar state was nothing more than an institution for the satisfaction of the most elementary social needs, a big police institution instead of the stronghold of inspiring communal life that a German state ought to be. There was the feeling that the Republic was weak and did not defend itself and always cast friendly and admiring glances at those who were about to destroy it; a feeling for which these years provided plenty of grotesque examples. Hitler made much of the persecution which he had suffered, fully aware that this was all ballyhoo; that not even Social Democratic Prussia ever really cracked down, and that the 'Reich' and the other *Länder* had for years spared and protected him as much as they could. There was the feeling that the Germans were by far the strongest European nation in spite of 1918, and that the republican governments had not known how to exploit this strength. Instead they had put their faith in 'understanding' and the League of Nations; but this organization had been too much an instrument of conservative French power politics to be able to fulfil the hopes of the German rulers. There were the old 'greater German' and pan-German dreams – which went much further than the aims of the Weimar Republic. There was the antisemitism of the lower middle class, not very strong at first but whipped up by propaganda not only against the Jews as such but also vaguely against big banks, big stores, Marxism and 'international capitalism'. Then there was what a Nazi speaker called the 'anti-capitalist yearning of the people'; and the Social Democratic Republic had done almost nothing against capitalism. This, too, was exploited with success by the Nazi Party. What matter that the while Hitler was receiving money from some of the biggest German industrialists and that from the summer of 1931 onwards he courted the Rhenish industrialists. One could be both, for and against capitalism, at the same time. Everything went into the stewpot. The irrational 'movement', which had no programme, which gained strength from its own strength, which pushed ahead for the sake of the power that would be reached through it, could absorb anything that strengthened it. It absorbed the misery of the poor, the wealth of the rich, the noble dreams of the young and the hard-hearted calculations of the old, the brainless irresponsibility of those who wanted 'something different', credulity and hysteria. It also absorbed hatred. Hatred of the 'November criminals', hatred of the world, hatred of the 'System', of the 'bosses', of the Social Democratic officials who still controlled the levers of power of the Prussian administration and who claimed to govern; this was the illusion they laboured under. How strong this hatred was and how people revelled in it! Those who experienced it in the days of their youth will never forget it. Those who grew up in the friendlier atmosphere of our time cannot imagine to what depth public life descended in those days.

What the Nazi leaders did not do because they were only interested in catching votes and because they were anyway cynically indifferent to any distinction between truth and falsehood, a few educated political writers tried to do for them. We have already discussed the set of ideas called the 'Conservative Revolution'. At that time its exponents stood at the centre of intellectual and political interest. In their papers they discussed what should be done, to what positive goals the masses assembled in the Nazi movement should be led. They really intended to bring about the union of nationalism and socialism, a union which in their view was fundamentally a natural one, hitherto obstructed by Marxist doctrine. Liberal capitalism and Marxism were both finished. Having been ruined by reparations and its involvement in the economy of the world Germany must draw the lesson and make itself independent of world markets; it must control its own production and its own consumption. But as Germany was too small other territories must become part of its economic sphere, particularly the Danube valley, south-eastern Europe. This could not be done without central planning. Here the Russian example had its effect; the Soviet Union alone among the great powers had not been affected by the economic crisis and was now successfully realizing its Five-Year Plan of industrialization, a fact which impressed some non-Communist Germans. Germany was small compared with Russia, but not even what Germany possessed, what its soil produced, what it could manufacture, was used, because people had no money. It was widely thought that this was an intolerable scandal which refuted 'capitalism' for ever. The world needed to be 'rebuilt', an historic turning-point had been reached, everything must be changed, economically, politically and morally. Those were the kind of ideas that were being put forward, and even such un-imaginative, superficial politicians as General Kurt von Schleicher did not refuse to listen to them. Hitler himself at times believed in confused revolutionary economic theories which he was quick to drop, however, when he noticed that they harmed his relations with the industrialists who held the purse strings. Being an opportunist he was not really interested in the economy. This was a secondary issue to be dealt with by experts – by those who could do nothing else. The chief thing on which everything else depended was politics. The chief thing was power.

The *Deutschnationalen*, Prussia-Germany's old Conservatives, were in a difficult position. Some of their cleverest spokesmen realized that the dictatorship of the Moderates had become the last stronghold of order, and so they gave Brüning feeble support. The majority, under the party leader, Alfred Hugenberg, entered into an alliance with the National Socialists whom they copied, though showing a little more restraint; they talked of the 'November criminals', of the 'outrage of Versailles', of the treachery and inefficiency of democracy and the rest. Hugenberg was a rich man, the owner of an enormous publishing and newspaper business; in his way he must have been able. But how blind he was to think that he could join the Nazis, compete with them and yet preserve the independence of his group. How deluded he was by vanity and hatred to regard this alliance as a conservative one. The concentration of all enemies of the Republic on the right was called the Harzburg Front after the spa where the whole gang, industrialists, generals, bankers and party leaders, met in 1931. What they had in common was hostility to the Republic. There were plenty of signs during the honeymoon which followed this multi-marriage that there was little else to hold them together and that Hitler's political ingenuity was ten times superior to that of all other groups, parties and associations. Hugenberg let it be known that he fully appreciated the dangers of the National Socialist movement; but like so many others he thought that he could make use of it.

Field-Marshal von Hindenburg was upset by this alliance of the right and extreme right against the Republic, against Brüning and undeniably also against him, President and patron saint of Brüning's government. All or almost all those who had elected him seven years earlier were now against him and almost all who had voted against him were now for him, the Republicans, the Catholic Democrats of the Centre, the Socialists and the trade unions. He was uncertain whether the right hand betrayed him or he the right; but something was wrong, and must, if possible, be put right. He did not think much of Hugenberg and, coming from a more solid century, he profoundly disliked the south German and *grossdeutsche* rabble-rouser, the 'Bohemian corporal', as he called him. Yet, if Germany wanted to abandon democracy was it his, the royal Prussian Field-Marshal's, business to stop it? Under the constitution a new President was due to be elected in March 1932. There were attempts to make the Reichstag prolong Hindenburg's term of office or to have him 'chosen' as candidate of the whole nation. The attempts failed; the nation was too disturbed and divided by hatred to agree on one idol. Although all-party committees, which included Conservative as well as other politicians, invited the President to be their candidate and Hindenburg attached the greatest importance to this form – on the grounds that he could after all not prevent the Socialists from voting for him – the election was more or less a repetition of the contest of 1925. The paradox was that Hindenburg was now the candidate of the 'popular bloc' and Hitler the candidate of the 'Reich bloc'. The crazy Austrian received the votes of the east-Elbian Junkers, the Rhenish industrialists, the majority of the aristocracy and the middle class; the Prussian general those of the Lower Bavarian peasants and the Socialist workers. In order to keep the dreaded enemy out of power, democracy sheltered behind the broad shoulders of the only man with whom it could still hope to defeat Hitler in the election. It won nothing although it won the presidential election. Hindenburg was not its President; there were plenty of warning signs in the winter of 1932 that this was the last thing he was. Democracy merely preserved a front of moderate parties which were neither in sympathy with it nor controlled by it and which depended on the good will of Hindenburg and the Army. This was the most hopeless political defensive battle ever fought.

Would a more genuine political division of the nation have been possible? Could a Social Democrat have stood against

Hitler instead of the old Junker? Yes, if the democratic state had still possessed the courage of its convictions. But then everything would have happened differently and the nation would never have entered the *cul-de-sac* of 1932. Discouraged, compromised and in effect excluded from politics, the left could no longer mount a political offensive. It is doubtful if even the Centre Party would have supported a really democratic candidate – certainly not one of whom the Communists would have approved. This was the point: the Communists refused to accept any democratic candidate at all. With their deluded and twisted minds they had calculated that Germany must pass through a short period of National Socialist dictatorship in order to end up more surely with Communism. 'Don't you see,' the Prussian Prime Minister, Braun, once said to them, 'that you are doing the work of the other side? You both want to destroy the democratic republic in order to establish your dictatorship on its ruins, each of you his *own* brand. Then you want to hang *them* and they want to hang *you*. I fear you will be the ones who will hang.' 'We shall hang *you* first,' they yelled, deluded as they were. In fact the Communists again put up their own candidate and worked together with the Nazis against the Republic to the bitter end.

Hindenburg won. The majority of the nation voted for him, only just over a third for Hitler. But this third was heart and soul behind its *Führer* whereas Hindenburg's supporters were only agreed on what they did not want. The old man was a symbol of their helplessness. They chose him as their policeman and he accepted their choice, but not the function, and gave them no promise whatsoever that he would henceforth act in the way they wanted. Therefore they hardly had the right to complain about a break of faith when, barely two months after the election, he dropped his ascetic Chancellor and asked the right to form a government.

At the time General von Schleicher claimed that Brüning was incapable of mastering the economic crisis, that his deflationary policy merely made the situation worse; and that he had also failed to fulfil his second main task, that he had not 'tamed' the Nazis. Schleicher argued that their party had grown in strength in every provincial election and that unless it was brought into the government and under its control it would engulf the state. There was something in these arguments. Probably, however, they were not the decisive ones and the intriguers round Hindenburg were less afraid of Brüning's failure than of his eventual success at home and abroad. The crisis could not last for ever. If it was coming to an end – and there were signs that it was – if Brüning succeeded in resolving it while remaining within the framework of republican legality, the opportunity to overthrow the democracy, offered by the misery of the masses and the Nazi movement, would probably be lost for ever. The Chancellor was given no chance to defend himself; this had been arranged. He was overthrown by the same handful of people – influential because of the terrible situation – who had brought him to the top; in their decisions they were more influenced by the general atmosphere and by corrupt pressure groups in the presidential palace than by factual arguments. Brüning had given substantial financial assistance to the east-Elbian landowners. Now, however, there was a scheme to divide those estates that could not be saved and to use them for the settlement of unemployed town dwellers. It seems that more than anything else this modest, overdue land reform cost Brüning his office. If this is so, it was the last occasion on which the Prussian Junkers – or more precisely a small, energetic section of them – were able to exert an evil influence on the course of German history. Their success did not help them. Hindenburg refused to sign further emergency decrees.

This was not a dismissal because the President had no authority to dismiss the Chancellor. Brüning could have said to the Reichstag: 'There will be no more emergency decrees. Instead of collaborating indirectly by carrying emergency decrees you will once more have to take a direct share in governing the country, as envisaged in the constitution. I appeal to the majority which has supported me so far and which knows the dangers of a change of government as well as I do.' He would have lost nothing by such an appeal to the common sense of the people. But Brüning, who saw himself as serving Hindenburg and depending on the will and mercy of this substitute monarch, was so surprised and deeply hurt by the old man's lack of loyalty that it never occurred to him to think of a return to the parliamentary system. He was 'dismissed' because he felt himself to be dismissed; the ex-lieutenant felt that he could not remain in command if the Field-Marshal did not wish him to remain. He retired immediately and refused with bitter pride to accept any office or favour from the new rulers.

There followed eight confused months during which Germany was continuously in the bright, unhealthy searchlights of politics. Almost nothing else was talked about. The country dillied and dallied like a bride facing an unprepossessing suitor; she wished to accept him and she did not wish to accept him and she performed the most curious contortions in order to avoid him. The left, particularly the Social Democrats, no longer had any influence at all on the course of events. They were still there, they held party congresses and electoral meetings, they kept the nucleus of their supporters together – not so long ago they had impressively tightened their organization into an 'Iron Front' – but everything happened as though they did not exist, and their loyal followers were seized by a feeling of profound isolation. As in a nightmare a man cannot lift his arm, the great party could not use its strength. The parties represented in the Reichstag were no longer of any importance, only two forces were, as Julius Leber remarked in retrospect: the President and the mob. The last remaining obstacle between Hitler and Germany, leaning on his walking stick, surrounded by legitimate and illegitimate advisers, was the aged Hindenburg. This was the position in which he found himself after he had betrayed and surrendered the only remaining stronghold, Brüning's government. Hindenburg did not want to suppress the Nazi movement which he might still have been able to do with the help of the Army and of the Prussian police. He thought too much of Nazis who, however unruly, at least belonged to the right and who were responsible for the complete elimination of the 'Marxists'. On the other hand he did not want Hitler to come to power because he did not trust the character of the 'Bohemian corporal'. Above all he did not want him to come to power alone. The desirable course of action to him still was to 'tame' the Nazis and to divide the power between them and the Conservatives. It was a question of having one's cake and eating it. With Hitler, however, power could not be divided.

Appeals were made to the spirit of the past, and there were attempts to rule with governments which, given their social character, would have fitted into the age of Frederick William IV. One of these was the 'Barons' Cabinet', the government of Franz von Papen, Brüning's successor. Schleicher had again been responsible for the choice of the Chancellor and Hindenburg had again accepted the advice of the political general, now also Minister of Defence. The appointment had been preceded by a secret agreement between Schleicher and Hitler: the Nazis would agree to 'tolerate' Papen as the Social Democrats had tolerated Brüning, and in return were promised complete freedom of activity and new elections, in effect a new victory at the polls. Papen was elegant and courageous, not bad, not really malevolent but irresponsible, vain, scheming and pitifully superficial. Nothing could be more characteristic of the decline of public life than the appointment of this well-bred buffoon, amateur horseman and orator who had vaguely heard something about the 'Conservative Revolution'. Anything was possible in the vacuum of power created because the Nazis on the one hand and Hindenburg and the Army on the other neutralized each other, and because the left was no longer of any account; the charming nobleman succeeded in ingratiating himself with Hindenburg and that was enough for the moment. This was how men had become Prime Ministers in the age of princely absolutism. Was this still possible, could this last, in the age of industrial democracy, in the furore of nation-wide political passion? A number of Junker reactionaries from the Wilhelminian age and one or two industrialists assisted the Chancellor by the grace of Hindenburg.

Papen set to work with a will. His idea was to keep the promise made to Hitler while quickly scoring some successes abroad and at home, and so to weaken the man with whom he would later have to share power. In the sphere of foreign policy Brüning had done good spade work; there Papen could reap what his predecessor had sown. He succeeded in having the reparations debts cancelled once and for all. At home, against Hitler, he played the game which Stresemann and Seeckt had played against him nine years previously: he himself struck the big blow against the left. There was no need for central government action against Saxony and Thuringia as there were no Communist governments in Germany now. In Prussia, however, there still existed the core of the Weimar Republic, the Centre–Social Democrat coalition, the government of Braun and Severing. Undeniably this was an anachronism now that the Weimar Republic no longer existed in reality; it reminded one of a big lump of snow that refuses to melt although the temperature has risen, that continues to lie there, strange and grey, proving nothing about the weather. Moreover, Braun's government was a minority government; it continued in office because although the Nazis and the Communists had a majority in the *Landtag* and voted and shouted together against the government they were unable to form one of their own. Thus the Social Democrats were still in office as the guardians of order and there were still rumours about the strength and republican loyalty of the Prussian police – an overestimate of this force. In July under a feeble pretext Papen dismissed the Prussian ministers and placed Prussia under the control of the central government. This was a *coup d'état*, an undoubted violation of the constitution, as the German Supreme Court later assured the ex-ministers in a helpless, cautiously veiled judgement. Papen probably had some truth on his side when he claimed that references to the constitution no longer made sense in this crisis. The Weimar Constitution, upheld in its rudiments by Brüning, had ceased to function after his fall. Lassalle's dictum that constitutional questions were questions of power now applied in its full force. It became clear that the Prussian Social Democrats were powerless or, what amounted to the same thing, that they lacked the courage to use their power. They announced that they were giving way to force, that the hour was an historic one, and disappeared. After ten years of fruitful and creative work which, however, had failed to measure up to the highest demands of politics, they retired unthanked and ridiculed into an opposition which everyone knew could not be an effective force.

After William II Prussia ceased to be a genuine state; it was merely the largest part of Germany, a fragment in which it was impossible to organize political power. What influence had 'Prussia' been able to exert during Brüning's term of office, during the most recent government crisis in the Reich? What had been its contribution to foreign policy, to economic policy? The fact that Prussia was now taken over by the Reich was hardly an event of historical importance; in fact fifteen years passed before it was dissolved formally, a legal step which failed to arouse the slightest interest. What was of historical significance was not Prussia's capitulation, but the final, meekly accepted defeat of the Social Democrats. Later people argued as to whether it was inevitable, listing the material and legal resources at the disposal of Braun's government in July 1932 which were not used. This is a question of taste. A person who has gone a long way in one direction usually goes on because if he were to turn back at all he should have turned back long before. The Social Democratic Party was isolated and exhausted by the two years of passive 'toleration' of Brüning, by the disappointment of the hopes which it had until recently placed in Hindenburg. The player who has already lost the game has no more use for his pawns. Otto Braun was a tired man, disappointed and disgusted by the spectacle offered by Germany. He thought that he would never get over the way in which he had been dismissed:

> To be sent packing like a domestic servant caught stealing, at the orders of a man whose sincerity and loyalty to the constitution I have recently defended body and soul, and who owes his reelection as President at least partly to this fact, is somewhat embittering. After forty years of political activity I know that there is no gratitude in politics; but a minimum of respect is the pre-requisite of political collaboration.

This is how he saw things and *he* always treated *his* Conservative opponents with respect; they nevertheless continued to see in him an upstart 'Red' who needed to be kept in his place. For this attitude they too later paid a price.

Papen's victory over Prussia was a pyrrhic victory. It was no achievement to remove an authority which, though already broken, still had the support of a very substantial part of the electorate and the most sensible, most loyal and most solid one in the country at that, namely the Social Democrats. All that Papen accomplished was to remove one more pillar supporting the crumbling order, to prevent a pact between the government and the moderate left and to heighten bitterness and passions. The campaign for the elections to the new Reichstag then in full swing assumed the form of a restricted, but terrible civil war. When the votes were counted it emerged that the Nazis had once more been able to double their number of seats and now entered parliament as by far the strongest party. Hitler's demands became wilder than ever; although he wanted to be given power 'legally' by the President he regarded it as far beneath his dignity to share it with any other party according to rules of the game of parliamentary democracy. What had happened in Italy must also happen in Germany. In a dramatic scene Hindenburg rejected Hitler's demand; he would be allowed to join the government and should do so, perhaps as the second man in a presidential cabinet; otherwise let him gain a majority in parliament. This was no longer possible. The disintegration of public life, terrible murders which Hitler was not ashamed to applaud, forced the Chancellor, Papen, to take more energetic counter-measures, to threaten legal action and to announce restrictions. Relations between the government and the National Socialists deteriorated rapidly. There was no more talk about the policy of 'toleration' on which General von Schleicher had built his plan. Whereas Brüning had still been able to rely on the support of half the Reichstag Papen had not a tenth of it behind him, and no sooner had the newly elected parliament met in September than it was dissolved again.

There was a new election campaign with meetings, marches, inflammatory posters, vituperation and lies, fighting and shooting. It was, if one wants to count up, the fifth election campaign in 1932; a foreign observer might have concluded that electing was the main occupation of the German people. Never has the *ultima ratio* of democracy, the appeal to the electorate, been so abused. The two elections with which Hindenburg's new period of office opened were won by the left, but the victory was not a real one for it decided nothing. The Prussian parliament, elected in May, was unable to form a government and could do nothing but offer the world a spectacle of bawling incompetence. The Reichstag elections in July and again in November gave the nation no chance of expressing confidence in the government because, apart from the Conservatives who had shrunk into insignificance, all competing groups fought against Papen. Although they fought each other with howling fury they were united in this hostility; their frantic activities seemed peripheral to the deadlock which the rulers of the moment had reached. These men did not believe in democracy, and it must be said in their defence that the state of affairs in Germany in 1932 might have made even the most convinced democrat despair. They drove the nation from one election to the next, not because they wanted to make democracy a reality – which was no longer possible – but to ruin it. The nation submitted. As a wild animal in a circus, although stronger than its tamer, obeys the whip, the great revolutionary and totalitarian parties, Nazis, Communists and all their militant associations, obediently complied with every demand to prepare themselves for a new election. The magic of legality which Chancellor and President dispensed was still very strong. It is difficult to see why it could not have been possible to continue this game, mad and destructive though it was compared with Brüning's policy, for some time yet. If there were five elections in one year why should there not be another five? Probably Papen's plan was to let the Nazis elect themselves to death.

That hope did not appear entirely unfounded. In November Hitler lost a substantial part of his support, and considerably more still in the subsequent elections in the individual *Länder* and towns. The nation seemed to be tiring of the man who kept it in suspense, who promised so much, who for long had been so close to power but who never got there. His opponents – he had always had many and serious opponents – breathed a sigh of relief for the first time since 1929. Would the spectre vanish without ever becoming a political reality? However, there was still no majority capable of governing, the Nazis were still by far the strongest party in parliament and Papen could rely on barely a tenth of the Reichstag. Legally this state of affairs made it impossible to govern even with emergency decrees – unless the Reichstag was dissolved every time during its first session, as actually happened in September. The situation therefore demanded action, a suspension of the constitution, and Papen would have had the courage to try it: the proscription of the extreme parties on the right and the left, the proclamation of a state of emergency and the use of the Army. But it was characteristic of this curious and painful story that whenever one wanted to take strong action against Hitler the other whose collaboration was needed did not co-operate; as though the participants had secretly conspired to prevent their energetic gestures and efforts from accomplishing anything. In November 1932 it was General von Schleicher who refused to follow Papen's line. The 'amateur horseman' had quarrelled with too many people and won over too few; even an 'authoritarian government' needed to be more broadly based in the people than the 'Barons' Cabinet'. Schleicher openly declared that the Army could not fight a civil war against Communists and National Socialists simultaneously. Hindenburg and the *Reichswehr* had been the pillars of every republican government since 1930, and although Hindenburg remained all too susceptible to Papen's charm, the Chancellor could not attack without being sure of the Army. Schleicher's vote forced Papen to resign.

The General and Minister of Defence who since 1928 had exerted so active, but irresponsible an influence on politics, who had elected and overthrown Brüning and Papen, was now compelled to emerge from the twilight of his office and shoulder the burden of the Chancellorship himself. Stresemann's democracy, Brüning's semi-democracy, Papen's gaudy authoritarianism, they were all finished. There remained, it seemed, only the Army itself, no longer as the discreetly effective marker on the weighing machine, but as the last and full weight in the scales. Von Schleicher disliked being in the limelight and the thought of using his 'supra-party' Army directly in the political struggle was repugnant to him. However, the President was determined not to go back to Brüning or to the Social Democrats, a step which was anyway no longer possible because not even Brüning could have achieved a majority in parliament now; yet it was necessary to govern the country somehow and to provide a counter-weight to Hitler's power which was still considerable. Therefore the only solution was a government of generals. Reluctantly the 'eminence in battle-grey' accepted the task. The 'Barons' Cabinet' was followed by the 'Socialistic General'.

It is one of the curious features of this terrible year that Germany, before finally throwing itself into the arms of the pan-German demagogue, quickly and vainly experimented with various past forms of government. Brüning – this was Catholic, conservative democracy and the spirit of loyal comradeship between King and Chancellor. Papen – this was a return to the old Prussian average, with a slight admixture of 'Conservative Revolution'. Schleicher wanted to be the democratic officer who is above class differences – this too recalled the proven past, Scharnhorst, Gneisenau and even Caprivi, Bismarck's successor. The new Chancellor airily informed the eagerly listening nation that he was not concerned with such rigid concepts as capitalism and socialism. Nor were constitutional reforms the most important issue – a pointed allusion to Papen. A strictly scientific financial policy was all very well – this was aimed at Brüning – but what was needed now was to create work and more work. People were bound to agree with him on this point. A wave of confidence rose towards the General from the tired, despairing nation. His dark past was willingly forgotten, provided he proved to be the strong man who at long last created order, peace and work; even the two politicians towards whom he had behaved so treacherously, Brüning and Groener, were prepared to help him. But Schleicher was not a strong man. Generals less often are in politics than one assumes; how can a man behave with confidence in a sphere with which he is not familiar and whose peculiarities can only be discovered after long training and experience? It was one thing to pursue a shabby, personal policy of intrigue from the Ministry of Defence, but another to lead the German Reich in the winter of 1932–3. The conflicts which were being fought over were bitterly real; they were not, as Schleicher wanted to believe, of the kind that could be settled with a little firm or sober, friendly talk. No sooner did he start vaguely to outline a programme of creating work than the Association of Industry attacked his allegedly inflationary and socialist policy. No sooner did the possibility of a return to Brüning's settlement plans appear on the horizon than the landowners of the *Landbund* raised a hue and cry about the General's Bolshevism. Papen and Schleicher were both playing with ideas which certainly had some bearing on Germany's political and social crisis. A constitutional reform, Papen's pet scheme, was in fact a necessity, regardless of the form it would take. A major re-organization of the economy, the nationalization of coal and steel – a brief dream of Schleicher's – also came close to the heart of the German problem. However, the constitutional and the economic issues were both difficult and serious ones where reforms could only be achieved against tremendous opposition. Neither Papen nor Schleicher was equal to the seriousness and the difficulties of the task. Neither had emerged gradually as the result of genuine political struggle, both had leapt to the top because of extraordinary circumstances; these false leaders would be removed as speedily as they had arrived, the one by the other or both by a third.

Even now Schleicher did not wish to use the Army, his real support; as a responsible statesman even less than before when he had been able to use the threat of military force from a distance. He did not want to be a dictator depending on bayonets, he felt incapable of playing this part. Instead he tried to find a broader, as it were democratic, basis for governing, fundamentally an old idea of his. If it was not possible to come to an arrangement with Hitler then perhaps it was possible to reach agreement with some of his powerful, popular followers who at the time had broken with the demagogue. Perhaps it was possible to form a front of all trade unions from the pro-labour groups within the Nazi Party to the Christian and the Social Democratic trade unions. Then there could be another dissolution of the Reichstag and government without parliament but with the sensible, moderate, unprejudiced world of labour led by the Socialistic General. The press discussed these questions at Christmas time, exploring a variety of new combinations and permutations; articles appeared giving inside information on who had received whom and who might enter whose cabinet. Here too possibilities existed. Yet again to translate them into reality would have needed more political experience and strength of person than possessed by General von Schleicher who hesitated, schemed and longed for the obscurity of the Ministry of Defence.

He had no luck. The parties did not encourage his efforts and the parties, though unable to govern, were the strongest political organizations. The free trade unions would not have minded working with Schleicher. The Social Democratic Party, suspicious and embittered by the experiences of the past year, resolutely refused to agree to any plan which amounted to even a temporary cold-shouldering of parliament; oblivious of the fact that parliament had long been cold-shouldered in practice and that very different dangers threatened. The constituton, in pieces and ruined, was still a sacred object to men like Wels and Breitscheidt and Braun. They were less averse to a constitutionally appointed cabinet headed by Hitler than to a general who ruled without parliament and who had not long ago treated them as enemies. All this was understandable and excusable; moreover, in retrospect it is also easier to see where it was leading. After six weeks Schleicher found himself in the same situation as Papen before him. He too had no alternative but once more to dissolve the Reichstag and to rely on the Army; that same Army of which he had said six weeks earlier that it was unsuitable for a *coup d'état* and a civil war. Even if he had found an extra-parliamentary bridge to the Centre and the Social Democrats it is likely that the forces to which he finally succumbed would have united still more purposefully against him and would have overwhelmed him somehow.

Nor did the apparent decline of the Nazis prove fortunate for the General-Chancellor. Threatened by internal schism, burdened with enormous debts and in danger of being deprived of the fruits of its long years of subversive activity on German soil, the Party was more prepared to compromise than in the previous summer and autumn. Greater elasticity in negotiation was a prerequisite for the victory which the Nazis wanted to achieve within the framework of 'legality'. There was *one* condition: two partners were needed and while Hindenburg allowed the General to govern the demagogue had no chance. But the men in the presidential palais had become so accustomed to intrigue and the overthrow of governments that they continued the game as soon as Schleicher had assumed office. It is distasteful to relate these things, the quarrels between the cunning, vain, dishonest and deluded noblemen, and the poet's words 'let them not be remembered' might well be applied to them if only their activities had not had such a terrible consequence for the world.

It was Franz von Papen who now assumed *vis-à-vis* his friend Schleicher the role which eight months previously Schleicher had played *vis-à-vis* Brüning. Whether for reasons of patriotic zeal or ambition and revenge we shall let his friends and his critics argue over; the motives are irrelevant and can anyway not be proved either way. What is worth reflection is only this, that such a lightweight person could for a short moment determine the course of world history. Papen was still the intimate adviser of the old President whose hard heart melted towards so few; no more was needed. An ambitious banker acted as intermediary between the Chancellor who had met with misfortune and the demagogue who was threatened by misfortune. The two met secretly but their meeting soon became known. They met once more and a third time, involved Hindenburg's son and his Secretary of State in their machinations, and gradually reached an understanding. They found an Army general who was prepared to take over the post of Minister of Defence in a government led by Hitler. They informed the *Deutschnationale Partei* and the *Stalhelm* of their plan and so, for the moment, restored the 'Harzburger Front'. They distributed offices – only three for the National Socialists and nine for the Conservatives, which to them seemed proof of Hitler's chastened mood. All this happened in the quiet of private houses and offices from which only rumours penetrated to the outside world. The attack on the President himself began only when they had agreed on the main issues, when all the intriguers around Hindenburg had been won over to the new course. It is a fact that the old soldier, who lacked intelligence but not instinct, objected to the last to Hitler's appointment as Chancellor. But all his life he had relied on his advisers and now all his advisers, public and secret, were unanimous in their advice. There was, they argued, no longer any other solution. With Papen as Vice-Chancellor and Commissar for Prussia, with the *Reichswehr* as before under Hindenburg's own command, with foreign and economic policy, agriculture and finance in sound conservative hands Hitler would be 'contained', even if given the title of Chancellor; the desirable objective, the exploitation of the 'constructive forces' of National Socialism without its exclusive rule would at last be achieved. Any other alternative was out of the question. Schleicher's plans were tantamount to socialism, to the ruin of the great landowners, the 'national state of emergency' recommended by him amounted to a breach of the constitution which Hitler was willing to uphold; until the moment when, again without violating the constitution, the Field-Marshal's life's work would at last be crowned by the restoration of the monarchy . . . Those were the kind of arguments put to the old man by his intimates, while civic organizations, agricultural and industrial associations, pressed him to try out the leader of the great popular movement. Isolated, confused, barely in control of his weary spirits, Hindenburg gave way. The familiar method, a refusal to dissolve the Reichstag, forced Schleicher to resign. The Socialistic General, the strong man, the experienced toppler of cabinets, powerless against the intrigues which he himself had once so successfully employed, was as easy to overthrow as the others before him and disappeared without serious thought of rebellion. Two days later Hindenburg appointed the leader of the National Socialist German Workers' Party as Chancellor. 'You are wrong, we have hired him,' Papen replied when his attention was drawn to the danger of this act. This was indeed how it looked on paper and this was how most people understood the situation; not only the schemers-in-chief but also the public critics, the left-wing journalists and the members of the republican parties which continued to survive. The distribution of power, or at least the distribution of offices, in fact seemed to favour the Conservatives in their partnership with the demagogue. Yet after six months only a few traces remained of all the clever safeguards and even those vanished after another twelve months.

7. *Reflection*

The Weimar Republic did not come to a definite end on 30 January 1933; there is just as good reason to say that it ended only in March. At first the new transition period seemed almost like a return to the coalition governments of the best Weimar days; the realization that what had begun was something quite different came only in the weeks and months that followed. Here first was merely one more in the pathetically long list of German Chancellors since 1917. But the man who was given the title occupied the centre of German and world events for a good ten years. This should never have happened. It is an episode as stupid as it is gruesome, designed to make us question the meaning of history. Yet it did happen; it followed on what went before and arose from it just as what exists today came out of what was there then. Therefore we must try to describe it and to understand its causes.

Even in retrospect people involved in politics usually do not wish to admit that they made mistakes. It was always somebody else, never they themselves. Just as there is no trace of self-criticism in the memoirs of the main characters of the First

World War, Tirpitz and Ludendorff, Poincaré and Lloyd George, the actors of the years 1932 and 1933 show no retrospective remorse. Franz von Papen, Secretary of State Meissner and Schacht, President of the *Reichsbank* as also Otto Braun and Karl Severing, have presented us with their memoirs; friends have spoken for others, for Alfred Hugenberg, the *Deutschnationale*, and for the murdered General von Schleicher. Something can be learned from all this. Yet it is always apology. It is always a distortion of perspectives, a refusal to admit what happened, a change of emphasis, if it is not just a so-called failure of memory. They could never have acted except as they did; they wanted the right things and they acted correctly; if nothing good came of it the fault lay with the situation or with his colleagues, never with the autobiographer. For someone to stand up and say: here, at this decisive moment I made a mistake, learn from it and do better – this seems contrary to human nature.

Hitler's appointment is defended in over-simple fashion by the schemers around Hindenburg. They say that everything happened 'legally', that what took place was intended as a return to constitutional conditions rather than as a *coup* and that nobody could have foreseen that the end would be different. Nor could anyone suggest what should have been done instead ... Another favourite line of argument is to stress the attitude of the parties and the masses. As a large section of the people wanted Hitler as its leader, his appointment was in accordance with a cardinal principle of democracy. The nation should criticize itself instead of accusing individuals. Furthermore the parties were to blame, first, for example during the Schleicher period, because of the clumsiness of their manoeuvres and then – we shall come to this – because of the weakness and cowardice with which they accepted their destruction and even hastened to destroy themselves before they were forced to do so. Critics reply that the issue was decided by schemers: Papen, the banker Schröder, Oskar von Hindenburg, Hindenburg's Secretary, Meissner, Hindenburg's landowning neighbour, von Oldenburg-Januschau and so on. What are we to make of these conflicting arguments?

It is true that a handful of men prepared the way for the 30

January. The negotiations were so secret and the number of those in the know was so small that even General von Schleicher with his excellent spy service did not know what was happening to him and to the end feared a new Papen government but not a Hitler government. No proof is needed to show that ambition, resentment and pomposity played their all-too-human part in the affair. How small the people sometimes are who are in a position to make history, how base their motives, their thoughts, their character. But why were they able to make history?

They stood in the no-man's land between the great German parties, democracy and the Nazis. This enmity, this paralysis of German politics caused by the conflict of the mass parties, gave them their chance. What was more, they themselves, Hindenburg, his circle and the Army, formed the last dam against the flood of Nazism. The forces of democracy were too weak to do so. If they had been able or had dared to do so, they should in 1932 have nominated their own candidate for the all-important presidential office instead of hiding behind the Field-Marshal. They sought protection from Hindenburg and Hindenburg's men rendered them this service but at the bitter price of excluding the left from all spheres of influence. Then, when they formed the dam against the radical right alone, without the left they were not strong enough to support it; their plan, to use the National Socialists to do away with socially-minded democracy without allowing Hitler to gain power, could never in the long run succeed. An industrial society in a state of great political excitement could be ruled either democratically or demagogically and tyrannically; it could certainly not for any length of time be ruled by a few backward-looking aristocrats supported by nothing but an army of 100,000 men also in a state of political ferment. How could a Papen and a Schleicher succeed where half a century previously a Bismarck had failed in much less difficult circumstances? The alternative solutions, to 'tame' or 'contain' the Nazi Party – Papen and Schleicher's idea – or to split it – Schleicher's idea – were illusory because as a politician Hitler towered high above both his own followers and the Conservative dilettanti. This was not known at the time and retrospective prophecy is easy; but today we do know it and what one knows one should say. Democracy itself, and this means mainly the parties of the Weimar Coalition, should have been stronger and have had a greater political and moral influence on the people than Nazism. Because they failed during the vital years Hitler's victory became practically inevitable. How can one seriously believe that men like Hindenburg, Papen and Schleicher could have saved the Republic? Had *they* been made for this, was this *their* function? If one answers these questions as one must, the distasteful history of the intrigues of January 1933 loses much of its significance. In the end there was nothing sinister about the way in which Hitler came to power, because he was politically the strongest and had the most vehement popular movement behind him. Once such a movement exists its victory is always likely, according to the rules of democracy and according to the rules of history. Therefore the individual scenes of the last act are not of great importance. Schleicher wanted to 'tame' the Nazis, to share power with Hitler as early as the summer of 1932, and at that time Hindenburg and Papen held different views. However, if at the point when the Nazi movement had reached its moment of greatest impetus an agreement had been reached with Hitler, if there had been a coalition government even with Schleicher as Minister of Defence, it only means that the Nazi revolution would have started half a year earlier than it in fact did. The same applies if Schleicher instead of Papen had come to terms with Hitler in December 1932 or January 1933. We have little reason to assume that the General would have been more of a match for the crafty devil than the 'amateur horseman'. There is equally little reason to assume that a government consisting of a Centre–National Socialist coalition would have come to a different end in 1932 from that of the Conservative–National Socialist government in 1933. The parties' powers of resistance or lack of it, including those of the Centre, showed themselves in 1933; and the vehemence, the sense of purpose, the tremendous ruthlessness of the Nazis could have been revealed in 1932. Hitler knew what he needed to turn shared power into absolute power: the office of Chancellor and the Ministries of

the Interior in the Reich and in Prussia; this would have satisfied him a little earlier, as it satisfied him a little later. Therefore
the attitude of the Social Democrats in January 1933, their refusal to enter into an alliance with Schleicher, can hardly be regarded as decisive. The left was exhausted, defeated since the
Prussian *coup d'état*; there is no historical mystery about the
fact that it was not called back to assume responsibility or that
it failed to answer the call which was not really made. Only
Brüning's system was solid and serious enough and sufficiently
well run – looked at in isolation – to have outlasted the crisis
and built a bridge to better days. But what purpose is served by
speculation which ignores reality. Not even Brüning's system
should have been set up. It was wrongly constructed; this we
know because of the way in which it collapsed. How can one
describe as solid something that depended on the whim of one
hard-hearted old man out of touch with his age? When he says
in his memoirs that democracy could have been saved if Hindenburg's physical and spiritual health had lasted five more years,
Brüning passes sentence as much as on his own system as on the
Weimar democracy. To argue whether Hitler was brought to
power by a few schemers or by the people is therefore unnecessary. It was because of Papen's activities that he became Chancellor in a particular way and this fact alone should have been
enough to make Papen remain forever silent in shame and remorse. But without the popular movement that existed Papen
could not have acted, nor would he have wanted to. With it
Hitler's victory was probable anyway, whether it happened with
the help of Papen or Schleicher or perhaps with that of Prelate
Kaas of the Centre Party; the end would always have remained
the same.

Various mixtures thought up by Schleicher or Papen did not
offer any real alternative to demagogic dictatorship. There was
only one: democracy. It did not need to take the form of the
Weimar Constitution for the forms in detail were not important;
a monarchy in the British – or south German – style would have
been much better for democracy than Hindenburg's presidential
rule. Democracy in this context means nothing more than the

free interplay of the main interests and opinions of society according to certain rules, so that there is no other obstacle to the will of the majority than the protection enjoyed by the minorities. Since the eighteen nineties the Germans had predominantly been a people of labourers and white-collar workers. The rest were numerically in the minority, particularly the so-called propertied classes. Within the framework of democracy this certainly did not imply the destruction of minority rights. Without law, without the protection of minorities, democracy itself deteriorates into demagogic dictatorship. Even after 1919 in a completely free vote, no majority could be found in Germany in favour of dispossessing the former princes; this was right because it is bad and not at all democratic to place a small, not essentially guilty minority outside the law. There was enough legal sense, enough regional tradition and loyalty to prevent this; and great spiritual organizations like the Catholic Church always prevented material class conflicts from becoming all important. On the other hand, in a true democracy small minorities threatened by economic disaster, like the Prussian landowners, could not expect any saving privileges, any corrupt subsidies such as those provided by the *Osthilfe* of 1932. And most certainly in a true democracy the great trade unions of the industrial and white-collar workers must gain a position at least equal to that of the employers and their associations. The beneficiaries of Bismarck's system, the east-Elbian landowners and the west German industrialists, were not prepared to accept such inevitable consequences of true democracy. A return to Bismarck's system was impossible; they were incapable of thinking out a third workable solution. But when a third possibility did appear and became a reality because of its own driving force, they agreed, willingly or unwillingly, to come to terms with it. Had they really accepted socially conscious democracy, had they reconciled themselves to it, the catastrophe of National Socialism could have been prevented in spite of all popular agitation; then it would have been possible to keep the Brüning government until the Nazi Party began to fade away naturally. But the upper middle class regarded the development since 1917 as illegitimate and thought that it could still be reversed. Hence its pact with the revolution of the desperate lower middle class, symbolized by the famous meeting in the banker's house; hence the 30 January 1933.

Otto Braun, the Prussian Social Democrat, reduced the causes of the failure of the Weimar Republic to two simple common factors: 'Versailles' and 'Moscow'. Versailles – this was the root of the German Republic in defeat, which from the start made it, together with all its symbols, an object of contempt for a large section of the population. This is where French policy *vis-à-vis* Germany must accept a substantial share of responsibility, at any rate until 1924. Moscow – this was the folly, surpassing all belief, of so-called Communists who, pursuing a worthless and destructive dream of the Day of Judgement, attacked everything that gave rise to hope for demoratic and social progress. Without the Communists the Republic would have begun more auspiciously, with less bloodshed, Hindenburg would not have become President and democracy would not have been harassed and suffocated from the left and the right simultaneously; even in 1933 the sole contribution of the Communists was to provide Hitler with a welcome pretext for establishing a dictatorship. Yet those historians who blame the catastrophe of 1933 to 1945 entirely on Versailles and Moscow and who see the economic crisis as its catalyst make life too easy for themselves. It is as true as it is trivial to say that the crisis hit Germany more than other nations, that it coincided with psychological conditions created by 'Versailles' and that the Communists did all they could to put a spoke in the wheels of the Republic. Why, however, were there so many Communists? Why were there so many National Socialists after 1929? Because the democratic state failed to integrate a large part of the population, failed to satisfy its political desires.

The Weimar Republic has notable achievements to its credit and also important constitutional innovations. Yet basically the Republic was the mutilated and weakened Empire without an emperor. The war had done much more to change German society than the revolution of 1918 and what followed from it; and

Hitler's Third Reich was to do much more still in that respect. The Conservatives or *Deutschnationalen*, the aged Hindenburg above all, had hoped for a return to the spirit and the things of the Wilhelminian Empire from the 30 January 1933. But the thirties and forties brought a movement which led right away from the Kaiser's Reich. Conversely the events of 1918 and 1919 had been expected to lead to revolutionary changes and the Weimar state had in fact brought mainly restoration; an interlude between the revolution of the war and the Nazi revolution. Faces and names alone speak a clear language. The politicians and economists of the Weimar Republic, Marx and Stegerwald, Ebert, Müller and Braun as much as Hugenberg and Westarp, Hergt and Keudell, Stresemann and Cuno and Rathenau, Seeckt and Groener, Kirdorf and Stinnes and Krupp all belong to the age of the Kaiser. The press which produced arguments for or against them was equally old and imperial: the *Norddeutsche Allgemeine*, the *Frankfurter*, the *Berliner Tageblatt*, the *Vossische* and *Vorwärts*. The old mental attitudes, the old feuds, the old faces remained. The new ones only came with the Nazis, not pleasant ones but new ones. The 'Weimar' parties were the opposition parties of the Bismarck era. The Centre joined the government even under William II, the Social Democrats under Max von Baden, only to return into customary opposition shortly afterwards. As far as parliamentary history is concerned the Weimar Republic belongs to the same period as the Kaiser's Reich. The nation was undermined by the same appetites and longings, divided by the same differences; only that now the view of the *Reichsfeinde*, of social welfare democracy, had allegedly become the official one and that this victory of the left was calumniously equated by its opponents with the defeat of 1918. It is necessary to express these things in such a complicated way because they were desperately complicated; because the Weimar Republic was at odds with itself. It was not recognized by a large part of the nation which refused to recognize the defeat or the abandonment of the old imperial colours.

In such a situation those who took over the leadership would have had to be very strong, very sure of themselves and very creative to shape the state according to their ideas against the will of so many. The Social Democrats were expected to be such men. At the 1919 elections to the National Assembly more Germans voted for them than voted for the National Socialists even at the time of their greatest popular triumph in the summer of 1932. The Social Democrats, sensible and peace-loving, honestly prepared to work with their opponents, but pessimistic, over-cautious and compelled long ago and under unfavourable auspices to share responsibility in the Wilhelminian Reich, lacked creative courage. They refused to govern because their mandate had come from forty or forty-five and not from fifty-one per cent of the electorate. They returned the mandate to the 'majority'; but there was no genuine majority capable of action. Majorities capable of action do not appear out of nothing; it is for the leaders to find, to create them, however discreetly and legitimately they set about their task. The will to rule was missing. As a result the people were disappointed and soon many deserted the Social Democrats again. They remained the largest party in the Reichstag; but they returned to their accustomed, thankless role of the last ten years of the Empire of being partly in the government and partly in opposition, leaving to the Centre its accustomed role of always having a finger in every pie. Soon everything was just as it had been before, except for the missing authority of the Crown which had once steadied the state. Again the Social Democrats were the *Reichsfeinde* in spite of all they had done for the Reich; the events of November 1918, the lie about the 'stab in the back', were cited as new proof. Because of the disappearance of the Crown which the 'national opposition' had never really dared to tackle, because official Germany was now democratic, republican and pacifist, the radical right found much greater support than before 1914. Whereas the number of pan-Germans had been small at that time a substantial part of the nation was now 'pan-German' in the sense that it rejected the system of government on chauvinist rather than on Socialist grounds. The parties negotiated with each other without the protection of the monarchy; if they failed to agree on some minor point Chancellor and government 'fell'. These follies repelled the Germans; the cabinet crisis became the symbol of the Republic. In Prussia things were different. What the Social Democrats had there was not, however, genuine power to govern; they were merely in control of the administrative machinery. In the biggest of the federal states they came to be identified with the policeman and the tax collector, not with the men who decided the taxes. They became mere administrators, undoubtedly very efficient ones, and mere defenders of 'legality'. They defended a system which they had not created and continued to defend it even when the majority of the people had come literally to hate it. The Social Democrat as police chief in a top hat – that was how it was possible to present the 'System' to the people in the last years. When the Social Democrats were driven out of the Prussian administration in the summer of 1932 all they did was to appeal to the law, to the precarious, unpopular legality which originated with the revolt of 1918. At the end of 1932 they were more afraid that General von Schleicher would violate the constitution than that Hitler could come to power. Even ten years later the aged Prime Minister, Braun, informed the Americans from exile that legally the Social Democratic government in Prussia still existed and that all that the Allies needed to do in order to restore legality was to reinstate it. This, it must be admitted, showed an exaggerated legal sense; and no sense of the force of the facts, the facts of history. With Hitler the reverse was true. He cared so little about the law that he never thought it worth while to get rid of the Weimar Constitution. What interested his black soul was real power.

As the Social Democrats did not shape the Weimar state nobody did. It was governed by men who had never wanted it, who did not believe in it and who, although they reluctantly sat in the saddle, cast their eyes at other horses that might perhaps be better after all. One is tempted to say that the thing which gradually disintegrated after 1930 and then collapsed within a few weeks in 1933, the 'Republic', never existed. What is curious is not so much the process of disintegration as the fact that so many people refused to believe in it for so long. What is curious is that something that had no reality lasted for so long, like the crumbling house to which Kant likened peace supported only by equilibrium: the sole reason why it did not collapse was because it did not know which way to fall. After 1930 only the Army and the President – two not very republican institutions – stood between the Nazis and the Republic. If one goes back further even Hitler's defeat in 1923 was not a republican victory. The young demagogue was thwarted by the Bavarian Army, by the Bavarian monarchists; in the long view by the fact that for reasons of foreign policy General von Seeckt regarded such *coups* as premature. We know how gently the unsuccessful revolutionary was dealt with. Later he made much of the persecution which he had endured and even tried to use the memory of it to heighten the pleasure aroused during the *Machtergreifung*, the take-over. In fact he was never seriously persecuted by anybody and the law suits brought against him and his followers by the Reich or the free state of Bavaria were never more than a polite pretence. Because the prosecuting authorities admired the man and felt that he was more or less right, if unfortunately somewhat violent in his methods. Among the organizers of extreme right-wing *coups* only Kapp was prosecuted with any degree of seriousness, and the suppression of his *coup* alone was something like a genuine victory for the Republic. But it happened early and had no lasting results.

The Weimar state was thus more an appendage of the Empire of William II or of Bismarck than it was a distinct historic epoch; it was an interregnum between two eras, the second of which was, as we know, infinitely worse. It was as terrible an adventure as Weimar was a feeble one, and it lasted even less long. The failure of the Republic proves nothing about the historical validity of what came after it and much too much honour is done to Hitler by historians who want us to believe that all that Germany did for hundreds of years was to prepare itself for the inevitable end, for National Socialism. Particular ideas and sentiments which Hitler used, pan-German nationalism, imperialism, desire to have a strong man and antisemitism had of course long been there in the German soul; yet such ideas alone did not constitute an historically effective force. Although we think that we can hear Hitler's voice in slogans of the pan-Germans, the late Bismarckians, the supporters of Ludendorff, the *Vaterlandspartie* and the *Freikorps* together do not add up to National Socialism. It is not identified by these elements. Other things were needed for its rise: the economic crisis and this unique individual. The economic crisis helped the breakthrough of the individual; in 1933 it therefore helped feelings to emerge which originated from the year 1919 and which basically were already out of date in 1933. Such perverse happenings are possible in history. What had in fact started with Bismarck and what the First World War brought to fruition was the interregnum: the inability of the nation to settle its internal conflicts according to the rules and to give its state a satisfying meaning. The rest was not predetermined. If the one man had not existed, anything might have happened, but not National Socialism as we knew it. *He happened to exist.* In an interregnum the strongest takes over and it was Hitler who happened to be the strongest.

Very many Germans did not want him until the end and even most of those who voted for him freely did not want what he finally brought. They did not want the Weimar Republic without knowing what they did want, or if they knew they lacked the courage to act. The Social Democrats lacked the courage to introduce socialism, the *Deutschnationalen* lacked the courage to offer effective resistance to 'Versailles', the Bavarian monarchists lacked the courage to restore their monarchy and the Army lacked the courage to do anything. For a long time it was thought that the *Reichswehr* actively encouraged Nazism and brought it to power. Historical science has destroyed this legend. If many young officers swore by Hitler their views were not shared by their superiors; the Army was part of the people and could not be isolated from what was happening among the people. The generals were deeply distrustful of this mob-raiser and did not want to see him in control, much less in unrestricted control. Yet they were opposed to the Republic and themselves incapable of replacing the Republic by anything else. The same is true of industry, particularly of the heavy industry of the Rhineland. It did not 'make' Hitler, as historians of the Marxist school have wanted to persuade us; the German steel magnates were not that imaginative. Only a few outsiders among them provided the Nazi Party with money during the period of struggle. It was not until 1931 that Hitler made a big attempt to gain the sympathies of industry, and he was only partially successful. Only very late, at the time of the Schleicher episode, did important industrial groups join his camp.

On the other hand industry too was opposed to the Republic, to democracy, to the degree of freedom given to the workers' party and the trade unions under the Weimar Republic. The industrialists again were totally incapable of producing a constructive policy. What else could they do in the long run except reluctantly to accept the strongest anti-republican offer? They were all in the same position, the opinionated professors, the old bureaucrats, the young romantics, the war veterans' associations, the *Herren* clubs, all those who refused real support to the Weimar democracy and who wanted something else without themselves knowing what, a return to what had been before or a step forward, a strong system, a strong lead, something national, something splendid. As they were incapable of producing it they allowed themselves to be carried away by the man who in his wild, rough way seemed both before and after January 1933 to offer it. Once in power Hitler therefore found it terrifyingly easy to assume absolute control, and the political parties in particular were reduced to dust at his touch. The conviction that he was the right man on the right road was widely held by the liberal or ex-liberal bourgeoisie at the time; let us add that this view was also widely held outside Germany and that many a Social Democrat felt himself defeated not only by criminals and terrorists but by history. The 'System' had failed; it had solved neither the problems of foreign policy nor the economic crisis; for years it had been unable to master a situation akin to civil war. What use was it to object that those who were now assuming power had in fact caused this situation? That the Social Democrats had not controlled the 'System'? They had been in power for fourteen years, Hitler scornfully said to them in the Reichstag. He was wrong: they had not been in power since 1920 and in the sense that Hitler understood the word nobody had been in power. But if they were dumbfounded and failed to reply it was because their reply would not have been a convincing one. We did not have power, they had to say to themselves, but in 1919 we could have had it. For reasons of decency, of good faith, of weakness we failed to grasp it and allowed events to take their course.

It was the feeling that Hitler was historically right which made a large part of the nation ignore the horrors of the Nazi take-over, which made it possible to pass the Enabling Law and allowed the parties to dissolve themselves. The strongest politician of the interregnum had a right to assume control, let him show what he could do; and if he had only shown a modicum of restraint a new, legitimate period of German history would have opened in 1933 and he would still be ruling today. People were ready for it. If Hitler must not be compared with Napoleon certain events can be compared in the abstract. Napoleon also seemed to have right on his side after the Eighteenth of Brumaire; France and a large part of Europe believed that he had. Later the situation changed and after 1805 the history of France was nothing but the mad adventure of one man. The same was true of Germany. The qualities which made Hitler the strongest man of the interregnum compelled him to go on. When he learnt how terribly easy it was to conquer Germany, when Europe revealed to him the same weakness as Germany, the same readiness to come to terms, to succumb, he lost his reason completely and the evil elements in his soul unknown even to him gained the upper hand. What seemed to begin as a new chapter in German history became the adventure of a villain who forced his will on Germany and through Germany on a large part of the world.

Part Eleven
The Darkest Chapter

'Hitherto,' writes Tacitus, 'no one who has acquired power criminally has used it for good ends.' In another place he says: 'Never have worse defeats, juster omens shown that the gods are concerned not with our safety but with revenge.' Observations of the kind that the Roman historians were given to making, tell us more about the next part of our story than the whole of modern sociology.

It will be difficult to find the right language. Nothing is accomplished by accusation, indignation or disgust. Equally it is impossible to continue the story quietly as if we were dealing with merely another chapter of German history. We might even ask to what extent we are still concerned with a chapter of *German* history and to what extent with disintegration of an international nature. Since Max Weber in the nineties had spoken of the longing of the German middle classes for a new Caesar, since the activities of the pan-Germans and the violence of the First World War *one* current of German life had been flowing towards the morass of Nazism. Hitler's revolution would be wholly German; unlike, for example, the movement of 1848 which was a revolution in imitation of the West and which was misjudged by Marx through the eyes of the West. On the other hand many elements of Nazism were of non-German origin; from the Roman origin of the title which the stranger, the newcomer, assumed, the salute with which he had himself greeted, to the whole machinery of the 'totalitarian' one-party state, copied from the Russians and the Italians. One sometimes suspects that problems and themes of German history – the class struggle and its suppression, the centralized state *versus* federalism, or 'greater' Germany – were used only because the powerhouse happened to be situated on German soil; that other themes might equally well have provided it with fuel. One can only draw attention to the question of which elements came from German history and which were of a contemporary, international nature; to answer it is impossible.

Nor is it possible to say whether we are dealing with the manifestation of a danger generally inherent in twentieth-century democracy. Whether there could be a repetition of these happenings, in Germany or elsewhere. Or whether they were unique, like the economic crisis of 1930, characteristic of a society which though industrialized was not industrialized enough. To ask whether such happenings *can* occur again seems meaningless to me. Do we *want* them to occur again or not – that would be a more sensible way of putting the question.

There remains the task of describing '*wie es eigentlich gewesen ist*' (what it was really like). There is no shortage of sources; German as well as Anglo-Saxon research has done excellent work in this field since 1945. Moreover, particularly as regards the events of the year 1933, the writer can draw on his own recollections. In this he differs from the young of today to whom the whole period with its garish banner headlines, its stupid ado about nothing, its deceptions and its murders is as unfamiliar as Tyre and Nineveh. How fortunate they are.

1. The Take-over

When Hitler was appointed Chancellor on 30 January 1933 the professional mouthpieces of German public opinion predicted that he would not be in office long. The conflicts within the new coalition were clearly apparent. Hitler, Papen and Hugenberg had fulminated too bitterly against each other in recent months for anyone to believe that they could now work honestly together. Moreover, the Conservatives in the cabinet were definitely in a strong position, first because they held many more offices, and secondly because behind them there were Hindenburg and the Army which was still regarded as by far the most reliable concentration of power in the state. Hitler would be given no chance to get too big for his boots and probably he would shortly be forced to resign again. The economic problems were there, they cried out for a solution. But where a serious economist like Brüning had failed those ignorant quacks, now made to show what they could do, would certainly not succeed. Only too soon would the contrast between their promises and achievements become clear to all. What then? No one knew, but at any rate it would be the end of the Nazis . . . This widely held view was quickly shaken. From the start the new government showed an energy the like of which had not been seen since the beginnings of German constitutional history.

The Reichstag was dissolved again. Hugenberg, the Conservative, had been opposed to this course of action because he suspected that the result would not be in his favour. Hitler wanted it and Hindenburg allowed himself to be persuaded once more, on the grounds that the Reichstag elected in November did not have a working majority and that the people must be given an opportunity to express themselves for or against the new government. If this was the pretext the purpose was a very different one. The Nazis knew that, given imagination and impudence, the power of the state could be used in the electoral battle to encourage their followers, intimidate the weak and gag their opponents. 'This campaign is easy to fight because we control the resources of the state,' noted the Party's chief of propaganda in his diary. 'With radio and press at our disposal we shall excel ourselves in rabble rousing. Nor, of course, is there any shortage of money this time.' Indeed not. A number of industrialists headed by Krupp allowed themselves to be persuaded to put an election fund of three million marks at the disposal of the government; the new Prussian Minister of the Interior, Göring, had explained to them that as this was the last election campaign for ten or probably a hundred years some evidence of generosity would not be misplaced. However, not only was the electorate wooed with a breathtaking succession of meetings and entertainments, promises and threats; the new rulers also demonstrated that they were in power and intended to stay there, and that therefore it was pointless to vote against the forces that had come to stay. One such demonstration occurred in the first week when Hindenburg signed a new emergency decree severely curtailing the right of assembly, freedom of speech and the press. It was in Prussia particularly that these demonstrations occurred. It was not the Prime Minister, von Papen, who was the strong man there as he imagined, but the National Socialist Minister of the Interior, Göring. He was strong because he was sufficiently ruthless, intelligent and malicious to exploit to the full the power at his disposal as master of the police. He dismissed officials and officers whom he regarded as unreliable and replaced them by his creatures. He ordered the police always to treat the members of the right, particularly the National Socialists, as allies of the state and not to molest them but to shoot at the left. Over-zealousness in shooting people would be excused; a lack of it would be punished. He organized the Party troops of the SA into an auxiliary police force, gangs of unemployed workers in brown shirts were authorized by the state to do what they liked to their political opponents. It had never happened before that the state itself, the guardian of the law, suddenly became a criminal, attacked its enemies – not even its own enemies but those of the ruling party – broke up their meetings, forced them to be silent, maltreated and killed them. But was this not in the nature of the situation? Although the man who had been made Chancellor had promised to 'obtain power by legal means' he had also promised repeatedly that he would never, never surrender the power given to him. What could one therefore expect?

Franz von Papen, the man directly responsible for the new situation, quickly began to have qualms. Having deliberately blown up the last dyke he now sought to undo his own deed by opening out his silver-handled umbrella against the murky floodwaters; these paid no attention to such elegant opposition. When he saw that nothing could be done he changed course and swam with the stream, as well and as long as he could. Of a 'Fighting Front Black-White-Red' which he founded with his

Conservative allies and which aimed not a few concealed blows at the head of the government hardly anything was heard during the campaign; after the elections it was silent.

At the other end of the scale the Communists now learnt too late that even for them the legal security of democracy had had its advantages. They had treated the Social Democrats as their main enemies, denied there was any difference between democracy and Fascism and until late in the winter of 1932–3 had collaborated practically and effectively with the Nazis. They had always spoken of the doomsday of revolution without making serious preparations for it, even for the protection of their own skins. Although they might still call for a general strike they were not heard; the feeble acts of terrorism which they committed here and there were merely a welcome pretext for the strong and successful Nazi terror. The old Weimar parties, the Centre and the Social Democrats, fought more effectively. They were still there, they kept their loyal followers together and bravely refuted the calumnious accusations made against them, but they found themselves in a pretty hopeless defensive position. When they attacked and announced that they wanted to 'come to power' it seemed like a pale imitation of what the Nazis had done until the day before. The arguments with which they rejected the accusation that they had been in power for fourteen years and had missed their opportunity lacked conviction. The strongest opposition came from southern Germany, particularly from Bavaria. There the regional variant of the Centre, the *Bayrische Volkspartei*, had governed for nine years in a moderate and increasingly sensible fashion, and there the resistance was both political and religious; political because National Socialism clearly aimed at the practical disfranchisement and abolition of the federal states, and religious because the Catholic Church regarded Hitler's national and racial idolatry as a heresy. The situation had thus become reversed since 1923. Whereas Berlin was already under the Austrian's dictatorship, a stronghold of injustice, Munich remained a bastion of order. Anybody who looked around in Germany at the time and despaired of the Berlin-Weimar Republic and its founders could still put his trust in Bavaria. It was possible to believe in the Bavarian state and federalism as bulwarks against Nazi centralism and dictatorship in Berlin at a time when the Weimar Constitution and democracy for the whole of Germany had ceased to hold out any promise.

At the climax of the election campaign, on 27 February, the Berlin Reichstag building was set on fire. The culprit, the only one found at the scene of the crime, was a Dutchman, who it was claimed was a Communist and had 'admitted to having links with the Social Democrats'. That very night thousands of Communist officials were arrested and all Communist and Socialist newspapers were banned; the next morning an emergency decree signed by Hindenburg suspended the basic rights of the constitution, protection from illegal arrest, secrecy of correspondence, freedom of the press and of assembly. It was said that the Communists, in alliance with the Social Democrats, had planned a civil war, a universal blood bath, for which setting fire to the Reichstag was to have been the signal; hence energetic countermeasures were justified. At this point the observer of German affairs held his breath for a moment. If the leaders of the opposition refused to accept this subterfuge apparent to any intelligent child, the President and the Army and the Conservatives would be compelled, whether they wished to do so or not, to reverse the decision of 30 January. What would have happened then is anybody's guess. If on the other hand the aristocracy and the middle classes accepted the outrage and pretended to believe in the mysterious conflagration, they would thereafter have to swallow what they were offered, even more extraordinary things, and their political acquisitions, parliamentarism, parties, rights of the states, rights of the civil service, protection in law generally, freedom of thought and freedom of action would be lost. They accepted. Even the Bavarians admitted that the Communists were now undoubtedly the greatest danger – the Communists who with childish innocence presented themselves at police stations in order to refute the accusation against them, who, instead of beginning their famous revolution, allowed themselves to be caught and led like lambs to the slaughter. Brüning alone let it be understood in an election speech that he was not completely convinced by the official version. Apart from that there were rumours, even secretly circulating broadsheets – or else, among many middle-class people, a surreptitious shrug of the shoulders and a smile. The feeling was that the fire, whoever the culprits, had had its effect; this was the end of the 'red scoundrels', Communists and Socialists. The latter put up a feeble struggle, protesting that they must not be lumped together with the Communists. To which Göring replied with a sneer that it was just a case of the pot calling the kettle black. There was terror and jubilation, cynicism, weakness and more jubilation, and above it all the inexhaustible crowing, triumphant, ingratiating and threatening voice of the *Führer*, as he now had himself called. No wonder that from this one-sided civil war against a fictitious enemy, from this ecstasy of victory without a preceding battle the Nazis emerged with another five million votes. What was surprising was that the old parties, the Centre and the Social Democrats, still survived and that half the nation was still not prepared to vote for the victors. In the new parliament the Nazis and their Nationalist satellites together disposed of fifty-two per cent of the votes; in practice they had considerably more because the eighty Communists no longer counted and any of the Social Democrats could be arrested or if need be murdered. '. . . what do numbers matter now? We rule the Reich and Prussia . . .'

A few days later they took over in southern Germany. Even in Bavaria the Nazis were now by far the strongest group. The claim of the Bavarian federalists to represent the right of their *Land* was invalidated by the attitude of their own people, if not all at any rate too many of them. The rulers in Berlin needed no more. As happened in the previous year in Prussia, the south German governments were replaced by Reich Commissars, their members arrested, killed or forced to flee abroad. It was a sure sign of the times that this could happen even in Munich, that there too the long prepared, often promised resistance of the loyal supporters of the state failed to materialize. Not everybody was happy about the new situation, but while those who were sad kept silent those who were pleased expressed themselves noisily and many who had so far supported the old system hastened to make their peace with the new one. After all it is safer and also better for the peace of one's soul to belong to the victors instead of the defeated; we all know how tempting it is to claim that the victor has historical right on his side and to despise his victim. Hence communal rejoicing was very much more in evidence than solitary misery and disgust. In prison cells men were tortured and every now and again the corpse of a victim was dragged out of some river; but in the streets bedecked with flags uniformed party officials with their ladies enjoyed the early spring, and the new rulers drove about in stolen cars, puffing cigars. The holiday mood, the feeling of liberation far surpassed the silent terror. Anyway the terror, as the saying went, was 'contrary to the *Führer's* intentions', and Hitler appealed to his comrades to show moderation, blaming the excesses which had occurred on 'Communist provocation'. The atmosphere of a great popular festival of liberation, unification and honour regained created a stronger impression even beyond the frontiers of the Reich than the crimes and the revelling, bawling brutality.

The 'Day of Potsdam' seemed to prove the optimists right. On that occasion, during a celebration in the *Garnisonkirche* at the tomb of Frederick the Great, the eighty-six-year-old Hindenburg was for the last time allowed to be the centre of interest. The old man was not displeased with the latest developments because they had taken place 'constitutionally' and he had therefore not broken his oath, which was all-important to him. Of the rest, of the lies, the murder and the agony, hardly anything penetrated into the growing confusion of his mind. Around him he saw familiar flags and uniforms, even familiar faces, the ex-Crown Prince and generals from the past. He was pleased because he believed that he had done right after all and that he had led Germany back on to the old road which it should never have left. In this conviction he was strengthened by Hitler who on that day gave a fine performance as the old man's admirer, as a Prussian, conciliatory and pious. Perhaps he was not play-acting because he had the gift of convincing himself at the moment of what was in his interest to seem and to say. For the moment he needed the confidence of the old man who was still powerful, and the confidence or at least the forbearance of the generals. Two days later, in the Reichstag which met in one of Berlin's opera houses, the tone was already much more modern. Hitler demanded a decree enabling the government for a period of four years to make and apply laws without the consent of parliament, including ones that conflicted with the Weimar Constitution. He added, however, that he intended to use the 'Enabling Law' only rarely, as the government had a safe majority in parliament, and that he had no intention of encroaching upon the rights of the Reichstag and the Reichsrat, of the *Länder* and still less of the President. But in view of what had happened in recent weeks no one could misunderstand the significance of the bill. It meant nothing less than complete and final dictatorship. The fact that Hitler threatened that he would take the power which he needed, with or without the consent of parliament, that he was free to do as he wished, might have made a vote against the bill seem like a gesture of senseless heroism. The police who were much in evidence in the hall, the gangs shouting outside the building – 'The law or bloody murder' – damped the spirit of the opposition. The Centre voted for the bill which needed a two-thirds majority. Later their leader, Heinrich Brüning, gave a detailed justification of his attitude. He said that at the time it no longer made any difference what his party did because Hitler could have as many deputies arrested as was necessary to give him a two-thirds majority in a rump parliament even without the Centre; that a dictatorship had in effect been established by the decree of 18 February and that the Enabling Law did not add much. Yet if that was the position it would have been better to risk a last, dignified, if no longer very effective protest, instead of giving subversion that semblance of legal continuity to which Hindenburg, and therefore Hitler also, attributed so much importance. The Social Democrats, those that were still at large, thought so. Wels, the chairman of the parliamentary party, had the courage to justify his party's refusal to vote for the bill; in measured words, but he justified it. This gave the *Führer* the opportunity to overwhelm his defeated, impotent opponents with biting sarcasm; he did not need their votes, they had had their day anyway. But let them be under no illusion, he was no bourgeois who provoked his enemies without destroying them . . . He received his two-thirds majority and far more.

It was not only the terror that was responsible for this voluntary abdication of the parties, especially the old Centre Party so deeply rooted in the political history of the new Germany. It was also the feeling that they had been beaten, had failed, become useless, and that in the confusion of this spring nothing remained but the dictatorship of those who, whatever their means, had proved strongest. What the means had been Heinrich Brüning knew very well; the *Deutschnationalen* knew it too and the chairman of their parliamentary group shot himself in the despair of an insoluble conflict of conscience. Most people ignored these individual tragedies and overlooked the moral blemishes of the 'revolution'. The 'new state' existed, or was in the making, there was nothing to be done, and anyone who tried to oppose it was a fool: order must be established, even if it was done by those who had so far brought the worst disorder. Work must be created for the unemployed because this crying problem still remained unsolved. Only united determination could solve it; the parliamentary parties had proved unequal to the task and would certainly prove unequal to it now. That was the mood which, more than anything else, explains why the deputies departed without a protest from their erstwhile scene of activity or inactivity.

Now things happened thick and fast. The National Socialists were systematic people, announced the new Minister of Propaganda with the cynical frankness and malicious relish which were characteristic of him; they would not bite off more than they could chew, but what they could chew they would bite off piece by piece and thus they would gobble up the whole of Germany in a few months. This was indeed what happened. In spite of Hitler's promise during the debate on the Enabling Law not to touch the rights of the *Länder* or of the Reichsrat which represented them, a week later there occurred the so-called *Gleichschaltung* (co-ordination) of the federal states and communes. To start with provincial parliaments, urban and rural district councils were co-ordinated according to a key provided by the Reichstag election of 5 March; this meant that everywhere from city to village there were mayors acceptable to the Nazis. This was followed by the appointment of *Reichsstatthalter* (Reich governors) in the federal states; highly paid party members who were meant to be the real heads of the *Land* governments. The *Länder* thus ceased to exist as members of a federal state and became mere administrative units. In 1934 this arrangement was confirmed by a new decree: 'The *Länder* will cease to have popular representation. The sovereign rights of the *Länder* are taken over by the Reich. The governments of the *Länder* are subordinate to the Reich government.' A law, allegedly for the 'restoration of the permanent civil service' decreed dismissal of all 'non-Aryan' government employees. Equally all those civil servants were to be dismissed who, because of their past attitude could not be expected 'to give wholehearted support to the national state'. As university professors, secondary school teachers, panel doctors and even members of state orchestras counted as civil servants thousands soon found themselves in distress. Painful though this was for them it was profitable for others. Because Germany was a poor, over-populated state, the individual's struggle was hard and there were plenty of applicants for every post; many who so far had not found success in life could now move in and up. Such people found nothing to criticize in the 'national state'. What the law laid down for the state, private firms did on their own account, particularly newspapers, theatrical and artistic concerns. Jewish influence in this sphere had undoubtedly been strong in the Wilhelminian Reich and the Weimar Republic. Now it was suddenly reduced to nothing. Many non-Jewish but politically unsound editors were also forced to go. Others fell into line, some with intentional, dignified slowness, others from one day to the next, if they had not secretly done so much earlier as a preventive measure, and now displayed the party badge in their buttonhole instead of carrying it in their pocket. This has happened in other periods and other countries. Let us not therefore be too proudly indignant over human weakness; let us rather praise those who remained loyal to their beliefs, unthanked, in increasingly difficult circumstances, at terrible cost.

The trade unions were destroyed. Originally the Nazis had treated them with some respect; they had been inclined to differentiate between the great professional organizations of the workers and the Social Democratic Party. There had been talk of a 'corporate state' in which the trade unions could find a place. What the new rulers really wanted, however, was less romantic. They wanted absolute power, to dominate and control the masses, an aim which conflicted with the existence and dignity of medieval corporations. Therefore the idea was quickly abandoned. On 1 May, the old Socialist holiday, a new form of popular entertainment was provided; the members of all concerns, private as well as national, assembled, and meetings were held everywhere at which speeches were made praising the value of labour and fireworks let off. The new masters knew how to manipulate the masses, how to make them express jubilation. Many a man who turned out reluctantly went home impressed and delighted; perhaps Hitler was well disposed towards the workers after all? The next day, however, showed that the diversions of 1 May had been intended as a prelude for action of a very different kind. All trade unions, Christian as well as free, were dissolved, their property, houses, banks, schools and holiday homes, taken over and looted and their leaders arrested. This was done in the now familiar manner, by a secretly prepared, sudden attack, which succeeded once more. What no Hohenzollern would have dared, what under the Kaiser would infallibly have produced a general strike and terrible unrest now encountered almost no resistance. The fight was fought by one side alone, the blows, symbolic and literal, fell on people who did not defend themselves. Such was the state of the nation three months after 30 January; in part it felt conquered and defeated and in part it felt that it was being swept along, liberated and well led at last. Let us not say that these conflicting emotions split the nation in two, into victors and vanquished, because in many – impossible to determine their number – the two feelings existed side by side or conflicted. The result was that people drifted along.

The trade unions were replaced by the Labour Front, a compulsory organization comprising all employees and employers. Its purpose was to control the workers and to influence them in the direction desired by the state; its methods included offers of advantages and amenities. The Nazi state was not 'hostile to the workers'. This phrase, applicable to certain groups of employers and parties in the nineteenth and early twentieth century, does not describe the Nazi state which is characterized by very different things.

The destruction of the political parties happened almost by itself, as a fish dies out of water, or ice melts in fire. The most honourable end was that of the Social Democrats because they were proscribed as a treasonable organization. There was something in this; many of the party's leaders had gone abroad and said there what could no longer be said in the Reich. The Centre disbanded itself voluntarily, maintaining that the party had never seen its existence as an end in itself and that, because Hitler's position was more powerful than that of any German emperor, parties had become superfluous. The Conservatives followed suit. Their leader and gravedigger, Hugenberg, the cunning, rich, powerful, deluded and bone-headed Hugenberg, soon found himself forced to give up his position in the cabinet; the 'coalition' supposedly intended for eternity thus lasted barely six months. Papen remained but his vice-chancellorship was merely a joke. Finally the National Socialist German Workers' Party was proclaimed Germany's 'only political party' and any attempt to preserve or found other parties was threatened with severe punishment. This happened seven months after the Weimar parties had refused to grant the Chancellor, von Schleicher, the very modest plenary powers – the mere adjournment of parliament – for which he had begged.

The process of *Gleichschaltung* was extended also to intellectual life. Let us not say that it was completely successful, either then or later. There were writers and scholars who retreated into their innermost self, avoided contact with the present and remained loyal to their readers. This was possible; but many others took a different course. They co-operated, 'reorientated themselves' and wrote the nonsense expected of them; either because of a spark of enthusiasm – the ready acceptance of success was after all an old vice of German intellectuals – or because of mere ambition or desire to earn money. Theatre, film, radio, press and publishing certainly were profitable in those days and as such they were an easy prey for the state. Like the Russian Communists before it the Nazi state was keenly aware of the potential of the arts as an instrument of power. Nothing must be written, shaped, performed or laughed at that did not please them. At first a newly established Ministry of Propaganda and Popular Enlightenment saw to it that press and radio struck the right note. When Party and state became one the Party propaganda chief became the official propagandist. A large number of newspapers remained in private hands, and the famous liberal papers of the past which survived tried to preserve a little of their tradition. In the non-political sections this was still possible for a while. In the political sections the press could only simulate freedom. In this sphere freedom *must* mean criticism and anyone who made even the most cautious attempt at political criticism disappeared into a concentration camp. An Office of Culture was founded with departments for every form of artistic and intellectual activity. Anyone who refused or was not allowed to join was forced to find another occupation. Jewish painters were not only forbidden on pain of punishment to sell their paintings but even to paint at all. If this hasty compulsory organization of artists and intellectuals placed high value on their political potential it also revealed a profound contempt for individuals.

The attempt to extend the process of *Gleichschaltung* to the churches, particularly the Protestant Church, did not succeed. The Association of German Christians which tried to square the circle and to combine Nazi ideology with Christianity was stillborn. The Protestant *Reichskirche* succeeded in controlling only a small number of clergy and parishes. The rebels, not against the state, but against the state church, united in a 'Confessional Church' and proved stronger. Hitler regarded Pastor Niemöller, the inspirer and spokesman of the Confessional Church, as a dangerous enemy. The Catholic Church was more conciliatory at first; the fact that it was a thousand years old, that it was both supra-national and had its roots deep in the community of the faithful allowed it to feel secure in secular matters. The Vatican was the first foreign power to let itself be persuaded by Catholic German politicians to conclude a treaty, a Concordat, with the Nazi government. But this readiness to negotiate concerned forms and legal matters, not questions of doctrine. The fortress of the faith stood at the centre of the German state, from the jubilant beginning to the bitter end, unconquered and virtually unassailable.

Meanwhile the creation of work for the unemployed remained the most urgent positive task for the new rulers. If they failed to keep their promises in this sphere, nothing else, talk, propaganda, executions, jubilation and terror, could have protected their system in the long run. In fact they did succeed. It was Hitler's conviction that mastering the economy was fundamentally a simple problem which required determination without much theory; and at first success proved him right. The Four-Year-Plan, which he proclaimed on the Russian model, did not exist; the Nazis had no economic programme. They proceeded to act without one. It was their good fortune that they could fall back on plans for the creation of work prepared by Brüning and Schleicher, and that they were aided by the gradually improving state of the world economy. However, it is an old truth that luck and merit go hand in hand. With this the Nazis undoubtedly scored a point, even a very substantial point in the eyes of those who were at last freed from the agony of idleness. The German employers for their part co-operated willingly; big government orders which they would have decried as Bolshevism had they come from Brüning or Schleicher, daring issues of discountable paper, creation of money, expenditure which could yield no profit now seemed justified to them, or at least acceptable. They too were more concerned with power and status than with theory. They gladly allowed the 'authoritarian' state, the mob-raiser who knew how to make them feel that at last they were masters in their own home again, to do things which they would never have allowed the hated 'Marxists', the trade unions, or even honourable, lonely Dr Brüning to do. Hitler was not interested in economic questions, he was interested in power. If one controlled the whole country one also controlled industry, from above, and one could leave boring details to the specialist. The doctrinaire quacks whom before 1933 he had allowed free expression of their views were sent packing and he surrounded himself instead with able men. One of these was indisputably Hjalmar Schacht who once more took charge of the *Reichsbank* and soon also of the Ministry of Economics. He had the confidence of German industry and international finance to whom he seemed to guarantee a moderate, if unorthodox, leadership of the German economy. His approach was certainly not orthodox. Politically an opportunist, shrewd and bold, a man of vitality and imagination, Schacht had understood what the conservative theorists of the period had still not grasped: that money had no absolute value, that it was a symbol and a means, an instrument for the distribution of goods. Where it was not available in sufficient quantities it could be created; and it failed to fulfil its purpose, it caused inflation only when more of it was allowed to circulate than was warranted by current production. In his first years in office Schacht did not cause inflation although he created money. How he did it was his professional secret, but he did it. The money went into repairing houses and machinery, into building remarkable roads, into new houses; and also into armaments, although not primarily into these at first. It was transformed into food, clothing and the pleasures of life. Manual and white-collar workers did not live better than in 1926, but soon much better than in 1932. For a long time the people as a whole had not been allowed to enjoy what they possessed, what they could make and harvest. This unnatural scandal came to an end, not from one day to the next but within two years; this was the eye-catching, the overwhelming achievement of the regime in its early days.

There was no miracle behind this. It could have been done by Hitler's predecessors. Only they had not done it and had left the dictator to think of the simple solution of bringing together unemployed labour and urgent work. To do this required a little common sense which Hitler possessed; it was one side of his character. It also required a little financial know-how which the new President of the *Reichsbank* possessed. There is no point in describing his methods of raising money as 'dubious manoeuvres', as was done for so long. There is no point either in playing down the credit due to the Nazi government for getting the economy moving again. Fundamentally it did what Franklin Roosevelt was doing in the United States at the same time; it did it more successfully and more quickly because it did not have to fight a Supreme Court which insisted that its actions conflicted with antiquated bits of legislation; it also chose the more correct way because from the start it concentrated on expansion and not on artificial restriction of production. If there was no miracle behind all this i t was nevertheless not surprising that millions of people to whom it brought relief regarded it as a miracle and were henceforth inclined blindly to put their faith in the man whose achievement it was.

Hitler was now the ruler of a state which had hitherto been regarded as a constitutional state and wanted to be regarded as such even now; the master of an orderly bureaucracy inherited largely from the Wilhelminian Reich. At the same time he was also the chief of a vast gang of adventurers and terrorists. Had he not been the latter he could not have become the former; naked, lawless force, SA and SS, the Reichstag fire and the concentration camps were contributory factors in the establishment of the dictatorship; they were not the only ones but they played an important part. Hitler had two faces: that of the Herr *Reichskanzler* complete with morning coat and top hat and that of the gangster surrounded by a heavily armed bodyguard of thugs. Germany itself had two faces, then and later: it was a thoroughly civilized country which in some respects remained civilized to the end and yet it was ruled by terrorists. From March to the middle of the summer of 1933 there was no conflict; the terrorists were conquering the state. Then, when the Nazi Party had, as the phrase went, become the state, when it had gained control of the political machinery, the bureaucracy and the police, came a period when the terrorists and the state wanted, momentarily at least, to go separate ways. Although the dictatorship was to remain with all the means needed to make it secure, propaganda, intellectual *Gleichschaltung*, prisons, concentration camps and the executioner's axe, the state could now do this itself, legally so to speak; the irresponsible party elements as distinct from the state were no longer needed to the same extent as before. Hitler wanted to establish order, to give the economy a feeling of reasonable legal security; he also wanted peace with the rest of the world and knew why. After the summer of 1933 the state uttered frequent warnings that the revolution was over and that everybody must behave accordingly.

The leaders of the fanatical party troops did not like this. For them the state as it gradually assumed shape was still too bourgeois, too orderly, too much under the control of the old powers. They did not find in it the place of which they had dreamt; they felt that they were becoming superfluous. *What* they had dreamt of, what they meant when they demanded a 'second revolution', they could not have said themselves; one does them too much honour if one believes that they were aiming at any kind of 'socialism'. They enjoyed permanent disorder, they revelled in looting, arresting and plundering on their own initiative and wanted to be outside the state but to dominate it. The Army, excellently disciplined and well equipped, was a particular thorn in their flesh. The leader of the S A, Captain Röhm, Hitler's old friend, wanted to amalgamate the S A and the Army into one great adventurous popular army with himself as its head. The *Reichswehr* generals objected.

The *Reichswehr* had not made Hitler, it had not helped him to become Chancellor, much less to become dictator. Hitler owed thanks to the new Minister of Defence, von Blomberg, not for active help in his 'revolution' but for toleration; the same toleration which the Army leadership had shown towards all German governments since the fall of the Hohenzollern. In the early days of the Republic the Army had intervened a few times against the Communists, otherwise it did not interfere in politics. It allowed there to be chaos, though disliking it, provided its own structure remained intact. Its strength, in republican times, had rested on the weakness of the republican governments, but it was only an apparent strength which was never put to the test. Hitler's government was the first strong government in Germany since Bismarck's fall. This weakened the position or apparent position of the Army; because it had never been as strong politically as the people and probably also the generals imagined. The fate of General von Schleicher provided a striking proof of this fact. Armies have never governed and cannot govern because of their very nature; where the military has ruled successfully it has soon ceased to represent the army. On the other hand it is impossible to govern *against* an unbroken army. The *Reichswehr* could still become disagreeable if its most cherished interests and traditions were threatened. It could do so particularly because the head of the state continued to be its friend; President von Hindenburg, a lonely man tottering towards the grave, his mental powers impaired, a vanishing myth, was yet the occupant of the highest office, and for millions of Germans his name was sacred. Hitler knew this. Since the start of his political career, particularly since his defeat in 1923, it had been his habit to be on good terms with solid powers, with industry, the Army and the President; powers which could be outwitted and got round, but not defeated in open battle. In the quarrel between the Army and the SA he was therefore inclined to support the Army if a clash became unavoidable.

The German Conservatives for their part saw in the mounting crisis of the early summer of 1934 a chance to undo some of the things which had happened after the Reichstag fire, and which they had disliked. A victory of the Army over the SA would be a victory of the state over the Party, of order over permanent disorder. Let Hitler remain Chancellor; the unperceptive view that he was a good, upright man who was much better than the majority of his Party, that it would be possible to change over 'with Hitler into the Fourth Reich', was widely held among the Conservative middle classes at the time. Cut off from his Party and his Party troops, the source of his power, Hitler would cease to be a dictator. His worst followers, the super-demagogues, Jew-baiters and sadistic police officials would disappear and the situation would be more or less what people had hoped for in January 1933. In spite of the undeniable successes of the dictatorship there was at the time much discontent among the German middle classes, not to mention the workers. All those who believed in justice and human dignity, and they were many, objected secretly to the boastful, brutal baseness of the rulers. Hitler therefore faced two threats: the 'second revolution' of the Party, and what the right wing of the Party called the 'reaction', the restraining programme of the Conservatives, aimed at weakening the dictatorship. If he turned against the first trend and suppressed it he seemed the more certain to become a prisoner of the second, the Conservative one.

The crisis was magnified and speeded up by the generally known fact that Hindenburg only had a few months to live. His disappearance would mean two things: it would no longer be possible to make use of his personal authority; the problem of his succession would arise. Therefore something must happen while Hindenburg was still alive.

Franz von Papen made a speech. He attacked the 'second revolution'; also the absence of a firm rule of law, the propaganda lies, the never-ending boasts and threats, the deification and self-deification of individuals, all of which had nothing to do with the true Prussian character. The speech, it must be said to the credit of this shifty individual, was good. But speeches or secret discussions were all that the various Conservative circles, Papen's circle, Schleicher's circle and Brüning's circle, had prepared. Not even the advocates of the 'second revolution', who ought to have known their Hitler, had really prepared for revolutionary action. They merely threatened it but postponed its execution about which they probably had no very clear idea.

The dictator acted two weeks later. On 30 June – with Hitler personally in charge in Upper Bavaria – Captain Röhm and hundreds of his friends were murdered, the whole leadership of the SA. This appeared to be a victory for the Army which during this period was in a state of alert. But it was not meant to be its victory and was not, because the Army did not act. Hitler acted by using the special, recently created SS units. In order to prove to the Army which had urged him to action who was the master, two high-ranking offcers, Schleicher and Bredow, political generals of the Hindenburg period, were murdered in the process. Brüning escaped the same fate by fleeing to England; Papen avoided it by the skin of his teeth; his adjutants and friends, the men who had drafted his speech of protest were murdered. This was Hitler's way of solving the crisis, his reply to the threat from the Conservatives; he had people murdered, not just on one side which would have made him the prisoner of the other but on all sides at once, so that he alone and his immediate circle were the victors. The occasion gave an opportunity to settle many old scores. In woods and swamps the bodies of those who had been beaten to death were found, disfigured beyond recognition; bodies of Catholic politicians and administrators, of writers and lawyers, of harmless citizens who years ago had incurred the displeasure of some Nazi leader. If the law of the jungle prevailed why not exploit it to indulge in the kind of murder that only a year ago the assassins would not have dared to commit. For a few days the rulers showed their true face. Only for a few days; then they slipped back into the frock coats of honourable civilians and began to explain and excuse: cases of murder unconnected with the main operation would be handed over to the courts – but this never happened – some of those killed had been the victims of misunderstandings or had resisted arrest and therefore regrettable consequences had been unavoidable, and so on. The cabinet which still contained a handful of 'bourgeois' ministers decided that the purge had been an act of 'self defence by the state' and therefore legal. Germany was a constitutional state, it must be one because without laws seventy million people cannot live cheek by jowl. Therefore the alternative was to say that what had been done was done legally or to try the Chancellor as a multi-murderer. Hitler himself was franker than the others. He accepted responsibility for Schleicher's murder which had at first been hushed up: anyone who met with foreign diplomats and conspired against him was shot on his orders. During those days he, as leader of the German people, had also been its supreme judge and had been entitled to administer justice on his own authority.

People listened, believing or disbelieving, enraged or indifferent, glad that they themselves had escaped, with the feeling that with such a government it was necessary to be careful in word and deed. They did not regret losing the insolent SA; the rest was bloody and sinister and could not be understood by the ordinary citizen. A well-known, learned political lawyer wrote an article on *The Führer Defends the Law*.

And Hindenburg? The deluded old man accepted even the murder of the generals, of his friend Schleicher, the whole series of brutish crimes. Isolated on his East Prussian estate, almost a prisoner, misled by faithless advisers, he sent congratulatory telegrams to Hitler and Göring: 'According to reports submitted to him' they had acted splendidly. It was the last service rendered to the rulers, by the dying myth, the final step in the old man's moral abdication which had in fact taken place long ago. A month later he died, as a Christian, and with the dignity which throughout his life had disguised his shortcomings of mind and character. However, Hindenburg's disappearance no longer signified a crisis, hardly even an occasion. The alliance between the Army and the dictator was sealed when the Army accepted the crime against itself and dishonoured itself in order to destroy its opponents; was it an alliance or the subjection of the one by the other? The 'supreme judge' of 30 June was master of the situation. Who still dared to oppose him? Was not even von Papen, the gentleman, the knight without fear or reproach, anxious to continue to serve the man who had been responsible for the murder of his closest collaborators? By decree the offices of President and Chancellor were merged. Legally this was still done on the strength of the Enabling Law of the spring of 1933. The Chancellor became the head of the state and thus also Commander-in-Chief of the armed forces. The Minister of War, von Blomberg, hastily made officers and soldiers swear the oath of allegiance to Hitler personally. Then the nation was invited to give its view in a 'free plebiscite' on what had been done and could not be undone – a trick employed with success by earlier dictators. Five million citizens voted 'no'; there were therefore at least – at the very least – five million unshakeable, courageous human beings in Germany at that time. This did not alter the facts. The process of *Machtergreifung*, the take-over, was finished in August 1934.

2. Intermediate Reflection

Had this been planned from the start or did it happen because surprising opportunities were seized? Goebbels boastfully claimed the first; others, Hindenburg's Secretary of State for example, want us to believe that Hitler originally pursued much more moderate aims and was pushed further partly by threats and partly by favourable developments. But it is the propaganda chief who is speaking the truth.

It began with the Reichstag fire. The suspicion that the conflagration had been started by those who derived such tremendous advantage from it immediately became widespread and this attitude was characteristic of the situation as a whole; people thought the Nazis capable of such a crime and many did not even mind. The trial which followed was not designed to allay this suspicion. Only *one* trail was followed and that was an obviously false, fabricated one. The German and Bulgarian Communists who were accused of starting the fire proved their innocence so convincingly that the court which consisted of men of the old school had to acquit them. The theory of the experts – bolstered up by complicated scientific evidence – was that van der Lubbe could not have acted alone. The figure which the Dutchman cut during his trial confirmed this view. He told the judge that he found the whole trial comic and behaved like a grinning idiot and not as expected like a political criminal of great physical and intellectual strength. Yet the case was brought to an end quickly and for all time and no further attempts were made to reopen it. Van der Lubbe's execution took place hurriedly and quietly; the press was not allowed to comment on it. What had begun with tremendous publicity ended with silence. No wonder that the theory has survived that the fire was started on the orders, if not of Hitler then of his henchmen. This has never been proved and it is not surprising, particularly if one remembers what has happened since and what has happened to those who could have known about it. However, twenty-eight years after the fire a book appeared which undertook to prove, with as much technical skill as the specialists had displayed to prove the contrary in 1933, that van der Lubbe alone was guilty. We can leave this quarrel to the pyrologists. For the historian it will continue to be obscure and can remain so particularly as its subject is of little importance. If the National Socialists caused the fire they only employed the means which they were to use frequently later: to simulate the threat which was the object of their well-planned counter-attack which would have been made in any case. If they did not start the fire they were helped by fortune, as so often during the years of their rise. To write history with arguments taken from pyrology is to misunderstand it. More interesting is the question of what use was made of the Reichstag fire. Even before the flames had been put out the fire was surrounded by a magic circle of political lies. It was said that the Communists were planning a *coup*. This was not true. The evidence, allegedly found at their headquarters, was never published. The fire was said to have been the starting signal for the *coup*. This was nonsense because nobody starts a *coup* with such a childish act, least of all trained Marxists. To say that the Social Democrats were in league with the Communists was an even more stupid lie; one could just as well have claimed that the Pope was in league with the Communists. These lies served to justify a venture which, as its planners later admitted and boasted, would have been carried out in any case. One is tempted to ask why in that case lies were necessary at all. What was needed was power and that the Nazis had anyway. For twelve years they remained loyal to the habit of using lies to justify what they did, could do and would do anyway.

The destruction, first of the radical left, then of the left in general and then of all political parties had been planned or at least desired. Chance came to the rescue of the intention. The permanent state of emergency had been planned. Never in recorded history has an historical individual done so exactly what he planned to do; an experience which was bound to make the man self-confident to the point of madness and blasphemy. Undoubtedly he expected generally more opposition than he found. One wonders how the road to personal dictatorship could have been so smooth and so short; much smoother than that of Lenin and Stalin; much shorter than that of Mussolini.

The Germans have no liking for the game of revolution and have usually behaved clumsily under lawless conditions. The men of 1848, like those of November 1918, were faced with a lack of constitutional continuity; they had to create their own authority. In 1848–9 the attempt failed and in 1918–19 it was not a success. The Social Democrats distrusted their authority just because it emanated from a revolution, and did not want to use it for revolutionary action. They saw as their most urgent task the speedy creation of a new system of legality. Hitler occupied a position of constitutional continuity; he was Chancellor by virtue of Paragraph 52 of the Weimar Constitution. But he, not Gagern, not Ebert, was the revolutionary, and he needed only few legal tricks to start a revolution 'legally'. In the first weeks, while Göring's police terror violated the constitution, the courts still dutifully proceeded against him; prisoners were ordered to be released, bans on newspapers were lifted. But then came the emergency decree of 28 February and then the Enabling Law; and these two tricks were enough to bring the whole vast machinery of the constitutional state under the control of the terrorists. For centuries the bureaucracy had been accustomed to obey those who had the right to give orders. The terrorists now had this right and they rarely omitted to appeal to this or that paragraph. What objections could a *Landrat*, a *Ministerialdirektor* or a commissioner of police raise? Added to the magic of the law there was the personal magic of the President. There was a deep-rooted belief among the people that Hindenburg and his Army would not accept anything criminal and that therefore anything that had their sanction could not be bad, even if it seemed so. The old man thus rendered the terrorists an invaluable service in establishing their dictatorship and did so for just as long as they needed him; when he finally lay down to die he was no longer needed.

A similar function was exercised by the 'bourgeois' ministers in the cabinet, whether they actually did some work like Hjalmar Schacht or merely served as a comforting symbol, like the Foreign Minister, von Neurath. They formed the bridge between the terrorists and peaceful Germany, the constitutional, bureaucratic state. In 1933 the Germans would not have been prepared to tolerate naked gangster dictatorship; the delicate organism in its highly concentrated condition would not have supported this. Anomaly and illegality were compelled to hide behind normality and legality, otherwise the bureaucracy without which Germany could not exist would not have co-operated. The Reichstag fire trial provided a curious illustration. It was not a dishonest show trial on Russian lines. The judges were men of the old type, honest lawyers from the time of the Kaiser. The Nazis, judging this type correctly and despising it, did not think it wise to put them in the picture; somehow the worthy judges would undoubtedly extricate the Nazis and themselves from the affair, which indeed they did. They refused to convict the accused Communists because they were clearly not guilty. Equally they refused to recognize the true state of affairs, which they suspected of course, and moved carefully in order not to destroy in sudden and terrible fashion the noble pretence of the constitutional state whose servants they were. The result was a carefully formulated nothing. The culprits for whom nobody had looked were not found; fortunately, it was said, they apparently had not been Germans ... This game of hide and seek between right and wrong, this continuation of normality and legality under the cloak of crime is typical of the whole period.

Civil war does not suit the German character either. The Germans have never had one. Even the Thirty Years War was a war between princes, not a civil war. One may call this a piece of good fortune. Had the Germans resembled the Spaniards there would have been no lack of inflammable matter for a real civil war in 1919 and again in 1932. The idea did not even appeal to the

Communists. Although they promised their revolution they never had any clear idea of how they would start it and relied on the law and on the very constitution which they intended to overthrow. When they were attacked they called for the police, because the attack was against the law and the constitution. Hitler could therefore fight his civil war not only with the help of the state but without any resistance. The war started with the unconditional surrender of his opponents who did not understand what was happening to them. The Reichstag fire was to have been the signal for battle, but the Nazis were forced to stage it themselves because their enemies did nothing. Therefore from the beginning until 1939 the dictatorship cost only a few thousand lives, in executions, murders and suicides; no one was killed in open battle. If there was something to be said for this compared with a genuine civil war there was also something peculiarly repulsive about this self-indulgent, mercilessly exploited but bloodless victory of one part of the nation over the other.

Hitler continued to employ the method of surprise attack which led to bloodless victories, first in Germany and then in Europe. The bloodbath of 30 June was not a battle but a slaughter. The new opponents, Conservatives and ultra-Nazis, behaved as the left had done before. They announced that it was time to bell the cat without making any serious attempt to do so. Hitler on the other hand did not joke where power was concerned, and that was the reason for his superiority. He was always at war and in war any advantage counted, whereas his opponents believed that they were living in peace, under laws. One need only consider how easily General von Schleicher, for example, allowed himself to be caught and killed, and did not believe the warnings which he had been given. Hitler was well aware of this attitude, made fun of it and challenged the world to follow his example. The world did not do so for a very long time and until it did he proceeded from triumph to triumph. When it finally decided to follow his example and to meet him with equal determination he was lost.

The method of surprise attack in fact robbed Hitler's victories of a good deal of their reality. Although he liked to talk about destruction, extermination and eradication his method was merely suppression. The *Länder*, even Bavaria, the oldest and strongest among them, seemed to have vanished for ever in 1933. Yet they exist again today. The same is true of the political parties and the trade unions. They reappeared, not always identical with their predecessors but continuing old traditions, as soon as the spell had been lifted from them. Remarkably few National Socialists were found in Germany after Hitler's collapse. How different was the situation in Russia where there had been a genuine, terrible civil war and where the old classes and institutions were indeed destroyed; there they cannot come back.

For the moment many of the vanquished joined the victors, either from opportunism or from conviction. The inglorious end of the parties seemed proof that they deserved their fate. The Republic itself, it must be admitted, had not been worth much. Was liberalism not really out of date, were party dictatorship and the 'totalitarian state' not more suited to the times? It was a nuisance to some people that they could no longer read uncensored leading articles, but on the other hand the state of the economy improved. Foreign policy also improved – a development which could not fail to please every patriot, Nazi or non-Nazi. In 1932 Germany's position in the world had still – allegedly – been threatened, weak and discredited. Two or three years later the situation was different. The Reich was wooed from all sides and concessions were made to it which nobody would have dreamt of in Stresemann's or Brüning's time.

3. Foreign Policy

Hitler lived by a few simple ideas: Nature is cruel. As part of nature man is justified in being cruel. Life is war. There is always war, only its form changes. As a predatory animal lives at the expense of other animals a nation lives at the expense of other nations. What it wants to enjoy it must take away from others. If it wants to enjoy safety it must either exterminate its neighbours or at least render them permanently impotent. Compassion, charity, truthfulness, loyalty to obligations, all the Christian virtues are inventions of cowards and weaklings. Nature does not know them; the strong man does not observe them. He kills the weak; he lies and breaks treaties where it is to his advantage. The world has always been like this, all great empires have risen in this way, the Roman, the British, and the German Empire too shall arise in this way . . .

The extent to which this view of the universe permeated the man's whole conscious life, to which he openly expressed it at all times, to which he acted in precise accordance with it must surprise anyone who has not lost all capacity for surprise. On the first page of his first book he had written: 'When the territory of the Reich embraces all the Germans and finds itself unable to assure them a livelihood, only then can the moral right arise, from the need of the people, to acquire foreign territory. The plough is then the sword; and the tears of war will produce the daily bread for centuries to come.' Twenty years later, a few months before the end, he philosophized in a speech to German officers:

Among the events which are fundamentally immutable, which remain the same in all ages and only vary with regard to the form of the means employed is war. Nature teaches us at every glance at its doings that it is dominated by the principle of selection, that the strong is victorious and the weak is defeated . . . Any other universal system, any other universal law is unthinkable in a universe in which the fixed stars force planets to circle round them and in which planets force moons into their orbits, in which suns are destroyed in a day and re-placed by others. Nature also teaches us that what applies in the macro-cosm is equally self-evident as a law in the microcosm. Above all Nature is unfamiliar with the concept of humanity which says that the weak must in all circumstances be preserved and assisted . . . We human beings have not created this world, we are merely small bacteria or bacilli on this planet. We cannot deny these laws, we cannot undo them . . . What appears cruel to man is self-evidently wise from the point of view of Nature. A nation that cannot maintain itself vanishes and another takes its place . . . Nature distributes living beings all over the world and lets them fight for their fodder, their daily bread; the strong keeps or gains his place and the weak loses it or fails to gain it. In other words war is inevitable. The fact that a state, a nation or a people is small does not fill Nature with pity, on the contrary, it will mercilessly do away with whatever is not strong enough and this apparently merciless cruelty in the last resort contains cold common sense.

This was the philosophy; crude naturalism, acquired from inferior followers of Darwin and transferred to politics. With its banal truths and banal falsehoods it would not be worth mentioning if its prophet, who was the German head of state, had not seriously set out to deal with the peoples of Europe in accordance with its concepts.

His practical plan was roughly divided into four stages, four thrusts each of which was meant to impart some of its impetus to the next. First Germany must, as the saying went, be freed from the 'fetters of the Versailles Treaty'. The aim was popular and plausible; we have seen that all was not well with the Versailles treaty. Hitler, however, regarded this aim as completely inadequate; the mere restoration of the frontiers of 1914 was not enough for the sacrifice of millions of German lives. Secondly it was necessary to make Bismarck's restricted national state into one which embraced Austria and Bohemia, which reached as far as German was spoken. Thirdly it had been realized since 1848 that such a pan-German Reich would have its own dynamic; it must expand and in one way or another rule the small Slav and Danube nations. Finally, there was the question of Russia. Hitler had calculated that Russia alone provided the space needed by Germany to become a nation of 200 million people, a *Herrenvolk*, a people that would rule the world; and that Bolshevism which he regarded as a Jewish, basically weak form of government offered the Germans a welcome opportunity to realize that ambition. Although there was nothing much to be gained in western Europe Germany must control it. Probably Germany would have to conquer western Europe which was unlikely to agree peacefully to German domination. Nevertheless western Europe was only a secondary theatre of conflict, Franco-German enmity could be settled quickly with the left hand when the occasion arose. With Britain Hitler would have preferred to be on good terms; if people there would listen, it might be possible to rule jointly with them up to a certain point. Those were Hitler's basic ideas. They were developed in *Mein Kampf*, published in 1925, and Hitler did not deviate from them for twenty years. Three days after becoming Chancellor he said in an address to the commanders of the armed forces that 'to conquer new *Lebensraum* in the East and ruthlessly to germanize this area' would be the aim of his policy.

The various ideas and emotions had come to him from different sources; from Austria came antisemitism, hatred of Slavs and pan-German nationalism; from the war years the concept of *Lebensraum*, the idea of almost unlimited conquest in all directions, particularly in the East; from German historians and philosophers the equation of might with right, the contempt for moral considerations. Hitler's own contribution lay in the determination and mad logic with which he set about achieving his aims. Added to this there was his evaluation of one historical event which he had witnessed. He was firmly convinced that given better leadership Germany could have won the war, that, in fact, no more would have been necessary than the early elimination of all 'Marxist traitors'. Now he wanted to govern Germany in such a way that, as he said a thousand times, there could be 'no second 1918'.

We are concerned with general history not biography and therefore need not delve into the dark recesses of the mind which produced these forces, these motives and judgements. Hitler's plan was not merely impractical, it was bound, if implemented, sooner or later to destroy itself; nor was it consistent or sincere; it was bad literature. Someone who hated humanity as much as he did and who wanted his nation to prosper at the expense of humanity could not love his nation bearing in mind that it too consisted of human beings. Hitler wanted to dominate his people, who happened to be the Germans, and through them the world; but not, as he persuaded himself and them, for their benefit. He wanted power in his own interest, in the interest of the devil. Hitler had many faces. Yet when he said in 1945 that he was indifferent to the fate of the Germans and that if they could not follow him to the end they deserved to go under, and acted accordingly – that was the moment when he showed his true face. For the time being, while Germany was not ready for war he was forced to hide many things, not only his innermost plans, nature and aims, but other things as well. The man of war was compelled to act the man of peace. This was difficult or should have been difficult because in his early years he had gone fairly far in revealing his dreams; his ideas were there, in black and white. But the world wants to be deceived, particularly if one tells it what it believes to be true, desirable and sensible. In that case it is only too happy to forget who the person is who tells it these things. Perhaps the hothead had become reasonable with the years and with the burden of responsibility. Apparently he had, because what he told peace-hungry Europe for five years in countless 'peace speeches' was all sensible: War was madness, it could only lead to the destruction of civilization; no nation was more in need of peace than the German nation; it only wanted, like any honourable person, to regain its honour, and it was ready to respect the honour and interests of other nations, great and small; his aim was not domination but equality, and so on – who could find fault with these sentiments? Step by step he moved towards his goal, towards war. Each step was more daring than the last. After each step he stopped and carefully restored the world's faith in him with more talk of peace and new offers, making sure that no effective action would be taken against him by interpreting all his actions in philosophical terms understood by the rest of the world, invoking justice, economic common sense, national self-determination and so on. This deceit must have given him tremendous pleasure and he probably had not believed himself that the world could be deceived so easily for so long. He also deceived his own people. This helped because if the Germans had known what was at stake it would have been impossible to deceive the world. A whole nation cannot play-act. But the overwhelming majority of Germans was as peace-loving as the French and the British. They liked to hear the things which their *Führer* told them about honour, equality and constructive work; they liked to hear them all the more because he used the occasions to display exactly as much masculine self-assertion as it was possible to display without danger. Only a very small circle knew Hitler's innermost ideas and even this circle learnt them only gradually. Others knew, without being told, by remembering what he had said and written earlier, and still more by direct and unmistakable aesthetic and moral observations. These people, whether they stayed at home or emigrated, shared Cassandra's unhappy fate.

When Hitler came to power the dictator or semi-dictator of Poland, Marshal Pilsudski, approached the French to ask whether it would not be best to act at once and to nip the rising danger in the bud. The French vacillated and after the new man's first big 'peace speech' it became much more difficult for them to decide on action. The pattern for all future diplomatic crises between 1933 and 1939 was set. If *one* power – France, Poland, Britain or Russia – was or seemed prepared to act the others were not, and as nobody wanted to act alone, nobody acted. Not *against* Germany; but each of the European powers was from time to time prepared to negotiate independently *with* Germany, so that their partners, friends and allies found themselves unpleasantly surprised by some bilateral statement or agreement; because no joint action could be agreed upon it was a case of each man for himself or *sauve qui peut*.

In the spring of 1933 the Reich and Austria became involved in a diplomatic conflict which was also a political or domestic one. The situation in Austria was more or less as it would have been if Bavaria had not surrendered in March 1933. Austria was, or professed to be, a German state. But it was not part of the Reich, it had not been co-ordinated. It was ruled by the Christian Socialists, a strongly Austrian-accentuated variant of the Centre. Tension in Austria was much greater than in Bavaria, not only between the Christian Socialist Party and the Austrian Nazis who in practice aimed at unification of the *Ostmark* with the Reich but also between the government party and the Social Democrats who ruled the capital, Vienna. There was therefore a twofold split of the nation in Austria. The Chancellor, Dollfuss, saw no way of avoiding the fate of Bavaria but dictatorship, exercised by his own party. When the Nazi organizations were proscribed Germany replied by pressure, by closing the frontiers; every German who wanted to travel to Austria bought permission with a large sum of money. Austria was poorer than Germany and took much longer to overcome the economic crisis. This fact, combined with the country's old, pan-German and antisemitic traditions made it possible for the proscribed Nazi Party to gain more and more followers.

In the autumn of 1933 a disarmament conference met in Geneva without achieving anything. In principle it had been recognized that Germany was entitled to equal rights. France, realizing that it was much inferior to the Germans in population, industry and vitality, did not seriously want to disarm but merely to talk about disarmament. This gave Hitler a welcome pretext; he claimed that he had not asked for arms for Germany but merely for equal rights, for disarmament by the others. Because this just demand had never been complied with, Germany was unfortunately compelled to leave the League of Nations. The gesture pleased the Germans. It was a gesture of freedom and pride, justified with well-sounding phrases. Hastily asked whether it approved of its government's foreign policy the nation gave an overwhelmingly positive reply, this time even without the need for much pressure from above. Meanwhile the government had already begun to re-arm secretly and openly, and to establish new divisions.

In January 1934 Poland and Germany announced that henceforth they would not use force against each other, that they would solve any difficulties that might arise by peaceful means and live together in friendship. The agreement was intended to be valid for ten years in the first instance. It was a clever move which helped to undermine the French system of alliances in the East and made possibilities of German–Polish collaboration against Russia appear on the distant horizon. It showed – or did it not? – that the new German rulers had incomparably more courage and power than the old Weimar government which would never have dared to enter into friendly relations with Poland as long as there was the 'Corridor' and Danzig and Upper Silesia. All this Hitler now seemed to accept, at least for ten years. Why, he asked in private, should I not sign a treaty today if it brings advantages, and break it tomorrow?

In February 1934 the Austrian Chancellor, Dollfuss, to demonstrate that he too was a strong man and no friends of the Marxists, aimed a blow at the Vienna Social Democrats. They defended themselves, more resolutely than the German Social Democrats; but the ruling party and its armed might were stronger. Austria now also had its one-party state, its bursting prisons and its murdered Socialists, though all only on a very small scale. In the background there was Mussolini's Italy which tried to gain the friendship of both Austria and Hungary and to play them off against Germany. In July 1934 the Austrian National Socialists attacked; they tried to gain power, not legally on the January 1933 pattern but more on the pattern of November 1923. Dollfuss, the dictator, was murdered in his official residence. But once again the state, provided it dared to defend itself, proved stronger than the insurgents. Although the Nazis had the support of at least a third of all the Austrians they could not conquer the state. And because Mussolini drew up his divisions on the Brenner as a threat or for protection, Hitler did not dare to help from outside. He rapidly extricated himself from the affair. It was announced that the Reich had nothing whatsoever to do with the regrettable happenings in Austria; anybody who had helped to create a contrary impression would not escape punishment. It is interesting to note how quickly Hitler gave way when he encountered determined opposition and people might have learnt from the occasion. However, it remained the only time between 1933 and 1938 when a foreign power stood up to Hitler.

In January 1935 the inhabitants of the Saar voted on whether they wanted to remain under the administration of the League of Nations or return to Germany. The Versailles treaty had provided for a referendum fifteen years after the peace treaty. The Social Democrats in the Saar fought for the *status quo*, from their point of view with good reason; but the natural feeling of being part of the great fatherland which was so visibly on the way up, together with Goebbels' propaganda, was stronger than all political stratagems. The Saar voted to return to Germany, and a new wave of emigrants, honest workers who had allowed themselves to be exploited or deceived by politics, spilt into France.

In 1934 and 1935 under the German threat Stalin's Russia moved closer to western Europe. To what extent the move was meant seriously nobody could say; nor did anybody know how serious were Hitler's rhetorical attacks on Communism. In any case the Soviet Union joined the League of Nations. In 1935 it even concluded a defensive treaty with France and Europe thus found itself at the point of departure of 1917: a strong country at the centre flanked by powers allied against it. But neither France nor Germany, nor Russia were what they had been in 1895; history does not repeat itself so simply. In France above all the political blocs, right and left, were evenly balanced and opinions, wishes and fears neutralized each other in such a way that action in one direction or another was impossible. Nationalistic and anti-German by tradition the right was attracted by Hitler's anti-Communism, feeling that France might perhaps co-operate with him in that. The left was by tradition pro-German and pacifist; although bound to see the German system as its enemy it nevertheless approved of many of the things which Hitler did or said; it did not know what it wanted. Internal conflict, excited inactivity, the gloomy suspicion that everything done in the past had been wrong and that what was being done now was still wrong – this was no soil for useful alliances. The Franco-Russian alliance remained a scrap of paper.

In March 1935 Hitler went a step further and proclaimed Germany's right to rearm; at the same time he announced conscription. This was nothing new; merely that the veil was dramatically pulled away from a state of affairs that had long existed. The *Reichswehr* became the *Wehrmacht*. It was said that it would serve the cause of peace, not war, and protect Europe from Bolshevism; and the Germans felt that this was true; why should Germany alone not be allowed to do what all the others did? The representatives of the Western powers, there for form's sake, could not spoil the grand military parade in front of the Berlin *Schloss*. Three months later Britain concluded a unilateral naval treaty with Germany, under the terms of which there was in principle to be one German naval vessel for every three British vessels except in the case of submarines where the proportion was to be one to one. With this step the other side, the victors, also finally renounced the armaments restrictions of the Treaty of Versailles. France shook its head anxiously and helplessly.

Perhaps France should try to win over Italy against Germany? After all in the previous year the head of the Italian government had demonstrated such successful energy in the Austrian affair. This might be possible, but at a price. Italy wanted to use the general disorder, the collapse of the system of Versailles, to acquire an empire in Africa; according to Mussolini, a great people needed an empire. This Italian one would be created in Abyssinia. The scheme was contrary to the Covenant of the League of Nations of which Abyssinia was a member. But what if Italy was needed against Germany? In that case France must secretly agree to let Italy have its war in Africa while protesting in public; it must allow Italy to break the law in the hope of winning its support against a future German breach of the law. Mussolini sent his army to Addis Ababa. The League of Nations decided on economic sanctions against the aggressor, but only of a variety which did not seriously impede his military activities, which insulted him in a welcome way without hurting him. The sanctions encouraged the Abyssinians to offer hopeless resistance but did not help them; France, by betraying what had so far been regarded as the basic idea of the League of Nations did not win Italy as an ally but merely weakened its own cause, and someone else took the opportunity to strike a hard blow at the international system of law.

In March 1936 Hitler tore up the Locarno Pact. In addition to providing various artificial guarantees the Pact had confirmed an invention thought up at Versailles, the 'demilitarization' of the Rhineland; Germany was not allowed to build fortifications west of the Rhine, or to have garrisons there. Demilitarization was a substitute for the buffer state which Clemenceau was not given in 1919; the demilitarized zone, it was hoped, would save France and Belgium from surprise attacks. But such 'neutralized' zones offer no protection. Hitler just sent a few battalions across the Rhine; a symbol to be followed by more important things, by the construction of fortifications along the frontier. It was the usual early spring surprise; the Germans liked it and why not, after all it merely redressed an old wrong, it contravened an antiquated, vindictive law? The Archbishop of Cologne personally sent the German garrison a telegram of congratulation.

In its way the occupation of the Rhineland was nevertheless as decisive an event as the Reichstag fire. If the Western powers allowed the Locarno Pact to be torn up they would accept more, they would let Germany become the dominating power at least in central and eastern Europe. Whereas acquiescence would mean the collapse of the French system of alliances if France reacted now, Hitler must quickly withdraw his battalions across the Rhine, and after that almost anything might happen, even the collapse of the dictatorship. The German generals, Blomberg, Fritsch and Beck, indeed expected the French to act and warned Hitler against his adventure. For three days it seemed as though this time he had overplayed his hand. The French moved troops and made really threatening speeches for the first time since 1933. Then, however, the French politicians started to negotiate, not at first with Germany but with their British friends, and thereafter, as Hitler observed happily, 'they could only talk it to shreds'. Once more France was paralysed by doubt: Why should the Germans not take for themselves a right which all other nations had? Why should they be prevented from marching against Russia, if that was really their intention? German propaganda performed its most impressive achievement so far. The venture, whose purpose was to isolate France and to cut it off from its allies in the East, was presented as an offer of eternal friendship between Germany and the Western powers; as the offer of a brother's outstretched hand across the Rhine. Again, as after Germany's withdrawal from the League of Nations, the nation was asked to express approval of Hitler's action in a plebiscite; the real issue was said to be whether the electorate wanted Europe to be united and to end the age-old Franco-German enmity or not. The 'electoral campaign' was conducted on this basis. After being inundated for some weeks with 'peace speeches' and at the end even treated to a minute's silence the nation went to the polls to the sound of bells and sirens; 'anyone who does not turn out to vote is a traitor'. It was therefore hardly surprising that ninety-nine per cent of the electorate voted for all the great things that were allegedly involved. At that moment Hitler's popularity had reached its zenith; it even infected the rest of the world. If only a few days previously the British had discussed what measures to take against the Reich, a wave of pro-German sympathy now swept across Britain affecting even the government. It was felt that here at last was an opportunity for a constructive new beginning, that a second, better 'Locarno' must replace the first. Hitler emerged triumphant from the most daring of his adventures so far, having taken on the whole world, despite his generals' warnings. It cannot be said that the experience changed his character; this was moulded before, just as his aims were by and large determined before. However, the episode convinced him still further that he was the chosen, the infallible one, and thus speeded up certain developments.

First of all, to quote the German Foreign Minister, it was necessary to 'digest' the Rhineland, that is to say to build the fortifications later called the West Wall; while this went on there was peace, a period of calm, of appeasement, as the new British Prime Minister, Neville Chamberlain, called it.

Although the Spanish civil war falls into this period it has no place in a history of Germany. It was Spanish in character and ought never to have become identified with the fluctuating and imprecise conflicts in Europe, between Germany and the Western powers, Germany and Russia, Fascism and Communism, capitalism and socialism. Spain was a lonely country and it ought to have been left to its solitude; its internal, purely Spanish conflict might then have been resolved more quickly and in a less terrible fashion. In fact the Germans and the Italians helped General Franco, and the Russians and the French aided the Republicans, a bloc consisting of a motley collection of moderate liberals, Social Democrats, regionalists, anarchists, Communists and gangs of murderers. Help was not given for philanthropic but for political and strategic reasons, and also purely to gain military experience. The fact that government and rebel forces in Spain could murder each other for years with European help throws a terrible light on the period of 'appeasement'. Nevertheless Spain was only a secondary stage for German, Italian and Russian politics; in the end it was only Spanish, not European decisions which were taken here.

Meanwhile the balance of power in Europe shifted from month to month. The German Reich was once more the centre of attention, not passively and plaintively as in the twenties, but actively as before 1914; a centre of unrest, of danger, of attraction. This state of affairs had come about even though Germany had not yet regained any of the territory lost in 1919, merely because of its internal energy and because of a leadership whose determined ability was in marked contrast to the weak, ineffectual behaviour of the West. On paper France still had alliances with Poland, Czechoslovakia, Rumania and Yugoslavia, added to which there was now also the Franco-Russian pact. This, however, confused the system of alliances instead of strengthening it; the small Eastern states feared Russia, and with good reason. The fact that the Franco-Russian pact existed on paper only did not help. As Germany's military position in the West grew stronger the fear increased that France had secretly already abandoned its central European allies; and the Danube and Balkan states, mostly ruled by corrupt semi-dictators, once so insolent and boastful, became increasingly anxious to please Germany. How could a nation maintain an effective system of alliances if it did not trust itself, if it did not know what it wanted and if it preferred to be left in peace by the world and to live alone. No dramatic blows were needed to break up the French alliance system; it gradually rotted away. Economic factors entered. Germany, not France, had always been the big buyer and seller on the central European markets. Under Hjalmar Schacht's so-called 'New Plan' this relationship assumed curious forms; in order to avoid spending foreign exchange Germany concluded a number of bilateral agreements, barter arrangements in effect, as a result of which the states of central and south-eastern Europe became increasingly dependent on Germany. As long as Germany paid with useful finished goods and not with loot there was little objection to this method. Britain, for example, regarded this development as fundamentally natural. Neville Chamberlain thought good-naturedly that there was no cause for anxiety if Germany wanted to revive its economy and that of the south-eastern states by intensive bilateral trade; sooner or later the British exporter would also somehow benefit.

This was the direction in which events seemed to be moving in the period of appeasement. The problems and conflicts of the war were out of date because Germany had long ceased to be the vanquished nation of 1918. It was as feared and powerful as under the Hohenzollern, even more powerful because France was weaker than before, because the whole European system was weaker, and because in central Europe there was no longer the Habsburg monarchy but a collection of artificial, small states distrustful and envious of each other. They all now fell under the political, economic and moral influence of the Reich. This happened without a great crisis, without a severe test of the French system of alliances. It was Europe's weakness which tempted Hitler to go further. He was not satisfied with the prospect of peaceful development, of unspectacular, gradual and indirect victory; this was not enough for him. He had conquered Germany in order to fight the war over again, with the right aims, avoiding all the mistakes which in his view had been made the first time; not in order to hand over to his successor the Reich with the frontiers of 1914, still less with those of 1919.

The attitude of the Czechs suited his plans. They alone, among all the nations living between Russia and Germany, did not participate in the new development, did not adapt themselves to the new tone. Under their Foreign Minister and future President, Eduard Beneš, they banked on the French alliance, flattering themselves that they formed a strategic and intellectual bridge between France and Russia, and clung to the visibly vanishing tradition of the League of Nations. One can understand their attitude. Rumania, Yugoslavia, Poland, states which had to some extent been tested by experience, thought that they could preserve their national existence even in a Europe overshadowed by Germany. The Czech politicians thought differently. Their state was too new, its establishment had cost too little, it extended too far into German territory and was too chequered in ethnic composition; there was no such thing as a Czechoslovak nation-state and the dominant nationality, the Czech one, was in a minority compared with the other nationalities, Germans, Slovaks, Ruthenes and Hungarians, inside its own straggling frontiers. Not, it must be admitted, a very reliable bridge between France and Russia. If anything, Czechoslovakia was a pawn in the European game, so weak, standing there astride, that it might well tempt the strong, the adventurer to push it over; if that happened the whole artificial system of Versailles would collapse.

Then there was always still the Austrian state. Another post-war creation which had come into life reluctantly, it was poor, cut off and full of social tensions. Since 1934 Austria was living under a dictatorship which imitated the Reich and even more so Italy. It is impossible to say how many supporters Hitler had there because they were never freely counted; moreover, people were not 'Nazis' for ever; it was possible not to have been one yesterday, to be one today and to cease being one tomorrow, according to the circumstances. The Austrian figures probably corresponded roughly to the German ones of before 1933; certain regions were more hardened in error than for example Bavaria or Württemberg or Hamburg. To ask whether this meant that Austria wanted the *Anschluss* would be to ask the wrong question. A country after all is not a single-minded living being, and Austria, split into religious groups and classes which had only recently literally been at war with each other, was even less single-minded than other nations. This much one can say metaphorically: whereas in 1919 it had in fact wanted to join a federalist Germany, later it gradually abandoned the idea and went its own way. Even the Austrian Fascists probably attached less importance to unification with Germany than to obtaining power in Austria which they expected to remain autonomous within Germany. In fact the country had come to a dead end. A large part of the population, the Social Democrats, was silenced politically, embittered and could no longer be mobilized for the country's defence. The government did not deny that Austria was German, the 'other German state', an 'independent, German, Christian Austria' and so on. This was a clumsy move because, if Austria was German there was really no reason why it should not be part of *one* great German state in which, according to fashionable theory, the nation would realize itself politically. Originally, moreover, Austria owed its existence not to its own determination but to France's desire for a balance of power, to the will of the victors, to the League of Nations. Now the League of Nations was only a legend, France was weak, unanxious to act and without sympathy for the clerical semi-Fascism which reigned in Austria. The people on whom independence had been forced, who even in 1931 had stupidly not been allowed to form a simple customs union with Germany, were now left to find themselves a protector. To their own surprise they found it in Italy. There was something sinister about this development because traditionally there was no love between Italy and Austria; nor could the boastful Mussolini be relied upon. Blinded by Hitler's rising star the Italian dictator in 1937 hastily linked the fate of his country with that of Germany. The name of the so-called 'Berlin–Rome Axis' implied that Europe turned round it; though not yet a treaty of alliance it was the prospect of one. Henceforth Austria's chances of emerging safely from the crisis were remote.

The states between Russia and Germany were weak from within, imitation nation-states, imitation democracies, imitation monarchies, founded on the temporary impotence of the Germans and the Russians. They were secretly prepared to come to terms with Germany, provided that they could preserve what they had, or acquire a little illicit gain. In the East there was the powerful Soviet Union, threatened by Germany and apparently afraid and looking for allies, but feared as well and thoroughly disliked; moreover, troubled by internal persecution, treason and witch-hunting trials it was unlikely to be a reliable ally. In the West the old victorious powers had long abandoned their victory. Britain, credulous and anxious to observe the letter of the law, was still hopeful that, provided Germany was allowed to have whatever it claimed, lasting peace might be obtainable after all. France, divided and torn, was incapable of making timely concessions or seriously prepared to defend what it wanted to preserve, pursuing a diplomacy of collecting allies without trusting them and of expecting help in need without wanting to give any. At the centre there was the Reich, governed by a man who knew what he wanted and who played the game in deadly earnest, to whom every combination was open and who was ready to use them all in turn and to abandon them again; a man who used ideas like weapons, suiting them to the political situation, 'equality of rights', 'liberation', 'unification of all Germans', *Lebensraum*', 'Europe'; a man whose contempt for the world grew as he came to know its tolerance, credulity, lack of purpose and impotence. There was the Reich, ruled by a man who was *always* at war whereas the others wanted the world now and for ever to be at peace, a man to whom even his partners' and opponents' desire for peace was a useful weapon. How well Hitler talked, how sensibly, how profoundly and chivalrously; how well he knew how to take his opponents' most attractive arguments and to serve them up as his very own, innermost convictions. A different note was sounded when he was alone with his followers. On 5 November 1937 he said to a small circle of military and political collaborators that the time for decision was approaching. The extra *Lebensraum* which the Germans needed could only be obtained at the expense of other nations, and only in Europe. There had to be a war. Germany must attack, at the latest in 1943, perhaps long before then, depending on circumstances. These remarks were received with dismay by the soldiers present. Yet they can hardly have come as a surprise to them.

4. The Nazi State

The time has come to take a look at the state that was to be led into the great adventure.

'National Socialism', its spokesman often said, was a *Weltanschauung*, an ideology. Basically, however, it was not; not in the sense that Communism for example was. Communism was an elaborate system of doctrines about the world, man and history; false science, false religion which many people seriously believed in. Many people died willingly for Communism, including German Communists. In places where the party was proscribed its followers went underground and when, years later, the pressure was lifted, they reappeared – genuine, indestructible fanatics that they were. The Nazis also boasted of their fanatical faith – they were very fond of the word 'fanatical' – but their fanaticism was only skin deep. Fanaticism demands faith, and what did the Nazis believe in? When Hitler's Reich was broken up almost no National Socialists were to be found. People claimed that they had never been Nazis, that they had known nothing, that they had been forced to join in or had joined in merely to prevent worse things from happening, not because they acted in accordance with their beliefs. Only in the disputed frontier regions where there was momentarily no distinction between the Nazi cause and the pan-German nationalistic one, as in Austria in 1934, were people ready to die for the cause. This was the exception, not the rule. Democrats, Socialists, students, conservative noblemen and trade unionists risked their lives in Germany for the sake of human decency. The Nazis wanted to live and enjoy life.

When these words were written people were saying that there were still or again 'National Socialists' in Germany. One wonders why they should be called thus. Because they believe that not everything that Hitler did was wrong; that Germany was entitled to tear up the Versailles treaty; that the West should not have stabbed Germany in the back when it was defending Europe against Bolshevism; that the Germans were the most industrious nation in Europe; that firm, secure government was needed; and more such things. These may have been sentiments and opinions which National Socialism made use of. But they were there before; they survived National Socialism, and their sum total does not by any means add up to the essence of National Socialism.

What then was National Socialism? It was an historically unique phenomenon, dependent on an individual and on a moment, a phenomenon which can never reappear in the same form. It was a state of intoxication produced by a gang of intoxicated experts, kept up for a few years. It was a machine for the manufacture of power, for the safeguarding of power and for the extension of power. The machine was located in Germany and therefore used to fuel German energies, German interests, passions and ideas. 'We want power' – this cry of the year 1932 was the essence of the new message. Power meant organization, indoctrination and the authority to give orders; it meant the suppression of all independent life, of anything capable of resistance. In that sense it was essentially a negative element. The power of National Socialism over Germany thus only became complete when the Reich was close to collapse, when its army had already been defeated.

The determination to have power was considerable; the doctrine was not. Who can say today what the Nazis 'taught'? The superiority of the Nordic race? They made fun of it, admitting when they were among themselves that it was a weapon not a truth. Few of them seemed to have seriously believed this nonsense. Antisemitism? This was probably the most genuine feeling of which Hitler was capable, but it was hardly a *Weltanschauung*. Nor did antisemitism arouse the imagination of the Germans among whom it was no stronger than among most other nations. Later, when the authorities ordered the murder of Europe's Jews there were people prepared to do this, just as they would have carried out any other order. Himmler himself said shortly before the end that it was time for Germans and Jews to bury the hatchet and to become reconciled. When he wanted to save himself and worm his way into the Allies' favour he pretended that the murder of the Jews was nothing but a regrettable misunderstanding. This was not an article of faith but crime produced by evil propaganda. The same was true of the old Party programme, abandoned as soon as the Nazis came to power, of the economic theories and the talk about the common good. One member of the gang, the President of the People's Court during the war years, said that the bond between National Socialism and Christianity was that both claimed the whole man. Yet even that was only evil propaganda, boasting, imitation of the Communists, of the Jacobins. He would not have been able to say for what National Socialism required the whole man. Relatively the most interesting formulations of the Nazi theory came from outsiders who were quick to place their talents at the disposal of the new rulers and to credit them with all sorts of refinements. Equally there were German scholars who did not find it difficult to avoid the whole mishmash and who followed their pursuits as before; much less difficult than it is under Communism. As personified in its leaders 'National Socialism' was a determination of tremendous intensity which cared for nothing but itself and was for that reason identical with cynical opportunism; without its leaders it did not exist at all. Hence it vanished with Hitler's death and at the time people looked at each other in surprise as though they had woken from a long period of bewitchment. If the Nazis believed in anything they believed in the great man. If he believed in anything it was in himself; in the last years of his life conviction that he was the chosen one assumed dimensions which can no longer be called human.

In the opportunist who used ideas without remaining loyal to them people saw what they wanted to see. Good citizens who in spite of excesses that unfortunately were undeniable felt all in all quite happy in the Third Reich, admired the man of order who had restored discipline. Erich Marcks, a Prussian historian of the national liberal school, a friend and pupil of Treitschke, a worshipper of Bismarck whom he had known personally, believed in his old age that he was in the presence of a second, greater Bismarck, and that the work of the Iron Chancellor was at last splendidly crowned. For others Hitler was the revolutionary nationalist, a Socialist, a man who had liberated the country from the burdens of the past; for others still he was the great internationalist and unifier of Europe. For very many people he was simply the man who was lucky and who always knew what to do, today one thing, tomorrow another. When he was successful and there was a dramatic but pleasant occurrence such as the annexation of Austria, the vast majority of Germans really were 'Nazis'. When nothing happened, when the situation became difficult, dangerous and finally desperate the number of Nazis declined rapidly and was much less than in 1932. At the end there were scarcely any Nazis.

In the thirties there was much scepticism in Germany, much cynicism and rootlessness. Most people did not believe what their rulers said but when asked officially whether they supported 'their government's policy' they voted 'yes'. Life was hard, how hard had recently been demonstrated by the years of economic crisis. Now that there was work again and opportunity of promotion and reasonable security people's attitude was that it would be foolish to risk everything for the sake of mere political differences. Success justified those at the top. People who resisted and who thought they knew better learnt in concentration camps or Gestapo cellars who was the master. No doubt they were unfortunate, but then why be so irresponsible and stubborn; for the others, for the vast majority who suffered no such experiences life was not bad all in all. People could live, earn money and, until the economy was placed completely in the service of the war effort, buy pleasant things with it. If Nazism isolated its opponents, uprooted them or benefited from the fact that they had long lost their roots, in its way it provided others with a home, with spiritual shelter. How attractive it could make itself, for instance at the Nuremberg Party rallies. There were marches past by hundreds of thousands of healthy young people, gymnastic displays in imposing arenas, torchlight processions and fireworks; true, the participants were made to listen to long speeches but those seemed of secondary importance. The Labour Front into which young people were conscripted was frequently a great experience for the middle-class citizen or the intellectual. It brought him into far closer contact with the 'community' than the Weimar Republic ever had done. People were happy to belong: as one of hundreds of thousands of Party officials, as youth leaders, student leaders and 'Strength through Joy' organizers, to bear whatever small share of responsibility they were given, to obey and to command. The nature of youth, the nature of the Germans, the nature of man which normally derives more satisfaction from helping than from oppressing and tormenting, was stronger than the mad orders from above; not always, but by and large. The Nazis behaved like foreign conquerors, exploiting the country, putting the people in their place with massive, vulgar monuments, with rallies and parades designed to make the individual feel small, with columns of enormous limousines occupied by black uniformed men and in the last resort with the prison camp watch towers and machine guns. They knew how to make power terrifying. But they also knew how to identify themselves with the masses whom they had conquered, how to make them shout themselves hoarse with enthusiasm and how to give the young a feeling of well-being and happiness. They could act the part of grim tyrants and of jolly buffoons, and knew how to make themselves more popular than any German monarch had ever been. If one says that their regime was alien to the country one is speaking the truth, and if one says that it was the most genuinely German, the most popular form of government in modern times, one is also speaking the truth. What Nazism was and what it did cannot be condensed into a single concept, unless it be one the formulation of which sounds highly artificial: it was a combination of identity and non-identity. Nazism was as German as anything could be, produced and supported by a wider cross-section of the population than any previous German system of government; this is the most serious accusation that one can make against the Germans. At the same time it was something foreign, reminiscent of the Hauptmann von Köpenick who disguised himself as the town's commander and whom the town obeyed because it was accustomed only to obedience. The town, those living nearby and even the outside world were deceived by the disguise. In 1938 Chamberlain firmly believed that Hitler was Germany's legitimate representative and that it was with him and not with any treacherous opposition that Britain must come to terms. Long after 1945 French historians specializing in German history were still delving into the prehistory of National Socialism in order to prove that for a hundred years German history had moved with unerring certainty towards this cataract. They saw the identity but overlooked the non-identity. It must be said that the non-identity did not harm the rulers; on the contrary, indirectly they benefited from it. Apart from the wartime conspiracies the feeling of not wanting to be identified with the regime and of disgust shared by many Germans did not express itself in treasonable activity. It found an outlet in useful achievement because the best form of escape from an authority and a public life held in contempt was the private pursuit of specialized skills. What the state needed to fulfil its most extravagant plans was exactly this: scholars, bureaucrats and technicians doing their duty. The Army provides the most telling example. Generals who despised their new overlord devoted themselves all the more seriously to their practical tasks. Young men, disgusted by the brutalities of the regime, volunteered for military service hoping to breathe cleaner air in the Army and to enjoy greater legal protection. They did their duty and did it well; this meant that they helped to prepare Hitler's great war.

Although the Nazis meant the power of Party and state to be total, to be homogeneous, in reality the situation was different. The influence of the man at the top was great and those who regarded him as the tool of particular interests were much mistaken. He alone decided on war and peace, and later on war strategy. Beneath him, however, there was confusion and violent rivalry with everybody grabbing as much power as he possibly could. The courtiers around Hitler and the strong men in the provinces, ministers, *Gauleiter*, *Statthalter* and police chiefs, they all constituted centres of power which governed against each other, with their own cultural policy, their own spy system and their own forms of blackmail. To some extent this was Hitler's intention; it is after all an old tyrant's trick to play people and forces off against each other. Here, however, the practice went far beyond what was in the interest of the central authority.

Moreover the Party was not the only power in the state. The statement that it had 'conquered' the state was justified. But it implied that the conquered state continued to exist, in contrast to Russia where the Bolsheviks began afresh after the brutal destruction of everything. It was impossible to do this with the civilized German state, with its sensitive, vital organisms. In spite of all corruption, of all 'directions from above' and Party intervention the civil service continued its traditional work and many an industrious administrator had the sort of career he would have had under the Kaiser or the Republic. The same applied to industry. It has been said that German industry under Hitler continued to follow the course on which it set out in the time of the Hohenzollern and the Weimar Republic: rationalization, concentration, more trusts and increasing dependence on government contracts. From this it has been assumed that the Nazi state, independent though it pretended to be, was basically in the service of industrial interests. Is this not a false conclusion? Life continued. It continued to follow the old track, from that there was no escape. What was new was the political line and it was this which interested Hitler. In the main he allowed industry to continue as before, provided it delivered the goods needed for his policy. There is no reason to assume therefore that political decisions were not arrived at independently or that they did not play a decisive part. There are of course historians who believe that Germany was forced into war, in 1914 as in 1939, because of the false structure of its economy. But this is a metaphysical argument which cannot be proved. The threads which are supposed to have linked industry with the decisions in Hitler's head cannot be shown. Nor is this hypothesis needed to understand what happened in 1939 and afterwards. The dictatorship was a political one. As the strength of Hitler's personal position increased his policy became more daring, impatient and shameless, and he came closer to the execution of his own plans. His position was strengthened by a succession of thrusts, one of which occurred in the summer of 1934, another in the spring of 1936. In the autumn of that year he announced a new 'Four-Year Plan' designed to make Germany largely independent of the import of raw materials by the production of synthetic or substitute materials at home. The plan lacked substance and the Party member entrusted with its execution, the corrupt Hermann Göring, understood nothing about economics. Nevertheless, the plan made it possible to subordinate industry more than ever before to Party and political aims. Schacht's 'New Plan' had been determined by economic considerations: the desire to reduce imports of finished goods in favour of the import of raw materials and food, and to increase exports. Even Schacht's policy was designed to aid German rearmament but lefthandedly, only within the limits he considered economically bearable. After 1936 the Nazis went beyond these limits. The rulers said in memoranda and at meetings that it was more important to deliver the goods somehow than to produce them on an economically sound basis; there was no such word as 'impossible' in the vocabulary of National Socialism; faced with Germany's need to have the best army in the world all specialist doubt must be silenced; the economy must be harnessed

without regard to private interests, profitability or whatever else. The Ministry of Economics will set the target; let private enterprise think of ways of fulfilling it. If it proves incapable of doing so the National Socialist state will solve the problems itself . . . It will not be Germany that is ruined but merely certain industrialists. Within four years the German army must be ready for action and German industry must be prepared to mobilize for war,

said one of Hitler's memoranda of the year 1936. Impatient boasts that were not without practical consequences. Henceforth industry received its orders increasingly from Göring. Enormous sums went into unprofitable ventures and there was a shortage of consumer goods. The policy of 'advance financing' gave way to unrestricted deficit financing. In all this industry did not dictate to the politicians. It was the politicians who dictated to industry; as indeed the people were to an even greater degree dictated to and frightened by the police, and 'propaganda' increasingly gagged and deceived public opinion.

As the tyrant's true plans were gradually revealed it became more difficult for people to remain neutral, to tolerate the regime or to confine themselves to non-political work. The early illusions vanished and secret centres of criticism, repugnance and hatred appeared. We have seen how small the opposition was in 1933, at the time of the Enabling Law; then only the Social Democrats – the Communists were no longer consulted – remained aloof from the universal exuberance. The Conservatives supported the new regime, and so did the once liberal middle class and the Army. Men like Schacht, like the Mayor of Leipzig, Carl Goerdeler, joined in happily, and not even the mass murders of 1934 made them appreciate the true nature of the dictatorship. Now there was a change. Schacht and Goerdeler resigned in 1937 and formed a kind of opposition. Their attitude was ambiguous; they were part of the regime and yet they were not; they speculated with a few friends about actions that might possibly be taken in certain circumstances, but at the same time remained in touch with the rulers or at least with men close to the inner circle of power whom they suspected of sharing their views, generals, secretaries of state, ambassadors and industrialists. If Hitler had been unable to overthrow the weak Weimar state from without, a few disappointed Conservatives, unsupported by any party or popular sympathy could certainly not overthrow the strong and ruthless Nazi state from without. All they might hope to do was to prevent the worst, war, by warnings, indirect influence and by providing the outside world with information and suggestions. Here again the generals seemed to be holding the key to the situation, as common sense suggested that war could not be waged without military experts.

The generals did not want war. It was their duty to prepare for it, as was happening more or less efficiently in all European countries. But they were afraid that in a war on two fronts Germany would fare worse than in 1918 and they expected such a war every time Hitler embarked on a new adventure. On the other hand the Army's political power was nothing like as great now as it had been in 1933 and even then, as we have seen, it was not great enough to intervene decisively. The politician dominated the military experts as much as he dominated industry. They had their hands full establishing new divisions and creating an army of millions. This task they mastered; against their own interest if they had political ambitions. The new mass army was bound to be an even less reliable instrument in their hands than the *Reichswehr* had been. They disapproved of having to strengthen the Army hastily and without sufficient thoroughness; they disliked the *Führer*'s bluff and the vulgarity of the Party bosses. They exchanged worried letters and expressed their technical reservations at conferences. But they did not govern, they were experts. Moreover, when it came to the point, they allowed themselves to be humiliated.

One such incident occurred in the winter of 1938 which brought Hitler another increase in power. The Minister of War and the Commander-in-Chief of the Army, von Fritsch, resigned; the latter because of an odious defamation campaign against him by the secret police. The generals knew that their colleague was innocent but they allowed him to go. Not without anger, not without threatening noises as in 1933 and again after the murder of Schleicher; the Chief of Staff of the Army, Ludwig Beck, was ready to aim a strong blow at the slanderers, the police and the Party bosses, if the generals would follow him. They did not follow. Fritsch's successor, von Brauchitsch, started his activities by allowing Hitler to make him a present of a large sum of money. The Ministry of War was replaced by a 'High Command' under the dictator's control: 'Henceforth I shall personally take direct charge of the entire armed forces.' Sixty senior officers were retired and a number of diplomats considered unreliable suffered the same fate. An arrogant and foolish Nazi took charge of the Foreign Office.

5. Cheap Victories

The result of the occupation of the Rhineland and rearmament had been to enable Germany to negotiate freely with the outside world and give Hitler control of the Army. Now things happened very rapidly. The goals had been decided; not the methods nor the dates. If after the Reichstag fire Hitler was able to dominate Germany more quickly than he had expected, he now gained control of central Europe sooner and more easily than he believed possible in November 1937. He watched and waited, deceived his victims with shrewd, honey-sweet words and then seized his opportunities with lightning speed.

First came the Austrian one. Certain of his prey he would in this instance have preferred gradual infiltration to conquest from outside. His calculations went wrong because of the energy with which Kurt von Schuschnigg's dictatorship resisted National Socialist conspiracies in Austria. In February 1938 Schuschnigg was summoned to Hitler's court in Upper Bavaria. Faced with the final threat he was forced to accept the German ultimatum: to take Austrian Nazis into the cabinet and to let them stir up unrest without restriction. With such desperate conditions in his pocket the Chancellor believed that he could still save his Austria. When he saw that this was impossible and that within weeks the new co-rulers were taking the ground from under his feet he called for a plebiscite to ask the Austrians whether they wanted a 'free, independent, German and Christian Austria'. It was an attempt to beat Hitler with his own method, a plebiscite in which the formulation of the question and other tricks made it difficult to answer 'no'. The mouse tried to copy the cat but when the cat saw that the mouse really intended to run away it pounced. The plebiscite was prohibited; the Nazis in Austria rose and German troops marched in. Not even the Austrian Nazi leaders had wanted this; it made what was to have been their moment of glory seem too much like conquest from outside. Now all dams broke. Deceit, brutality, terror, the pleasures of revenge, jubilation at being liberated, flags and flowers – this new mixture which characterized all triumphs of Nazism swept over the Danubian state. Behind the troops came Heinrich Himmler's police; in Vienna alone 67,000 people were arrested. But what happened in camps and prison cells was easily silenced by the dervish-like cry of the masses 'One people, one Reich, one *Führer*' which welcomed Hitler as he marched in. In Austria, as we know, there were at least as many Nazis as in southern Germany, and they included some of the most brutal, the most wicked. The fact that they had been forced to stay underground for so long intensified the virulence of their outburst. As usual the enthusiasm was vocal, sorrow and agony were silent and the neutrals and sceptics – a numerous tribe in Austria – quickly joined the winning side, with the result that a fairly uniform picture emerged. Europe was under the impression that what was happening to the Austrians was what they really wanted and that intervention was neither justified nor practicable. German and Italian troops exchanged vows of friendship at the Brenner Pass. France and Britain uttered the familiar protests which nobody took seriously. In 1919 and even in 1931 they had been adamantly opposed to a free and decent union between Austria and a federal Germany. Now when the Nazis poured into Austria and when murder, suicide and the ruin of many thousands accompanied an event which might otherwise have happened peacefully and with dignity they turned away indifferently. *The Times* solemnly said that 'greater' Germany and Great Britain had no cause to quarrel – an allusion to the fact that there had been an *Anschluss* between the Scots and the English 200 years before. Was it surprising that many Germans concluded that Hitler's behaviour was right and that Rathenau, Stresemann and Brüning's methods had been wrong. Obviously people did not listen to sensible arguments but were prepared to accept *faits accomplis* and force. Hitler returned to Berlin as the man who had enlarged the Reich. There was another plebiscite, this time in the 'greater' German Reich, with the expected result.

On closer inspection not everything went as well as the Austrians had hoped. It was the German not the Austrian Nazis who ruled the country. They grabbed the carefully hoarded gold of the

Vienna State Bank, confiscated the substantial estates of the Austrian Jews and occupied the most important posts. And although in the old Reich the *Länder* continued to exist as administrative units Austria was not annexed as a *Land* but placed directly under the control of the central government and its satraps, with the vague title *Alpen und Donaugaue*. Consumed by an old hatred against his native country, particularly against Vienna Hitler wanted to eradicate the very name of Austria from men's memory. A blemish, in the eyes of the Austrians if not of the Germans. However, what the Austrians felt was no longer important. Saved, liberated and caught they were forced to co-operate. The dazzling searchlight which had rested on them for a few weeks now quickly turned towards another area. It was easy to predict which that would be.

Hitler had made 'greater' Germany a reality. The dream of the men of 1848 had at last become a fact. In three days he had done what Bismarck had not attempted in thirty years. Not so long ago Hitler had asked not to be compared with Bismarck; he might well prove to be the greatest of all Germans; whatever he had planned he had carried out and that was how things would go on. Why therefore stop now when everything was going so beautifully according to plan? As envisaged by the men of the *Paulskirche* 'greater' Germany included Bohemia. Now Bohemia was the heart of a post-war state clumsily called Czechoslovakia in which there lived about four million German-speaking people. They enjoyed complete equality of civic status, were fully protected by the law and free to pursue their economic, cultural and political interests; but not in a state which satisfied them emotionally. The old game of disliking each other which the Czechs and the Germans had inherited from the Habsburg Empire found enthusiastic supporters in Czechoslovakia. But after 1918 the Czechs had the advantage. They were the rulers and they were in the majority; where they could hurt the Germans a little without actually breaking the law they did so. Now they were to pay for this attitude. Many 'Sudeten Germans' followed a leader who, having started on his own, quickly became a tool of Hitler and of the policy of the Reich. What his followers really wanted cannot be said with certainty because they were never asked; probably they did not want to become part of Germany but to have an autonomous existence within a Bohemian–Moravian state. However, it must not be thought that the individual citizen knows exactly what he wants in such a crisis; in the end he is inclined to want what a vociferous leadership tells him to want. When Eduard Beneš, President of the Czechoslovak Republic, summoned the Sudeten German leaders to his castle in order to grant any and every wish they might have, they extricated themselves from the discussions and broke them off under a flimsy pretext. They were now more anxious to break away than to obtain advantages within the Czech state.

The German dictator did not particularly want the Sudeten Germans to break away from Czechoslovakia. The great philanthropist cared little about the happiness of the Sudeten Germans or about the ideal of the pan-German state. The real or alleged emotions of the Germans in Bohemia, their real or alleged plight, were an opportunity for him, nothing more. Nationalism was an instrument which he would employ as long as it was useful, in this case to smash and then to swallow the whole Czech state. This was his next aim. Meanwhile let Europe's and America's star journalists rush to northern Bohemia in order to study the living conditions and demands of the Sudeten Germans on the spot; let those duped people enjoy the limelight and let them feel that they were at the centre of history, just as a few months previously the Austrians, now swallowed up by the grey everyday life of the Nazi Reich had felt that they occupied the centre of the world stage. A glance at the map, moreover, showed that to take away the Germans in practice meant the end of the Czechoslovak state. Without the industries of northern and eastern Bohemia, the fortifications and the lines of communications the Prague republic ceased anyway to be a state; it could only have lived out an impotent satellite existence in the shadow of the Reich, almost completely encircled by it. The Western powers had accepted the annexation of Austria as an internal German affair. They could not do the same in the case of Czechoslovakia.

For that the republic had after all played too important an

international role for twenty years. Here was a people which even in the most generously interpreted sense of the word could not be called 'German', a people which had an alliance with France, a similar form of association with Russia, an 'Entente' with the Balkan states, which enjoyed considerable popularity in America, possessed an up-to-date Army and occupied a strategic position of classical importance – on this occasion the world could not pretend to be unconcerned. In May therefore French diplomacy began to spread the word that an attack on Czechoslovakia would spark off a European war. The Russians supported this attitude and even Britain, uncommitted by any treaty, made warning representations in Berlin. Confronted with what seemed to be a defensive front Hitler drew back on 23 May and announced that no one planned to attack the Czechs. Exactly a week later he issued a directive to his generals: 'It is my irrevocable determination to smash Czechoslovakia by military action in the foreseeable future. To await or to create a suitable opportunity from the political and military point of view is a matter for the political leadership.'

The method was always the same: to create disorder, if necessary to use terror in order to produce counter-terror and then to intervene, allegedly with the aim of preventing civil war and chaos and of helping one's friends. The method was used first in Germany and then in Austria; now it was used, not for the last time either, on the Czechs and, as always, it was adapted to the local peculiarities of the case. As planned the crisis reached boiling point in the late summer. At the Nuremberg Party rally Hitler screamed threats against Beneš: he would not tolerate a second Palestine 'in the heart of Germany', he would come to the aid of his German brothers in distress whatever the cost. Disturbances in Eger and Carlsbad were suppressed by the Czechs. The Sudeten German leaders expected German intervention, and rightly; the German attack on Czechoslovakia was planned to start on 28 September. Hitler for his part was right in maintaining that the Czechs were asserting themselves because they were relying on their Western allies. Eduard Bencš wanted a general war as the only way to save his state, more or less as the Serbs had done in

1914. But whereas in 1914 the Serbs had been on the offensive in 1938 the Czechs were on the defensive.

They were mistaken in their hopes. The French had helped to found the Czechoslovak state because it seemed to bring them political and military advantages, and as long as it did this it was a genuine, a necessary state. Now it brought no more advantages. Because of the sheer necessity of having to defend it, Czechoslovakia threatened to draw France into a second world war for which the French had little inclination. As a result Czechoslovakia now seemed to them to be a pretty unnatural state. France was anxious, if it could be done, to extricate itself honourably or at least not completely discreditably. The mood in Britain was similar, except that here the public spirit was stronger and juster, less corrupted by momentary influences. If Hitler wanted to conquer Europe the British were morally prepared to oppose him by force as they had, by tradition, opposed Napoleon and William II. However, let Hitler first prove that this was really his intention. If his aim was merely, as he maintained, to gather together in one nation-state all those Germans who *wanted* to belong to it, that was a different matter. Then there was nothing to be done, however tiresome effects such an action might have on the European balance of power. If the Sudeten Germans really wanted to 'return to the Reich' it was wrong to prevent them by means of a world war and it was better to let nature, which in this instance was probably identical with right anyway, take its course. The best, said *The Times* on 7 September, would be if the Sudetenland were taken from Czechoslovakia and made part of Germany. When Neville Chamberlain made his surprise flight to Berchtesgaden two weeks later he carried the same proposal in his pocket.

Hitler had expected to be allowed to attack Czechoslovakia, as he had been allowed to attack Austria six months earlier, putting up with the risk of a major war. What now happened took him completely by surprise: the Western powers intervened, for the first time before and not after the event, not to prevent him from doing what he wanted to do but merely to give it a peaceful form and to offer him a colossal gain without any risk; alternatively to threaten him with war if he refused the offer and acted on his own.

At the discussions which followed in Berchtesgaden, in Godesberg and finally in Munich this grotesque question only was at stake: should the Germans march into the predominantly German-speaking regions of Czechoslovakia with the consent of the European powers, on agreed days and in agreed states or should Germany attack at once, without Europe and against Europe. The second alternative appealed more to Hitler's emotions and for a few days it seemed as though he would choose it. His frenzy revealed itself; he was ready to unleash war, not over a matter of substance but because of minute details of a question decided in principle. With heavy hearts France and Britain belatedly did what they could to prepare for war. The Germans too saw war approaching and, like the British and the French, disliked what they saw; where troops appeared they were greeted not with the enthusiasm of 1914 but with a gloomy indifference. It seems that this mood left an impression on Hitler. Faced with a threat coupled with an offer unique in the diplomatic history of Europe, and also urged to moderation by his Italian ally, Hitler finally decided to accept the huge, incomplete offer and to postpone the rest until later. As a result agreement was quickly reached at Munich. The Czechs were not asked. These bogus vitors of 1918 were forced to accept an arrangement the harshness of which far exceeded that of the Treaty of Versailles. Not even the Sudeten Germans were asked, although the Munich Agreement promised plebiscites in the disputed regions. Many of them did not really know what was happening to them; they were surprised and confused when German troops moved in with the consent of Europe to liberate them from Czechoslovakia. Besides it was impossible to separate the two peoples without employing the barbarous method of an exchange of 'populations'. Almost one million Czechs now came under German sovereignty together with the Sudeten Germans.

Hitler was sufficiently perverse and mad to be profoundly annoyed by the conclusion of the affair. By agreeing to more than his allegedly just demands the Western powers had prevented him from carrying out his real aim. 'The fellow,' he said of Chamberlain, 'has spoilt my entry into Prague.' In reality the fellow had hoped for a lessening of tension in Europe and Germany as a result of the incredible concessions of the Munich Agreement. However, the atmosphere in Germany remained tense. Screams, barks and offended threats went on coming through the loud-speakers at public meetings even after Munich. And as if to show the world with whom it was dealing and to destroy any illusion about the nature of the German regime, the most terrible pogrom thus far against the Jews was staged in November; in one night all synagogues were destroyed, thousands of Jews were dragged into camps and tortured and finally a 'fine' of one milliard marks was imposed on the German Jews. Chamberlain had said toler-antly at Munich, that like Britain, Germany had the political system which appeared to suit it and which it should certainly keep. Could one say this of a government which of its own free will indulged in such activities while the mass of the people watched, indifferently or bitterly, without taking part in these crimes? Only a few weeks after Munich even the most confirmed British supporters of the policy of appeasement began to wonder whether they were on the right road and whether they could follow it much longer.

The Munich Agreement was ambiguous. By sacrificing the Czechoslovak bastion without even consulting France's so-called main ally in the East, Russia, and by abandoning the 'Little Entente' of the south-eastern states the Western powers seemed to be giving Hitler a free hand in the East. That was more or less how the event was understood in Germany because the Germans understood nothing but power politics anyway. This view, how-ever, assumed that the West thought more logically than it did. The main motive of the French had been the desire not 'to die for the Czechs'; they had followed the British who had not made a conscious gesture of abdication of political power but had wanted once more, for the last time, to be just. They fully realized that this act of justice would considerably strengthen Germany's position. J. L. Garvin said in the *Observer* that, since Napoleon, perhaps even since Charlemagne, no man had been as powerful in Europe as Hitler after Munich. Henceforth the small central and eastern European states would revolve around Germany and indirectly receive their laws from Germany, more or less as the kingdom of Portugal had done for centuries from Britain. It was possible to put up with this state of affairs provided things were done in a civilized manner, provided these peoples retained control at least of their internal affairs and were allowed a certain degree of diplomatic latitude. Let Germany establish its centre of gravity in central and eastern Europe by natural and peaceful means; there must be no more *coups*, no more aggression, deceit or lightning wars. In the end Britain broke with Hitler over a question of form. However, it is form which enables people to live together and the form which Hitler chose derived from his nature.

He could have had central and eastern Europe as a German sphere of influence. He had it already. An attitude of *sauve qui peut* spread across the old crown lands of Austria, as well as a mood of 'take what you can' – by relying on Germany at the expense of one's neighbours. The rulers of Poland did not spurn a share of the Czech booty and annexed the industrial region of Teschen, forgetting that what had happened to the Czechs today might happen to them tomorrow. Hungary too let Germany and Italy cede it a piece of Slovakia. The Czechs themselves probably hoped to build a modest little house from the ruins of their grandiose edifice, although they were clever enough to see who would henceforth be the real master. They abandoned the policy of Masaryk and Beneš, allowed the President to go into exile without regrets at his departure, gave the Slovaks and Ruthenes the autonomy which Germany demanded for its new protégés, allowed the Reich to build a road, meant to be extra-territorial, across Czechoslovakia and dismissed Jews from office – in short they accepted the role they had been given. All they asked was to keep up the pretence that they had a state, an army, a foreign service and a modicum of dignity. One might have thought that the most extravagant German imperialist would have been satisfied with this.

Not so the man in Berchtesgaden. As a morphine addict cannot give up his poison he could not do without plans for new aggression, surprise attacks, secret marching orders and colourful entries into conquered towns. He could not forget that in Munich he had been served up with only part of the state which he had wanted to swallow whole; spoilt and puffed up by easy victories and corrupted by cheap philosophy, he was not interested in spheres of influence, in peaceful collaboration and similar unspectacular matters. Before 'Munich' he had sworn that the Sudetenland was his last demand. At Munich he had agreed to guarantee together with the other great powers the existence of rump-Czechoslovakia. During the winter he avoided fulfilling this promise in spite of France's polite insistence. In March it became clear why. There was a disagreement between Czechs and Slovaks, a repetition of the Austrian and the Sudeten-German crisis, only that this time it was not Germans among themselves, or Germans and Slavs but Slavs among themselves who irritated each other with German encouragement. Again it was necessary to restore order. The weak old President of Czechoslovakia was told to come to Berlin and confronted with choosing between a German invasion, the destruction of Prague by bomber squadrons, and entrusting his people to German protection. The President signed; the Protectorate of Bohemia and Moravia was proclaimed; German tanks entered Prague and Brünn without encountering any resistance and Hitler enjoyed a night in the castle of the ancient kings of Bohemia.

This event did not much affect the balance of power. If it is a characteristic of a genuine state to resist aggression however poor the chances of success, Czechoslovakia had ceased to be a genuine state after Munich and had perhaps never been one. All the more reason why it should have been in Germany's interests to preserve appearances. Because of the sheer pleasure of seeing the hated Czechs completely at his feet and of being called 'Protector of Bohemia' Hitler rent the veil which had barely covered his policy hitherto. It was no longer the glorious aims of redressing the injustice of Versailles, of gathering all Germans and only Germans into one state, that were at stake. The dictator stood revealed to the world as a man who broke his word, as a liar. Anyone vaguely familiar with Hitler's character, with the contents of *Mein Kampf*, who knew how he had come to power and what his methods were, was not surprised; Neville Chamberlain, however, was. After a brief moment of hesitation Britain's long-standing policy of appeasement collapsed, amid the sound of furious indignation. If the Western powers did nothing about the Prague *coup* at least they did not recognize the Protectorate, as they had recognized Hitler's 'bloodless conquests' in the past. Consequently there followed an interim between peace and war, with a *de facto* order which was no longer legitimate. One might add that if Hitler had been satisfied with the Protectorate and had stopped there the arrangement would probably in time have worked. Time legitimatizes many things and Britain and France would finally have accepted a situation which they could not change. Of course the suggestion that Hitler might have stopped there is so absurd as not to be worth speculating about.

Until March 1939 he operated with aims which, pursued by other men with other means might have been just. To seek to eliminate the stupidities of the Treaty of Versailles, to want Austria and German Bohemia to be free to determine their own political system, were on paper just demands in the Anglo-Saxon tradition. Nevertheless it is not legitimate to distinguish between a just German foreign policy up to the Munich Agreement and a transition to the rape of foreign nations after March 1939. Such a distinction merely explains, or helps to explain, why until 1939 the Western powers, with a bad conscience about the past and full of goodwill for the future, offered so little resistance. They wanted to be just. Hitler, however, was never just; he did not know the difference between right and wrong. Whatever he touched went bad; the Austrian *Anschluss*, from which good might have come, became a fraud and the people were degraded into a hysterically howling mob in which no clear will could be discerned or even develop. As in Germany Hitler had used democracy to destroy democracy, he destroyed the European Anglo-Saxon order with its own idea that peoples had the right to determine their own fate. He encountered in Europe the same tolerant weakness, the same helplessness and confusion as in Germany.

Britain's appeasement policy became a tragedy or tragicomedy of errors not only because it was persuading someone to keep the peace who admitted that to him there was no difference between peace and war. Neville Chamberlain and his friends were also mistaken about Hitler's position in Germany. They thought that they were making their concessions to all good Germans, whereas in reality they strengthened Hitler's position among his own people and helped to nip in the bud the resistance of the best. The Sudeten German crisis was a case in point. Many Germans then believed that the Western powers would not abandon the Czech state and that Hitler's policy was leading straight to a major war. The fear was exorcized at Munich. But linked with the fear of war in the minds of some distinguished men were hope and determination to act; these were strangled at Munich. Unfortunately nothing went beyond the stage of secret discussion, travelling and planning. Yet the picture of Germany in those days would be incomplete without reference to these activities.

German resistance to Hitler reached its greatest intensity in August and September 1938. This did not mean much; the masses, big parties and organizations, were not part of it; they could not be part of it, given the nature of the totalitarian state. But the initiated and those ready for action occupied important positions or were close to people who did, in the general staff, in the *Abwehr*, the military intelligence service in central Army staffs, at the control centre of the Berlin police and in the Foreign Office. Because of their position, serving the system which they opposed, their attitude inevitably fluctuated between the permissible warning criticism – to the extent that there still was any criticism – and actual conspiracy; the frontiers between loyal service to the state and opposition were fluid. Many German diplomats, military attachés, the Secretary of State of the Foreign Office himself, gave advice and hints to the British which Hitler would have regarded as treasonable. Almost all senior generals uttered warnings to the effect that Germany was militarily and economically unequal to a major war. The Chief of Staff of the Army, Ludwig Beck, composed memorandum after memorandum, pointing out that Hitler's policy was isolating and endangering the Reich. While this was still 'legal' opposition Beck secretly went further, particularly after his resignation in August 1938. For him it was no longer a question of preventing war but of seizing a chance to overthrow the corrupt Party dictatorship at the last moment. At first he still wanted to save Hitler himself and to aim his blow only against the secret police and the Party bosses in Berlin. His successor as Chief of Staff, Halder, took over these plans and pushed them further. What generals Halder, Witzleben, Hoeppner, Beck, Oster and their civilian helpers finally prepared was a military *coup*, the arrest of Hitler and all his helpers in the first hour after the declaration of war. A protest, the material for which was prepared and ready, would prove to the nation the crimes of the regime; a temporary military government would establish the foundations of a democratic constitution. The sorrow which one still feels today when one examines the plans, reads the appeals, the letters, the subsequent accounts and the eye-witness reports, is moderated only by the admiration commanded by the stature of those concerned, particularly General Beck. They were very lonely, they acted under terrible danger to themselves in a sphere which was as alien to their education and social background as the jungle. The envoys whom they sent to London were treated with the utmost coolness by the Prime Minister. Neville Chamberlain thought that Britain must work with the German government, not with its private enemies and visionaries who had nothing behind them. Nevertheless the conspirators were ready to attack and in the days after Godesberg it seemed again as though the decisive hour was near. At the last moment Hitler gave way and the Western powers gave way even further. The extent of the victory which German diplomacy by blackmail achieved at Munich made action impossible. The pusillanimous had been wrong. It must be said that at that time it would have been easier for Britain, a free, civilized power, to break off relations with Hitler than for German officers to rise against their supreme commander. They had relied on Britain for the break. When instead there was a ceremonious reconciliation, when Britain and Germany promised never to fight each other again internal German resistance collapsed. The conspirators went their separate ways; some retired into private life, others concentrated dutifully but unhappily on their work. The passionate hopes and tensions of September were succeeded by the dull, fatalistically accepted sultriness of the August that followed.

6. Unleashing the Second World War

The big, but indifferently governed, amorphous Polish nation-state had expanded in 1919 at the expense of the Germans and the Russians; some of the settlements made in the flush of cheap victory might better have been avoided. The so-called Corridor dividing East Prussia from the Reich was an awkward instance of abstract justice which ignored reality; the Free City of Danzig was a piece of pure nonsense. Danzig was German. The Poles thought that they needed the harbour and could plead that until 1793 Danzig had been part of Poland. The victors in Paris in their wisdom had decided that Danzig should be neither German nor Polish but independent under the control of the League of Nations and part of the Polish economy.

Meanwhile the vanquished of 1918 had in practice become the victor. Those Polish acquisitions no longer quite fitted into the picture of a German controlled central Europe. On the other hand as Germany's power had recently increased so tremendously and as the Reich had gained more than had been lost at Versailles, it might have allowed the few remains of the Versailles order to survive. Poland would then inevitably have been drawn more deeply into the German sphere of influence than was already the case in 1938, and the question of the exact line of the frontier would have lost its sting. It is pointless, though, to speak of sensible alternatives in a case where all arguments were only pretexts, hiding the madness of a boundless determination to dominate and to destroy. Soon after 'Munich' Hitler made a suggestion to the Poles which on paper seemed tolerable. They should surrender Danzig, allow an 'extra-territorial' road across the Corridor and participate more closely than before in Germany's anti-Russian policy. The misfortune of the Poles was that they were a stronger, older and more genuine nation than the Czechs and could not retire voluntarily. Yet every renunciation that the Poles made was the beginning of a renunciation of their independent political existence. Their state occupied former Russian and former German or Habsburg territory, and it was a

Prussian-German tradition to regard the whole Polish state, not just a monstrosity like Danzig, as intolerable in the long run. In 1919 Poland had spread farther to the West and to the East than it should have done; in its ambition it had been as intoxicated by victory and as blind as the other small nations. Yet even a more modest attitude then would not have helped it later. Poland owed its existence as a state to weakness, to the temporary collapse of Russia and Germany. Therefore it was forced to pretend that nothing had changed since 1919 and bravely to insist on the rights acquired at that time – or to surrender. The first German demands would have been followed by others. Then what? The Poles would have been drawn as satellites into ˙Hitler's Russian catastrophe like the Rumanians and the Hungarians; or at some moment a Polish revolt against German rule would have given the Nazis sufficient cause to embark on the same course of extermination as that for which Poland's diplomatic resistance provided the excuse in 1939. It was impossible for Poland to emerge unscathed from the crisis of those years, however it behaved.

When it chose resistance, the diplomatic 'No', it determined the form and time of its catastrophe. In May 1939 Hitler said in front of his most important generals that war was inevitable. 'Danzig is not the object at stake. For us it is a matter of expansion in the East . . . Therefore the question of sparing Poland does not arise and the decision remains to attack Poland at the first suitable opportunity.' He did not expect a repetition of the 'Czech affair'. There would be a war, against Poland˙alone or against Poland and the Western powers. All boats would be burnt and nobody would ask any more about right or wrong.

Surprisingly, Neville Chamberlain at the end of March strengthened Poland's position by a promise of help. This was Britain's reply to the annexation of Prague and a reversal of its policy: from appeasement to threats, from insular neutrality to links with the Continent. Dictated by indignation and disappointment, belated, hasty and lacking a firm foundation, this first British step nevertheless showed where the line would be drawn. At Munich Britain had made the last justifiable concessions, it had not given Germany *carte blanche* to commit whatever outrage it willed in eastern Europe. Britain was tired of blackmail and deceit and was still in principle committed to the old policy of preserving the balance of power which did not allow the domination of Europe by one power. As Britain committed itself to Poland the almost forgotten Franco-Polish alliance came to life again. Hesitantly, without much conviction, France followed the British lead. Having abandoned their strongest position in Central Europe, Czechoslovakia, in order to be fair, the Western powers prepared to defend the rest with gestures if not with deeds.

Gestures, however, were not enough. If there was to be a repetition of 1914 – and the historical imagination was so impoverished that this was what it seemed to amount to – then Poland was an inadequate substitute for Russia, and the Soviet Union was needed for the effective encirclement of Germany. Although the unsuspecting Chamberlain thought that Poland was stronger than Tsarist Russia, the French knew better, and so did many Britons, Winston Churchill among them. They called for an alliance with Russia, which on the part of the French existed on paper. The pity, however, was that the eastern states which felt threatened by Germany, from the Baltic to the Black Sea, also felt threatened by Russia, at whose expense they had been founded or enlarged in 1919, and therefore rightly did not put much faith in Russian help. Chamberlain did not trust Russia either; he underestimated its military strength – as did almost everybody – and treated the Kremlin with restrained hauteur. Let Russia intervene when it was needed and only to the extent that it was needed. Let it help to defend an order established at its expense in 1919; the order of Brest-Litovsk, which the Germans had fought for and which the Western victors had taken over. Let Russia defend that order but only when summoned, not before; it must not be allowed to establish in peacetime a foothold in the border states, the only way in which it would have been in a position to put up an effective defence when the crisis came. This was the nemesis of 1919. For a very long time there had been a territorial order in eastern Europe satisfactory to both the Germans and the Russians and this was the most solid arrangement possible. Perhaps there could also be an order which satisfied only one of the two great powers, but an order which satisfied neither was too just to be durable. And this precisely was the order which France and Britain now feebly tried to preserve.

On top of it there was the nemesis of Munich. After Britain had abandoned Czechoslovakia without even informing Russia, the Kremlin was profoundly and vindictively suspicious of Western policy. One can understand this, particularly as to Russians the 'just' motives which had led to the Munich Agreement were laughable fabrications. Stalin himself was not the man to surrender anything concrete merely in order to be just; and he did not believe that others could do what he regarded as unthinkable. Consequently the reports, offers and demands which passed between London and Moscow in the early summer of 1939 were as fumbling as, for example, General von Schleicher's parliamentary negotiations in December 1932. And let it be emphasized again: on the other side there was someone who may have been blasphemous in boasting of his powers of decision but who had good reason to boast. Hitler watched the negotiations between Russia and the West. Intuitively he divined how badly they were going. And gradually – to determine the precise moment is unimportant for our purpose and will never be possible – the idea came to him that he might do with one stroke what the Western powers were working towards hesitatingly and clumsily: he himself might come to terms with the Russians. For twenty years he had thundered against Bolshevism, founded 'anti-Comintern' fronts and presented himself as the defender of the West against Asiatic barbarism; moreover he had selected in Russia the regions which were one day to be German *Lebensraum*. Let this wait; the time would come to see to it. Hitler was as determined in the pursuit of his long-term aims as he was opportunist at the moment, a tactician who rapidly reversed course. He had always succeeded in isolating one victim by liberally distributing promises, peace pledges and non-aggression pacts in every other direction. His chosen victim now was Poland. Why not deal it a lethal blow by coming suddenly to far reaching terms with Russia? Friendship with Russia was a traditional Prussian policy. But such traditions meant nothing to Hitler, or meant something only momentarily because the attitudes of the Army and of the Prussian aristocracy, still influential in the Army, simplified his incredible *volte face*. Traditions, general trends and basic possibilities were all one to this rootless individual; he manipulated them as he manipulated ideas – using one today, another tomorrow, then all of them until there was nothing left.

While the negotiations between Russia and the Western powers were jolting along negotiations of another kind went on secretly between Berlin and Moscow. They too progressed slowly; there were no discussions of concrete proposals, only gentle hints, attempts by each side to sound out the other, a game in the dark. At the beginning of August the Germans became more explicit and more insistent with their offers. If the war against Poland was to begin at the time of year when wars traditionally began, it was necessary to settle the Russian affair by the middle of the summer. Stalin for his part, seeing that the Western powers did not want what he wanted, and convinced that there would be a war, decided to direct the fury of Germany's military power against Poland and the West instead of against Russia. The bombshell, the biggest in Europe's long diplomatic history, exploded on 23 August: a non-aggression pact between Germany and the Soviet Union. That much emerged from what was published of the treaty at the time. Although the unpublished part was not known – the secret agreement by which Germany and Russia shared out vital regions of eastern Europe, Poland and the Baltic states – the general importance of the event was clear at once. In three weeks the two tyrants had achieved what the scrupulous Western powers could not bring themselves to do in thirty months. The tyrant in the East had given the tyrant at the centre the green light, in the West generally, and in the East to an unknown frontier. 'Now I have the world in my pocket,' Hitler rejoiced when he learnt of the signing of the pact in Moscow.

Now the barriers were down. This was no diplomatic crisis as in 1914. It was not a case of one country being motivated by fear of another, a case of being in the dark about the other's plans, a case of a tangle of misunderstandings, obligations, promises and military plans from which all powers were desperately seeking to free themselves. Only one state acted, the German Reich, and only one man in Germany, the dictator. He was not pushed on by popular feeling as the weak Kaiser had been in 1914; he was free to choose, but he had chosen long ago. During the dogdays the campaign against Poland, the Poland which only six months ago had been 'our friend', assumed dimensions unparalleled even in the campaign against the Czechs in the previous year. There was no way back because there was not meant to be one. Hitler still wanted to have his war against Poland alone; it seems that he was hoping to the last day that the Western powers would keep out and that their solemn assurances to the contrary were only bluff. But, as he calmly informed his people, he was prepared for their intervention. Again he threw out promises: if only he was allowed to crush Poland he would keep the peace for ever and would willingly defend the British Empire against all its enemies. His tricks no longer worked; he had cheated too often. The British replied that they did not want to derive any advantage from the abandonment of an ally. It was not too late for negotiations but they must take place between Berlin and Warsaw, not between Berlin and London, and not under the threat of force. In vain did some venturesome private individuals try to mediate; in vain did Italy, unwilling and unprepared for war, implore Germany to desist. The order to attack Poland was given for the morning of 26 August. On the evening of 25 August, when the troops were already on the move Hitler withdrew the order because Mussolini had sent unwelcome word that he would not be able to join in at once. Hitler thought out new plans, new short-lived manoeuvres to deceive the enemy; he decided that the attack should start on 1 September. There was a last sham offer which Poland never received, of which Britain was informed only orally and of which Hitler later said that he had needed an alibi for his own people. On 1 September the Germans crossed the Polish frontier and on 3 September the Western powers issued an ultimatum demanding Germany's immediate withdrawal; when the Germans refused Britain and France declared war on Germany. In all this there was hardly any tension, not as in 1914, not even as in the days of Munich: only a feeling of gloomy, almost boring inevitability. If a man says that he wants to make war and makes war, if the others say that they will intervene if he does and then really do intervene; if a man eternally repeats the same game of incitement, threat, false offers, honeyed words of peace and bellicose screams – how can there be any tension.

During the Czech crisis the British Ambassador had reported from Berlin that the mood was definitely against the war but that the nation found itself helpless in the grip of the Nazi system. People were like sheep being led to the slaughter. If war broke out they would march and do their duty, at least for a time. This observation was as true for 1939 as it had been for the preceding year. Isolated, excited and deceived as they were, some Germans – only some of them – fell for Hitler's 'alibi' which nobody else in the world believed; they really thought that an acceptable offer had been made at the last moment, and that it had been rejected by the fanatical Poles. No doubt they also believed in the Polish attack staged by Hitler with convicted criminals who were dressed up in Polish uniforms and put to death on the spot with lethal injections. Yet even without believing all this incredible filth they would still have obeyed and each one of them would have done his allotted task. This was the state of affairs that things had reached after six years in which the Nazis had tightened their hold on everything; one man could command as he wished and seventy-five million people obeyed. They obeyed without pleasure, they believed without pleasure. The start of the war was not a relief as in 1914, it was only the extension of the familiar crisis into a new, unknown and dangerous dimension. The war was so distasteful to the German nation that in the first days the ruling psychologists-in-chief avoided the word itself and spoke of a police action or of purely 'punitive measures' against Poland. There was no change of attitude during this long, last, most terrible and most stupid of European wars. Victories gave no joy in spite of intensive propaganda attempts to arouse pride and hatred; they were accepted with indifference. Defeat confirmed what most people had dimly suspected from the beginning. Only such victories as seemed to bring the end closer were received with interest; rumours of peace alone produced genuine rejoicing.

7. Reflection

As regards the start of the Second World War there is no 'war guilt question'. Even confirmed nationalists and long-standing supporters of Hitler who abandoned him late or not at all, like Hjalmar Schacht or Franz von Papen, tell us in their memoirs that Hitler alone was responsible for the war. He himself claimed this readily and proudly among his intimates in 1939. And Göring knew it when he remarked on the first day, as though appalled by what they had done: 'God help Germany if it loses this war.' The straightforward origin of the war was no source of comfort during the war years. Later it proved convenient, saving us from the scientific and pseudo-scientific controversy about responsibility for the war which poisoned the post-1918 period. All that remains to do is to list the errors which encouraged the criminal to commit his crimes. There were errors at all levels; from the superficial mistake of a false judgement of history and the lessons drawn from it to the basic error of blasphemous self-adulation and madness.

From the start Hitler was determined to fight the First World War again, and this time correctly. Above all there must not be another 9 November 1918, a promise which he made not once but a thousand times. He was never more fanatical and his face was never more contorted than when he made this promise. To prevent a repetition of 9 November 1918, to govern Germany accordingly and to fight the war accordingly – this was a *leitmotif* of all his actions; it came from the conviction that without 9 November Germany could have continued and finally have won the First World War. This was an error, but the most terrible experiment was needed to prove that it was an error. No other historical misjudgement has ever been paid for with so much blood.

Why had Germany fought the First World War? Why had its objectives been wrong? What were the right objectives for which the war must be repeated? This was where *Lebensraum*, the theory of living space, entered. Germany, so Hitler believed, needed more space, needed it in Europe and at the expense of other nations. General Beck had rightly objected in 1937 that 'the population situation in Europe has been stable for a thousand years or more and that far-reaching changes therefore seem impossible without severe repercussions, the long-term effects of which are impossible to predict . . .' To make more room for the Germans on the old Continent by conquest, limitation or extermination of other peoples, to play at barbarian invasions after fifteen hundred years was an impossible, childish dream which not even the most terrible crimes could transform into a reality. The problem of how to feed themselves, how to preserve their high standard of living, existed for the Germans as much as for the British, the Italians and the Japanese. But this was not the way to solve it. In fact at the time of this writing the Germans live incomparably better than they did when they were plundering Poland and the Ukraine and the Balkan peninsula.

It was not against Bolshevism that Hitler went to war. On the contrary, so that he could start the war he allowed Bolshevism to penetrate far to the West, surrendering to it eastern Poland and the three Baltic states, doing precisely what the Western powers were not prepared to do in 1939. When two years later he attacked Russia it was not because he thought that Bolshevism was strong and threatened his Europe. On the contrary, he fell back on his old theory that Bolshevik Russia was weak and destined to become Germany's booty, and thought that he could finish it off in five months. Only in the winter of 1942 when he came up against Russia's terrible strength, did he change his tune and presented the war as a necessary defensive war of German-speaking Europe against Muscovite barbarism. Many Germans finally came to accept this aspect of the war as its most real and serious one. But this was an interpretation made possible by later experiences, which had nothing to do with the real actions and motives of 1939.

Hitler's most personal idea, and about the only one which he really believed in, was that of the world conspiracy and danger of Judaism. Behind the resistance of Europe, Britain, Russia and America, everywhere he found the Jews. In reality the Jews were anything but a world power, certainly not a conspiratorial one. They were weak and helpless, each community in its country. Hitler's persecution of the German Jews did not prevent Britain from pursuing its appeasement policy for five years. The Jews remained in Germany, most of them, because they did not know where to go and also because they were good patriots who could not believe in the sentence which threatened them, and they stayed until they found a terrible end. Nor was Bolshevism under Jewish influence as Hitler claimed. If in Lenin's day a few Jews had occupied leading positions in Russia they had all long been dismissed and exterminated by Stalin. The world conspiracy of Judaism was a chimera. Hitler attacked the most defenceless people of the world, no, not a people but millions of individuals who felt part of the most diverse nations, and he murdered them because of their 'race', because of their name.

The philosophy behind Hitler's actions was that in war everything was permitted, that nature was always at war and that man was part of nature. 'Close your hearts to pity. Proceed brutally. Eighty million men and women must be given what is theirs by right. Their existence must be safeguarded. The stronger has right on his side. Show the utmost hardness.' To sign a treaty today and to break it tomorrow, to cheat, to deceive, to exterminate whole races – men had always done this; Hitler thought that the man who had the courage to use such tricks and to use them logically would win. If one looks at history, not as it should be according to Christian ethics, but as it is, one cannot deny that there is some truth in this theory. Injustice is often done to nations as to individuals and there are instances of great injustice being triumphant and becoming part of history unpunished. That was what Machiavelli and Thucydides taught. One must also grant the German tyrant that he had a keen eye for the wrong done by others, for the hypocrisy of the Christian, Western democracies. He recognized the contradiction between their words and deeds. But even here he made a mistake, moral issues quite apart. His practical mistake was to exaggerate. Although wrong has always been done there was done in this twentieth century of ours, in the heart of Europe, by one of the most civilized nations on earth, so much wrong that the world could not stand it. Hitler went so far that in the end nobody wanted to negotiate with him any more; proud, upright Britain refused to do so after September 1939 and after June 1941 everybody refused. He went so far that in the end he united the whole world against him, Americans, British, Russians and Indians. This unnatural alliance did not last a day longer than he himself, but while it lasted its sole purpose was to get rid of this one, unbearable man. He ruined himself with the very tricks which he had used to climb to the top. He had gained control of Germany and then of Europe by being more ruthless than the others. In the end the world became as ruthless as he, in its actions against him and against the nation which he had made the instrument of his will. Then the trick ceased to be effective and the Allies could use the right of the stronger against him and his Germans. How could the world not be stronger than one man and one nation? It is a simple story, in spite of its horror.

Finally Hitler overestimated himself. He had intelligence, intuition, imagination and willpower, and he knew it. Also he was lucky for a long time. From this he concluded that he was one of the greatest men of all times and that on the other side there were only small fry. 'The enemy has not reckoned with my great powers of decision. Our enemies are wormlets. I saw them at Munich.' His enemies, however, were not as feeble as he thought, mistaking their patience and goodwill for weakness. In Churchill, Roosevelt and Stalin he found opponents who were his equals even as far as willpower went.

In a sense the game which Britain and France played in 1939 was as out of date as Hitler's own game. It no longer corresponded to the realities of Europe and to Europe's changed position in the world. But the one went well with the other. Hitler's plan to dominate Europe in the Napoleonic style, to exploit it for the Germans, to use Europe to make Germany a world force, was nothing but a barbaric piece of childishness in the middle of our century. The Western powers replied by pursuing, in the old British anti-Napoleonic style, a policy of preserving the political balance of power; a hastily prepared system of alliances to encircle Germany, the 'Great Coalition'. They resumed where they had left off in 1918; the British their blockade and the French their trench warfare. But as Europe lacked the vitality of 1813 or 1914 in dealing with the world it also lacked vitality in dealing with domestic issues; it did not have enough energy to preserve ‚the European balance of power. The French made the accustomed gestures and in the autumn of 1939 spoke in the old diplomatic language, but there was no strength, no enthusiasm, no hope behind their gestures. The system of alliances in the East collapsed like a house of cards. Britain still had pride and courage but lacked power. It could never decide the war, it could only survive until the war became something completely different, until it ceased to be a European war, a war to preserve the balance of power. The European order which the Allies had wanted to save was not after all restored in 1945, and to that extent the war had been in vain. For six years his enemies had tried to satisfy Hitler; then for six years they had shot and thrown bombs in order to get rid of him. This they achieved, but not much else.

8. Character and Course of the War

Germany like the other peoples of Europe had greatly enjoyed the First World War at the beginning. It was started with enthusiasm and style, with tremendous clashes; and although even this war spread because Italy, the Balkan states and finally America joined in, it was very much a war from the start. It remained what it was, a European conflict with unimportant secondary theatres of war in other continents, in the places where Europe ruled. The basic character of the struggle did not change during the four years of its duration, however much its intensity increased; at the end it was decided more or less with the arms with which it had been begun.

Nobody except Hitler and his cronies really wanted the second war and even Hitler knew in his heart of hearts what he was letting himself in for. In 1939 Europe was sad, consumed by the knowledge that the exercise must be repeated, and that, if it had not been done right the first time in spite of all the sacrifices, probably no good would come of it the second time. In France that feeling led to emotional paralysis and defeat. Although the Germans started the war they were not enthusiastic, neither the civilians, nor the soldiers, least of all the generals. Never has a general staff been so little to blame for a war as the German General Staff of the Second World War, and never has it approached its task with so much distaste; never have the politicians been so firmly in the saddle with the Army reduced to the role of the horse. The dictatorship had made the war; it was *its* war. The great majority of senior officers viewed the dictatorship with doubt and detached indifference, if not with hatred and contempt. Yet generals, Army and people kept the war going as long as it was physically possible to do so.

There were specific reasons, which we shall come to later, for this perseverance to the bitter end. In general it is true to say that a healthy nation – not to mention the particular talents of the German one – regards war, once it is there, as a serious matter, to be fought seriously. Soldiers fight because they have no choice; officers know their duty. To remain aloof and to sabotage is against human nature; it requires an abnormal or very strong character. For better or for worse people want to share the fate of the others. Most Germans, not all but probably the majority, accepted the war as the fate of the nation, as the task which it had to master, without asking why or how the task came to be given. In the last resort they treated it as a non-political matter. They did not regard it as a Nazi affair however much Nazi policy was responsible for the start of the war and the terrible way in which it was fought.

The relationship between the 'regime' and the nation during the war was therefore a complex one. The war was Hitler's war; even more than before 1939 this man stood at the centre of events. But even more than before 1939 the war needed the people; logically this situation ought to have led to a new, even stronger bond between the dictatorship and the people. But human activity is not logical. In practice the distinction, separation and hostility between the regime and the people, at least in the later war years, were more marked than in peacetime. While the people fought Hitler's war at the fronts and worked for Hitler's war in the towns, the regime fought a war against its own people, butchering thousands of them. In 1944 the defeats of the German armies by the enemy enabled the Nazi Party to achieve its complete and final conquest of the Army; one might say that the regime was never stronger than just before the end, and that it even benefited from the approaching collapse of the Reich. The dictatorship meanwhile sought to keep control of the people by making it jointly responsible for the Nazi crimes, and by threatening that a victorious enemy would impose vindictive peace terms. 'We are now,' was the propaganda line, 'committed to each other for better or for worse. If we fall you also fall, because the enemy will make no distinction between us and you.' This persuasive argument began to be advanced as soon as the possibility of defeat appeared on the distant horizon; and the Allies did almost nothing to refute it.

Anyway let us be honest and note that most people were reasonably content while things went well and there was no need for much sacrifice. There was also a great deal of loose talk at the time, for instance that the war had been inevitable because Germany had not been allowed to become a world power, or that it was the great clash between Socialism and Capitalism and similar nonsense. Later such talk ceased.

Least unpopular was the war against Poland, as long as it remained restricted to Poland. Prussia-Germany had been anti-Polish since 1848 and 1918. There was a feeling that the impudent Slavs who imagined that they were the equals of the Reich must be made to suffer for their presumption. The generals did not want a war; but if there had to be one Poland was the enemy on which they preferred to test their skill. In the event everything went very smoothly. Brave, but with antiquated equipment and badly led, the Poles could not withstand the onrush of the German armoured divisions for even a fortnight. A French offensive aimed at the Rhine could, of course, have changed the situation completely at a time when Germany had concentrated its forces against Poland and was almost defenceless in the West. But the French did not dare to attack; they wanted to wait until they were attacked. In practice they did not keep their promise to the Poles because a mere declaration of war was of no help. Thereby they once again abandoned an eastern ally, as the Czechs had been abandoned the year before. This was indicative of the whole situation; a surrender the consequences of which could never be undone. The Russians were more punctilious in keeping their new commitments. On 17 September they marched into the eastern regions of Poland which they had been given under the terms of the Moscow Pact. On 5 October Hitler held his victory parade in Warsaw.

Then he made a peace offer to the Western powers. He would keep Poland, the whole of Poland, less the predominantly non-Polish Ukrainian and White Russian regions annexed by Stalin. Germany must also be given back its African colonies. Otherwise he had no claims on the West and saw no reason for further bloodshed ... This was the German peace offer of 1916 over again; the peace offer of the victor who would be content with his booty, provided he was allowed to keep it. Britain could not accept. It would have lost its standing, the respect of the world, imponderable but vital assets. Hitler's peace offensive had much less chance of success than the German offers duringt he First World War. The Kaiser and Bethmann Hollweg had been God-fearing men of honour, not proven defaulters and scoundrels. We know anyway that Hitler himself did not take his offer at all seriously, however reasonable it sounded. Three days after making it he wrote: 'The German war aim must be the final military liquidation of the West ... As regards the world this avowed objective must, however, undergo such propagandistic corrections as are psychologically necessary from instance to instance.' Between Nazi Germany and what remained of free Europe peace was no longer possible.

On the other hand the Allies did not want an active war. According to a memorandum of their Commander-in-Chief, General Gamelin, they could take the offensive only in 1941. In fact the French were incapable of doing so because the nation lacked the necessary enthusiasm – an attitude which endears it from the human point of view but one which did not help to preserve the balance of power or to simplify strategy. The Allies did not live up to the claim made by the declaration of war of 3 September. They wanted to wait, to find supporters. Hence the curious episode which the West called the 'phoney' war, when the protagonists faced each other inactively on the Western front and searched clumsily for other theatres of war and other enemies. Twice, over Finland and over Turkey, the Allies nearly forced the Soviet Union into the war on Germany's side – a piece of stupidity which proved their helplessness. In France the feeling was widespread that the whole affair was pointless and that Europe would do well to resign itself to the inevitable, to German control, instead of serving British interests. The French did in fact resuscitate the war aims of Napoleon and Marshal Foch: the partition of Germany into its historic parts, and the Rhine as France's frontier. But few people believed in these objectives. Nor was the slightest thing done to make such dreams a reality.

Hitler had no war plan. His aims were definite: the 'liquidation' of all European states, including the Russian, one after the other, avoiding a war on several fronts. The method, the means, the sequence were matters for improvisation. Being at once monarch, politician-in-chief, supreme commander and his own chief of general staff, Hitler played off against each other two planning organizations under his control, the high command of the entire armed forces and that of the Army; he moved from opportunity to opportunity, concentrating each time on one venture, one attack, one victim and leaving the future to take care of itself. That was the manner in which he had operated at home and abroad; now he conducted the war on the same lines. The great empire which he wanted to found was to be German, not European, but he wanted to found it on European soil. This meant the conquest of all the European peoples. Nothing less was meant by their 'military liquidation'; Hitler would not have agreed to anything approaching free federation, even under German domination. But the conquest, even if it succeeded, could not last. To transform the majority of Europeans into second-class nations or helots was impossible. At the time the Belgians, the Dutch and even the French were discussing the need for a united Europe and the fact that the age of the small states was past, ideas which would have found a certain degree of support if attempts had been made to translate them into action. What Hitler offered could never command any support.

Even if one made allowances for his distinction between Slav and Germanic peoples the fate of Poland after September 1939 showed what Hitler offered. His orders regarding Poland were known only to a few people at the time. He himself delighted in describing them as devilish. And devilish they were, for they amounted to the extinction of all forms of higher civilization, the murder of the ruling classes, and to 'racial extermination'. The Poles who had dared to say no to a German claim were henceforth to be unskilled workers for German culture, nothing else. The Polish Jews, millions of them, were to be murdered. The execution of this play began during the campaign or shortly afterwards. A German officer who owned an estate in Poznán asked in his will for a cross to be erected there in memory of those murdered in the late autumn of 1939 with the inscription: 'Here lie between fourteen and fifteen hundred Christians and Jews. May God have mercy on their souls and on their murderers.' A young soldier wrote home from the campaign: 'Never shall I tell what I have experienced and seen.' These are comments of Germans who were there. Poland was isolated in its agony, but such misdeeds cannot be kept completely secret. From refugees, from German soldiers, the world heard something of the fate of the defeated Poles. This would finally have ruled out negotiations with Hitler had they not been out of the question already. Europe found itself unable or unwilling to take serious action against the ascendancy which Hitler's Germany had gained in Europe without being able to suggest any other real solution of the European problem (because France's war aims were simply ludicrous); yet it could never accept Hitler's solution of which he had given a demonstration in Poland.

The way out of the impasse was a new, real war. Again, as a dozen times since 1933, Germany took the initiative. Europe must be made to accept what it was not prepared to agree to voluntarily and in so doing Germany would treat the 'so-called neutrals' – as Hitler put it – like the avowed enemy. Already in October the decision had been taken to invade France, circumventing the Maginot Line and mopping up Belgium and Holland in the process. Again the Army High Command warned against any early venture of this kind, pointing to the numerical superiority of the enemy; once more Hitler contemptuously ignored the warnings, claiming that he knew the French better. Although General von Manstein who, like many of his colleagues, describes the occasion in his memoirs, says that the Army High Command was 'overpowered', it must be admitted that the High Command had not much authority left, and that the crises after 1933 in which it lost more and more of its authority are too numerous to be counted. The execution of the plan, originally timed for November, was put off several times. Other projects intervened. In April 1940 German troops invaded Denmark and Norway with the aim of protecting ore supplies from Sweden by the sea route and safeguarding Europe's northern coasts against a possible British attack. Norway collapsed in three weeks in spite of hastily improvised Allied help – a lightning campaign to Hitler's taste, with all the tricks and the cruelty of his *Machtergreifung*. Although Norway escaped the fate of Poland and kept its own puppet government, the German occupation caused much misery and sowed the seeds of a hatred which even today, after so many years, has not died away completely. Moreover, after the Scandinavian affair and the way in which it was carried out, the remaining neutrals knew what they might expect. The second great war of the twentieth century had started carefully, hesitatingly. After the fall of Norway it was clear that in the end no law would be observed in this war.

The great offensive in the West began in May 1940. It was over by June and was the most mystifying event in the history of modern war. The Dutch Army capitulated after three days, the Belgian after three weeks and the French after six weeks. Here too the Germans used a strategy of terror; the bombardment of Rotterdam, culminating in the destruction of the town centre one hour after the surrender of Holland, started a type of warfare which was later to back-fire upon Germany. By and large, however, these fantastic victories were achieved straightforwardly. They were won because of the superiority of German leadership, troops and arms over an enemy who had no wish for a repetition of the sacrifices of the First World War. The French fell into every trap of strategy and propaganda. When the be-all and end-all of their war plan, their great line of fortifications, was outflanked and broken, they had nothing left. Their own panic and collapse, the flight of countless millions across the country to the south, caused them more misery than the victor who was interested in preserving order and who behaved in a comparatively disciplined manner. In the summer of 1940 France presented a picture of ignorance, cynicism, merry-making indifference, secret readiness to make common cause with a superior enemy who seemed to have history on his side, dislike of the world which disturbed its peace, and class conflict; there was the awareness that France had technically 'declared' war and was in this sense responsible for what had happened; only in the hearts of a minority was there shame and despair. The generals were aged, stubborn men from a glorious past, with strong Fascist sympathies; having proved incapable of fighting the war, they offered an armistice and managed to get their own people to approve of it. They could do this because it was what the vast majority wanted. Hitler accepted rapidly and had the armistice signed on the very spot and in the very railway carriage in which twenty-two years before the unhappy German parliamentarians had met Marshal Foch.

This act of revenge and self-gratification could not make the event more real than it was; it could only symbolize the senselessness of the see-saw of victory and defeat in the history of Franco-German enmity. As Hitler's victories became impressive and unprecedented they also became more shadowy. Nor did they give much pleasure to the German people, satiated as it was with historical wishes come true – 'greater' Germany, victory in Czechoslovakia, victory in Poland and now victory in France; if they gave pleasure it was only because they seemed to bring the end nearer. Western Europe no longer had the will to fight

Europe's strongest military power. Yet it was not really willing to submit; nations with the traditions of the Dutch and the French could not do so. They pretended to fight and pretended to submit. The settlement differed in each of the four western states, depending on whether king and government had gone into exile or remained. In general what happened everywhere was an aping of German, Italian or Spanish Fascism, which was impotence incarnate. 'Fascism' must at least be sovereign, must be able to make big gestures and have the nation and glory behind it. The various types of west European Fascism were the outcome of defeat, represented by men who lacked the support of their people and who profited from its misery. The power which they possessed was everywhere that of the German Army, a power not theirs but above them. It was impossible to establish a 'European order' on such foundations. Yet Berlin made merry and thought that the end of the affair was near. Field-marshals were appointed by the dozen, troops were demobilized and the 'greatest commander of all times' was fêted. In fact nothing had been decided.

We have said that at the time there was among the peoples of Europe a readiness to give up old political habits and to accept new social and inter-state forms of existence. But Nazi Germany had done nothing to prepare for such a change and could not do so. 'Europe' and the 'Reich', Europe and the power of the German tyrant were conflicting entities, and even if Hitler had wanted to offer the Western peoples an acceptable, free order – which he and his system were by their very nature incapable of doing – Britain's big 'no' would have been enough to make it impossible. Whatever happened, there could be no true peace on the Continent while Britain did not make peace and continued to offer example and hope to all European resistance. Britain did not make peace and failed to hear the contemptuously thrown out offer which Hitler repeated in July. A new note was struck. The campaign in the East had been terrible for the Poles, but it was a local, isolated affair, an overture after which the curtain did not rise for a long time. The war in the West had ended almost ridiculously. Britain meant business. Winston Churchill, warrior, artist, adventurer and statesman saw Hitler for what he was:

'That wicked man, that repository and embodiment of so many soul-destroying hatreds, that monstrous product of former wrong and shame . . .' He swore that Britain would not rest until the worst blot that had ever sullied the face of humanity had been obliterated. Churchill brought meaning and magnificence and moral greatness to the war. Britain did not fight for itself for it could have had peace at once; it fought for itself only to the extent that on its existence depended the survival of human rights. Let us add that there was an element of danger in this grand gesture. A political war became a crusade of right against wrong. Later this had unfortunate consequences. But could the trend have been avoided at this stage? Was Hitler's cause, given his nature and the way in which he pursued his aims, not really the wrong one? Enough attempts had been made to use diplomatic methods and to treat him as an ordinary power.

Britain's 'no' was impressive, the only great human event of the period. Unfortunately it could not be followed up by action. At Dunkirk the British Army, inadequate in numbers, had saved its bare skin, no more, from the collapse in France. It was impossible to think of a liberation of the Continent for years to come, and then only if Britain gained allies. The unreality of the British position during the following year lay in the fact that the British claimed to be fighting for a victory which was completely beyond their grasp until other, stronger powers intervened. Who this would eventually be was an open secret.

Hitler, master of Europe from the North Cape to the Spanish frontier and through his Italian ally to Sicily and Africa, had not at first worried about the continuation of the game. As always, from May to June he had concentrated on one victim. When Britain refused to admit defeat he was forced to ask 'what now?' and, very belatedly, gave orders to prepare for the invasion of Britain. For this purpose he thought that he must first eliminate the British Air Force. In the first really serious battle of the war, the Battle of Britain, he failed to do so. Thereupon he decided to ignore Britain for the time being.

As after the Polish campaign there followed a period of war without theatres of war or only with subsidiary ones, a period of exploration and manoeuvre. The Italians, whose intervention in France had come too late to gain them glory, sought laurels by attacking the British in Egypt; a venture which did them no good. Then they tried to gain them by attacking Greece; another venture which did them no good. Mussolini gave Hitler the idea of cutting off Britain from Suez; hence the German landing in Africa. From Mussolini also he inherited for better or for worse the war against Greece. This went together with an action against Yugoslavia. Hungary, Bulgaria and Rumania submitted to German leadership, produced what was demanded of them, and when asked even participated in Germany's campaigns. The Serbs alone rebelled in March, breaking the treaty imposed upon them. Hitler tolerated no rebellion in Europe since rebellion is contagious. Yugoslavia was conquered and then Greece. Once more the British had given what help they could, as in Norway and in France; again they had been driven out.

There were German troops in Oslo and on the frontiers of Egypt, in Bayonne, in Warsaw and in Athens. The whole continent, with the exception of Sweden and Spain, was directly or indirectly under German control; Spain too and even Sweden were ready to give the help expected from them. This was a fantastic adventure, a tremendous national effort. The sheer territorial expansion already went far beyond anything that had been achieved in the First World War; whether the same could be said of the conquest of real opposition is another question. Europe was flabbier and more undermined in 1941 than in 1916, readier to surrender. Hitherto everything had gone incredibly easily, except for the landing in Britain; and that had not been attempted.

There was talk of the invincible 'fortress Europe'. A German professor lectured on 'closed areas in which intervention is prohibited', of which the German was one. How could it be conquered as long as its rulers did not intervene in other similar areas? In the spring of 1941 there was near peace from the Atlantic to the Pacific coast of Eurasia; a Japanese diplomat travelled comfortably in his private railway carriage from China via Moscow to Berlin and Rome. What he heard there was less peaceful.

It is impossible to determine when exactly Hitler decided to attack Russia. Such an issue is not decided in a day. Although it had never really been in doubt Hitler toyed with other, conflicting plans; he may have been sincere when in November 1940 he made grandiose proposals to the Russian Foreign Minister for the partition of the British Empire. Sincerity is a word without firm meaning in such a context. There were indications as early as July 1940 that the peace with Russia would not last long. There was the order in November to prepare action 'Barbarossa'. There was also the chapter in *Mein Kampf* in which Hitler elaborated the theme that in Russia and there alone Germany could find the *Lebensraum* which it needed. In this he was correct to the extent that it could certainly not be found in Belgium or Denmark.

There was no compulsion to attack the Soviet Union. It did not threaten Germany. Or rather, it threatened Germany only in the sense that it existed, that it was an important industrial and military power which in the last resort could not be trusted, particularly as treaties no longer counted; therefore Hitler could not concentrate completely on Britain as long as there was a sovereign state and an undefeated army in the East. It was the situation which in 1812 allegedly forced Napoleon to turn against Russia. But was Napoleon really forced to march to Moscow, was his a rational political act? There have always been historians who have doubted it. Furthermore, Stalin fulfilled his obligations towards Hitler much more punctiliously than Tsar Alexander his towards Napoleon. The Tsar cast inquiring glances at Britain, broke the rules of the continental blockade and saw the great clash approaching. Stalin cast no glances at all in the direction of Britain, supplied the Germans faithfully the goods which he was committed to supply and had no inkling of the approaching clash. He contemptuously ignored Britain's and America's well-founded warnings; while Hitler uttered sweet words to the last day, Stalin went through veritable contortions of appeasement, putting those of poor Neville Chamberlain absolutely in the shade. It is impossible to do more than speculate whether Russia would ever have attacked Germany. Such a move was against the character of the Russian nation, against traditional Russian strategy, Communist doctrine and against Stalin's cautious, even cowardly nature and his respect for Germany's military strength. When Hitler sent his troops across the Russian frontier this was the free decision of a single man. Once more he won his first victories because the enemy was surprised and very badly prepared.

There were German military men who held Russia's strength in less contempt than the supreme commander. But as so far their warnings had always proved wrong and as they had almost completely lost any influence on policy making and the direction of the war, their voice was very feeble; yet in Germany's interest on this occasion it should have been strong and decisive. Hitler claimed that the information about Russia's strength was a fiction and was certain that he could end the venture before the onset of winter. The best informed American military counted on a campaign of 'at least a month and at best three months'.

A greater technical task has never been tackled; because and to the extent that it was technical and a task for masculine skill, the flower of the German nation, the Army, set to work with a will. Napoleon had marched into Russia with half a million men in a single column, weakly flanked by auxiliary troops to the south and the north. Now millions were thrown forward in three offensives: against Leningrad, against Moscow and against the south-east. Experts assure us that this three-pronged offensive without a 'centre of gravity' was a mistake; Germany should have concentrated on the enemy instead of occupying territory. But Hitler was the sole planner of German strategy and he was given to large-scale outflanking manoeuvres, to the conquest of towns with symbolic names, to spectacular gains which produced loot.

What he wanted was the destruction of the Russian state and people. How this was to be done and how far he wanted to go he was not really clear about; after all it was impossible to kill 180 million people with the technical means available at the time. Probably he was prepared to allow the majority of Russian-speaking people to live, but not as a nation. He said that everybody who even looked discontented must be shot. All active Bolshevists must be liquidated. The Asiatics must be treated as they deserved to be. 'Only *one* people will survive this struggle and that will be the Germans. You, gentlemen, and your brave soldiers shall answer for that. Hammer into them what is at stake. Make them hard and counter any humane and soft ideas among them.' And later in a speech to the nation: 'We have been entrusted by our Maker with an historical revision of unique dimensions which we are committed to carrying out.' The extermination of the Russian state and people would have been a considerable 'historical revision'. In no war in Christian times was the alternative 'you or us' put so shamelessly. The German generals saw the situation in a different light. They tell us how they tried to avoid carrying out Hitler's criminal commands, to preserve 'soldierly decency', to save prisoners from starving to death, and if possible to gain the sympathies of the population. There is no reason to disbelieve them; they were not barbarians. Nor need one think that the German Army as a whole behaved more brutally than other armies. Pleasure in cruelty exists in every nation; it flourishes wherever people are given the chance to practise it that war provides; these are temptations which individuals succumb to everywhere, but not the majority. Thrown into a far-off, alien and hostile country, harassed by partisans behind his own front lines, frightened by the behaviour of an enemy who knew no mercy towards the invader, the German private did his hard duty because he had to, and made life as tolerable as possible for himself. Tolstoy in *War and Peace* expressed the feeling of those caught up in such migrations; one individual, the emperor, the dictator, cannot really have been responsible for this fate of millions; it happens because it has to happen ... The German soldier certainly wanted to win, that was part of it all. The difficult and tortuous idea that Germany's victory would be Hitler's victory and that this was undesirable could only occur to a few independent minds.

Such was the attitude of the officers and men. It did not alter the fact that the great mass of sensible and sane people served a few criminals, that by their brave action they made a devilish undertaking possible. Germany had had a double face since 1933; the man who was Chancellor, head of state and in this case supreme commander over his generals, could if he wished, talk sensibly; yet at the same time he gave insane orders which were punctually carried out; if not by the Army then by specially drilled 'commandos'. Just as the Army looked the other way and did not want to know about these things, the historian also does not like to speak of them. These are deeds and figures which the imagination cannot grasp, which the mind refuses to believe, however clearly they can be proved by reason. They are true. We have the orders, the speeches of the 'Reich Commissar for the Consolidation of the German Heritage' to his henchmen; we have the reports of eye witnesses, the evidence of the commandants of the extermination camps in court; we have the photographs. There can be no doubt about a crime which happened in our time and which will cast a shadow on the image of man and his story for ever. The worst, the gas chambers in the extermination camps in Poland where Europe's Jews, millions of them, were killed, was then known only to a very small number of criminals. The Allies, much better informed than the German Army and people, knew nothing exact about these camps. The story was different as regards the mass murders of Jews or Communist officials which took place publicly during the Russian war. A German officer reported in 1942 from the Ukraine that he had been an 'eye-witness to a mass extermination during the "final solution of the Jewish question" and he did not wish such an experience for his worst enemy'. Carl Goerdeler wrote to General Kluge in 1943: 'Last week I heard an 18½ year-old SS soldier, once a decent boy, say calmly that it was "not exactly pleasant" to machine-gun ditches filled with thousands of Jews and then to throw earth on bodies that were still moving. What have they done to the proud army of the wars of Liberation and William I.' These were the lowest depths of Hitler's venture. And in this instance the lowest depth and greatest crimes determined the character of the whole.

At another level also, not quite so close to hell and not at all secret, Germany's war policy destroyed its own aims and possibilities. In Russia, particularly in the non-Russian districts of the Soviet Union, in the Baltic provinces and the Ukraine, the

German Army had been received with sympathy. Here was a chance which the German generals saw and wished to use. But Hitler made no distinction between Ukrainians and Poles; in future the Germans must be the masters and the Slavs the out-lawed serfs, whether Great Russians, Little Russians or Czechs. The Party bosses who had established themselves and their staffs in the occupied territories governed in their master's interest and their own, not in the interest of the Army; their purpose was to establish themselves securely and to exploit. 'In the old days', said Göring, 'this was called plundering. Perhaps the forms have become more humane. Be that as it may, I intend to plunder, and extensively at that . . .' One form of plunder was that of human beings. Over five million men were captured in the conquered territories and taken to work in Germany; it would be wrong to say that they were all made to work under barbaric conditions; some later stayed on voluntarily; but the conditions of the great majority were nevertheless wretched and degrading. The Russian prisoners of war who at the beginning had surrendered in vast numbers because they had no desire to fight for the despot in the Kremlin, were left to starve to death. 'In the prisoner-of-war camps,' Göring said to the Italian Foreign Minister in the winter of 1942, 'the Russians have started to eat each other. This year between twenty and thirty million people will die of hunger in Russia. Perhaps this is a good thing . . .'

Faced with such an enemy there was in the long run only one possible reaction. The people of Russia, confused in 1941, at odds with themselves and easily defeated, during the following year united in hatred against the invader; and, as there was no other, they united under the leadership of the Kremlin.

Germany lost its Russian opportunity, having long lost its European one. After starting his war against Moscow Hitler liked to present himself as a European, defending freedom, defending Europe's ancient civilization against the Huns of the twentieth century. Europe ignored the call and could but ignore it. Again through no fault of the Army leadership. In 1940 the German Army had shown more restraint in France and Belgium than in 1914 and its commanders were full of goodwill. At first they in turn had the goodwill of a large part of the population. But as the political leadership made it impossible for them to keep their promises the occupation regime and its local 'collaborators' quickly incurred the deadly hatred of the people. The exploitation of the occupied countries for the German war effort; the unwillingness for five years to send prisoners of war home and the deportation of forced labour; Germany's refusal to make peace and to recognize existing frontiers because it did not want to recognize any frontiers and wanted to break up the old states of western Europe or incorporate them in some fantastic medieval form into the Reich; intrigues to incite one section of a people against another; the filling of government posts with weak Fascists without popular support; and finally the cruel suppression of all opposition, the police terror, the shooting of hostages and the torture – these were not the means to unite Europe. Not even if it had been true that Europe could not be united without a central authority and without a degree of force. The Europeans did not regard Germany's struggle against Russia as their own. Even the voluntary legions of the French and the Spaniards could not hide this fact. They achieved almost nothing, nor did the troops of the states considered Germany's full fledged allies, Rumania, Italy and Hungary, achieve much. As Europe watched the German–Russian duel from afar its hopes were predominantly with Russia.

One may say that this was a tragedy, another late chapter in the history of Europe's self-destruction. If at the time Germany had been what it owed itself and the world to be then its cause would indeed have been that of Europe. It would have been its task, as it was for hundreds of years the task of Austria and Prussia, to counterbalance the power of Russia and to keep it in check. Hitler's Europeanism was a belated, hastily improvised, blatant lie. He and the Nazi ideology could not unite Europe, neither against an external enemy nor internally, nor defend Christian civilization.

Nobody was free from guilt. The walls of the prison in which Europe languished were built with many bricks: the Russo-German Pact of August 1939, Poland's boastful manner, France's insistence on alliances and on preserving the balance of power without wanting to act when the need arose, Britain's prolonged appeasement policy, the neutral or uncommitted attitude of the small nations, as though it was still possible to be neutral towards Hitler, the inability of all to show up Hitler's solution of the European problem by putting forward a better and real solution, the universal egoism and the long years of futile talk. Not even the great neutral power across the Atlantic was free from guilt. Having decided the First World War, America had hastily vanished, pretending that it was not concerned with Europe. It was as if by its attitude it had invalidated the result of the war; because in spite of all the clever follies of the Treaty of Versailles, Germany was and remained by far the strongest power in Europe, and if the Continent was left to itself Germany was bound to gain a dominant position in it. In Hitler's time, before and during the war, President Roosevelt had played the great arbiter who was both involved in and above Europe's problems; who encouraged the Continent's struggle against Germany, supporting it by a number of elaborate tricks, yet unable to throw the weight of his own nation into the scales at the right moment. Convinced that the world could not live with Hitler but tied by the American constitution, by the traditional neutrality of the United States, he approached his goal by small, methodical steps; he provided Britain with useful supplies, assisted the British fleet, made treaties with European governments in exile, and in the end even ordered American ships to shoot at sight at German submarines. Roosevelt's actions formed a chain of provocations. As yet, however, America was placing only a small part of its resources at the service of the European war, and Germany had no interest in increasing the American effort tenfold by a formal declaration of war. Things might have gone on like that for a long time because, according to a cherished myth, Americans never start a war, nor do they voluntarily take part in one; someone must force them to do so. On this occasion it was Japan which did America this terrible favour. Far advanced in its imperialistic adventure in east Asia, apparently close to its aim of founding on that continent and the big Pacific islands an empire roughly corresponding to

Hitler's Reich in Eurasia, Japan had recognized in America the enemy which it must first eliminate. The moment seemed favourable. Russia, fighting for its life, could take no action, Britain's energies were tied, and even those of America were already strongly committed in Europe. On 7 December 1941 the Japanese bombed the American Navy in Pearl Harbor. As they also attacked the British possessions in the Pacific, and Britain and America therefore became allies against Japan, the circle would in any case soon have been complete. Hitler, however, did not wait for the natural outcome. On 11 December he ordered 'the American chargé d'affaires to be handed his passports', to use an expression from a bygone diplomatic age. On the same day Germany, Italy and Japan concluded a triple war alliance. What had begun as a German 'reprisal against Poland' now spanned the earth; it had become a double war and a world war in a sense in which the war of 1914 never had been.

Fate played on miscalculation, on men's ignorance. When in November the Japanese decided on their blow against Pearl Harbor they believed what all the world believed then: that Russia was finished, that it could therefore safely be left to the Germans and that Japan was free to fight with America. This, we know, was an error. If the Japanese had wisely forborne to attack America President Roosevelt could not have brought his country into the war so soon, however much he wanted to do so. If instead they had concentrated their whole strength against Russia the Bolshevik state would probably have collapsed. The world would then look different today; not better, but different.

Although in the first months of its war in the Pacific Japan scored most remarkable victories, after December 1941 no one in the Anglo-Saxon camp had any real doubts about the end of the affair. Both Germany and Japan were strong. But physically far apart, fighting different enemies and with over-extended fronts, they did not constitute a genuine alliance. Neither did the Russians and the Anglo-Americans in the sense of trusting each other wholeheartedly. But at least they fought against the same enemy and gave each other effective support. The Anglo-Saxon alliance, the partnership of Americans, Canadians, British and Australians was the most intimate there has ever been; a world-wide network of bases, sources of raw materials, centres of production, information, opportunities to exert diplomatic influence and prestige, at the heart of which there was North America, incalculably rich, fresh and spoilt by fortune. Once more the United States could do what it had done in the first war and what no state will ever be able to do again: in the midst of war it could, safe from attack, prepare in comfort for war and then appear on the scene, supplied abundantly with means to kill and to save people. The Allies decided that Germany was the main enemy which must be dealt with first, before Japan; they decided to approach the main enemy methodically, step by step: to attack him in Africa, in the Mediterranean, in Italy and only then in France. Meanwhile they would torment German towns with bombs but let the Russians carry the main burden. Their plan was methodical and cruel, designed to protect the lives of their own people, without feeling for the lives and sufferings of the enemy nations.

That a great war must have great aims was also part of the American tradition. Americans only went to war when they were attacked or could claim to have been attacked, but then they went far beyond the aim of mere defence and protection of rights. Roosevelt and his friends were lavish with their promises for the post-war period: there would be eternal peace and social justice; freedom from fear, force, hunger and want; the 'aggressor nations' only needed to be brought to their knees to achieve such an ideal condition. There were three, or rather two, aggressor nations, because the Italians were not to be taken seriously. All other nations were good and all other governments (for example the Russian) were good. The good, peace-loving nations must form themselves into a great league, 'the United Nations', which they did at Christmas 1941. With some changes, additions and omissions the American plan was a revival of Wilson's programme.

However, this time it aroused no pious enthusiasm among the Anglo-Saxon peoples. In 1941 mankind was more sceptical than in 1914. During the Second World War Germany gave more genuine cause for hatred than during the First, yet it was hated much less in America, really not at all. German citizens living there were hardly molested. The Americans read the atrocity stories without much emotion, and in any case they only heard the worst after 1945. They worked, earned money and sent their sons overseas. These fought well, but more or less as the Germans fought well, because there was a great technical task to be mastered and because one did one's duty among comrades. They did not fight for Roosevelt's 'four freedoms'.

But if America's war was not a serious crusade for a good cause it became a serious struggle against a bad cause. That was the character which it was given by the political leadership, a development which had tangible political consequences. Roosevelt, like Churchill, was convinced that Hitler was an enemy of humanity with whom there must be no negotiation. Therefore, the argument went, one could not negotiate with Germany since Hitler and nobody else governed Germany and led the German Army. 'Hitler is Germany and Germany is Hitler', had been the Nazi cry long before the war. This mad principle was now in practice taken over by the Allies. Hitler, Nazi Germany and Germany, these three seemed to them synonymous. Indeed, they had been synonymous long before Hitler. The Second World War was the direct continuation of the First, merely a last link in the long chain of German attempts at hegemony over Europe and a large part of the world. The real enemy was 'German militarism'; it was this which must be destroyed, not just the man who after all could never have committed his crimes without the general staff and without the people. The Allies must avoid a repetition of the mistake of 1918. On that occasion fine promises had been made to the Germans, some of which were kept and some of which were broken. As a result of those that were kept the Reich and its Army were let off lightly, and Germany's military power was able to rise again quickly. Those promises that were not kept had given the Germans an excuse to claim that they had been deceived, that they could have gone on fighting for a long time and could have won if they had not been taken in by Wilson's fine promises. This time the Allies were going to do things differently. There would be no more promises, no peace programme to whose idealistic articles the defeated enemy might be entitled to appeal. 'Unconditional surrender' – that was the demand which the Americans and British made after January 1943 and which they offered their enemy day in day out in leaflets and over the radio as the only alternative to continued bombing and killing. It is easy to commit a new mistake in wanting to avoid the repetition of an old one and to learn from history. Wilson's promises had been too generous. Roosevelt's promises as far as they concerned the enemy were too simple, too brutal, too lacking in imagination. They positively invited Germany to go on fighting as long as possible. To equate the spirit of Hitler with the spirit of Prussia, the guilt of the Nazis with the guilt of the general staff, and to find in German history a straight line of brutal imperialism leading from Frederick the Great to Hitler – these were simplifications that were scientifically untenable and harmful in practice. We know from past experience that war makes people stupid. They see only one goal, victory, and nothing else. An intelligent, historically educated man like Churchill must have known this in his more lucid moments. When he decided in June 1941 to give the Russians every possible assistance he said that thanks to Hitler his task had been greatly simplified. He wanted to destroy Hitler; and if the devil were fighting Hitler then he, Churchill, would address a few nice words in Parliament to the devil.

The attitude of the Allies matched that of the German tyrant. The worst that can be said of them is that, during the last years of the war, they sometimes descended to his level, that in their rage, their just horror and their impatience, they too sometimes did things which Hitler had been the first to do. Both Hitler and the Allies were obsessed by the experience of 1918. Hitler screamed that there must not be another 9 November 1918, Germany must not again fall for enemy promises, there must be no capitulation, Germany must fight on until five minutes past twelve. The Allies replied that there must be no more 'Fourteen Points', the guilty must not be spared, there must be no stopping at the frontiers of the enemy state, there must be a march to Berlin and Germany must be broken up. They drew exactly opposite lessons from the story of 1918 and the years that followed. As they had been taken in by Hitler, the evangelist of peace, they were now taken in by the man of total war. The two attitudes, that of Hitler and that of Roosevelt and Churchill, complemented and reinforced each other. Both renounced politics and only made war for the sake of war.

But if they had acted differently and encouraged the German opposition by sensible proposals, they would probably have fared no better. Hitler had everybody murdered who criticized his policy, everybody who even thought of negotiating with the enemy. The grip of tyranny on the German nation was such that it was no longer accessible even to the most sensible voices from abroad because merely listening to foreign broadcasts was punishable with death. Nevertheless the Allies should have tried, although it is probable that even without the mistaken, over-simplifying demand for 'unconditional surrender' the whole thing would have ended as it did.

Let us return to the course of events. The winter of 1941-2 brought the great non-European powers, America and Japan, into the war. It brought Japan's great triumphal procession in the Far East – shocks which although they could not preserve the Japanese Empire were in some way irreversible. For the German armed forces the same winter brought the first terrible setback, or the second if we regard the Battle of Britain as the first. It appeared that Russia's resistance was unbroken and it was capable of mounting a counter-offensive.

This had not been expected in Germany, at any rate not by Hitler and his henchmen. The *Führer*'s headquarters had claimed as early as November that the Russian state had collapsed and had described its armies as 'shattered remnants', contemptuously ignoring any warning that there still existed vast centres of production and military training grounds east of the Urals. Then came the winter, the coldest for a hundred years, at a time when no winter campaign had been planned and nothing had been prepared. Then came the Russian counter-attack, fought by troops equipped for the weather and supplied with all necessities. The German front held; but the losses and suffering were such that those who were there have no wish to describe them. At the height of the crisis Hitler took over direct command of the Army. Convinced that any withdrawal spelt catastrophe and that will-power – his willpower – could accomplish anything, he commanded that no inch of soil must be yielded; cashierment from the Army and deterrent courts martial helped to ensure that the order was carried out, so that the positions were held that could serve as the springboard for new large-scale offensives in the spring. If any further proof had been needed to convince Hitler of his infinite superiority over the professional soldiers, of the fact that he was one of the chosen whom providence always protected, it was this achievement. At that time he was fond of comparing himself to Napoleon, claiming that he had avoided the fate which had befallen 'another man' a hundred and thirty years earlier.

Then came the campaign of 1942, the last great conquest of Hitler's war. In spite of recent experiences Hitler's judgement of the previous autumn was not revised; the enemy was exhausted and finished and the efforts which he had made in the winter had been the last he was capable of. Therefore it was less important to destroy the remains of his armed forces than to occupy large areas, reaching the centres of Russian industry and raw material production in order to make Russian grain, oil, ore and coal available to Germany. There were two offensives, one against the Caucasus and one across the Don towards the Volga. The Volga was reached at Stalingrad and the Germans occupied the northern Caucasus. Hitler rightly boasted about the technical achievements which made this advance possible and enabled the economic harvest to be reaped. In the same speech he swore that Stalingrad would be taken and that then nobody could drive the German troops from their positions which cut across the enemy's most important supply route. But as he talked and boasted the two offensives came to a halt, as in the previous year. The German fronts in Russia were extremely extended, one to the south and one to the east, weakly linked and badly protected against break-throughs and outflanking movements. Again Hitler ordered that not a foot of territory was to be evacuated, leaving the commanders on the spot no freedom of manoeuvre; and again the enemy, allegedly exhausted and bled white, launched a winter offensive with immense materials and an immense superiority in men. In vain did the generals warn Hitler to abandon the advanced position at Stalingrad. The German Sixth Army, between two and three hundred thousand men, was encircled by the Russians, advancing from the south and the north-east. The promise to supply the besieged army by air could only be partially kept. Hitler's order prevented the troops from breaking out while they still had the strength to do so. The circle became smaller, the Russian artillery fire assumed a concentration unknown even in the First World War and there was hunger, cold and death; Napoleon's losses during his retreat from Russia were only a little in excess of those of the Germans at Stalingrad alone. On 1 February 1943 the German commander surrendered with what he had left, about ninety thousand men. 'For Stalingrad,' Hitler proudly said, 'I alone am responsible.'

Coinciding with the catastrophe in southern Russia there was a catastrophe in North Africa. In November General Rommel's *Afrikakorps* was decisively defeated by the British; what was left of it withdrew in the direction of Tunis. But they were not safe there because in November American and British troops had landed in Morocco. Squeezed from east and west, harassed by well supplied, fresh troops, cut off from Europe by the Allied air force, without supplies and without hope the Axis forces surrendered in Tunis in May 1943. In the summer the Allies occupied Sicily and landed in southern Italy. Mussolini, Germany's irreplaceable ally in his heyday, for whom the war had begun so hurriedly four years before, was removed by a *coup*. Italy capitulated in September and disappeared as an active source of energy – if it had ever been one; quick action however enabled the Germans to secure the greater part of the peninsula and to torment the country for almost two years with their defensive war. The last attempt to advance on the Eastern front failed in the summer of 1943. Henceforth the initiative rested with the Allies; the Germans retreated everywhere, step by step, abandoning their conquests; retreated although their troops behaved heroically and were well led by their local commanders. But they always withdrew too late, to lines which could not be defended because nothing had been prepared to defend them – 'otherwise the troops would cast longing glances backwards'. They never evacuated any region freely and according to a plan, while it was possible to do so without catastrophe. The strategy of the self-appointed 'greatest commander of all times' now amounted to keeping his armies where they stood, in non-existent fortresses, in countries the occupation of which had long lost its earlier purpose, from Norway to Greece, while superior enemies broke in from all sides.

Polite attempts were made to induce Hitler to give up direct military leadership. But he absolutely refused on the ground that he was more capable than anyone else. The despised western democracies developed an organization which worked well; for the planned Anglo-American invasion of France there was a supreme commander with an internationally constituted staff. Hitler wanted Germany, people and army, to be led according to the dictates of his iron will alone; but among his subordinates there was confusion, a struggle for power, distrust and envious conflict. There were continual changes of command. Field-marshals were appointed and dismissed, so-called *Führer* orders conflicted with orders given by the regular authorities. The German Air Force – what was left of it – and the German Navy – what was left of it – obeyed the whims of their commander. Heinrich Himmler's *Waffen-SS*, an independent army, was privileged, securing the best troop replacements and accepting orders only from the executioner-in-chief, the *Reichsführer SS*. In the occupied territories the agents of the *Beauftragte für den Arbeitseinsatz* (Commissioners of the Planned Distribution of Labour) pursued their policy of seizing manpower while senior SS and police officers gave their criminal orders without paying attention to the somewhat less inhumane attitude of the military governors.

After Russia's entry into the war the Communists organized rebellion against Germany, assassinations and acts of sabotage, in all conquered territories, from Greece to France. There was also a non-Communist resistance which gained in importance as liberation by the Western Allies approached or seemed to approach. In France these resistance troops were para-military units claiming the rights of combatants and causing the Germans serious worry. The occupying power replied as threatened conquerors always have replied to resistance from the defeated enemy: with terror. Fifty Frenchmen, a hundred Italians for one murdered German. The military governors also ordered the shooting of hostages, but they did so with a heavy heart and in their reports warned against the effects of such barbarism. The worst crimes were committed by units of the SS and the SD (Security Service). Let us not describe and list these things. But let us not think either that inhuman cruelty is a specifically German characteristic. The French under Napoleon did similar things in Spain – one need only look at Goya's drawings. If the leaders erect a system out of bestiality there will always be a minority willing to obey. This has been so everywhere at all times. The number of victims in the Second World War was greater than in other wars because all numbers were greater. They were small in the West compared with what happened in Poland and Russia.

Europe did not want the kind of unity which Hitler forced upon it. It reacted, it could not but react; and it reacted all the more strongly because the Allies encouraged it to do so and because it saw the day of liberation approaching. The occupying power reacted in turn, believing that it must safeguard its security and authority. Terror heightened terror. In the East the situation was different. There had never been any talk of collaboration there, only of extermination, and the numbers of the victims were ten or a hundred times greater. In addition there was the special madness of the Nazi Party, pathological Jew-hatred. This was not a reaction because the Jewish attitude towards the conqueror was one of unresisting, fearful willingness. It was a one-sided act of extermination which took the same form everywhere. The Jews in France and in the Netherlands were treated in the same way as the Jews in the East. One does not like to speak of things which one has not experienced and which, though they were done by human beings, one cannot imagine: either the agony or the numbers. It has been impossible to ascertain with certainty how many

Jews were killed; estimates vary between four and six million. What is the difference? Who can visualize four or six million human beings, men, women and children, picked up at random, in the devilish gas chambers of Auschwitz and Maidanek? Darkness hides this vilest crime ever perpetrated by man against man.

Standards generally deteriorated. Even the Western Allies, civilized, well governed and eloquent though they were, were not immune. They fought the European war slowly and methodically, and until the summer of 1944 they fought it with troops only in the Mediterranean area. Elsewhere for the moment they fought it only in the air. Allied air strategy aimed at spreading terror and wearing down enemy morale. The conviction was widespread that against Nazi Germany any means was justified and that the will of the Germans must be broken somehow. A rain of fire descended nightly on Germany's towns and what was hit were not so much strategic targets and industry – which continued to produce and even managed to raise its output of war material until 1944 – as the life of the population and the architectural glories of the past. The world quickly seemed to descend to the level which the fiend had intrepidly chosen on the first day of war.

Between air raids the Western radio stations relayed the sonorous and self-satisfied voices of propagandists inviting the German people to surrender unconditionally as the only alternative to further 'senseless destruction'. Sound advice, but easier given in editorial offices in New York and London than carried out on the spot. The Germans now lived between two terrors, enemy attacks from the air and the People's Courts which passed sentence of death on Hitler's Germans. Who has counted them? Students and professors, soldiers, workers, apprentices of seventeen, society women, clergymen, nurses, industrialists, writers, Germans of all classes, occupations and ages – they lost their lives because of a carelessly uttered word. The nation which seemed to terrorize Europe lived itself under the same terror; the men of the French Resistance found support among their people and died proudly as patriots whereas every one of the Germans went to his execution alone, abused and expelled from the national community This was the ultimate consequence of the pledge that there would not be another 9 November 1918. In 1943 and also in 1944 one side said: we shall never capitulate, and the other replied: we demand unconditional surrender. Armies fought each other in Russia and Italy; bombs fell on towns, and in concentration camps prisoners died from hunger, overwork, medical experiments or torture. Allied statesmen met at conferences, in good humour, elated and intoxicated by the problems and world-wide perspectives of 'this amazing war', as Churchill called it.

9. Resistance

If history is worth telling because of the noble things which men have done or tried to do then it is worth telling the story of the last years of the war because of the German resistance. In the darkness it was a shining light.

It was now no longer the propaganda, the tricks and the achievements that worked; their time was past. The tyrant's voice was heard less and less frequently – once or twice a year only and when he spoke it was to threaten, not to cajole. There were no more plebiscites, no 'elections to the Reichstag'; nobody was asked: 'Do you, German man, and you, German woman, approve of your government's policy?' Those days were over. The German citizen was obliged to approve of the actions of his government. Disapproval brought death and open resistance seemed as doomed as the mortal creature's opposition to all-powerful elemental forces. Nevertheless there was resistance, the most glorious achievement of German history, if the dictatorship of Hitler and Himmler was the most inglorious.

The Munich students who in February 1943 distributed leaflets telling the truth about the tyranny and calling for sabotage in the armaments factories, were no politicians. They were young, happy Christians; stemming from the Catholic youth movement, at one time even taken in by the cheerful community spirit which the Nazi movement provided for the young, they had gradually come to recognize the true character of Nazism. With their bare hands, with their faith, with their pathetic duplicating machine they fought the omnipotent state. Their efforts were doomed from the start and their time was short. Yet even if German resistance had consisted of nobody but the Scholls and their friends, their actions would have been enough to save a little of the honour of those whose tongue is German. There were many more, clergymen, professors, trade unionists, mayors, landowners and bureaucrats. They were found in the Christian churches, among the proscribed but secretly continuing Social Democratic Party, among the middle class and among the aristocracy. Here I do not mean those who rejected and hated the regime but said so only among their closest friends, nor the great preachers, the bishops who could dare to accuse false gods without actually indulging in politics. Resistance was political activity, the attempt to overthrow the state which was so strong, so terrible, so ruthless that it could not be overthrown from within. There were various circles, Socialist and Conservative, preparing the ground intellectually and pressing for action. At the centre the story-teller must place the military opposition because without it civilians like Julius Leber and Wilhelm Leuschner, Carl Goerdeler and Ulrich von Hassell could not have thought of a *coup*. After 1934 the only way of getting rid of Hitler was by military force. Not for the purpose of establishing a military dictatorship. The generals wanted to overthrow a dictatorship, not to set up one. But their co-operation was essential. The civilians could provide ideas, political plans and contacts with the masses, but the shooting must be done by the soldiers.

However, their occupation in wartime was to make war not indulge in politics, much less to overthrow their own government. That art the German generals had never learned, never practised; it was against their tradition. More difficult still was to fight Hitler's war, to equip and safeguard the Army but at the same time to curse the war and to think of ways of removing the man who had started it. Active senior officers, for example the Chief of Staff of the Army, Franz Halder, could not resolve this conflict. They went far in their opposition, thought, planned and held secret discussions but stopped short of the action which alone could have historical results. Let those who think they could have done better in a similar situation blame these men for their attitude. Others felt no conflict, no scruples. A senior intelligence officer on each occasion informed the victims of future German invasions, the Norwegians, the Dutch, of the proposed date of the attack, to the extent that he knew it. His actions were dictated by his conscience, his hatred of the Nazis; here too it seems idle to ask in retrospect if such an attitude was permissible or not. There were no rules that could be observed under Hitler's criminal dictatorship.

We saw that in August 1939 the military opposition took no serious action. Partly because it was still paralysed by the disappointment of Munich; partly also probably because the war against Poland was as popular with the German Army as any war could be. But soon after the Polish campaign when Hitler ordered the preparation of an offensive in the West secret opposition and planning started again. At its centre was the former Chief of the General Staff, Ludwig Beck. From him threads went to Halder, even to the weak Commander-in-Chief of the Army, Brauchitsch, to the commanders of the intelligence service, Admiral Canaris and General Oster, and to outstanding civilians like the former mayor of Leipzig, Carl Goerdeler. At that period, with the Pope as intermediary, the German opposition and the British were in touch in Rome and the British government showed understanding for the efforts of Hitler's opponents, letting it be known that if they succeeded in overthrowing the dictator before the start of the offensive in the West it might be possible to arrange a peace in which all reasonable German demands would be met. Hitler's opponents did not succeed. No serious attempt was made to delay the signal for the start of the offensive. And it must be said that the general mood in Germany at the time was such that it could not be made. The attack on Poland had been too easy, too triumphant; the Germans were not badly off during the 'phoney war'. Finally, after frequent postponements the Germans attacked in the West. Again their offensive was so successful, German losses were so small and the generals who had feared a second

1916 – a terrible halt in front of the Maginot Line – were proved so wrong and Hitler's judgement emerged as so accurate, that for a long time there could be no question of active opposition. It was the misfortune of the German resistance that while Hitler was victorious there was no psychological opportunity to attack him. Yet when the final victories were immediately followed by the first ominous defeats the Allies had lost their interest in a compromise peace, in negotiations with unknown and dubious so-called 'militarists'; now they thought that they could end the affair in their own way. The story of the German conspiracy against Hitler is a chain of disappointments; his peaceful triumphs, his victories and his defeats in turn perplexed the conspirators. Events never offered them a genuine, promising initiative. Yet the words written by Carl Goerdeler a few weeks after the defeat of France show that the spirit of German resistance never flagged, even at the height of military victory: 'A system which in Germany is based on financial madness, economic pressure, political terror, illegality and immorality can not establish a constructive community of free nations under German leadership.' Under such a system collapse was certain, whether it came soon or later. 'No nation lives alone in the world; God has also created other nations and allowed them to develop ...' 'Everlasting oppression of others is as contrary to the law of God as it is contrary to that of the sensible ... awareness that only free human beings accomplish the highest achievements and that continual free interchange alone preserves and enhances life.' German resistance once more became a possibility and an urgent necessity during the Russian campaign, particularly after the first terrible winter had revealed the lack of preparation, the impudent underestimate of the enemy and the inhumanity of the aims of the German leaders. The conspirators had long been convinced that Hitler must go. Now there was an opportunity of justifying such action to the nation; if men could be found to do it, the man who had misled the people could be arrested, tried or, if need be, murdered; to take such action against the victorious *Führer* would have been impossible because the greater part of the nation would not have understood it. After 1942 there was a succession of plots, some unplanned, others well planned and prepared technically down to the last detail but frustrated by some devilish accident.

To the degree that the opposition spread, that its activity became more marked, more obvious and more excited, the danger which threatened it also increased. It was impossible to hide what so many people thought and planned. There was wave after wave of arrests. Central figures of the conspiracy were awaiting trial in prisons and camps long before the last, most open act was risked.

It was now very late for such an act, too late as some of the participants thought. Or only not too late in the sense of saving Germany's honour without achieving any practical gain. As Colonel Tresckow put it in a message which he sent from the Eastern front to Count Stauffenberg in Berlin:

> The attempt must be made, *coûte que coûte*. Even if it is not successful there must be action in Berlin. It is no longer a question of practical purpose but of demonstrating to the world and to history that the German resistance movement dared to take the vital step. By comparison nothing else matters.

What in 1938 and 1939 and even in 1942 was meant to have been a decisive act could now only be a demonstration of honourable intent. The Allies no longer cared what happened in Germany. They had an inkling of what was going on and could through their agents in Madrid, Berne, Stockholm and Ankara have had much more than an inkling. But they were not interested. The longer the Anglo-Saxons delayed the promised offensive in the West, the longer they waited before they gave decisive military assistance to the Russians, the more anxious they were to come to terms politically with the Kremlin. They put their faith in the unity of the coalition and the loyalty of Russian policy, nothing else. Their self-righteous and short-sighted simplifications were on a par with Hitler's heinous simplifications. To them the 'Prussian Junkers', 'German militarism', the 'general staff' and 'Nazism' were one and the same thing which must this time be eradicated root and branch. Anyone who was against Hitler in Germany now was against him only because he wanted to save his own skin or the Army and prepare the next war, as had been the case with Ludendorff in 1918. There must be unconditional surrender in the East and in the West. Such were the simple lessons which these politicians drew from history; so poisoned was the present by error and pride and blindness on all sides.

On 6 June after unique technical preparations the Allies landed in northern France. Their superiority, at first in the air and then on the ground, proved so overwhelming that it could only be a matter of weeks before the German front crumbled. General Rommel, commander of an Army group in France, knew this in advance and was determined to end the war in the West, with or without Hitler's agreement. That Rommel was no politician is revealed by the purely military arguments of the 'ultimata' which he sent to the tyrant in Berchtesgaden. But this strong, simple soldier, who was worshipped by the Army and the people and who was also thought of highly by the Allies, would probably have been the man most capable of bearing 'the terrible double weight of war and civil war', as Ernst Jünger has expressed it. Whether the Allies would have accepted his offer to withdraw the German Army to the old frontiers of the Reich if they stopped the air raids is another question. The issue was not put to the test. In the middle of July the general was seriously injured; when, to his misfortune, he recovered, everything had been decided. On 17 June the Russians started a big attack on the middle of the German front, broke it and surged irresistibly towards the German frontier. Hitler, in Berchtesgaden, spoke of the impending collapse of Britain, of 'dead certain final victory'; his statements lapsed into fantasy. What was much more probable by then was that the war would end by the early autumn with the occupation of the whole of Germany.

On 20 July, at the daily conference at the *Führer*'s headquarters in East Prussia Colonel Stauffenberg placed a bomb with a time-fuse under the table at which Hitler and his advisers were standing. Stauffenberg left under a pretext, saw the explosion, thought that Hitler must be dead, flew to Berlin and brought the conspirators the expected news. Then the long-prepared steps were taken. General Witzleben, announcing that he had assumed command of the armed forces, ordered the arrest of Party and SS leaders in Vienna, Paris and Prague and had the government district sealed off by the Berlin 'watch battalion'. But Hitler was not dead. Several of his collaborators had been killed by the explosion but he had suffered only minor injuries. Nor had the conspirators succeeded in destroying communications at his headquarters as planned. There followed a clash between Berlin and East Prussia, between the orders signed by Hitler's creatures and those signed by Witzleben; the battle was won by the Nazis within a few hours. Even in this period of universal military catastrophe the state still held together, and the magic of the pale-faced tyrant, trembling like a leaf and thirsting for revenge and for the death of all traitors, still worked. At this period his regime would not have survived him by one day. But as he was alive all those for whom it was still possible and some for whom it was too late hastened to disavow the rebellion and to turn against it; troops and officers in and near Berlin, commanders in the occupied territories and commanders at the fronts. The band of genuine conspirators held out; but for them there remained only death. The more fortunate ones committed suicide; on the others Hitler's executioners closed in.

Where the rule of the party was based on a selection of inferior people, the resistance was based on a real élite from all classes, traditions and regions. The good genius of the nation had come together in opposition, in the fight against the monster. Now that its action had failed it stood hopelessly revealed, a victim of the People's Courts, of the butchers and stranglers. They all met with the same fate, the Socialists, the trade unionists, the democratic politicians, Leber, Leuschner, Haubach, Reichwein, Bolz and Letterhaus; the administrators and lawyers, Goerdeler, Planck, Harnack and Dohnanyi; the theologians and writers, Delp, Bonhoeffer and Haushofer; the aristocrats, the south Germans, Stauffenberg, Guttenberg, Redwitz and Drechsel, and the north and east Germans, Witzleben, Dohna, York, Moltke, Schwerin, Kleist, Lynar and Schulenburg. If at the period before the Nazi take-over the East Elbian aristocracy, or part of it, had burdened itself with grave guilt it made amends with the sacrifice of 20 July; and the German aristocracy as a whole acted honourably in this great crisis. This suited the tyrant; he raged against the 'gang of aristocrats' whom he had long come to loathe, pretended that the affair had been organized by reactionaries and thereby sought to discredit it in the eyes of the people. But the names of the victims spoke too clear a language. They were all aristocrats, *aristoi*, the best; not tied by class or caste.

One could ask, in retrospect, whether the country and people for whom they sacrificed themselves still deserved this sacrifice. They believed in their fatherland, and one of the most spirited of them, Count Stauffenberg, died crying, 'Long live holy Germany'. By then, however, Germany had long ceased to be anything holy and could never be holy again; the idea was outmoded, the concept of the fatherland had been destroyed. These men still took history seriously and were concerned about the threat to the nation; the near future was to show that the 'decline' of 1945 was anything but final. Thus they have been doubly ignored and forgotten. Confused and numbed the nation ignored them in the chaos of the final stages of the war; at that time no one grasped the loss of human material which Germany suffered with the catastrophe of 20 July. Nor did the Germans wish to be reminded of it in the hustle and bustle of economic recovery a few years later. Streets were named after men of 20 July, but who remembers today who these people were? The indifference of the nation strangled the living and forgot the dead. Their attempt to save the meaning, the continuity and the honour of German history at a time when these could no longer be saved, made them part of a vanished past and makes their glory before God greater than that which a well-meaning authority is seeking to ensure for them with posterity.

10. The End

After this abortive effort the agony, the redemption of the pledge that there would not be another 9 November 1918, continued for nine more months. Blasphemous madness made Hitler believe that the failure to assassinate him had proved once more that he had been brought into the world to fulfil a mission. Officers and soldiers were now made to use the Hitler salute. The police chief-executioner became commander of the reserve army and then also of an Army group. This act put the final seal on the subjection of the Army begun on 30 January 1933 – the more terrible the defeats on all fronts, the more completely victorious the Nazi Party. The nation was never more firmly in the Party's grasp than in the second half of 1944. The terror had achieved its purpose.

New war efforts were made, new divisions were squeezed out of the exhausted nation, boys and old men were called up into a *Volkssturm*. It was now said that the war was a national war to defend Germany's frontiers. For three years the Germans had advanced continuously, for two years they had fallen back continuously; they had fought for limitless *Lebensraum*, had carried the war from the North Cape to the Caucasus and to Egypt; now, after five such fantastic years the war was said to be in defence of the old, limited frontiers of the Reich. The chaos and the agony did not stop the people from sensing that there was something amiss in this argument. Nor could Hitler bring himself to behave in accordance with the new defence theme. He still brooded over new offensives. He still refused to evacuate any territory occupied by German troops before they were thrown out with terrible losses; even in March 1945 he refused, in spite of the pleas of his advisers, to bring back the German divisions from the Baltic provinces or Norway, on the grounds that he could not do so for economic, strategic or political reasons. His gaze was still riveted on the phantom of victory.

German propaganda wisely dropped any mention of conquest. It now operated with fear, with the punishment which the victors would mete out to Germany and thereby played upon feelings which were prevalent anyway. Many of the soldiers knew only too well what had happened in Russia and that from this enemy, if he won, no mercy could be expected. The Atlantic Allies revealed nothing about their war aims except the demand that their spokesman mellifluously reiterated for 'unconditional surrender'. There were rumours about a plan to take away Germany's heavy industry and to turn the Germans into a nation of peasants and fishermen – a piece of nonsense which American politicians had really thought up and which on a hot summer's day they had made palatable to President Roosevelt. German propaganda could have received no better assistance.

After the Allies had overrun the whole of France in the summer and pushed the Germans back to the old frontiers of the Reich, the war came once more to a standstill in the autumn. The Americans were careful. They halted where five years earlier the French had halted, and from where, five years earlier a spirited offensive could have put an end to the whole affair, at the legendary, scarcely manned, scarcely existing *Westwall*. There they stopped, and once more for months used only the barbarous argument of aerial bombardment. It was at that time, very shortly before the end, that the heaviest raids took place, hitting towns which had so far been spared and which believed themselves safe because they had no industry, like Darmstadt and Dresden; these nightly mass murders of civilian populations showed the depth to which public morality had sunk generally. 'Combatants', an historian wrote long ago, 'exchange qualities'. Hitler had adopted nothing from the Anglo-Saxons but the Anglo-Saxons had adopted characteristics of Hitler's. Allowing themselves and their bombs time, they met for conferences at which they made grand and vague plans for the future. Germany was to be divided into occupation zones, the German Army and general staff were to be done away with for ever and there were to be fantastic frontier changes in the East: Poland was to be compensated with German territory for regions which it would cede to Russia.

In December Hitler used the freezing of the front in the West for a last counter-blow. The plan was a good one, and it was assisted by the element of surprise. The American front trembled; but only for a moment. How could it have been otherwise, given such a distribution of strength. At the beginning of January the Germans were compelled to give up the '*Führer*'s Christmas present', as the propagandists called it. If the Allies had suffered heavy losses, those of the Germans were irrecoverable; and this last flicker of German aggressiveness only served to intensify the victors' impatience, rage and simplifying brutality. Thereafter German resistance collapsed everywhere. The Balkan peninsula had already been lost during the autumn and winter. In January the Russians began their last big offensive from the Baltic to the Carpathians, penetrated into Silesia and threatened Vienna. At the Oder the Germans succeeded once more in halting them. In March the Allies crossed the Rhine, and there now began a wild chase of motorized units across Germany, similar to that of the Germans across France five years earlier. Millions of German soldiers were herded together in improvised prison camps. In the middle of April the Americans reached the Elbe; at the same time the Russians broke through the Oder line and advanced on Berlin. Yet the madman's orders were still obeyed, or were obeyed where sensible officers and courageous citizens did not refuse obedience at the risk of their lives. As before deserters and 'defeatists', soldiers who had returned without being ordered to do so, were murdered, bridges were blown up, industrial installations destroyed and towns in which there was nothing to defend drawn into the fighting; with the result that enemy artillery now destroyed what the bombs from the air had spared. Hitler had wanted to revise the Peace of Westphalia; now Germany looked and people lived as described by the chroniclers of the Thirty Years War. And still the conspirators of 20 July went their solitary way to execution.

The man responsible for this mass nightmare turned reality sat in the air raid shelter of the Berlin Chancellery. An old man at fifty-six, unable to sleep, living on drugs and poisons, trembling, his face an ashen grey, with restless eyes, he held his military conferences which no longer bore any relation to reality. Braving dangers and difficulties which defied all description, senior officers even now made their way to him; and it is one of the strangest facts in this whole strange story that even now they bowed down before this trembling wreck of a man and carried out his devilish, senseless orders. Until late March, perhaps even until April, he seems to have believed in the 'triumph of will', in holding out until the final victory. For a long time so-called 'new weapons' had been his hope; then he waited for a split in the enemy coalition which would enable him to do one of the rapid about-turns in which his career had been so rich: with the Western Allies against Russia or vice versa. Always before his eyes was the example of Frederick the Great who after seven years of war had been saved by the sudden death of one of his enemies, the Russian Tsarina. In Roosevelt's sudden death on 12 April Hitler saw a hopeful parallel. In vain; for the moment Roosevelt's death produced no change. Later, soon, the great coalition was to fall apart, but not while the man was alive who alone had created it and who alone kept it intact. Until Hitler's death or capture the secretly smouldering conflict between Russia and America could not break out. At last Hitler understood that everything was finished. His will had not been enough to make the impossible possible. He drew no conclusions from this fact. He uttered no word of remorse or regret; nothing to say that he had been wrong and that the providence to which he had so often blasphemously appealed had after all not intended him to be the victor. His conscience was clear. The country resembled a burnt-out volcano; its citizens lived in ruins and cellars; from the eastern provinces refugees streamed in hundreds of thousands to the West, the guilty and the innocent, decent people who had done their work and who had never pursued Nazi aims, deprived of their possessions, without help, children without parents, the sick and the dying being pushed in handcarts; in the concentration camps the horrified Allies found mountains of corpses of people who had starved to death. But Hitler felt sorry only for himself. In his view he had sacrificed his health for his people, had renounced the pleasures of life for five years, had not seen a film or heard a concert, and look at the thanks he got. Treason, nothing but treason all around him had been the only cause for the temporary failure of his well-meant war, which, anyway, had been started not by him but by the Jews. In March already he had ordered one of his Ministers, Speer, to destroy all vital installations, factories, dams, means of transport and supply depots, before they fell into enemy hands. Speer objected that if the orders were carried out the nation must starve and freeze to death after the war. That was as it should be, replied the man who loved Germany so dearly. If the nation did not know how to be victorious it had failed the test and did not deserve to survive. Anyway, its best sons had been killed and only the inferior ones remained.

This was Adolf Hitler's last wish. And it would be correct to say that it had really been his innermost wish for decades. We know that even in the days before he came to power he spoke in lurid tones of a universal doom of this kind, a struggle in the burning hall on the Nibelungen model, a *Götterdämmerung* of death and fire. That was what he was striving for; consciously or subconsciously his whole incredible career in the last analysis served only to realize this dream. He wanted to drag Germany down with him, to celebrate with his funeral the end of the world. At the same time he dictated a last will full of lachrymose dispositions: although he was not a rich man he had enough to allow his relatives to live in modest comfort; his collection of pictures was to go to his beloved birthplace, Linz on the Danube. Furthermore, in the sight of death he now wished to enter into the marriage which in life he had to deny himself because of his un-flagging toil for the German people ... The Russians had long penetrated into the vast city of ruins. When they had made their way to the centre of Berlin and their shells began to fall near the Chancellery, Hitler decided that the hour had come. In the airless chambers of his bunker he entered into belated marriage with his mistress, strictly according to the rules, with a marriage contract, witnesses and champagne. Then the couple retired and com-mitted suicide as painlessly as possible.

Hitler went a long way in the career which he had mapped out, but never far enough to satisfy himself. There were still countries in which people were free and did not believe in his mission; this to him was unpardonable. 'The Jews,' he said during the war, 'once laughed at me; I don't know whether they are still laughing or whether they have stopped!' This was the urge which made him achieve his successes and commit his crimes: to force himself on the world, to make life a misery for those who had dared to take him less seriously than he took himself. His attempt to found the great German empire had failed and was bound to fail. But he triumphed in death to the extent that finally the whole world took him seriously, that the whole world united against him, against one individual; and that he left the world which he had been unable to conquer in a much altered, brutalized state.

As soon as this man's orgiastic dream of power had come to an end the nation awoke as though from a long period of stupor. There was no suggestion that regime and Party might live on after him; not even if the foreign victors had not been the masters in Germany. The wicked spell did not outlast the magician. With unbelieving amazement the Allies found almost no National Socialists in a country governed for twelve years by National Socialists. The whole episode was reminiscent of a comedy in the style of Hauptmann von Köpenick, more criminal than any previous nuisance in history, but nevertheless only a nuisance, a fraud which now that it had been unmasked was disowned by practically everybody. And this was not really the essence of the whole painful story: the story of an imposter who had used great but morally blind, indifferent national ability like a machine and had made it work for himself, punctually, effectively and lethally until, surrounded by ruins, it broke down.

The message which Admiral Dönitz, who had been appointed Reich President, addressed to the people was lost in the confusion of the collapse. Equally illusory proved the attempts of two of Hitler's most faithful followers, Himmler and Göring, initiated while Hitler was still alive, to negotiate with the Western powers. Now they wanted to do what the men of 20 July had wanted to do for the right reasons at the right time and for which Himmler had had them murdered in thousands. Now it was too late; the peace feelers of *these* men deserved the contempt with which they were received by the victors. The capitulation which was signed on

7 May 1945 placed the whole of Germany's armed forces in the hands of the victors and put an end to German sovereignty. There had been no new 9 November 1918. Germany had fought as long as it could, as long as Hitler had wanted. Then it had surrendered unconditionally, as the Allies had wanted. Both sides had had their wish.

Part Twelve

What Has Happened Since

1. Potsdam and the Partition

'Treaties are the expression of the relationship between the moral and material forces of the partners to them that exists when they are entered into. Their durability is determined by the accuracy with which these forces are judged, with which their origins and future developments are evaluated, and whether more attention is paid to the timeless political character of states and nations than to momentary factors. The rights to which they lay claim never outlive the conditions in which these rights were established.'

If one accepts these criteria, put forward by the historian Albert Sorel, was it likely that the Potsdam Agreement (2 August 1945) would last long?

The victors took over the administration of conquered Germany, which they decided should have no autochthonous government until further notice. This step presupposed that they would remain united. But the main reason why so far the uneasy union of the Allies had kept together, Adolf Hitler, had disappeared. There had been signs in the spring that with his disappearance the coalition would fall apart and there were further signs of it during the meeting of the heads of state and government in Potsdam. In the long run it was therefore improbable that an undivided Germany would be harmoniously administered by the three or four victorious powers.

The Potsdam Agreement reduced the area of Germany by about a quarter, by placing the German territory east of the rivers Oder and Neisse under Polish civil administration, and the northern part of East Prussia under Russian administration. The final settlement of Germany's eastern frontiers was to be reserved for the peace treaty. But as the expulsion of the German population from the regions to be administered by Poland was accepted as a *fait accompli* – which it was not at the time of the Agreement – and as the hastily improvised West German authorities were ordered to feed and house the millions of refugees from the East the provisional arrangement seemed from the start as final as it proved in the coming years. It was difficult to refute the argument of the Russian Foreign Minister, Molotov, that these millions would hardly have been expelled and resettled only to bring them back to their old homes soon afterwards. In practice, if not yet in international law, the Agreement amounted to the annexation by Poland of several old German provinces – East Prussia, Silesia, parts of Pomerania and Brandenburg. Such a terrible mutilation of the conquered state presupposed that it would in the long run remain as helpless as it was at that moment. This again presupposed that the victors would remain united and would continue to treat Germany as the enemy. We know how shaky were the foundations on which the first assumption was based. Therefore the second also lacked a firm basis; unless the victors remained united they must shortly start to court the defeated enemy – to court all Germany, or the part which they occupied. Moreover the victors, at any rate the Anglo-Saxons, were unlikely to keep up for long the attitude of the merciless oppressor because it was against their nature. And finally, however pitiful Germany appeared at the moment, there was no reason to suppose that its vitality had been broken for ever. If it was not broken for ever, if the German state was not permanently occupied, if the victorious coalition collapsed, what consequences, bearing in mind Sorel's observation, could be expected from the way in which the eastern frontiers had been drawn?

Using the argument of power alone there was only one positive answer to this question, and this still holds true today. The hundred-year struggle between Slavs and Germans, Stalin said in 1945, had ended with a Slav victory. He argued that the decision differed from earlier ones, for example that of 1917, in that it was irreversible. The Germans could not do again to the Russians what they had done in 1941. Therefore, provided Poland remained under Russia's tyrannical but effective protection, the new frontiers could last, however much they ran counter to the 'distant origins' and the history of 500 years. Germany might become strong again, but not strong enough to challenge Russia.

As for the moral aspect of the question, the *Economist* thought that the Allies had ended the war against Hitler with a peace in Hitler's style. In 1945 it could look like that. The recommendation that the expulsion of the German-speaking people from Poland, Bohemia, Hungary and Rumania – about twelve million in all – and their resettlement in the overcrowded ruins of Western Germany should proceed in an 'orderly and humane' fashion was somewhat reminiscent of the request of the Holy Inquisition that its victims should be put to death 'as gently as possible and without bloodshed'. Measures to keep down German industrial production – of which there was little to keep down at the time; the dismantling of industrial installations either simply as loot or as regular reparations; the deportation for indefinite periods of further millions as prisoners of war to Russia and France, an activity which began only after the end of the war; the Anglo-American order forbidding all human contact between the occupation troops and the population – these and other measures created a relationship so mercilessly gloomy as had never existed in Christian or post-Christian times between victor and vanquished. To be precise: it had existed only once before, in Hitler's Europe; not fully in the West, but certainly in the East. In Poland and in the conquered parts of Russia conditions had been infinitely worse. Whatever the victors decreed in Germany was designed as punishment to ensure that the Germans would never be powerful again, and to place them temporarily under Allied supervision; whereas Hitler's aim in Poland and Russia had been to destroy the nation, to reduce it to a state of illiterate slavery. This was not the aim of even the Russians. It would not have been in character either with their elementary humanity or with their philosophy. It was true that their soldiers behaved terribly while the fighting lasted, but the Germans, given the way in which they had fought in Russia, could hardly expect the Russians to fight humanely on German soil. As soon as the fighting was over the Russian government, whose attitude was basically constructive, began to have its way against its own soldiery. Berlin lay in ruins, like Leningrad. But whereas Hitler had given orders not to accept the capitulation of Leningrad and to shell the city until nothing remained, food was distributed among the Berlin population by the conquerors. Soon afterwards the first orders were issued to re-establish cultural and political activity: to form parties and trade unions, to open schools, clubs and theatres. These are differences on the basis of which the *Economist*'s view ought at least to be qualified. In fact the Germans themselves expected worse. They knew full well what their own people had done and planned to do in eastern Europe. Their *Führer* had taught them about 'an eye for an eye and a tooth for a tooth'. As we know, towards the end he had regarded the 'downfall' of the nation as the natural, even desirable conclusion of the war, particularly as the Germans had failed the test and it was the law of nature that the weak deserved to die.

One ought to look upon events and decisions between 1939 and 1947 as a chain of evil actions and evil reactions. There is little to be said for the historical arguments with which the Poles justified their annexation of the 'regained territories'; they are silly. Nor is there very much to be said for the argument of 'compensation': that because the Russians had taken land from the Poles in the East, they were entitled to a similar amount of German land in the West at the expense of a defeated enemy who deserved punishment, so that they should emerge from their agony without territorial loss. If the territory which Russia had taken in the East was Polish it should have remained Polish; if it was not Polish the Poles were not entitled to compensation. In fact the population of the provinces annexed by Russia was not predominantly Polish but Lithuanian, Ukrainian and White Russian; only about two million Poles from there were settled in the 'regained' western territories. This monstrous displacement of people and frontiers was irrational. It was an act of revenge on the part of the Poles; an act of compensation for terrible losses and sufferings in every sphere; an act of fulfilment of age-old imperial dreams which the Poles thought that they had a right to indulge in after so much suffering and as the victor. Stalin may have had other ideas; for example to create everlasting and thoroughly reliable enmity between the Germans and the Poles (but was it not already reliable enough?); or to make the citizens of rump Germany ripe for Communism by forcing them to find room for ten or twelve million penniless refugees. So far it must be said that this cruel operation has had very different results. But we do not know the end.

The other peoples of eastern Europe saw no reason to lag behind where the Poles led the way. They too wanted to get rid of their Germans. From Bohemia, Hungary and Rumania they were forced to go, the heirs of ancient migrations, of colonization, of merchant settlements, heirs of peasants, artisans and founders of cities. The extensive German sphere of activity in the East, imperilled long ago by rising Slav nationalism, was suddenly destroyed; the dream of the men of 1848, the dream of the 'imperial mission', was over. A terrible counterblow had hit those who had wanted to become the masters of eastern Europe. There were no complicated frontier disputes as in 1919, no plebiscites, no protection of 'minorities' – they disappeared. This happened in a state of physical anguish and mental numbness which prevented the main sufferer, the German nation, from understanding what was happening; by the time they understood, it was accomplished. The Germans could no more grasp this than they could grasp the full truth about the murder of the Jews, which now began to be revealed – crimes and figures which the mind could not visualize.

Of National Socialists the Allies found remarkably few. It is difficult to be precise, but there certainly were times, 1938 or 1940, when the great majority of the nation believed in its *Führer*. During the war it had shown a cohesion which may have had a variety of causes: patriotism, habits of obedience, fear and cynicism. The Germans had shown very little sympathy for the conspirators of 20 July and had obeyed the madman's orders to the end, always or almost always. Now everything looked completely different, the past as well as the present. It was not what Adolf Hitler had done to other nations that was held against him; people might have got over that. It was the situation into which he had led his own people which condemned him for ever. Those who could do so rapidly disowned his heritage; as did others who, on closer inspection, could not do so. The readiness to work with the victors, to carry out their orders, to accept their advice and their help was genuine; of the resistance which the Allies had expected in the way of 'werewolf' units and nocturnal guerrilla activities, there was no sign.

The German officials installed by the Allies in local government, and later in the re-established or newly created *Länder*, were survivors of the Weimar period who had not compromised themselves with Hitler, men of the defunct Centre Party, of the Social Democratic Party and to begin with even in the West, of the Communist Party. They were joined by emigrés returning from America, Britain, Russia and Switzerland. They were nominated by and responsible to the 'military governments' alone. As it was the task of these governments to educate the Germans in democracy, elections were held as early as 1946; political authorities were then appointed in accordance with the election results. One can see this democracy imposed from above as a paradox; a double one, because it had been German democracy that had brought Hitler to power, and because the repetition of such behaviour was strictly prohibited. In fact, however, the ideas and wishes of the Germans now corresponded more or less to those of the Allies. They would not have elected another Hitler, even if they had been allowed to do so. Food and housing, work, legal security and peace, those were the only things they longed for.

The Allies assumed responsibility for the punishment of the 'major criminals' whose guilt they demonstrated at a monster trial. No doubt the victors administered the law as they interpreted it and their justice was impaired by the fact that nobody was allowed to inquire into their own 'war crimes', but who else could have conducted the trial? The German population endured the nightly reports of the trial in Nuremberg, city of Nazi Party congresses, without much interest, without much hatred against either side. Let the defeated leaders of yesterday, pathetic figures that they now were, suffer their well-deserved fate; the burning question was what there would be to eat tomorrow. The prosecution of the 'minor' criminals, their exclusion from public life, was left to the German authorities, using methods prescribed by the military governments. The enterprise which went by the ugly name of 'denazification', was as necessary as it was impossible. Necessary because it was out of the question to have a democracy in which the officials, administrators, lawyers and teachers remained the same as those who had proved such willing pupils under Hitler. Impossible because roughly half the nation could not sit in judgement over roughly the other half, nor could the majority of those with special qualifications be excluded from their sphere of occupation. Even a proper revolution could not have achieved this, and the mood of the Germans was anything but revolutionary. The past remained and was shameful enough for those who had shame: but it was impossible to banish into the void of unskilled labour all those who had helped to make it. In addition it must be said that the occupying powers themselves were not entirely honest in their determination to 'denazify'. They were attracted for practical reasons by those who had skills, and for human reasons by those who lived in undamaged houses, had good manners, spoke foreign languages and detested Communism; that is to say by the upper class, particularly in industry. But this class, with or without Party membership, had been heavily embroiled in the adventure of the Third Reich. It had not created Hitler's regime, but it had supported it and had not suffered by doing so. As things worked out it was chance whether a person ended up in the dock or on an intimate footing with the military governments.

Docile, orderly and anxious for peace, the occupied country created no difficulties for the victors. It was they themselves who created them. The development of the following years can be explained fully only by the quarrel which arose among them and which the vanquished copied with customary obedience.

The quarrel was inherent in the nature of the situation and was easily foreseeable. Not the least of its causes was the fact that it had been predicted all along; both sides expected it, prepared for it, interpreted events accordingly and reacted in a way which soon justified the mutual distrust of the two main partners, Russia and America. Both saw the German situation from their own viewpoint; the Americans and their Western allies mainly from a political and moral one, and the Russians from a sociological one. The Russian doctrine was that Hitlerism had not been a voluntary, human aberration, but an inevitable expression of the German class structure. Therefore it was necessary to overthrow this structure and to eliminate both the Junker and the capitalist class. The fact that they confiscated all estates in excess of 250 acres without compensation, that they nationalized the banks, the insurance companies and at least half the factories during the first year of occupation did not necessarily mean that they intended to introduce their economic system directly and completely. For a while their German stooges continued to speak of private property, private enterprise and a mixed economy as being the only system suitable for Germany. In fact, however, life in the 'Soviet Zone' very quickly became markedly different from that in the three Western zones. The two resurrected 'Marxist' parties, the Social Democrats and the Communists, were made to merge into a 'Socialist Unity Party', the leadership of which was inevitably in the hands of the Communists. Party members were not allowed to vote on this step, which was put to the vote only in the three Western sectors of Berlin, where it was rejected by an enormous majority. By refusing to merge with the Communists in the places where they still had a free choice, the German Social Democrats rejected the system which the Russians had intended for the whole of Germany, thereby taking the decisive step towards the partition of the country and of Berlin.

Neither the three Western powers nor the Russians had planned this. The partition of Germany was not in the interest of the latter because they firmly controlled their own zone anyway; influence over the rest, particularly the Ruhr, in which they were especially interested, they could only gain if Germany remained united. Had they wanted or foreseen the division of Germany they would never have agreed to make Berlin the seat of the four occupying powers, an arrangement which they later found so inconvenient. Conversely, if they could have foreseen what would happen the Americans would not have evacuated the part of central Germany, Thuringia and Saxony, which they had conquered. They had all wanted to be correct; to keep the agreements made in the last year of the war and to govern jointly from Berlin. Of course they were not very surprised when the tricky programme proved impracticable. Maybe they were not very sad either.

After all, it must not be forgotten that until late in 1945 the Allies toyed with plans for dividing Germany not into two but into many parts. The idea was to undo the work of Bismarck, which allegedly had been the root of all the evil. Stalin too had toyed with this idea, but had dropped it abruptly in the spring. As late as the Potsdam Conference President Truman presented a curious plan for a south German–Austrian federation which would include even Hungary, and a west German state with the Ruhr as its centre. What was decided at Potsdam was something quite different; what began to emerge, the partition of Germany into two, had no logical connection with the fantasies of the last year of the war. But if there seemed to be no logical connection, deep down there may have been one after all. What is certain is that the three Western powers, particularly France, were not greatly concerned to preserve German unity. If they had been, they might have acted differently in the crises that followed.

Once the separation of the Russian zone from the three Western zones seemed probable everything worked towards that end. It had been intended that Germany should remain an economic entity, if only because it was to pay reparations as a whole, partly in the form of industrial plant and partly from current production. Whether this demand was economically sensible does not concern us here; morally it was justified, just as much as the demand that Russia should receive the lion's share. But as the territories east of the Oder and the Neisse were in practice lost to Germany and alone represented an enormous, incalculable compensation and as the Russians in their zone took what they liked, claiming it as war booty, the Americans changed course as early as the Potsdam Conference at which they proposed that the Soviet zone should be Russia's reparation territory, while the Western Allies would help themselves from their zones and hand over only ten per cent to the East. This solution in practice meant abandoning the economic unity of Germany which the victors had wanted to preserve. Each commander-in-chief now took charge also of the economic life of his zone and ordered the dismantling of whatever he considered right, while at the same time being responsible for seeing that the population did not starve to death. In May 1946 the American Commandant interrupted deliveries to the Russians on the grounds that there was not enough to supply the population with the bare essentials; in 1948 deliveries were stopped for good. Altogether the Russians received very little from the Western zones and incalculable quantities from their own. However, it is equally impossible to calculate what this was worth to them in practice. Much of the dismantled machinery rusted away alongside the Russian railway lines. This was why the Russians during the next years kept on pressing for an increase in German production at a time when the Americans were still artificially restricting it. Moscow wanted to get as much by way of useful goods as possible.

It would be academic to ask if the 'cold war' began over Germany or if it was transferred to Germany from elsewhere. What the Russians did in their zone of occupation they also did in the whole of the belt of countries between Germany and Russia; they bolshevized Rumania, Poland, Hungary and Bulgaria. Everywhere the stages were more or less the same: at first a bloc of all 'democratic', 'anti-fascist', 'peace-loving' forces under Communist leadership; then 'people's democracies' in which the non-Communist parties were no longer allowed to play anything but a sham role; then a one-party dictatorship. From the beginning this was how they had understood freedom, democracy and friendship with the Soviet Union; while using the same words West and East had always talked past each other. The West thus felt cheated and began to see in Communist imperialism the enemy of tomorrow, of today.

The Germans benefited as well as suffered from the split of the world into two camps. Inevitably both parties to the Cold War began to woo Germany and to adopt a more conciliatory attitude in word and deed towards the Germans. This new relationship could not prevent the partition of the country – on the contrary, it was bound to deepen it. Yet in various ways the separated regions benefited: in the Western zones people as a whole, in the Russian the social stratum to which power had been delegated. As early as September 1946 the American Secretary of State, Byrnes, struck a new note, saying that Germany must not become an almshouse for ever, that its economic recovery was essential for the recovery of Europe, that as things were the country was governed neither by the Allied Control Council nor was it able to rule itself, that this was an intolerable state of affairs, and so on. The road which led to the foundation of the Federal Republic was here hinted at for the first time. It was a long but predictable road. So predictable that one might ask why it was not taken sooner and why efforts continued to be made to achieve something so unnatural as the artificial limitation of German production when everybody could feel that the wind was blowing from a very different direction.

The attempts of the victorious powers to reach some measure of agreement at the Foreign Ministers' Conferences of 1947 followed a monotonously regular pattern. Each side insisted on its point of view and no longer tried seriously to make allowances for the other. 'Appeasement', the Americans had learnt during the Hitler period, certainly did not lead to the desired goal, and this negative rule they applied with decisive simplicity. The Russians wanted a unitary German state in the style of 'Weimar' with democracy of their own type, as well as reparations from increased 'current production'; the Americans wanted a strongly federalist Germany with democracy in their style;

and the French wanted a loose federation of German states. Partial agreement on words could not disguise the insoluble conflict.

Parallel with the separation of the two parts of the country went the gradual consolidation of the Western zones. The fusion of the American and British zones in January 1947 was logical. The military zones of occupation had never been intended to be more than their name indicated. Because the administration of Germany as a whole had collapsed the only possible procedure was to bring about the economic and then the political unification of those zones whose rulers were prepared to co-operate. At the moment it was the Americans and the British. The French followed late and reluctantly; the Russians never. Soon afterwards German executive organs and a joint parliamentary representation – the 'Economic Council' – were set up in the 'Bi-zone'. The Russians realized that this was the beginning of a West German state, and for some time to come the dissolution of the Bi-zone remained one of their standard demands. Naturally they would have been free to make their territory part of the Bi-zone. What they demanded instead was a return to the Potsdam Agreements and the Allied Control Council which had ceased to function in 1947 and never met again after March 1948. What they wanted in fact was that the three Western zones should join their own zone, to extend their own economic and political style to the whole of Germany, not the other way round. In a conversation with Bulgarian and Yugoslav friends, Stalin said early in 1948: 'The West will take over Western Germany and we shall make East Germany into our state.' Milovan Djilas, who reports the remark, adds: 'This idea of his was new but easy to grasp . . .'

The currency reform of 1948 which put an end to the inflation by withdrawing the *Reichmark* and replacing it by the *Deutsche Mark* at a ratio of 6.5 to 100 was another step towards partition as well as consolidation. Its success proved how long overdue the reform had been; it was the start of West Germany's economic recovery. In the first six months after the introduction of the *Deutsche Mark* production doubled. The Control Council had not been able to agree on a currency reform for the whole of Germany. What alternative was there but to introduce it in the three Western zones? It is undeniable that it was the owners of real values, including shares bought at the right time with inflation money who benefited from the way in which the currency was reformed, whereas those who owned nothing but a little cash were compelled to rebuild their lives from the start. Many succeeded admirably; great fortunes were made in a short time from nothing and rarely has it been more accurate to speak of giving 'the green light to efficiency' than in the Germany of the early fifties. On the whole, however, the reform meant renewed concentration of private property, that is the opposite of what was happening meanwhile in the Russian sphere of influence. Therefore the currency reform must be seen as playing roughly the same role as the founding of the Socialist Unity Party in the Soviet zone, that of an act of separation; like the foundation of the SED it was also ordered by the occupying power.

The Russians replied with a currency reform in their zone and then with the blockade of Berlin, where the *West-Mark* had been introduced. The plan – after all, a plan there must have been – was, now that there no longer was a single German state, to drive the Allies out of Berlin and to annex the whole of the old capital to the Russian zone. Undeniably the purpose which had brought the Americans, the British and the French to Berlin had ceased to exist; undeniably the city was situated in the middle of the Russian zone. But the Berliners had demonstrated too clearly that they were determined not to be part of the Russian system, and the honour of the Allies was too much committed; also they had earlier surrendered extensive stretches of Germany for the sake of their presence in Berlin, territories which by right belonged to them if they evacuated Berlin. They did not evacuate Berlin but for a year supplied themselves and the population of their sectors from the air. During that year the three Western zones became the 'Federal Republic'. The principle had been agreed upon between the Allies and the German politicians since July 1948; the Parliamentary Council charged with drafting the constitution of the state met in September; it concluded its work on

8 May 1949, four years to the day after Germany's unconditional surrender.

The Americans were more enthusiastic about these developments than the Germans who, as General Clay complained, instead of grasping the opportunity to become masters in their own home again, were curiously slow and reluctant. The German premiers wrote to the Allied governors that the new organization must not become a proper state. They did not want to give the other side the right or apparent right to accuse them of having taken the final step in the partition of the country; they sensed what they were doing and did not want to do it while nevertheless doing it. Hence Western Germany was given a 'Parliamentary Council' – delegates of the chambers of the *Länder* – instead of a national assembly in the classical style and a Basic Law instead of a constitution. Hence the declaration at the beginning of the Basic Law that it would remain in force only until such time as the whole nation could give itself a constitution under freedom conditions.

But as events had their own momentum up to the foundation of the Federal Republic and that of the German Democratic Republic which followed exactly a week later, they continued to have their own momentum. After May 1945 they moved in one direction only. Whenever a decision was required it was predictable what it would be. The Federal Republic would have become a state even if, as a German journalist had suggested, it had been called 'emergency association of German *Länder*'. The name was of no importance. 'The very short period,' said Albert Sorel of the situation of France in 1795, 'and within that period the fleeting moments in which nations are masters of their destiny were over for the French Republic.' For Germany they were over at the very latest in 1949; it is a matter for speculation whether the Germans were ever masters of their fate after 1945, whether in the first post-war years they could have chosen another road and preserved their country from the results of the Cold War. It cannot be said, however, that they tried very hard or very intelligently.

2. The Federal Republic

The Federal Republic was created by the nation or that part of the nation to which the Western powers gave an as yet limited right of self-determination; formally, however, it was not created directly by the nation but by the *Länder*. Representatives of the *Landtage* considered and adopted the Basic Law; it was ratified by the *Landtage*, not by a national assembly, still less by a plebiscite.

Organizing the *Länder* was one of the earliest acts of the occupation forces and not a bad one, although they were established within and only within the individual zones, a fact which made their frontiers, particularly in the French occupied South-West, rather peculiar. Later there were modifications. With the exception of Bavaria, of old the most vigorous of the German states, and the city republics of Hamburg and Bremen, the new creations had no or only shadowy historical identity. There were many reasons for this; above all the dissolution of Prussia by the Allied Control Council in 1947. The Control Council bestowed on this step an historical significance which it did not truly possess; because we know that Prussia – what was understood by it – had long been swallowed up by Germany, that the Prussian state had ceased to exist at the latest in 1933. In any case it would have been impossible to restore it, as East Prussia, Pomerania and part of the Mark of Brandenburg had been given to Poland and the frontier between the Russian and Western zones cut through the rest. But as the victors were wedded to the erroneous view that Prussia bore the main guilt for Germany's historical errors and crimes they ceremoniously carried out a posthumous execution of the dead kingdom. Its place was taken by the completely unhistorical 'North-Rhine-Westphalia', 'Lower Saxony', which had Hanover as its core but also included some miniature principalities of the past, such as Lippe and Oldenburg, and 'Schleswig-Holstein' whose autonomy Bismarck had suppressed in 1866; other principalities confiscated at that time, Kassel and Nassau, became part of Hesse, a unification that was historically meaningful. 'Lower Saxony' and 'Hesse' at any rate were fine old names. A new *Land*, Rhineland-Palatinate, composed of fragments of Bavarian, Prussian and Hessian territory on the left bank of the Rhine, owed its existence more to French wisdom than to history. Another result of the arbitrary manner in which zonal frontiers had been drawn was the union of Baden and Württemberg; in 1949 this union was approved by a plebiscite which many people in Baden still claim to have been unfair. Arbitrary or accidental in detail this curious set-up of *Länder* has by and large proved a success; just as the Napoleonic system did after 1805. The new *Länder* had some historical *raisons d'être*; they had almost no connection with the German 'tribes', no more than the territorial states of the princes. If the Allies were of the opinion that *Länder*, regardless of where they were situated or what they were called, corresponded to a good German tradition, they were right. They also corresponded to real needs of self-administration, at any rate as long as there was no united Germany. In 1919 Max Weber had regarded the bureaucracies of the *Länder* as a vital element which it was impossible to dispense with; the same was true in 1945. As the Reich, which had done all the damage, emerged broken from its orgy, it was in the *Länder*, manageable units, that life was resumed and people began to deal with their predicament. Unequal in size, population and wealth the new *Länder* were nevertheless roughly of the same order of magnitude; both the pygmy states and the Prussian giant had disappeared. Among the German politicians who warmly approved of the foundation of the *Land* North-Rhine-Westphalia and thus of the dissolution of Prussia, was the former mayor of Cologne, Konrad Adenauer. Another German politician, Kurt Schumacher, the leader of the Social Democratic Party, who had come to Berlin with Adenauer to discuss the organization of the new *Land* with the British Commandant, was against the move.

The re-establishment of political parties happened spontaneously, in several regions at once, under the leadership of politicians of the Weimar period who had suffered – some of them greatly – under Hitler Of the Weimar parties only one reappeared, the Social Democrats. It was the only party which had not covered itself with shame in 1933 and could rely on old loyal members. Its spokesman, Schumacher, had spent twelve years in Hitler's concentration camps and rightly held the view that the victors had nothing to teach him; broken in body but not in spirit, stemming from the East Prussian middle classes, very German, very Prussian in the tradition of Bebel, a patriot and a democrat, Schumacher had no doubt that *Reich*, nation, state and socialism would naturally continue in conjunction with one another. He and his friends were convinced that the hour of the bourgeoisie which had served Hitler was over and that the turn of the Social Democrats had come at last; that the reconstruction of the German economy was a matter for the state – the whole German state. But by making enormous efforts to prevent the amalgamation of Social Democrats and Communists in the Western zones and in West Berlin, and by seeing in Communism the real enemy Schumacher himself encouraged the split of Germany which he was passionately determined to prevent. He placed national unity above all but one consideration. National unity must not be *à la russe*. In 1946 the German Social Democrats did once again what they had done in 1919: as far as lay within their power they saved Germany from Communism. As if to demonstrate that it was the same old ill-fated party the German middle class once again failed to appreciate their action. As in 1919 the Social Democrats were convinced that they would be called upon to govern, allied with the party which governed in Britain, allied with the strongest tendencies of the age. As in 1920 they were disappointed.

The Christian Democratic Union which originated in Berlin and the Rhineland and which quickly spread to the whole of Germany was new as a party although among its members were many politicians of the defunct Centre Party as well as *Deutschnationale* and Prussian Conservatives. It was designed to be a collective party of the middle classes, markedly religious but not clerical, differing in this way from the Centre. Some founders of the Centre had wanted a Protestant wing as early as the eighteen sixties. The CDU accepted Protestants, mindful of the hardships which members of both creeds had suffered under Hitler. The first programme of this collective middle-class party said that Germany's future economy must have a marked Socialist flavour and that at least the basic industries must be nationalized. At the time this view was almost universally accepted in Europe. By 1948 at the latest, however, the CDU had ceased to think so; programmes, as the party's most influential politician, Konrad Adenauer, philosophically remarked, do not have eternal validity.

Of the smaller parties founded after 1945 only one survived, the *Freidemokratische*, which vaguely continued the traditions of the old National Liberals and the south-west German *Freisinnige*. Other groupings, partly nostalgic and regional, partly aimed at exploiting particular protest feelings, continued to lose in importance until they vanished. The Communist Party, which, given the way in which German society and politics were developing, would not possibly have kept in the running, was declared illegal in 1956.

What showed itself in the second and third post-war years was the strength of the middle classes or of the 'restorative forces', as they were called. The exaltation which had led to the belief that everything could and must be started completely afresh did not last long. The growing anti-Communism of the Americans was directed also against what people vaguely thought of as socialism; the Americans, not the British Labour government, were by far the strongest occupation power. Their assistance to Europe, the 'Marshall Plan' announced in 1947, extended to Western Germany, although conditionally. In the Bi-zone, thanks to American protection but also on the basis of election results, the CDU succeeded in getting hold of the key economic positions. After the currency reform the economic director of the Bi-zone, Ludwig Erhard, at one sweep abolished the whole system of rationing and controls and gave the green light to acquisitive instinct; let everyone produce, buy and sell as much as he could. The result of this daring decision soon surpassed the highest expectations. What was later called the 'German economic miracle' began while the constitution of the Federal

Republic was being discussed. It had its influence on these discussions and still more on the elections which followed. The average German was still very poor; but for the first time for years he could eat and buy something for his money – a memorable experience.

The Basic Law of the German Federal Republic – in reality a fully fledged constitution – reflected little of Kurt Schumacher's Jacobin spirit. It was influenced by the experiences of the recent past, of Weimar even more than of National Socialism, although little was to be learnt from them as far as political law was concerned. The result was a democratic federalist constitution, as the Allies had ordered, with a strong admixture of pessimism. The Basic Law said – and it could say nothing else – that political power emanated from the people. The very next sentence qualified this statement: the people exercised their power through elections and through the special organs of the legislature, the executive and the judiciary. This meant that they would not exercise their power directly; there would be no more plebiscites and the President, instead of being elected by the people, would be chosen by a national assembly consisting half of national deputies and half of deputies from the *Länder*. This meant the replacement of the 'substitute Kaiser' of the Weimar Republic, of Max Weber's 'charismatic' leader of the people, by a friendly, pale *pouvoir neutre*. The President lost the right to dissolve parliament of which the old Hindenburg had made such plentiful use, except on occasions when parliament proved incapable of producing a working majority; in that eventuality, as for any kind of emergency decree, the agreement of the *Länder* governments was necessary. These were represented in the *Bundesrat*, a kind of upper house, as in the Weimar period, and also part of the executive, as in Bismarck's day. On principle no constitutional changes curtailing the rights of the *Länder* were allowed.

The course that recommended itself after the experience of National Socialism was to limit power, to prevent the people from taking direct action; the lesson learnt from the history of the Weimar Republic would lead to the stabilization of power. This aim was to be served by one of the most original inventions of the founding fathers in Bonn, the 'constructive vote of no-confidence'. A government could only be overthrown if parliament chose another head of government. It was necessary for a negative coalition to prove that it was capable of positive work. In order to prevent a proliferation of parties a subsequent law required parties to win at least five per cent of all votes cast; if they obtained less their electors failed to be represented. Both provisions, the constructive vote of no-confidence and the 'five per cent clause' were designed to prevent an undisciplined, ineffective parliament.

The weakness of the Federal President was the strength of the head of the executive, the Federal Chancellor. He was elected by parliament, the Federal President being entitled to make the first proposal; the other members of the cabinet were appointed by the head of the state. Such constitutional justification as there was for 'Chancellor democracy' was based on the fact that the Chancellor was the only elected minister, that, as laid down in the constitution, it was for him to 'determine the guiding lines of policy', and that he could only be overthrown by an election. The personality of the first Federal Chancellor did the rest, and perhaps this was the main factor.

The new Republic was designed to be a federal, democratic, socially just state. Although there were some articles giving the state the right of expropriation in the interest of the community, very little use was made of them. In another sense, however, the new Germany really became a socially just state.

The constitution began with an imposing list of fundamental rights of the German citizen, with nineteen articles not connected with the constitution or any form of positive legislation. Nothing thought up by Anglo-Saxon, French or German philosophy in the course of 700 years was omitted; nothing taught by the bloody lessons of the Hitler period. Five years earlier 'enemies of the people', men and women who listened to foreign broadcasts, 'defeatists' who doubted the German victory, had been executed in thousands. Now the death penalty was abolished. Five years earlier children of fourteen and old men of sixty had been pressed into military service; now the German citizen was expressly given the right to refuse war service; the right to persecute men for their creed, race or language was expressly denied. Then there were guaranteed freedoms: of creed, of opinion, of the press, of speech and of development of talent. But what if these noble things were misused? With the experience of 1932 in mind and with somewhat less of the Rousseauesque faith of 1919, the makers of the constitution provided for this danger. A citizen who misused his basic rights in order to undermine the free democratic order, lost them. Political parties whose objectives clashed with the spirit of the constitution would be proscribed, as would-be organizations which endangered the peace of the world. 'I have defeated them with their own madness', Hitler had boasted in 1933. Now Germany swore not to have a similar experience again. The self-restriction of democracy, originally imposed on the nation by the victors, was taken over by the new autonomous German state. Although its logic cannot be faulted the question of who provides the guarantee for the guarantor can never be answered with certainty.

All in all the constitution was good, better than that of Weimar, more cautious and more sceptical. The fact that it has also stood the test of time better cannot be entirely attributed to its qualities. For how long should it remain in force? Until the whole nation was free to give itself a constitution. To which territory should it apply? To territory to which it could apply now, including the western part of Berlin; theoretically, however, the constitution was intended also for those who had not been allowed to share in drafting it, that is to say it was intended for the whole of Germany. How far did the whole of Germany extend? It extended as far as it had done before. Hitler's conquests, from Vienna to the Volga, were invalid, but so were the conquests of the others. Had the victors themselves not confirmed this by deciding to administer Germany jointly within the frontiers of 1937, as they had been before the *Anschluss*; by placing the territory east of the Oder and the Neisse under Polish administration until the conclusion of a peace treaty but not for ever? If the victors themselves decreed the continuation of the German

Reich who were the vanquished Germans to deny it? Such were the somewhat vague conclusions reached by the fathers of the constitution on this delicate and difficult issue. In international law they had a case. There had been no peace treaty in 1945 because there was no German government with which to conclude one and the intention was that there should be none; also because at the time no German politician would have dared to belong to a government whose first act would have had to be the signing of such a treaty. People remembered only too well the fate of those who had signed the armistice of 1918 and the treaty of 1919; and 'Versailles' had been child's play compared with the treaty likely to be drawn up on this occasion. Therefore, as nothing had been legally decided, that on which no decision had been taken, the German Reich with all its provinces, eastern and western, continued to exist in law. The argument gave the new state, the Federal Republic, both a very provisional character and one whose claim went beyond reality; what remained uncertain was not only how the claim was to be met but how claim and reality were related.

Nothing lasts longer than a makeshift arrangement. The pragmatic, provisional character of the Federal Republic, its slow, organic growth, the manner in which it gradually became a reality, proved an advantage compared with the Weimar Republic whose theoretical existence had been carefully thought out and created in one sweep but whose real existence was confused and shadowy. The disadvantage was, and has remained until today, that the phantom of the German Reich prevented the new reality, the Federal Republic, from freely acknowledging its own identity.

In fact the problem was insoluble. If the German politicians had said that in fact, if not yet in international law, Bismarck's Reich was no more, that, half broken in 1919, it had been twice destroyed under Hitler, first by his limitless conquests and then by Germany's defeat; if they had added that in future Berlin, situated at the eastern fringe of the German settlement area, could no longer be the capital, their observations would have corresponded to the facts while at the same time endangering two things: the legal basis of the Allied presence in Berlin and the claim to reunification, the right of the eighteen million Germans in the Soviet zone to national self-determination. The German politicians clung with words to the phantom while in fact building the new state.

The seat of the government was moved to Bonn, the small, idyllic university town on the Rhine. This decision too was open to more than one interpretation. It could serve to underline the provisional character of the Federal Republic; the other town under consideration, the much larger Frankfurt, centrally situated and offering memories of the Reich, would have been the more solid choice. But the man who had just managed to push Bonn through, the Rhineland politician Konrad Adenauer, may well have had other ideas on the subject which characteristically he did not voice. One, however, he did express: that the German capital must be 'situated among vineyards, not among potato fields'. The further to the west, the closer to France it was situated the happier he was; that much one may assume.

The constitution was ratified by the parliaments of the *Länder*. Bavaria, as always more self-assured than the rest, did not ratify but recognized, thinking as always, that it could not remain apart ; in any case it was not allowed by the victors to do so.

In accordance with the constitution elections to the *Bundestag* took place in which the Christian Democratic Union gained a narrow lead over the Social Democrats, 139 against 131 seats; in addition there were a number of smaller, predominantly right-wing groups. The man who was chosen as head of the state was a liberal, elderly native of Württemberg with a politically impeccable past and semi-scholarly, semi-literary and artistic interests, Professor Theodor Heuss. When it came to choosing the head of government Konrad Adenauer was elected by exactly the required number of votes and not one more; as his critics pointed out with arithmetical accuracy, by his own vote. This was not a strong basis for a government and nobody could have predicted that it would support him for fourteen years.

Fourteen years, during which German society changed more profoundly than in the preceding century. Not that the Federal

Chancellor caused this change; no man could do this, Adenauer least of all. But he presided over it; he did much to shape the form it took in domestic policy and everything to determine the form it took in foreign policy, its relationship with western Europe and America. For four or five years the Germans had been without a *Führer*. Now, so soon, they had another, but of a new kind.

3. Adenauer

With Adenauer the West German middle class came to power for the first time. It is true that the chancellors of the Weimar Republic had also belonged to the middle class but their power had been limited and they had looked up with secret or open admiration to the old hierarchy and had therefore regarded their own position as only barely legitimate. Like them, Adenauer, who belonged to their age group, came from a modest family of civil servants. Industry, considerable adroitness, an inborn air of authority strengthened by bitter experience had brought him high office as long ago as the days of the Kaiser. He became chief burgomaster of Cologne, a member of the royal Prussian Upper House and under the Republic President of the Prussian Privy Council. But this middle-class German felt no sympathy whatsoever for his country's feudal past, its royal, Prussian, military past. One might say that his approach was almost unhistorical; so much so that the incredibly long period of history – from Bismarck to Khrushchev and John Kennedy – which he had lived through, made little impression on him. In his speeches there was no mention of the past; if he was all too inclined to forgive those who served Hitler and to use the best bureaucrats among them it was not because of sympathy for their past but because he was interested only in the present and in practical issues. In the First World War he had foreseen the fall of the monarchy without regret, after the war he had spoken in favour of the dissolution of Prussia, of the foundation of a Rhenish state, which while being part of Germany – Adenauer was no 'separatist' – would help to orientate German policy towards the West and to give the French positive peace guarantees. In the Weimar Republic Adenauer was one of the most creative local administrators, no more because he did not want to be more; at one point he could have become Chancellor but refused because he did not trust the conditions of the offer and preferred to play safe. There are indications of his political insight during this period, particularly the fact that at the height of the economic crisis he should have urged his party colleague, Brüning, to set afoot a great programme of creating work, on the argument that otherwise German democracy would be lost. Brüning, hamstrung as he was and mesmerized by the fear of inflation, thought the idea fantastic.

The Third Reich brought Adenauer ignominious dismissal, obscure and dangerous retirement, prison and the contempt of his fellow citizens. It was difficult to know men and not to despise them, he remarked at that time. And in 1947 he said in a speech in Luxembourg: 'During the years of National Socialism the Germans behaved so as to make me despise them. But since 1945 I have learnt to respect my people again.' He was bound to add the qualification and to believe it, for otherwise the great effort which he put into his vision of Germany would have been in vain.

Do democracy and contempt for the human race go together? In theory no; in practice easily and often. Adenauer became a demagogue when it came to winning an election and there is evidence to support the remark of his rival, Kurt Schumacher, that he had a 'very reserved relationship with truth and honesty'. From a bygone age he brought with him the concepts of patriarchal order which existed in his family and which had existed in the city of Cologne when he had been in charge. His idea was to help the people, to keep them on a tight rein and to do as much as possible himself. Humanized by suffering and by nature rather delicate his thought processes were unsubtle, lacking in generosity and anything but literary; the simplifications he permitted himself in his speeches as well as in his actions were of classic dimensions. He was greedy for power, though relaxed, jovial, cynical and with a sense of humour which hid the hard core. Although a religious man he distinguished between the things of this world and the next like a Lutheran; while fundamentally modest and opposed to theatrical poses he was cunning and impudent when it concerned the leadership of his party which he secured, almost usurped. If politics, to quote an American senator of the age of Lincoln, is not a struggle for ideas but 'the management of men' Adenauer was a politician of first rank; he was cleverer than Bismarck, as is shown by a comparison of his brilliant departure and the bitter darkness of Bismarck's decline and fall. Then he took over the Chancellorship he was as old or nearly, as Bismarck when he retired. But the eighty-year-old Adenauer was more part of his age than Bismarck at sixty; again because he was completely without historical sense and class ties.

Naturally he was concerned about his country and its sullied honour. To regain for it a degree of autonomy, a respected place in the world, order at home, prosperity, and above all peace – that was about as far as his conscious aims went. He had observed that his nation could do nothing sensible with great, absolutely independent power and therefore he did not want it to have such power again. As a German citizen he could not approve of the terrible loss of German territory in the East. But he neither loved nor knew the lost provinces; they were strange to him, the more so as people there had been predominantly Protestant and more radical in politics than in Western Germany. As for the partition of Germany two facts are certain: in a German state united up to the Oder Adenauer would never have become Chancellor; with such a state neither he nor anyone else could have pursued the policy which he wanted to pursue, that of close links with western Europe. Let the reader draw what conclusions he likes from these two facts. The present author does not claim to have penetrated the innermost thoughts and feelings of this eminent politician.

Adenauer had no love for socialism, as a member of the

middle class, as one who was himself not averse to the accumulation of property and who liked to consort with financiers and industrialists. His arguments against socialism were simple and characteristic: for the workers it made no difference whether they worked in nationalized factories or in private undertakings; concentration of power was one of the dangers of the age and therefore it was always preferable to keep political and economic power apart; the vital element in economic life was free enterprise and competition not orders from above, and so on. The fact that, as the Social Democrats suspected, the middle class and capitalism might have played some part in Hitler's rise did not worry him; he was no sociologist. Moreover, he had no desire to restore certain past conditions; he only wanted to return to what to him seemed natural and God-given, to law and order, Christian morals and manners, and property. He thought the Social Democrats capable of putting national unity before freedom (from Russian influence) and neutrality before links with Europe. Kurt Schumacher replied by calling Adenauer ‘the Allies’ Chancellor’. Both insinuations were unfair; neither was wholly unjustified. However inflexible Schumacher's anti-Communism, it was true that his aim, the restoration of the ‘Reich’, could, if at all, only have been achieved by Germany's neutralization together with some opening of doors towards the East. However busily Adenauer tried to clear Germany's name the fact remained that in helping to establish the sovereignty of the new Federal Republic, he limited it, because its political, moral, economic and finally military links with western Europe and America, which he created, literally made the much vaunted ‘reunification’ impossible.

He must have known this; there is no reason to think him stupid. As a result a certain element of dishonesty entered into his policy; not in his dealings with the West in which his loyalty was determined, constant and beyond any doubt, but towards his own people to whom he made promises which probably nobody, least of all he with his diplomacy, could fulfil. He resided in Bonn but took a vigorous part in the cult of the Reich capital, Berlin; he served the fragment called the Federal Republic which under his leadership with incredible rapidity became a flourishing community, and claimed to be serving the phantom of the vanished 'Reich'. He claimed this because it helped him to win elections; perhaps also because he was so essentially a practical man that he found no time to think about the basis of his policy.

So much for the man who from 1949 to 1963 directed the fate of the Federal Republic. Of 'direction' one can, of course, speak only in matters of foreign policy. In the social sphere Adenauer allowed events to take their course, while placing himself in a position where developments favoured him and gave his diplomacy free rein.

Towards the West this diplomacy was amazingly successful. It was not completely successful because Adenauer and his government sincerely wanted to regain German sovereignty only to merge it with that of Europe; because he aimed at establishing a United States of Europe, and for a time at least had the great majority of Germans behind him in this. The feeling that they had lost their national home, the desire to replace it by a wider, European one, was strong in Germany in the late forties and early fifties. This desire was not fulfilled, or only indirectly. Instead there were other satisfactions, some of them more old-fashioned. Beyond the Federal Republic's eastern frontiers Adenauer's policy was unsuccessful. Constantly and inevitably unsuccessful to such a degree that it is permissible to ask if it seriously sought what it pretended to seek.

The phases of Germany's western policy are quickly described. Every step towards the autonomy of the Federal Republic was accompanied by a new link with western Europe or America or both.

1948 saw the creation of an international Ruhr Authority (to which the Russians would dearly have liked to belong) designed to regulate the production of north-west Germany's heavy industry and the distribution of its products. The Federal Republic itself became a member of this organization whose purpose was to control German industry, feared even now. In 1949 the powers of the victors were restricted by an 'occupation statute'. In 1950 the war in Korea provided Germany's economy with a considerable stimulus and German policy with a considerable opportunity. Was Germany not divided like Korea? Might the German Communists not do what the North Korean Communists had done? Should Germany itself not make a contribution to counter this threat? Konrad Adenauer offered the Allies German auxiliary troops for the defence of Europe. There were long discussions on the subject. The Allies would have liked Germany's help but many people were still afraid of it and the awkward point was that less than five years ago it had been decided to demilitarize Germany for ever. In Germany itself there was strong opposition to the establishment of an army. The Germans remembered the political role played by the *Reichswehr*; they remembered the horrors of the last war, a mere five or six years away; they also remembered the verdict of 'guilty' which the victors had passed on the German generals in Nuremberg, and the ruins, the humiliation. Must this happen again so soon? Must there be an army intended for direct use against another part of Germany, against the 'zone', the DDR, in which, by the way, there already existed something called *kasernierte Volkspolizei* (people's police lodged in barracks) suspiciously resembling an army? The Social Democrats toyed with this opposition without completely identifying themselves with it. They were dominated to the point of bewitchment by one thought: not to be accused, as in 1918, of having betrayed their country, of not caring whether their country was powerful or not. Hence their insistence on unification as the task overshadowing everything else, their oath never to recognize the new eastern frontier, their arrogant tone towards the Western powers. Hence now their attitude towards the problem of rearmament: let there be a German military contribution, but only if Germany was given complete political and military equality, only if the Allies developed a 'go-ahead strategy' aimed at carrying the war across the Vistula into former Polish territory. The last demand at least was decidedly impractical; it fitted in with the concept 'Reich' which Schumacher never abandoned, but not with the concepts 'Federal Republic' and 'West' which were the terms in which Adenauer thought. Certain of his parliamentary majority he allowed the ailing Schumacher to thunder away while spinning threads between Bonn, Paris and Washington.

Adenauer who had seen not only Seeckt but also Schlieffen and Moltke at work, did not himself want an autonomous army. He gladly took up an idea suggested to him in Paris and which had the approval of Washington, that of a 'European Defence Community'. In addition to the Coal and Steel Community (of which more later) which the six European states were about to set up, there was to be a joint military organization, six contingents under one command. Such an arrangement would have given the Federal Republic triple protection: against a Communist attack; against remaining forever the vanquished enemy; and also – and this was what particularly attracted Adenauer – against a repetition of the experience of the *Reichswehr*, against a German army as a 'state within the state'. At the same time this was to be a guarantee for the enemies of yesterday, the allies of tomorrow. With agreement on the 'defence community' about to be reached the international standing of the Federal Republic improved noticeably. It was given the right to establish diplomatic relations of its own; Adenauer could take for himself the title of Foreign Secretary. The Federal Republic joined the Council of Europe, western Europe's parliamentary representation vested with vaguely defined rights, located in Strasbourg. The state of war between Germany and the Allies was formally terminated, though 'peace' was not concluded in the normal manner. The Allies could not sign a peace treaty because to do so would have deprived them of the responsibilities and rights which they had *vis-à-vis* the Russians, or jointly with the Russians for the whole of Germany and in particular for Berlin. Finally, in 1952, the legally somewhat confused relationship between the conquered, occupied country and its erstwhile enemies was made the subject of a wholesale agreement, the Bonn Treaty or the 'General Treaty'. The Federal Republic became a sovereign state but the Allied troops remained on its territory on their own authority. They remained not, as yesterday, to control or to 'educate' the Germans but to protect them. Their task was 'the defence of the free world of which the Federal Republic and Berlin form part'. One of the aims of Allied policy remained the 'peaceful reunification' of the two parts of Germany. A re-united Germany should have a 'free democratic constitution similar to that of the Federal Republic' and remain 'integrated into the European Community'. Further it should in no way interfere with the 'rights of the three Powers as laid down in the treaties'. In other words, in the original wording of this important article, the Federal Republic would not desert Europe, not be neutral even if it extended over the whole of Germany. It is self-evident that this clause was not designed to make 'peaceful reunification' any easier.

The Bonn treaties were linked with the Paris treaties on the European Defence Community; they would come into force only when the latter had been ratified. After a heated debate they were adopted by the *Bundestag*, against the votes of the Social Democrats. An historic event, so it seemed. *The Times* spoke of a *renversement des alliances* in the style of 1756. France's enemy for a hundred years and Britain's for fifty years had become their ally against the power which in two world wars had kept the balance against Germany. The treaties, as they stood, never came into force. France regretted its own idea, that of the European Defence Community, and did not want to abandon its military and political autonomy to the extent envisaged. This refusal, definite in August 1954, temporarily profoundly embarrassed American–German policy. But where there is a will there is a way. In place of the European Defence Community the Federal Republic joined both the Great American–European military alliance, the Atlantic Treaty, and the formally more closely knit West European alliance, the Brussels Pact. There was no complete merger of military forces. The German *Bundeswehr*, established with German thoroughness and promptness, was a national army, exactly what Konrad Adenauer did not want; and for the moment the Federal Chancellor was very unhappy about this. Nevertheless its twelve divisions were placed at the disposal of the North Atlantic Treaty Organization under an American commander; they joined in manoeuvres with their allies, often on their territory, and exchanged arms and secrets with them. The intention was to establish a considerable though restricted force, of about 500,000 men, and it was stipulated that the Federal Republic must explicitly forgo the manufacture of nuclear weapons. The German army was not a new *Reichswehr*. Nor did its leaders who had been in Russian prison camps and had learnt from experience have much ambition in this direction. The young men called up under the new conscription laws had even less of it. They moved into the barracks because they had no choice, but without enthusiasm. The uniform had lost its old glamour.

Once Germany's 'military contribution' was thus legally tied up no obstacle stood in the way of ending the Occupation Statute. Its place was taken by the treaties of 1954. The Federal Republic became sovereign; as sovereign that is as a European state, particularly one so delicately placed and burdened with such a past, could be. Restrictions that were discussed the Federal Republic voluntarily imposed upon itself: the presence of Allied troops on its territory was given a 'contractual basis. The right of the Allies in an emergency to assume ultimate control disappeared once Germany itself had made legislative provision for a 'state of emergency'. The clause binding the whole of Germany to treaties concluded by the Federal Republic was dropped; a change of formal rather than of practical importance. The fact that there had once been such a clause was to characterize German policy in the decade to come.

There for the moment ended Germany's political and military emancipation and integration. It had been predictable at least since 1948, a logical product of the Cold War. If anything it is surprising that it took so long. The new constellation, the new reality, was there but the old still existed and prevented the new one from emerging straightaway.

The same emancipation and integration occurred in the economic sphere, simultaneously and closely linked with the one in the diplomatic and military sphere. As a recipient of Marshall Aid the Federal Republic joined the Organization for European Economic Co-operation and within its framework helped to liberalize European trade. The Ruhr Statute was replaced in 1951 by the European Coal and Steel Community, an imaginatively conceived organization which consciously restricted the sovereignty of its six European members; the High Authority, controlled by a Council of Ministers on basic issues only, was entitled to give directives and, in cases of dispute, a court of arbitration decided independently of the law of member states. Although the aim was an economic one, the creation of a common market for the steel industry, the abolition of tariffs, of import restrictions, of export subsidies, and of discriminatory freight rates, there was also a political aim: closer union of the continental states, fusion of German and French heavy industry in order to prevent for ever the recurrence of experiments in autarchy such as took place in 1933, or the invention of industrial 'war aims' such as occurred in 1916. Also political in essence was the meaning of the Treaty of Rome which, after initial crises and disappointments, was signed by the same states in 1957 and which extended the principle of the Common Market to the whole of economic life. 'The task of giving economic freedom of action and movement to the countries of our European zone is difficult but not insoluble,' Walther Rathenau had written in 1913.

. . . The result would be an economic unit equal or perhaps superior to that of America and within the federation there would be no more retarded, stagnating or unproductive regions. At the same time nationalistic hatred would lose its sharpest sting . . . If the countries of Europe join forces economically and this will happen sooner than we think, they will also join forces politically . . .

Later than he may have thought, after two world wars, Rathenau's prophesy came true.

In all this activity Adenauer's Germany participated, at times playing a delaying role, particularly when the interests of its strongly organized agricultural community were at stake; by and large, however, it co-operated loyally and enthusiastically, sometimes leading the way. The internal opposition, the Social Democrats, had rejected the Coal and Steel Community as 'conservative, clerical, capitalist and creating a cartel'. Since then things had changed: they too supported the European Economic Community. What was accomplished was not what Adenauer had hoped for at the start, the merging of German sovereignty into that of Europe. But the achievement went part of the way and if one remembers that the Treaty of Rome was signed only twelve years after the *finis Germaniae* of 1945 it was evidence of remarkable success.

The Cold War and its Western protagonist, the United States, contributed to this achievement. So did the terrible experiences which Europe had endured between 1920 and 1945; although it is the exception rather than the rule for politicians to learn from experience. On the German side the Federal Chancellor contributed. The authority which the old man acquired at home, his unchanging, completely reliable behaviour towards the outside world, his refusal to play the power game with East or West, were part of the process of European integration, of fitting Germany into a west European–Atlantic community. This was his success; a very great one and, as far as he personally was concerned, achieved very late in life. No wonder that he did not advance beyond it.

Adenauer showed the same confidence-inspiring unequivocal attitude in a matter which weighed upon Germany only morally: the question of compensating the Jews. As most European Jews were dead there was of course nothing or very little to be done by way of compensation. The little that could be done the Chancellor succeeded in getting done, both at home and in the Arab world which offered vitriolic nationalist opposition to his suggestions. Under a treaty between Germany and Israel, concluded in 1952, the new state of the Jews received payments in the form of goods worth three milliard marks, to be made within twelve years. The formal basis for this treaty was the fact that during the Hitler period hundreds of thousands of refugees had arrived in Palestine deprived of their possessions. Behind it was the determination not to atone for – that was impossible – the worst crime in Europe's long and bloody history, but to make a gesture in that direction. The *Bundestag* solemnly ratified the treaty and the government carried out its provisions, in spite of the trouble which it thereby created for itself in the Arab world.

The agreement with Israel formed only a small part of an extensive system of 'reparations'. In his *Weltgeschichtliche Betrachtungen* (Historical Reflections) Jacob Burckhardt comments that emigrants should never return, or if they do, should never demand back their lost property. The Federal Republic paid the surviving Jews, those who returned and those who did not, compensation which all in all amounted to about eleven milliard dollars. This was much less than what had been lost by those who had been murdered or had fled; it was much more than the victims had thought possible in their wildest dreams. If much in the history of the Third Reich was unfortunately unique this restitution too was unique; we look in vain for comparisons in the history of revolutions. The Germans had been thorough in their crimes; they were thorough also in seeing that justice was re-established. One of the more curious features of the affair was that these reparations did not arouse in people anything like the anger which the much smaller payments of the twenties had caused. The electorate, without interest and without anger, allowed its representatives to pass the necessary legislation the implementation of which was made possible by the annual expansion of the economy.

Those were the achievements, the successes of the 'golden fifties', as they became retrospectively known, not without melancholy. As regards foreign policy they certainly were easy years for West Germany, in spite of all crises, which originated elsewhere; years of gradual reconciliation, of growing ties, of dependence on the over-powerful American protector. In one of his last speeches to the Reichstag Bismarck had said about the distant days of the Holy Alliance: 'At the time of the Holy Alliance . . . those were patriarchal times, we had plenty of handrails to grip and many dykes to protect us from the raging European floods.' Bismarck had pulled his Prussia-Germany out of this order and had fought to give it an autonomy which, though in the end he was afraid of it, he never wanted to abandon again. Adenauer was no Bismarck and it was not in his nature to keep six balls in the air simultaneously. At the period when this was written the ninety-year-old ex-Premier was longing for the safe handrails and dykes, for the conditions of 1955.

Hand in hand with the diplomatic advances went a change of atmosphere. One cannot say that in 1945 Germany had been isolated; quite the contrary. But it was ostracized and despised, and the life of its citizens was so restricted that they could hardly move from one town to another; the whole country was a prison. The Americans were the first to invite favoured Germans across the Atlantic in order to teach them something of the 'American way of life'. Tourist travel began after the currency reform; at first it was combined with complications but as the mark became stronger all restrictions were lifted. In the fifties millions of German tourists began to flood Europe every summer, more freely than at any time since the summer of 1914 and in much greater numbers. In addition to the pleasures of holiday travel there were international meetings on a scale hitherto unknown: politicians and parliamentarians, members of the new European economic bureaucracies, local administrators whose respective cities had established special links, businessmen, trade unionists, soldiers, journalists, scholars, professors and groups of young people. The universities, German as well as French, British and American, became multi-lingual centres of education where the word 'nation' almost took on again the meaning which it had had in the late Middle Ages. And finally there developed a migration on an even larger scale: of those who looked for work, or better working conditions, who came from Italy, Spain, Greece, Turkey and finally from Africa to settle in Germany – in the very country where a few years earlier permanent poverty and permanent unemployment had been expected.

Although this remarkable process enabled the Germans rapidly to recover their self-confidence which had reached its nadir in 1945, their attitude was on the whole no longer nationalistic in the old sense; wider horizons and new knowledge worked in the opposite direction. Whereas fourteen years after 'Versailles' the Germans had still suffered from hate and inferiority complexes, 'Potsdam' was practically forgotten after fourteen years. An agreeably relaxed attitude characterized the atmosphere in 1960, both in the Federal Republic's domestic life and in its relations with western Europe, which for the first time in modern history were made up not only of official links but of contacts between countless human beings. Who would have thought this possible in 1945? Who, seeing this and having seen the twenties and thirties, could but rejoice? The spectacle was almost too good to be true; perhaps it never was.

4. Germany and Eastern Europe

What happened when the German ship of state burst asunder in 1945 was that the western, bigger half, the Federal Republic, proved in the long run to be not a wreck but a remarkably seaworthy vessel. It sailed off in a new direction: towards western Europe, towards the Coal and Steel Community, the Atlantic Pact, the European Economic Community and so on, a voyage which a united Germany could not have made. And this voyage took it further and further from the much less happy fragment, the 'Soviet occupied zone'. It is true that in moments of crisis there were passionate appeals of: 'We belong together, we are still one ship'; but the direction taken by the Federal Republic did not confirm the truth of this.

Perhaps with the end of the war the country was predestined to be partitioned. It is possible to argue for and against this thesis; but anyway one can do no more than speculate. Whether the Federal Republic chose its road voluntarily or was forced to take it does not affect the result. Voluntarily or otherwise it took decisions, not one but a succession of them, which literally made it impossible to have 'reunification' on the classic lines of free elections in the whole of Germany and the establishment of a nation-state. In consequence the Germans should have been honest enough to reach conclusions which they did not reach for too long. At the moment of writing the German politicians seem at least to be more aware of the situation than before.

The 'German Democratic Republic' – in Germany it is always necessary to add 'so-called' – formally came into existence exactly one week after the adoption of the Bonn Basic Law. The Russians really had no choice but to transform their share of the booty into a state or pseudo-state. As sheer booty they could not in the long run keep it. Neither could they permit unification with an already completely Western-orientated Federal Republic. This could not be the intent of their victory of 1945 gained with such terrible sacrifices. Having once created a state they were compelled to continue to 'communize' it in order to give it some kind of identity, since this state did not really want to exist. What they permitted the Finns who were a nation they could not permit the East Germans who were not. Only its Communist structure could keep the 'DDR' apart from the Federal Republic. From the beginning it has thus been the unhappy, second-born twin of the more fortunate Federal Republic. 'Under the first we are free, under the second we are slaves.' The establishment and controlled development of the DDR involved more slavery than is generally assumed. The Russians took the first, from a Western point of view false, steps without wanting them to lead to the partition of Germany which was not at all in their interest. The Americans reacted; from then on it was a circle of predictable reactions and increasingly feeble, increasingly unconvincing attempts to break the spell. With tedious monotony each side repeated the demands which it knew the other would reject.

Until 1952 the Russians demanded a return to the Potsdam Agreement, to the Four Power Control Council which had proved unworkable. In their note of 10 March 1952 – much discussed later – they abandoned this demand. But the Germany which they envisaged – without treaty obligations and with a limited military force – would have had to give up all its west European and American links and organizations, both actual and planned; things that is, which had meanwhile become a reality and represented the progress of five years. In addition at the heart of the proposal, as seen by the Russians and the rulers of the DDR, there was always a 'council' containing the same numbers of representatives from both parts of the country; elections to a national assembly would come later and be organized by this council. This meant that the DDR in its existing form intended to join the new united Germany and to contribute to its development, not to allow itself to be eliminated.

Both the United States and Federal Republic insisted that a united Germany must be free to enter into or preserve whatever alliances it wished; this meant that the territory of the DDR would become part of the Atlantic Pact system. Further both the Anglo-American and the West German proposals on reunification regularly envisaged not a council composed of the same number of members from the two parts of the country but a national assembly chosen in free, internationally controlled elections; this meant that first of all the DDR with all its institutions would be removed from the scene by the vote of its liberated citizens. Here lay the difference both of political interest and of philosophical concept between the two camps which no exchange of notes could overcome. The only question then was which point of view was the more legitimate according to modern traditions of international law, democracy and human rights, and to that question the answer was clear. But justice is one thing and political interests and power politics are another.

The development of the DDR resembled that of the new 'people's democracies' or satellite states, while being both drearier and slower. It was drearier because the foreign origin of the pressure was more evident. In Poland even during Stalin's worst period it was possible to compare conditions very favourably with those during the German occupation; later, willingly or otherwise, the nation could be identified with the political system. In the DDR no such comparison was possible. Instead there was the comparison with life in the Federal Republic, a contrast which annually drove hundreds of thousands via Berlin into the Federal Republic. Nor was it possible to regard the rulers as the managers of the nation because there was no nation; only the reluctantly severed fragment of a nation. As the rulers had no illusions about the extent to which they were hated, the pressure of the Ministry of State Security was even greater, and street and house wardens were even more active informers than elsewhere. The 'construction of Socialism' progressed more slowly than elsewhere. In addition to the nationalized industries privately owned enterprises continued to exist for a long time; perhaps because of the continuing hope of 'reunification' (Russian style). The East German governments pretended to be coalitions of parties, some with reputable bourgeois names. It was only in 1953 that the citizens of the DDR learnt that they had been living under the 'dictatorship of the proletariat'. Only after that date was necessity made into a virtue and the booty from which the Russians had intended to squeeze every possible drop, and – perhaps – thereafter to drop it again, became an economic and political partner of the Soviet Union.

The alliance between the ruling Socialist Unity Party and the Kremlin was less ambitious than that between the West German rulers and Paris, London and Washington. The West German government could have survived without Allied protection, not the East German one. On the other hand, the attitude of the Russian victors was more brutal because they themselves were poor and had suffered most in the war. The 'zone' went on paying reparations until 1954, in all between fifty and one hundred milliard marks; this relatively – compared with Western Germany – unfavourable starting basis of the zonal economy provides some if not the whole explanation for the lower standard of living in the DDR. It also explains the pride with which many of its citizens look today at what has been achieved.

Formally the development of the relationship between the new state and its great friend and enemy more or less resembled that of the Federal Republic and the Western powers: the Russian control commission was transformed first into a High Commission and then into an embassy; an army was established 'for the defence of the country', Eastern Germany joined the Council for Mutual Economic Assistance and the Warsaw Pact, and so on. It was the road which the Federal Republic was taking in the opposite direction; only that the Russian creations did not prosper as well as those of the West.

The foreign policy of the DDR – to the extent that it is possible to speak of such – was characterized by friendship not only with the Soviet Union but with all the people's democracies; there were technical and cultural agreements with Poland, Czechoslovakia, Rumania and Bulgaria. The decisive difference was that the DDR recognized as final, just and good what the Federal Republic always refused to recognize, the new German–Polish frontiers and the expulsion of the Germans from Bohemia. This was one reason why Poland and Czechoslovakia preferred to have this neighbour. It seems that the pedestrian and stuffy East Berlin was not, nor is today, much respected by the more intelligent Communists of eastern Europe. However, in view of past experience, the safety of its new western frontiers is to Poland the most vital question of all. Given the sphinx-like behaviour of the Federal Republic which swore on the one hand not to use force and on the other promised to change what could obviously no longer be changed without force, Poland had no alternative but warmly to embrace the East Berlin regime which it secretly despised.

Both German governments made accusations against each other which overshot the mark. East Berlin claimed that Bonn was 'revanchist, imperialist, and Fascist'. This was unjust; such descriptions did not and do not apply to the Federal Republic. What was correct, however, was that it continued traditions of the old Reich, some good, others less so; that the Bonn bureaucracy was at heart the old bureaucracy of the Reich and that only too many of its senior administrators had loyally served Adolf Hitler. Bonn maintained that the rulers of the DDR were the representatives of a despotic and hated foreign system, without a shadow of democratic legality, that they were usurpers with whom West Germany must have no relations whatsoever. Although there was a good deal of truth in this thesis it carefully ignored all the progress which was being made in East Germany and which gradually transformed barely tolerable conditions of life into tolerable ones. It overlooked all nuances which distinguished men and men, rulers and rulers, by lumping them together as 'Communists', a concept which had become a bugbear. This attitude made it impossible for West Germany to establish any contact with more willing, liberal elements in the DDR which might have been anxious for such contacts. Every letter from East Berlin to Bonn was returned unopened. All proposals for joint consultation – which at times might have been worth examination – remained unanswered or were answered publicly with contempt. It was a question of all or nothing. The DDR must disappear completely at one blow or remain what it was. Perhaps – some Bonn politicians adopted this attitude – the worse it was the better.

With sails set Konrad Adenauer steered the course promised by his American friends and protectors, President Eisenhower and Secretary of State Dulles, and which was called a 'policy of strength'. In order to parley with the Soviet Union, Adenauer once said, it was necessary to 'be armed to the teeth'. He who at the beginning had been sincerely afraid of a national German army, together with his assistants missed no opportunity of asking for the creation of this army to be speeded up and for its size to be increased; in order to defend the West the Germans needed rockets and nuclear weapons. He and his assistants missed no opportunity of warning against an international *détente*. They argued that the devilish character of the Communists was immutable; that it was impossible to come to terms with them. Anti-Communism thus became a negative force in the life of the Federal Republic. One sympathizes wholeheartedly with the West Germans for not wanting to be under Communist rule; it is not a social system which brings great joy. But it is doubtful whether, given the manner in which Hitler had used the Communist bugbear and what he had done to Russia, it behoved them a few years after the end of the war once more to stake everything on military strength, and verbally to fight the Cold War with even more ardour than America; it is doubtful whether this helped the Federal Republic's cause at home or abroad.

It helped the party leader. Konrad Adenauer, because he defeated the opposition party, the Social Democrats, with the same arguments with which they had been defeated in the past. He made Bismarck's *Reichsfeinde* into enemies of the Federal Republic, into friends of the Communists. We know that this was not at all what they were, during Kurt Schumacher's lifetime or after his death. But as the Social Democrats continued to believe in reunification they opposed Germany's membership of the Atlantic Treaty system, the introduction of conscription, and later the equipment of the *Bundeswehr* with nuclear weapons. They did this because they wanted to pursue a national policy, because this time they did not wish to appear as *Reichsfeinde*. But they again faced an insoluble dilemma: anybody who sincerely wanted to restore the 'Reich' was bound to want a measure of contact with the Communists who occupied part of the Reich, and was bound to reject the transformation of the fragment of the Reich called the Federal Republic into an aggressive, well armed force. Thus they gave Adenauer a chance to accuse them of being friends of the Communists and of betraying their threatened country. The Social Democrats failed to resolve this dilemma. They evaded it more and more, to a point where it became impossible to see any difference between the policy recommended by them and Adenauer's.

As regards the 'policy of strength', it became increasingly noticeable with the years that while lip-service was paid to it nothing was done to practise it and that it did not bring the promised fruits. What was successful were the peaceful West European creations. The militant efforts were successful in so far as they were designed to defend the *status quo* of 1946; they went no further and only verbal attempts to go further were made even when opportunities seemed to offer themselves. In June 1953 the workers of East Berlin rebelled against their masters, or to be more precise against an increase in the 'norms' decreed by their masters. While the rebellion was put down by Russian tanks the Allied troops beyond the sector frontier stood with their arms at the ready. That day, 17 June, was later made into a national holiday in the Federal Republic – recalling, not the storming of the Bastille, but its successful defence and the manifest failure of West Germany's own policy. A few months after this defeat Adenauer gained a triumphal victory in the *Bundestag* elections; his party now had half as many seats again as in 1949. The next elections took place in 1957, a year after the bloody suppression of the Hungarian revolt; an event which like no other should have called for an American 'policy of strength' and like no other demonstrated the hollowness of this policy. With an absolute majority for his party Adenauer was even more successful in the elections than four years before. What had the German electorate voted for? Certainly for the so-called 'economic miracle', shown in its true light by such banal and effective election slogans as 'no experiments' or 'what you have, you have'. Certainly also for the Federal Republic as a new state, as a great power, for the new army, for the American alliance. Certainly not for the mass protests of the Social Democrats against the American alliance, against the army and against nuclear weapons for the army. Certainly not for reunification by means of a policy of strength. The effectiveness of this policy was now plain for all to see.

Germany continued to follow the same path during the next four years which brought the perfecting of the army and the coming into force of the Rome Treaties. They also brought confusing events; for example political changes in France and America. What Charles de Gaulle's return to power would mean was not immediately clear; he was known to be a determined nationalist, a statesman who thought in historical terms, who would gladly accept the Federal Republic as junior partner but who would put obstacles in its path as a major European power, as a nuclear force, as America's continental sword. With characteristic realism de Gaulle hastened to recognize, if not the DDR, at least Germany's new eastern frontiers, the Oder-Neisse line, as *de facto* irrevocable. This recognition was deliberately ignored in Bonn. The victory of the Democrats in the American Presidential election of 1960 brought to the top a young team likely to look for new approaches in foreign policy. Indeed it later set out to relax the hardened attitudes of the Cold War and to prepare a 'strategy of peace'. President Kennedy was admired for this the world over, except by the officials of the Federal Republic who had nothing but suspicion and contempt for his attempts to reduce tension. The aged Konrad Adenauer, in the fifties perhaps the most influential man in the Atlantic alliance, became isolated and lost contact with reality. The confusing and shameful spectacle which he presented in 1959 by first announcing that he would give up the office of Chancellor and retire to that of President of the Republic only to take back his promise after some weeks, confirmed the impression that his once firm but subtle hand had become unsure.

Yet it was in those years of slow crumbling of rigid fronts, when Adenauer's course proved to be what it had basically always been, successful in the West and unsuccessful to the point of hopelessness in the East, that the Social Democrats adopted the same course; their criticism, their plans for Germany and their fantasies about reunification had brought them too little gratitude. They were tired of everlasting opposition; a role only too reminiscent of that which they had played under William II and again in the Weimar Republic; capable at local government level but without influence in the places where fate was decided. Why, Max Weber had asked over half a century earlier, did the Social Democrats not take the consequences and turn to the right if the way to the left was blocked or regarded as blocked? The Godesberg party programme of 1959, discretely prepared some time ago, finally and completely took the consequences and turned to the right. Expressions like 'Marxism', 'working class' and 'class struggle' no longer appeared; their place was taken by the sonorous slogans of a liberal social policy. Germany thus finally reached the point which the American parties had reached decades ago: each claimed to do what the other was doing, only better. The final surrender of age-old doctrines corresponded to the development of German society. But did the success of German diplomacy correspond to the volte-face in foreign policy now also made by the Social Democrats? They accepted everything they had criticized hitherto, the army, the American alliance, the policy of strength. They, who a few years before had organized vain protest movements against 'atomic death', even accepted the curious project of the Multilateral Force – the artificial plan thought up by the Americans to let the Europeans share their nuclear power without letting them do so at all, a scheme which had its still-birth written all over.

If the Godesberg Programme meant the acceptance of the

Federal Republic, together with its military defence, as a powerful reality, it was the recognition of irreversible facts. If it was an expression of approval of the 'policy of strength' and of the 'reunification' which followed from it, it was mere rhetoric; the kind of rhetoric which Adenauer and his followers had indulged in for ten years. August 1961 was to bring melancholy proof of this fact. Hard pushed by the loss of their best scientific and technically qualified elements, by the increasing defection of their citizens to the Federal Republic via West Berlin, the rulers of the DDR took the final step to seal off their territory: overnight they built a wall across Berlin. Under the terms of the Potsdam Agreement concluded sixteen years earlier the step was as illegal as it was cruel from a human point of view. But as it did not change the *status quo* the Western allies behaved as they had always behaved: they accepted what had happened.

In Germany feeling ran higher than in June 1953 and the authorities did their bit to fan it. The Germans suspected that a firm seal had been placed on the partition of their nation. However, Konrad A'denauer, the advocate of the policy of strength, remained silent for a remarkably long time. When he finally appeared on the television screen it was to explain why it had not been possible to do anything: the danger of a nuclear war had been too great. It may have been; it certainly was during the whole Dulles–Adenauer period as soon as attempts were made to transgress the *status quo* of 1945. The old man's words, if one listened carefully, were a declaration of bankruptcy.

Not that the majority of his followers wanted to see the matter in this light or regarded it as of decisive importance. In the *Bundestag* elections in September 1961 – four weeks after the wall had gone up – the balance shifted for the first time against the CDU in favour of the Social Democrats who had presented themselves as a 'people's party' under a new leadership. But the government coalition could and did remain the same; the SPD continued to play the role of the barely opposing opposition. For two more years his party friends allowed the founder of the Federal Republic – now approaching his ninetieth birthday – to continue in office. They were politically barren years, enlivened only by a separate Franco-German alliance and by a spectacular French state visit. Adenauer saw the treaty as the fulfilment of an age-old dream, the crowning of his life's work. There can be no doubt that he was always more interested in establishing ties with the West than in finding an opening to the East, in restoring the 'Reich'. The ties between the Federal Republic and western Europe were indeed many and close. So close that it was hardly possible to single out one of them and to proclaim it ceremoniously as the most significant. In the years to come the Franco-German treaty did not play as important a role as expected in the enthusiasm of 1963. General de Gaulle behaved as a correct ally over the Berlin question, paying lip-service to 'reunification'; this he found all the easier to do as he knew that reunification now lay in the very distant future. He could not want it wholeheartedly, a fact which every German who was honest with himself was bound to realize. De Gaulle thought in terms of the European balance of power. France might act as a counterweight to fifty-seven million Germans but not to seventy-five million Germans, not to the unification of the third biggest industrial state in the world with another which had also been an important industrial state. It is curious how they all kept from each other what they all knew. It is curious on how much repressed conflict and un-thought-out, unrealistic promises Adenauer's friendships were based.

The same was also true of his friendship with the Germans who had been resettled in Western Germany after being expelled from the provinces east of the Oder and the Neisse. Not only did Adenauer's Federal Republic treat the other, unhappy Germany, the DDR, as non-existent although at the same time it made trade agreements with the DDR and in order to do so indulged in the most artificial contortions and mutual games of hide and seek. Not only did it presume to break with any state that recognized the DDR, it also refused to reconsider Germany's eastern frontiers, the frontiers of the Reich, as they had been in 1937. The explanation of this position was not consistent; it veered between the argument that nothing must be given up in law in order to regain at least part of it in subsequent negotiations and the other that the Germans had an inalienable right to the whole of the country. Behind all this was the political power of the refugees who had organized themselves in remarkably strong and active associations. After a difficult start they had been very successfully integrated into the economy of the new Germany; they had done their bit to make the economic miracle a reality and for the most part were materially better-off than they ever had been at home. Every big city had its new districts whose street names recalled the old home. The children of the refugees went to school in their new home and soon became indistinguishable from those of their fellow pupils who had been born there. As soon as it was in a position to do so, the state gave generous help to the new citizens in their efforts to establish themselves. Their economic integration took place more quickly and successfully than had ever been dreamt of in the years of disaster.

That their political and moral integration should have been somewhat less successful was not surprising. Silesia and Prussia had been regions with a marked civilization and a character of their own; if as German provinces both were a thousand years younger than the Rhineland and Suabia they were no less German for all that. Nobody could blame the refugees for bitterly opposing formal recognition or approval of the wrong done to them. A less pleasant side of the picture was the lack of interest displayed by them in the German crimes which had preceded their expulsion and which alone could explain it. There were associations which organized their loyalty to their home land, their memories, their links with their compatriots, their interests and their political influence. Serious issues were involved: the question of whether it was ever possible to approve of the expulsion of twelve million people or to regard it as final without thereby sanctioning any barbarity. There were also more questionable motives: to pick up jobs, to keep alight a flame the purpose of which became to warm its guardians, to build up a political force which regarded itself as entitled to veto German foreign policy. Any political party that made the slightest gesture towards recognition of the new eastern frontier – that was the theory – lost the refugee votes, millions of them. None of the three parties ever dared to put this theory to the test; they all made repeated promises to the refugees, which they realized could not be kept.

The temporizing, the intellectual timidity which characterized various aspects of Adenauer's foreign policy was in evidence here too. The refugee politicians swore that they wanted reconciliation with the Poles and the Czechs, that they did not wish to achieve their aims by force. Yet what was the point of proclaiming non-violent aims which could never be attained without violence; that this was so became more obvious as the years passed and as the former German territories were developed and settled by the Poles. The aim, it was said, was to regain the 'frontiers of 1937'. But while it had them Germany had never wholeheartedly recognized the frontiers of 1937. They had been the very frontiers of the 'shameful dictated peace of Versailles', for the revision of which Germany had thought it worthwhile to embark upon a war which became a world war. Would Germany stop this time at the frontiers of 1937? In the light of past experiences would the Poles, even if they did the impossible and conceded the frontiers of 1937, have reason to feel safe behind these frontiers? Indeed, among the more extreme refugee spokesmen there were those who announced that the frontiers of 1937 were an insufficient goal. Journalists, theologians and even politicians occasionally and tentatively suggested that there must be a new approach to the Slavs instead of a repetition of the old game of nationalism and frontier change; but the idea was never seriously thought through, never seriously followed up because of the iron veto of the refugee organizations. Finally – to complete the web of contradictions – it was highly doubtful whether the majority of the refugees would return to their old homes if they were free to do so. Surveys revealed very different and humanly plausible ideas on the subject. Over the years people lose touch with their old home, particularly if the new home offers advantages such as they have never enjoyed before. The effectiveness of the refugee organizations was therefore part of an element which characterized the whole of Adenauer's eastern policy the secret of which was the negation of the *status quo* for the purpose of maintaining that *status quo*. The refusal to accept the existing situation had become a factor which helped to maintain that situation. But whether it is possible to claim that it helped to perpetuate the situation is doubtful because there is explosive material in such a supporting pillar and no one knows how much.

If Adenauer's eastern policy had any result at all it was that the Poles and the Czechs attached themselves even more closely to the Russians from whom alone they could expect protection against Bonn's 'peaceful revisionism'. This attachment had been inherent in the political situation since 1945. It would have taken place in any case and was unavoidable; but it could have been modified. This the United States, Britain and France tried to do, but not Adenauer's Federal Republic.

These then were the shadows on the foreign policy which the Chancellor bequeathed to his successor when he finally retired in the autumn of 1963 under pressure from his friends. The whole Federal Republic said farewell to the old man more ceremoniously than Germany had done to any of its politicians, including and particularly Bismarck. The left had never forgiven Bismarck. It forgave Adenauer, for the moment, and did not refuse to attend the celebrations in honour of his departure. The present writer would not have refused either. Because whatever must be said against Adenauer in the end more can be said in his favour as is shown by a comparison between Germany in 1945 and in 1965. There remained the problem of continuing to develop Adenauer's heritage in the West and of overcoming it in the East. In fairness it must be added that it was by no means *his* heritage alone.

5. The New Society

It is said of Dostoevsky that he never worked better than after his orgies at the gambling table or his epileptic fits. Something similar is true of the Germans; they never worked with more economic success than after their wars, and with most success after Hitler's war.

Adenauer's foreign policy, in so far as it was constructive, was carried out against the background of Germany's economic boom. The fact that the nation, for the first time in eighty years, gave up politics as its main occupation, abandoned its impassioned concern with internal and external conflicts and concentrated on the production of wealth, gave him the elbow room which he needed for his diplomacy. The 'economic miracle' on the other hand needed this diplomacy. Without the confidence which Adenauer gained for the Federal Republic in the Western world, without the relaxation of international tension to which he contributed substantially, German exports could never have reached the unparalleled heights attained at the end of the fifties. Germany, in 1945 a robber robbed in turn, a beggar in deepest misery, fifteen years later possessed more gold per head of population than the United States, had an export surplus of almost two milliard dollars and a national income roughly three times as big as before the war. The Federal Republic had become the third most important industrial power and the second most important trading power in the world.

The expression 'economic miracle' is criticized on the grounds that there was no miracle. Certainly not, only luck and achievement. It was lucky that Germany received American aid and that it could participate in the world-wide boom, the breakthrough to universal affluence which occurred to a varying degree everywhere in the Western world, partly thanks to the war. From an economic point of view certain things proved fortunate which from a human point of view were less so: the destruction and dismantling which forced German industry to begin completely anew and to do so in the most modern manner; the enormous demands of the home market; the expulsions the victims of which brought nothing to West Germany except their skill and their desperate determination to succeed once more and then never to become poor again. After 1945 the Germans liked to refer to the 'blessing of the year zero', treasuring the intellectual sphere where this blessing did not exist to the extent that people believed. It did exist in the economic sphere. As for the achievement there is no need to waste words on it, particularly as plenty of words are wasted on it in Germany.

That the Germans should be proud of what they have accomplished is not altogether unnatural.

In the poorer DDR a little of the charm of the nineteenth and early twentieth century can still be found. In the Federal Republic almost nothing of it remains except where it has been artificially kept alive and in a few aristocratic oases in the country. Herded together in a confined space, active, anxious for better houses and more mobility the Germans transformed the face of the country beyond recognition. This process took place everywhere in the West but in Germany it was more radical because the size of the population had increased more abruptly and because the war had destroyed more than elsewhere. A few piously re-erected monuments apart the reconstructed cities had nothing in common with the old ones except the name; the small towns, mostly well preserved, were linked to the cities by the industries which settled in their area, by cars, television and the new arts of salesmanship. The distinctions between town and country, long sentimentally misused, broke down; the old attitudes, good ones and less good ones, which had characterized German provincial life gave way to a uniform desire for gain which pervaded the whole country What began with the currency reform of 1948 was called 'reconstruction' only for a short time. In the literal sense of the word, the replacement of destroyed buildings, the 'reconstruction' was completed in under ten years; in the sense of reaching the pre-war level of production it was completed after only three. Since then it has no longer been a question of restoration but of increasing production and consumption, of turning an ever greater number of things into necessities of life, of making existence easy and enjoyable to a hitherto undreamt of degree.

The fact that the small, crippled Germany became incomparably richer than the big one had ever been, confused or should have confused the arguments of the refugee organizations. They were apt to recall that a quarter of the nation had been fed from the lost territories. They might have been fed, was the answer, but badly and expensively, whereas now the market was flooded with every conceivable kind of food from the Continent and the world. The Germans had lost their conquests, the most recent as well as the earliest. Instead they could buy land, in France, in Ireland, in Madeira and in Florida, and some availed themselves boldly of the opportunity.

The position on the labour market, its exploitation by energetic trade union leaders, brought about not only a two or threefold increase in the workers' net incomes but resulted in a considerable rise in their relative share of the national income. To this critics from the Social Democratic opposition and still more from the groups that felt disappointed by the new 'popular party', opportunist course of the Social Democrats, objected that although the workers' consumption might have risen and although they could – if still only to a very limited extent – share in the new amenities of life while in employment, nothing had changed as regards their state of dependence, their want in old age; they could not save enough to guarantee them a minimum of independence. In spite of the glitter of the shopping streets and the car parks the German class structure remained fundamentally the same. The administration, science, the legal profession, industry and trade still recruited from the upper and middle ranks, that is from among themselves. The new state once again favoured not the poor but the rich; at first by the currency reform and then by fiscal legislation. Enormous private fortunes were amassed within a few years. As in the age of the Kaiser, or more so, the economy was controlled by vast industrial concentrations in the form of companies with up to 200,000 employees or of open or secret alliances and associations; their managers were more powerful than the members of the government and corrupted political life. The determination of the Allies to 'disentangle' German industry was made a mockery and the chance of social revolution was lost once more.

Such criticism, true though it was in some respects, must in turn be questioned. Was it possible to enjoy the advantages of the boom without putting up with its darker sides? Were the workers materially better off if the factories 'were owned by the people' or, perhaps more important still, were they freer to influence public life? Was there any reason to object to a concern merely because of its size? It was true, for example, that each of the three companies into which the Allies had divided the chemical giant, *I. G. Farben*, soon achieved a bigger turnover than the parent body had ever reached and that the heads of these concerns had considerable power. It was impossible to give a snap judgement on whether they used it to the advantage or the disadvantage of the nation. The fact that a person had acquired power by successfully competing in the economic field offered no guarantee of his virtues. But neither did the fact that another had risen to power by the democratic process, an observation which can be illustrated by examples; it was desirable that there should be competition between the two forms of advancement. Moreover, the German industrialists, and in particular the more eminent among them, could not remain aloof from the social changes. They no longer are sworn fighters for their class, imperialists and brutal overlords; the type personified in the age of the Kaiser by the Krupp of that day and by Kirdorf has disappeared. Symptomatic of the change is the fact that in the Adenauer and post-Adenauer era it was the House of Krupp – once so active in thinking up 'war aims' – which identified itself with a constructive and realistic East European policy. The workers for their part have gained a right to consultation which in the coal industry goes beyond mere questions of wages and work. The boards of directors in that industry consist of equal numbers of representatives of workers and shareholders and there is a member of the management who represents those interests which are no longer called 'proletarian'. Such institutions are capable of expansion and a future chapter of social history will deal with their future expansion. If they do not signify a radical change in class structure, à 'revolution', it may be because the time of revolutions is past, because we live in an age of permanent revolution which it is impossible any longer to guide by a single Utopian idea.

Nor is it possible seriously to uphold the often heard claim that the German class structure has not changed or has been 'restored'. It is possible to restore a throne, not a social order. The German state, whose ruling class – civil service, judiciary, church, army and aristocracy – had survived the fall of the Hohenzollern dynasty and helped to ruin the Weimar democracy broke down during the years of Adolf Hitler. It came to grief during the period of a powerful, rootless, popular and totalitarian dictatorship which, supported by the lowest elements, overthrew the class hierarchy because it had no connection with the old authority and little with the old hierarchy. The most powerful representative of the old authority, the Prussian aristocracy, was ruined three times over in that period: by the war in which it lost thousands of its members; by its resistance against Hitler, the chain of conspiracies which resulted in the murder of hundreds of them; and finally by the Poles and the Russians, who drove the Junkers off their estates – how many of them died no one has counted – razed their castles and distributed their possessions. The survivors disappeared in the flood of refugees from East Germany; and, although some of them re-emerged from the stream and because of their vitality again held office, the Junker class as a social entity and force can never reappear. This was the tragedy, the more cruel because it happened so very late and was hardly noticed in the confusion of the first post-war years. Its most eloquent symbol is the suicide of Bismarck's daughter-in-law who was also his niece, the widow of his son Bill, in her castle, Varzin, a few hours before the arrival of the soldiers of the Red Army.

The final ruin of the old powers-that-be left the Germans in 1945 without any authority except that given them by the victors. As the victors withdrew the new picture became clear: that of a bourgeois society, completely freed from the old hierarchy. It was, moreover, a purely capitalist society, because now and only now did German industry no longer take its system of values from the old authorities or expect protection and recognition from them. If it is true that democracy is the form of government which corresponds to a capitalist economy, Germany in 1949 was ready for the first time really to develop democratic habits: to hammer out laws between several parties, interested groups, associations and religious communities. In that sense Konrad Adenauer was a democrat; he was perfect at playing the mediator, at ensuring that all groups received their share or one which satisfied them, thus giving himself a free hand in the sphere which interested him most, that of foreign policy. Adenauer's outmoded, Bismarckian verbal attacks on the Social Democrats were not in keeping with the new society. Nor were they taken very seriously. Capitalism without an admixture of feudalism, democracy and socially-minded democracy came to the fore simultaneously in the Germany of the fifties, and in the process capitalism was brought under the control not of the authorities but of a socially-minded democracy. The extent of this control was and will be disputed. Although the old 'ideologies' still serve for Sunday speechifying they are useless for weekday compromises.

Also democratic were the new governments, both in Bonn and in the *Länder*. Germany was no longer ruled, as during the Weimar Republic, by the Wilhelminian bourgeoisie with its respect for authority nor by gangsters, as in the Third Reich, but by a solid middle class. Adenauer stemmed from this class, although from an earlier vintage, a fact to which his distinguished, hard features bore witness. His younger colleagues were of different appearance; they looked like provincial worthies in their Sunday best, typically middle class. The aristocracy, in so far as it survived in West Germany, played roughly the part that it had long played in France: in the country it still retained a little of its role of patriarchal ruler, in the capitals it occasionally played a social one and in politics none at all. With sound instinct it had withdrawn from that sphere. The same was true of the old dynasties. They had become sufficiently harmless to start being liked again, and their modest pomp, to the extent that they could afford it, was produced to entertain the public – a sign that many old quarrels had ceased to be of interest. These, one might think, were far-reaching changes which may go further still. But they will never satisfy the ideologists, as long as there are such.

The character of a society is determined not only by the distribution of economic and political power, not only by the distribution of the national income. There are psychological factors which affect a society as much as they are affected by it. The Germans of the late fifties were no longer 'subjects'. They had lost their old respect for authority, both public and private. The officers of the new *Bundeswehr* could tell a tale about this. It was true that university students still came predominantly from the middle classes and that talent among the lower classes was insufficiently mobilized. But whereas the universities of the Weimar period had been centres of reactionary and romantic protest, in the fifties they were, as in America, Britain, Japan and Spain, centres of vigilant, sober criticism, centres of progressive restiveness – a difference worth mentioning. Where it came from nobody can say. Why did the German professors who for three-quarters of a century had been agents of an intolerant nationalism now appear as critics in the opposite sense and why did the students follow those who issued the strongest warnings: against nuclear weapons for the army, against the excesses of a nationalistic gutter press, against overbearing actions by the state if and when such actions violated the constitution? One can only point out that this change occurred; one cannot explain it. But was it not more significant than the class composition of the universities? What is important in the last resort is not that there are social classes – they exist everywhere – but how they behave.

In the legal profession too recruits continued to be drawn from the same classes as before. Moreover, application of the principle that judges could not be dismissed allowed too many of them who had disgraced themselves during the Hitler period to remain in office and to retire too late with too much honour. It would have been better if this scandal had been prevented. Yet German justice is no longer class justice. Instead of passing judgements shamelessly inspired by political malice, as in the twenties, it defended the new state as best it could with the means at its disposal. It protected the spirit of the constitution against the state, it protected the *Länder* against the centralism of the Federal government, the freedom of the press against encroachments by vindictive ministers, and soldiers against the brutality of their superiors. In old democracies such behaviour would have been natural; in such a new one, founded in such inauspicious circumstances as the German, it was not at all natural. Past experience had not led the world to expect to find in Germany a judiciary philosophically concerned with discovering the truth, making judgements loyally in accordance with the new laws.

The transition from the authoritarian state to democracy can be defined by another observation. The Germans of the fifties expected from the state not the fulfilment of life which service to the community provides but advantages. The state itself, government and parties, no longer appealed to the wish to be of service to the community but to group egoism, particularly at election time. Hence the new and telling expression 'election gifts'. As the Germans are inclined to extremes they went also in this to the limit of what is wise, and sometimes beyond. It became difficult – as in America – to pass laws and to obtain money for measures not in the interest of groups but only of the community as a whole. The profound difference which exists in this sphere between the public spirit of West Germany and that of East Germany would be difficult to overcome even after a reunification.

But such observations do not give a complete picture. As everywhere and always there are conflicting tendencies. Old traditions have been weakened but they are not dead. The very lack of feeling of the average citizen for the *res publica*, in so far as it concerned the whole community, gave the government a chance to re-establish the authority of the state as a distinct factor over and above a variety of group interests; it was helped in this by being able to refer to such issues of universal concern as the 'Communist danger' or 'reunification'. Let us be precise and add that to emphasize the importance of the state *vis-à-vis* society need not be bad, that it is even necessary up to a certain point. A nation cannot exist in the long run – or emerge successfully from the tests which it will have to face if it is concerned only with gain. But then it is a characteristic of the human predicament that the correct, well-balanced solution is never to be had, or only for fleeting moments. The Germans have had too much authority for most of the time; now they have very little. They could have too much of it again. They will certainly have too much of it if they permit armed force to assume the function which Adenauer and his energetic assistants claimed for it.

6. The 'Unconquered Past'

The rise to unparalleled wealth, the establishment of unparalleled links between Europe and America took place against a historical background of which the Germans had reason to be profoundly ashamed. Many were honestly ashamed; others said they were, within limits; many were not. They thought that the only thing which Hitler had done wrong was to have been defeated; they did not object to the acts which had led to his defeat and which had made it morally well deserved. They were helped by the new confusion of world developments; by Stalin's brutal imperialism, by America's anti-Communism which took over some of the arguments once used by Propaganda Minister Goebbels. They were helped by the fact that the Allies had been able to win the war but had not been able to make a good peace, neither in Germany nor elsewhere; that might continued to go before right, that more money and ingenuity went into the preparation of war than had ever been spent on it by Hitler; and that this time the fault lay not with the Germans.

Roughly thrown on to an entirely new level of existence they turned away from the cult of their past. The old 'success myth' which had stretched from Bismarck to Hitler was broken. The Italians could reject Mussolini's adventure while taking pride in the Risorgimento and even in the doubtful glory of the First World War. In Germany a much older development which for long had been enthusiastically approved of had seemingly ended in nothing. It had been possible to regard the outcome of the First World War as historically illegitimate and transitory. The outcome of the Second had conclusive force. Its victim was the glory of the early twentieth, the nineteenth and even the eighteenth century; the *kleindeutsch* Reich and Bismarck and Frederick whose anniversaries were celebrated hesitatingly or not at all. Theodor Heuss, the first President of the Federal Republic, by origin an historian, tried to save a little continuity and at least 1848. The Germans were proud to have such a learned President but what he said passed over the heads of his listeners.

The National Liberal historians had seen a continuation of Bismarck in the Kaiser, in the First World War, negatively in the Weimar Republic, half doubtfully and half enthusiastically in Hitler. They were silent now, because they were dead or because they were at their discredited wits' end. Some, it must be said, showed an admirable ability for self-criticism and development even in their later years; as a result there developed a fairly fruitful discussion of German history of the last eighty years. In so far as it included a critical examination of the principle of the German nation-state it assisted Adenauer's European policy; the Chancellor himself of course paid little attention to what the historians did. The young ones who gradually came to the fore no longer participated with passion in this discussion. For them the twenties were part of history and very strange; as the years passed even the shame of the Third Reich became part of history. They set out to examine it in a highly objective, expert manner, without fear of the truth, and the result of their work received the approval even of Polish critics. They did not continue any tradition, least of all that of the recent past; a pleasant illustration of the fact that in intellectual life it is possible to generate ideas not connected with anything pre-existing. The first big general examinations of the Hitler period came from the Anglo-Saxon countries; the detailed research which quickly superseded these came mainly from Germany itself. Inevitably a certain continuity was established between what had gone before, the age of the Kaiser, the First World War and Weimar, and the earlier periods were dragged into the catastrophe of the later one or at any rate spattered by its murky waters. The links and first symptoms – the antisemitism of the nineties, the imperialism of the pan-Germans, the class struggle conducted mainly by the right against the Social Democrats, the war aims of 1917 – were presented in the light of subsequent events.

As a whole the German historians ceased to be prophets. They no longer felt themselves carried along on the crest of a strong wave of good fortune, they no longer knew where the journey would end or where it should end. Consequently they no longer had the same close contact with public opinion as in the past.

Formerly they had been the spokesmen of the nation in political as well as in moral matters; no other branch of learning had expressed the alliance between the monarchy and the national bourgeoisie in such eloquent language. There is no longer a dominant branch of learning of this kind in Germany today. And if there were it would be physics not history. On the occasions when philosophically inclined physicists have commented on topical matters they have been listened to as were formerly the historians. If the comings and goings of the latter still find their way into newspapers and television they no longer arouse the same interest among the 'propertied and educated' classes as in the past. History no longer forms the public conscience; it has again become a specialist science and on the whole remains restricted in its effect to the lecture room and the learned congress. The past has ceased to determine the identity of democratic society.

There is also the question to what extent the research into the German crimes, which has been carried out and published for example in Poland, has affected the public. A liberal, sensibly organized television system has certainly told the Germans a great deal, often in the effective way made possible by the preservation of sound and pictorial records. Moreover, the attitude of the first two Federal Presidents was exemplary. But who wants to know things the knowledge of which arouses feelings of shame? The full picture is a complex one. There was a completely reliable scholarship which served truth and only truth; a dignified remorseful officialdom; a judiciary which partly through its own fault started much too late to take proceedings against Hitler's mass murderers but which then did about as much as it could do; there was a conscientious, liberal element in the big mass media, television and the press, or at any rate a large part of the press. At a lower level there was gloomy obstinacy, cynical indifference, a desire not to know, white-washing and a great readiness to seize on justifications of Hitler which these people did not dare to voice themselves but which they were now offered by rabid Americans and Britons. The young generation of West Germans which so much resembles the youth of western Europe and

America adopts a somewhat different position. Those born shortly before or after the end need no justification. They want to know the truth to the extent that they want to know anything about the dim and distant past. They laugh at Hitler's recorded voice and cannot understand how their parents could have failed to laugh when those speeches were made. The parents refer to the 'unconquered past'. The children ask what there is to conquer. Their attitude is that great folly was committed which cannot be undone but which will gradually go the way of all crime and suffering in history.

The period as it developed did not favour prophets, historical or others. The Federal Republic produced no Nietzsche, no Spengler and no successors to the 'great contemporary critics' of the past. Immediately after 1945 there were people who thought that they could continue where they left off in 1933 and new prophecies about the end of the world, theories about the destruction of humanity through technology and other popular visions of the twenties appeared on the market. But as on this occasion the apocalyptists encountered little interest they were compelled to devote themselves to more constructive ways of proceeding. There was plenty of ground for apocalyptic fears, but the mind reacts as it wants not as it must, and it is not known in advance how it will react. Criticism certainly exists in present-day German literature; criticism of the welfare society, of conformism, of corruption and also of 'alienation', more or less as in other Western countries. The fantasies which had arisen in the first thirty-three years of the century from the morass of social conflict – on the subject of left-wing revolution and 'conservative revolution', glorification of war, of power, of an heroic going under – did not reappear. It was as though Germany was as tired of intellectual as of political orgies.

7. Les Allemagnes

For a long time the French for 'Germany' was a plural word: *Les Allemagnes*. This was an allusion to the political and cultural complexity which characterized the nation during most of its existence.

This complexity disappeared at first only gradually in the nineteenth century, and then suddenly though not wholly since Bismarck did not want it to disappear wholly. Complete national unity was established only under Adolf Hitler. Then it led to conditions which made it understandable that the European allies of the Federal Republic, as also those of the German Democratic Republic, were not as anxious for 'reunification' as they claimed. We have already quoted the lines which Franz Grillparzer wrote in the middle of the nineteenth century:

> *Oh Herr, lass Dich herbei*
> *und mach die Deutschen frei,*
> *dass endlich das Geschrei*
> *hernach zu Ende sei*.*

That they should have had again to clamour for freedom over a hundred years later was only because of considerable historical lapses of tact on their part. German energy in the late nineteenth and twentieth century was very great. It would have sufficed to preserve unity and freedom if it had been used sensibly.

In retrospect the political complexity of *Les Allemagnes* of the past seems more organic and fruitful than the division which exists today. But what does 'organic' mean in history? Force was used to establish the many German principalities no less than the unity of France, Spain or of the North American Union. Terrible wars, like the war that lasted thirty years, had to happen to make the map of Germany what it was at the time of the French Revolution. Dynastic and religious factors kept the civilization of Bavaria firmly apart from that of Prussia or Saxony until well into

---

* Oh Lord, deign to set the Germans free so that their clamour for freedom shall cease at last.

the nineteenth century. Despotism, operating in a wider field, separated Austria from the 'Reich'. If in the early seventeenth century the Austrian estates had had their way – who knows – Austria might have become an arch-Protestant, arch-German state, as much as or more so than Prussia. Obviously there is a difference between the gradual development of the Habsburg monarchy which for centuries did sensible and useful work and the compulsory establishment of the lower middle-class school-master state of East Berlin. Yet force was involved in both cases. There is also an indisputable difference between the intellectual quality of the Counter-Reformation and the musty chimera called Marxism. Yet systems of ideas were involved in both cases.

The *Anschluss* between Austria and Germany lasted for seven terrible years. This is a very short time compared with the centuries during which Austria was increasingly separated from Germany, and it is a short time even compared with the period which has followed and in which the separation was reconfirmed. Whether the Austrians are Germans or not, whether they are a nation or not is still debated in Vienna. To the foreign observer the discussion seems futile. Why compare an historically confirmed fact with an uncertain general concept?

Not that the fate of the Austrians after 1945 was an easy one. They too were made to pay the Russians a heavy price for Hitler and the punishment was not altogether unjust because too many inhabitants of the liberated country had behaved very badly during the *Anschluss*. But Austria was spared partition for several reasons. Seven million people were less important than seventy million and the little country was not worth a Cold War. The fact that formally it had not been 'conquered' but 'liberated' made more than a formal difference. Unlike Germany it was at once allowed to have a national central government. In the case of Austria it was the veto of the four liberators which had to be unanimous whereas in the case of Germany unanimity was needed for positive decisions by the Four. Therefore, the central government in Austria was able to preserve or gradually to restore the unity of the country which had been divided into occupation zones. Personal factors counted. In their dealing with the Russians the new representatives of Austria, Conservative and Socialist, showed a malleability, a confidence-inspiring ability, a modest intelligence with which they succeeded in extracting concession after concession from the victors, culminating in 1955 in the withdrawal of all troops, full sovereignty and neutrality. We wish to imply not that Germany could have had the same by exercising the same skills but that the Germans lacked these skills.

In Germany not only the 'zones' but the political parties fell apart and they did the same in the new Federal Republic: there was a permanent Christian Democratic government and permanent Social Democratic opposition. In Austria neither the occupation zones nor the parties fell apart. The two facts are connected; the task of restoring the unity of the state could only be solved jointly by the great parties. In the Federal Republic no party dared to recognize the new realities, particularly the new eastern frontiers, because the competing party would have benefited. In Austria the two great parties did jointly what needed to be done in order to liquidate Hitler's heritage. The coalition between the Socialists and the old Christian Socialist Party who rechristened themselves the Austrian People's Party was difficult. Between them stood the memory of the bitter civil war of 1934 and the Catholic dictatorship of the pre-*Anschluss* years. The two parties now seemed to be locked in permanent embrace in order to prevent the repetition of similar catastrophes. The result was a unique form of government: the development of a new democratic hierarchy from the two parties and their numerous allied organizations, and the distribution of many thousands of posts in the state and the nationalized industries strictly in accordance with the principle of proportional party representation. The new Austrian society was a semi-political, semi-professional society which lacked elasticity but in which everybody, or almost everybody, received his due. Austria's distinct fate, as also the nature of its political and social structure, helped to strengthen its separate identity. From the past this identity could not derive much strength. For the Hàbsburg monarchy had died long ago and it was best to ignore the twenties and thirties. If Austria also had its 'unconquered past' it managed its present with skill. Of the broken tradition of the Habsburgs there remained at least this that Vienna could discreetly maintain such contact with Budapest, Prague and Warsaw as circumstances allowed. The question of what is the area covered by 'German history' cannot be answered more clearly at the end of our story than at its beginning. If one accepts the concept of *Les Allemagnes* the most recent Austrian development would form part of it. If one accepts the nineteenth century concept of the nation-state – and it is this which the Federal Republic does not want to abandon – one must let Austria go its way without paying further attention to it.

The old Austria had not consciously wanted to break away from Germany. In fact the Habsburg whose policy in effect did most to further the break, Ferdinand II, took the unity of the Empire tremendously seriously and tried to save it or to restore it under the banner of the Catholic Counter-Reformation. Although he was successful in the hereditary Habsburg territories he failed in the rest of the Reich, and the two portions fell asunder.

A similar fate befell the Russian and the German Communists. They above all had wanted to preserve Germany's unity. They had not wanted to make Germany 'Communist' immediately and completely; that would come later. But as they had no influence beyond their zone, as the country beyond their zone developed political and social forms opposed to them, they hesitatingly began to transform into a Communist state the territory allocated to them solely for occupation purposes. The character of its inhabitants, its geography, its fluvial system, its road and rail network linked as it was to the West and its shortage of mineral resources made it singularly unsuitable for the purpose. But political power can do anything given time, and it needs less time today than the Habsburgs needed. At first only a piece of Russian loot, the DDR gradually became a junior partner of the Soviet Union. Its economy, the most unnatural in the world, developed as it became almost entirely linked to that of the Eastern bloc. Communist doctrine, still the official religion, took second place to the principle of productivity in the interest of the DDR and its great protector. A vast bureaucracy has grown up which administers not only the state but industry and agriculture. It is concerned more with technical know-how than with doctrine and has learnt to identify its own advantages with the preservation of the regime. There are possibilities of advancement and they are made use of even by those who are indifferent or hostile to the monstrosity of the accidentally and arbitrarily created new state.

Its officialdom sees the DDR as a new state. Although it makes clumsy, sentimental attempts to establish links with certain episodes in German and Prussian history it regards the German Reich as dissolved and must do so because otherwise its state would have no legal basis. Therefore it is very ready to recognize the Federal Republic; it advocates the theory of 'two German states'. The Federal Republic does not do this. It is not prepared to recognize the DDR and regards itself as the representative of the German Reich which exists *de jure* and must be restored *de facto*.

What has happened since 1949 has led West Germany away from rather than towards this theoretical standpoint; the Federal Republic has developed a strong identity which is not that of the Reich. The focal point of its foreign policy is not the whole of Germany but the Rhineland and southern Germany. An all-German foreign policy would have necessitated an Eastern policy, and the Federal Republic had no such policy. Had the 'Reich' been restored in the late forties politics and society would present a very different picture. Germany would be ruled by a Social Democratic party which would not be a 'popular party' but doctrinally Marxist and which would battle with hate-filled enemies, as in 1920. Capital would not have the power which it has. The aristocracy would not sit happily and prosperously in its castles but would have fallen victim to a land reform; and there would be much less prosperity than there is. There would be no friendship with France, much less internationalism, no rejoicing at visits of Western potentates the like of which the 'Reich' never saw.

But the Federal Republic refuses to recognize its identity, to see the source of its success. More confusing still: it is its very success which blocks the Federal Republic's view of its identity and of the source of its success. Originally West Germany wanted prosperity not power. This it succeeded in obtaining; and with prosperity power re-entered by the back door. A surprising guest, yet for many people not an unwelcome one. The economic and military power of the Federal Republic is seen simply as a product of German achievement, simply as German power. Politicians can be heard to say that Germany has not been so powerful since 1914. Consequently the temptation increases to regard the results of the Second World War, even to the east, as temporary and invalid, and to aim at least – at least – at the restoration of the Reich of 1937. One can think of no reason why once this has been achieved, Germany should stop there, why the whole gruesome film should not be shown all over again. There are various trends working towards the restoration of the old, complete nation-state.

German politicians and political theorists had conceived the Federal Republic as an organism composed of the federal states. Although today the *Länder* still exert a beneficent influence as guardians of the constitution and have plenty of useful as well as decorative functions, the emphasis has rapidly shifted towards the centre, towards 'Bonn'. The same energies have swept the whole country and have made all regions more like one another. The millions of refugees could not be expected to feel themselves Bavarians or Hessians. Too many problems could only be solved centrally, both those that resulted from Germany's particular situation and those that the Federal Republic had in common with other developed industrial societies. In 1965 the Federal Republic was not a federation of states but a state divided into regions; it reached exactly as far as it was allowed to. It was easy to conclude that it *ought* to reach further; to the frontiers to which it had once reached. Whether the Reich still existed legally or not, it was clearly the nation which here, as so often since 1866, asserted itself.

The same conclusion was forced upon the Germans by the rest of the world. For in 'Europe' too success led to paradoxical results. In the late forties the nations of the Continent had joined forces in order to improve their lot and to meet the threat of Russian imperialism. At the time it was thought that the union would be forever, that the day of European nation-states was past; this belief was most fervently held in Germany but it also existed elsewhere. A joint economic policy and a joint military and foreign policy quickly made the sap of life rise again; and with it returned courage and the feeling that in the end all had not been quite so tragic and final and that each nation could struggle once more on its own as before. In France Charles de Gaulle made this feeling the guiding principle of his policy, partly in theory and partly in practice. It never occurred to him that what was sauce for the French goose could equally be sauce for the German gander, that in fact it must be so in the long run. 'Germany has changed', he used to say airily. But if, as he claimed, France had not changed but pursued the same unvarying national interests, how should, how could Germany have changed?

Perhaps the General was wrong. Perhaps both countries have changed, as regards the structure of their societies and as regards their position in the world; changes which, if the sociologists are right, cannot fail to have a lasting effect on foreign policy.

For the time being two conflicting trends exist. There are those who want to continue the European work and those who want to return to the old virtues and vices of the nation-state.

In the course of our long story the present writer hopes to have shown that he favours the middle of the road, that he dislikes false extremes and false alternatives. The continuation of the European work does not preclude the defence of specific national interests. This would involve the establishment of clear and constructive ties with eastern Europe and the creation of an atmosphere in which the ice of the Communist dictatorship in East Berlin must melt. Then it would be possible to set up a confederation of the 'two Germanies' and the process of estrangement between the two populations could be reversed. The two partners of the confederation would preserve the commitments to the East and the West which they had entered into in the past but would together form a kind of bridge and a centrepiece. This would need a good deal of statesmanship. But who can hope to achieve anything without statesmanship in such a situation?

In fact Adenauer's successors have made hesitant attempts to establish contact with the states of eastern Europe. Hitherto these attempts have not progressed very far; partly because the mood in eastern Europe has worked against them and partly because the Federal Republic is committed to principles and taboos which its politicians have not had the courage to ignore. Their argument has been that Germany would only clarify its attitude to eastern Europe when it was reunited; only then would it be prepared to negotiate about peace, make demands and, perhaps, enter into compromises. But there will never be a 'reunification' or 'peace negotiations' unless Germany states in advance what it wants, unless it makes certain renunciations beforehand. The situation is reminiscent of that of the First World War, of the time when Germany offered peace, and not dishonesty, but cloaked its peace conditions in cunning, sinister ambiguity. Because Germany wanted to 'retain some trumps' no peace negotiations ever took place; the trumps vanished in Germany's hand. It is curious how certain national inclinations, certain abortive practices reappear in spite of completely changed conditions.

If one wants to speculate about the future it is possible to foresee the repetition of other, worse happenings. In modern German history periods of peace, of sensible adaptation alternate with periods of explosion. The Holy Alliance, the time of 'hand rails and dykes' was followed by the militant revolutionary age of Bismarck; after the conciliatory policy of the aged Bismarck came William's imperialism and Ludendorff's war; after Stresemann came Hitler. This last succession contains the most topical warnings. What happened was not that Stresemann deceived western Europe with his reconciliation policy; he was honest. It was the nation which, unconsciously, deceived the outside world through Stresemann. It allowed him to do what he wanted to do as long as nothing else could be done; it would have chased him off later had he not died in time. In 1933 the Germans pushed away the ladder which they had used to climb to new power because they had no more need of it. Certain of Adenauer's utterances make it seem likely that he himself was afraid of giving a repeat performance of Stresemann's historical role. Hence the links, the new additional links of his Germany with western Europe on which he worked so busily. In the last resort the

Atlantic allies did something very dangerous and irrational; they caused or permitted the terrible mutilation of Germany, a truly Carthaginian peace. But instead of destroying Carthage they rushed to rebuild it and to make it as rich and militarily powerful as possible. Did they not thereby put the wisdom of the Germans to too hard a test? Was it possible to imagine greater naïvety, blinder confidence? It was hoped that the German nation would undergo a moral purification, but the success of such a process is doubtful with any nation. The structure of society has changed but who knows whether its basic character has changed. What has characterized the German nature for a hundred years is its lack of form, its unreliability.

There are journalists today who recommend Germany to return to a policy of national autonomy, to play off the great power blocs or the parts of the disintegrating power blocs against each other, and at the suitable moment to evict the Poles from their 'regained' territories. If that were possible and done very different things would also be possible and would also be done. Germany would no more stop at the 'frontiers of 1937' than it had stopped there in 1939. Will this happen?

I do not know. I do know that even for a German the eventuality is not desirable. A second 'greater' Germany would bring no more happiness to the Germans than the first one, not to mention other nations.

However, there are strong forces at work to prevent such a development. Although Carthage has not been destroyed it has been shackled. It has very little room for manoeuvre and the majority of its inhabitants know this. Eastern Europe – Poland, Bohemia and Russia itself – is no longer what it was in 1939. The whole world is no longer the same. War is not the same. The might of the mightiest is restricted by factors which did not exist in Adolf Hitler's day and which can be ignored only at the risk of deadly danger. It was incredible that Germany could twice within twenty-five years seek to dominate Europe by force of arms. History is long-suffering. Our reason, however modest it may have become, refuses to let us believe that Germany could be allowed to make a third attempt.

Finally, German society has changed. A glance at leading German newspapers, a glance at television programmes demonstrates this daily. The stuffy, ignorant Germano-centric, spiteful tone of the twenties has gone. The general attitude of the press is incomparably more open to the world, more urbane, sober and critical. This applies particularly to the generations which, if all goes well, will occupy the key position in ten or twenty years' time. Among the older people there are incorrigible cases. The young generation is new. If in present-day Germany there is a struggle between a reactionary trend – back to nationalism, to the vicious circle of frontier disputes, to the authoritarian state, to an overestimate of military matter, to intolerance – and a really modern trend, the latter has an incomparably better chance than in 1927. Anyone who knows the past and therefore realizes that he cannot know the future, will say no more.

The German nation has been endowed with great gifts; others which would have been equally important it was not given. It has made serious mistakes, the most serious ones while it was stronger than ever before. It cannot go back to forms of its political existence which it wantonly destroyed itself. It will not again be able to play the role which it played during the first half of the twentieth century, and this is not a misfortune either for Germany or for the rest of the world. If it has learnt from its mistakes – and much, though not everything, indicates that it has – then it will assert its weight to its own advantage without in the process inflicting new suffering on its neighbours.

Bibliography

KONRAD ADENAUER: *Erinnerungen*, Vol. I (1965); Vol. II (1966). Vol. I translated as *Memoirs, 1945–1953* (London 1966)

WILLY ANDREAS: *Das Zeitalter Napoleons und die Erhebung der Völker* (1955)

PRINCE MAX VON BADEN: *Erinnerungen und Dokumente* (1927)

MICHAEL BALFOUR: *The Kaiser and His Times* (London 1964)

GEOFFREY BARRACLOUGH: *The Origins of Modern Germany* (Oxford, 2nd ed. 1947)

LUDWIG BECK: *Studien*. Edited by Hans Speidel (1955)

AUGUST BEBEL: *Aus meinem Leben* (1914)

LUDWIG BERGSTRAESSER: *Geschichte der politischen Parteien in Deutschland* (1952)

THEOBALD VON BETHMANN HOLLWEG: *Betrachtungen zum Weltkriege* (1922)

M J. BONN: *So macht man Weltgeschichte. Bilanz eines Lebens* (1953)

HANS BOOMS: *Die Konservative Partei, Preussischer Charakter, Reichsauffassung, Nationalbegriff* (1954)

KARL DIETRICH BRACHER: *Die Auflösung der Weimarer Republik* (1955) The account of the crisis of 1932 leans heavily on this excellent book.

OTTO BRAUN: *Von Weimar zu Hitler* (1949)

KARL BUCHHEIM: *Die Christlichen Parteien in Deutschland* (1953)

PRINCE BERNHARD VON BÜLOW: *Denkwürdigkeiten*

ALAN BULLOCK: *Hitler: A Study in Tyranny* (London, new ed. 1964)

E H. CARR: *German–Soviet Relations Between the Two World Wars, 1919–1939* (Oxford 1952)

RALF DAHRENDORF: *Gesellschaft und Demokratie in Deutschland* (1965)

LUDWIG DEHIO: *Gleichgewicht oder Hegemonie. Betrachtungen über ein Grundproblem der neueren Staatengeschichte* (1948)

HANS DELBRÜCK: *Krieg und Politik* (1919)

JOHANN GUSTAV DROYSEN: *Politische Schriften.* Edited by F. Gilbert (1933)

KLAUS EPSTEIN: *Matthias Erzberger and the Dilemma of German Democracy* (Oxford 1959)

MATTHIAS ERZBERGER: *Erlebnisse im Weltkrieg* (1920)

THEODOR ESCHENBURG: *Staat und Gesellschaft in Deutschland* (1956)

ERICH EYCK: *Bismarck, Leben und Werk* (1941)
Das persönliche Regiment Wilhelms II, Politische Geschichte des Deutschen Kaiserreiches von 1890–1914
Geschichte der Weimarer Republik (1954, 1956)

JOACHIM C. FEST: *Das Gesicht des Dritten Reiches. Profil einer totalitären Herrschaft* (1963)

OSSIP K. FLECHTHEIM: *Die Kommunistische Partei Deutschlands in der Weimarer Republik* (1948)

FRITZ FISCHER: *Der Griff nach der Weltmacht* (1961). Translated as *Germany's Aims in the First World War* (London 1967)

CONSTANTIN FRANTZ: *Deutschland und der Föderalismus* (1917)

FERDINAND FRIEDENSBURG: *Die Weimarer Republik* (1946)

H. W. GATZKE: *Germany's Drive to the West. A Study of Germany's Western War Aims During the First World War* (Baltimore, Md., 1950)

IMANUEL GEISS: *Julikrise und Kriegsausbruch*, 2 vols. (1963)

JOSEPH GOEBBELS: *Vom Kaiserhof zur Reichskanzlei* (1937)

HELMUT GOLLWITZER/KÄTHE KUHN/REINHOLD SCHNEIDER: *Du hast mich heimgesucht bei Nacht. Abschiedsbriefe und Aufzeichnungen des Widerstandes 1933–1945*

G. P. GOOCH: *Studies in German History* (London 1948)

WILHELM G. GREWE: *Deutsche Aussenpolitik der Nachkriegszeit* (1960)

BERNHARD GUTTMANN: *Schattenriss einer Generation 1888–1919* (1950)

GEORGE F. W. HALLGARTEN: *Hitler, Reichswehr und Industrie. Zur Geschichte der Jahre 1918–1933* (1955)
Imperialismus vor 1914 (1951). Without agreeing with Hallgarten's theories, the author has learnt much from this comprehensive work, and some of the quotations in Part Eight are taken from it.

FRITZ HARTUNG: *Deutsche Verfassungsgeschichte vom 15. Jahrhundert bis zur Gegenwart* (1933)

HEINRICH HEFFTER: *Die deutsche Selbstverwaltung im 19. Jahrhundert* (1950)

HERMANN HEIDEGGER: *Die deutsche Sozialdemokratie und der nationale Staat 1870–1920* (1956)

KONRAD HEIDEN: *Geburt des Dritten Reiches: Die Geschichte des Nationalsozialismus bis Herbst 1933* (1934)
Hitler. Das Leben eines Diktators, Eine Biographie (1936)
Ein Mann gegen Europa (1937)

ADOLF HEUSINGER: *Befehl im Widerstreit. Schicksalsstunden der deutschen Armee 1923–1945* (1951)

ALFRED HEUSS: *Theodor Mommsen und das 19. Jahrhundert* (1956)

THEODOR HEUSS: *Friedrich Naumann, der Mann, das Werk, die Zeit* (1949)

WALTER HOFER: *Die Entfesselung des Zweiten Weltkrieges* (1954)

[MAX HOFFMANN]: *Die Aufzeichnungen des Generalmajors Max Hoffmann*. Edited by F. Nowak (1929)

PRINCE CHLODWIG ZU HOHENLOHE-SCHILLINGSFÜRST: *Denkwürdigkeiten des Fürsten Chlodwig zu Hohenlohe-Schillingsfürst* (1906)
Denkwürdigkeiten der Reichskanzlerzeit. Edited by Alexander von Mueller (1931)

JOHANNES HOHLFELD: *Deutsche Reichsgeschichte in Dokumenten, 1849 bis 1934. Urkunden und Aktenstücke zur inneren und äusseren Politik des Deutschen Reiches* (1934)

GEORG KAUFMANN: *Geschichte Deutschlands im Neunzehnten Jahrhundert* (1912)

SIEGFRIED VON KARDORFF: *Bismarck. Ein Beitrag zur deutschen Parteigeschichte* (1929)

LIONEL KOCHAN: *Russland und die Weimarer Republik* (1954)

HELMUT KRAUSNICK: *Vorgeschichte und Beginn des militärischen Widerstandes gegen Hitler* (1956)

ALFRED KRUCK: *Geschichte des Alldeutschen Verbandes* (1954)

ANNEDORE LEBER: *Das Gewissen steht auf. 64 Lebensbilder aus dem deutschen Widerstand 1933–1945* (1953)

GEORG LEDEBOUR: *Mensch und Kämpfer*. Collected by Minna Ledebour (1954)

ERICH LUDENDORFF: *Meine Kriegserinnerungen 1914–1918* (1919)

HENDRIK DE MAN: *Gegen den Strom. Memoiren eines europäischen Sozialisten* (1953)

ERICH VON MANSTEIN: *Verlorene Siege* (1955)

ERICH MATTHIAS and RUDOLF MORSEY: *Der Interfraktionelle Ausschuss 1917–1918*. Quellen zur Geschichte des Parlamentarismus und der politischen Parteien (1959)

Die Regierung des Prinzen Max von Baden. Quellen zur Geschichte des Parlamentarismus und der politischen Parteien (1962)

FRANZ MEHRING: *Geschichte der Deutschen Sozialdemokratie* (1913)

OTTO MEISSNER: *Staatssekretär unter Ebert, Hindenburg, Hitler* (1950)

BERNHARD MENNE: *Krupp, Deutschlands Kanonenkönige* (1936)

ARNOLD OSKAR MEYER: *Bismarck, der Mensch und der Staatsmann* (1949)

HENRY C. MEYER: *Mitteleuropa in German Thought and Action 1815–1945* (The Hague 1955)

ARMIN MOHLER: *Die Konservative Revolution in Deutschland 1918 bis 1932, Grundriss ihrer Weltanschauungen* (1950)

WILHELM MOMMSEN: *Deutsche Parteiprogramme* (1952)

FRIEDRICH NAUMANN: *Mitteleuropa* (1915)

GUSTAV NOSKE: *Von Kiel bis Kapp. Zur Geschichte der deutschen Revolution* (1920)

Erlebtes aus Aufstieg und Niedergang einer Demokratie (1947)

HERMANN ONCKEN: *Rudolf von Bennigsen. Ein deutscher liberaler Politiker* (1910)

Lassalle. Eine politische Biographie (1920)

FRANZ VON PAPEN: *Der Wahrheit eine Gasse* (1952)

THEO PIRKER: *Die S.P.D. nach Hitler* (1965)

WALTHER RATHENAU: *Von kommenden Dingen* (1917)

Politische Briefe (1929)

HANS ULRICH RENTSCH: *Bismarck im Urteil der schweizerischen Presse 1862–1898* (1945)

ERNST RIECHERT: *Das zweite Deutschland. Ein Staat, der nicht sein darf* (1964)

GERHARD RITTER: *Carl Goerdeler und die deutsche Widerstandsbewegung* (1955)

ARTHUR ROSENBERG: *Geschichte der Weimarer Republik* (1955)

HANS ROTHFELS: *Bismarck und der Staat. Ausgewählte Dokumente* (1953)

Die Opposition gegen Hitler (1958)

LORD RUSSELL OF LIVERPOOL: *The Scourge of the Swastika* (London 1954). Published in German as *Geissel der Menschheit. Kurze Geschichte der Nazikriegsverbrechen* (1955)

HJALMAR SCHACHT: *76 Jahre meines Lebens* (1953)

PHILIPP SCHEIDEMANN: *Der Zusammenbruch* (1921)

Memoiren eines Sozialdemokraten (1928)

FRANZ SCHNABEL: *Deutsche Geschichte im neunzehnten Jahrhundert* (1948, 1949)

OTTO-ERNST SCHUEDDEKOPF: *Das Heer und die Republik.* Quellen zur Politik der Reichswehrführung 1918–1933 (1955)

WILHELM SCHUESSLER: *Bismarcks Sturz* (1921)

CARL SCHURZ: *Lebenserinnerungen.* Revised by S. von Radecki.

KURT SENDTNER: *Rupprecht von Wittelsbach, Kronprinz von Bayern* (1954)

HEINZ-OTTO SIEBURG: *Deutschland und Frankreich in der Geschichtsschreibung des neunzehnten Jahrhunderts* (1954)

WERNER VON SIEMENS: *Lebenserinnerungen* (1942)

WERNER SOMBART: *Die deutsche Volkswirtschaft im neunzehnten Jahrhundert und im Anfang des zwanzigsten Jahrhunderts* (1919)

HANS SPEIDEL: *Invasion, 1944. Ein Beitrag zu Rommels und des Reiches Schicksal*

HEINRICH RITTER VON SRBIK: *Deutsche Einheit, Idee und Wirklichkeit vom Heiligen Reich bis Königgrätz* (1942)

RUDOLF STADELMANN: *Soziale und politische Geschichte der Revolution von 1848* (1948)

FRITZ STAMPFER: *Die ersten 14 Jahre der deutschen Republik* (1947)

FRIEDRICH STIEVE: *Deutschland und Europa 1890–1914. Ein Handbuch zur Vorgeschichte des Weltkrieges* (1927)

A. J. P. TAYLOR: *The Course of German History* (London 1945) *The Habsburg Monarchy, 1809–1918* (London 1948)

ALFRED VON TIRPITZ: *Erinnerungen* (1919)

HEINRICH VON TREITSCHKE: *Historische und politische Aufsätze* (1917)

Die Ursachen des deutschen Zusammenbruchs im Jahre 1918. 12 vols. (Untersuchungsausschuss der deutschen Nationalversammlung, 1925–1929)

VEIT VALENTIN: *Geschichte der Deutschen Revolution von 1848 bis 1849* (1930)

EDMOND VERMEIL: *L'Allemagne Contemporaine, Sociale, Politique et Culturelle, 1890–1950* (1953)

[ALEXANDER VON VILLERS]: *Briefe eines Unbekannten. Aus dessen Nachlass neu herausgegeben von K. Graf Lankoronski und Wilhelm Weigand* (1910)

MAX WEBER: *Gesammelte Politische Schriften* (1921)

COUNT KUNO VON WESTARP: *Die Konservative Partei im letzten Jahrzehnt des Kaiserreiches* (1935)

J. W. WHEELER-BENNETT: *Nemesis of Power: The German Army in Politics, 1918–45* (London 1953)

Index